THE
SPEAKER
AND
HIS
AUDIENCE

S0-CYF-858

Under the advisory editorship of J. Jeffery Auer

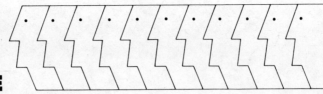

THE SPEAKER AND HIS AUDIENCE

Dynamic
Interpersonal
Communication

SECOND EDITION

MARTIN P. ANDERSEN
E. RAY NICHOLS, JR.
HERBERT W. BOOTH

California State University
Fullerton

Harper & Row, Publishers

New York
Evanston
San Francisco
London

Sponsoring Editor: John G. Ryden
Project Editor: Duncan R. Hazard
Designer: Michel Craig
Production Supervisor: Stefania J. Taflinska

The Speaker and His Audience: Dynamic Interpersonal Communication,
Second Edition
Copyright © 1964, 1974 by Harper & Row, Publishers, Inc.
All rights reserved. Printed in the United States of America. No part of this book
may be used or reproduced in any manner whatsoever without written permission
except in the case of brief quotations embodied in critical articles and reviews. For
information address Harper & Row, Publishers, Inc., 10 East 53rd Street, New
York, N.Y. 10022.

Library of Congress Cataloging in Publication Data
Andersen, Martin P
    The speaker and his audience.
    1. Public speaking.   I. Nichols, E. Ray,
joint author.   II. Booth, Herbert W., joint
author.   III. Title.   IV. Title: Dynamic
interpersonal communication.
PN4121.A664 1974 808.5'1 73-7477
ISBN 0-06-040261-X

CONTENTS

PREFACE

Although this second edition of *The Speaker and His Audience* has
been extensively rewritten, its primary purpose is the same as that of
the first edition, namely to direct the reader to the theory and practice
of audience-oriented speech communication. The content applies not
only to the formal speaking occasion but also to the many informal
communicative situations in which each individual participates daily.
The authors believe that productive communication can be achieved
only if both the speaker and the listener understand that the process of
communication is a transaction, in which both participate as partners.
The book has six specific purposes: (1) to help the student understand
the process of speech communication and its role in the conduct of the
social, political, and vocational affairs of individuals at all levels of their
interpersonal relations; (2) to make the student aware of the roles of
both partners in the communicative act; (3) to explain the ways in
which the listener is motivated and to show why he does not at all
times act as the speaker desires; (4) to instruct the student in what he
must do, as a speaker, to relate his message to the need-value systems of
the listener as a means of reinforcing or changing the latter's attitudes
and behavior; (5) to help the student develop proficiency in the preparation and presentation of messages that will create meaningful relationships between communicators and respondents; and (6) to help the student develop critical standards that will guide him in ethical and efficient communication. To achieve these aims we have written a text that
has a fivefold basis in content and philosophy.

First, we have incorporated in the text essential and pertinent—
and currently accepted—theories of learning, motivation, group process,

perceptual psychology, semantics and linguistics, communication, and rhetorical criticism. Thus the text has a behavioral-science orientation which in turn is based on traditional rhetorical theory. In recent years research, practice, and theoretical formulations in speech communication have increasingly drawn upon the social and psychological sciences for understandings about ways to change human attitudes and behavior.

Second, the functional nature of speech communication is stressed throughout. Effective communication is presented as a means to the achievement of individual and group goals. We perceive communication as the basic tool in the conduct of each individual's developmental tasks and interpersonal activities. It is also the primary instrument by which the affairs of business, government, civic organizations, community groups, education, and the church are conducted. Communication is, further, the essential ingredient in the solution of many of the vital problems facing this country and the world today: the generation gap, the confrontation with police, citizen apathy, racial discrimination, minority-group demands, preservation of the environment, and the credibility gap between the government and the people, to mention just a few. Serving so widely as a tool of social control and adaptation, communication must, therefore, be relevant to the need-value systems of the partners in the communicative situation.

Third, the authors have sought to take the student beyond first principles in both the theory and practice of speech communication. Although we recognize that for many students this course will be their first exposure to a fundamental, organized theory of speech communication and its training and practice, we also believe that most students prefer a text providing content in depth. Hence, each chapter deals comprehensively with advanced areas of study, while not overlooking guides for the beginning student. The text combines fundamentals with advanced theory, blends traditional classical concepts with the latest findings of the behavioral sciences, and points out the applications of rhetorical principles in many communicative situations. The student is provided ample opportunity to explore each topic in depth.

Fourth, while recognizing that speech communication can be divisive, the authors have sought to focus on its positive value in building accord and cooperative action. Historically this has been the aim of responsible persuasive speaking. Today, too, we have even greater need to stress the unifying values of the spoken word. We must focus on the services that speech can perform for the individual and society. We must recognize that when speech is used ethically and efficiently, it is capable of achieving lasting goals and of releasing man's potential for building and preserving democratic values and cooperation.

Finally, our aim has been to present speech training as in harmony with the objectives of a liberal education, while serving as an increasingly essential tool in achieving personal and group development, adjustment, and cooperation. We believe that speech education makes a positive contribution to the development of a liberally educated man. Such a person must be capable of logical thought, must have a broad understanding of human nature—of how and why people interact—must have a knowledgeable awareness of the problems affecting him and society, and must be articulate in his promotion of goals mutually beneficial to the groups of which he is a part.

The pattern of organization of the book follows that of the first edition. The three parts help the student understand, prepare for, and participate in different communicative situations. Part One considers the nature of the communicative transaction, the ways communication serves individuals and groups, the roles of the participants in the process, how respondents are motivated, and the functions of listening and style as links between the speaker and his listeners. Part Two deals with the basic principles of speech preparation. Part Three covers the theory and practice of communicating in the interview and in small groups.

The content and format of the book differ from the first edition in a number of respects. Several chapters have been completely rewritten, and all others have been revised and updated. More than in the previous edition, the text stresses the transactional nature of communication, in which communicator and respondent act as partners. Greater emphasis is placed on the functional values of communication in achieving individual and group goals. We have carefully selected from classical rhetoric those principles which have made major contributions to current speech communication theory.

Chapters One and Twelve contain material not found in other speech communication texts. Chapter One has been designed to help the student realize that he is a member of thousands of overlapping communication networks, that he is forever in the midst of communication. Chapter Twelve treats not only the basic elements of reasoning but also examines the theory on which reasoning is based, so the student will know the "why" as well as the "how." An actual speech is analyzed, showing applications of both Aristotelian and Toulminian methods of reasoning. Many chapters, such as those on audiovisual aids and interviewing, have been expanded and improved.

In the interest of clarity and brevity, in four instances content formerly treated in two separate chapters has been combined into a single chapter. This applies to the subject matter on language and style, vocal and physical behavior, attention and motivation, and the selection and organization of materials. We have deleted the chapter "Speaking on Special Occasions" and have completely reorganized the material in Part Three, "Participating in the Speaking Situation." The reference materials and exercises at the end of each chapter have been updated.

Several other innovations are included in this revision. A new speech communication model is presented in Chapter Four. To assist the student in comprehending the various elements and their relationships to each other and to the entire communicative situation, he is led through progressive steps in the construction of the model. An approach to style that is not found in other current textbooks, that of the "whole man communicating," is presented and explained in Chapter Seven. We devote one complete chapter to the importance and necessity of a carefully thought-out thesis statement or central idea. Departing from the usual procedure of considering several general purposes in the communicative act, we believe that there is one general purpose: to elicit some sort of behavioral response in the listeners, and we have treated purpose with this approach.

Throughout the text we have considered participation in the communicative act in a somewhat unique manner. Our focus is not so much on the format of the speech as on the process of communication. We feel that if the student understands the process involved, he can adapt to any speech occasion. Only the unique characteristics of communicating in the interview and small groups, not treated in the previous chapters, are considered in Part Three. Overall, we have sought to write a text that stresses the behavioral bases and implications of speech communication, that reflects the best of traditional rhetoric, and that still maintains an audience-oriented approach to the study and practice of speech communication.

The text is designed to meet the requirements of students who are taking a one- or two-semester first course in speech communication. The references for collateral reading, exercises and projects, illustrations, and sample speeches all have been selected with the students' needs and interests in mind. Without sacrificing simplicity or brevity we have sought to present in a thorough manner what the student needs to know about the many facets of speech communication.

Many influences have contributed to the writing of this book. We acknowledge gratefully the encouragement and helpful suggestions given by the teachers and students who have used the first edition. We are especially indebted to seven of our colleagues at California State University, Fullerton—Professors Louis Cockerham, Seth Fessenden, Joyce Flocken, Kay Good, Lee Granell, Lucy Keele, and Philip Schreiner—who have made valuable suggestions for modifications of selected chapters.

Professors Earl Cain of California State University, Long Beach, and Jack B. Holland of Orange Coast College, Costa Mesa, California, have contributed freely in the preparation of this second edition.

Our wives, Margaret M. Andersen, Marion Nichols, and Beverly Booth, have given helpful advice and needed encouragement.

A special word of thanks goes to Voras D. Meeks, Speech Editor of Harper & Row, and Dr. J. Jeffery Auer for their editorial advice and encouragement.

We are grateful to Mrs. Salene Borenstein and Miss Cathy Brambley for their assistance in the typing of the manuscript. Our appreciation also goes to Mrs. Leta M. Shattuck and Mrs. Vedia Goodell for their special assistance in the preparation of the manuscript.

To the host of professional colleagues in our own and other institutions who have influenced our thinking, we express our thanks. We have tried to indicate other sources of influence in footnotes and references. We alone are responsible for errors of fact or opinion.

MARTIN P. ANDERSEN
E. RAY NICHOLS, JR.
HERBERT W. BOOTH

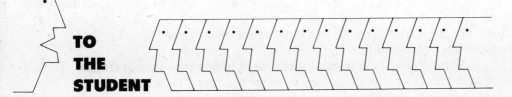

TO THE STUDENT

Students have many different reactions to enrollment in a speech course, from that of a young lady bubbling over from her triumphs in speech activities at her high school who said, "Oh, I just love speech! You know, you just get up and talk and . . ." to that of another, somewhat less gregarious, freshman who felt quite differently: "I can't get up there before all those people. I'd be scared to death!" In between there are many other attitudes toward what is thought of as the traditional speech class.

"Why should I take speech? I'm not going to make public speeches."
"Obviously it's a snap course. All you have to do is get up and talk."

These opinions come from students who may or may not be sure that they have found satisfactory answers to such questions as, "What am I going to do in life?" "How is what I'm doing here going to help me when I'm not sure where I'm going?" "What's this communication jazz all about anyway?"

Whatever your attitude may be, this book has a message for you. It is concerned with you and the student who sits next to you, whether he be your best friend or someone you don't even know. It is concerned with how you get on together. It is concerned with the human beings you are going to meet every step of the way as long as you live on Planet Earth, for your interaction with these people, their ability to communicate with you, your ability to communicate with them, are going to determine to a large extent whether or not you achieve your goals in life.

Some young people suffer because they feel they do not relate well to others. They are nagged by such thoughts as, "Other people get along so easily. They have no trouble talking. They seem to get everything they want. I'm often afraid to speak up, and so I generally go along with my friends, even though I don't believe their ideas are any better than mine." Unfortunately, when we berate ourselves in this manner, we are usually striking out at some void or lack in our personalities, which we are unable to identify and, consequently, are unable to improve. We continue to hold a vague concept that something is wrong with us.

The first purpose of this book, then, is to help you understand yourself and your relationships to other people through the primary functional means of interaction—communication. This understanding will enable you to get your mind off yourself and your supposed inadequacies and focus on the means by which we influence others and they influence us. This focus may also enable you to see that many, if not most, of our limitations are self-imposed. We therefore become vulnerable to the influences of others. After all, this is the name of the game. If you don't influence your friends, they will influence you. Unfortunately, if we do not register our opinions, we place ourselves in the position of being used by the dominant ones, when all we had hoped for was to be liked and respected—a status we can achieve only through the use of our influence.

Another purpose of this book is to help you understand other people. You will learn how to motivate them by changing their attitudes and values and appealing to their needs and desires. You will learn the rhetorical principles employed in bringing about behavioral change. You will learn that it is possible to influence others. Were this not so, American businesses would not spend millions of dollars every year attempting to influence the public. Political polls also testify to the fact that people do change their opinions on both issues and candidates. They change as a result of a number of influences. Each one of us has the potential to be a part of that influence.

Finally, if we are to be part of that influence, we must discover that it is necessary to become mutual problem solvers. This may require that we become more analytical than we have been in the past. It is necessary for us to learn that it is not possible for one person to have his desires fulfilled, at least to some extent, unless this same privilege is granted to others. This means, then, that we need a communicative process by which men solve problems together. Such a system exists and has existed for 2,300 years. It is designed to apply reason rather than force to solving the problems that exist among people. If we accept it, become skilled in using it, we may discover that, whatever our vocation may be, we shall have an approach to solving the social, the humanistic, problems wherever we go or whatever we do.

Actually, then, this book is about the things that you desire and the methods that you can use to influence other people, so that they will view your desires, your achievement, your efficiency, and your sense of values as worth their while, worth their attention, and perhaps even worth their wholehearted acceptance.

A complete understanding of the theory and skill in the practice of effective speech communication ordinarily would require a great deal of time and study. If this is your first course in communication, and if you are to participate in platform speaking situations early in the semester, you will need some help in planning your first speeches. Furthermore, those of you who have already had some training in speaking may wish to review the principles studied previously. Hence, we present a brief overview of the steps you should follow in speech preparation. If your instructor asks you to participate early in the semester in an interview or a discussion, it is suggested that you read Chapter Fifteen, "Communicating in the Interview," or Chapter Sixteen, "Communicating in Discussion Groups." Certain of the suggestions given below are applicable in the interview and discussion.

It is a good idea to follow the steps given below in preparing for any group situation in which you will be speaking. With these steps in speech preparation we conclude our foreword to you.

1. *Analyze the communicative situation.* The initial step in preparing to participate in any speaking situation involves an analysis of the audience and the occasion.

Throughout this book we emphasize the need for starting the preparation for any speaking situation with an analysis of the listening audience, whatever its size. Find out as much as you can about the age, social backgrounds, economic status, educational level, and beliefs and attitudes of your listeners. Discover, if you can, their interest in and attitude toward the subject under consideration and toward you as a speaker. To what extent and in what ways are the listeners involved in and committed to the goals of the speaking situation?

You should next consider the occasion for the communication, be it a speech, interview, or discussion. Consider both the physical setting and the backgrounds of the occasion. Is there a public-address system? If not, will your voice carry to all parts of the room? Is needed equipment available? Will the listeners be comfortable? Do other speakers appear on the program? What is the order of speaking? What is the attitude of the other speakers toward the purpose of the meeting? Does the meeting have immediate and local or far-reaching roots and implications? If you have the answers to these questions and others suggested in Chapter Nine, adaptation to the speaking situation will be easier.

2. *Select the subject of the communication.* We point out in Chapter Ten that the speech subject must be in the area of your expertise, must be related in some way to your capabilities, knowledge, interests, and beliefs. That is, you should usually speak only on those topics on which you have or can get needed information, in which you have a vital interest, and which you can conscientiously defend or attack.

The task of selecting the subject of the communication also should be approached from the point of view of the audience. The subject should be based on or appeal to the listeners' "need-value systems." By this term we refer to the configuration of forces that motivate an individual to action. These forces may be needs, the things which he wants or desires, or values, the standards or norms which guide behavior.

3. *Determine the specific audience response desired.* The speech occasion and the subject largely will determine the specific response you anticipate from your audience. This desired response, in turn, will govern your selection of materials, organizational patterns, speaking style, and manner of delivery. We state in Chapter Three, "The Purpose of Speech Communication," that the objective of all communication is to bring about some behavioral response in listeners. The behavioral change may be overt or covert, it may increase understanding, it may change attitudes and beliefs, and it may take the form of some specific action.

4. *Determine the central idea of the communication.* Once you determine the specific audience response desired, you are ready to prepare the statement of the central idea of your speech. This statement, called the thesis statement, is formulated only after a careful study of the particular audience has been made and after the topic selected has been sufficiently limited and narrowed to one central idea. A thesis statement might be, "The sponsors of the Santa Ana Scout Troop 234 should vote the extra money needed to send the troop on a two-week outing next July." Further treatment of narrowing the subject and formulating the thesis statement is found in Chapter Ten.

5. *Gather needed speech materials.* You are now ready to start the actual preparation for your speech, interview, or discussion. Review and make notes of what you already know about the topic. Then do the necessary study to find additional pertinent material for a comprehensive development of your speech subject or your part in the inter-

view or discussion. Always research your subject in depth. You may wish to scan Chapters Ten, Eleven, Fifteen, and Sixteen in carrying out this step in your preparation.

6. *Plan the organization of your speech.* The organization of the speech, the agenda for an interview, or the outline of the discussion refer to the sequence of major and subordinate points, the amount and type of supporting detail, and the content of the introduction and conclusion.

The introduction contains the statements needed to arouse and hold the listeners' attention, establish the speaker's right to speak, provide a background for what is to follow, and clarify the purpose.

The body of the speech—or interview or discussion—contains the main ideas that develop the thesis. These ideas should be arranged in a clear, orderly, and meaningful sequence. In an interview that is unstructured or in a discussion in which it is not always possible to keep all participants "on the beam" at all times, it may be difficult to follow exactly the sequence planned. Try to stay as close to it as the situation demands.

You should employ ample supporting material, such as testimony, statistics, analogies, and illustrations to develop the main points and the subpoints. Audiovisual aids should be used when pertinent and helpful.

The conclusion should contain a brief restatement of the main ideas of the speech—or the conclusions reached in the interview or discussion—or suggest action to be taken or heighten any emotional state you wish to arouse in your listeners. In a discussion or interview the plans for the next meeting, if any, should always be made before concluding.

The most effective way to be sure you have covered the subject adequately is to make a detailed outline of the speech, a list of possible questions to ask in the interview, or an outline of the discussion content.

Chapters Eleven, Fifteen, and Sixteen offer suggestions for this preparation step.

7. *Consider the style of the speech.* We consider language to be a basic ingredient of the speaker's style. In fact, all that you do verbally and nonverbally when communicating is a part of your style. Style, then, is the whole man communicating.

When considering the element of language, ask yourself questions such as these: "Does the topic call largely for factual material, or should the method be narrative or descriptive?" "What level of language is indicated?" "What degree of formality or informality is required by the occasion?" "To what extent would the use of selected figures of speech contribute to emphasis, heightened emotional states, and understanding?"

We do not recommend that you write out your speech as a means of planning the language to be used. If you do, you are apt to rely too heavily on the written speech during delivery. We do, however, suggest that you think carefully about your use of language, perhaps writing out *brief* parts that are particularly complex, and then practicing aloud, until these passages become a natural part of your presentation.

The concept of style that we present in Chapter Seven suggests that style has many components. Language is one. It also has all those characteristics, qualities, or abilities which make up a speaker's charisma. Ask yourself these questions: "Do I appear to be confident, enthusiastic, and objective?" "Do I identify with, and am I friendly toward, the audience?" "Does my physical action contribute in a positive way to the achievement of my speaking goal?" "Do I have an 'in-depth' understanding of my subject so that I can make adaptations that the occasion may demand?"

In preparing for a discussion there is less that you can do in planning the verbal and nonverbal aspects of communicative style. Try to be courteous in everything you do or say. Use language that is clear, at the level of the group, and generally nontechnical, yet do not avoid figures of speech when they contribute to meaningfulness. Avoid arrogance and indifference in physical manner.

8. *Plan the physical aspects of the presentation.* You must give some consideration to the ways in which you will use your voice and body in delivering a speech or in participating in an interview or discussion. "Does the occasion call for overt physical action?" "Can the objective be achieved in a more unobtrusive manner?" "Should vocal delivery be forceful or quiet?" "How can I adapt physically to the conditions of the meeting room?"

The following guidelines may help in planning the physical aspects of your presentation: (1) be relaxed, yet remain in control of your vocal and bodily action, (2) make your physical action congruent with the speech purpose, the occasion, and the audience's expectations, and (3) do only physical things that contribute to the speech goals, and avoid doing things that may detract.

Chapter Thirteen treats the physical and vocal aspects of delivery.

9. *Rehearse the speech.* A final step is the rehearsal of the speech. If a speech is to be given in the extemporaneous mode (not from manuscript or memorization of a written speech), rehearsing it

does not mean using the same words in each rehearsal. Rehearse by vocalizing the *ideas* and the supporting materials to be presented. You will discover that with each successive oral rehearsal (do not rely on silent rehearsals) the ideas will form themselves into verbal language more easily, even though the words used in successive rehearsals may be quite different.

Be sure to practice the handling of visual aids so that your physical action does not appear ungainly or awkward.

M. P. A.
E. R. N.
H. W. B.

PART ONE

UNDERSTANDING THE COMMUNICATIVE SITUATION

Part One of this text presents the theoretical principles that the student must understand before he can begin his speech preparation. The content identifies the myriads of communicative situations of which he is a part. In succession the text then outlines the purposes of speech communication, explains the nature of the communication transaction as a two-way partnership, shows how the individual listener perceives, thinks, and learns, presents in some detail the ways in which listeners may be motivated, and finally explains the nature of style and listening and how they serve to relate the speaker and listener.

The principles treated in Part One apply to all speaking situations, whether one, several, or many listeners are involved. Although the content is largely theoretical, it is also functional. That is, the discerning student can make immediate application—in his day-to-day relations with other people—of the content presented. This section is functional in still another way. It helps the student understand both himself and his listeners. In many speaking situations—perhaps the majority in which any person participates—the individual is alternately a speaker and a listener. Therefore, every potential speaker must know how he performs in a communicative situation, whether he be a sender or a receiver.

Every chapter in Part One treats the subject matter in depth. The content is based on traditionally oriented rhetoric as well as on recent findings of the behavioral sciences. Part One gives the reader a thorough grounding in the psychology of speech communication.

CHAPTER ONE
HOW COMMUNICATION SERVES THE INDIVIDUAL

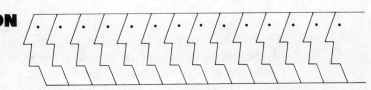

*Speech is the great instrument
by which man becomes beneficial to man.*
　　　Hugh Blair

Communication is the supreme relationship among people who, by the very nature of living, are forced to solve problems together. It is supreme because in every social act the bonding element of communication makes a relationship satisfactory or unsatisfactory.

What is this process which affects all humans so significantly? We define it as *the purposeful, transactional process by which one person, through the use of audible and visible symbols, engenders meanings in the minds of his listeners.*

THE SIGNIFICANCE OF COMMUNICATION

In the nuclear age nations are faced with a problem that has never existed before: surprise attack and retaliation so devastating that civilization could be destroyed. To make this catastrophic exchange as remote as possible, the President of the United States and the Premier of Russia are linked by the "hot line," to be used in cases of extreme urgency, in which a successful communication is the difference between human survival and holocaust. Although this particular communication line is vital to every one of us, it still may seem somewhat remote to all but the President and the Premier, who are chained to it.

We may never have thought of it in this fashion, but each of us has numerous little hot lines that may be brought into play in specific emergencies—emergencies that might not have arisen had it not been for the inadequacy of our routine efforts to communicate. We operate these lines at times successfully and at times unsuccessfully. Occasionally they are short-circuited altogether, and a precipitate action takes place instead of a communication that might have solved the problem.

You or some of your school friends may have experienced some of these successes or failures in communication. For example, when you *did* get your instructor to raise a grade, when you were assigned to an adviser who *took time* to "advise" and with whom you could talk about mutual interests, when you convinced your parents that you really did not want to take over the family business as your life's career, or when you and your girl decided that you could make out financially and your lives would be happier if you married even though you hadn't finished school. Or perhaps—because of breakdowns in communication—in the instances cited above none of the responses you sought were achieved.

Consider some other situations in which communication failed.

Probation officers at juvenile reception centers in counties all over America would not be returning runaway children under duress to their parents in faraway places if communication breakdowns had not occurred long before the child ran away. Their leaving illustrates a precipitate action taken when the hot line either could not be put into effect or failed.

The use of drugs by juveniles and adults in both civilian and military areas presents a ready-made example of how failure to communicate at the rational level can contribute partly to a serious national problem. Our culture has long since reached the point at which many adults govern their activities through the use of drugs of one kind or another: vitamins for energy, barbiturates for sleep, amphetamines for stimulation, tranquilizers for relaxation—some under prescription, some not. Many children who have observed this process and have resorted to "uppers" or "downers" themselves have frequently received little meaningful help from adults, although in recent years school, church, and parents are beginning to recognize the need to understand and to take action to prevent or remedy some of the problems facing young people. Communication that has failed has underlined the need for effective interaction, as in city after city volunteer and professional groups, civic agencies, and individuals have set up emergency hot lines for both children and adults who need immediate help on some personal problem. Where communication has been reciprocal, both within and among groups, there is some likelihood that the results of the communication will be positive.

On the other hand, in some situations no communication has occurred, and disaster has resulted, or communication has been primarily one-way, the voices of the opposition, loyal or not, having been ignored, stifled, or treated as irrelevant. Consider the following situations, which have had broad repercussions. During the late 1960s and early 1970s a number of colleges were closed down, temporarily at least. Many college buildings, including ROTC offices, were burned. Numerous branches of "establishment" businesses, including the Bank of America, were bombed. Marchers chanting "Burn, baby, burn!" have been stimulated to violence. On many campuses violent confrontations between students—in most instances the minority—and the college administration or the police have resulted in deaths, property damage, and increased emotional rancor. In many of these instances communication was, in a sense, effective; however, the vigorous or weak voices of nonviolence did not become a part of the chain of communication, which should have avoided the precipitate action.

Although some of the illustrations presented above may not specifically relate to you, it might be well to realize that the communicative transactions that you accumulate each day, each week, and each month, run into the thousands. They determine how you will satisfy your everyday physical needs and make important and complex decisions such as where you will go to college, what professional objectives you will develop, how you will get the courses you need, and whether or not you will make friends with your professors and fellow students. Beyond your campus life they will determine the nature of your family relationships, the candidates you will vote for, the attitudes you will develop toward such things as religion, marriage, and the importance of money in your life.

The instances cited above indicate specific situations in which communication affects your life. You should be a skilled communicator, so that the single hot lines or the communication networks of which you are a part are employed in a mutually beneficial way for the participants in the communicative transaction.

Because we wish you to share with us a recognition of the significance of speech communication in the conduct of human affairs before looking at the ways it serves you as an individual, we wish to comment on some of the general characteristics of communication.

There are many positive facets of communication that are not immediately apparent but are significant and should be commonly understood.

Communication is a "time binding" tool; through it historians, anthropologists, and archeologists bring to us facts about past cultures and predict our future. Because of recent developments in scientific technology and theory, human engineering (exemplified by cybernetics and mass-motivation research), linguistics, psychological conceptualizations, content analysis, and learning theory, the field of communication is now recognized as a highly useful scientific tool. Improved methods of data processing, the contributions of field and perceptual psychology to interpersonal training techniques, propaganda analysis, and what has been almost an explosion in research in communication as a behavioral science, all bear witness to the increasing use of communication as a scientific methodology.

Despite some negative instances the influence of communication as a democratic decision-making tool is growing. This is evident in the successes of the Women's Liberation movement, new voting privileges for young people, and the slow gains in civil rights in meeting minority-group needs.

Communication is the main artery in the life stream of business and industry. The stock market, wage negotiations, price fixing, the internal administrative efficiency of any given business, the development of productive work teams, meeting sales quotas, and effective public relations, all depend largely on communicative processes.

Finally, communication at the level of the mass media is mainly responsible for the wide and almost instantaneous expansion of knowledge today. The increase in knowledge and the modern mass media combine to make each individual truly a citizen of the world.

Our point of view is aptly summed up in these words:[1]

Speech communication is man's most significant behavior and constitutes the basis of social interaction. A failure to understand its significance and to seek effective development of the processes may inhibit the viability of our society—a frightening, complex society of both technological advances and social disorder.

THE NEED FOR THE STUDY OF COMMUNICATION

If you are not already convinced that speech communication plays an important role in the conduct of the social, political, and vocational affairs of all humans, let us direct our attention briefly to the matter of your need to study communication.

To make adjustments in life's developmental tasks—learning a language and adjusting to a family situation, adapting to the norms of peer groups as a youth and young adult, assuming the responsibilities of adulthood, and making the necessary life changes as a senior citizen— one must develop a flexible personality of many dimensions. One of these dimensions is your communicative ability.

It is the purpose of this book to assist you in establishing your communicative identity and abilities: first, by enabling you to perceive yourself as a communicator and respondent within the circle of your close relationships, such as your family and friends, and by giving you a means of analyzing how well you are meeting the demands of the communicative process, and, second, by helping you understand the importance of your voice in solving the issues of our time.

Man can survive and, in the process, nurture his environment and his fellow human beings only to the extent that he is able to initiate and sustain effective communication. Man has organized a society in which the individual must respond almost immediately, not only to the urgent messages within his own family, neighborhood, or city, but to divergent and important messages originating at any point on the earth.

Ruesch and Bateson have emphasized man's need in the field of communication as follows:[2]

The human being's need for social action is the moving force which compels him to master the tools of communication. Without these his ability to gather information is imperiled and gratification of needs is threatened. The superiority of a person within his group is determined in the first instance by skillful use of his means of communication; to receive information and to give that which others need, to possess a workable concept of events, and to act accordingly, marks the successful man.

This precise statement of our need and our goal forces us to examine our responsibility for successful communication. Our medium for the most part is speech with its accompanying patterns of visual and auditory signals. Our problem is understanding the complex nature of a successful message transaction. Our goal is to interact creatively with others, not only to receive the immediate rewards of this contact, but in the long run to encourage the self-development that continually emerges from the process.

Most of us have observed in numerous instances the malfunctioning of the speech communication process. The range of this malfunctioning is tremendous. It lies at the root of many failures in our most desired relationships—with our friends, our families, our business associates. To assume that the deficiencies in a process as complicated as communication can be solved by amateur methods of constructing "in" vocabularies for "in" groups, by a sprinkling of four-letter words, by insisting that we "tell it like it is," or by taking refuge in the inviolability of a so-called "generation gap" is to fail to understand the real significance of communication.

The twin problems of lack of understanding and lack of skill in communication are not new. Rhetoricians were struggling with them long before Aristotle provided the first systematic treatise on rhetoric. Generation after generation has contributed to our knowledge of communication, and such names as Cicero, Quintilian, St. Augustine, Francis Bacon, George Campbell, Richard Whately, and James Winans, among others, have made significant contributions.

We are fortunate, therefore, as we face the communication explosion of our times, that systems of rhetoric not only exist but continue to be the subject of extensive experimental and field research.

It is beyond the scope of this textbook to review the specific theories of the classical rhetoricians. However, selected traditional conceptualizations should be mentioned briefly for three reasons: they are basic to the content of this text, and they suggest emphatically the need to study communication.

First, we study communication to learn about the respondents. Aristotle's *Rhetoric* consists of three books, of which Book II deals primarily with the audience. He believed that the audience determines the speech's goal, that the speaker should learn how emotions of the audience can be evoked, and that the speaker-audience relationship was important. We too believe that your study of communication will help you understand and adapt to the people who are at the other end of your hot lines of communication.

Second, we study communication to learn about the various aspects of speech preparation and presentation. They are essentially the five canons of rhetoric: invention (subject matter), disposition (arrangement), style, memory, and delivery. They have been treated by Plato, Aristotle, Quintilian, Whately, Winans, and others.

Third, we study communication to become better critics of our own speaking and that of others.

Diligent study of the theory and practice of communication will increase the number of successful message transactions and decrease the number of failures. We ask you to make the effort.

THE TRANSACTIONAL NATURE OF COMMUNICATION

In Chapter Four we will study in detail the nature of the communication process. At this point we need to look at one dimension of communication, namely that it is a transactional relationship. As we view the speaker and his audience, recognizing that he performs not only in formal platform situations but also in small groups, we must realize that he alternates as communicator and respondent. He plays the roles of speaker and listener at both intra- and interpersonal levels. Understanding the communicative transaction, therefore, is a key to success in relating to others.

Because we sometimes do not understand the nature of speech communication and forget that the gift of speech must be nurtured, we frequently use it shamefully, frequently without wisdom, without beauty, without friendliness, and without awareness or sensitivity to the needs of our partner in communication.

The decisive factor in effective communication is audience orientation. This is a crucial point, since the result of speaking always occurs in the listener. Successful communicators, in conversation or on the platform, are audience-oriented. They perceive communication as a tool for involving listeners in a mutually satisfying interaction. The student leader will assure his success by demonstrating his interest in the needs and desires of his fellow students.

John F. Kennedy knew that listeners like the opportunity to participate, to become partners in solving perplexing national problems. He appealed to this desire when he issued his challenge: "And so, my fellow Americans, ask not what your country can do for you; ask what you can do for your country."

Martin Luther King is remembered for his great dream, projected not only to his own people but to all races and sects:[3]

When we allow freedom to ring, when we let it ring from every village and every hamlet, from every state and every city, we will be able to speed up that day when all of God's children, black men and white men, Jews and Gentiles, Protestants and Catholics, will be able to join hands and sing in the words of the old Negro spiritual, "Free at last, thank God Almighty, we are free at last!"

Such speakers were audience-oriented communicators. The imagery of their language, the personal quality of their illustrations, with which their listeners could identify, and the congruity of their appeals with the needs and values of the audience, reflect the communicators' thorough understanding of the speaker-audience transaction.

As you become aware of some of the blocks to effective communication, you will recognize that the mere utterance of words does not necessarily establish in the minds of your listeners the reality and values that those words represent to you. Each person has his own way of viewing the world. You will soon appreciate the symbolic nature of communication and the need to adapt your speech to the perceptions of individual audiences.

THE VALUES OF COMMUNICATION TO THE INDIVIDUAL

We have now seen that communication is a means of keeping the lines of interaction open among individuals, that the study of communication will enable you to play your roles as speaker and respondent more effectively, and that, whatever role you play, it is as a partner in a transactional relationship. We now consider three general values of effective communication to the individual: it is essential in the processes of learning and thinking, it is the primary means of influencing others, and it aids in personal adjustment. Without communication these processes would be impossible.

As a Basis of Learning and Thinking

Speech communication—language in oral form—is a form of discourse that serves as the essential medium of exchange of ideas in all vocational activities and academic disciplines. This is so even in areas containing special symbol systems of their own, such as mathematics, music, and logic. However, regardless of the subject area involved, speech is a necessary tool in the transmission of knowledge. This fact makes communication the keystone in the processes of learning and thinking.

Learning and thinking are closely related processes. Learning is generally defined as the process that results in a change in the person's behavior, as a result either of past experience or of practice. Thus, when we learn, we adjust to our environment. This is essentially the point of view of John Dewey who, in one of his major theoretical contributions to education, describes learning as problem-solving, or making discriminations that result in either success or failure in achieving desired goals.[4] Ruesch and Bateson make essentially the same point when they say,[5] "The individual is said to have learned when discriminating reactions as well as anticipation of events indicate mastery of self and surroundings."

We make these discriminating reactions in part, at least, through the process of thinking, which psychologist Ruch describes as "using symbols to manipulate implicitly ideas or objects not physically present to the senses."[6] What we think about is said to be representative of previous experiences, so that we may think—use language symbols silently—about what we have learned in the past.

What we learn or think about may be divided into four general categories:

1. Concepts that are abstract and therefore can be learned in part only through a set of symbols.
2. Interrelationships with people that depend upon the perception and interpretation of meanings partially conveyed through a symbol system.
3. The development of skills acquired in part through language conceptualizations.
4. The discovery of new insights that result from the ability to combine conceptualizations and skills—usually referred to as creativity.

The Development of Concepts

When we use the word *concept* we refer to the name of a class of objects or of some property that objects have in common. Thus, we speak of the concepts "house" or "split-level," "apple" or "red," "demonstration" or "nonviolent," and "examination" or "midterm." We develop these concepts because repeated experiences establish within our minds some common property that many objects have in common.

To illustrate the role that communication, or symbolic language, has in the development of concepts, let us examine a concept having both a reasonably concrete aspect and a high level of abstraction. The concept "depth" may be acquired in the first place only through actual experience with objects that have depth: a jewel box, a wading pool, a cistern, or the Grand Canyon. The concept of depth may be understood readily in a frame of reference of common measures or measuring tools. Before diving one might ask "What is the depth of the water?" and easily resolve the question.

Not only can the word *depth* involve us in the use of accurate measuring instruments, it can also take us into the world of abstraction when someone remarks, "I wonder what the real depth of his feeling is in this matter." Man has not yet come up with a satisfactory means of measuring or communicating depth at the abstract level. He can measure in a rather clumsy fashion. He can detect an area of shallowness by observing another person whose actions or words reveal little "depth."

Obviously, the more concrete the concept, the more likely it is that we can measure and talk about it accurately. But whether concrete or abstract, a symbol system is required for the process either of learning or of thinking.

We can make the role of communication in concept formation and perception more apparent by examining the nature of speech development in the child. Speech in the normal child develops at an early age and is a tool of learning throughout life. Through trial and error, conditioning, rote memory, and actual sensory experiences the child continues to learn language and speech and how communication helps him to meet his needs. He learns that words "stand for" things, events, persons, or their attributes, such as *food, father, toy,* and *hot.* This is the beginning of his concept formation. As he begins to see relationships in terms of his own experience, he starts to form concepts. These concepts are expressed in language symbols. Langer states:[7]

Language always expresses relations among acts or things, or their aspects. It always makes reference to reality—that is, makes assertions or denials—either explicitly or implicitly . . . But no language consists of signs that only call attention to things without saying anything about them—that is, without asserting or denying something.

It might be added that, as the child matures, the store of concepts and language symbols grows. The symbols and the way in which he uses them are the principal means by which all later thinking and learning takes place.

The relationship between thinking and learning and speech may be indicated in the following way. Thinking stems from some inner need to resolve a problem; learning is the resultant adjustment. The materials with which thinking deals are symbols, mostly verbal ones. A person comprehends meanings or resolves problems by ordering these symbols in some sequential and functional pattern.

Precision in thinking depends on exactness in speaking; conversely, skill in speech is a function of proficiency in thought.

Again, Langer points out,[7] image making depends upon a brain capable of receiving countless stimuli from many threshholds, which must be dealt with at Operation Central—the brain. There are too many, even, to store. Of those which are placed in the Memory Bank, many will never come out again, but the brain as an organism has dealt in some fashion with all the stimuli, and a few have been tabulated as sufficiently urgent in meaning for our symbol system to be activated and a communication to be undertaken for the purpose of making some adjustment in the organism or its environment.

The adjustments the individual makes depend largely upon the quality and quantity of the language symbols and concepts stored in his brain. The level of his conceptualizations in turn reflect the quality of the language used by the persons responsible for the individual's early speech training. To a large extent the communicative abilities of a child in the formative years of his life are a function of his interactions in his primary groups, chiefly the family.

The lessons of our own experience, the examination of the development of speech and thought in the child, and the testimony of modern and eminent psychologists and anthropologists force us to the conclusion that speech and thought are inescapably interrelated.

Interpersonal Relationships

Having explored the learning-thinking process as it relates to concepts, we may see that our second category depends upon the ability of one person to communicate a concept to another. To do so, the communicator must use a symbol system as a bridge to the respondent. The bridge will be meaningless unless both communicator and respondent view the symbol in similar fashions.

How is this accomplished? To answer this question it is necessary to understand that communication takes place at two levels: the *denotative level*, or the level of literal content, and the *metacommunicative level*, or the level where additional, but meaningful information is provided and received. *Metacommunication* means messages about messages.[8] As we have previously indicated, each message has a purpose. It is designed to adjust the environment so as to bring it more in keeping with the needs and desires of the communicator. The communicator needs to assure himself that the respondent will understand his intention. Conversely, the respondent needs to assure himself that he understands the communicator's intention. When the message and the meta-communication about the message are dissonant in some respect—in conflict, inconsistent, or at variance—then confusion, misunderstanding, or an undesired response or interaction may result.

Let us illustrate how communication at both those levels affects relationships between people. Let us say that a husband and his wife are sitting in the living room watching a television program. Suddenly the husband exclaims "It's too hot in here!" The wife may agree or disagree, for she will have her own sensory image of whether the room is hot or cold. If she agrees, there is still the question of what her husband intended by the remark. Was it made to suggest that she get up and open a window? Turn on the air conditioner? Bring him a bottle of beer from the refrigerator?

The only conceivable way she can determine how he wished to affect the environment is through her ability to assimilate and evaluate what we have called metacommunication. Thus it will be necessary for her to ask herself what kind of intonation accompanied her husband's statement. Perhaps he said it in a fashion indicating that he recognized a hopeless situation: everything had already been done that could be done to cool the room. Then he is merely recognizing a state of affairs and hopes for agreement; this means, if she interprets him correctly, that she needs only to respond affirmatively, to share his feeling. If, on the other hand, he speaks with some irritation about the heat in the room, and they both know that the solution is that one of them get up and turn on the air conditioner, then the respondent probably will recognize, perhaps with irritation, that her husband wishes her to get up and turn the knob.

It should be clear that meaning is only partially established by the symbol system. Without messages about messages we are unable to make the finer discriminations that illuminate the communicator's real intent.

Metacommunication, however, cannot wholly fill in the mortar between the bricks of a message. A frame of reference must also be established. This frame of reference will depend on previous relationships, understandings, and perceptions that contribute to further extensions of meaning.

For instance, if, in the example above, there had already been a discussion of the temperature in the room, and the wife had taken the position that it was not hot but actually a little too cool for her comfort, a frame of reference would have been established that would have affected all further messages. Thus the respondent might have reacted in a fashion in keeping with the previous context: "Why don't you take your coat off?" or "All right, I'll go get a sweater."

Whatever may have been the outcome of the situation we have described, it would always be a function of all aspects of the total communicative situation. When we consider that attitudes, beliefs, and feelings—all of which have an effect on our relationships with people— are developed through a process as imprecise as much human communication is bound to be, there should be little wonder about some of the results. If we are to improve our communications and resulting relations with other people, we must fully understand the importance of the message content, metacommunication, the frame of reference, and the level of abstraction (a topic that will be examined later).

The Development of Skills

Although language symbols are essential in almost all types of learning, the extent to which they are involved in the learning of skills depends upon the particular occupation of the individual. A relatively small amount of oral instruction is needed to acquire many vocational skills, practice being more essential. Even here, however, the worker must be able to communicate to others about his trade.

The point was made by Mr. Paxton Blair, former justice of the Supreme Court of New York, in a speech to the New York State Bar Association, dealing with needed improvements in our educational system:[9]

I should advise that recipients of vocational training be required to submit to some instruction in the use of language. Nothing is more pitiful to hear than a competent workman who has discovered what is wrong with the article of yours he's working on . . . but who is unable to describe to you what the matter is. Viewing the workman in another environment, we may observe concerning him that one of the most effective ways of securing advancement is to show his employer that he can express himself well, can formulate a set of instructions clearly and understandably and can in consequence be safely entrusted with a position of responsibility above his fellows.

In some professions, too, as in many of the arts, manual dexterity is essential, and here learning may be a matter both of physical development and of language skill. Whatever the skill may be, even though practice is of primary importance, its development relies to some extent upon the ability of the learner to interpret his language-symbol system.

As a Basis of Influencing People

As modern life becomes more complex, we as individuals become less the masters of our fate. We depend upon others to fulfill most of the needs of our daily lives, and it is mainly through speech that these needs are expressed.

In college your skill in oral communication may determine the results of a job interview, the outcome of a campus election, grades in courses, and acceptance in social groups. In later life the need to use speech to influence others may be even greater. Communication is a means of gaining acceptance in professional groups, of solving family problems, and of counseling others in personal decisions. Political affairs are conducted largely through oral communication: candidates seek the support of voters, pressure groups seek to influence legislators, and legislators seek to sway their colleagues and impress their constituents. In business and industry the ability to lead others through speech is of top importance. In almost every occupational group some skill in effective persuasion is essential. In a democratic society persuasive speaking is a necessity: minority views must be supported, differing views clarified, the majority viewpoint endorsed, accused persons permitted to present their defense, and special-interest groups given a hearing. These are proper functions of persuasive speech.

We must, however, keep the use of persuasion within ethical bounds. The admonition of Quintilian still holds true: the orator is the *good* man trained in speaking. Persuasion that is not completely ethical is found in many walks of life. Advertising in business is frequently found to be misleading or inaccurate.[10] Leaders of some religious groups have used speech for personal gain. In politics we still have demagogues and rabble rousers. Pharmaceutical quacks have gained notoriety and wealth through television and radio. A few labor leaders have built great personal power through persuasive skill and strong-arm methods.

Emphasizing the concept of social responsibility in influencing others, Mr. Virgil L. Baker, chairman of the Department of Speech at the University of Arkansas, made this positive statement:

Democracy not only implies freedom of speech, but it also implies moral and ethical responsibility. Under a democratic system, the individual must work not alone for his own best interests, but must work also for the best interests of all. The public speaker in a democracy is a public servant.[11]

As a Basis of Personal Adjustment and Therapy

As we have already shown, speech is the primary means by which the individual adjusts to the group and through which the group exerts its influence on the individual. Speech communication further serves the individual as a means of personal adjustment and, in some cases, of needed therapy.

A child engages in a great deal of imitative activity in which he takes on—plays—the roles of persons with whom he comes in contact. From this "reflexive" activity (one in which the individual is an object to himself) the child gains a myriad of symbolic self-perceptions. He sees himself as "good," "brave," "shy," "unwanted," "powerful," and so forth. Gradually his self-perceptions become organized into patterns that establish more or less permanent ways of looking at himself throughout life. In the words of Combs and Snygg:[12]

The development of language and the ability to communicate by means of words opens new frontiers of experience. Language makes it possible to experience vicariously what would otherwise have to be experienced slowly and painfully. It even makes possible experiences one could never otherwise have. . . . Language provides a "shorthand" by which experience can be symbolized, manipulated, and understood with tremendous efficiency. Above all, the possession of language vastly facilitates the differentiation of self and the world about.

The verbal experience that the individual has as he develops to maturity and out of which his perception of self largely arises is the major determinant of his skill in adapting his personality to life's situations. If his verbal experiences have given him a feeling of adequacy and have been varied, he usually will have the capacity for acceptance of self and of others. On the other hand, if his verbal experiences have been limited or unrealistic or have developed self-perceptions of inadequacy, his adjustment to others becomes difficult or is not made at all.

Once we have acquired the basic skills of speech and our self-perceptions have become fairly clear, speech enables us both to modify our interpersonal situations and to adapt our personalities to them.

Consider some of the situations that may challenge your skill in adjustment through speech: a sorority rushing party, a counseling session with a twelve-year-old at a scout camp, an oral examination, or an appearance before a traffic court. Some situations call for little skill in speaking; others demand that you draw on every aspect of verbal proficiency. There are times when speech serves merely as "phatic communion," described by Bronislaw Malinowski as speech in which bonds of social communion are created by a mere exchange of words. "How are you?", "How is the family?", and "How was the trip?" are often asked without the expectation of a detailed or literal reply; rather, they are verbal contributions to a situation in which tradition and courtesy require some exchange of *oral* pleasantries.

Not only does speech serve as a medium for the development of personal adjustment, but it has long been essential in the fields of therapy and counseling. The primary tools and techniques of clinical psychologists, psychiatrists, and counselors are forms of oral exchange. The "nondirective counseling" technique is a process of *verbal* interchange. In the Rorschach ink-blot test an individual is required to *tell* what he sees in the ink blots. Word association tests require the counselee to make instant *oral* or written reactions to selected lists of words. In "free association" tests, which require oral reactions in nondirective situations, patients are urged to *talk freely* about whatever comes to mind. In each instance what the individual says as he responds to the test provides clues to his personality structure.

Overstreet and Overstreet describe the relationship between emotional distress and speech:[13]

Any acute emotional disturbance, whether temporary or chronic, has some effect on the speech of the person who suffers it; some effect on what he says and how he says it. We all know this from experience. We know that when we are frightened or nervous or suddenly angry, it pays for us to watch our words; and even if we watch them they may betray us, so intimate is the tie-up between feeling and speech.

Minor forms of maladjustment tend to reveal themselves orally through such symptoms as criticism of others, self-pity, excuses, contradictions, bragging, denials, defense of personal failures, and "slips of the tongue."

Persons for whom society has no meaning—those with serious mental and emotional disturbances—build through their own symbolic systems tight little universes from which unacceptable relationships are excluded. Not all who are afflicted in this fashion are in mental hospitals: some are in prisons, but others are still spinning the web of exclusion that will isolate them from meaningful communicative transactions so that they must be rescued ultimately by a psychiatrist or be doomed to face society's inclination to incarcerate the unmanageable. How do such conditions arise? Maltz says:[14]

Many doctors believe that "confusion" is the basic element in neurosis. To deal effectively with a problem, you must have some understanding of its true nature. Most of our failures in human relations are due to "misunderstandings."

We expect other people to react and respond and come to the same conclusions as we do from a given set of "facts" or "circumstances." No one reacts to "things as they are," but to his own mental images.

In part parents contribute to the development of either normal or pathological behavior in their children through their speech as well as through their actions. They may exert too much or too little control or set standards of achievement far beyond the ability of their child, or they may fail to provide adequate challenge. They may hold personal values at variance with accepted norms, or they may create a total family behavioral configuration that prevents the development of such normal personality traits as self-reliance, responsiveness, flexibility, sensitivity, and confidence in the stability of others' actions; on the other hand, they may create a family atmosphere in which sound mental and emotional health can develop.

Besides being used in therapy, in counseling, and in creating the essential conditions for healthy day-to-day living in the home, speech is used in many other situations to ensure effective adjustment to the realities of living. The "leaderless discussion group" is now used extensively as a method of research and group interviewing. "Role playing" and "psychodrama" are used for training, for therapy, for improving large-group communication, for stimulating discussion, and for improving interpersonal relations skills. The "confessional" is as old as the Christian Church. The basic premise in all these techniques is that "talking it through" can serve as an aid in personal therapy.

THE INDIVIDUAL AS COMMUNICATOR AND RESPONDENT
Having observed some of the values obtained through the communication process, let us resume our analysis of your role as sender and receiver. To begin with, you are the center of a number of communication networks.

Identifying Respondents in Communication Networks
In each network you are connected to several respondents. Some may be your family—brothers, sisters, mother, father, aunt, uncle—any relatives with whom you are closely associated. Others, almost as intimate, may be close friends, associates in school, influential teachers, and respected doctors and clergymen. Others, in a much more loosely fashioned part of the network, may be casual acquaintances, such as a service-station operator, a checker at the supermarket, a parking attendant, a switchboard operator, a waitress in a restaurant. Still others may be an employer, a supervisor, fellow workers, and subordinates.

For a given individual there will be variants or intermixtures of the network parts described. Whatever the case, you must view yourself as both a communicator and a respondent in these nets. You must also accept the fact that messages are transacted between other members of the net, some of which involve you, although the members may not contact you. The full recognition of this fact as natural in any network is important to the stability of every person.

You will soon recognize that in these nets are people with whom you do not associate well and others with whom you associate very well. If you examine these situations more analytically, you will discover some of the signs, the clues to your success in some channels and your ineffectiveness in others.

The Messages Exchanged

In a later chapter we shall consider in detail the general and specific purposes for which people exchange messages. We shall discover that message contents are as numerous as the reasons that people interact. Messages may be related to people's needs, attitudes, beliefs, or experiences. Some messages are exploratory in nature; others are informative, narrative, descriptive, or imperative. Sometimes messages contain expressions of praise, commendation, blame, acrimony, vituperation, or hatred. At times the content of a message is clear and focused; at other times the meaning is unclear and diffusive. A message may be brief or long, continuous or not. What is said may be unifying or divisive, appropriate or inappropriate, well-timed or poorly timed. The messages we send and receive in the nets of which we are a part have many qualities. However, there are a few characteristics that all messages have in common. We shall now look at a selected number of these characteristics.

Characteristics of Verbal Messages

We may use some of the external characteristics of oral communication as guidelines in analyzing our proficiency as communicators and respondents, but first we need to know how to identify message units. Although the unit of sound has been established as the phoneme, and the unit of language has been established as the word, no one, despite the number of communication models that have been drawn, has yet made more than a tentative formulation of the boundaries of a verbal message.[15] Does it begin when I, the source, become slightly aware of the desire or need to formulate a message? Or when I turn to a respondent and make clear to him through various bodily movements and facial expressions that I have a message to deliver? Or when I open my mouth to speak? Or when the respondent gets some indication of the meaning of my message?

Because of the intricacy of the many stages and aspects involved in the formulation and transmission of the message we refer the student to Chapter Four, where he will be able to study more in depth the models of the communication cycle. For our purposes we arbitrarily define a message unit as including the inception of the message in the speaker's mind, its presentation, and the assimilation of the feedback pertaining to it. With this definition we proceed to the identification and explanation of four selected characteristics of verbal messages.

Frequency

The frequency of exchanges is the number of verbal exchanges necessary to complete a given communicative act. A topic may be handled adequately with a minimal number of message units, and a transaction may then be completed, but the reverse is also possible. The extremes in frequency of exchange are found in the two contrasting situations: an accepted group leader often may get desired action by a single, meaningful message, but in another group the leader who proposes action new to a group or contrary to its current wishes may have to repeat his message often before it is accepted and acted upon.

Intensity

The intensity of a verbal message indicates the importance that you or your respondent places upon the message. This is a judgment that will depend upon the acute perception of both parties in reading a number of both visual and vocal cues. It will be noted, of course, that there is not always agreement on the importance of the message.

Duration

The duration of a message is the length of time it takes to complete a verbal message unit as defined above. Although a transaction may be completed in one unit, usually there are a number of units in each transaction. When the feedback accumulates to such a point that it becomes verbal response, a reciprocal, or new, message unit has begun. The message transaction, however, does not terminate until it has been completed, until the intent of the communicator has been realized or exhausted.

Subject Matter

The subject matter is the topic of the communicative act. A given topic may be handled with a minimal number of message units, and a transaction may then be completed. However, the reverse is also possible. A large number of subjects may be covered without a transaction's being completed on any of them. Hence, in speaking it is desirable to limit the number of subject-matter message units to those which pertain to a given transaction only. That is, try to keep on the subject. In evaluating the content of your messages it will be helpful to separate those message units which relate to a specific topic from others which were merely a digression or which related to another transaction.

The Outcomes of Communicative Exchange

In the assessment of outcomes you will understand that it will be necessary to restrict your analysis to message units and transactions with one person bearing on one topic. The outcomes must always be related to your specific purpose and may be evaluated on such a scale as shown in the accompanying diagram.

The characteristics of verbal messages we have listed may be used to analyze the message units involved in the transmission. Frequency and duration tell you a lot about who has dominated a given conversation. Intensity suggests the amount of emotional involvement. Subject matter enables you to sort the messages that relate to the prime purpose.

THE MUTUAL EFFECTS OF COMMUNICATION ON PARTICIPANTS

As a result of your analysis of these factors you might discover whether you said too much, whether your message units were too repetitious, whether you became too emotional, whether you allowed yourself too much digression, or whether you failed adequately to interpret feedback and respond to it. By exploring a number of communicative acts you can learn a great deal about yourself, both as source and respondent. How many orders, requests, demands did you initiate? How often was your intent fulfilled? How many times were demands made of you? How fully did you resolve them? How often did you brush them off, procrastinate, or simply refuse?

Through our communication, verbal and nonverbal, we are continually affecting others and being affected. Those with whom we associate most we affect the most. We analyze them, we assume them to be predictable, we take them for granted, we disagree, we invent devious methods of getting our own way—all of this we do and at the same time rarely accept the fact that our obstinate friend, wife, husband, father, or daughter is in part that way because we affected him. The reverse is also true. Each one of us is affected in the same way and often without much conscious recognition of the process. Once we recognize fully that a joint partnership exists in matters of communication—that we are continually affecting each other—the sooner it is possible for us to make the adjustments that help to solve problems and prevent the kind of dangerous personal isolation we discussed before.

The Personal Nature of Perceptions

Popular as the concept may be that one ought to "tell it like it is," no person can tell it except as he perceives it. The assumed objectivity or honesty of "telling it like it is" turns out to be a myth:[16]

You act, and feel, not according to what things are really like, but according to the image your mind holds of what they are like. You have certain mental images of yourself, your world, and the people around you, and you behave as though these images were the truth, the reality, rather than the things they represent.

We must recognize that not all children raised in comfortable homes necessarily perceive their status as their parents might wish them to, just as we must realize that not all children raised in a ghetto perceive their environment in the same ways, that some might like to improve it and some simply like to get out of it. If we are to communicate, then, with any degree of satisfaction, we must fully appreciate the personal nature of mutual perceptions.

The Personal Nature of Purpose

We are confronted even more fully with the concept of personalization when we attempt to assess someone else's purpose. A communicative transaction may or may not reveal the purpose of either the source or the respondent. If it does reveal a purpose, we next ask, "Is this the *real* purpose?" We cannot assume that a purpose is always candidly stated. It may be difficult to understand the intensity of another person's plea if he has a strong hidden purpose.

It is hardly wise to assume that unrevealed motives indicate dishonesty. Often in the given circumstance the motivations are sufficiently complex to make it fruitless to try explaining them. We may therefore be faced with judging whether we can comfortably accept the stated purpose at face value.

Assessment of purpose also depends upon our image of the other person. If he has done nothing to cause us to distrust his motives, we will have little reason not to accept his message. If, on the other hand, we always question his motives, we are likely to find ourselves demanding a further statement of purpose, thinking, "This time I'm going to pin him down"—futile as that may be.

Knowledge of purpose is basic to the understanding of a communication. However, as we have just pointed out, purpose is not always obvious. We can only be reasonably certain of it when other visual and audible factors seem to be consistent with it.

The Reciprocal Assessment of Ethos

The term *ethos* is used here to refer to the configuration of factors that establish the speaker's *credibility*. By using this term we mean to indicate that a receiver evaluates the source as he perceives the source's authority and character. If the receiver's perception is positive, the source has credibility for the receiver. Since we are viewing the communicator and respondent as operating reciprocally, we may extend our perception of ethos to include either party.

Traditionally ethos has been considered the speaker's trustworthiness, expertness, and good will. Recent empirical studies tend to confirm the first two items. In some studies the dynamism of the speaker has been substituted for the Aristotelian concept of good will.

The communicator wants to know how he is being received, and the respondent wants to know whether the communicator's apparent intent is in accord with his ethos. Therefore, a reciprocal scrutinization is going on. Our assessment of this situation will be aided if we analyze both communicator and respondent on the basis of relative status and position, emotional states, and clarity of reasoning. These subjects are separately discussed in the following paragraphs.

Relative Status and Position

Implicit in the communicative situation are each person's views of status and position, whether it be father talking to son, employee to boss, teacher to student, or student to student. This relationship will, perhaps, not be viewed in the same fashion by both parties. Consequently it may inhibit successful communication. The party with higher relative status may lower that status voluntarily and in so doing improve the exchange of views. Reversing the process is not likely to improve the exchange.

Whether we like it or not, in this world higher relative status implies a power factor. If one is to challenge this power factor, he should be well aware of the risks involved. Free speech is guaranteed in the First Amendment. However, anyone who takes the concept too literally is running a risk. If this were not so, labor unions would be nonexistent. A power structure is created by employees to enable them to speak on an equal level with management.

On the campus a similar situation exists in the view of many students. It is exemplified in such expressions as "The administration does not listen to us," or "I try to make appointments with the President, but he refuses to see me." The complaint becomes even more specific when more militant students address an administration in such terms as "We will not end our strike until such and such demands are granted." Upon inspection it turns out that these demands are designed to rectify the difference in power status between the administration and the students. The students are recognizing implicitly that the power structure does exist, that, in order to cope with it in terms they would consider adequate, they must equalize it before discussion can proceed.

Such demands, when fully carried out, have caused the notable crises at Columbia, Harvard, San Francisco State, and a number of other educational institutions. Carried to its extreme, this type of demand challenges the ultimate source of the power structure, which resides in the political system and the taxpayer. Such action involves risks that should be thoroughly scrutinized when a student—or anyone else, for that matter—determines to bid against a strongly established structure.

The importance of status and position has been reinforced by a number of studies in the field. A study made in 1968, among others, provides rather conclusive proof that the status structure of a group will even be allowed to outweigh our personal observation.[17] In this study, which used twenty-nine adolescent boys in a camping situation in which the status structure of the group was known, it was demonstrated that when each camper was asked to judge the performance of those with whom he associated, in target shooting and canoe handling, his answers did not reflect the actual skill of the individuals involved but, rather, their rank status. You must be aware, therefore, that you are judged by your fellows, not on the basis of whether you can handle the canoe better, but whether they perceive you as handling it better.

There are certain areas such as government, the armed services, and business, where status is well defined. There are other areas such as marriage, voluntary service, and student-teacher relationships, where the utmost care needs to be exerted to determine the exact nature of the relationship as each participant sees it.

Regardless of whether status is set forth clearly or not, it exists in the perceptions which the communicators and the respondents have of each other's ethos, and therefore it cannot be disregarded.

Emotional Status

Ethos is affected, not only by an understanding of status and position, but also by the emotional states observable in the participants in the communication transaction. It has been shown that intense emotional reactions may prevent the communicator's intended message from getting through to the respondent, but the respondent may be quite alert to the signals that indicate the communicator's emotional state, whether they are intended or not. The communicator and the respondent must be aware of the effect that an emotional state is having on the transmission or the reception of a message.

One cannot communicate rationally with a person who is excessively angry until his anger has subsided. Neither can one console someone who is in the throes of grief or emotional stress.

In most offices word gets around quickly on those days that the boss is surly. This is not the day to ask for a raise or demand a change in procedure or ask for the afternoon off. Whether you approve of the boss' attitude or not, you have the option of letting your reaction to his emotional state interfere with the quality of your performance—a choice which, if you make it, will only increase the difficulties of the situation. Your knowledge of the communicator or respondent's ethos will help you to interpret his emotional state and thus communicate more effectively. Conversely, if you know little of his ethos, his emotional state will be a factor in your assessment of him and the nature of the messages he transmits.

This may be illustrated in the relationship between professor and student. All too frequently the professor, in handling his class, fails to take into account the effect that his mood will have upon the students. Such comments, although immature, as "I don't care whether I make a good grade in this class or not," convey the feeling of the student that the professor's attitude has failed to stimulate the student's interest and desire to learn.

Reasoning and Clarity

In viewing the relationship of communicator and respondent we must also consider the clarity of the reasoning embodied in the message. We are concerned with two things at this point. Is the message clear? Is the message reasonable? The more concrete the message is, the easier it is to determine its clarity. If the message is, "Meet me tomorrow noon at the May Company," it is not entirely clear, for in order that this communication may be successful, two questions will have to be asked: "Which May Company?" and "Where in that May Company?"

As the message becomes more abstract, it may be more difficult to ask the questions that will properly clarify it. For example, should minority students be allowed to enter college if they have substandard academic records? In attempting to understand the meaning of this query we might ask a number of relevant questions without fully or even adequately extracting the communicator's meaning. What is a "minority" student? What is the range of the substandard level? Is this not a handicap instead of an asset? Will he be provided additional help?

Once we have established clarity to the best of our ability, the reasonableness of the idea or request must be considered. In all likelihood it will seem most reasonable to the hearer if it does not require anything very difficult, if it seems of some value or use, and if it seems to have no hidden implication that might be injurious.

We must admit that the streets are full of people who appear to do unreasonable things. Consequently, we can only judge that these things do not seem unreasonable to them. What is reasonable to a given person may be only a whim of the moment, unless that person has been saturated at some point in his life with the principles that apply to the logical gathering of evidence and the application of reason. This is a subject that cannot be treated adequately here, but it will receive additional treatment in Chapters Eleven and Twelve.

The Reciprocal Assessment of Credibility

Although a message may seem reasonable, this does not necessarily ensure its credibility. Two tests may be applied to assure ourselves of a message's credibility.

First, we ask whether the message is internally consistent. We are asking the question "Does the message in any way invalidate itself?" Consider the following.

"I didn't have the money for a new car, but the deal was just so good I couldn't pass it up."

"I have nothing against him; I just don't like the way he wears his hair."

"I'd give my right arm for that job, but it's just too far to drive."

As can be easily observed, each of these messages contradicts itself. What is not, perhaps, so easily observed is that each sentence contains a hidden message, which tells the perceptive respondent something about the communicator's way of thinking.

The second test asks the question "Is the message externally consistent?" External consistency deals with those things clearly outside the message but relating environmentally to the message, either to substantiate it or to invalidate it. The following examples will illustrate.

"I know I'm overweight, but there's nothing I can do about it."

"I really don't know how I got an A in that course in history. I hardly ever read a thing."

"A poor boy doesn't have a chance today."

"I'm not in any danger; this cliff has never given way before."

In cases such as these the external fact gives the lie to the statement. The hidden message is in the refusal to face up to the external reality.

Your task and mine in making our communications effective is to reduce as much as possible the internal and external inconsistencies to be found in our messages, so that the perceptions of the respondent will not be filled with incongruity but, instead, will blend into a consistent whole.

The Reciprocal Assessment of Meaning

The assessment of a message's meaning hinges first on an analysis of the purpose, which we have already considered. Analysis of purpose alone, however, does not provide sufficient basis for judging the meaning of a message. We are all prone to judge messages on the basis of whether they meet our expectations and whether the benefits we desire appear to accrue. Our tendency in reacting to any message is to ask the question "What's in it for me?" If we do not like the answer to this question, the tendency will be to reject the message. Conversely, if we like the answer, we will tend to accept it and revel in the benefits we are about to obtain.

Given the complex and contradictory nature of attitudes, needs, and desires, the effect of many messages will not be so clear-cut, and the problem of determining values will not be easily accomplished.

Our task, then, in assuring ourselves that there will be mutually acceptable assessments of message meanings by both communicator and respondent depends, first, upon our ability to make our purpose clear and unequivocal. It depends, second, on our realization that the respondent has expectations brought to the surface by the stimulus of our message, expectations that require satisfaction. It depends, third, on the fact that the respondent hopes for some benefit from the communication. If we analyze his stake in the issue involved in our message, we shall then be better able to provide the benefit that will cause him to accept it.

IMPLICATIONS

1. Since communication is necessary to meet every individual's need for social action, the concepts and the processes you will be studying in this book are relevant to everyday activity.
2. Adequate understanding and the development of your ability to handle the problems of communication will determine your success as an individual.
3. It is possible to become a successful communicator only when you realize that the transactional nature of communication is the great determining factor in effective communication.
4. Learning and thinking are processes dependent upon communication.
5. Creativity is the result of your ability to see new relationships through communication.
6. Communication is a method of reordering the environment through influencing people.
7. Successful handling of communication will assist you in personal adjustment.
8. By visualizing yourself as the center of a number of small communication networks you may increase your understanding of the process of communication.

9. Examination of the characteristics of verbal messages can be of assistance in analyzing the effectiveness of your communication.
10. You must realize the importance of the fact that mutual perceptions are highly personalized.
11. You must realize the importance of the fact that each individual's assessment of purpose is highly personalized.
12. Your credibility as a communicator has a significant relationship to your status and position.
13. Successful communication cannot take place without an understanding of the inhibitions and the stimuli created by varying emotional states.
14. Adequate communication cannot take place without clarity of reasoning.
15. The credibility of your message depends on whether it seems internally and externally consistent to the hearer.
16. You must evaluate your message in terms of the expectations and benefits predictable for both yourself and the respondent.

EXERCISES

1. Consider some of the instances in which you have tried to exert influence over others through speech and have failed. Consider also some instances in which you were successful in influencing others. What were the reasons for your failures? For your successes?
2. Can you think of the ways in which others have influenced you through speech? Have their contributions been of a positive or negative nature?
3. What learning experiences have you had that have not involved the use of oral language? Has any form of symbolism been involved? Explain. Can you have learning without the involvement of some type of symbol?
4. Make a list of the ways in which speech has served you individually. Add to this list ways in which speech serves some of the groups of which you are a member. Does your analysis give you some indication of the importance of speech and speech training? Plan to comment on this question in class.
5. Make a short talk in which you explain the groups or nets in which you are a communicator-respondent. Illustrate with a chart in which you show the four characteristics of message units. Be sure your chart is large enough for your audience.
6. Give a short talk in which you explain the messages exchanged between you and one other person on a given topic. What were the outcomes? Whose intent was fulfilled? Illustrate with a chart showing how you traced the message units over a period of time.
7. Try to observe some communicators who seem to be lively and effective when they speak. Do they have the qualities of ethos mentioned in this chapter?
8. Prepare to discuss "the ethics of communication" in class. Can speakers be ethical every time they speak? Under what conditions is a speaker apt to be unethical? Are you always aware of your ethical responsibility when you speak? If not, why not?
9. In this chapter we gave illustrations of relatively informal communication situations. Comment on how the components of these communication situa-

tions differ from more formal situations, as when a lecturer is giving a talk before a luncheon club.

10. Think of some recent speaking situation in which you were the speaker. What was the nature and extent of your awareness of the audience? Could you see them? As individuals? Only as a group? Could you feel how they reacted to your speech and to you? Did you make any changes because of their reactions? What were they? Be prepared to discuss your analysis in class.

ADDITIONAL READINGS

Baird, A. Craig, "Responsibilities of free communication," *Vital Speeches*, 18 (no. 22, Sept. 1, 1952), 699–701.

Brigance, William Norwood, "Demagogues, 'good' people, and teachers of speech," *The Speech Teacher*, 1 (no. 3, Sept., 1952), 157–162.

Chase, Stuart, *Power of Words*, New York, Harcourt, Brace Jovanovich, 1954, chaps. 1, 8.

Gibson, James W., *A Reader in Speech Communication*, New York, McGraw-Hill, 1971, pp. 44–49.

Giffin, Kim, and Bobby R. Patton, *Basic Readings in Interpersonal Communication*, New York, Harper & Row, 1971, chaps. 1, 6.

Holtzman, Paul D., *The Psychology of Speaker's Audiences*, Glenview, Ill., Scott Foresman, 1970, chaps. 1, 3.

Johnson, Wendell, *People in Quandaries*, New York, Harper & Row, 1946, chaps. 11, 14.

Katz, Elihu, and Paul F. Lazarsfeld, *Personal Influence*, New York, Free Press, 1955, chap. 6.

McCroskey, James C., *An Introduction to Rhetorical Communication*, Englewood Cliffs, N. J., Prentice-Hall, 1968, chap. 4.

Morris, Frederick K., "Let us think clearly," *Vital Speeches*, 22 (no. 23, Sept. 15, 1956), 734–735.

NOTES

[1] John W. Keltner, *Interpersonal Speech-Communication: Elements and Structures*, Belmont, Calif., Wadsworth, 1970, preface.

[2] Jurgen Ruesch and Gregory Bateson, *Communication, The Social Matrix of Psychiatry*, New York, Norton, 1951, p. 38.

[3] Martin Luther King, Jr., "The American Dream," an address delivered at Plymouth Church of the Pilgrims, Brooklyn, Mass., Feb. 10, 1963; used by special permission.

[4] See Henry Clay Lindgren, *Educational Psychology in the Classroom*, New York, Wiley, 1956, p. 212.

[5] Reusch and Bateson, *op. cit.*, p. 34.

[6] Floyd L. Ruch, *Psychology and Life*, 5th ed., Chicago, Scott, Foresman, 1958, p. 349.

[7] Susanne K. Langer, "The origins of speech and its communicative function," in James W. Gibson, *A Reader in Speech Communication*, New York, McGraw-Hill, 1971, p. 87.

[8] See Virginia Satir, "Communication: A verbal and nonverbal process of making requests of the receiver," in Kim Giffin and Bobby R. Patton, eds., *Basic Readings in Interpersonal Communication*, New York, Harper & Row, 1971, pp. 21–39; also Kim Giffin and Bobby R. Patton, *Fundamentals of Interpersonal Communication*, New York, Harper & Row, 1971, pp. 188–190.

[9] Paxton Blair, "Lawyers and education," *Vital Speeches*, 17 (no. 24, Oct. 1, 1951), 760.

[10] For an excellent essay on the problems of ethical persuasion in business see Franklyn S. Haiman, "Democratic ethics and the hidden persuaders," *Quart. J. Speech*, 44 (no. 4, Dec. 1958), 385–392.

[11]Virgil L. Baker, "The art of public speaking," *Vital Speeches*, 18 (no. 10, Mar. 1, 1952), 318.

[12]Arthur W. Combs and Donald Snygg, *Individual Behavior: A Perceptual Approach to Behavior*, rev. ed., New York, Harper & Row, 1959, pp. 133–134.

[13]Harry Overstreet and Bonaro Overstreet, *The Mind Alive*, New York, Norton, 1954, p. 34.

[14]Maxwell Maltz, *Psycho-Cybernetics*, Englewood Cliffs, N. J., Prentice-Hall, 1960, pp. 105–106.

[15]Langer, *op. cit.* See also Karl Wallace, *Understanding Discourse: The Speech Act and Rhetorical Action*, Baton Rouge, Louisiana State Univ. Press, 1970, chap. 3.

[16]Maltz, *op. cit.*, p. 31.

[17]A study by Koslin, Haarlow, Karling, and Pargament reported in Haig A. Bosmajian, *Readings in Speech*, New York, Harper & Row, 1971, p. 95.

CHAPTER TWO

THE COMMUNICATOR IN SOCIETY

THE SCOPE OF COMMUNICATION IN SOCIETY

The generation to whom this book speaks—the undergraduates of the 1970s—will, like most other college generations, attend to the stimuli that have the most meaning to them. These stimuli are of several different types. One type includes activities that develop the feelings of the "in group," such as rock and folk music festivals, unique modes of dress and grooming, and support of the currently "in" idol of music, stage, screen, or recording. A second type includes the appeals made to support causes that reflect "new" sets of values: pollution control, preservation of the environment, "free" speech, experimentation with drugs, and greater sexual freedom, to mention a few. A third type includes all those appeals and activities that reflect the efforts of younger people to gain greater control of their own destinies. This category would include the struggle to lower the voting age to eighteen, to gain greater control over college curricula, to participate more actively in all aspects of governmental administration, and to make religion more relevant to the need-value systems of young people.

We pointed out in Chapter One that every young person is involved in many communication networks, where he participates both as sender and respondent. In all the situations mentioned above communication is involved in one way or another. Rock music, the efforts made by younger people to preserve the environment, the organization of the Jesus People, and such groups as Nader's Raiders are all forms of, or responses to, communicative messages. They reflect the need of an age group for identification, for involvement in meaningful causes, or for the establishment of "new" and relevant values. The messages that young people—and older persons—send and react to are related to all kinds of problems: economic, social, religious, racial, political, and cultural. These messages are literally in the thousands and shoot through the air at a pace exceeding the ability of any one person to attend to them. If he tries, he is overwhelmed, not only by their tremendous number, but also by the dissonance that frequently accompanies them.

In Chapter One, in talking about the significance of communication, we indicated only a few of the ways in which communication is used, sometimes successfully and sometimes unsuccessfully. Each person participates daily in countless communicative situations in the home, school, church, business, labor, and many vocational areas. Some idea of the wide use of communications can be seen when we consider the great number of different work activities that are communication-oriented: public relations, education, space exploration, television, radio, the press, religious education, governmental administration, the courts, psychotherapy, and politics.

If we look at the communications industry alone we get some idea of the magnitude of communication. To illustrate, three of the ten largest companies in this country deal primarily with the production of electrical equipment and the transmission of messages. One of these three, the American Telephone and Telegraph, is the third largest in terms of revenue.

Another way of viewing the magnitude of communicative activity is indicated by Briand, who states:[1]

Two thirds of all Americans depend on television for their information; and in turn, easily that many advertisers depend on that 2/3 for the purchase of their products in a kind of two-way umbilical cord for survival.

It is difficult to comprehend the magnitude of this communication barrage and the diversity of communication methods that have developed in recent years. Turner comments on the growth of communication in this way:[2]

In the fifty-year span just before and immediately after the first voyage Columbus undertook, modern communication began. Movable type made its European debut (by way of China) and was introduced into the new world (via Mexico). With this step man launched interpersonal communication; with the addition of mechanical power, mass communication had begun. . . .

Chiefly in the latter part of the nineteenth and the early years of the twentieth centuries came the telegraph, telephone, phonograph, motion pictures, the radio vacuum tube of de Forest, and major new developments in all of the graphic arts. These brought tremendous changes in all directions, but the principal ones were the shift in initiative from receiver to sender and the creation of machines able to see and to listen. . . .

Now a further new stage is upon us! Machines do for men's minds what mechanical power earlier did for their muscles. . . . We bounce radio beams off the moon and the planet Venus, and propel satellites millions of miles into space to gather scientific data. From attention to communication media that was limited to a few minutes daily only a few years ago, we and our contemporaries are now devoting several hours each day.

The quantitative figures of daily communication interchanges in our nation alone are of astronomical magnitude.

Trapped in a communication hurricane of major proportions, the individual is inclined to feel that his voice is of little value and cannot possibly be heard against the roaring tumult. However, despite the traumatic nature of our highly technological communicative environment, our society does have ways in which the individual can have a voice in the control of his social, political, and vocational affairs—and this at all levels of interaction. It is important, therefore, that each individual be competent in his use of communicative techniques, if he is to contribute maximally to his own well-being and that of society.

SOCIETY'S USE OF COMMUNICATION IN DECISION MAKING
One of the situations in which the skilled communicator can participate effectively is in the decision-making process, which is a part of almost every group activity. Sometimes this decision making is conducted democratically, sometimes only partially so.

Communication in Democratic Processes
Democratic decision making usually is carried on through discussion, in which each individual can express his opinion, influencing others, who in turn influence many more. When the voice of one individual is added to that of another, either in informal groups, such as neighborhood political gatherings, protest meetings, ad hoc committee sessions, and the more formal governmental hearings, organization conventions, and gatherings of taxpayers, it is possible to influence City Hall, state legislatures, and the Congress. Such gatherings have prevented undesirable zone changes, brought about the development of waste-disposal areas, prevented oil drilling in residential neighborhoods, launched and influenced political candidates, reduced discriminatory housing, and promoted legislation for traffic safety. Discussion in these meetings is

one of our better means of disseminating information, crystallizing opinion, and committing others to action.

One of the outstanding examples of the success of group effort is the nationally recognized work of Alcoholics Anonymous in the rehabilitation of those who cannot control their drinking. The techniques developed here have been adapted to other similar problems.

Additional evidence of the effectiveness of discussion and one-to-one communication is seen in products that are unadvertised but sold in great volume by word of mouth, and in fads that are taken up by each of us because a friend has influenced us to do so, and in rap sessions, which enable students to get together among themselves or with amenable professors to probe the problems of the academic environment.

The complaint that "my voice will not be heard" is very often more a rationalization than a truth. Many in colleges find that when they attempt to open the paths of communication to students, insufficient numbers are interested in participating and thus completing the communication cycle.

Recently a lobbyist who works in the state capital of one of our larger states made the comment that if any of the legislators with whom she worked were to receive thirty letters in one day from a group of interested constituents, he would probably fly home to see what was going on.

Although he might not change his opinion or his commitment, few legislators care to have the image of being completely unreceptive. It is not reasonable to assume that thirty letters on a major policy problem will change the ultimate decision, but there have been many occasions on which the spontaneous activity of a small group has spread until large organizations have been influenced.

The individual and his effort is important because any movement must start somewhere. The leadership of one individual is often the deciding factor in whether or not a group is formed and, if formed, whether it has the stamina to reach its objective.

It is doubtful that the free Negro who used the pseudonym "Othello" would have believed that his speech against slavery, one of the first ever given by a black man in America, could have helped initiate the antislavery movements that followed and the resulting war and the Emancipation Proclamation. In the following paragraph he chides the colonists for failing to live up to the principle of freedom for which they revolted in 1776.[3]

When the united colonies revolted from Great Britain, they did it upon this principle, "that all men are by nature and of right ought to be free." . . . After a long, successful, and glorious struggle for liberty,

*during which they manifested the firmest attachment to the rights of
mankind, can they so soon forget the principles that then governed
their determinations? Can Americans, after the noble contempt they
expressed for tyrants, meanly descend to take up the scourge? Blush, ye
revolted colonies, for having apostatized from your own principles!*

A democratic society has many methods of using communication. All are rooted in the First Amendment to the Constitution, which
guarantees freedom of religion, speech, press, assembly, and redress of
grievances. We report the news through media. We editorialize on it, for
we have a right to express our opinions. We advertise, even to the point
of incredulity, so long as it will sell the product. Those who benefit
from this process tend to support and upgrade it, while those who feel
they have been unjustly treated will tend to degrade it, attempt change,
and even use force to frustrate it.

The democratic process demands that a voice be given to
everyone, but we are continually faced with the problem of determining which voices will make policy and carry it out. Such decisions are
not easy and must be made and remade without destroying the process
that allows them to be made. For, when this happens, all efforts at
improving the democratic process are lost. It is an ongoing effort to
maintain a balance between too much order on the one hand and chaos
on the other.

Democratic processes demand open discussion, the hearing of
all voices concerned, the acceptance of majority rule, and the protection of the rights of the minority. In such situations advocacy is the
means by which we promote our points of view, and the counting of
votes is the means by which we make our decisions. It is obvious that
not all decisions made in this fashion are satisfactory to everyone, nor
are they necessarily the best decisions, but we are continually forced to
settle for that to which the majority will agree.

Communication in Pseudodemocratic Discussions

We must observe that not all our institutions and organizations operate
in the spirit of the democratic process described above. Many operate
with a much greater limitation on the number of voices to be heard and
on the openness with which they are heard. What we might describe as
pseudodemocratic discussions are usually power-centered processes.
They are cloaked, however, with an aura of democratic procedure. The
members know that, although they are part of the organization, their
vote has limitations and that in many or all cases the vital decisions are
made by a few people who represent the higher echelons of status or
prestige.

For example, corporations are controlled by a board of directors that determines operational policies. Usually only limited issues are placed before the stockholders. Some churches place the ruling power in the hands of a small board of elders, giving the congregation only a limited range of decision.

In the area of politics we are aware that this process is frequently used. Despite the voting privilege of the members at large, often basic decisions are made in sequestered, smoke-filled rooms. When such usage constitutes abuse of the democratic privilege, members of organizations are forced to assert their rights and to modify the method of operation.

College and university campuses frequently offer an example that is most discouraging to students. In the classroom they are taught the importance of democratic procedures. It is with considerable disillusionment that they learn that many institutions of higher education are not democratically controlled but governed rather by a self-perpetuating board of trustees. Student requests for changes or increased flexibility in curriculum or academic relationships are not easily granted, because the administrators report to the board, not to the students.

Jerrel Smith, a black student in a class in advanced public speaking at California State University, Fullerton, presented a discourse entitled "Opening up communication with the administration." His first point was the need for raising the power status of the students. He said in part:

Communication with the administration that's going to mean anything is out. It's out until we get some power—so first thing you got to do is stand up and say, "We are all somebody that has to be listened to! . . ." and we've got to believe it, for that's the way you get power.

In many instances the effort to gain a bargaining position has resulted in struggle and violence, which have been counterproductive to both the academic community and the general public.

Communication in Secret Parleys

It is obvious that some organizations make no pretense of using democratic methods. All decisions are formulated privately by those who have established among themselves the power to do so. Communication is effective but is limited to members of the "in" group or to those who conform to its decisions. Sometimes, when communication is not open, the power held by the few may not be abused but is used in such fashion as to make the constituents feel that it is benevolent. Characteristic of this type of rule are many labor unions, family-dominated businesses, religious and educational institutions with self-perpetuating boards, and bureaucracies with appointed rather than elected leadership.

No society is completely free from the use of any of these three methods. However, governments built on democratic standards tend to make more use of the first two procedures. Governing bodies that have not been forced by their constituents to conform to democratic standards are free to make almost total use of private, secret decision making.

SOCIAL ACHIEVEMENTS RESULTING FROM COMMUNICATION

Society's methods of using communication are responsible for our everchanging way of life and for the organizations and institutions that have developed. Before the printing press, communication was chiefly oral. When it became possible to disseminate the written word easily, a great change took place, affecting all facets of society. The electronic age suggests to us that the oral-visual process will receive greater emphasis in the future. McLuhan and Carpenter put it this way:[4]

Until WRITING was invented, we lived in acoustic space, where the Eskimo now lives: boundless, directionless, horizonless, the dark of the mind, the world of emotion, primordial intuition, terror. Speech is a social chart of this dark bog.

SPEECH structures the abyss of mental and acoustic space shrouding the race; it is a cosmic, invisible architecture of the human dark. Speak that I may see you.

WRITING turned a spotlight on the high, dim Sierras of speech; writing was the visualization of acoustic space. It lit up the dark. . . .

A goose's quill put an end to talk, abolished mystery, gave architecture and towns, brought roads and armies, bureaucracies. It was the basic metaphor with which the cycle of CIVILIZATION began, the step from the dark into the light of the mind. The hand that filled a paper built a city.

The handwriting is on the celluloid walls of Hollywood; the Age of Writing has passed. We must invent a NEW METAPHOR, restructure our thoughts and feelings. The new media are not bridges between man and nature: they are nature.

An understanding of the historical role played by communication in developing civilizations should impress on us its significance and value in our own age. Sometimes communication has been used with varying intensities; again, for varying purposes; and sometimes it has been misused. We now look briefly at the results.

Varying Intensities of Interaction

As speech communication became a viable means of interaction among people, the life of the tribe became more sophisticated, and the resulting village or gathering-place soon elevated itself to what the ancient Greeks described as the *polis,* a word from which we obtain *metropolis.*

For the Greek, the *polis* was more than just a village. It had all the elements of a national state gathered into a city. It was a place in which to live and know people, to make a living, to participate in governmental affairs, to conduct courts in which the law might be upheld, to raise armies and to fight wars and, above all, to carry out a way of living in which the individual was involved with all processes of society and government. In this environment the first recorded experiments in democracy were made. Plato and Aristotle set up their academies. Plato's academy preempted the study of philosophy. Aristotle's academy observed and catalogued scientific phenomena and taught that the process of speaking well to influence others was of prime importance.

The level of interaction among the Greeks was very high. There was much demand for the writing of speeches and the development of good arguments, for each individual was subject to defending himself in court without a lawyer. If he wished to influence the *ecclesia,* or governing body, it was necessary to speak his opinions in the forum. It was the observation of such speech processes at work that formed the basis of Aristotle's monumental analysis, the *Rhetoric,* which dealt with oral communication so thoroughly and accurately that its contents remain important today.

Aristotle observed that rhetorical communication was a psychological process that influenced people by assessing their needs, desires, and value systems and by discovering the verbal stimuli that would cause them to be affected. A large portion of the *Rhetoric* is concerned with audience analysis and human motivation. Aristotle believed that the rhetorical system applied in all areas that had no technical field of subject matter, especially the law courts, the legislature, and special occasions devoted to praise and blame.

As cities grew and empires spread, the sanctity of the *polis,* as understood by the Greek, was lost except in a few outstanding instances. In Rome under the Republic the pattern of Greek polity held sway for a time. Through his training as a lawyer, his facility in debate, and the impact of his style, Cicero was able to dominate the Roman forum and to demonstrate that it was possible to become a consul without the credentials of a soldier and the force of an army at his back.

The importance of Cicero's achievement should never be underrated. With the Aristotelian system as a base and his own sense of style as an added persuasive factor, Cicero demonstrated that the power of oral communication was as valuable an asset as military prowess. Even Julius Caesar was wary of his contemporary's ability in the forum.

It must be noted, however, that the periods in history in which speech communication could be the viable means of holding a society together are quite rare. Generation after generation has been forced to return to the same battlefields to enforce its desire for democratic process. Military rule and dictatorial power have for the most part dominated the history of the world, although printing did contribute to international understanding. McLuhan and Carpenter point out the significance of the invention of the printing press, which made possible the dissemination of information to all who could read:[4]

Gutenberg made all history SIMULTANEOUS: the transportable book brought the world of the dead into the space of the gentleman's library; the telegraph brought the entire world of the living to the workman's breakfast table.

Although Gutenberg made the printed page available to all civilized societies, the tool that he provided could not guarantee the democratic process. Nevertheless, there have been bright periods in which the intensity of interaction among people has been sufficiently strong to revive the voice of the people in a number of more modern environments. Examples of the results of this interaction are the establishment of the British Parliament and the development of the Constitution of the United States.

To be sure, there have been many people who refused to accept the enlargement of the *polis* to a highly structured society and desired to live in small rural communities or even in isolation. We also have involuntary social islands where people have been forced to gather because the outside environment was unwilling or unable to absorb them. Despite the fact that not all have gathered in the *polis,* which we have developed into the metropolis, it is here that interaction among people has reached its greatest intensity.

Varying Purposes of Interaction

Out of the communication-centered interaction of past societies the blueprints of many of the systems with which we live have been put together. Although we would like to think that the concept of interpersonal relations is new, history would force us to concede that it is as old as the gathering of men into groups. However, in the pages of history human conflict tends to receive more attention than the methods by which men achieved amicable settlement of their difficulties. As societies grew in size, informal, interpersonal methods became inadequate.

Judicial Systems

The desire to achieve equity in the settlements of wrongs resulted in the development of judicial systems. The roots of our judicial system are deep, extending into British common law and fixed firmly in the codes developed by Rome centuries ago. The forms that evolved and the reforms that were adopted were possible only because people sensitive to injustice were willing to speak in their own behalf to secure an equitable society. Such famous doctrines as *habeas corpus*, trial by a jury of peers, and innocence until proven guilty were established to protect the innocent from the flamboyant abuses of those with power.

Former Attorney General John N. Mitchell describes the process of social change in America as it relates to the Supreme Court:[5]

If one scans American history, it is the rule and not the exception that the Court has found itself in the center of almost every significant political and social debate—the great debates over federalism, the slavery controversy, reconstruction and nineteenth century economic reform, the dissent and syndicalism controversies of the First World War period, and the New Deal programs of President Roosevelt, and most recently, desegregation, crime, obscenity and reapportionment.

As Mr. Mitchell indicates, our court system is in a continuous process of evolvement. Such frequently discussed subjects as prison reform, capital punishment, and the rehabilitation of prisoners will occupy the attention of the immediate future. The reforms and improvements that are being made and that will continue to be made will be the result of the communication process in action.

Educational Systems

For the fifth grader or the high school student the building in which the tenuous threads of learning are woven may appear as an impenetrable, if not threatening, establishment, for it is difficult for him to perceive education as an evolving process similar to the judicial system. Let us refer back to the inquisitive minds of classical Rome and Greece. The first academies began, long before the birth of Christ, as private gatherings of tutor and pupils under the olive trees in Athens. The inevitable questions of why, how, and of what value occupied the dialogues, but the state felt no compulsion to subsidize learning. Popular teachers got rich, and rich students were polarized in groups around them.

In Rome much the same pattern followed, but the groupings included girls as well as boys. Quintilian, a contemporary of St. Paul and one of the most famous teachers of all time, was the first man ever to be hired by a state to instruct the youth. After a career of teaching public speaking, law, and rhetoric he retired, and in his eighties he wrote *The Institutes of Oratory*, which includes an entire system of education for the citizen of his day. Although Quintilian was the chief influence in education for generations to come, many of his precepts are only now being rediscovered and considered to be most contemporary in terms of the teacher-student relationship.

It is a big jump from Quintilian to education in the United States today. In between existed the monastery schools of the Middle Ages, many of which did as much to misinform as to inform. In the Renaissance Quintilian's principles were rediscovered, but they were so badly applied that philosophers such as John Locke and rhetoricians such as George Campbell revolted against the classic principles. Today's classroom, mandatory through the twelfth grade, is by no means the exciting place of inquiry envisioned by Quintilian.

Mr. Max Rafferty, formerly Superintendent of Public Instruction in California, has expressed the view that individualism is stifled in our elementary and secondary schools and that our colleges function as huge factories.[6]

Some writers believe that much of what our younger students learn today comes from outside the classroom. McLuhan and Carpenter state:[7]

Before the printing press, the young learned by listening, watching, doing. So, until recently, our own rural children learned the language and skills of their elders. Learning took place outside the classroom. Only those aiming at professional careers went to school at all. Today in our cities, most learning occurs outside the classroom. The sheer quantity of information conveyed by press-magazines-film-TV-radio far exceeds the quantity of information conveyed by school instruction and texts. This challenge has destroyed the monopoly of the book as a teaching aid and cracked the very walls of the classroom so suddenly that we're confused, baffled.

Because our educational system has been so greatly affected by the revolution in communication, many are in a quandary about the direction education should take. However, as is the judicial system, education is still evolving. Many changes have come about in recent years. Some are obvious to the student, such as the newly evolved experimental colleges, often created at the demand of students, and the development of the "free" schools, often housed in abandoned shops. Demands for free child care for the children of students, coeducational dormitories, and unstructured classes are indicative of rapidly changing concepts among many students.

McLuhan and Carpenter attribute to electronic media much of the change that has come about in young people who have been raised under the tutelage of television. They say:[8]

This simultaneous sharing of experiences as in a village or tribe creates a village or tribal outlook, and puts a premium on togetherness. In this new tribal juxtaposition of people, nobody strives for individual excellence, which would be socially suicidal and is therefore taboo. Teenagers deliberately seek mediocrity as a means of achieving togetherness. They are strengthened in this tendency by the goading of the adult world, which is essentially individualistic. Teenagers want to be artists, but they cannot stay "together" if they are exceptional; therefore, they boycott the exceptional.

All around us, at all levels, education is changing but, regardless of the direction in which the changes may tend, the chief instrument of change is communication.

Political Systems

Not only do we interact to obtain justice and instruction, but much communicative effort is expended in the political arena. We have already suggested how political systems arose in centuries past and have indicated that in history truly democratic societies have been a rarity. As a consequence any formidable study of the history of public address is limited to classical Greece and Rome, Great Britain, the United States, and a few western democracies.

We have already mentioned the United States Constitution. Let us examine the use of communication among the delegates who gathered in 1787 in Philadelphia for the Constitutional Convention. Little reason existed to bring them together as a national entity except a desire on the part of the delegates to fuse the frequently opposing and contradictory opinions into a document that would provide a political foundation for themselves and millions of people yet to come.

Such men as James Madison of Virginia, Alexander Hamilton of New York, Gouverneur Morris of Pennsylvania, Elbridge Gerry of Massachusetts, and the two Pinckneys from South Carolina had strong beliefs about government, which were nearly as diverse as the attitudes in England and the colonies that had caused the Revolution. It was no simple thing to bring together the views of these men. Tensions rose, members absented themselves from sessions, and Alexander Hamilton went home in disgust. The process of hammering out a constitution was not easy.

Their method was little different from what would be used today. They met as a committee of the whole; they met as small committees who reported back. Investigation took place, discussions were held, speeches were made, compromises were effected. And the final outcome of the interaction was a document that satisfied no one but could be accepted by everyone.

Social Movements

It is difficult to separate the social from the political arena, for most issues ultimately reach political status. Some social needs are not met until sufficient social pressures force the government to deal with them. The movement to achieve suffrage for women is an illustration. The Women's Rights movement began in the early part of the nineteenth century, but it was not until 1920 that suffrage was granted by the federal government. In the meantime thousands of words were expended in speeches, dialogues, and discussions to promote the cause of women. Today, too, communication is a major tool in furthering the goals of the Women's Liberation movement. Concern about the aged was not manifested in governmental action until the passage of the Social Security Act in 1935, after many years of debate and discussion.

In contrast with the movements for securing suffrage for women and positive aid for the aged, social issues today are acted upon in somewhat shorter periods of time, in part because radio and television provide a new rapid forum for the exchange of ideas. Suffrage for eighteen-year-olds is an example of a need that was acted upon after a relatively short period of public discussion. The problems of abortion, sex education, protection of the consumer, high insurances costs for automobile drivers, and school desegration have moved from concern among a few to action among private or governmental agencies in a short period of years. Another excellent example is the furor raised over the deterioration of our ecological balance. The average person had not heard the term *ecology* until about the late sixties. Now, in the early seventies, action is being taken at all levels of government.

Many people frequently feel that the voice of a single person has little effect in securing action for the needs of the many. This is not always the case. We have many examples of the power of a single voice: Ralph Nader, as an advocate of consumer protection; Paul Erlich of Stanford University, who was instrumental in rousing interest in ecology; and Thurgood Marshall, who almost single-handedly brought about the school-desegregation decision of the Supreme Court.

We have named only a few of the many who, as advocates, have made headlines throughout the nation. Thousands of others are unlisted and perhaps will always be unsung. Our conclusion must be that when the rhetorical audience is ready and a stimulated speaker rises to the occasion, the result can be a torrent of communication resulting in political action.

International Systems

Communication does not cease at national boundaries. One of the first and most important treaties subscribed to by almost all nations resulted in the setting up of the International Commission on Communication, which publishes the Berne listings of all radio frequencies and call signs allotted to the various nations.

Another international system, but one that operates on private rather than governmental funds, is the International Red Cross. Its activities in situations of disaster and war are well known.

Within the United Nations such agencies as UNICEF and UNESCO perform very important services. Here, as in the other systems we have mentioned, communication is the vital factor, and it operates under the even greater handicap of multilingual channels. We must not underestimate the importance of the communication revolution to international affairs. Seymour stated it very well in a speech delivered to the International Advertising Association:[9]

No nation can escape this wonderful and terrible new immediacy. And no nation or institution has yet really learned how to use this wonderful and terrible new power of mass international communications. . . .

What we have, therefore, as the result of all the connections, and through television, is a new kind of international unity. It is fragile, it is formless, it shifts like water; it has no body or structure; but it is there—it is really there. It is the start of the formation of world opinion, of a world audience. And it is momentous, because it is the beginning of the first true unity the world has ever had.

All nations are involved in dozens of talks with other nations or groups of nations on specific subjects such as limitation of arms, control of fisheries, trade concessions, boundary disputes, and no end of other subjects. The difference between the present and the past is, as Seymour pointed out, the need to meet the demands of a new world opinion based on a simultaneously alert world audience.

Varying Misuses of Interaction

It is important at this point to identify one of the vital factors in the process of communication: it must be a two-way process. It is not enough for the communicator to initiate all of the messages and the receiver simply to adjust to them. Such a method inhibits response and assumes that the transmitting party has all the information. This type of one-way process in communication results in a significant misuse of interaction.

On the contrary, given the basic belief that the people should have an ultimate check on government, a communication system is then established that operates in the true sense of the word: movement of messages in both directions. Without this guarantee, which obtains for more than half the population of the world, the communication system is one-way: that is, government to people, a method that can maintain itself only if it exercises controls that people dare not confront. Such policies result in isolation, as indicated by the East German Wall and the Iron Curtain. It is difficult to control politically people who have uninhibited ability to travel and communicate.

IMPLICATIONS OF CURRENT
DEVELOPMENTS IN COMMUNICATION

It is important to stress the fact that over the centuries, through democratic processes, people have established many of the great institutions of our time but that these institutions must continually be inspected and revised in terms of the changing environment and that these changes come about through the same democratic processes. We have emphasized the importance of the individual advocate in bringing about social movements that result in political change. Finally, we must reiterate that because of the increasing rapidity of communication there has been a continual shortening of the time required to initiate, develop, and pressurize a social movement to the point at which political action must be taken.

As we consider the future in terms of the many rapidly developing systems utilizing computers and instant-communication channels, such as COMSAT, we can begin to appreciate that instant reporting of news from almost any part of the globe is nearly achieved. The simultaneous availability of this information will increase as the number of memory banks increases—rapidly. Everything that man knows will ultimately find its place in a memory bank.

What qualitative effect will this have upon our society? Two areas of importance suggest themselves immediately. Man's rapidly changing criteria for evaluating social needs will tend to change even faster, and this in turn will create an even greater need for individual responsibility. These rapidly changing criteria will mean a greater reliance on consensual evidence, as people attempt to make up their minds. Polls have already established themselves as a potent factor in public opinion, an example of which may be seen in the issue of the Vietnamese War, where public opinion was cited more frequently than substantive evidence as a reason for withdrawal of troops.

The rise in use of consensual evidence means an even greater demand for opinion leadership, which faces us directly with the problem of who is most likely to be formulating public opinion on the issues of the present decade.

Judge Learned Hand expresses it very well in his speech "The Spirit of Liberty":[10]

The hand that rules the press, the radio, the screen and the far-spread magazine rules the country. Whether we like it or not, we must learn to accept it.

And yet it is the power of reiterated suggestion and consecrated platitude that at this moment has brought our entire civilization to imminent peril of destruction. The individual is as helpless against it as the child is helpless against the formulas with which he is indoctrinated.

Not only is it possible by these means to shape his tastes, his feelings, his desires and his hopes, but it is possible to convert him into a fanatical zealot, ready to torture and destroy and to suffer mutilation and death for an obscene faith, baseless in fact and morally monstrous.

There is little doubt but that the leaders of the future will be those best able to comprehend the unique nature of the communication system and use it to the advantage of the causes they espouse. Whether in the future there are many such opinion leaders or few, their responsibility as individuals becomes even more important.

NEEDED FUNCTIONS OF COMMUNICATION IN SOCIETY

In the previous section we noted that communication has been an important instrument in shaping the systems that society uses to carry out its varied functions. Sometimes communication is used widely and efficiently; sometimes the contrary is true. As we consider the roles that communication should play in the future, two stand out as being significant: communication should be instrumental in closing the relevance gap between the needs of society and what is being done to meet them, and communication should also serve to balance conflicting individual and group goals.

Closing the Gap Between Society's Problems and Solutions

For a large number of citizens, including many of the young, there appears to be little relevance between society's needs and its ability or willingness to cope with those needs. Such people point to a failure to grapple adequately with the problem of ecology. They lead protests; they go on marches, they commemorate days for ecology; they lambaste institutions for their failure to clean up their engines, furnaces, and disposal systems; they point to the inflexibility that exists within institutions. Within education the goals are at times unclear; at times they are clear, but the leaders cannot or will not act to achieve them. Within the church some attempts are being made to make religion relevant to the everyday needs of the members. Inequities in the administration of our judicial system seem apparent, yet solutions come slowly. Needed changes in our political systems—greater representation of minorities in our political parties, for example—are just beginning to occur. It has taken both nonviolent and violent efforts on the part of a minority to get, at best, partial solutions to some of their problems. Much more needs to be done. Our communication systems and our individual communication skills will play an important part in making proposed solutions relevant to our problems.

Serving As a Balance Between Conflicting Goals

From the daily papers, the radio and television newscasts, and personal experience we learn about conflicting goals of individuals and groups. As communicators our first task is to help identify these conflicting goals and then use our communication skills in achieving mutually satisfactory solutions. We need to be skilled in discussion, debate, and persuasive speaking. We must also learn the importance of compromise and be willing to make some concessions in the solutions we are willing to accept. For no one individual nor any one group will obtain everything it wants. Instead, the divisive groups will be forced to adjust their goals and settle for the best modified plan that can be approved by all. In the case of relations between labor and management the disputes over wages, working conditions, and fringe benefits may not be settled until all the processes of injunction, strike, labor-management talks, and government pressure have run their full course. But ultimate settlements are the result of two-way communication, finally sifting down from overall demands to the final minimum for which each side is willing to settle, and balance is once more achieved.

For the Negro who feels discrimination within an institution, the problem is more difficult, for in most cases he does not have behind him the power of the union. He may find himself accepting inferior jobs and inferior pay until he is able to rally the support that he needs through court decisions and equal-opportunity laws. Again communication is the means by which he settles his dispute, whether it be with management or with labor unions.

There are many functions that institutions and individuals may perform in solving conflicting goals, but the most important is opening up two-way channels of communication through which employees and management may confer without inhibition or fear of retaliation.

CURRENT METHODS OF COMMUNICATION FOR MODIFYING SOCIETY

Observation of the communication process as it is being used to modify our society indicates that four methods are being used: that of subversion, that of dissent, that of avoidance, and that of persuasion. We shall examine these in the following paragraphs.

Subversion

Subversive techniques and their revolutionary counterparts are not new in society; they are as old as the first government. The rule of the people is also an ancient concept and one designed to obviate the need of either subversion or revolution, for, if the people rule, changes can be made peacefully.

Obviously there are a great many people in the United States today who do not believe this or refuse to accept the terms under which democracy is practiced. Nevertheless, the communicative influence of a small minority can have a strong effect. It can have a coded language and the "in" people know themselves as "in" people, for they know how to use the "in" words. A rhetoric of revolution could be established, but such a rhetoric cannot mature where the burden of oppression reduces men's minds to a single objective, that of destroying what exists. Under such circumstances a rhetoric is no longer needed.

The method of subversion and revolution not only has failed to identify convincingly an oppressor; it has failed to establish a constructive objective.

Dissent

The method of dissent is clearly a recognized constitutional right of individuals and groups in our society. To dissent means to disagree and even to demand redress of grievances, whether it be through the courts or legal assemblage. But we must reiterate that dissent must be a law-abiding process. If it is not, it is no longer "dissent," and "rebellion," "civil disturbance," and "riot" become more appropriate terms.

Recent history demonstrates that attempts to exercise constitutional rights by large assemblies have frequently resulted in civil disorder. The evolution of a law-abiding assembly into a rioting mob is a quick and easy transition, and when it occurs, the leaders of the assembly are quick to blame the police, and the police to blame hard-core leadership, which has not been content with the method of dissent. The method of dissent has an identifiable rhetoric, which can be traced through the pages of American history, and its leaders have often become the grass-roots advocates of social movements that have later gained social respect and political approval.

Abraham Lincoln is not often thought of as a dissenter, but his maiden speech in the House of Representatives was an attack upon the war policy of President Harrison, which challenged the President's justification of the Mexican War. But Lincoln in turn as President heard the voices of dissenters. Among them was that of Frederick Douglass, who carried the battle for the Emancipation Proclamation literally into the parlor of the White House. His speech entitled "Our work is not done" drove home his view that the war between the states, fought for any other purpose than that of freeing the Negro slave, was utterly futile.

Avoidance

The method of avoidance is often associated with the lethargy of the average person. We can see it statistically when we are told how few people have participated in an election. We hear it referred to in such a term as the "silent majority." In principle, avoidance is the strategy of refusing to recognize an issue until actually being confronted with it.

Since the great majority is made up of many smaller minorities, it is hardly surprising that it is difficult to interpret and to shape the will of the majority without tremendous and repeated communicative onslaughts. Avoidance does not help solve problems; it merely adds to the problems of those who attempt to communicate solutions.

Persuasion

We have left to the last the method of persuasion, which is the discovery of the means by which a respondent can be stimulated to consider favorably a point of view. This is the rhetorical process, which works for the advocate in many types of human communication—in person-to-person conversation, in small conferences, in group discussions, and in public address. It is with the means of discovering and using this ability to persuade for the benefit of the individual and society that the remainder of this book will deal.

IMPLICATIONS

1. We must be aware of the enormous world of communication, which exists in our environment and governs much of our activity.
2. We as individuals can participate in the decision-making process through the available situations—the dyad, the small group, the larger listening audience.
3. Many of the processes by which our institutions make decisions are not democratic and require adjustments of our communication to this fact.
4. Despite the size, complexity, and nondemocratic nature of some of our decision making, the individual voice can still be heard in our society.
5. Individuals and small groups have a strong record in influencing social and political change.
6. Our basic social philosophy not only guarantees everyone a voice but demands that he use it effectively.
7. Human interaction, although as old as man's primordial ability to associate, has now through speech become a keystone of our culture.
8. Aristotle's observation, made 2200 years ago, is fundamental today: rhetorical communication is a psychological process that influences people by assessing their needs, desires, and value systems and discovers the means by which they can be influenced through speaking.

9. Cicero's demonstration to the world that the power of speech was as valuable an asset as military prowess or any other source of power must be demonstrated in every age.

10. The printing press, although it could not guarantee democracy, made possible the recording of historical events for everyone.

11. Our most important institutions, such as our judicial, educational, and political systems, were made possible by communication and must be continually revised and updated through the communication process.

12. Because of the communication explosion of our times social movements can culminate faster in political action than ever before.

13. Of the various means of social control and change, the method of persuasion is the most equitable and constructive.

EXERCISES

1. Keep a log for several days of the various attempts that are made in our communicative environment to influence you. How many ideas were thrust at you via the radio, television, informal conversation, and so forth? Note how you reacted to them. Present the results to your class.

2. Make a three-way list of organizations that you feel make their decisions on democratic, pseudodemocratic, and secret bases. Can you find arguments to justify their methods? Can you find arguments to support a need for change? Be prepared to present your analysis in class.

3. Make a list of small groups or individuals who have acquired public recognition through their support for specific causes or changes in our society. Discuss your findings with other members of the class.

4. Read Book I of Aristotle's *Rhetoric* and report to the class on his observations of people and how they are motivated.

5. Read Book I of Aristotle's *Rhetoric* and report on his observations of the importance of political action.

6. Read as much as you can about Cicero and his career. Make a report to class in which you compare him to an ambitious pre-law student today.

7. Read McLuhan's *Gutenberg Galaxy*. Support or oppose his theory of the influence of communication in social change in a presentation to your class.

8. Read an account of the Constitutional Convention of 1787. Report on the methods of communication used by the delegates.

ADDITIONAL READINGS

Aristotle, *Rhetoric*, New York, Modern Library, 1954.

Bowers, Claude G., *The Tragic Era: The Revolution after Lincoln*, New York, Blue Ribbon Books, 1929.

Corbett, Edward P. J., *Classical Rhetoric for the Modern Student*, New York, Oxford Univ. Press, 1965.

Fawcett, Dame Millicent (Garrett), *Women's Suffrage: A Short History of a Great Movement*, (reprint of 1912 ed.), New York, Source Book Press, 1970.

Gwynn, Aubrey, *Roman Education from Cicero to Quintilian*, Oxford, Clarendon Press, 1926.

Hecker, Eugene Arthur, *A Short History of Women's Rights from the Days of Augustus to the Present Time*, Westport, Conn., Greenwood Press, 1971.

Hendrick, Burton J., *Bulwark of the Republic: A Biography of the Constitution*, Boston, Little, Brown, 1937.

Hobbs, Lisa, *Love and Liberation: Up Front with The Feminists*, New York, McGraw-Hill, 1970.

Hofstadter, Richard, ed., *Great Issues in American History*, New York, Vintage Books, 1958.

Hunt, Gaillard, and James B. Scott, eds., *The Debates in the Federal Convention of 1787 Which Framed the Constitution of the United States of America*, New York, Oxford Univ. Press, 1920.

Kennedy, George, *The Art of Persuasion in Greece*, Princeton, Princeton Univ., 1963.

Kennedy, John F., *Profiles in Courage*, New York, Harper & Row, 1956.

McLuhan, Marshall, *The Gutenberg Galaxy: The Making of Typographic Man*, Toronto, Univ. Toronto Press, 1962.

Parrington, Vernon Louis, *Main Currents in American Thought*, New York, Harcourt, 1930.

Voorhis, Jerry, "Effective speaking in Congress," *Quart. J. Speech*, 34 (no. 4, Dec. 1948), 462–463.

Walter, Otis M., "The teaching of speech as a force in Western culture," *Speech Teacher*, 11 (no. 1, Jan. 1962), 1–9.

NOTES

[1] Paul L. Briand, Jr., "America, the Violent," *Vital Speeches*, 36 (no. 22, Sept. 1, 1970), p. 678.

[2] W. Homer Turner, "In the beginning was the Word: The responsibility for good communication," in James W. Gibson, *A Reader in Speech Communication*, New York, McGraw-Hill, 1971, pp. 83–84.

[3] Carter G. Woodson, ed., *Negro Orators and Their Orations*, Washington, D.C., Associated Publishers, 1925, pp. 14–15. Speech delivered circa 1788.

[4] Marshall McLuhan and Edmund Carpenter, eds., *Explorations in Communication*, Boston, Beacon, 1960, pp. 207–208.

[5] John N. Mitchell, "The Supreme Court," *Vital Speeches*, 36 (no. 17, June 15, 1970), 515.

[6] Max Rafferty, "What's going to happen to us individuals?" *Vital Speeches*, 36 (no. 24, Oct. 1, 1970), 752.

[7] McLuhan and Carpenter, *op. cit.*, p. 1.

[8] *Ibid.*, p. xi.

[9] Dan Seymour, "The new responsibilities of business," *Vital Speeches*, 36 (no. 22, Sept. 1, 1970), 680.

[10] Judge Learned Hand, as quoted in *U.S. News*, May 24, 1971, p. 61.

CHAPTER THREE
THE
PURPOSE
OF
SPEECH
COMMUNICATION

*The modes of persuasion are
the only true constituents of
the art [of rhetoric]: everything else is merely accessory.*
Aristotle

We have already pointed out that every communicative act grows out of a specific communicative situation in which the participants—communicator and respondent—respectively have a need to speak and to listen. That is, every communicative transaction is purposeful.

THE COMPLEXITY OF COMMUNICATIVE PURPOSE
The fact that communication is transactional in nature, involving a reciprocal relationship between speaker and listener, makes the purpose of any speech act highly complex. Consider the following illustrations.

In a State of the Union address presented over television, the President of the United States desires to achieve a favorable audience response. In doing so, however, he may have a number of specific goals. He seeks to *inform* when he reports on the economy of the country, to *convince* when he reasons that any gains in economic conditions are due to his policies, to *stimulate* when he assures his viewers that the economic programs he hopes to implement will be "in the best American tradition" and will unify the diverse segments of the nation, and to *actuate* when he urges his listeners to "work together" to achieve better economic opportunities and rewards for all. In each instance he is attempting to effect some change in his viewers. Although a change may be perceived only when there is some behavioral response, whatever change occurs will relate to modifications in the listeners' understanding, beliefs, and attitudes.

The motivations of the viewers in listening to the President's address, however, will vary, depending in part on their political backgrounds and degree of involvement in political affairs. A layman of the same party as the President may want nothing more than to have his current beliefs about the country's economy reinforced; a legislator, differing in political beliefs from the President, probably will be listening for reasoning fallacies or for inconsistencies that may be attacked at some later time.

In the college classroom the teacher usually seeks to inform his students, to stimulate their thinking, and to create an atmosphere conducive to the free exchange of ideas. At the same time he may be motivated to speak because of a complex of personal goals of which he is partially or even totally unaware. He may unconsciously be trying to display his knowledge, build his stature in comparison with his teaching colleagues, or ensure a high "student rating" of his teaching skills. The students, too, will have various goals, usually reflected in their mode of listening and other classroom behavior. They seek to be informed, to impress the teacher with the extent of their present knowledge and eagerness to learn, or to compete with their classmates for a "good grade."

Protest and confrontation meetings became common occurrences in America during the 1960s and 1970s. In these we find another complex of speaker and listener purposes. The militant speaker usually has two or more clear goals in mind: to reinforce the listeners' attitudes toward the cause for which he is speaking and to get the audience to act violently or nonviolently upon some suggestion or exhortation. Most of the listeners in the audience at a protest meeting also have relatively clear goals in participating in the communicative situation: to reinforce or renew predetermined attitudes, to gain a sort of emotional rededication to a cause and, secondarily, to seek information, show solidarity by their attendance, and indicate their support of the speaker.

An outstanding example of a communicative situation in which we find a complexity of speaker-audience goals occurred in 1958, when Edward R. Murrow, noted commentator and reporter, who was well known for his courage in defending controversial causes and attacking sacred cows, in a speech delivered before the Radio and Television News Directors Association, zeroed in on the abuses in radio and television broadcasting, his own industry. In his speech he commented:[1]

It may be that the present system, with no modifications and no experiments, can survive. Perhaps the money-making machine has some kind of built-in perpetual motion, but I do not think so. To a very considerable extent the media of mass communication reflect the political, economic, and social climate in which they flourish. . . . We are currently wealthy, fat, comfortable, and complacent. We have currently a built-in allergy to unpleasant or disturbing information. Our mass media reflect this. But unless we get up off our fat surpluses and recognize that tele-vision in the main is being used to distract, delude, amuse, and insulate us, then television and those who finance it and those who work at it may see a totally different picture too late.

These illustrations suggest the difficulty, if not the impossibil-ity, of devising definitive and mutually exclusive classifications of speech purposes. In any given communicative situation the speech purpose usually is a network of relationships, reflecting the personal desires and needs, the communicative skills, and the relevant expectan-cies of the participants in the transaction. The authors of a recent speech textbook[2] state that "communicative purposes are multiple; they overlap; they may contradict one another; and speakers and listeners do not always share mutual purposes."

To this we may add that communicative goals are frequently hidden, sometimes exist only at a subconscious level, and always reflect the need-value systems of the participants. The authors quoted above continue by saying,[2] "Without understanding this complex network of personal and social communicative motives, it is difficult to compre-hend the communicative tasks of either speaking or listening." This comprehension of the communicative tasks of the speaker and the listener is precisely, however, the aim of this book. This chapter will give you guidelines in the determination of speech purpose.

APPROACHES TO DETERMINING SPEECH PURPOSE

Your purpose in speaking will largely determine the materials and methods you employ in preparing for and participating in any commu-nicative act. Your approach to the determination of speech purpose has, therefore, immediate practical value.

In the past the purpose of oral discourse has been classified in the following ways:

1. On the basis of speaker intent: that is, to entertain (or to interest), to inform, to impress (or to stimulate or arouse emotional awareness), to convince, and to persuade (or to actuate). At times these five classifications are reduced to two: to inform and to persuade.
2. On the basis of speaker-audience relationship: that is, to be utilitarian, aesthetic, and therapeutic.[3]
3. On the basis of message content: that is, to be expository, persuasive, entertaining, and inspirational.

None of these approaches is audience-oriented. We believe that such a classification has great merit, but we prefer to consider the purpose of communication in terms of the response of the listeners. Listener response is, after all, the ultimate goal of all meaningful communication. Aristotle, considered perhaps the greatest classical rhetorician, wrote, in the fourth century B.C.,[4] "The end or object of the speech is determined . . . by the audience."

We believe that all communication has a singular goal, namely to secure some behavioral change in the listeners. This approach has many values when you are a communicator. For one thing, it encourages you to approach the overall task of speech preparation with your listeners uppermost in mind. If you are concerned with changing their behavior by increasing their understanding on some subject, you will naturally start with what they now know about the subject, how they perceive it, and how they think and learn. If you wish to change their behavior by affecting their needs or attitudes, you will be concerned foremost with discovering the attitudes they currently hold and selecting appeals that will be motivating. You must realize, however, that no matter how selective in specific goal the speaker may be, the listener does not respond piecemeal but as a total organism. Thus, when the rhetorical purpose is audience-oriented, you are apt to select and organize your supporting material less on the basis of what is readily available and more on the basis of what will affect your listeners.

To state the general purpose of speech communication in terms of what happens in the listeners is sound both pedagogically and psychologically. Educators tell us that changes in an individual's understanding, attitudes, and behavior take place only when these processes are meaningful within the individual's perceptual field.[5] This means that listeners will respond in ways the speaker wants when they perceive that their response has some reality (is acceptable and meets some personal goal) for them.

Everything you will do in preparing to participate in a communicative situation—the planning of a pattern of organization, the selection of supporting materials, the choice of language, the mode of delivery, and the appeals to make—is a function of the response you seek from your listeners.

BEHAVIORAL RESPONSE: THE PURPOSE OF SPEECH COMMUNICATION

It is evident that as communicators we must first know the nature of the response sought before we can set about achieving it. An architect must first know the purpose of a building before he drafts plans. A student must first know his goals before he can select a program of courses leading to them. Just so when you are a speaker: you cannot select the means until you have determined the desired listener response.

The general purpose of every communicative transaction is to effect some change in the listener. This change will manifest itself in behavior, from acts only slightly apparent or delayed, to acts that are physical or are otherwise immediately overt. They will always be based upon (1) new perceptions or understandings, (2) modification of attitudes or beliefs, or (3) expected fulfillment of needs and desires. That is to say, the basis of change—or the change itself—will be oriented around psychological processes that are essentially and progressively cognitive, affective, and motivational. It must be understood that these three bases of behavioral change in listeners are closely related and cannot operate except in conjunction with each other. That is, new perceptions always precede changes in attitudes and beliefs and these changes usually precede fulfillment of satisfaction of needs.

In order to understand better the tasks that the communicator must plan, to achieve a desired listener response, it is advantageous to consider the three bases of behavioral change separately. First, however, let us examine the nature of our general purpose, the behavioral response that we expect as the result of rhetorical communication. We shall then consider the means by which we achieve the purpose: by introducing new understandings, by affecting attitudes and beliefs, or by adapting to the listeners' needs and desires.

Behavioral response means any action taken by the listener, covert or overt, conscious or unconscious, immediate or delayed, for which the communicator and his message bear some responsibility. This situations the observable response usually will fall at the "barely observable" feedback, such as small body movements or changes in facial expression, to "clearly observable" action, such as an overt effort to perform some physical task advocated by the speaker. In learning situations the observable response usually will fall at the "barely observable" end of the continuum. For example, a child or an adult may not do more than nod his head, smile, or frown, to indicate whether or not he understands. The silent mental activity—the cognitive restructuring—that occurs in the listener can, of course, only be inferred, unless the "amount of learning" can be determined at some later time. Response that falls at the "clearly observable" end of the continuum is, of course, easy to determine.

The specific type of response you may seek in any given speaking situation will vary widely from other responses. We shall consider some of the different classifications of listener response later in this chapter.

The occasions on which you will seek responses falling at either end of the continuum from "barely observable" to "clearly observable" are legion. To name a couple: you appeal to your friends to join a religious movement, such as the "Crusade for Christ," or you ask others to join you in actively supporting political candidates who have had great appeal to youth, such as Eugene McCarthy, the Young Republicans, or the late Robert Kennedy in the 1968 presidential campaign. Sometimes you communicate in many different modes, as through speeches or in discussions and interviews, seeking to get your student colleagues to join some confrontation movement or activity on campus. These are instances in which you seek clearly observable response.

By contrast, there are situations in which you will be seeking a response that will be manifested in a much less observable fashion. If you are active in student government or participate on some faculty-student committee—and the amount of student participation in academic decision making is on the increase—you may find yourself seeking to change the attitudes of either faculty or students on such topics as student evaluation of teaching, fraternity hazing, Black Studies programs, total student control of disciplinary action, or the Pill. In these instances the response sought may not be observable at all, or it may be delayed.

Outside the classroom the occasions on which we seek to change the behavior of others may be formal or informal, private or public, in interviews, in larger discussion groups, or in social or business situations. In family conferences, in church, at political rallies, in legislative assemblies, at conventions of professional organizations, in the doctor's consulting room, in the locker room between halves, or over television and on the radio, appeals are made to people to respond in some way that the speaker perceives as desirable.

Whatever change we seek, we must always consider the specific response sought or expected, the character of the audience, and the occasion, when we plan the content and presentation of a speech or other form of communicative act. We must not speak at a level beyond the age, education, and interests of the listeners. We must study the motives that impel them to action and start our speech preparation at that point. Further, we must remember that a response sought in the form of immediate action will require different rhetorical techniques from those used when delayed action is sought.

It is important to note that, since behavioral change, or audience response in any of its degrees or forms, is the ultimate goal of all speaking, speech communication must be considered essentially persuasive. If your speech is basically informative, the information given usually serves only as a means to some more important behavioral goal of the listener: to solve a problem, speed up some mental process, or improve a physical skill. In any informative speaking situation the listener must already perceive a need for the information or be persuaded of such need. Thus, the speaker rarely gives information for its own sake alone but, rather, to achieve some related behavioral response.

Similarly, when your speech deals with the attitudes and beliefs or needs and desires of your listeners, your goal is still persuasive in nature: that is, you wish to bring about some desired listener response.

In concluding our comments on behavioral response as the general purpose of speech, we should emphasize the fact that, to determine the success of your message, you must be able to measure or gauge the response in some way. Sometimes the only indication you have of success or failure is in the audience feedback during your speech; sometimes you can tell by the actions taken by the audience immediately after the speech; at still other times you may not know until long after the speech has been given.

Increasing Understanding

One of the most frequent reasons you will have for communicating with other persons is to increase your listeners' understanding as a basis for some change in their behavior. This increased understanding may lead directly to the behavioral change, as when instruction in a foreign language results in improved reading or speaking ability in that language. At other times increased listener understanding—achieved by giving factual data, explaining, showing applications, and so on—may be only a preliminary to changing the attitudes of your listeners or persuading them that they should act as you suggest, because your proposal will meet some of their needs. Understanding is a part of all speaking, and some change always occurs when a person understands.

The speaker who wishes to induce response by increasing the understanding of his listeners is essentially providing a meaningful learning experience for them. That is, the transaction occurring between a speaker and his audience is a teaching-learning one, since the speaker wants the listeners to perform one or more of the mental activities involved in thinking and learning. His ability to do this will be revealed by the behavioral response of the listeners. If that response challenges the speaker's data or conclusion, he is then placed in the position of demonstrating his rightness—a persuasive undertaking. He uses the rhetorical methods originally systematized by Aristotle and refined by rhetoricians over the centuries. Those rhetorical methods apply in the teaching-learning transaction, as they do in all rhetorical situations.

While educational psychologists and educators describe the learning (understanding) process in many ways, the major kinds of learning (understanding) activity upon which they agree are included in the following list. Except for two or three items, they reflect rhetorical practices identified by Aristotle and long since established as part of the content of rhetoric.[6]

1. Cognition: the awareness of a new image, idea, fact, or concept.
2. Selective recall: the recall of a known fact or concept from memory.
3. Classification: the placing of a fact or concept in groups of similar facts and concepts.
4. Perception of relationships: comprehension of how one fact or concept is dependent upon or linked to another.
5. Perception of comparisons and contrasts: the noting of similarities and differences between two facts, events, persons, or concepts.
6. Generalization: the formation of conclusions from known facts and concepts.
7. Making applications: the discovery or awareness of how a principle or theory functions in practice.
8. Cumulation: the storing of a number of facts or concepts.
9. Sensitization: sensitivity to events, self, and other people, and their relationships.
10. Memorization: the memorization of facts, principles, or relationships.
11. Sequential cognition: the perception or awareness of the sequence of steps in a process or story.
12. Problem solving: inquiring, creating, synthesizing.

Although these varieties of learning are not mutually exclusive, the rhetorical methods the speaker will use will vary somewhat according to the kind of learning and the responses sought.[7] For example, suppose you wish your audience to memorize certain principles or facts; then you will undoubtedly use restatement and repetition throughout the speech. If you wish your listeners to perceive new relationships, you will use illustrations, comparisons, and contrasts and employ to full value metaphor and analogy. Hence, as you set about the preparation of a speech heavily dependent upon increasing the audience's understanding of a topic, keep in mind the particular ways in which that understanding may occur.

In our daily lives there is a continual need to gratify requests for instruction, to define terms, to analyze concepts and relationships, to share and report experiences accurately, to explain processes, and to describe sensory images. Teachers need to help students to learn; students in turn fulfill requests for reports to their teachers. Clergymen explain religious doctrines to their congregations; church members give testimonials on the importance of religion in their lives. Judges need to instruct juries in order to ensure justice. Civic officials are required to report to their constituents on public matters. Foremen in industrial shops are requested to explain processes to their workmen. Military leaders brief their men, to prevent miscalculation on an important mission. Selected members of almost every profession give talks at their annual conventions on matters of interest to the membership. The public lecturer, teacher, shop foreman, newscaster, scout leader, luncheon-club guest speaker, administrator, sales director, member of a study club, and innumerable others are all concerned at one time or another with the general rhetorical purpose of effecting behavioral changes by increasing their listeners' understanding. Their purpose is achieved in each case to the extent that their listeners have understood and responded to the content of the communication.

Changing Attitudes and Beliefs

We stated earlier in this chapter that the purpose of speaking in any communicative situation is usually a complex network of overlapping speaker and listener desires and expectancies. However, as far as the speaker is concerned, the ultimate goal is to induce a behavioral change that accords with the response he hopes the listener will make. The means used to bring about that response may be an increased understanding, which we considered in the previous section, or a change in the listener's attitudes or beliefs. Neither of these two means to an end, however, can be completely separated from the other. New perceptions always affect our attitudes or beliefs in some way, and any change in attitudes and beliefs must be preceded by an awareness or understanding of new ways of looking at an object, person, or concept.

The speaker whose purpose is to get a response based on a modification of attitudes or beliefs must (1) know something about the nature of these internal states ("sets") of the individual, (2) understand how they are formed, and (3) have some skill in the use of the rhetorical techniques employed in changing them. We shall consider these matters in detail in Chapter Six.

At this point we present a brief statement of what beliefs and attitudes are, since we need to know what it is that we seek to change. Fortunately, there is wide agreement among psychologists on the meaning of the words *attitude* and *belief*.

Krech, Crutchfield, and Livson[8] state that an attitude is "an enduring system of positive or negative evaluations, feelings, and tendencies with respect to a social object." In another work[9] attitudes are described as "either mental readinesses or implied predispositions which exert some general and consistent influence on a fairly large class of evaluative responses." Briefly, we may say that an attitude is a learned, enduring, generalized, and energizing tendency of an individual to respond in a given way toward some object, person, or group. Attitudes concern themselves with the affective (feeling) processes of an individual—those processes which attribute goodness or badness to something. They are generalized in nature.

By contrast, a *belief* is a specific proposition with which we may agree or disagree. One writer puts it this way:[10] "A belief is the acceptance of a proposition as true. Beliefs are not necessarily *for* or *against* anything but are merely statements that something is *so* or *not so.*" Beliefs usually involve some thinking, or the results of thinking, whereas attitudes frequently develop without our conscious awareness. Beliefs concern themselves with the cognitive (thinking) processes of an individual, those processes which deal with evidence, testimony, or reliance on authority. Of course, some beliefs are not subject to proof but are held only in the hope that they are true.

Although bringing about a modification of a listener's attitudes or beliefs may be a complex task, it has been achieved in a single stimulus-evaluation-response communicative situation. For example, numerous experiments have shown that attitudes toward food, certain ethnic groups, and federal aid to education have been changed to a statistically significant extent by a single speech advocating change. On the other hand, consider the possible difficulty in changing some commonly held beliefs about religion, politics, the use of drugs, or the "establishment."

Psychologists generally agree that attitudes and beliefs are the products of an individual's experiences and general culture. Thus, as a person matures, his stockpile of attitudes and beliefs also grows. As an adult a person literally will find that his way of living is shaped by his attitudes and beliefs. Further, because of the commonality of social mores, experiences, and regulations for living, many attitudes and beliefs will be shared by large numbers of people. Thus, in our dealings with others we constantly find the need to reinforce or change their attitudes or beliefs. Almost everyone who works in any way to influence others—students, teachers, preachers, salesmen, protest leaders, lawyers, or members of a family—will need to know something about the ways in which attitudinal change occurs.

Glancing at the articles in any daily college newspaper or, better still, eavesdropping in a college bull session, will reveal countless numbers of topics on which you will wish to share your attitudes with others or change those of your peers: the use of drugs, marital and sexual relations, the crisis in Indochina, the problems of the Chicanos, credibility gaps in many areas of national life, the Israeli-Arab situation, relevance of college courses, or (two personal matters) women's styles and men's haircuts. On most of these topics you will probably have both attitudes of a general nature and firm beliefs on specific aspects of each. Your feelings and convictions will be of so pervasive a nature that usually you will seek to bring others to your point of view.

When the aim of your communication is to change behavior by affecting the attitudes and beliefs of your listeners, you will use all the rhetorical tools available. You must, of course, first make your proposition clear; it must be understood by your audience. You will depend largely on your own prestige and credibility as the speaker; you will organize your material appropriately to your goals; you will use substantiated evidence and sound reasoning; your language will be carefully selected; finally, you will employ appeals that are consonant with the needs and desires of your listeners. In short, you will employ the tools of ethos, invention, arrangement, and delivery as effectively as you can.

Appealing to Needs and Desires

A third basis of inducing behavioral change in listeners is by making appeals to the fundamental needs and desires, inherent or acquired, in human nature. The need for self-preservation and security, the desire to be wanted and to belong, the urge for physical well-being, the will to accomplish, and the desire for personal recognition are but a few of these concerns. Progress for individuals, groups, communities, and social institutions is a function of change, and the incentive for change is usually sparked by appeals to human needs and desires.

The needs and desires, sometimes called "drives," of the human being are the motivating forces that impel him to action. These impelling forces, or motives, are many and varied. Some are said to be instinctive, or common to all humans, such as the physiological needs to satisfy thirst and hunger and to avoid pain. Other motives are learned and so are held only by the people within a given culture, age group, or economic stratum. Included in this category would be the desire of the Chicanos to change their "image," of teenagers to gain the approval of their peers, or of some self-made members of the "affluent society" to be listed in the Social Register. Finally, because they are in part the result of experience, some motives are unique to individuals. Perhaps because of these facts there is no accepted and definitive classification of motives. We know, however, that all motives are related to the individual's ego or to his relations with other people or to his physiological needs. Because of the importance of motive appeals in inducing behavioral change in a speaker's audience, we shall consider in Chapter Six some of the salient human motives.

The greater the behavioral change you seek in your listeners, the greater the stress you will usually place on showing the relevance of your suggested action to their need-value systems. To act as you suggest, a listener must see some reward or the absence of some punishment resulting from the action. Motive appeals to human needs and desires are an integral part of almost every communicative act. Thus, if he is to listen carefully so as to understand, to give up some cherished belief, to change some attitude, or to perform some overt act, the listener must also see how that cognitive, attitudinal, or behavioral change will better his situation in some way.

Motivation, or the lack of it, is perhaps the greatest force in bringing about or preventing behavioral change in individuals, in groups, and in institutions. This is especially true with respect to education. Teachers are always concerned with the problem of motivation, of making the subjects they teach "relevant" to the needs of their students. Because of this need for relevance, higher educational institutions throughout the country have started programs of "Black Studies," "Chicano Studies," and "Ethnic Studies." The leaders of those minority groups based their demands for the new programs primarily on the plea for courses of study that more nearly coincided with the perceived needs of the students. In most other areas of human activity where change has occurred, it has occurred because someone has shown how the change would meet some existing human need. In religion, government, business, labor, agriculture, and community life this reciprocal action is taking place. Demands for change are based on appeals to human needs and desires, and changes occur because they appear to meet people's unfilled needs.

As a speaker, when you seek to change human behavior by employing appeals to human needs and desires, it is important that you know something about the needs and desires of your listeners and also have the rhetorical skills that will motivate them to act as you propose. Not only will you use logical techniques—sound reasoning, facts, and authoritative opinion—but also you may wish to depend heavily on such psychological tools as suggestion, rationalization, group pressures, and your own ethos, as much as factors that are intrinsic in your speech.

Finally, as in speeches by which the hoped-for listener response is achieved through learning or attitudinal change, so also, in a speech in which the emphasis is on appeals to human needs and desires, you must always adapt your rhetorical techniques and speech content to the particular speech situation. The nature of the adaptation you must make will depend in part on certain judgmental factors that will be kept in mind by a particular audience. We consider the most important of these factors in the next section.

FACTORS AFFECTING AUDIENCE RESPONSE

Among other considerations, the listener's impression of you as a person—and as a speaker—will be an important influence on his response. Do you identify with the listeners? Do you appear to share common beliefs and ideals with your audience, even if you are not a member of the particular organization or group to which you are speaking? Do you appear sincere and objective, and confident that what you are proposing is in the best interests of your listeners? Do you appear credible and knowledgeable? In other words, do you appear as a "good man skilled in speaking"?

The listener's impression of the occasion is a second factor affecting the nature of his response. Listeners may be classified in many ways, but one thing that every speaker must determine is whether his audience is attending voluntarily or because of some obligation. If attending voluntarily, the audience will be somewhat more likely to listen receptively than if it had been forced to attend. In either case, you will need to know whether your listeners perceive the occasion as one that will better their personal lives in some way. If the meeting is some memorable occasion, do the listeners have longtime associations with the sponsoring organization? Do they perceive the occasion as having widespread, even national, implications or as of local interest only? How important is it that the listeners be *seen* as members of the audience? You should plan carefully the ways in which you can increase the importance of the occasion in the minds of the listeners.

In a speech designed to increase the understanding of the audience on some subject you probably will employ some form of emotional (psychological) appeal. This constitutes a third factor affecting the ways in which an audience will respond. The emotional reactions to a speech may range from highly aroused physico-neurological states to mild and covert feelings or to a total lack of interest. The effective speaker seeks to develop in his listeners emotional states that fall between these extremes. Minnick puts it this way:[11] "As one approaches either of these extremes, intelligent behavior is inhibited—in one case because there is no motivation (no concern) at all, in the other because the motivation (concern for the outcome) is overpowering. The desirability of some emotional involvement in other than habitually experienced events is indicated, but too great an involvement is manifestly undesirable." The conclusion is that hyperemotionality results in overaction, and lethargy results in inaction.

Another caution that you should keep in mind in making emotional appeals: be sure that your audience is in fairly strong agreement with you, if you plan to use strong appeals in your conclusion.

The way in which your audience views your use of intellectual content must also be considered in estimating the audience's response. By intellectual content we refer to your evidence and reasoning. Obviously, you should not indulge in specious reasoning or use unsupported evidence and testimony. The conclusions you draw should be easily perceived, credible, and acceptable. The authorities you quote should have good status in their fields; it is unwise to quote from persons who are inexperienced in your subject matter. Obviously, too, in employing intellectual content you should not appear to be superior to your listeners; the tendency to be overbearing is not usually rewarded.

Another important factor that will affect the manner in which your listeners respond to the purpose of your speech will be their expectation of the extent to which your proposals will provide a satisfaction of their needs or an avoidance of some danger. As we have already stated, human needs and desires are many and varied. When a need is unsatisfied, the individual seeks some goal that will satisfy that need; conversely, if some personal attainment is threatened or some danger appears imminent, the individual will take measures to avoid that danger. For example, the holder of poorly-paying stocks may switch to tax-free municipal bonds, and the student who is in danger of getting a low grade in a course may study harder to ensure better grades.

The lesson for you as a speaker is to realize that your proposals must appear to conform to and to satisfy the need-value systems of your listeners. That is why we say, throughout this text: Start your speech preparation with a careful analysis of your listeners. For it is there that you will find your response.

AUDIENCE RESPONSE MANIFESTATIONS

We have already pointed out that the purpose of every communicative act is to secure some form of audience response, which can be said to fall on a continuum ranging from "barely observable" to "clearly observable." This, however, is a general description of response. We need to look at the more specific categories of response to give us some guidelines for speech preparation and presentation. Therefore, we now suggest some of the specific ways in which response may be manifested. There are six different bases for classifying the responses an audience may make:

> Observability—overt or covert
> Timing—immediate, delayed, or continuous
> Listeners' awareness—conscious or subconscious
> Mode of Participation—individual or concerted
> Degree and direction—favorable, neutral, or unfavorable
> Quality of response—habitual, emotional, or intellectual

These we now take up in the following sections. After them we shall discuss the stopping of action and the concordance between speaker and listener.

Overt or Covert Responses

Many times we seek observable responses from our listeners. We try to get them to clap, stomp their feet, cry out in some fashion, or be quiet, appear reverent, or repeat phrases, such as "Amen, Amen!" We also seek changes in the study habits of students, larger pledges from church or party members, signatures on insurance applications, purchase of the new style of dress instead of last year's, or larger contributions to the Community Chest. We may seek such overt responses when talking in either formal or informal face-to-face situations, as in an interview or over the sales counter or when speaking to larger groups in public. Riding with a careless driver, self-preservation may prompt us to ask him to slow down, watch the traffic, observe highway signs, or let us drive. Or, as a representative of a student action group, we may appeal to the college Academic Senate to give greater control to minority students over the content of the Black Studies Program.

If a student at California State University, Fullerton, for example, were seeking observable action in concluding a talk before the Student Senate on the subject of a larger budget for the football program, he might use these words:

The facts are clear! Chicano members of the football squad—most of whom are first string players—do not receive as much in room and board and incidental allowances as do the Blacks and Caucasians. Since we in the Student Assembly have control over the football budget, I urge you to withhold all funds for football until these inequities are removed. Vote "No!" on the football budget!

Sometimes we seek responses that are not so observable and that cannot be made clearly evident by the listeners. We try to get people to change their attitudes on some political issue, accept the logic of an argument supporting a proposed bond issue, or believe that a certain public official is honest and concerned about reducing property taxes. We may seek this covert response in either formal or informal speaking situations, in which the final resolution of the matter by the respondent may never be made known to us.

As communicators, then, whether before an audience or in a discussion or conversation, we must realize that the covert response may be as significant as the overt. The prime difference is that as speaker we do not have the satisfaction of seeing the behavioral change. We must content ourselves with the knowledge that we have made the best appeals possible and leave the rest to the respondent. He is the only one who can be fully aware of why his response will be covert rather than overt.

Immediate, Delayed, or Continuous Responses

The teenager who asks his parents for the use of the family car usually wants an immediate reply. The insurance salesman wants a sale today, not tomorrow. The political candidate knows that he must first get the nomination at the convention. Each seeks an immediate response.

We may also seek delayed or future listener response. Occasionally teenagers use the technique of a slow build-up before asking for the family car; the actual touch comes later. The smart insurance salesman knows that he may lose a sale if he pushes too hard; some people want to think it over. The political candidate who has won his party's endorsement keeps in mind that voting comes later and plans his campaign accordingly.

Sometimes we seek action extending over a period of time. The teenager who wants to use the family car on several occasions, the insurance salesman who seeks commissions earned over the lifetime of a policy, and the successful political candidate who desires the support of his constituents at the succeeding elections, all seek continuous response.

In February, 1971, the General Motors Corporation held a conference for a group of prominent educators and representatives of foundations and investment institutions. The conference was called to explain the progress General Motors had made in a number of areas of public concern, such as automotive emission control, industrial pollution control, urban transportation, and minority-group employment opportunities. Mr. Richard C. Gerstenberg, then a General Motors vice president, made the closing talk of the conference. He sought continuous future response from his audience in his final comment:[12]

In GM we are making progress in many areas of broad social concern— more progress than most people know. You have seen some of it today and you have also seen some of our great problems. We need your understanding. For it is upon your understanding—and the understanding of all of those who are the owners of this business—that all our future progress depends.

Continuous response is sought by the minister who preaches on tithing, by the scout leader who talks about "preparedness" to his troop before the two-week camping trip, and by the mutual-fund broker who tries to get his client to start buying a certain fund "in a small way."

The teaching situation is one in which the speaker seeks all three types of response suggested in this section: immediate, delayed, and continuous. This is particularly true of the teacher of communication: he wants his students to apply the principles of effective rhetoric in the immediate classroom situation and to think about them and apply them whenever they communicate outside the classroom.

Conscious or Subconscious Responses

Usually listeners know both the response a speaker seeks and the response they will actually make. That is, the speaker-listener transaction, including the listener's response, is at a conscious level. In each of the three examples given above the listener (parent, buyer, and voter) is aware both of what the speaker wants and what his own action is.

Sometimes, however, listeners respond, either overtly or covertly, in ways of which they are not aware. We call these subliminal responses, or those which occur below the threshold of consciousness. Many of us, without being aware of it, buy products because of the subtle influence of radio or television advertising. Sometimes, as a result of a barrage from close friends, newspaper editorials, and public speeches, we change our attitudes on basic public issues without being conscious of the change. When we chat with friends, we respond unconsciously in both observable and unobservable ways. We nod, move closer to the center of conversation, ask a question, keep silent when pleased, or disagree. Much of this physical and mental activity is below or just at our threshold of consciousness.

An excellent example of a speech (unpublished) seeking behavioral change through subconscious response was given by Dr. Wallace H. Wulfeck, a psychologist and businessman, before the 1959 annual convention of the American Hardware Manufacturers Association at Atlantic City. Mr. Wulfeck talked about behavior dynamics and gave a large number of pointed examples of why people act the way they do. Although the speaker said in conclusion that he hoped the insights into human behavior he had presented would make his listeners more understanding of their associates in business and more efficient in dealing with them, it was quite obvious that he also sought to give his listeners an understanding of themselves, which would perhaps modify their relations with their associates. If such changes did occur, it is unlikely that the individuals were aware of them.

Individual or Concerted Responses

Sometimes we seek individual response and commitment to action. This was the goal of the President of West Virginia University in a speech at the 1958 Annual Commencement of the institution:[13]

Set a high standard for your own conduct and live up to it. Then you will be in a better position to exact high standards of others—in govern-

*ment, in business, in labor, in education, and in other activities. You
can never successfully impose a higher standard on others than you are
prepared to accept for yourself. And each of you must face for himself
the age-old question, "For what shall it profit a man, if he shall gain the
whole world, and lose his own soul?"*

*Our future will become your present. The shape it takes will follow
the mold you make.*

Door-to-door salesmen, pollsters, preachers, television commercial announcers, teachers, psychiatrists, and probation officers usually seek individual responses, even though some may speak to groups.

By contrast, Mr. Henry Cabot Lodge, the United States Representative to the United Nations, sought group action in a speech before one of the United Nations' subcommittees when he concluded with this statement:[14]

*The resolution offered by India, Sweden, and Yugoslavia . . . is a serious
resolution, without trick phrases. It is a worthy vehicle for our hopes.
We should adopt it. Not only should we adopt it, but we should do so
unanimously, and with sincerity, and then, Mr. Chairman, we should all
set about carrying it out.*

Concerted action can also be a goal, as when a coach gives a between-the-halves pep talk to his team, a drill sergeant gives orders to a platoon of trainees, or an American Legion Commander urges his local post to approve some matter of national policy.

Favorable, Neutral, or Unfavorable Responses

Sometimes one is concerned with the direction of a response, favorable or unfavorable, and the extent to which it goes. Sometimes you may speak before a hostile audience, one unfavorable to the point of view you express. Your task, then, as we shall point out in later chapters, is somewhat more difficult than when you seek to reinforce the attitudes of a friendly audience. On some occasions you will talk to an audience containing persons both favorable and unfavorable to your cause. If you are a trial lawyer, you will try to convince jury members, assumed to be influenced by the opposing side, to accept your point of view. In many other situations, including political ones, the best you can hope for in one talk is to neutralize the extremes; for example, in the give and take of labor-management negotiations we have a situation in which, at times, the best that can be achieved is comparable to a neutral position. It is necessary, therefore, in analyzing the audience and situation, to estimate realistically the amount of favorable response that can be anticipated.

Habitual, Emotional, or Intellectual Responses

In a later chapter we consider in some detail man's habitual, emotional, and intellectual ways of acting. This is another way of looking at the nature of response a listener may make to a speech. While most human action contains elements of all three, at times the speaker tries to evoke one type of response only. Man is in part a creature of habit and likes the comfort of responding in a manner to which he is accustomed. For instance, the filling station attendant's "Fill 'er up?" is effective indirect suggestion and will usually elicit an habitual affirmative reply. The church elder who argues for a change in the Sunday service ritual may frequently meet with resistance from his colleagues because of a desire to preserve ways that have now become a habit. It is relatively easy for the Fuller Brush man to sell a new product to a customer who has bought his products for many years.

The cheerleader at a championship football game, the revivalist, the agitator, and the demagogue seek emotional responses mainly. Cheers, amens, intensifications of hate and prejudice, unsupported and slanderous accusations, and frequent fallacies in reasoning are some of the earmarks of a highly emotional appeal. It is quite apparent that George C. Wallace, in a Fourth of July address attacking the civil rights program, delivered in Atlanta, Georgia, in 1964, was at least partially concerned with the arousal of the emotions of his listeners when he proclaimed:[15]

It is therefore a cruel irony that the President of the United States has only yesterday signed into law the most monstrous piece of legislation ever enacted by the United States Congress.

It is a fraud, a sham, and a hoax.

This bill will live in infamy. To sign it into law at any time is tragic. To do so upon the eve of the celebration of our independence insults the intelligence of the American people. . . .

This bill is fraudulent in intent, in design, and in execution. . . . Yet there are those who call this a good bill.

It is people like Senator Hubert Humphrey and other members of Americans for Democratic Action. It is people like Ralph McGill and other left-wing radical apologists. . . .

I do not call the members of the United States Supreme Court Communists. But I do say, and I submit for your judgment the fact that every single decision of the Court in the past ten years which related in any way to each of these objectives has been decided against freedom and in favor of tyranny. . . .

The record reveals, for the past number of years, that the chief, if not the only beneficiaries of the present Court's rulings, have been duly

*and lawfully convicted criminals, Communists, atheists, and clients of
vociferous left-wing minority groups.*

At the other extreme, of course, speakers seek emotional responses that are less intense or less obvious: feelings of love or remorse,
intensification of personal resolutions, or unconscious readiness to act
on some later stimulus.

We also seek intellectual responses from our listeners. This may
merely be understanding and action on simple directions or instructions; it may also be reflective thinking at its best or action based on
logical analysis, valid evidence, and reasonable inference.

Other: Stopping Action and Concordance of Purpose

We now see that when the listener responds to the speaker's purpose,
this response may have a number of different dimensions or characteristics. You as communicator may seek overt action, such as voting in a
certain way, that is immediate or delayed, individual, or group. You
may seek a change in attitudes, a response that may be covert, conscious, and immediate. Or you may seek to increase understanding, a
response that could be continuous, conscious, intellectual, and individual.

In these classifications we have been concerned primarily with
responses that involve doing something: giving consent, making a contribution, making a commitment to later action, changing attitudes, or
performing some physical action. There are times, however, when we
want our listeners to stop acting in a certain way. In the home some
parents seek this type of response. From the public platform and
around the conference table speakers also seek responses that involve
the stopping of action.

We are familiar with the cease-fire conferences held in many
trouble spots throughout the world. On many national issues our public
leaders argue that our national government should *stop* spending so
much money on the space program, *stop* off-shore oil drilling in Texas
and California, *stop* providing more than our share of financial support
to the United Nations, *stop* spending so much money on farm subsidies,
stop involvements in Southeastern Asia, or *stop* industrial pollution.

Concordance Between Speaker and Listener

We have tried to indicate clearly that the speaker must determine in
advance the exact purpose of his communication; he must know the
listener response he wants. He must also know, to the extent possible,
the expectancies of his listeners, their purpose in participating in the
communicative situation. Effective communication is usually ensured

when the purposes of both listener and speaker are understood by both parties, and when the mutual motivations are shared. Consider the following illustration.

The Mother Church, The First Church of Christ, Scientist, in Boston, frequently sends its representatives—teachers of Christian Science—throughout the country to speak at member churches in the larger cities. The speakers are usually very articulate, knowledgeable, and respected, and many have a charisma that enhances the dignity of the speaking occasion. Usually about ninety-five percent of the listeners are members of the Christian Science faith. They come to the lecture seeking information, inspiration, and reinforcement of their existing religious beliefs. Here is a situation in which the speaker tries to do what the listeners expect and want him to do. There is a concordance of purpose.

When the purposes of the speaker and listeners are unknown to each other, and when they are in direct or partial opposition, success for either party is less likely. Usually the speaker should make his purpose clear to his listeners, and vice versa. There may be instances in which, for strategic reasons, this is not desirable. However, mutual understanding of purposes, similar motivational patterns, and a willingness to work as partners in the communication transaction, all contribute to more meaningful communication.

IMPLICATIONS

What are the implications for the speaker of this consideration of the purpose of speech communication? We may list at least the following:

1. Every communicative situation is purposeful. There is a need to speak and a need to listen.
2. The purposes of the speaker and listener usually are multiple, usually overlap, frequently are hidden by one or both parties, and always reflect the need-value systems of the participants.
3. There are many ways in which the general purpose of speech has been classified: on the basis of the intent of the speaker, the relationships between speaker and listener, the content of the communicative message, and the nature of the response sought in the listener.
4. Our view of the general speech purpose is based on the behavioral response sought in the listeners as a result of new perceptions and changes in cognitions, attitudes, and beliefs.
5. This purpose has practical value for the speaker, since it forces him to start his speech planning, preparation, and presentation with his audience uppermost in mind. It is sound pedagogically and psychologically.
6. Although the bases of change in the listener that are sought are treated in this book separately—for academic purposes only—we must realize that they are

not mutually exclusive and perhaps cannot operate separately in any communicative transaction.

7. "Influencing behavior" deals with all the ways in which humans act: on the basis of habit, emotion, and intellect.

8. "Influencing behavior by changing cognitive structure" deals with the perceptual processes of the listeners. It seeks to provide a meaningful learning experience, in which such mental processes as classification, selective recall, perception of comparisons, generalizations, or making applications can occur.

9. "Influencing behavior by changing attitudes and beliefs" deals with both the affective and cognitive process of the listener. Because attitudes and beliefs are products of the individual's experience and culture, the speaker must make his proposal appear consistent with the need-value systems of his listeners.

10. The speaker must keep in mind that the responses of his listeners will be determined by a number of factors: (1) the listener's impression of the speaker, (2) his impression of the occasion, (3) his reaction to the emotional appeals, (4) his estimate of the intellectual appeals, and (5) the extent to which he perceives the proposal as providing satisfaction of a need or avoidance of danger.

11. Audience responses may be manifested variously: (1) overt or covert, (2) immediate, delayed, or continued, (3) conscious or subconscious, (4) individual or concerted, (5) favorable, neutral, or unfavorable, (6) habitual, emotional, or intellectual, and (7) action-stopping.

12. To the extent that it is possible and strategically desirable, the purposes of speaker and listener in participating in the communicative act should be mutually understood. Further, the motivational patterns of each should be concordant. Effective communication is enhanced when these conditions pertain.

EXERCISES

1. Make a list of some of the specific responses you might want to bring about in others. For example, you may wish to borrow twenty dollars from a friend, get your teacher to change a grade, join with friends in a "rap session" on the use of drugs, get the Academic Senate of your college to approve, in reality, freedom of the press in the college daily paper, or try to get the Student Senate to do something about the quality of the food in the Commons. Take five items from your list and write down the appeals you could use to attain your specific goals.

2. What do you consider to be the values to the speaker in stating the general purpose of speaking in terms of listener response? Prepare to support your conclusions in class.

3. Select six speeches printed in *Vital Speeches of the Day* and determine the major purpose of each. Select one and determine whether there are multiple additional goals. Are the purpose and subordinate goals, if more than one, difficult to isolate? Do they make the main purpose clearer or more obscure?

4. With the purpose of influencing behavior through increasing understanding, prepare a short speech using a title such as one of the examples in the list

below. Be sure in your speech that you do the following things: (1) make clear to your audience the nature of the responses you are seeking, (2) be certain that your audience knows why and how the information you are providing has value for them, and (3) be certain that you demonstrate that your information is credible.

 a. Steps in training "Seeing Eye" dogs.
 b. North of the Arctic Circle: living in Barrow, Alaska.
 c. Industrial uses of fiber glass.
 d. What happened to me when I stopped smoking.
 e. How to "watch the girls go by" on the Via Veneto.
 f. What "farm parity" actually is.
 g. Ski equipment: costs and kinds.
 h. How to do an "About face!"
 i. How to operate a slide rule.
 j. I spent a night in an English castle.
 k. What an anthropologist really does.
 l. A comparison of two beaches: Waikiki and Copacabana
 m. The world's fastest game: jai alai.

5. With the purpose of influencing behavioral response by changing attitudes or beliefs, prepare a short speech on one of the following topics:
 a. Men's attitudes toward women are changing.
 b. Why the Vietnam War has been too costly.
 c. The "credibility gap" between the government and the people is increasing.
 d. Traditional religion is a "lost cause"!
 e. Why I believe there is ESP.
 f. Off-track horse-race betting would be good for my state.
 g. Open-mindedness is the first step to wisdom.
 h. Are we spending too much money on space exploration?
 i. The American Indians are still the *lost* Americans.
 j. *Jesus Christ Superstar* was needed.
 k. Pop art was needed a long time ago.
 l. Andy Warhol is a hero.
 m. Daniel Ellsberg was a brave man.

6. With the purpose in mind of securing overt action, prepare a short speech on one of the following topics:
 a. Now that eighteen-year-olds can vote, they should!
 b. Let's stop meddling in the Israeli-Arab squabble.
 c. Join the Crusade for Christ!
 d. See America first!
 e. If you're overweight, you can do something about it.
 f. Why you should join the college "swingers" club.
 g. Why women should learn judo and karate.
 h. Why a teenager should go to church and tithe.
 i. What you can write "letters to the editor" about.
 j. Two can live as cheaply as one, if both work.
 k. What the college student can do to help depressed countries.
 l. You, too, can own a "dune buggy."

7. Refer to the list of twelve categories of learnings in the section headed

Increasing Understanding in this chapter. Under each heading list two topics on which you might give a speech. Compare your list with the lists of two of your classmates. In what ways are the topics, taken as a whole, different from those about which you might speak if your purpose were to create change in attitudes and beliefs?

8. Prepare to discuss in class the reasons for a mutual understanding of purpose between speaker and listener and for motivational concordance.

9. Listen to a visiting speaker on your campus. Is his general purpose clear? If the audience is composed of students and faculty, are the types of response sought for each group different? Why?

10. Think of a recent situation in which you have participated as a listener. In this chapter we have listed five things that usually affect the nature of the response made by a listener. Did any of these factors affect your response? Which one? Why? Did several? Why? What other factors affected your response?

11. Considering that the purpose of rhetorical communication is to influence the respondent, can you list five situations in which you as communicator were able to discern that you had succeeded in influencing your respondent? Can you list five situations in which you as respondent were influenced? In either case are you able to distinguish situations in which attitudes were changed or understanding was increased?

ADDITIONAL READINGS

Baird, A. Craig, and Franklin H. Knower, *General Speech*, 3rd ed., New York, McGraw-Hill, 1963, pp. 47–49.

Berlo, David K., *The Process of Communication*, New York, Holt, Rinehart & Winston, 1960, pp. 1–22.

Cronkhite, Gary, *Persuasion: Speech and Behavioral Change*, Indianapolis, Bobbs-Merrill, 1969, chap. 1.

Eisenson, Jon, J. Jeffery Auer, and John V. Irwin, *The Psychology of Communication*, New York, Appleton, 1963, pp. 20–29, 230–235.

Keltner, John W., *Interpersonal Speech-Communication*, Belmont, Calif., Wadsworth, 1970, pp. 10–11, 328–334.

Morgan, Clifford T., *Introduction to Psychology*, 2nd ed., New York, McGraw-Hill, 1961, pp. 526–538.

Nadeau, Ray E., *A Basic Rhetoric of Speech-Communication*, Reading, Mass., Addison-Wesley, 1969, chap. 1.

Oliver, Robert T., Harold P. Zelko, and Paul D. Holtsman, *Communicative Speaking and Listening*, 4th ed., New York, Holt, Rinehart & Winston, 1968, pp. 73–92.

Smith, Donald K., *Man Speaking: A Rhetoric of Public Speech*, New York, Dodd, Mead, 1969, pp. 35–37.

NOTES

[1]Edward R. Murrow, "A broadcaster talks to his colleagues," in Floyd W. Matson, ed., *Voices of Crises*, New York, Odyssey, 1967, pp. 274–275.

[2]Robert T. Oliver, Harold P. Zelko, and Paul D. Holtzman, *Communicative Speaking and Listening*, New York, Holt, Rinehart & Winston, 1968, p. 79.

[3]John W. Keltner, *Interpersonal Speech-Communication: Elements and Structures*, Belmont, Calif., Wadsworth, 1970, p. 10.

[4]Aristotle, *Rhetoric*, trans. by J. E. C. Welldon, New York, Macmillan, 1886, p. 22.

[5]We comment in detail on the meaning of *perceptual field* in Chapter 4, note 10 at the end of the chapter.

[6]See Glenn Myers Blair, R. Stewart Jones, and Ray H. Simpson, *Educational Psychology*, 3rd ed., New York, Macmillan, 1968, pp. 107–122; Henry Clay Lindgren, *Educational Psychology in the Classroom*, New York, Wiley, 1956, pp. 4–18; Gardner Lindzey and Elliot Aronson, eds., *The Handbook of Social Psychology*, vol. 1, 2nd ed., Reading, Mass., Addison-Wesley, 1968, pp. 453, 546–547.

[7]See Chapters 6 and 11 of this text.

[8]David Krech, Richard S. Crutchfield, and Norman Livson, *Elements of Psychology*, 2nd ed., rev., New York, Knopf, 1969, p. 823.

[9]Philip Zimbardo and Ebbe E. Ebbesen, *Influencing Attitudes and Changing Behavior*, Reading, Mass., Addison-Wesley, 1969, p. 6.

[10]Albert A. Branca, *Psychology, The Science of Behavior*, Boston, Allyn & Bacon, 1968, p. 319.

[11]Wayne C. Minnick, *The Art of Persuasion*, Boston, Houghton Mifflin, 1957, pp. 225–226.

[12]Progress in Areas of Public Concern, report of a conference held at GM Proving Ground, Milford, Michigan, February, 1971, published and distributed to stockholders in General Motors Corporation.

[13]Irvin Stewart, "Set high standards," *Vital Speeches*, 24 (no. 21, Aug. 15, 1958), 670.

[14]Henry Cabot Lodge, "Peaceful and neighborly relations," *Vital Speeches*, 24 (no. 7, Jan. 15, 1958), 209.

[15]George C. Wallace, "Fraud, sham and hoax," in Matson, *Voices of Crises, op. cit.* (note 1), pp. 178–187.

CHAPTER FOUR

THE NATURE OF THE COMMUNICATIVE TRANSACTION

There is more than a verbal tie between the words common, community, and communication. Men live in a community by virtue of the things which they have in common; and communication is the way in which they come to possess things in common. . . . To be a recipient of a communication is to have an enlarged . . . experience. One shares in what another has thought and felt . . . has his own attitude modified. Nor is the one who communicates left un-affected . . . one has to assimilate, imaginatively, something of another's experience in order to tell him intelligently of one's own experience. All communication is like art.

Leo Lowenthal

For variety we have used the terms *speech communication, communication, oral communication, speech,* and *rhetorical communication* synonymously in this text; they may all be defined as the *purposeful, transactional process by which one person, through the use of audible and visible symbols, engenders meanings in the minds of his listeners.* Several words in this definition are critical: "purposeful," "transactional process," "symbols," and "engenders meanings."

To say speech communication is purposeful means that it is always goal-centered. Emphasis is thereby focused on outcomes. We do not consider accidental (nonintentional) or unilateral (self-expressional) communication as falling within the purview of this definition.

To say communication is a transactional process implies that a partnership, or at least a relationship, exists between the parties involved, the communicator and the respondents, and that the transaction is not static but is flexible, changing, and continuous.

Calling communication symbolic suggests that a code is used, one that is made by the participants.

Finally, and perhaps most importantly, communication engenders meanings. This denotes that there are *brought into being within the listener* meanings or understandings that parallel or duplicate those of the speaker. This result—the creation of meaning—takes place completely within the listener.

There is no physical transfer in communication. Rather, the speaker starts a process that evokes some recognition or modification of the cognitive structure of the listener—the facts, images, ideas, beliefs, and needs each individual carries with him—so that the process is in conformity with, or approximates, the cognitive structure of the speaker. It is as if the listener *assigned a meaning* to each communicative stimulus that comes to him from others. But since this meaning is personal to him and exists only within him, as speakers we can never be sure that our meaning is the same as his. At best, it probably is a close approximation.

Although it is not essential to an understanding of our definition of communication, it is important for the reader to know the sense in which we say "one or more listeners." This phrase denotes the audience, which is quite frequently large numbers of persons regimentally facing the speaker, sometimes smaller groups in a face-to-face situation, and at other times a single person. Whether we say "listeners," "audience," "receivers," or "respondents," we refer to the one or more persons whom we hope will assign the same meaning to our message that we had intended.

The function of speech communication, then, becomes that of creating messages that stimulate in listeners meanings that bring about desired responses. Hence, if our speaking is to be effective, it must reflect our understanding of and adaptation to the separate components of the process as well as the relationships among them. In this chapter, therefore, we shall consider selected models of the communication process, the characteristics of the process, the stages of the process itself, and its components.

VALUES OF UNDERSTANDING THE COMMUNICATIVE TRANSACTION

The question is frequently asked by students, "But why *study* speech communication? I've always been able to talk." This is an understandable question, but it usually results from numerous misconceptions about oral communication. Some are listed below.

> "The study of speech communication is too difficult and seldom pays off."
> "The study of speech communication won't teach me more than I now know. I've always been a good speaker."
> "Speech training means the memorization of a lot of rules."
> "Few people ever become *public* speakers, so why waste the time studying something that may not be useful?"

"Learning by trial and error is, after all, the best way."

"Speech training involves the learning of a lot of tricks."

"What a person does is, after all, more important than his words. Personality is what counts in getting along with others."

"Getting over stage fright is more important than spending a lot of time studying rhetoric."

Space is not available to refute each of these assumptions. The many obvious breakdowns in communication in present-day life certainly should suggest that some study is needed. The use of more effective communication skills would do much to reduce the generation gap, solve at least some of the problems of minority groups, increase credibility between the government and the public, and bring about some understanding between local law-enforcement groups and the communities in which they work. The college student of speech communication needs to become skilled in speaking because of the great advantages of improved rhetorical abilities for him now and later in life. Let us look at some of the benefits that may come from the study of speech communication.

One value of understanding the nature of the communicative transaction is the heightened awareness one develops of the complexity of the process. Once you know something about its many components, the notion that if only you speak you will be understood is dispelled. A second value is that you become aware that the process involves both a communicator and a respondent. Your study of communication will force you to look more closely at the roles the two partners in the speech act play. Further, knowing something about the process will help you to understand where breakdowns may occur, how they can be avoided, and how people can be motivated to respond as you desire.

Later in this chapter you will learn of the difficulties incurred in communication and the ways to ensure that the message sent and the message received coincide. Finally, knowledge of the process—knowing the sequence and nature of the stages in the process—will make your speech preparation more efficient. Your preparation will be speeded up, you will focus more on essentials, and you will have greater confidence in your ability to be an effective communicator.

THE COMMUNICATION PROCESS

One way of studying the parts of a process and their relationships is through the use of models. A model is a representation of an existing structure or process by means of a set of symbols and rules of operation. This definition has two important implications: there is a structural correspondence between the model and the thing or process it

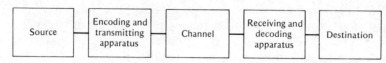

FIGURE 4-1. Elements of a communication system.

WHO → SAYS WHAT → IN WHAT CHANNEL → TO WHOM → WITH WHAT EFFECT

FIGURE 4-2. The Lasswell model of communication.

represents, and the configuration itself reflects value judgments about the relative importance of each aspect of the thing or process it represents. These implications point up the following five values of the study of models, which should aid in our understanding of the communicative process.

1. The *organizational* value: The model brings together isolated bits of information and relates them in a meaningful pattern. Structural, temporal, procedural, and experimental relations can be shown.
2. The *descriptive* value: The model may be used to describe and delimit or to establish the boundaries of the process or thing being modeled. It establishes dimensions.
3. The *predictive* value: The model may serve as a guide to qualitative and quantitative predictions. It may serve to answer questions like "Will it work?" "Under what conditions will it work?" and "How effectively will it work?"
4. The *theory-construction* value: The study of the components and relationships in the model can aid in the development of a theory relative to the thing modeled.
5. The *problem-solving* value: If the model bears essentially a one-to-one relationship to the thing modeled, it can aid in solving problems resulting from malfunctions of the thing modeled.

In the following section we describe a number of communication models, including our own, in considerable detail. Only if you understand the complete nature of the communication process can you avoid the pitfalls that trap many speakers. Too frequently speakers assume that what they say is always understood, are self-oriented in their approach to speech preparation and delivery, and ignore the feedback from their audiences. Your thorough understanding of the

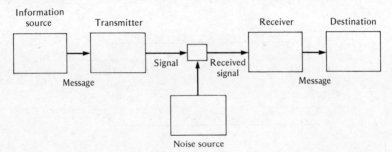

FIGURE 4-3. The Shannon-Weaver model of communication. (From C. E. Shannon and W. Weaver, *The Mathematical Theory of Communication,* Urbana, Illinois, University of Illinois Press, 1949.)

nature of communication should enable you to develop a real partnership between yourself and your listeners.

As you study the communication models, keep in mind the definition of speech communication we gave early in this chapter: The *purposeful, transactional process by which one person, through the use of audible and visible symbols, engenders meanings in the minds of his listeners.* In what ways do the models conform to this definition? What are the elements of structural correspondence? Also ask yourself, "To what extent do the models provide the five listed values?" Try to apply each value to each model.

Models of the Process

Before we look at selected models of the communication process, we should understand that all communication operates over or through a communication system. See Figure 4-1, and note that there are five elements: source, encoding and transmitting apparatus, channel, receiving and decoding apparatus, and destination. If any part is missing, communication cannot take place. When all are present, a message can be sent from the source to the destination. Note, as you study the models, the ways in which the elements of the system are utilized.

An early, verbal model is Figure 4-2; Harold Lasswell, a public-opinion expert, devised it.[1] Note that this model includes the components sender and receiver, message, channel, and response. It stresses the human factor in the process and concerns itself with the effect of the message.

A slightly different focus is found in Figure 4-3, a model devised by Shannon and Weaver,[2] two pioneers in communication and information theory. This is a verbal-graphic model. It adds a significant factor to the communication process, namely noise. We may define *noise* briefly as any stimulus that detracts from the meaning intended in any communication situation. Thus, noise may occur at any point in the communication process. The source may send an incomplete mes-

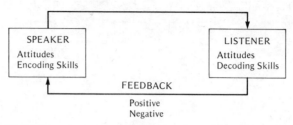

FIGURE 4-4. The Miller model of communication. From *Speech Communication: A Behavioral Approach* by Gerald R. Miller, copyright © 1966, by The Bobbs-Merrill Company, Inc. Reprinted by permission of the publisher.

sage; the transmitter may have some mechanical malfunction; or the destination, if a human being, may be biased and misinterpret the intended meaning.

You will note that the Shannon-Weaver model does not explicitly refer to the "effect" of the communication nor to its "meaning." Both these concepts are, as we shall see, essential components of the process of communication. Although it is mechanically and technically oriented,[3] the Shannon-Weaver model has been an impetus for many later diagrammatic models of communication.

By contrast, Miller's model, Figure 4-4, is oriented to human communication and indicates that certain personal characteristics of the speaker and listener must be considered. More important, however, is Miller's addition of the concept of feedback, suggesting that communication always moves in two directions, is truly a transaction between or among involved parties. Miller explains positive and negative feedback as follows:[4]

. . . those responses that are likely to be perceived as rewarding (applause, nods of agreement, apparent close attention to the message, and so forth) are labeled positive feedback, whereas those responses likely to be perceived as punishing (boos and catcalls, inattention, yawns, frowns, and so forth) are labeled negative feedback.

Still more important components are developed in the models constructed by Berlo, Johnson, and Schramm; we shall now examine them.

Berlo's model is called the SMCR model, the initials standing for *source, message, channel,* and *receiver;* see Figure 4-5.[5] Although the model does not specifically contain references to the concepts of feedback, included in the Miller model, or noise, included in the Shannon-Weaver model, Berlo refers to both of these concepts in his description of the communication process. He defines feedback as the process that *"provides the source with information concerning his*

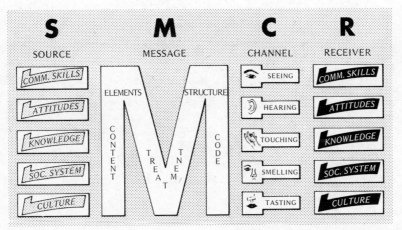

FIGURE 4-5. Berlo's "SMCR" model of communication. From *The Process of Communication: An Introduction to Theory and Practice* by David K. Berlo. Copyright © 1960 by Holt, Rinehart and Winston, Inc. Reprinted by permission of Holt, Rinehart and Winston, Inc.

success in accomplishing his objective. In doing this, it exerts control over future messages which the source encodes;" and he states that noise may be considered to include those "factors in each of the ingredients of communication that can reduce effectiveness."[6]

Besides calling our attention to the many channels through or over which communication may take place, Berlo's model focuses on the need for striving to obtain fidelity in communication. By "fidelity" we mean the extent to which the message sent by the source is replicated in the receiver. Berlo states that the five factors within the source—and also within the receiver—that determine the effectiveness of communication may be reduced to four: communication skills, attitudes, knowledge level, and the *sociocultural* system.

The last factor is more important than we are sometimes led to believe. However, Franklin Fearing, in writing on the psychology of communication,[7] stressed the importance of considering the sociocultural environment. He described communication as a cognitive and perceptual process dynamically related to the need-value systems of the communicators (senders) and interpreters (receivers). As the need-value systems of senders and receivers interact with the environment, disequilibriums (tensions) are created within the individuals. The result is a need to communicate. The messages sent and interpreted are presumed to meet these needs.

One of the significant aspects of Fearing's theory of human communication is that the communicative transaction takes place in a situation, or "field," the parts of which are interdependent upon each

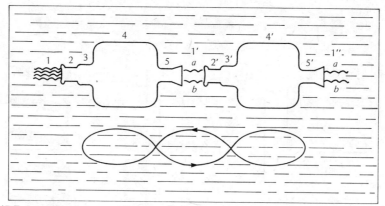

FIGURE 4-6. The Johnson diagram of stages in communication.

other. This concept of a "total communication environment" within which speech occurs is important for the student to understand.

Wendell Johnson was one of the country's foremost authorities in the area of speech pathology and audiology. We reproduce in Figure 4-6 his model.[8] Johnson stresses that an understanding of the total process of communication must encompass a consideration of the internal neurophysiological states of the participants. An explanation of this model is as follows.

Stage 1 is the event, or source of stimulation, which is external to the sensory end organs of the speaker; stage 2 is sensory stimulation; stage 3 is a preverbal, neurophysiological state; stage 4 is the transformation of the preverbal state into symbolic forms; stage 5 is the verbal formulations, in "final draft" as it were, for overt expression; stage 1' is the transformation of verbal formulations into air waves, *a*, and light waves, *b*, which serve as sources of stimulation for the listener (who may be either the speaker himself or another person); stages 2' to 1" correspond, in the listener, to Stages 2 to 1' in the speaker. The arrowed loops represent the functional interrelationships of the stages in the process as a whole.

Wilbur Schramm, although an authority in the field of *mass* communication, has given us several models of person-to-person communication, two of which are shown in Figure 4-7.[9] The first diagram indicates that for both sender and receiver communication occurs within their fields of experience. Schramm states that the two large ovals represent the accumulated experiences of the two individuals trying to communicate. It seems apparent that the greater the overlap of accumulated experiences, sometimes called *common ground*, between the source and destination, the more likely it is that the message received will coincide with the message sent. The lower diagram calls attention to the cyclical nature of the process and to the sorts of

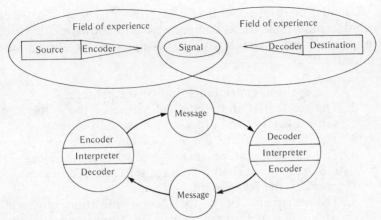

FIGURE 4-7. The Schramm models of communication. (From Wilbur Schramm, *The Process and Effects of Mass Communication*, Urbana, Illinois, Illinois University Press, 1971.)

activities that go on within an individual when he communicates. In his explanation of this diagram Schramm states:[9]

You are constantly decoding signs from your environment, interpreting these signs, and encoding something as a result. In fact it is misleading to think of the communication process as starting somewhere and ending somewhere. It is really endless.

Our examination of the models given in this chapter reveals that, among its other characteristics and components, communication encompasses at least the following elements:

1. A source and destination, both of which are affected in their attitudes, and social, cultural, and educational backgrounds.
2. A message.
3. One or more channels through which the message is sent.
4. An encoding apparatus and process.
5. A transmitting apparatus and process.
6. A receiving apparatus and process.
7. A decoding apparatus and process.
8. Noise, which affects the fidelity of transmission and reception.
9. Feedback.
10. A response, or the effect of the communication.
11. The total perceptual environment in which the communicative transaction takes place.

A model of total communication (which we shall shortly examine) would combine all these components and show, in addition, the following significant characteristics and elements of the process of communication:

1. The cyclical, continuous flow of the process.
2. The sequential and reciprocal nature of the influences that various parts of the process have on each other.
3. The direction of the communication flow.
4. The existence of an area of mutual understanding. This is the area in which the message sent has been exactly replicated by the respondent.
5. The existence of a total communication environment, which is acted upon by outside forces and contains the perceptual fields of both sender and receiver.
6. The existence of precommunication intrapersonal inputs of sender and receiver. These inputs take information from the environment, assess it in the light of the communication situation, select, encode or decode, and transmit or receive the message accordingly.
7. The positions in the process at which noise may occur.

In our examination of the communication process we shall first look at its several elements and then view it *in toto*.

Total Communication Environment

The total communicative environment, which is a constant consideration in the communication process, is shown in Figure 4-8. This is the situation that gives rise to the need to communicate and in which the communicative act occurs. The "communication environment" is composed of the perceptual fields of both sender and receiver and all the environmental influences that affect them in any way.[10] These perceptual fields are constantly being bombarded by stimuli or influences that originate from either the "total communication environment" or the world at large. For example, consider what frequently happens at a social affair. You are visiting with four or five persons, talking about sports, politics, a planned Sunday outing, or your school work. Several other small groups in the room also are conversing on various subjects. You are so engrossed in what is taking place in your own perceptual field that you ignore what the other groups are saying. You also ignore other stimuli in the total environment. Suddenly, some word, some phrase, the name of some person, or a complete sentence from another group catches your attention—enters your total communication en-

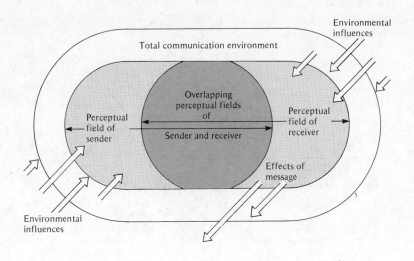

FIGURE 4-8. The total communication environment.

vironment and then your perceptual field—and you feel the need to communicate with or listen to the person in the nearby group.

The stimuli that impinge upon the environments in which we communicate are numerous. Some come from the physical world, some come from other people, and some are intrapersonal, coming from ourselves. Because these stimuli have varying strengths, they may or may not enter our perceptual fields.

Sender and Receiver
Another element of the communication process is twofold: it includes the sender, or source and communicator, and the receiver, or listener and respondent. It also includes the overlapping perceptual fields of both. In Figure 4-9 the left half represents the sender and the right half the receiver. Let us first turn our attention to the sender.

In any communicative act the sender performs three functions. He (1) acts as a source of the message, (2) communicates the message, and (3) adapts to any feedback he gets from the receiver when the receiver responds. These functions are indicated by areas 1, 2, and 3 in the figure.

Acting as the *source* of a message, the sender is affected by five "inputs." The first is his communication skills, including all the capabilities he has in speaking, listening, reading, writing, thinking, and per-

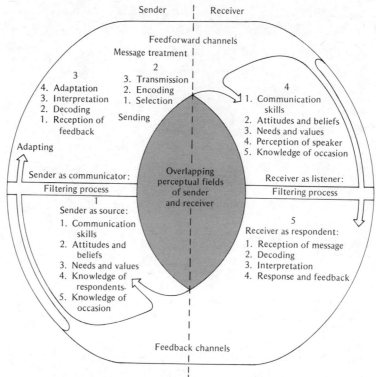

FIGURE 4-9. The sender and the receiver.

ceiving.[11] These skills aid him in planning, preparing, and presenting his message (see area 2) and in receiving and adapting to any feedback (see area 3).

The second and third inputs of the sender include the attitudes, beliefs, needs, and values of the individual. These are the acquired physiological and psychological states, predispositions, and characteristics of the individual that provide the driving force, the motivation for the individual to act in some way, including the act of speaking itself.

An example will illustrate how the second and third inputs function in the communicative act. Let us consider a person's values. A value is a learned goal and may have either positive or negative strength. That is, you may value something highly or just a little. Wrench[12] defines *value* as a "positive or negative sentiment toward something which is broad enough to serve as a criterion for evaluating attitudes and courses of action in a wide variety of areas." Thus, if ethnic pride is a value for you, and you are a Mexican-American, this value will influence you in many ways: besides joining the League of United Latin American Citizens and taking a course in Latin-American studies at college, you probably will express the opinion frequently that Mexican-Americans should not be treated as "second-class" citizens.

The fourth and fifth inputs include all that the sender knows about the audience and the occasion. This knowledge is a factor in determining the "why," "what," and "how" of the speaker's message.

These five inputs of the source are the factors out of which the message content arises. That is, they serve as filters, which screen out everything except that content which is deemed appropriate to the particular communicative transaction.

The second function of the sender is as *communicator;* see area 2 in the figure. The three parts of this function are the selection of the content, the encoding of this content into a meaningful set of understandable symbols, and the transmission of the message over the feed-forward channels. The message then is acted upon by the receiver. The planning, preparation, and presentation of any message involve both content and process, and these we shall consider, as "message treatment," in detail in the next section.

The third function of the sender is as *adapter* to the feedback that comes from the receiver when the latter reacts overtly. Let us say that one or more members of the audience react physically in some way. The speaker notes this action (reception), interprets it (say, as lack of interest), and makes some adaptation of content or delivery. When the feedback from the audience is verbal, the speaker must also decode the feedback before he can make his adaptation.

Let us now turn our attention to the right-hand part of Figure 4-9. The receiver performs the functions of listening (area 4) and responding (area 5). First, as listener the receiver is affected by essentially the same factors that determined the message sent. The receiver has certain communication skills: hearing acuity, thinking ability, and knowledge of the subject matter. What he hears is also affected by his attitudes, beliefs, needs and values. The listener's perception of the speaker also is affected by what he hears. For example, research has demonstrated that a speaker with high status will be believed more readily than one with low status; likewise, if a speaker is respected, liked, or perceived as in some way identified with the audience, his message will receive greater attention.

Second, the listener functions as communicator (respondent) when he acts upon the message received. One form of response may be feedback to the speaker. The nature of this feedback will be determined by the functions we have just mentioned. Once a message has been received, it must be decoded and interpreted in some way, and by overt physical action the respondent may feed back to the speaker some indication of his reaction to the message and what his later response may be.

Message Treatment

Message treatment deals with both the communication aspects and the procedures that the sender employs in preparing and presenting a message.

The communication aspects of message treatment are (1) the code, (2) the content, (3) the neurosensory and physiological speech structure of the sender, and (4) the channels of transmission.

Code refers to the symbols used to make a message meaningful to a receiver. In human speech communication, besides the verbal language employed, we sometimes use other visible symbols, such as gestures and body movements and supplementary visual aids.

Content refers to the rhetorical materials that compose the message. These may be facts, assertions, evidence, reasoning, illustrations, motive appeals, arguments, and the language of the message.

Neurosensory and physiological speech structure enables the sender to select, encode, and transmit his message. No communication is possible unless the communication system employed has an apparatus for encoding and transmitting the message. The receiver has a similar structure, which enables him to receive, decode, interpret, and respond in some way to the message received. The importance of this internal structure for processing messages was indicated in the Johnson model (Figure 4-6, p. 84).

Channels over which the message is transmitted and received usually are the sight and sound waves over which the signal—the symbols used—passes.

The receiver employs the same communication aspects in his handling of a message. He must understand the code used, interpret the content, and use all the parts of the human body and communication channels necessary to hear, decode, and perceive the meaning of the message.

We said earlier that message treatment deals with both communication aspects, just described, and procedures for preparing and presenting the message. Let us now look briefly at the procedures used in the treatment of a message. They are essentially those to which Johnson refers in the explanation of his model of the communication process (Figure 4-6, p. 84). The procedures are somewhat as follows. First, as a result of the interaction between the sender and the "total communication environment" an event, external to the sense organs of the sender, occurs and stimulates the sender. This event, which may be considered the motivation for speaking, sets up a preverbal neurophysiological state (Johnson's stage 3) within the speaker. This state is then translated into a symbolic form and overtly expressed (transmitted) over sight and sound waves, which serve as sources of stimulation for the receiver. The reverse process occurs in the respondent as he hears, decodes, and interprets the message.

It should be noted that the receiver, when acting as respondent, uses the same communication aspects and procedures when he prepares and transmits feedback to the speaker, as those that the speaker does when he originally selects, prepares, and transmits a message. Of course, the sender, too, becomes a receiver and respondent when he adapts to the feedback he has received and interpreted.

Message Replication

At the beginning of this chapter we defined speech communication as *the transactional process by which one person, through the use of audible and visible symbols, engenders meanings in the mind of his listener.* The ultimate goal would be, of course, to have the meaning of a message sent exactly replicated in the mind of the receiver. Although this goal is rarely, if ever, achieved, usually some degree of coincidence between message sent and message perceived is assured.

The amount of message replication is largely determined by two factors, as follows.

The first is the number of experiences and cognitions held in common by the speaker and receiver. For example, physicians, because of their training and experience, can understand the terminology of other physicians. Because of their common experiences, a football coach and his team members can communicate readily. An Air Force pilot just returned from a tour of active duty would find an understanding audience at the Air Force Academy. The more perceptions the speaker and his audience hold in common, the greater will be the likelihood of mutual message understanding.

The second factor is the rhetorical treatment of the message. For example, if a speaker uses language and supporting materials that his listeners understand, uses evidence and reasoning that they accept, and employs motive appeals that fall within the need-value systems of his listeners, then the possibility of message understanding will be enhanced.

Noise

The last element in the communication model we consider is that of noise. Noise is any unwanted stimulus, occurring within a communication system and transaction, that detracts from the meaning intended. The result is a decrease in message replication. We show the places at which noise may occur by the stars in Figure 4-10, which is a representation of the "total communication" model. We have indicated, in our explanation of Figure 4-3 (p. 81), that noise may occur in all areas of

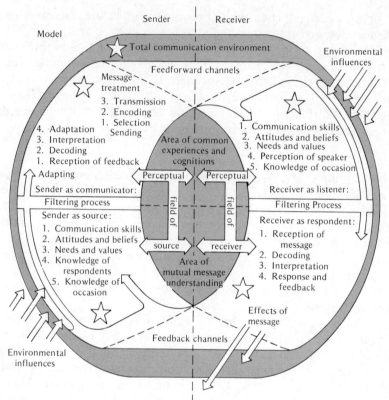

FIGURE 4-10. Model of the total communication process.

the model except the central position, that of common experiences and cognitions and mutual message understanding, or message replication. Obviously, if the speaker and listener hold common experiences, and if the intended message has been replicated exactly in the mind of the respondent, there can be little distortion of meaning. In speaking of noise Wilbur Schramm states:[13]

In engineering terms, there may be filtering or distortion at any stage. In human terms, if the source does not have adequate or clear information; if the message is not encoded fully, accurately, effectively in transmittible signs; if these are not transmitted fast enough and accurately enough, despite interference and competition, to the desired receiver; if the message is not decoded in a pattern that corresponds to the encoding; and finally, if the destination is unable to handle the decoded message so as to produce the desired response—then, obviously, the system is working at less than top efficiency. When we realize that all these steps must be accomplished with relatively high efficiency if any com-

munication is to be successful, the everyday act of explaining something to a stranger, or writing a letter, seems a minor miracle.

Noise may literally be mechanical noise, that is, outside interfering sounds, static, feedback in a public address system, or sounds of moving chairs or squeaking doors in an assembly hall. Noise, or its causes, may exist within the sender or receiver, be primarily personal, and relate to one or more of the message aspects we have described. Thus, the nature of the sender's need-value system may be such that he uses the wrong appeals in attempting to motivate his listeners. Noise may also occur in the message treatment, as when the sender does not understand how to select supporting materials that are acceptable to his listeners, when his material is improperly arranged, when his language is not adapted to his audience, or when his delivery is bombastic instead of quiet and dignified. Noise may also occur in the receiver when he acts as respondent and does not interpret the message as the speaker intended it to be interpreted. This may be due to any number of things: poor hearing, unfamiliarity with the symbol system used by the speaker, or personal bias that prevents the listener from accepting either the speaker or his arguments as credible. Finally, noise may occur in the channel, as when the power is weak or the channels are overloaded; this happens when a speaker who is "gung ho" on the use of audiovisual aids shows too many visuals at the same time. The audience is getting an oral message from the speaker while trying to attend to several messages from the visuals displayed.

It is impossible to remove all noise from the communication process; some is always present, and frequently it is found to a degree in all the aspects of the process, except in the central area in our diagram. Since this is the area in which the message received is replicated as sent, we may assume that interfering forces have been eliminated. Or, at the least, that should be your aim in speaking.

We have considered the values and nature of a number of models of the communication process in detail, because we believe that the more you know about the communication process, the more you will be able to overcome much of the noise you will encounter in any speaking situation.

Characteristics of the Communication Process
As we review the models of the communication process, certain characteristics seem to be explicit.

Function
First, the communication process is functional. It serves some of the mutual goals of sender and receiver. As we have pointed out in previous

chapters, these goals are specific. They may be overt or covert, single or multiple, but they should all be governed by the speaker's overall intent to influence behavior in a predetermined way.

A combination of openly stated and hidden speech purposes is common. It happens every day in speech classes. For example, you have been asked to give a three-minute speech to inform your classmates about some subject; this is your overt purpose. But in your own mind you have a second purpose, which may be the more important of the two: namely, to impress the teacher that you deserve an A in your grades. Open and hidden purposes are found in some of the speaking that goes on outside the classroom. Instances are readily found in advertising, administration in governmental and private areas, and in labor-management negotiations.

In Chapter Three we pointed out that giving information is invariably a necessary adjunct to influencing people. DeLaguna states:[14]

Speech is the great medium through which human cooperation is brought about. It is the means by which the diverse activities of men are coordinated and correlated with each other for attainment of common and reciprocal ends.

It is important that as intelligent citizens we participate in some constructive way in democratic decision making and problem solving. We have several modes of participation open to us: dissent, nonviolent but vocal protest, pressure, or one-to-one persuasion. History has provided many illustrations of what can happen when a group of persons, either through their own volition or because of force, fail to fulfill the obligations of citizenship. Conversely, the acceptance of these responsibilities serves the welfare of all.

Bower Aly, one of the country's foremost speech educators, in a speech delivered at the dedication of the Speech Building at Ohio University, Athens, Ohio, stated succinctly the role of speech in democratic decision-making as follows:[15]

. . . in a free society the welfare of all the citizens depends ultimately upon public opinion. If citizens do not have the ability to form sound judgments from the information and arguments presented to them, then the wise and the unwise must suffer together the consequences of their mutual failure to present and to prepare sound courses of action. That all Americans should be able to conceive policies effectively, to communicate them readily, to understand them thoroughly is a matter of first importance.

Symbolism

In our definition of speech communication we indicated that audible and visible codes were employed. Burke states[16] that communication is "the use of words by human agents to form attitudes or to induce actions in other human agents." Ross stresses its symbolic nature by defining communication as[17] "a process involving the sorting, selecting, and sending of symbols in such a way as to help a listener recreate in his own mind the meaning contained in the mind of the communicator." Because of the nature of human beings it is obvious that all messages must be sent in some code. All events, mores, objects, persons, concepts, and ways of acting that are common to persons of a given culture carry meaning and hence are symbolic codes. Writing on the role of communication in culture, Smith says:[18]

Meaning is a product of coding, and coding is a form of behavior that is learned and shared by members of a communicating group. A Burmese learns to code like other Burmese and a Bushman learns to code like other Bushmen. This is how words, gestures, and other forms of communication can carry any meaning. . . . To look at the world around us is a form of behavior. Each of us learns to look at it in the way that other members of our communicating group have learned to look at it. We . . . look at it through learned concepts, categories, and labels: animal, vegetable, and mineral; eatable, drinkable, and desirable; good, bad, and indifferent. Our perception is behavior that is learned and shared, and it is mediated by symbols. Culture is a code we learn and share, and learning and sharing require communication. And communication requires coding and symbols, which must be learned and shared. Communication and culture are inseparable.

Complexity

By now it should be obvious that communication is a complex set of interrelated processes. It is partly intrapersonal, partly interpersonal, and partly extrapersonal. The intrapersonal process consists of a myriad of neuromuscular adjustments that take place within both sender and respondent as they participate in the transaction, interacting with the total communication environment and with each other. The sender and respondent must receive, internalize, and store inputs (sensory stimuli) from the outside world, operate on the stimuli through neuroanatomical connections within themselves, and in turn translate the perceived stimuli into signs for transmission through the neurophysical organs of speech.

The interpersonal process involves a source (sender) and receiver (respondent). Both parties to the communicative act are in continuous, reciprocal interaction.

The extrapersonal process involves, and is affected by, the larger social, cultural, and physical milieu. Each communication situation has its own physical setting, unique audience, rules of procedure, social backgrounds, and patterns of verbal interaction. That is to say, communication takes place within a "total communication environment."

Reciprocity and Continuity

You can never stop a communicative act, although in our analysis of communication we have, in order to understand the process better, looked at its parts and procedures. One writer has said that communication is not something that exists, it is something that occurs. It is continuous, once started; it is reciprocal, at least in those situations in which the respondents feed back some indication of their reactions to the message received; and it is cyclical or two-way.

Stages in the Process

To illustrate how the communication process works, let us consider a typical speech act, one with which most students are familiar, and follow it by means of the accompanying diagram, left-hand column. The setting is a college classroom. The subject is "The rhetoric of Black revolt" and is taught by a speech-communication staff member who himself is a Black. The instructor is knowledgeable, serious but not bitter in his beliefs about racial discrimination, at times humorous, but always dynamic and forceful. He is well liked by his students, about a third of whom are Black. The instructor adjusts his notes on the lectern and begins by saying: "Today we shall consider briefly the ethnological argument advanced by Negro writers since the early eighteenth century in America, namely, that environment, rather than heredity, has been the main factor in keeping Blacks from realizing their full potential." There is some bustle as the instructor begins; the students open notebooks, sit up, begin writing and, as the lecture continues, overtly reflect various degrees of interest. Shortly one student raises his hand and is recognized by the instructor.

This brief illustration shows the stages in the communication process. The diagram also shows the *application* of those stages to our classroom situation (right column). Keep in mind our model of the communication process as you follow the sequence of steps in the brief communication transaction. You can easily picture mentally the nature of the "total communication environment," you can sense the nature of the interactions of the perceptual fields of the sender and respondents, and you can easily see the feedback and response.

Stages in the communication process	Application of the process to a specific communicative act
A speaker (or source)	The instructor
involved in	
some event occurring in a given setting	assigned to teach a speech communication course
recognizes	
a purpose in speaking	is to lecture on ethnological argument in Black rhetoric.
and plans	
the content of a message	He uses a chronological pattern of his subject material
which is	
encoded into aural and visual speech symbols and transmitted	and opens the lecture.
over	
sound and sight waves (channels)	There is unseen movement of sight and sound vibrations.
to	
one or more listeners (the destination)	All members of the class
who	
hear and see the audible and visible stimuli and translate them into thoughts	listen to and watch the lecturer and decode the sensory stimuli
which	
the listener then interprets	which they then intepret
and subsequently	
feeds back in oral and visual cues	and react to, mainly with physical acts and questions,
which suggest or indicate	
the immediate or intended future response.	which reflect interest in, or apathy to, the lecture.

Components of the Process

In any act of communication we go through the stages shown in the diagram referred to in the last paragraph. We might have selected the first oral exchange between the instructor and a student as the communicative act to describe. Then the student would be the sender, the respondent, the instructor. Different aspects of the interaction would assume different significances, the purpose would be changed, the content of the student's question and the instructor's answer would perhaps be brief and impromptu, and both student and instructor would be affected in their participation by their perceptions of each other.

Whatever the speaking situation, there are certain components that must be understood and considered in speech preparation. We shall now review those of greatest significance to the speaker, starting with audience.

The Respondents

"If *I* looked at the audience I'd probably faint." "I try to organize what I know about a topic as best I can and then just talk." "I probably know better than my audience what they should hear about my subject, and that's what I tell them." Comments such as these are frequently made by speakers, both beginners and experienced. They reflect an approach to speech preparation and delivery that is the greatest possible barrier to meaningful communication: self-orientation. It is the thesis of this text that *audience-orientation* is the first requisite of effective speech.

Obvious as the need of such audience awareness should be, it is not unnatural that a speaker should be concerned first with himself. He is expressing *his* idea, *his* point of view, *his* feeling. Think how often you miss what someone says because you are busy thinking what you will say next.

To achieve listener orientation does not mean that the speaker must become a specialist in the fields of psychology and social behavior. Rather, he should be able to apply a number of common-sense principles based on sound research, theory, and practice. As speakers we need to know that no two listeners live in exactly the same perceptual fields, social, psychological, or physical. Hence, the way any two listeners perceive a speaker, his purpose, and the subject matter, and the way in which their attitudes, needs, and values affect their reactions to a speech, will vary greatly. Let us look at some of the forces that make people different.

Kinds of Stimulus. We have already pointed out that forces that bombard the "total communication environment" in any communication transaction come from three worlds: the physical, the social, and the psychological. These same stimuli impinge upon both speaker and listener, once communication has begun. At this point we are concerned only with the ways in which these stimuli affect listeners.

Stimuli from the physical world frequently are significant barriers to effective listening and understanding, even for the most well-intentioned listener. The temperature and acoustics of the room, outside traffic noises, movements of restless auditors, persons walking in and out of the room, and uncomfortable seats are but a few of the external stimuli that compete with the speaker for attention. Pleasant surroundings, comfortable chairs, and absence of distractions, on the other hand, can be great aids to him.

A second type of stimulus comes to the listener from those around him, from other members of the listening audience. The messages that come from these persons may be both verbal and nonverbal. For example, a person attending a political rally is affected by the enthusiasm of other party members; a child gets cues about deportment from his older brothers and sisters, a person attending a commencement exercise usually is guided in his actions by those around him.

Finally, there are the psychological stimuli which come from the listener's personal world. These are his thoughts, wishes, loyalties, desires, knowledge, fears, beliefs, attitudes, and drives. These are things a person keeps within himself, but they determine how he thinks and feels and reacts to the messages he receives. Because man can store up sensory experiences, and because his stockpile of thoughts and feelings is constantly with him, the messages he, as listener, sends himself are of great significance. These stimuli constitute a force with which the speaker must reckon. If he understands them, they can be his allies; if he does not, they may well be his enemies. At times these internal stimuli are at a subliminal level; that is, they may be within the "total communication environment" but have not reached a level of consciousness in his perceptual field. At other times they rise to a level of awareness and determine his response to a speaker. Thus, loyalty to a political party may counteract the reasoning and evidence of an opposing party speaker. A desire to "be somebody" has caused many to succumb to a salesman's appeal. The still, small voice of conscience has kept many out of trouble. The inner messages that a listener sends himself can be so strong that he refuses to accept the proof presented by a speaker. Many a speaker has been branded a liar or a careless scholar merely because his facts contradicted the beliefs of his listeners.

Varying Interests. The increasing complexity of modern living, the tendency to specialization in almost every vocation, greater opportunities for cultural and recreational activities, developments in transportation and communication, and expansion of the use of mass media are but a few of the factors that affect an individual's interests, attitudes, and behavior. They have created a more intense, varied, and cosmopolitan life than was known a century ago. Increased travel, television, and the press have tended to combat provincialism. Attitudes, interests, and beliefs today reflect both diversity and unity. Our divergent political opinions are grounded upon basic beliefs in the democratic process. We have widely different views of how to achieve the "good life" for all citizens, but most of us believe that everyone deserves to be treated as a "first-class citizen." We believe that each has a right to hold a job for which he is trained and to receive the freedoms and rights enjoyed by others. In this country we have many different religious faiths, but at the same time we hold a common belief in freedom to worship, or not to, as we choose. Thus, though the diversity of life experiences represented by the listeners in any one audience is almost infinite, in certain respects most audiences are homogeneous.

Degrees of Orientation. If you are to speak to an audience that is highly oriented toward you, your subject, and your purpose, your task is made easy. But many audiences do not have such orientation. They must first be won over. It is well, therefore, to know the degree of orientation, or attention, in your audience. A useful classification of the degree of audience attention is that given by Hollingworth;[19] it is outlined as follows.

The audience showing the least initial unified attention is the *casual* audience; it is sometimes called "pedestrian." Loafers or passersby in a public square, people in a hotel lobby, sightseers on a midway and, frequently, television viewers, illustrate this type of audience. Its members have no speaker-listener orientation. Their reaction to a speaker, if they are even aware of him, lacks any unity. Here the first task of the speaker is to get attention.

A second type is the *passive,* or partly oriented, audience. This type is most frequently composed of captive listeners, those who are present under compulsion. Partly oriented audiences are found in many college classrooms, church congregations, service clubs, and public lectures. The members of these groups are aware of the speech situation, though their attention at first may not be entirely centered on the speaker. The speaker's first task with this group is to establish interest.

A third type is the *selected* audience, gathered for some common, known purpose. A labor union meeting, a prayer meeting, a legislative assembly, or the meeting of a professional organization is of this type. Here the speaker usually has the interest of his listeners; his first task is to impress them.

A *concerted* audience has a high degree of integrated orientation toward speaker and purpose, with a unified speaker-audience relationship. Some classes are of this type, as are research teams in industry, sales training groups, seminars, and some political groups. The primary tasks of the speaker in these groups are to persuade and direct action.

The *organized* audience has the highest degree of unified attention and dedication to the purpose of the speaking situation. Political conventions, fraternal meetings, military units, and athletic groups are of this type. The members of these groups are completely polarized toward the speaker, though sometimes because of compulsion. The speaker's task is to direct the specific action to be taken.

From the casual to the organized audience there is a progressive increase in the amount of information about the audience that can be determined in advance.

Setting

We look next at the setting in which we find our audience. This includes the background (the immediate and historical factors which gave rise to the speech occasion), matters of procedure, and the physical aspects of the meeting place.

Background. The immediate and historical factors giving rise to a speaking occasion often need to be considered by the speaker. One of the principal criteria of the effectiveness of a speech is its influence on the listeners (or on its readers, if the speech is printed). The history of public address in America is a history of debates on great issues, speeches on topics of popular interest, and countless discussions of both significant and trivial matters with which people are concerned in day-to-day living.

In studying the speech background the speaker is concerned with such questions as these: Must the speech content conform to the traditions surrounding the speech occasion? Does the occasion have epochal, far-flung ramifications, or is it local in nature? Do the antecedents of the occasion demand a speech suggesting immediate or delayed action? Is no action required?

Procedural Factors. On many occasions procedural factors should be considered. Among these are the length of the program, the order of speakers or discussion participants, the extent and nature of audience participation, and the probable action following the speaker or discussion. (The procedural factors affecting an interview are presented in Chapter Fifteen.)

The position of a particular speech, discussion, or interview in a larger frame of reference frequently affects procedure: Is the conduct of business a part of the communicative occasion? Will some social function precede or follow? Is the speech setting cultural, ritualistic, commemorative, or religious?

The Meeting Place. The physical aspects of the room in which the speech, discussion, or interview is to be held can contribute to or detract from effective communication. Acoustics is one factor, this depends on size, type of construction, outside noises, and size of the audience. The comfort of the listeners is also important. Physical features determine whether the listeners can see and hear the speaker or discussants. Also to be considered are facilities for the use of audio-visual aids, the adaptability of the meeting place to the size of the audience, the nature of the discussion formats to be followed and, sometimes, the availability of auxiliary services such as convenient transportation and parking. Many of these factors cannot be altered, but if you are the speaker or a participant in a discussion, you should be aware of them and their possible effect on the communication. Here we consider the platform-speaking situation primarily; in Chapters Fifteen and Sixteen we shall consider the effect of the physical appointments in the interview or discussion situation.

Whether the impact of the meeting place on the effectiveness of the communication is great or small, it should be considered in advance.

The Purpose

A third component of every communicative act is its purpose. Purpose is (1) the *general* response, or rhetorical purpose, and (2) the *specific* purpose, which is the immediate goal of a given speech on a particular occasion.

In Chapter Three we showed that the general purpose of speaking is to secure some form of response from the listeners; we also indicated in that chapter that any behavioral change that results from speaking will occur because the speaker has modified in some way the understanding of his hearers, has changed their attitudes or beliefs, or has appealed effectively to their needs and values. Whatever response occurs will be the result of having affected the listeners in one of these three ways.

When you speak you must also be concerned about your specific goal. This usually is different for every speech, every audience, and every occasion. For example, suppose you are talking on the subject of drug abuse. Your specific goal will differ according to whether you are talking to returned Vietnam veterans, to teenagers, to members of Synanon, or to trainees at a police academy.

Speech purposes, both general and specific, usually affect and are affected by all the other components of a communicative transaction.

The Subject Matter

An important component of the communication situation is content—the general statements and the supporting details that give them substance. The speaker must select his subject matter for a given speech both from his analysis of the listeners' experience and from his own interests and information. Both are important, but there is often a danger of placing too great an emphasis on the speaker's experiences and interests, rather than on the listeners' experiences, interests, and ability to understand.

In later chapters we shall consider at some length certain principles related to perception and learning. The point here is that we perceive and learn only in terms of what we may already know. In other words, listeners understand, learn, or accept only what their experience has prepared them to accept. For example, the student who makes straight A's finds it difficult to understand why the dullard must plod and strive for C's. The educator who believes in the traditional lecture method looks upon "group dynamics" with suspicion. The student activist views with scorn those students who will not join protest marches, take part in sit-ins, or otherwise interrupt the normal functioning of college life.

Meaningful communication in any situation can occur only if the subject matter has been developed in terms of the listener's perceptual field. That is—as we pointed out in the explanation of our model of the communication process—message replication is possible when sender and receiver are dealing with some common ground of ideas.

Instances of failure to find a common ground in communication are almost endless: the so-called generation gap, the traditional Anglo concept of the "typical" Black or Mexican-American, and the inability on the part of the general public—the taxpayers—to understand the need for greater financial support of education and to provide that support. These are but a few. To communicate effectively on these problems the protagonists must acquire greater understanding of the other's perceptual fields.

Encoder and Transmitter, Receiver and Decoder

We consider certain components of the communication process—encoding, transmitting, receiving, and decoding—as a unit, because together they include all the parts of the human body the speaker uses when he puts ideas into words and that a listener uses when he hears those words and translates them into ideas. These two stages in communication are neurophysiological in nature, involving certain sense organs, the brain, and all of the speech and hearing mechanisms. We are not concerned in this text with a study of the neurological and physiological bases of speech and hearing; that is the primary concern of the speech pathologist. However, we should of course recognize that, since speech is a "total body activity," the way our bodies function or malfunction affects the way we speak and listen.

Encoding and transmitting are both verbal and nonverbal steps in the communicative act. Encoding is the process of converting a message into transmittable energy units of visual sight and speech sounds. The conversion of message ideas of verbal and nonverbal sensory stimuli occurs as a result of activity of the nervous system and the anatomical speech mechanism. Signals or "signs" are then transmitted over the communication channels as sight and sound waves.

Assuming you have no physical defects, your major concerns in encoding relate to language use and skill in speaking. Suggestions for improving your skill in this stage of communication are given in Chapters Seven and Thirteen.

The bridge between the sender and the receiver is the channel—the sight and sound vibrations created in the air when you speak and act. These waves reach the listener, where the next stage in the communication process occurs.

Receiving and decoding are stages somewhat comparable to encoding and transmitting. The sight and sound waves travel invisibly through the air and stimulate the sense organs of the respondents. These sensory stimuli are transmitted as nervous impulses to the brain and there are decoded into words and thoughts. It is important for the respondent to be aware of both the aural and visual stimuli coming from the sender if he is to respond to and interpret the message as the sender desires.

At this point in communication your major concern as a speaker is with your listeners' skills in language use and listening. Aids to listening are considered in Chapters Seven and Eight.

Feedback and Response

Feedback from the audience is the only immediate indication available that you as a speaker have secured the desired response. Feedback is therefore an extremely important component of communication. Its value is threefold. First, it is a barometer of the listeners' acceptance of the speech purpose. Second, it serves as a governor of subsequent behavior of the speaker. If the feedback is positive, or favorable—as when the listeners laugh at a joke—the speaker continues in the same vein, states the relation of the joke to the point being made, or assumes that the point has been made and takes up a subsequent one. If the feedback is negative, or unfavorable, the speaker may modify his content or delivery until more rewarding response is evident. Third, feedback has an effect on the audience itself. This may be either favorable or unfavorable to the speaker. Suppose the speaker has been building up to a climax in a persuasive speech and has made a point that leads most members of the audience to applaud heartily. The few who have not reacted in this manner note the feedback given the speaker, begin to question their own inaction, and perhaps give greater attention to what the speaker is saying or even begin covertly to accept his message.

Most speakers should give greater attention to audience feedback than they normally do. All speakers should use feedback as a guide to on-the-spot audience adaptation.

After you have made the best possible preparation for a speaking situation and have adapted effectively to audience feedback, your fate is in the minds and hearts of your listeners. They will understand, react emotionally, or act as you wish, only if they perceive your message as a sufficient and necessary motivation for the desired response.

The Sender

We now come to the last component of every communicative act, the speaker (communicator), whether the situation is platform speaking, a discussion, or an interview. The speaker's skills largely determine the success of the communication; he has a major share of responsibility in creating a meaningful speaker-audience relationship.

Because the aim of all speaking is to secure some response from the listeners, the speaker's preparation must be audience-oriented. He analyzes the speaking situation, expands his knowledge of the subject matter, and plans the manner of presentation in relation to his prospective audience. Also, because communication is two-way, he adapts to that audience while speaking.

Foremost among the many questions the speaker must consider in his preparation are the following. What is his relationship to the audience, once he knows its characteristic? Is he aware of the reasons the listeners (discussants) are in attendance? To what extent do his and the listeners' goals coincide? Does he wish to be regarded as an "out-group" member? Is he accepted as an authority? Respected? Liked? Or will he first have to demonstrate his competence and goodwill?

The communicator must also determine his specific purpose in speaking and make this reasonably clear quite early. His answers to the following questions will modify the speech content. Is he seeking to advance his personal interests or is he concerned primarily with the welfare of others? Is he merely presenting the ideas, beliefs, and actions proposed, or does he personally support them?

The communicator must consider his command of subject matter. Is he familiar with it? Is he an authority? Can he secure needed information? Does he have time to make adequate preparation? In what ways will his own personal convictions affect his preparation?

Finally, no speaker can achieve meaningful communication unless he can present his ideas effectively. While he constantly seeks to achieve the lively, urgent sense of communication that we described earlier in this chapter, he must always adapt to the demands of the immediate situation. Does the occasion call for more or less formality? Should his vocal style be made more forceful, intimate, relaxed, or impressive? In what ways can he modify his physical activity to suit the actual speaking situation?

Any needed changes will be made most easily if the speaker has a real understanding of the role of the audience and a clear picture of his purpose, has selected and organized his subject matter effectively, and has anticipated adaptations he may have to make during the speech.

Horace G. Rahskopf, a former president of the Speech Association of America, spoke at the annual convention of that organization on December 28, 1950, and expressed concisely the point of view set forth in this chapter:[20]

Speech is a distinctive and unified process and its distinctiveness as well as its unity may be described in terms of its elements.

Again, the distinctive pattern which characterizes any act of speech, no matter in what varied form it occurs, may be described in terms of the setting. Let us remind ourselves of the familiar truth that every act of speech involves speaker, listener or listeners, time and place, body of things meant or potential things meant, and body of commonly understood symbolic processes. Speech as a primary process in human life may be described in terms of the interaction among these elements. Again the relationships are as inseparable as the elements in a chemical union and as dynamic as the particles of an atom.

IMPLICATIONS

1. We define communication as the *purposeful, transactional process by which one person, through the use of audible and visible symbols, engenders meanings in the mind* of one or more listeners. Among other implications of this definition the speaker must realize that the communication process is a two-way partnership, is symbolic, and seeks response from the listener.
2. Contrary to the belief of some, that training in speech communication is of little value, diligent study and practice will aid the student to (1) become aware of the complexity of the process, (2) recognize that *two* or more parties are involved, (3) understand where breakdowns may occur and how to avoid them, and (4) make speech preparation more efficient.
3. The study of models of the communication process will show the parts of the process and their relationships, outline its boundaries, provide guidelines to the workability of the process, suggest theoretical concepts, and aid in solving problems resulting from malfunctions in communication.

4. The speaker must be aware that all communication takes place in a communication system, the essential parts of which are a source, an encoding and transmitting apparatus, a channel, a receiving and decoding apparatus, and a destination.

5. An analysis of a number of models of the communication process and of a simple communication transaction reveals that the essential elements in a communication transaction are these: (1) a total communication environment or situation from which the need to communicate arises, (2) a speaker or sender whose participation is a function of the interactions among his personal communication skills, his need-value systems, sociocultural backgrounds, and his knowledge of his listeners, (3) a purpose in speaking, (4) a message, including both its content and code, (5) the encoding and transmitting of the message, (6) a channel or channels over which the message is sent, (7) a destination of one or more listeners, whose participation is a function of the same four interacting factors that determine the nature of the sender's participation, (8) the reception and decoding of the message by the listeners, (9) interpretation of the message, (10) oral and visual feedback from the respondent to the sender, and (11) some form of response.

6. A thorough understanding of a communicative transaction should suggest the need for concern about the factors affecting the listeners: their widely differing backgrounds and interests, variations in their degrees of speaker-orientation, the effects of the total speech setting, and their attitudes toward the general purpose of the speaker.

7. The speaker must recognize that understanding of his message (message replication) will occur only when some part of the perceptual fields of sender and respondent is held in common.

EXERCISES

1. Write your own definition of speech communication. How does it differ from that given by the authors? Be prepared to defend your definition in a class discussion.

2. Make a list of factors that warrant calling communication a transactional process. Compare your list with those of two other students. How do they differ?

3. Prepare to give a three-minute speech entitled "My misgivings about studying speech communication."

4. Think of some adult out of school or a classmate who has had some speech training. Be prepared to discuss in class what have been the values of this training.

5. Try to think of some communication situations in which you failed because you had not established common ground with your listeners. What could you have done to achieve effective communication?

6. Pick one of the models of the communication process presented in this chapter and compare it with that presented by the authors. Explain the differences. Is the authors' model too complicated? In what ways? How would you like to see it changed?

7. Think of a communication situation in which several kinds of "noise" detracted from understanding. What could have been done to eliminate or diminish them? What is the significance to a speaker of understanding the concept of noise?

8. Make a list of the physical factors that may affect the attentiveness of an audience during a speech.

9. Make a list of cues that constitute the type of feedback a speaker would receive in a face-to-face discussion situation. In a platform speaking situation. In an interview. What cues are found in all situations?

10. Think of some recent speaking situation in which you were the speaker. What was the nature and extent of your awareness of the audience? Could you see them? As individuals? Only as a group? Could you feel how they reacted to your speech and to you? Did you make any changes because of their reactions? What were they? Be prepared to discuss your analysis in class.

11. How does an awareness of the three worlds of stimuli to which listeners are subjected aid the speaker?

12. As you prepare for your next speech, try to make a mental list of the cognitive and affective components of your perceptual field. Is the list large? In what ways do these elements of your self as source affect your "message treatment"?

13. Think of some communicative situation in which you believe you achieved a high degree of message replication. What factors contributed to this effective communicative transaction? Explain them briefly in class.

14. Make a list of some codes of communication used by humans, such as signal flags, the Morse code, and religious symbolism. In what ways is speech communication, including both its verbal and nonverbal aspects, a more effective method of communicating?

15. In what sense is the expression "audience orientation" used in this chapter? Are you occasionally guilty of too great a degree of "self-orientation" in your speech preparation and delivery?

16. Conduct a conversation or interview with someone whose attitudes and beliefs on some subject are in direct opposition to your own. Probe to determine what background factors or experiences have led the other person to his point of view. If you were to give a speech to an audience made up of persons with views similar to those of the person interviewed, could you win them to your viewpoint? How would you go about doing this?

17. We have stated that the process of speech communication is functional, symbolic, complex, cyclical, and continuous. What additional characteristics would you add? Discuss your findings in class.

18. Think of two or three of your classmates whose ethnic, cultural, and educational backgrounds are different from yours. How are these differences manifested in the way each of you speaks? Are you all as effective in communication? If not, why not?

19. Pick a pair of antithetical groups, such as labor and management, parents and children, Catholics and Protestants, Hawks and Doves, or some other pair of your choice. Make a list of as many items of knowledge, experience, language, values, and so on, that might be considered common ground. Comment on your list in class.

20. Prepare a short speech on one of the following statements. If you can, relate your comments to the material of this chapter.

   a. More is meant than meets the eye. (Milton)
   b. The less men think, the more they talk. (Montesquieu)
   c. Never seem more learned than the people you are with. (Chesterfield)
   d. Better the feet slip than the tongue. (Herbert)
   e. We are less convinced by what we hear than by what we see. (Herodotus)
   f. It is hard for the happy to understand misery. (Quintilian)
   g. Speech is the gift of all, but thought of few. (Cato)
   h. A fine cage won't feed the bird. —Anonymous
   i. I pause and gaze at life from my small window. (Gibran)
   j. We must take care never to counterfeit warmth without feeling it. (Hugh Blair)

ADDITIONAL READINGS

Berlo, David K., *The Process of Communication*, New York, Holt, Rinehart & Winston, 1960, chaps. 1, 2, 3.

Branca, Albert A., *Psychology: The Science of Behavior*, rev. ed., Boston, Allyn & Bacon, 1968, chap. 12.

Brown, Charles T., *Introduction to Speech*, Boston, Houghton Mifflin, 1955, chaps. 1, 3.

Combs, Arthur W., and Donald Snygg, *Individual Behavior: A Perceptual Approach to Behavior*, rev. ed., New York, Harper & Row, 1959, chaps. 2, 3, 7, 12.

Fearing, Franklin, "Toward a psychological theory of human communication," in Dean C. Barnlund, *Interpersonal Communication: Survey and Studies*, Boston, Houghton Mifflin, 1968, pp. 30–44.

Keltner, John W., *Interpersonal Speech-Communication: Elements and Structures*, Belmont, Calif., Wadsworth, 1970, chap. 1.

Miller, George A., *Language and Communication*, New York, McGraw-Hill, 1951, chap. 1.

Miller, Gerald R., *Speech Communication: A Behavioral Approach*, Indianapolis, Bobbs-Merrill, 1966, chap. 4.

Minnick, Wayne C., *The Art of Persuasion*, Boston, Houghton Mifflin, 1957, chap. 12.

Nilsen, Thomas R., "On defining communication," in Kenneth K. Sereno and C. David Mortensen, *Foundations of Communication Theory*, New York, Harper & Row, 1970, pp. 15–24.

Oliver, Robert T., *The Psychology of Persuasive Speech*, New York, Longmans, Green, 1942, chaps. 4, 9.

Ross, R. S., "Fundamental processes and principles of communication," in Keith Brooks, ed., *The Communicative Arts and Sciences of Speech*, Columbus, Merrill, 1967, chap. 8.

Ruesch, Jurgen, and Gregory Bateson, *Communication: The Social Matrix of Psychiatry*, New York, Norton, 1951, chap. 11.

Schramm, Wilbur, "How communication works," in Wilbur Schramm, ed., *The Process and Effects of Mass Communication*, Urbana, Univ. Illinois Press, 1961, pp. 3–26.

Winans, James A., *Speech Making*, New York, Appleton, 1938, chap. 1.

Zelko, Harold P., and Frank E. X. Dance, *Business and Professional Communication*, New York, Holt, Rinehart & Winston, 1965, chap. 1.

NOTES

[1] H. D. Lasswell, "The structure and functions of communication in society," in Lyman Bryson, ed., *The Communication of Ideas*, New York, Harper & Row, 1947, p. 37.

[2] C. E. Shannon and W. Weaver, *The Mathematical Theory of Communication*, Urbana, Univ. Illinois Press, 1949, p. 98.

[3]The process of communication, according to the Shannon-Weaver model is as follows. A source, which might be a machine or a human, produces a message, which is operated on by the transmitter so as to produce a signal as, for example, the "dot" and "dash" of the Morse code. The signal is transmitted over a channel, and a perceived signal is again operated on, this time by the receiver, which reconstructs the signal as a message for the destination, that is, whoever is to take action.

[4]Gerald R. Miller, *Speech Communication: A Behavioral Approach*, Indianapolis, Bobbs-Merrill, 1966, p. 55.

[5]David K. Berlo, *The Process of Communication*, New York, Holt, Rinehart & Winston, 1960, p. 72.

[6]*Ibid.*, pp. 40, 111–112.

[7]Franklin Fearing, "Toward a psychological theory of human communication," *J. Personality*, 22 (no. 1, Sept. 1953), 71–88.

[8]Wendell Johnson, "The Spoken Word and the Great Unsaid," *Quart. J. Speech*, 37 (no. 4, Dec. 1951), 419–429.

[9]Wilbur Schramm, "How communication works," in Wilbur Schramm, ed., *The Process and Effects of Mass Communication*, Urbana, Univ. Illinois Press, 1961, pp. 6, 8.

[10]See Arthur W. Combs and Donald Snygg, *Individual Behavior: A Perceptual Approach to Behavior*, rev. ed., New York, Harper & Row, 1959, pp. 16–36. Among other things, these authors state: "By the perceptual field, we mean the entire universe, including himself, as it is experienced by the individual at the instant of action." They also say: "No matter what we are told, our own perceptual field will always seem real, substantial, and solid to us. It is the only field and the only reality we can directly experience. It includes all the universe of which we are aware—including not only the physical entities which exist for us but such other entities as justice, injustice, and public opinion. It also includes experiences of love and hate, or fear, anger, and human compassion which do not exist outside the experience of people. So strong is our feeling of reality with respect to our perceptual field that we seldom question it. . . .

The unique set of developmental experiences—homelife, peer group activities, vocational and avocational interests, and cultural and educational backgrounds—are the forces which help in the formation of the individual's needs, attitudes, and beliefs. This configuration of cognitive and affective material, interacting with his physical environment at any point in time, is roughly equivalent to 'perceptual field.' "

We believe that no effective communication can be achieved unless subject matter and purpose are consistent with, and developed out of, the reality of the world as the listener perceives it. This point is stressed throughout our text and is basic to our communication model.

[11]See Berlo, *op. cit.*, pp. 41–52.

[12]David F. Wrench, *Psychology: A Social Approach*, New York, McGraw-Hill, 1969, p. 253.

[13]Schramm, *op. cit.*, pp. 4–5.

[14]Grace Andrus de Laguna, *Speech: Its Function and Development*, New Haven, Yale Univ. Press, 1927, p. 19.

[15]Bower Aly, "Crisis in Christendom," *Vital Speeches*, 18 (no. 6, Jan. 1, 1952), 181.

[16]Kenneth Burke, *A Rhetoric of Motives*, Englewood Cliffs, N.J., Prentice-Hall, 1950, p. 41.

[17]Raymond S. Ross, *Speech Communication*, Englewood Cliffs, N.J., Prentice-Hall, 1965, p. 4.

[18]Alfred G. Smith, ed., *Communication and Culture*, New York, Holt, Rinehart & Winston, 1966, pp. 6–7.

[19]H. L. Hollingworth, *The Psychology of the Audience*, New York, American Book, 1935, pp. 19–31.

[20]Horace G. Rahskopf, "Effective speech," *Vital Speeches*, 17 (no. 11, Mar. 15, 1951), 346.

CHAPTER FIVE
UNDERSTANDING YOUR LISTENERS

Rhetoric, as was observed already, not only considers the subject, but also the hearers and the speaker. The hearers must be considered in a two-fold view, as men in general, and as such men in particular.
George Campbell

In this book we stress constantly that the most important element in the communication situation is the listener, the person we wish to respond in some way to our message. In this chapter our concern is with this listener as an individual. We view selected aspects of man's behavior; his habitual, emotional, and intellectual ways of acting; the nature of his perception and how he perceives himself and the world about him; how he learns and thinks; and the nature of his attention as he relates to people, things, and events. We also look briefly at some of the ways he behaves as a member of a group. In a word, then, we will learn many of the things we need to know about the individual or individuals who may become our partners in some communicative transaction.

MODES OF HUMAN BEHAVIOR

To adapt himself to the world in which he lives, man behaves in three different ways: as a creature of habit, of emotion, and of mind. Although one type of behavior predominates at any given instant, any individual action usually has elements of all three. Each type is important; each serves man continuously; each develops and manifests itself in different ways.

All behavior is purposeful. Whatever we do serves some biological, social, or intellectual goal. Lindgren describes the psychologist's concern with the purposive nature of behavior as follows:[1]

All Behavior is Purposive. *This idea strikes at the very roots of "common sense," which perceives much of human behavior as senseless and purposeless. If we follow the dictates of "common sense" in this matter, we are faced with the necessity of surrendering to what appears to be the inevitable stupidity of mankind, or becoming cynical, or taking steps to force people to act sensibly in spite of their perverse nature. The psychologist's approach, on the other hand, is quite different. Since he assumes that all behavior has a purpose, his task is to uncover that purpose. No matter how senseless and unreasonable human behavior appears, he knows that it serves some purpose or purposes for the doers; he knows that if he can discover the purposes, he can understand and predict the occurrence of this and perhaps even undertake to control and redirect it.*

Writing on educational psychology in the classroom, Lindgren again stresses the purposeful nature of behavior and suggests its complexity:[2]

. . . all behavior, however irrational it may seem, has purpose . . . that . . . results from a multiplicity of causes.

The speaker, faced with this realization, must understand not only human behavior but also the forms it takes. Habit, a form of human behavior, will be examined first.

Man a Creature of Habit

The essence of what is meant by *habit* may be extracted from these statements:

When we say that a man has a habit, we mean that he has the tendency to act in specific ways under specific circumstances.[3]

When an activity has been practiced until it is well integrated and until one does not have to pay close attention to it to perform it, that activity is called a habit.[4]

In everyday speech the word habit *refers mainly to extensively practiced and well-established modes of response.*[5]

A habit, therefore, may be described as a learned, seemingly automatic, situationally oriented, and useful behavior pattern. It is a form of conditioned response; it serves as a shortcut in problem solving, as a means of adjustment in critical life situations, and as a way of conserving the energy needed for day-to-day living. Habits result from adjusting to or overcoming obstacles and situations that require some reaction on the part of the individual. When the response first occurs, it may be innate, reflexive, emotional, or intellectual, but with repetition of the situation-stimulus it becomes habitual.

One aspect of habit that has special significance for the speaker is its motivational character. John Dewey described this character of habit in the following passages:[6]

We may think of habits as means, waiting, like tools in a box, to be used by conscious resolve. But they are something more than that. They are active means, means that project themselves, energetic and dominating ways of acting. . . .

Habit means special sensitiveness or accessibility to certain classes of stimuli, standing predilictions and aversions, rather than bare recurrence of specific acts. It means will.

In other words, the individual has what may be termed a habitual way of reacting to certain situations. He attributes certain physical, social, and intellectual characteristics to certain groups of people; he dislikes to break with tradition; he will listen more frequently to speakers he likes than to those he dislikes or does not know about. In short, he is a creature of habit.

Consider the ways in which habit affects your own life. There is probably much regularity in the time you get up, the places you study on campus, the persons with whom you eat your meals, the time at which you read the daily campus paper, and the type of campus activities in which you participate.

It is safe to say that habits constitute a significant force in all social behavior. The social psychologist Kimball Young describes the role of habit in these terms:[7]

But the term habit comprehends more than merely acquiring these proficiencies (manual dexterities). It applies to the development of fundamental traits of personality: attitudes toward oneself, toward others, and toward the physical universe. It involves acquisition of behavior patterns which lie at the root of curiosity, acquisitiveness, desire for prestige, desire for new experience, and all sorts of wishes expressed in social interaction and participation. It is basic to one's conception of oneself.

The attitudes we have toward people, our prejudices, our beliefs, the way we use language, the way we solve problems, and many physical actions are all greatly affected by our habits.

Man an Emotional Organism
The emotional behavior of man has long been of concern to speakers

and speech educators. As students of speech communication we need to understand this psychological phenomenon.

Characteristics of Emotional Behavior
In one of the earliest treatises on speaking, Aristotle, in his *Rhetoric*, devotes a large part of Book II to the emotions and how the speaker may employ them to his advantage. Here is an example:[8]

Take, for instance, the emotion of anger: here we must discover (1) what the state of mind of angry people is, (2) who the people are with whom they usually get angry, and (3) on what grounds they get angry with them. It is not enough to know one or even two of these points; unless we know all three, we shall be unable to arouse anger in any one. The same is true of the other emotions.

If the speaker wishes to affect the emotions of others, control his own to achieve desired goals, or employ emotional language and behavior in communicating, he must understand the nature of the concept of emotion. There is no ready answer to the question "What is an emotion?" However, by studying the descriptions of this concept we can begin to see its general and salient characteristics. Morgan suggests some of its many facets in this statement:[9]

We all know in general what we mean by it [emotion], but we find it difficult to say precisely what we mean. That is because emotion has several different aspects. For one, it is a stirred-up bodily state in which changes occur in our breathing, heart rate, circulation, and other physiological functions. It is also a pattern of expression—smiling, laughing, crying, cringing, and so on; it is something we do. Thirdly, it is something we feel—happiness, disappointment, unpleasantness, elation. And finally, emotion is also a motive: it keeps us working toward some goals and avoiding others.

The physiological states that are a part of emotions are mentioned in the following definition:[10]

An emotion can be considered to be an affective experience that is accompanied by generalized inner adjustment and physiological and stirred-up states, and that expresses itself in overt behavior.

Another important aspect of emotion is suggested in this definition by psychologists Arthur W. Combs and Donald Snygg:[11]

. . . emotion is a state of tension or readiness to act. This tension repre-

*sents the reaction of the organism to the perception of the possibility
of need satisfaction (self-enhancement) or the perception of threat
(maintenance of self).*

Branca says that we cannot observe all the changes taking place
within an individual when he experiences an emotion but that there are
at least three aspects of importance:[12]

*First, emotion is usually thought of as the way one may feel about
something. This view of emotion is that of conscious experience, or the
"state of mind" one is feeling.*

*A second aspect of emotion is the physiological. This view ap-
proaches emotion through the physiological changes that take place in
our organs as part of the emotional response.*

*The third aspect is the behavioral, the organism's observable reac-
tions toward objects and people.*

In brief, we may describe an emotion as a conscious, generalized, internal tension and readiness to act, usually manifesting itself in
overt action. It manifests itself in our feelings, physiological states, and
behavior. It is both a pattern of expression and a form of total bodily
behavior that motivates both our intellectual and habitual ways of
acting. Emotions occur because of some "arousing situation."

Some writers make a distinction between what they call primary, or main, *emotions*, essentially disruptive in nature, such as fear,
anger, grief, and joy, and *affective states*, less intense in nature, such as
sympathy, pity, envy, well-being, reverence, and adoration.[13]

Causation of Emotions

The onset of emotion has significance for the communicator. Writing
on this point a psychologist, Harold S. Tuttle, says:[14]

*The point at which emotion begins is in clear view. It is not in the stim-
ulating situation. Meaningful sensations arouse feelings and awaken
imagination; if the imagined sequence is unpleasant, reflective thinking
is set up, and plans are formulated. Emotion ensues if no adequate
plans can be thought of or if plans are frustrated. No emotion occurs if
adequate adjustments are provided by habit or by reflection based on
available data. It is the lack of a completely satisfactory plan of action
that sets up the emotional state.*

Thus, an emotional state may result, not only from a sudden
shock, but from an intellectual insight into all the implications of a
perplexing situation. That is, the thwarting that frequently results from

a reflective analysis of a problem situation can be the cause of an emotional state. The situation must have some significance before an emotional state is aroused. It is generally accepted that emotions result from objects, people, events, or situations that either threaten or promise some benefit to the individual. We are emotionally aroused because of things we fear, things that make us angry, and things or persons we love. In a milder sense we are frequently annoyed, worried, or sympathetic.

We get some notion of the wide range of emotional causation from the terms we use to describe our emotions. Emotions reflecting a negative connection or repulsion between persons or between a person and an object are hate, envy, jealousy, disgust, displeasure, grief, and revenge. Emotions reflecting a positive bond or attraction are passion, love, friendship, congeniality, and sympathy. Emotions reflecting internal causation primarily are sorrow, grief, shame, remorse, and regret. One psychologist collected more than twenty-one thousand descriptions of situations said to be annoying (a milder type of emotion) by large groups of people.

Whenever we confront a perplexing situation or one giving satisfaction, some emotional state is likely to result. In fact, during our waking hours most of the things that happen to us evoke behavior having some emotional accompaniments.

Intensity of Emotions

Closely related to causation is the intensity of our emotions. At times our emotions "consume" us and again we are "unmoved." Love may range from intense passion to covert adoration; hate may range from unbridled enmity to controlled contempt. Our reactions to a speech, too, frequently are emotional and may range from intense feelings and physical manifestations of approval to covert and mild acceptance, disapproval, or total lack of interest.

The effective speaker seeks to develop in his listeners emotional states that fall between these extremes. Minnick puts it this way:[15]

As one approaches either of these extremes, intelligent behavior is inhibited—in one case because there is no motivation (no concern) at all, in the other because the motivation (concern for the outcome) is overpowering. The desirability of some emotional involvement in other than habitually experienced events is indicated, but too great an involvement is manifestly undesirable.

An admirable example of a speech in which the speaker sought controlled and directed emotional response is the "War Message" of Woodrow Wilson, presented to Congress on April 2, 1917. At that time

America had suffered great losses from unrestricted attacks on American shipping and passenger vessels. Tension against Germany was mounting. Wilson recognized that the United States could not remain neutral, and Congressional approval of his recommendation to declare war was needed. At the same time he realized that a declaration of war might result in acts of hostility against loyal Germans living in this country. Consequently, he directed his charges against the German Empire rather than the German people and urged any sacrifice necessary to make political liberty a reality, while cautioning against unwarranted action against American citizens of German birth. His speech proposed action under conditions of considered judgment and controlled emotional involvement:[16]

It is a war against all nations. American ships have been sunk, American lives taken, in ways which it has stirred us very deeply to learn of, but the ships and people of other neutral and friendly nations have been sunk and overwhelmed in the waters in the same way. There has been no discrimination. The challenge is to all mankind. Each nation must decide for itself how it will meet it. The choice we make for ourselves must be made with a moderation of counsel and a temperateness of judgment befitting our character and our motives as a nation. We must put excited feeling away. Our motive will not be revenge or the victorious assertion of the physical might of the nation, but only the vindication of right, of human right, of which we are only a single champion.

In recent years the question of racism and equal rights for minority groups has been discussed, talked of, and written about and has been reflected in the actions of Blacks and Whites alike. Some Blacks advocate assimilation, some advocate nonviolent separatism, and a smaller number advocate the overthrow of the existing government. The wide variance in emotional appeals made by Black leaders is seen in the following two excerpts from speeches by Robert C. Weaver and James Forman. Weaver had been appointed by President Johnson in 1966, the first secretary of the newly created Department of Housing and Urban Development, and was the first Black to serve in the Cabinet. As a veteran leader in the civil rights movement he gave a speech in Chicago in 1963 in a program sponsored by the Fund for the Republic. Following is part of what he said about Negro leadership:[17]

Most Negroes in leadership capacities have articulated the fact that they and those who follow them are a part of America. They have striven for the realization of the American dream. Most recognize their responsibilities as citizens and urge others to follow their example. Sophisticated whites realize that the status of Negroes in our society depends not

*only upon what the Negro does to achieve his goals and prepare himself
for opportunities but, even more, upon what all America does to expand these opportunities. And the quality and nature of future Negro
leadership depends upon how effective those leaders who relate to the
total society can be in satisfying the yearnings for human dignity which
reside in the hearts of all Americans.*

The excerpt quoted above was the conclusion of a speech that
was moderate yet forceful in tone. Contrast it in degree of emotional
intensity with the following summary of the type of Negro leadership
needed in this country, as stated by James Forman in *The Black
Manifesto,* first presented at the National Black Economic Development
Conference held at the Wayne State University campus in April, 1969.
The *Manifesto* demanded the payment of $500,000,000 by the Chris-
tian churches and Jewish synagogues of the country to the Blacks. The
money was to be used in implementing the parts of the *Manifesto.* The
Black leadership needed is described as follows:[18]

*To implement these demands we must have a fearless leadership. We
must have a leadership which is willing to battle the church establishment to implement these demands. To win our demands we will have to
declare war on the white Christian churches and this means we may
have to fight the government structure of this country. Let no one here
think that these demands will be met by our mere stating them. For the
sake of the churches and synagogues we hope that they have the wisdom to understand that these demands are modest and reasonable. But
if the white Christians and Jews are not willing to meet our demands
through peace and goodwill, then we declare war and are prepared to
fight by whatever means necessary.*

Control of Listeners' Emotional Behavior

Two primary factors in both the control and the development of
emotional behavior are maturation and learning. The infant's responses
to emotional stimuli (tension) are usually vigorous, uncontrolled, and
undifferentiated. As the child grows older and has more experiences, he
loses many of his childhood fears and begins to reach, as Ruch says,[19]

*. . . the level of physical and psychological development where he must
learn to bear frustration—to give up the complete satisfaction of his
own needs and begin meeting the demands of his particular culture.
One lesson he learns is that violent, uncontrolled expression is not acceptable. Thus while a growing number of social restrictions increase
the child's emotional tensions, they also impose rules on the way he can
release them. Fortunately, by sacrificing some of his demands, he is*

able to gain the positive emotional satisfaction of approval, praise, at-
tention, and affection.

By the time the child is an adult he controls his emotional reactions—in accordance with the culture in which he lives—or, if the stimulus giving rise to the emotion is intense, he too may express his emotions through violent physical action, by invective, or by withdrawal. The person who is emotionally mature, however, has learned to keep his emotions under control. But the individual is left with the decision about when and how and under what conditions he can engage in emotional behavior.

The significance to the speaker of what we have just stated lies in the nature of the factors that determine the degree of emotional intensity of a stimulus. They are (1) the physical and psychological immediacy of the event, (2) the clarity of the perception of the event, and (3) the feelings of ability to cope with the event.

The first of these factors is the nearness of the event to us in time or space and the extent and way in which it affects us directly. The general public was greatly aroused when in May, 1970, during a mass demonstration four Kent State University students were fatally shot by members of the National Guard. Today concerned officials are still trying to attach the blame for the shooting, but the event has lost its emotional force, except perhaps at the University itself. In Wisconsin people reacted violently to the bombings that took place on the Madison campus in 1970; these bombings were of less concern to the students at the University of California, Santa Barbara, where, in the student living center at Isla Vista, about the same time, the branch bank building of the Bank of America was twice burned to the ground. We react more violently to emotional stimuli near to us. When the stocks we own begin to decrease in value, when a friend begins to use drugs, when our own grades begin to go down, then we start to worry. We are most aroused by events that affect us directly.

Weaver, in a speech at Chicago on June 13, 1963, sought to bring the reality of the problems of the Negro home to his audience—to make those problems meaningful to a largely white audience—in the following manner:[20]

The Negro here—as he has so frequently and eloquently demonstrated—
is an American. And his status, no less than his aspirations, can be mea-
sured meaningfully only in terms of American standards.

Viewed from this point of view what are the facts?

Median family income among non-whites was slightly less than 55
percent of that for whites in 1959; for individuals the figure was 50 per-
cent.

Only a third of the Negro families in 1959 earned sufficient to sustain an acceptable American standard of living. Yet this involved well over a million Negro families, of which 6,000 earned $25,000 or more. . . .

Over two-thirds of our colored workers are still concentrated in five major unskilled and semi-skilled occupations, as contrasted to slightly over a third of the white labor force.

In 1959 non-white males who were high school graduates earned on the average, 32 percent less than whites; for non-white college graduates the figure was 38 percent less.

The second factor, the clarity of the perception of the event, is a matter of the degree to which it appears satisfying or threatening. Many parachutists see no danger in free falls of thousands of feet; they know the safeguards they must take to protect themselves. Many automobile racers report that they think less of the dangers of their sport than of the testing of the man and the machine. Likewise, listeners are more willing to adopt a course of action if the goal is clear, if possible risks are noted, and if ways of averting or protecting against them are known.

The third factor affecting the intensity of an emotional state is our feeling adequate to handle the event causing the emotion. When we feel that we have things "well in hand," our approach to a problem is calm and collected; when we feel inadequate, we have feelings of insecurity, shame, and resentment, and even despair.

President Nixon, as have many Presidents before him, used the approach "We have things well in hand" in the last year of his first term in office, to gain favorable acceptance of many of his policies. In several public statements he assured the citizens of this country that the pull-out from Vietnam was on or ahead of schedule, that his price control and monetary programs were stabilizing the country's economy, and that his overtures to the leaders of Red China were in the best interests of the total world. In other words, everything was under control.

The speaker controls the emotional intensity of his audience through the use of the three factors mentioned above. Think for a moment about some of the events, the speech topics, that you have discussed with other students. We mention just a few reported to us by some of our students: the right of eighteen-year-olds to vote, relaxing the abortion laws, dress codes in schools, the use of drugs by persons of all ages, the problem of credibility in high places, the Pill, censorship, pornography, pollution control, the Vietnam war, the relevance of religion to everyday living, and the difficulty of paying the increasing costs of an education. Ask yourself these questions about the topics or about others you have discussed: "Is this a problem I have been concerned about, either physically or psychologically?" "If I have been concerned about the topic, do I see clearly how it might be solved to my satisfaction?" "Could I solve it by myself or with the help of others?" As you think about such problems, try to determine whether you feel emotionally involved. Would you act on one of these topics as some speaker suggested, if the proposal seemed to conform to your needs or values?

Man an Intellectual Being

We have seen that man may act because of habit or because he has been aroused emotionally. Both ways of acting may give either pleasure or pain. However, as the individual grows older, he learns to control to some degree both forms of behavior.

It should be noted that we said the individual *learns* to control his behavior. We may rightly ask "What do we mean by learning?" and "What is the relation of learning to communication?" We consider these questions now.

Nature and Principles of Learning

From the millions of words written about the process of learning we can glean certain concepts and principles that aid in our study of communication. Morgan calls learning *"any relatively permanent change in behavior that is the result of past experience."*[21] Learning may occur as the result of observation, study, experience, practice, instruction, identification, or insight. Lindgren comments on the nature of learning this way:[22]

Learning is a natural outcome of the individual's attempts to meet basic and normal needs and to ward off anxiety. Inasmuch as we function as changing organisms in a changing environment, we must continually make adjustments in our behavior if we are to meet our needs. Some adjustments we make because we want to ward off actual or potential threats to the satisfaction of our needs. Some adjustments we make in an effort to meet our needs more effectively. When we find ways of adjusting our behavior satisfactorily, we are learning something. If behaving in a certain way in a certain situation results in satisfaction, it will probably result in satisfaction again. Hence we are inclined to repeat the behavior if circumstances make it seem appropriate.

Learning is obviously complex. It is engaged in both consciously and unconsciously, and it involves both a cognitive and a motivational component. Learning is a function of the maturation of the individual in the culture in which he lives. It has its roots in the need to resolve some problem. It involves the totality of the individual's past experience. Each occasion for learning involves the restructuring of this learning potential in terms of the perceived needs of the situation. Learning is an active process, resulting in the development of needed habit patterns, skills, and cognition.[23]

Having looked briefly at the "what" of learning, let us now consider the "how"—the things that take place when we learn. Certain of these principles of learning have significance for the speaker.

Motivation. Little learning, and hence little understanding, result without motivation. As Dewey says, there must be some perplexity to be resolved, a "forked-road situation." This motivation may be either external and overt—that is, the individual may be told he should learn certain things—or it may be internal and covert. The prominent educator May V. Seagoe states:[24]

The learner himself need not be aware of his motivations or that he is learning or of the component acts of learning: in other words, it is not essential that he consciously "intend" to learn. But it is essential that some motivation be operative, even if it is only a tendency to try to understand.

Involvement of the Learner. As we have seen, learning is an active process. The theory that "being told is learning," widely held at one time, has few supporters today. The amount of learning is in proportion to the participation by the learner; mental and physical activity increases the effectiveness of the learning process.

Rewards. "Learning takes place only when the act that is performed is reinforced or rewarded," says Percival M. Symonds of Teachers College, Columbia University.[25] This is essentially the point of Thorndike's Law of Effect, which states that the connection between a stimulus and a response is strengthened when the outcome of an act is perceived as rewarding. Empirical evidence supports the application of this principle to the speaker-listener relationship. When a listener is persuaded that a proposed action will help in the achievement of some desired goal, the bond between action and goal will be reinforced, learning will be increased, and commitment to the action will be that much greater.

Readiness to Learn. E. L. Thorndike was one of the first educators to advance the principle of readiness: when an individual is ready to do something, to do it is satisfying, and not to do it is annoying.

One of the criticisms leveled at our educational system is that much of what the students are asked to learn has no relevance to their immediate needs and personal experiences. This criticism is partly valid. It is a primary reason for the development of Black and Chicano Studies in colleges and universities across the country in recent years. Readiness to learn has been a partial factor in what success the training programs for the hardcore unemployed have had. Training programs in the military, union apprentice programs, technical trade-school courses, and even review lectures, as given by some college instructors before exams, are based on the assumption that a "need to know" will increase readiness to learn.

Focus on Content. Many speakers, and especially beginning student speakers, ignore these facts: that the target of a speech (its specific purpose) must be clearly conceived by the speaker and clearly perceived by the listener, and that the means of hitting the target (the pertinence of the materials of the speech) must be instantly apparent to the listener. The most frequent criticisms made of the content of speeches of college students are that they are discursive, that the thesis is not always clear, and that the point of the speech is not obvious.

Perception in the Learning Process
Before a person can engage in the learning process, he must perceive the elements of the learning stimulus and situation. Perception in the learning process thus becomes important to the speaker. He needs to know what occurs when people "perceive."

Here is what a psychologist has to say about the process of perception:[26]

Perceptions are orientative *reactions to stimuli. They have in part been determined by the past history and present attitude of the perceiver. When a person perceives an object (or a symbol for an object), he becomes oriented to it with respect to its present setting and with respect to his past experience with the particular object or with similar objects.*

The most important element in distinguishing between sensation and perception is the amount of participation of the person in the sensory experience. If the stimulus object dominates and determines the whole experience, we are considering a sensation. If the person's past experience provides information or comparative material, and if the person's attitude at the moment lends some meaning or feeling to the sensing experience, we are dealing with perception. . . .

Merely naming an object or a sensation, as when we say a color is red, is a perceptual function, because we are designating the object or color by a word name. The association of the word with the color or the object has occurred before in our history.

A statement by Ruch gives further understanding of the concept of perception:[27]

The process of perception stands midway along a continuum from sensing to thinking. In its purest, perhaps hypothetical form, sensing does not involve the use of learning based on past experience. Thinking, at the other end of the continuum, is independent of stimuli from physically present objects; it is accomplished through the use of symbols which represent absent objects and the relationships among them.

We may summarize these writings and describe perception as a mental process that involves several stages. (1) An awareness of the thing perceived: the object, event, or concept must become a part of the learner's perceptual field[28] through some sensory impression. (2) Differentiation: the thing perceived is set apart from other stimuli. (3) An understanding recognition: the thing perceived is assigned meaning. This reaction to a stimulus—awareness, differentiation, and meaning—is the perception.[29] It is our discriminating understanding of objects, qualities, relationships, persons, and events, whether any of these life facts are objectively present or not.

Three facts are of importance to the speaker. (1) The way a person behaves is determined by the way he perceives. (2) The way he perceives is the only reality he can understand. (3) The way a person perceives and behaves is a function of his background and experience. Members of labor and management perceive and may act differently on a proposal for a wage increase, yet each believes his point of view is *right*. Differences in religious backgrounds will make two people seek salvation in entirely different ways; yet each will claim his to be the only way, and each will be unable to understand the other's point of view.

Perception always takes place in a frame of reference that is uniquely personal to the perceiver. It is usually difficult for a student to understand why he gets a poor grade in a course. It is also difficult for those of us who are instructors to understand why students don't understand why they got the poor grades, especially after we have explained the reasons—to our satisfaction. Our inability to understand that another person's way of perceiving life around him is "reality" for that person is a basic reason for our inability as Americans to act realistically toward communism. This failure was explained in the following terms by Senator Dodd of Connecticut:[30]

A detailed knowledge of communism in all the aspects is available; indeed it is abundant. But the evil of communism is so alien, so appalling,

*so far removed from anything in our own experience, that our intellec-
tuals and our people ignore the evidence.*

*By and large, men believe what they are prepared to believe, what is
familiar to them, what jibes with their own experience. We ignore the
clear sign in order to retain our familiar conceptions. We shield our eyes
from the reality of communism or we lack the intellectual curiosity to
inquire into it.*

A highly respected member of the speech profession, Waldo W.
Braden, of the Louisiana State University, in a speech given before Phi
Kappa Phi on his own campus on April 29, 1971, pointed out that
listeners perceive only in terms of their own experiences. The speech
dealt with the problems the education profession has in communicating
with persons outside that profession. He said:[31]

*Let me remind you. We communicate—not by what we are, but by
what listeners think we are. We communicate—not by what we know,
but by what listeners understand. We communicate—not by what we
intend to say, but by what listeners see, hear and are willing to accept.
We communicate—not by what we say, but by what listeners hear.*

The speaker will find it easier to sell his ideas if he keeps in
mind the possible great diversity between what reality is to himself and
what it may be to his listeners. Much conflict and many breakdowns in
communication result from inevitable differences in the "private realities" of the persons involved. We frequently call others prejudiced,
obstinate, or perverse, when they merely have different frames of
reference from our own. The person who tells the driver of a car,
"You're going too fast," may be thinking of a recent accident, even
though the driver may be staying within the legal limit. In 1971
President Nixon, when he announced his plans to go to Peking by May
of 1972 to visit Mao Tse-tung and Premier Chou En-lai of the People's
Republic of China, set off a wave of questioning reassessment on the
part of many leading Americans—who had opposed increasing contacts
with Red China—concerning the reality of their beliefs. Could it be that
for years many Americans had been viewing China incorrectly, through
their own peculiarly red-tinted glasses?

The following remarks were made in a speech delivered in 1971
at the 59th annual meeting of the Chamber of Commerce of the United
States, in Washington, D.C., by Mr. Charles M. Brooks, the Corporate
Manager of Labor Relations for Texaco, Inc. His remarks reflect a
perceptual field somewhat different from that represented by the
leaders of labor unions in this country.[32]

If we concede—as I think we must—that the high wage increases are causing the inflationary conditions, the question presented is whether union power is at fault. I think the evidence is overwhelming that union power does cause this cancerous condition of inflation.

This awesome power of the unions is the power to shut down railroads, silence telephones, stop fire-fighting, interfere with police and other essential services—the power to stop mail service—the power to do many things that are not allowed to any other being, organization or institution.

These were his final remarks:

It seems to me that in order to break the shackles that threaten to enslave us in inflation, we must dare to reason our way into legislation and attitudes that will curb the power of the unions to coerce, intimidate, threaten, commit acts of violence, control manpower supply and overpower all who oppose them.

Let us dare to require that the behavior of labor unions be in the public interest. Let us dare to insist that America be for all Americans.

One significant aspect of perception is that it is selective. Of the countless stimuli impinging on an individual at any given moment, only a few stand out clearly, while the rest either are ignored or form a hazy background. In other words, attention is a part of perception. Speakers, therefore, need to know and use the factors that determine the amount of attention their listeners are likely to give to any single stimulus. We shall consider a number of these factors.

Expectancy also plays an important part in what we perceive. The doting mother cannot believe that her darling, perhaps a brat in the opinion of others, could have caused "all that trouble." When we expect to find "good" or "bad" in others we usually do. Crossword-puzzle fans are keenly aware of how plaguing this "set" in perception can be: when a word is first thought of as a noun, it is hard to think of it as a verb. Students who have experienced nothing but the lecture method in college classes find it difficult to adjust to discussion. Such expectancy is an aid to the speaker if the content of the early part of his speech leads his listeners toward a predisposition to accept his climax.

Tendency toward stability is also characteristic of perception. An impression once obtained is difficult to change, even when one is presented with an array of "opposing" facts. If we like the Steve Allen or Woody Allen type of humor, we usually laugh when they appear on television. We might turn off Phyllis Diller or Jack Benny. We characterize people by such expressions as "eggheads," "pigs," "Uncle Toms," "pampered egotists," "raised-eyebrow cynics," "churchgoers," "hippies," "members of the establishment," or "too dumb to learn," and are reluctant to change our perception of the person so classified, even when we have contrary evidence.

A final characteristic of perception is what is called its whole-part relationship. Although the sensory percepts resulting from a stimulus may be in terms of color, size, texture, and so on, we perceive the object as a whole. When we enter the supermarket, we identify the various types of fruit, not in terms of their color, shape, and relationships of parts, but as "oranges," "lemons," or "grapes." This tendency to perceive objects as "whole" configurations also applies to speaking, when the stimuli are words. Politicians seek to create a favorable public "image." The breadwinner in a family wants a good "credit rating," and many students try to become campus "leaders." All of the separate things a person does combine to give others a total impression, which is the thing perceived, not the individual parts.

As we have seen, perception must occur in the process of learning. What happens when we perceive also happens when we learn, because in learning there always is stimulus, discrimination, and meaning.

Thinking in the Learning Process

Like many abstract and complex concepts, the nature of thinking—intellectual behavior—is explained in many different ways. It develops in the individual somewhat as follows. The earliest acts of the child are reflexive, random, isolated movements, which later become integrated into coordinated patterns. These patterns, in turn, aid the individual in adjusting to his environment. At times this adjustment can be achieved through habitual or emotional behavior. With maturity, however, we discover that these ways of acting do not always resolve our problems. At times we must act intellectually: habit and emotion must be under the control of our ability to think and make rational judgments. In effect, when we talk about intellectual behavior, we refer to the process of thinking and the resulting acts. McKeller says:[33]

The word "thinking" is frequently confined . . . to processes of reasoning, logical and reality-adjusted. . . . The second kind, or other end of the scale of thinking—is represented by dreaming, waking fantasy, and occurrences that sometimes accompany falling asleep and waking up, hallucination, and certain other phenomena that are prominent in psychosis. This antithesis between reality-adjusted thinking on one hand and fantasy-dominated thinking on the other has often been made.

As speakers, we are primarily concerned with reality-adjusted thinking. However, we must be aware of the fact that the intellectual behavior of some listeners falls closer to the other end of the continuum.

Some of the common characteristics of thinking and its relationship to language and learning are indicated in the following two statements. Crow and Crow state:[34]

Thinking involves the manipulation of symbols that represent images of objects not present to the senses, and complex concepts or ideas. In thinking, these symbols are recognized in their existing relationships, and are manipulated and organized into different or new relationship for the purpose of attaining a desired goal. . . . Essentially, thinking is problem solving.

Broudy and Freel say:[35]

However, we can also learn by thinking, that is, by going from what we know to what we do not know. From a set of clues, the detective infers who the murderer is. From a set of axioms, postulates, and theorems, we prove or demonstrate new theorems. From a set of facts, the scientist develops a hypothesis or theory.

These statements indicate the symbolic and goal-centered nature of thinking, the role of inferred connections, and the relation of thinking to other forms of learning. The problem-solving nature of thinking is also considered by the philosopher John Dewey, who states:[36]

. . . reflective thinking, in distinction from other operations to which we apply the name of thought, involves (1) a state of doubt, hesitation, perplexity, mental difficulty, in which thinking originates, and (2) an act of searching, hunting, inquiring, to find material that will resolve the doubt, settle and dispose of the perplexity.

Obviously there are imperfections in intellectual behavior, in the sense that an orderly sequence is always followed in resolving a perplexity. Many of the causes of imperfect thinking lie in the process itself. Thinking is a symbolic process, and few of us have more than an average skill in the use of the symbols.

Since intellectual behavior can so easily be imperfect, it is helpful to look briefly at the types of error we are likely to make. Ewbank and Auer divide thinking into two types: logical and nonlogical. Their description of logical thinking follows the steps outlined by

Dewey. Nonlogical thinking is characterized by the following tendencies or errors:[37]

> We tend to think in random fashion.
> We tend to rationalize.
> We tend to confuse desire and conviction.
> We tend to be suggestible.
> We tend to succumb to personal appeals.
> We tend to accept specious arguments.
> We tend to ignore intellectual appeals.

To this list of tendencies in nonlogical thinking we should like to add the following:

> We tend to interpret appeals from a personal viewpoint.
> We tend to err through hasty thinking.
> We tend to oversimplify in thinking.
> We tend to act without thinking.

As speakers and listeners we need to keep our intellectual behavior within the realm of logical reality. This means that our reflective thinking should approximate the well-known problem-solving sequence originally outlined by Dewey:[38]

1. A difficulty (an indeterminate situation or problem) is experienced.
2. The difficulty is located and defined. (The indeterminate situation is transformed into a determinate situation.)
3. Possible solutions are suggested.
4. The possible solutions are elaborated and their ramifications examined and compared.
5. Further observation and experimentation is conducted, which leads to the acceptance or rejection of each solution.

We may simplify this process by stating its successive stages. First we become aware of a problem, then define it, then suggest avenues of attack or proposed solutions, then evaluate each possible solution, and finally act upon the solution accepted.

These steps in reflective thinking are those usually followed in decision-making and problem-solving discussion; they also form the pattern of organization in many speeches that seek to convince. Therefore they will be referred to frequently in this text.

In this chapter we have considered ways in which each individual acts: habitually, emotionally, and intellectually. We have also looked at the role of perception in learning and understanding. Knowing how an individual behaves under differing circumstances is important to the speaker, because this knowledge aids him in motivating his listeners to respond in a desired manner. Another aspect of individual behavior, namely attention, must also be given some consideration because, unless the listener attends to what the speaker is saying, the speaker cannot expect later action.

ATTENTION IN INDIVIDUAL MOTIVATION
A flashing red light, a colorful billboard, a screaming siren, or an extremely "out" dress receive attention almost automatically. The attention given a speaker, however, is not completely automatic. Listeners are preoccupied with their own concerns, and even the best intentioned of them involuntarily resist giving a speaker their undivided attention. The speaker must compete with many internal and external stimuli. We shall look now at the importance and nature of attention and how to get and hold it.

The Nature of Attention
It is obvious that if an audience does not attend to what a speaker says, it cannot be expected to act on his message. Further, there is little point in speaking at all, if the speaker does not get the early attention of his listeners. That is his first task in every speaking situation.

To see how attention may be secured we first need to understand what it is. In an earlier chapter we noted that each member of an audience receives stimuli from three worlds: his physical surroundings, other people, and his personal world. Because there are literally thousands of these stimuli at any given moment, the individual ignores many of them while focusing on a few. That is, he becomes aware of certain stimuli while the majority fade into the background. This process of giving attention thus divides an individual's field of experience into a "center" and a "margin." In the center, or focus, we perceive events clearly; in the margin we perceive events indistinctly or not at all. This phenomenon is described by psychologists as the division of one's perceptual field into "figure" and "ground," the one dominant and unified, becoming the focus of attention, and the other more ambiguous and diffuse. It is important for the speaker to know that frequently what is the figure—the focus of attention at the moment—may become the ground—that to which we do not attend. Figure 5-1 shows this clearly. The diagram can be seen either as a vase or two faces in profile. If you stare at the figure for a few moments, the figure-ground relationship automatically changes back and forth.

Can you see both the vase and the two profiles?

Attention involves physiological changes. It is accompanied by

FIGURE 5-1. Figure-ground relationship.

the development of a coordinated, focused, muscular "set," which increases our sensitivity to the stimulus and heightens our readiness to respond. Ruch makes this statement about attention:[39]

We may regard attention as having three interrelated aspects, all of which are part of a single complex act. Attention is (1) an adjustment of the body and its sense organs; (2) clearness and vividness in consciousness; and (3) a set toward action.

What happens when we attend to something is this: There is a bodily muscular adjustment that enables the sense organs to receive selected stimuli more readily; these heightened stimuli come more sharply into focus and are perceived; the perceptions in turn are retained in our minds to provide a readiness for immediate or delayed action. Attention is both a physiological and psychological phenomenon. It is the first step in gaining acceptance of a speaker's message.

Characteristics of Attention
We are told by speech educators that if we get the attention of an audience, we can be sure that its members will act. We cannot assume, however, that once attention is secured, it will be retained without effort on the speaker's part. The attention span of most people is extremely short; concentrated attention lasts for no more than a few seconds. Hence, the speaker must constantly be alert to responses that indicate that attention may be lagging.

Further, our attention span constantly shifts. Some time, when you are studying or reading, keep a record for a two-minute period of the number of times your attention moves away from the center of your interest. Sounds, memories, future plans, and sensations will get momentary attention even during a brief period. The limited duration and constant shifting of attention usually work against the speaker. Consequently, he must use every reasonable means to get continued attention.

A third characteristic of attention—its selectivity—usually can be made to work for the speaker. People attend to things that satisfy their needs, and so they are disposed to listen carefully to a speaker who can show that his message is vital to his hearers. Of all the things to which they could attend, listeners focus on that which seems to fulfill their need.

Kinds of Attention

The kinds of attention are three in number: involuntary, voluntary, and habitual. We shall examine them in the following paragraphs.

Involuntary. Because of their characteristics certain stimuli get our attention with very little effort on our part. A loud noise will get involuntary attention unless we have become accustomed to it. The stranger in Chicago or New York hears the sounds of the "L" and subway; the resident in these cities does not hear these noises, or at least tries to ignore them. The dropping of a book, a clap of thunder, and the ringing of a doorbell are noises to which we attend involuntarily.

Voluntary. Sometimes we give attention only when we exert effort to do so. Other stimuli force into the background the things we wish to keep in our focus, and we must make a conscious effort to prevent this shift. Voluntary attention results from an individual's need to accomplish or understand certain things. The attention a student gives a lecture of an instructor usually is of this type. When we give voluntary attention for too long, we usually become disinterested or tired because of mental or physical strain.

Habitual. Habitual attention is the result of continued voluntary attention. That is, it results from practice. When a person gives habitual attention, he is set to attend and hence can do so with no conscious effort. It partakes of involuntary attention in this respect, and of voluntary attention in that it is related to a person's needs. Examples of habitual attention are the bowing of heads when the pastor indicates prayer, the immediate caution displayed by golfers when the cry

"Fore!" is heard, or the physical and mental alertness manifested by students when a popular and knowledgeable teacher enters a classroom to begin a lecture.

In a speaking situation we may make judicious use of involuntary attention and hope that the voluntary attention that listeners usually give takes on the characteristics of habitual attention, which entails a minimum of effort.

The Control of Attention

The attention given to any stimulus is generally controlled by three factors: (1) the qualities of the stimulus itself, (2) the external conditions of the environment, and (3) the internal state of the listener.

We have already noted that under certain circumstances we give involuntary attention to a stimulus because of its unique characteristics. When a stimulus is intense, is in sharp contrast with stimuli to which we have been attending for some time, is sudden or unexpected, or is novel, we pay immediate attention. Qualities such as these give a stimulus priority over others.

The condition of the environment is a second controlling factor. Have you ever walked into a cluttered shop and discovered that it was almost impossible to focus on anything? By contrast, the symbolic simplicity of a church interior or the careful staging and timing of a television spectacular contributes to heightened attention.

The internal states of the listener also control attention. The listener who is concerned with personal worries or physical discomforts is not ready to give proper attention to a speaker.

It is obvious that there is no positive way of getting every member of an audience to pay attention all the time. However, if your message has relevance to the listeners' needs, if it is clear and well presented, if the conditions of the room contribute to comfort and audibility, and if the listeners have a minimum of personal problems at the time, the probability of attention will be so much the greater.

Keeping in mind these conditions, let us now consider some of the specific things that may be done to keep our listeners' attention.

Factors Internal to Content and Delivery

The factors that are internal to content and delivery are ten in number: vital interests, conflict and competition, suspense and uncertainty, novelty and contrast, movement and change, repetition and restatement, intensity and size, familiarity, humor, and order.

Vital Interests. When a speaker is able to relate his message to the immediate or the deep-seated desires of his audience, he has a key to their attention. References to one's livelihood, medical needs, home life, professional and vocational advancement, and religious beliefs will command the attention of most listeners. The following excerpt from a speech by Admiral E. R. Zumwalt, Jr., Chief of Naval Operations, delivered to the graduates of the U.S. Naval Academy on June 9, 1971, is an example dealing with a matter of vital interest to his listeners:[40]

By 1985, 250 of you will have reached the grade of commander, and between 1991 and 1992, 148 of those will become captains. Well before the new century dawns, many of you will be wearing the stars of flag rank.

The Navy promotion system now has the capacity to move ahead as many as 15 percent of the truly outstanding officers of this class at an even faster pace. Such officers, if selected at the first opportunity at each point, can reach the grade of Captain in their 15th year and can be considered for flag rank by their 20th year of commissioned service—in 1991, in time to lead our Navy through the final decade of the 20th century.

Note the vital nature of the speech content suggested by the following titles of some speeches in a single issue of *Vital Speeches of the Day.*[41]

> Global Poverty and Underdevelopment
> Hysteria on the Campus
> Germany and Her Eastern Neighbors
> The Demise of Rural Medicine
> Cancer
> Freedom and Enterprise

We know that man must satisfy his physical needs. He becomes hungry and thirsty, has sex drives, needs rest, seeks health, provides shelter for himself and his family, and tries to maintain his body in physiological balance. Besides doing all this he seeks approval, love and affection, security, personal achievement and recognition, freedom from worry, and new experiences. In varying degree all these goals are vital to his existence, and he will therefore act upon them.

Conflict and Competition. American history is the story of conflict and competition, and both forms of opposition exist today. The War of Independence, the Civil War, World War II, the Korean War, and the Vietnam War, are examples from one area of our national life. In the area of human rights we have witnessed the freeing of the slaves, voting rights for women, the Womens' Liberation movement, voting rights for eighteen-year-olds, and the struggles of the Blacks and Chicanos for recognition. The extent to which some form of conflict commands attention in this country is reflected in the headlines in any daily paper. The following are taken from the *Los Angeles Times* of August 3, 1971.

> U.S. Backs Red China in U.N. but Will Oppose Taiwan Ouster
> Trainmen Win 42% Raise as Rail Strike Ends
> Lockheed Rescued; Nixon Hails Action
> Sudan Orders 2 Red Envoys Out of Country
> Reds Having Trouble Influencing Arab World
> Labor Settlements Lift Cloud but Many Remain
> Forests and Public Interest

Needless to say, the speaker who employs elements of conflict and competition in his speech is likely to get attention.

Suspense and Uncertainty. The sale of "whodunits" suggests the almost universal interest in suspense. Suspense programs on television usually receive a high rating. The outcome of Saturday's football game, a heavyweight championship fight, and the seventh game in a World Series, are matters of real concern. Many of us find it difficult to wait until the morning paper comes to find out the President's last statement, the latest "ultimatum" from the Soviets, the most recent development in our relations with Red China or in the Vietnam War, what happened in the stock market, or the most recent public statements of Senators Proxmire, Mansfield, Ford, or Javits.

The speaker achieves attention through suspense and uncertainty and apprehension—which few individuals can ignore—by building to a climax, by suggesting early in a speech that important information will be presented later, by telling stories, by using unusual figures of speech, or by suggesting the uncertain consequences of some action.

Novelty and Contrast. Speech titles with elements of novelty will catch and hold attention. Note the following, taken from recent student speeches:

> Living in a Computerized World
> Conning the Consumer
> Jesus Christ: Superstar and Bit Player
> Swinging is for Singles
> When Will Babe Ruth Lose His Record
> Nudism in Our Times

Novel expressions in a speech capture attention.

I believe in the discipline of silence and could talk for hours about it. *(George Bernard Shaw)*

There are several good protections against temptation, but the surest is cowardice. *(Mark Twain)*

In a sense we have come to our nation's capital to cash a check. *(Martin Luther King, Jr.)*

Carl Sandburg makes excellent use of contrast in the opening of a speech about Abraham Lincoln:[42]

Not often in the history of mankind does a man arrive on earth who is both steel and velvet, who is as hard as rock and as soft as drifting fog, who holds in his heart and mind the paradox of terrible storm and peace unspeakable and perfect.

Note the impact the contrasting figures in the following excerpt have on the listener. The speech was given in support of greater effort in dealing with cancer at a meeting of a Round Table forum in Lincoln, Nebraska, April 5, 1971.[43]

The amount spent on cancer research is grossly inadequate today. For every man, woman, and child in the United States, we spent in the year 1969:

$410 on national defense;

$125 on the war in Vietnam;

$19 on the space program;

$19 on foreign aid; and only $0.89 cents on cancer research

Cancer deaths during the year 1969 alone were:

(i) 8 times the number of lives lost in 6 years in Vietnam;

(ii) 5½ times the number killed in automobile accidents during the year;

(iii) greater than the number of Americans killed in battle in all 4 years of World War II.

The allocation of national priorities seems open to serious question.

Movement and Change. Other things being equal, movement and variation will catch and hold attention more readily than immobility and uniformity. The speaker needs to apply this principle to his physical action, voice, language, and speech content. In Chapter Thirteen we examine these matters more thoroughly.

Variety and movement in physical action through the use of dynamic, controlled, and appropriate bodily movement and gesture aid in getting and holding attention. Immobility and repetitious action detract from speaking effectiveness.

Vocal changes in pitch, force, timing, and quality aid in getting attention and in contributing to a greater understanding by the audience. A responsive voice is a tremendous aid to effective communication.

Variety in language and content also contribute to attention. We are likely to listen intently when language and thought move swiftly, are enriched with images of action, suggest contrasts, or create changes in mood.

Repetition and Restatement. We attend to things that are repeated. We find it difficult to avoid listening to often repeated phrases, words, and jingles of television and radio advertising. Such advertising provides an illustration of the value of repetition at both its best and its worst. In spite of ourselves we remember many of these phrases, and sometimes act on them at a later time.

Much of the impact of the speech made by Dr. Martin Luther King, Jr., at Washington in August, 1963, came from his repeated use of the phrases "I have a dream" and "Let freedom ring."

The impact of restatement and contrast is seen in the following excerpt from a eulogistic prize-winning speech given by a student from Ripon College, Ripon, Wisconsin, in 1957:[44]

The January 17 issue of the New York Times carried the headline, "Arturo Toscanini is dead." Newspaper boys shouted from the street corners of Milan, "The Maestro is Dead." The NBC Symphony in Radio City gave a concert in his honor—The Maestro is dead. La Scala in Milan was closed down, and a special mass was said in St. Peter's—the Maestro is dead. But death is such a final term to apply here. For Arturo Toscanini was more than an existing organism. He was a living man, alive in his music. Music was Toscanini, and death killed him only physically. The greatest part of Arturo Toscanini will live as long as man occupies a position on the universe.

Intensity and Size. We attend to big things. For decades Texas was the largest state in the Union, and most of us still willingly listen to a Texas "tall tale." Averages interest us less than "peak sales," "banner years," "bumper crops," or programs that "go over the top."

In commenting on our nation's economy, writers and speakers use such expressions as "superbooms," "major expansion programs," "best year ever," and "spending spree" to get our attention. Our economy is geared to the principle of exceeding last year's record; we are satisfied with nothing less.

When a stimulus is of long duration, intense in sound, large in size, or amplified, we are likely to attend to it. The speaker needs to apply this principle in both content and delivery. The developed example is frequently better than the undeveloped one. Large visual aids attract more attention than small ones. Broad, full, and sweeping gestures are more effective than confined, restricted ones. Any visual or audible stimulus that has characteristics of great size or intensity will secure attention.

Familiarity. When a speaker mentions places, events, people, or objects with which his listeners are well acquainted, he is likely to get immediate attention. Below we present some lists; as you read the lists, see whether you do not give greater attention to items with which you are familiar.

Persons	*Places*
Angela Davis	Via Veneto, Rome
Senator Allan Cranston	The Blue Grotto, Naples
Alfred M. Worden	Nome, Alaska
George Meany	Canal Street, New Orleans
Lee Trevino	Hennepin Avenue, Minneapolis
Cesar Chavez	Copocabana, Rio de Janeiro
Al Capp	Malaga, Costa del Sol
Daniel Ellsberg	Acapulco, Mexico

Events	*Objects*
Establishment of the U.S. Postal Service as an independent agency	United Nations Building, N.Y.
	Eiffel Tower
	Panama Canal
Governmental loan of $250,000,000 to Lockheed Aircraft Corporation	The Astrodome
	L-1011 TriStar
	Caesar's Palace, Las Vegas
Epidemic of Venezuelan equine encephalomyelitis in U.S. in 1971	Dune Buggy
	LRV (Lunar Roving Vehicle)
32-day round-the-world trip of Spiro Agnew in 1971	
Concerts of the American Wind Symphony Orchestra playing at Ravenswood, W. Va., in 1971	

Old friends, favorite television shows, Bible quotations learned as a child, and many other familiar things get our attention. However, in making use of the familiar, the speaker must put the commonplace in a new setting, contrast it with the unfamiliar, or show some significance of which the listener is unaware.

Humor. In a serious speech humor may often provide the light touch that sparks and holds attention. It can recapture lagging interest, relieve tension, provide emphasis, and diminish the force of opposing views. The following excerpts illustrate the effective use of humor.

In a speech given in 1957 before the American Forensic Association in Boston, the Governor of Maine, expressing his doubts about giving the speech, said: "Facing these doubts, I feel very much like the mosquito who found himself unexpectedly in a nudist colony. I don't know where to begin."[45]

Dr. William B. Langsdorf, then President of the California State University, Fullerton, told the following story at the opening of a summer conference of fifty teachers of elementary and secondary school from all over the United States. The story was told in the summer of 1969, when college presidents throughout the country were being harassed by sit-ins, teach-ins, violence, demands from protesting groups, and even threats on their persons. The story went something like this: "A certain college president died and—as sometimes happens—went to Hell. It was six months before he realized that he was not still working at his former job." His listeners got the message and enjoyed the fact that Dr. Langsdorf could laugh at himself.

This caution should be noted: humor that does not make a point, has little humorous impact, or is off-color can boomerang and be a handicap to the speaker. The moral is: Don't tell humorous stories unless they are appropriate, preferably tied to the context, and funny, and unless you tell them well.

Order. Order is essential in our lives. We depend on it in practically everything we do: names in a telephone directory are arranged alphabetically, schedules in a timetable are given in a chronological sequence, the table of contents and index are in the same relative positions in all books. We usually adjust our recreation and work hours and activities to a satisfactory schedule; for most of us our daily activity follows a patterned routine. More important, we look for patterns in things about us. Because the familiar events in our lives are more or less ordered, we expect and look for order in new experiences. Thus, when we listen to a speech, we try to discover a pattern of organization with which we are familiar. If we do not find such a pattern, our attention and interest wane.

Factors External to Content and Delivery

A number of factors external to content and delivery may be modified
by the speaker to increase the listeners' attention. The speaker's action
may be to remove, to minimize, or to heighten the factor involved,
depending on its nature.

Competing Stimuli. Care in removing competing stimuli before speaking will pay big dividends in greater audience attention. In Chapter
Eight we show the importance to the speaker of discovering in advance
the physical conditions under which he is expected to speak. Potential
distractions frequently can be removed. Seats may be arranged to bring
the audience closer to the speaker; scattered hearers may be asked to
form a compact group; for a discussion seats may be arranged in a
circle; temperature, lighting, and ventilation often may be improved;
the public-address system and projection equipment can be tested;
arrangements may be made to cut down outside noises; and the speaker
can familiarize himself with the platform setup.

At times it is inadvisable to compete with distracting stimuli.
Passing trains or planes may be so disturbing that the speaker should
stop talking for a moment. Since after-dinner speaking and the rattling
of dishes seem to be inseparable, a speaker is well advised to wait until
the dishes are removed before starting. At times one is forced to choose
between closing the window and having poor ventilation, or leaving it
open and being bothered by noise. Whatever choice is made, one should
seek to keep distractions to a minimum.

Audience Involvement. Audience participation is an important factor
in learning. It is important, therefore, that the listeners be involved in
some way as actual partners in the speaking situation—physically,
mentally, or emotionally, and, if possible, all three.

Physical involvement might be effected by asking the audience
to perform some physical action, such as raising hands or looking at
some object. Emotional involvement may often be secured by dramatic
narratives, exciting visual aids, and intense vocal quality. Questions,
startling statements, vital and current illustrations, and startling statistical data all help to keep an audience mentally alert. Except when the
activity gets out of hand, an active audience is usually an attentive one.

Social Facilitation. A salesman recently remarked to us that he always
liked to have in every audience at least one listener who frequently
nodded his head in agreement with the speaker's remarks. Usually the
persons nearby joined in nodding their heads or gave other evidences of
approval. This awareness of the actions of others in a group and the

tendency to act in like manner are called social facilitation.[46] When a speaker can get one or more members of an audience to show approval or to act as he wishes, he may expect others to follow suit.

Factors Within the Listener
Besides the attention factors found within the stimulus itself and those external to the content and delivery, the speaker needs to take into account a number of predisposing states of attention within the listener.

Motivation. Our interests, needs, and values govern not only what attracts our attention but what holds it. If you are hungry—and depending on how "flush" you are—you will look for MacDonald's, Colonel Sanders, a Hyatt House, a Sheraton Inn, or a Hilton International Hotel. If you are just starting your family and need to plan for the future, you will listen to what a speaker has to say about "term insurance," "planning an estate," "why it pays to own your house," and how to "save now, spend later." If your instructor assigns a term paper to be turned in at the end of the semester, and if you are wise, you will be looking for material for the paper throughout the semester. We are motivated to do those things which satisfy our individual needs.

Expectancy. The psychologists tell us that if we are "set" to respond to a certain stimulus we usually will do so. The mother reacts immediately to her crying baby, the fireman automatically takes certain action when he hears the fire alarm, the defensive football team tries to anticipate what the next play of the offense will be so as to be set for it, and if you have heard that a certain "prof" is a tough grader, you will either avoid his class or plan to study harder than you usually do.

In speaking we use the principle of expectancy in various ways:

1. In the introduction to a speech we try to build a favorable "set" toward ourselves, our purpose, and the subject.
2. We try to identify ourselves with the audience in terms of mutual reference groups, experiences, or need-goal systems.
3. We outline our main points in the introduction so that the listener may know what to expect and thus be set to hear the main points.
4. We use oral markers, such as "This is important," "Remember this point," and "Now hear this!" Our listeners expect what we say next to be important.
5. We get the audience to say "Yes" to a series of questions to which we know they will agree, in order that they may be set to accept our final proposal.

6. We select illustrations that are within the experience of our listeners.
7. We try to gauge the moment when our listeners are ready to act, so that we do not lose their attention by overselling.
8. We use jokes in which the punch line is unexpected.

Habit. Closely related to the factor of expectancy is that of habit. Because habitual behavior is partly the result of practice and partly the result of learning, habit functions in two ways in attention. First, we attend—in some circumstances—to things to which we are accustomed. The person who has some skill in music will attend to a professional musician or to good music more readily than the person who is unskilled. The professional golfer notes and appreciates the difficult shot more than does the duffer. The music, art, or movie critic can differentiate between professional and amateur efforts; he is trained to do so, attends to both extremes of quality, and can make value judgments that reflect his longtime experience. Likewise, the trained speaker and, more importantly, the trained listener, attend to and react favorably to quality in speaking.

Habit also functions in a different manner. The person who habitually acts in certain ways will also attend to any stimulus that is a variation in a familiar pattern. The forest ranger is quick to react to a fire that breaks out in his area. The orchestra conductor attends immediately to the mistake of a player. If you are in the habit of giving well-prepared speeches in a communication class, your classmates and, worse, your instructor, will note when you do poorly. Members of closely knit organizations such as neighborhood gangs, the Senate of the United States, some church groups, the Black Panthers, and Hell's Angels, have an established set of rules of behavior, some written and some unwritten. The membership is quick to note deviations from these rules and, more frequently than not, takes punitive action. The foregoing principle also has applications for the speaker.

Most listeners habitually expect speakers to do certain things in a speech, such as outlining the talk early in the speech, supporting generalizations with illustrations, building up to a climax, and giving indications of closing. Because of this they usually fail to give attention when these expectations are not met. To see the operation of the factor of habit in attention, note the action of a congregation when the preacher talks too long.

IMPLICATIONS
*The significance to the communicator-respondent
of the concept of habit is eightfold:*

1. The overt physical actions of some members of most audiences may actually be long-standing habit patterns, not necessarily responses to the particular speaking situation. The reason some of your listeners may not be attending to you may be because, if they are women, they must see what other women in the audience are wearing, and, if they are men, they are "girl watching." Lassitude after a meal or when the hour is late is a natural, habitual behavior pattern, not necessarily caused by what you have said. You must recognize that the actions of some listeners are habits. At the same time you must be alert to the need for greater effort under such circumstances.
2. Since habits result from the satisfaction of needs, they can frequently be changed by more effective ways of satisfying the needs. It is the speaker's responsibility to show that his proposal provides that more effective way.
3. Since habits are learned, new ways of acting also can be learned, to replace those we wish to change. To accomplish this the speaker must understand and utilize in his speech the basic principles of learning theory.
4. We have noted that attitudes are in part the result of habitual patterns of behavior. Hence, when we seek to change attitudes, we are actually seeking to change what may be a habitual way of looking at things. Although the holder of an attitude may not be aware of, or may have forgotten, its original cause, you must seek to discover all you can about the experiential factors basic to the attitude.
5. We have seen that our habits provide shortcuts for intellectual behavior, emotional response, and physical action. The effective speaker uses appeals that he hopes the listeners will perceive as more effective avenues to desired goals.
6. Keep in mind that a habit may be an impression that results from a single experience. Try to get favorable reactions from your listeners early in your speech: silent expressions that indicate such agreements as "That's my opinion, too" and "How right he is" or, when overt expressions are appropriate, "Amen, amen!", "Hear, hear!", and "More, more."
7. If your goal is to get your listeners to continue doing something that has become habitual, then your major task is to provide reasons for continuing that action.
8. If you wish to change a habitual behavioral pattern, then you may wish to stimulate deliberative thinking leading to a realization of the wisdom of a change.

The significance to the communicator-respondent
of the concept of emotion is ninefold:

1. Since emotions are "energizers": they may be utilized by the speaker in getting his listeners to act. The action proposed may serve as a release to the stirred-up body state that is the emotion, or at least part of it.
2. Emotions are motives. They keep us working toward goals and away from known or possible threats. When feelings of love or hate are high, we are aggressive and energetic in pursuing goals related to these emotions. When emotional states are weak, inactivity usually results.

3. Emotions often develop from conscious reflection on an event that threatens or favors an individual. A speaker can therefore arouse emotions by using language that depicts situations contributing to feelings of fear, anger, or pleasure.

4. When seeking to arouse emotions, aim for moderate intensity. An audience with little or no emotion is impossible to arouse to action; an overly emotional audience may be impossible to control, or it may act in a way that was not planned by the speaker.

5. Since emotional states result in part from learning, the speaker can sometimes arouse them by pointing out unsuspected dangers or pleasures in a situation.

6. Because increasing age brings a lessening of emotional excitability and greater control over the emotions, the speaker frequently will find older audiences less susceptible to emotional appeals than younger ones.

7. Because emotions are aroused when an individual sees no satisfactory outcome to a situation, a speaker may develop desired emotional states within his listeners by presenting a problem situation in such a way that his audience can see no possible solution. On the other hand, when an audience has been emotionally aroused over a topic before hearing the speaker, it is sometimes possible to overcome the emotional states by presenting a "means of escape" from the thwarting situation.

8. Stage fright—a malady of most beginning speakers—is a form of emotion. Since the stirred-up body state of an emotion can be lessened if the individual feels able to cope with the emotional situation, a thorough analysis of the causation of stage fright and planning to control it can sometimes remove the excessive fear and concern that frequently harass a speaker.

9. The speaker should recognize that often an audience needs to drain off excessive emotions through physical activity. Do not be disturbed if an audience does express itself overtly.

The significance to the communicator-respondent of the concept of perception is tenfold:

1. Because learning has its roots in the need to resolve a problem, the speaker's proposal must be presented as a solution to the problem.

2. Since learning is motivated, the value of a speaker's subject must be perceived as rewarding by his listeners.

3. Learning and understanding are increased when the speaker can involve his audience intellectually, emotionally, and physically in the learning process.

4. When understanding is the speaker's aim, he must adapt his materials to the intellectual level of his auditors, move from simple to complex concepts, and show his listeners the immediate values of his proposals.

5. The speaker must constantly keep his goal before his listeners, avoid irrelevant considerations, employ a coherent organization, and maintain constant interest.

6. Because understanding always takes place within the listeners' perceptual fields, the speaker must avoid content that is not perceived as reality by his listeners.

7. The speaker must adapt his content to the factor of expectancy. He recognizes

that the listener perceives what he expects to perceive and finds it difficult to perceive the unexpected.

8. Certain factors heighten the attention value of a given stimulus. The effective speaker employs these factors to speed up and clarify perception.

9. Because people have a tendency to perceive wholes rather than parts, the speaker should employ language that focuses on the image he seeks to create in the listeners.

10. Because of the principle of readiness to learn, the speaker should time his proposals for action when that action fits in with the needs of his listeners.

The significance to the communicator-respondent
of the concept of intellectual behavior is sevenfold:

1. Since thinking consists largely of language symbols, speakers must be sure that the symbols they use are understood by the listeners.

2. Since thinking is a process of looking at symbols or ideas in a given relationship and manipulating them into new relationships for the purpose of achieving a goal, the speaker must be sure that his listeners see both the original and the new sets of relationships and the connections between the two.

3. The wide range of activities included in the concept of thinking requires that the speaker try to discover the level of thinking of his listeners and make the necessary adaptations.

4. If a problem-solving pattern of organization is used in a speech, Dewey's steps in reflective thinking may provide a pattern for outlining the speech.

5. Since learning and thinking usually proceed from the known to the unknown, from the simple to the complex, from the accepted to the unaccepted, and from the experienced to the unexperienced, the speaker must follow these sequences in presenting message content that is *new* to his listeners.

6. As speakers we need to be especially wary of the pitfalls of nonlogical thinking.

7. As speakers we must realize that people seldom act entirely on a rational basis. We must be aware of the fact that human beings are also affected by their habits and emotions.

EXERCISES

1. In what ways does habitual behavior save you time? Are some of your habits wasteful of time? How? Prepare a brief speech in which you comment on time-saving devices you use.

2. Make a list of the ways in which a speaker could employ your habitual forms of behavior in motivating you to action. Discuss your suggestions in class.

3. Reread the first quotation from Lindgren found on page 111, which states that all behavior is purposive. Make a list of specific ways in which your habitual emotional, and intellectual behaviors are helpful to you, that is, serve you in some purposeful way.

4. Prepare a three-minute speech describing a situation in which members of the audience have manifested all four aspects of emotional behavior: stirred-up body states, overt action, expression of feeling, and motivation to later action.

5. Think of several situations in which you have been intensely aroused emotionally. What were the causes of the emotional states?
6. Discuss the types of mental activity that take place when you think. Give a
   three-minute speech in which you describe some act of thought, from the
   awareness of the problem-situation to its mental resolution.
7. Prepare to give a four-minute speech in which you illustrate how a speaker may
   apply the three factors (see page 119) that determine the degree of emotional
   intensity of an event or stimulus.
8. Comment on the following statements about learning:
   a. All learning must be painful.
   b. The most important factor in learning is motivation.
   c. Most people stop learning after they become thirty years of age.
   d. Many of the things we learn in school must be unlearned in later life.
9. Are the physical conditions in the room in which you do most of your
   studying conducive to effective learning? In what ways could classrooms be
   changed to improve learning conditions? Apply your observations on physical
   conditions as aids to learning in the classroom to other speaking situations.
10. a. Write down four or five of your social, political, religious, or economic
       beliefs.
    b. Now write down opposing beliefs held by your acquaintances. Explain why
       you think they hold these beliefs.
    c. Prepare to give a five-minute talk in which you examine a single belief in the
       light of the reasons why two people should hold opposite views of it.
11. From the following list of general topics select one, and prepare to give a
    three-minute speech in which you follow the thinking sequence outlined on
    page 129. Be sure that your subject is made more specific than the topic listed
    below.

Pollution control	Making education relevant
The effects of a computerized society	The future of professional sports
The value of dating machines	More education and fewer jobs
Let's have safer, not bigger, planes	The Alaskan Oil Fiasco
Students have a place in college academic adminis-tration	What education ought to do for a student
	Making integration really work

12. Do you concur with the statements made by Dr. Braden and quoted on page
    123? Why?
13. Have you had any contacts with students in the Upward Bound program? In
    what ways have their perceptions of the values, problems, and interests in
    schooling differed from yours? Why?
14. Get several copies of *Vital Speeches* from your library, and try to locate
    instances of the types of nonlogical thinking described on page 129. Hand in
    your list to your instructor.
15. Make a list of the things a speaker does that attract your attention. Try to
    classify them meaningfully. Which things contribute to meaningful communica-
    tion? Which do not?

16. Do you find that you can give attention to a stimulus when you are slightly tensed physically better than when you are completely relaxed? What application does this have in the speaking situation?
17. Prepare to discuss in class the implication of the figure-ground principle for the speaker.
18. Make a list of ideas, events, people, or things to which the members of your class would give selective attention. Give a three-minute speech in which you employ as many of these attention-getting stimuli as you can.
19. List several examples of involuntary attention, voluntary attention, and habitual attention. From a study of these examples what conclusions can you draw that have application to a speaking situation?
20. What do you consider to be some significant reasons for fluctuation in attention? What applications can you make to the speaking situation?
21. On pages 133–139 we list ten attention-getting devices that are internal to the content and delivery of a speech. Select any five of these categories, and under each category make a list of four items that might be employed in a speech to your class.
22. Give a two-minute speech in which you try to hold the complete and continuous attention of your audience. Use every device that will aid you in getting and holding attention. The other class members will be asked to note the points at which their attention wavered, even if only slightly.
23. Think of a speech you recently attended voluntarily. How did your motivation help in maintaining attention to what the speaker was saying?

ADDITIONAL READINGS

Branca, Albert A., *Psychology: The Science of Behavior*, Boston, Allyn & Bacon, 1968, chaps. 6, 7, 8, 10, 13.

Brembeck, Winston L., and William S. Howell, *Persuasion: A Means of Social Control*, Englewood Cliffs, N. J., Prentice-Hall, 1952, chap. 14.

Cantor, Nathanial F., *The Teaching-Learning Transaction*, New York, Holt, Rinehart & Winston, 1953.

Coffey, Hubert S., "What we know about changing attitudes in individuals," in *Human Attitudes: How They Develop and Change*, Committee on Civil Rights, United Steelworkers of America, 1954, pp. 37–51.

Combs, Arthur W., and Donald Snygg, *Individual Behavior*, rev. ed., New York, Harper & Row, 1959, chap. 3

Crow, Lester D., and Alice Crow, *Human Development and Learning*, New York, American, 1956, chaps. 6, 9, 10, 12.

Deese, James, *Principles of Psychology*, Boston, Allyn & Bacon, 1964, chaps. 2, 5, 8.

Hilgard, E. R., *Theories of Learning*, New York, Appleton, 1956, chap. 1.

Hollingworth, H. L., *The Psychology of the Audience*, New York, American Book, 1935, chap. 6.

Kidd, J. R., *How Adults Learn*, New York, Association Press, 1959, chaps. 1, 5, 6.

Lindzey, Gardner, and Elliot Aronson, eds., *The Handbook of Social Psychology*, 2nd ed., vol. III, Reading, Mass., Addison-Wesley, 1969, chap. 23.

McKeachie, Wilbert James, and Charlotte Lackner Doyle, *Psychology*, Reading, Mass., Addison-Wesley, 1966, chaps. 5, 6, 10.

Minnick, Wayne C., *The Art of Persuasion*, Boston, Houghton Mifflin, 1957, chap. 3.

Ruch, Floyd L., *Psychology and Life*, 5th ed., Chicago, Scott, Foresman, 1958, chap. 10.

Sargent, S. Stansfeld, and Robert C. Williamson, *Social Psychology*, 2nd ed., New York, Ronald, 1958, chap. 7.

Stevens, Walter W., "Polarization, social facilitation, and listening," *Western Speech*, 25 (no. 3, Summer, 1961), 170–174.

Upton, Albert, *Design for Thinking*, Palo Alto, Calif., Stanford Univ. Press, 1961, chaps. 3, 4, 5, 9.

NOTES

[1] Henry Clay Lindgren, *Psychology of Personal and Social Adjustment*, New York, American Book, 1953, p. 15.

[2] Henry Clay Lindgren, *Educational Psychology in the Classroom*, New York, Wiley, 1956, p. 41.

[3] Wilbert James McKeachie, and Charollotte Lackner Doyle, *Psychology*, Reading, Mass., Addison-Wesley, 1966, p. 28.

[4] Albert A. Branca, *Psychology: The Science of Behavior*, rev. ed., Boston, Allyn & Bacon, 1968, p. 46.

[5] Floyd L. Ruch, *Psychology and Life*, 5th ed., Chicago, Scott, Foresman, 1958, p. 298.

[6] John Dewey, *Human Nature and Conduct: An Introduction to Social Psychology*, New York, Holt, Rinehart & Winston, 1922, pp. 25, 42.

[7] Kimball Young, *Social Psychology*, New York, Appleton, 1930, p. 75.

[8] Aristotle, *Rhetoric and Poetics*, trans. by W. Rhys Roberts and Ingram Bywater, The Modern Library, New York, 1954, p. 92.

[9] Clifford T. Morgan, *Introduction to Psychology*, New York, McGraw-Hill, 1956, pp. 88–89.

[10] Lester D. Crow and Alice Crow, *Human Development and Learning*, New York, American Book, 1956, p. 52.

[11] Arthur W. Combs and Donald Snygg, *Individual Behavior: A Perceptual Approach to Behavior*, rev. ed., New York, Harper & Row, 1959, p. 228.

[12] Branca, *op. cit.*, p. 406.

[13] See Jon Eisenson, J. Jeffery Auer, and John V. Irwin, *The Psychology of Communication*, New York, Appleton, 1963, pp. 74–75.

[14] Harold S. Tuttle, *Dynamic Psychology and Conduct*, New York, Harper & Row, 1949, p. 377.

[15] Wayne C. Minnick, *The Art of Persuasion*, Boston, Houghton Mifflin, 1957, pp. 225–226.

[16] Woodrow Wilson, "War Message," *Congressional Record*, 65th Cong., 45 (April 2, 1917), pp. 103–104.

[17] Robert C. Weaver, "The Negro as an American," in Floyd W. Matson, ed., *Voices of Crisis*, New York, Odyssey, 1967, p. 174.

[18] James Forman, "To the White Christian churches and the Jewish synagogues in the United States of America and all other racist institutions: Black Manifesto," in James L. Golden, and Richard D. Rieke, *The Rhetoric of Black Americans*, Columbus, Merrill, 1971, pp. 543–545.

[19] Ruch, *op. cit.*, p. 166.

[20] Weaver, *op. cit.*, pp. 164–165.

[21] Morgan, *op. cit.*, p. 107.

[22] Lindgren, *op. cit.*, p. 225.

[23] This oversimplified and eclectic statement about learning is meant to be descriptive only. It is obviously incomplete and makes no attempt to reconcile differences between the viewpoint which claims that learning must be explained in terms of what may be observed and that which interprets learning in terms of what is conceived to be going on while learning is taking place. This dichotomy need not concern the speaker.

[24] May V. Seagoe, *A Teacher's Guide to the Learning Process*, Dubuque, Ia., Brown, 1956, p. 180.

[25]Percival M. Symonds, "What Education Has to Learn from Psychology, II. Reward," Teachers College Record, 57 (No. 1, Oct. 1955) 15.

[26]Branca, *op. cit.*, p. 215 (the parenthetical words are ours).

[27]Ruch, *op. cit.*, pp. 265, 266.

[28]*Perceptual field* is defined as "the entire universe, including himself, as it is experienced by the individual at the instant of action."

[29]See also Floyd H. Allport, *Theories of Perception and the Concept of Structure*, New York, 1955, pp. 14–66; Arthur W. Combs and Donald Snygg, *Individual Behavior*, New York, Harper & Row, 1949, pp. 16–36; and Gardner Lindzey and Elliot Aronson, eds., *The Handbook of Social Psychology*, 2nd ed., Vol., III, Reading, Mass., Addison-Wesley, 1969, pp. 315–449.

[30]Thomas J. Dodd, "Do we value our free civilization?" *Vital Speeches*, 26 (no. 18, July 1, 1969), 557.

[31]Waldo W. Braden, "Beyond the campus gate," *Vital Speeches*, 37 (no. 18, July 1, 1971), 573–574.

[32]Charles M. Brooks, "The need for legislation," *Vital Speeches*, 37 (no. 18, July 1, 1971), 563–566.

[33]Peter McKeller, *Imagination and Thinking*, New York, Basic Books, 1957, p. 4.

[34]Crow and Crow, *op. cit.*, p. 303.

[35]Harry S. Broudy and Eugene L. Freel, *Psychology for General Education*, New York, Longmans, Green, 1956, p. 281.

[36]John Dewey, *How We Think*, Boston, Heath, 1933, p. 12.

[37]Henry L. Ewbank and J. Jeffery Auer, *Discussion and Debate*, 2nd ed., New York, Appleton, 1951, pp. 45–53.

[38]John Dewey, *Logic: The Theory of Inquiry*, New York, Holt, Rinehart & Winston, 1938, pp. 101–119.

[39]Ruch, *op. cit.*, p. 267.

[40]E. R. Zumwalt, Jr., "Personal accountability: The demand of new approaches," *Vital Speeches*, 37 (no. 19, July 15, 1971), 605.

[41]*Vital Speeches*, 37, 1971.

[42]Carl Sandburg, "Abraham Lincoln," *Vital Speeches*, 25 (no. 10, Mar. 1, 1959), 293.

[43]William I. Aitken, "Cancer: Problems and progress," *Vital Speeches*, 37 (no. 18, July 1, 1971), 552.

[44]Elizabeth Langer, "An instrument of revelation," in Wil A. Linkugel, R. R. Allen, and Richard L. Johannesen, eds., *Contemporary American Speeches*, 2nd ed., Belmont, Calif., Wadsworth, 1969, p. 304.

[45]Edmund S. Muskie, "The influence of debating," *Vital Speeches*, 24 (no. 1, Oct. 15, 1957), 30.

[46]Floyd Allport, *Social Psychology*, Boston, Houghton Mifflin, 1924, p. 261. See also F. H. Allport, "Behavior and experiment in social psychology," *J. Abnormal Psychol.*, 14 (no. 5, Dec., 1919), 297–306.

CHAPTER SIX
MOTIVATING
BEHAVIOR

Nothing is so easy as to deceive one's self; for what we wish, that we readily believe.
Demosthenes

The needs of men are exceeded only by their desires.
Benjamin Franklin

In previous chapters we learned that perception and communication are highly personal processes. Individuals perceive and react to a message according to their own perceptual fields, at the center of which are their needs and desires, beliefs and attitudes. Hence, to motivate a listener we must show that our message is consistent with and triggers these wellsprings of action.

THE NATURE OF NEEDS
The student needs an A in most of his courses; the housewife needs a replacement for a broken kitchen appliance; the "hard-core unemployed" person needs a skill training course to get a job; the political candidate needs to become better known by the public. People everywhere have an infinite number of needs they seek to satisfy, and they attend to matters that seem to be means to satisfying these needs. This is significant for the speaker, for the response to his proposal will depend largely on whether it is perceived as something the listener needs or is, at least, related to his needs. In this section we shall examine the nature of needs, consider certain basic human needs, and look at the role of needs in stimulating behavior.

The Motivational Nature of Needs
Human needs are always present, are ever changing, and exert varying degrees of influence on behavior. They seem to be involved in everything an individual believes and does. What are they? What is their function? How are they satisfied?

It may help us to understand the motivational nature of needs to note that the human body always seeks a condition of equilibrium, or homeostasis. This condition is seldom perfectly achieved. Usually the individual is aware of and acts to allay some perceived psychological or physiological disturbance. Such disturbances concern the self alone, the self as related to other people, or the self as related to the environment. For example, a person feeling some physical deficiency may need nourishment or sleep. A disturbance related to other people might be perceived when one feels unappreciated, unwanted, or ignored, or when one perceives a small child in some potential danger. The disturbing factor may exist in the environment, as when a fire or storm has destroyed one's property. The perception of these disturbances does not in itself constitute a need; there must also be a feeling of necessity to do something—to remove, correct, or satisfy the condition. This *feeling of necessity is the need* and provides the motivation for action.

Man's behavior reflects a wide range of human needs. He wants food and water, clothing and shelter, sexual gratification, and rest if he is fatigued. In contrast with these needs are pleasurable sensory experiences, self-respect, satisfactory group memberships, and the esteem of others. The first group of needs relates primarily to body deficiency or imbalance; these needs are primary, unlearned, and physiological in nature. The second group deals primarily with interpersonal relations and less with physiological necessities; they are secondary, learned, and social.

There are numerous ways in which needs have been classified. One classification that has practical value for the communicator and reflects the twofold grouping suggested above is the deficiency-abundancy theory of the psychologists David Krech, Richard S. Crutchfield, and Norman Livson. They state:[1]

Behavior as a response to biological deficiency can be viewed as behavior under the influence of survival and security motives. Sexual activity, eating, running from danger or pain, building nests or homes to avoid extremes in temperature—all these activities clearly increase the probability of the survival or security of the individual or its species. And it makes good sense to say that survival or security motives are tension-reductive: They seek to remove *deficiencies or discomforts and to* avoid *anxiety or danger.*

Opposed to these survival and security motives is another type, which might be called "satisfaction and stimulation motives." The yearning to explore or to understand, to create or to achieve, to love or feel self-respect—all these desires are clearly not in the service of removing discomfort or danger. Their source does not seem to be tension reduction. Rather, they appear to involve tension increase *and a state of abundancy beyond the needs for immediate survival and security.*

Depending on whether he is appealing to deficiency or abundancy needs, the speaker will vary his supporting materials, select different patterns of organization, employ a controlled or vigorous style, or make appropriate changes in his mode of delivery. In the one case the communicator relates his message to goals that may appear necessary and essential to the listener; in the other case the message of the speaker must appear attractive and pleasurable, and provide some ego-satisfaction to the listener.

To aid further in understanding the rhetorical implications of motivation, we turn to a brief consideration of what psychologists Clifford T. Morgan and Richard A. King state about the *motivational cycle.* They say that motivation has three aspects, or stages, which are related to each other in cyclical fashion.[2] The first stage comprises *need, drive,* and *motive. Need is a lack or deficit within the individual;* it may be either physiological or derived. *Drive* suggests that the need provides incentive to behavior. *Motive* implies that a drive has direction toward a particular goal. The second stage in the motivational cycle of Morgan and King is called *instrumental behavior,* or any behavior that is instigated by the motive. The third stage is *reduction or satisfaction.* When a goal is reached, the need is satisfied.

The function of the motivational cycle for the speaker is clear. To be effective in communication the speaker must (1) understand the needs or motives that affect his listeners, (2) show how the action proposed will serve as instrumental behavior and, when taken by the listener, will (3) help that person achieve his goal. Recognition of the cyclical nature of motivation should make the speaker more audience-oriented in his speech preparation.

Types of Need

Human beings are complex organisms, and the things that motivate them, be they called needs, wants, drives, desires, or motives,[3] are rooted in both physiological and social sources. Some result from basic biological drives, and others are learned. Some occur earlier than others in the human developmental process. Maslow, whose work has been influential in this field, sees five levels of needs; a need on a lower level must be at least partially satisfied before one on the next level up may be met. His classification is as follows:[4]

1. Physiological needs, including hunger, thirst and sex.
2. Safety needs, including security, self-preservation, and stability.
3. Belongingness and love needs, including affection, friendship, identification and love.

4. Esteem needs, including prestige, self-respect, success and pride.
5. Self-actualization needs, including all forms of personal achievement.

In one way or another these needs influence or control every act of human behavior. They vary in their effect on individuals, however, depending on the intensity of the needs, their immediacy, the expectation of fulfillment, and whether several are in conflict.

While we need to be familiar with the general classifications of needs, such as that presented by Maslow, we should recognize, and be able to employ in speech preparation, the specific needs that activate behavior. The remainder of this section describes and illustrates the most significant activating motives of human behavior.

Self-preservation and Security

History is a record of man's struggle to preserve the race and keep his family and himself secure. The drive for self-preservation makes everyone interested in and concerned about such matters as protection from fallout, family size, and food production and distribution. We do everything we can to see that our family, our group, and our culture will survive. We are concerned that, as President Franklin D. Roosevelt once said, "one third of the nation has inadequate clothing, food and shelter." Great industries are built to satisfy our need to be secure. In 1970 we spent $62 billion on clothing, $143 billion on food and tobacco, and $91 billion on housing.

The motives of self-preservation and security operate in many other ways. We carry on continuous research to combat disease. The best minds in the country are constantly at work on the development of nuclear weapons to protect us against our enemies. Many of our best-selling books deal with mental and physical health. We buy good health for the entire family on the monthly plan or on a lifetime basis. As individuals we install safety belts in our cars or follow commonsense precautions in the use of firearms as matters of self-preservation. We also support organizations and programs that contribute to our security.

Self-Respect and Pride

"*I*" is not only the smallest word in the dictionary but also the biggest. To each individual the "I" is the most important thing in the world. We are concerned about our appearance, about our progress in our profession or business, about being in the know, and about the accomplishments of our children. Pride makes us do both foolish and wise things.

It makes us hide our hurts and at times keeps us from hurting others. Out of his wisdom about human nature Benjamin Franklin said: "Pride is as loud a beggar as want, and a great deal more saucy. When you have bought one fine thing, you must buy ten more, that your appearance may be all of a piece; but it is easier to suppress the first desire than to satisfy all that follow it."

Many of the leaders in the struggle for "equal rights" in America have tried to develop within the Blacks a pride in being Black. In this statement, Whitney Young illustrates aspects of self-respect and pride among Black Americans.[5]

It is up to black people to make black beautiful—by voting, working, studying and creating model communities across this country. . . .

When the Urban League builds into the ghettos of America the community and economic institutions needed to bring about change, it helps prepare the way for the realizations of a truly Open Society.

For real integration can only take place among equals, and our efforts will be directed at building a community which can exercise quality—a community that has pride in itself and its heritage.

Pride comes from standing straight and tall—and knowing that black is beautiful through the positive achievements of black people.

Pride is bringing home a decent paycheck and being able to house and clothe your family.

Pride is when little three and four-year-old kids don't try to wash the color from their hands because they've been brainwashed to believe that white's all right—but black keeps them back.

Pride is being what American society has always tried to keep blacks from becoming. Pride is being a Man.

Speakers can employ these motives in two ways. First, relate your proposals to your listeners' feelings of pride and self-respect: show them that what you propose will contribute to something in which they can take pride. Second, avoid doing anything likely to offend your listeners. By all means shun such belittling expressions as "Of course, you could not be expected to know . . .," "This is difficult, but I hope I can make you understand," and "Probably none of you realize the significance. . . ."

Property and Material Wealth

From the time we are children and collect dolls, toy guns, and story books, until we are old and collect "dolls," guns, and first editions, we never stop adding to our possessions. Even though we can't take it with us, we feel proud if we can turn over to our children a large estate. We are a nation whose people can be roughly divided into two classes, those whose aim is "to have and to hold" and those who seek "to get and to give." Both groups want property.

Usually the desire for property and material wealth is an admirable one, for the economic worth of a nation is one index of its standard of living. This is the motive appealed to by many of the candidates for political office at all levels. A candidate might say "Vote for me because I will exert every effort to provide jobs for the unemployed and increase the 'take-home' pay of the employed. I want every individual in this country to be able to own his own home, keep his family adequately clothed, and enjoy the material comforts which are his just due."

We strike out against forces we fear might destroy our material wealth and possessions. An example of a speaker's expression of concern for the protection of this nation's material wealth is found in a speech presented by J. L. Robertson, Vice-Chairman of the Board of Governors of the Federal Reserve System, before the Board of Directors of the Federal Reserve Bank of San Francisco, May 14, 1970. The speaker attacked inflation, one of the threats to a sound monetary policy.[6]

Put more specifically, people must understand that maintenance of the integrity of the dollar is of foremost importance. Without it we are in for trouble—trouble from which even our bright younger generation will not be able to extricate us. Consequently, one of the most important services we can perform is to educate the public about the evils of inflation and the necessary measures to prevent it.

H. E. Markley, the president of the Timken Company, in a speech given at Mount Union College of Alliance, Ohio, suggested that increased productivity was essential in the maintenance of a healthy economy in this country. In part, he blamed foreign competition as an important factor in the decline of the nation's productivity. He stated:[7]

Since the 1950's, our average growth rate has been the lowest among 21 leading countries. From 1965 through 1970, it has averaged only 2.1 per cent. Japan's has averaged 14.2 percent—nearly seven times better. The United Kingdom, Italy, Germany, France, Sweden, and the Netherlands also surpassed us during that same period.

What does this mean to the American consumer? Our share of the world's automobile production has been cut in half in less than 20 years. For decades, we were the world's leading producer of machine tools. We are now in fourth place. Last year, we produced only 20 per cent of the world's steel. Nine out of ten home radios that Americans buy are imported. One of every six new cars is imported. Two of every five pairs of shoes sold are imported. One of every two black-and-white television sets bought are imported.

Hundreds of other examples could be mentioned. What all this amounts to, however, is quite clear. We are being out-produced. And we have no one to blame but ourselves. . . .

We can no longer afford to have a declining rate of productivity. Our national economy cannot accept it economically nor can we afford it socially.

Recognition and Respect

Winning recognition and respect from others is one of the most important motives found in human nature. Evidence of this is found everywhere. In fact, the need for esteem and social approval is so great that those who do not experience it in some way often become maladjusted persons and problems to themselves and society. Without recognition we wither, as the vine withers without sunshine and rain.

Individually and collectively we want our achievements to be recognized, and we are prone to believe and act in conformity with the expressed opinions of those who give us this recognition. Public recognition of the work of the American Legion was stressed by General Douglas MacArthur in the introduction to a speech in October, 1951, before the Legion's national convention. The theme was that the counsel of veterans was needed in the determination of national military policies:[8]

No fraternity of men ever rested upon a more noble concept than does The American Legion. The indestructable bonds which unite its members were welded in a heat of battle by those who laid life and limb upon the altar of self-sacrifice.

From its very inception, it pledged itself to those high principles which form the preamble to its constitution. "For God and Country" it reads, and to these it has remained invincibly faithful. It has a written record of service to the nation which commands the gratitude of every citizen. . . .

Of all the issues which today confront our people, possibly none is of more immediate concern to the Legion than is the direction of our military policy.

James A. Farley, then Chairman of the Board of The Coca-Cola Export Corporation, gave a speech before an annual Brand Names dinner in New York on April 16, 1952. In his speech he stressed that American brand-name products are a force in expanding world trade and are recognized and esteemed throughout the world:[9]

To any world traveler it is heartening to see how widespread American products are distributed. You will find them in every corner of the globe. It may be an International Harvester combine at work in the wheat fields of Argentina. It may be a GMC truck along the dikes in Holland. Or perhaps it is a Singer sewing machine, humming busily away in a little Italian tailor shop. In Brisbane, in Calcutta . . . in Rio, Rome or Paris . . . American brand names may be found by the hundreds. And wherever you find them they are making friends for America.

Implicit in every American product is the idea of fair dealing . . . of identification and responsibility . . . the idea of a contract entered into in good faith and performed in good faith . . . the idea of a promise, freely made and faithfully kept. These ideas and associations are recognized by people everywhere in the world. Therefore, the distribution of American products in world trade is more important than ever before.

We pursue certain occupations because they are viewed as having prestige. Vance Packard's *The Status Seekers* describes the so-called pecking order in America. The drive for status and recognition is seen constantly: the ensign wants to become a lieutenant j.g., the associate professor wants to become a professor, the salesperson wants to be a sales manager, and the vice-president wants to become president. Status is achieved partly by what we do, but it is also essential that others recognize our abilities. That people want their abilities to be recognized is a principal operative in all walks of life.

Love, Affection, and Friendship

From birth to death man never has a feeling of completeness without love and friendship. These are necessities; we need both to give and to receive affection. The interplay of love and affection in the family circle forms the strongest bond of our social structure and gives meaning to the word "home." Lack of love gives rise to some of our most pressing social problems, such as divorce and juvenile delinquency. Although some people are egocentric in demanding and not returning affection, for the most part the force of love and affection is sociocentric. That is, love of country and loyalty to church, lodge, or friends is largely outgoing and selfless.

The nature of love and affection makes us protect and provide for our families and friends, endure great hazards for noble causes, have civic pride, take part in worthy movements, and participate in groups in which we can love and be loved.

On many college campuses special projects are supported and carried out entirely by the students. On the campus of the University of California, Los Angeles, one such project is UniCamp, a summer camp for underprivileged children in the Los Angeles County area. One student made the following appeal in soliciting funds for this program:

The main reason you should contribute I call love—the love which you should have for kids who haven't had your good luck and the love which the kids who attend these summer camps have for all of us who help to send them. Every dime, quarter, or half-dollar you give is tangible evidence that college students do think about kids who really need help. But more than that, your contribution will win the undying gratitude of kids who have precious little love in their lives. I was a counselor at Unicamp last summer—and as you know there is one counselor for every ten campers—and the ways in which these kids expressed their affection for their benefactors—you students here at UCLA—were many and varied indeed. A few said they wanted to write letters to "the university," a few asked me to tell "all" the students how they felt, some hoped that they could camp next year, and others showed their appreciation in smaller ways which made me realize these kids did appreciate what the university students had done for them.

Won't you give a little money and share in a lot of love? You may be unnamed but you will not be unsung.

At times friendship can transcend state, national, sectional, and even racial boundaries, when the appeal is simple, honest, and frank, as was Charles Evers' speech to a white audience in New York City, soon after he was elected Mayor of Fayette, Mississippi:[10]

Maybe what we do in Mississippi will help our black brothers and our white brothers all over the country. I'm only here to say: Let's help ourselves. Let's not cast anybody off, and let's not hate anybody. I'm not even going to hate that old chief of police, whom I'm going to fire on July the eighth.

It can be done. It's got to be done. We got no choice. Please, any of you here who are sitting on the fence, get down off it on the right side. Thank you so much. Come visit us in Fayette. Have no fear.

Adventure and New Experience

Man's life is a quest into the unknown. He will climb the highest mountain or swim the widest river to satisfy his craving for adventure and new experience. We put astronauts into space, fly faster than the speed of sound, explore the depths of the ocean, and chart the regions of the world that are still unknown, partly because we are adventurous and partly because we wish to expand the horizons of knowledge.

Millions of Americans travel many millions of miles each year in quest of new experiences. Depending on time, money, and inclination, we "Travel the Polar Route to Europe," "See America First," or take the family to the park. When we cannot travel, we gain new experiences vicariously through books, from television, by listening to travel talks, or from friends.

When things are new, they have an irresistible appeal. Any new method of dieting is better than the old-fashioned one of eating less. A new bomb, a new computing machine, a medical discovery, or a food fad attracts our fancy. We change styles in clothes and cars each year; in other things less frequently. We are curious, adventurous, and restless. We will listen and act if a speaker presents ways of satisfying these drives.

Sometimes the challenge is to accept new ideas. Each June brings its flood of commencement speeches, many of which exhort graduates to accept the challenges their graduation places upon them. In a speech given to the graduates of the U.S. Naval Academy in June, 1971, the Chief of Naval Operations commented in this manner about the challenge facing these new naval officers:[11]

Those who would command ships or men should hold indelibly in their consciousness these words from out of the past:

"Accountability is not for the intentions but for the deed. The Captain of a ship, like the Captain of a state, is given honor and privileges and trust beyond other men. But let him set the wrong course, let him touch ground, let him bring disaster to his ship or his men, and he must answer for what he has done. No matter what, he cannot escape. . . .

It is in the absolute nature of this challenge that the true rewards and satisfactions of a naval career can be found. The path which brought me to this platform on this occasion now lies open before you—it is a path as individual and personal as that which led to your own presence here today—each step along the way can be as challenging and full of potential for personal reward and satisfaction as you choose to make it.

Freedom from Restraint and the Need to Belong

We consider finally two contrasting but closely related drives that exist in all of us—in the small child in a crib, in the young boy growing into manhood, in the lawbreaker who has been jailed, and in the aged person. All seek to escape from the restrictions placed on their freedom. All seek to belong.

The desire for freedom from restraint is manifested in individuals, in groups, and in nations. Few of us want to be "low man on the totem pole"; it is much more fun when we are on the top, with no one above to impose his wishes on us. The scholar wants to be unfettered in his search for new knowledge. Teenage gangs constantly seek to be free from the restraints imposed by law, convention, and their peers in other gangs. They carry on many of their activities outside the law, to show their independence. Nations, too, want independence, freedom, and the right to do as they choose. Freedom from the restraints that for years have kept them second-rate citizens has been the goal of Black Americans during the sixties and seventies. It was within the framework of the desire for freedom that Martin Luther King, Jr., made his great appeal to the American people on February 10, 1963. He ended his address with these stimulating words:[12]

With this faith we will be able to hear out of the mountains of despair a tone of hope. With this faith we will be able to transform the jangling discords of our nation into a beautiful symphony of brotherhood . . . We will be able to speed up that day when all of God's children—black men and white men, Jews and Gentiles, Protestants and Catholics—will be able to join hands and sing in the words of the old Negro Spiritual, "Free at last, free at last, thank God Almighty, we are free at last!"

Man also has a need to belong. This is the need that makes him a member of "the gang" in the first place. He wants to be seen with like-minded persons, do what they do, and support their values. This need to join with others for the common good also is expressed in Dr. King's speech:[12]

. . . many of our white brothers, as evidenced by their presence here today, have come to realize that their destiny is tied up with our destiny and they have come to realize that their freedom is inextricably bound to our freedom. This offense we share mounted to storm the battlements of injustice must be carried forth by a bi-racial army. We cannot walk alone.

The motivating effect of the desires considered in this chapter depends in part on their intensity. Thus, basic physical needs are more potent and more urgent when hunger, thirst, and extremes of heat and cold and pain are felt. For example, we need bread and water for life; this achieved, we can cultivate our taste for crêpes suzette and caviar. Adequate shelter is a universal want, but four bedrooms, a den, and a swimming pool are luxuries that usually can be postponed. Our perception of the intensity and urgency of our listeners needs will aid in our speech preparation.

THE NATURE OF BELIEFS AND ATTITUDES

Many people believe in the Ten Commandments and try to act accordingly. Many have democratic beliefs that they try to implement in their daily lives. Some Americans belong to the Republican Party, others to the Democratic, depending upon their beliefs; and they act accordingly. In America some people believe in aid to underprivileged countries, in abortion, in capital punishment; others do not.

Attitudes differ widely, are held with varying degrees of intensity, and change over time. Polls reveal some of these differences. For example, consider the attitudes of Americans on such topics as "womens' lib," relations with Red China, the Vietnam War, offshore oil drilling, the "relevancy" of college education, or "street children."

We may rightly ask, "What are beliefs and attitudes?" "How do they develop?" "How can they be changed?" The effective communicator must have answers to these questions.

The Nature of Beliefs

A belief is the conviction that something is true. It implies trust, reliance, confidence, and assurance that the thing believed can be accepted. We can define it as the acceptance of a proposition, statement, or fact, on the basis of evidence, authority, experience, or mental predisposition. A person may believe, for example, in the value of a college education because of evidence that indicates its benefits. Belief in certain forms of church worship may result from authoritative direction. One may believe that he should avoid certain foods because of unhappy after-effects he has experienced. Some people believe that aggressiveness is necessary in interpersonal relations, merely because they have a predisposition toward authoritarianism. In each case, to those who hole it the belief always appears to be justified.

The conviction that we are justified in any belief we hold is a significant characteristic of beliefs. Many are entirely without logical support; they may be based on false or incomplete data; they may be distorted by emotion; they may be held because of tradition; still others are forced on us. Other factors may also operate to instill within us beliefs that most people would not consider valid by objective standards. As a result, many of us hold unsupported beliefs: superstitions, delusions, prejudices, stereotyped notions, and the like.[13] Such beliefs are hard to change. Furthermore, the varying degrees of intensity with which beliefs are held cause people to act in support of some of them but not of others. As speakers we need to gauge the intensity with which beliefs are held if we would change the convictions of our listeners.

Sources of Beliefs

Beliefs arise from experience and may be accepted either critically or uncritically. Eventually they become fixed in our value systems and influence our actions. Knowing the sources of beliefs helps the speaker appeal to his hearers and influence their actions.

Primary-Group Experiences. Probably the first important source of beliefs is our experience in primary groups, especially the family, play groups, and classroom. Most of the beliefs we learn in these groups are held with varying degrees of conviction throughout life. Many we accept uncritically, though that does not necessarily make them undesirable. Our actions in later life quite frequently support the beliefs developed in our formative years. Thus we may pass religious beliefs on to our children. Beliefs about sportsmanship and loyalty, learned in play groups and gangs, help to shape our adult personalities. Many of the things we are taught to believe early in life will determine adult patterns of family behavior.

Cultural Influences. A second source of beliefs is the culture in which a person lives. Though at times the influence of specific cultural factors may be slight, the influence of religious beliefs, for instance, on such matters as war, birth control, and personal habits is well recognized. Widely traveled persons tend to be less provincial in their beliefs than stay-at-homes. Various nationality groups in America have very different views about such matters as the place of women in the home, the education of children, the use of modern conveniences, and what constitutes proper clothing.

Intellectual Factors. Beliefs are established in some individuals by intellectual means: reasoning, evidence, logic, and empirical data. This fact is very important in many instances. Some people accept nothing unless it can be proven; their attitude is "Show me!" Others ask for proof only occasionally, or believe anything they read "in the paper." At one extreme the designers and builders of the Polaris-firing nuclear submarine had ample tested and scientific support for their belief in its capabilities; at the other extreme a sick person's belief in the curative values of a certain medicine is based solely on faith. Obviously, objective means of arriving at beliefs assures somewhat more constructive decisions and actions.

To many people it makes a very slight difference whether or not they have proof for their beliefs. Their beliefs are personal and hence represent reality for them, even if not based on proof or truth as they are perceived by others.

Nonrational Factors. Although many beliefs have intellectual sources, many others grow out of our tendency to think illogically, to rationalize, to use stereotypes, and to accept specious reasoning. Through rationalization we fix and protect our beliefs. If we want a new car we set out to convince ourselves that we should buy one now, as prices may go up next year; some of our friends have recently purchased new cars, and if they can we can; buying now would cut repair costs; the longer we keep the old car the less will be the trade-in value. And so on. This process of rationalization—thinking up reasons for a desired act—continues until we believe that we must act. Whether the action is logical is beside the point; we act because we believe we should. In most people this formation of belief through rationalization goes on continually.

Indicators of Beliefs

As speakers we need to know as much as we can about what our listeners believe. We may discover this in several ways.

Behavior. We get some indication of a person's beliefs from his behavior. If he attends church regularly, sings in a choir, or teaches Sunday School, we assume he accepts the religious beliefs of his church. If he joins Rotary, Lions, Kiwanis, or some other luncheon service club, we infer that he believes in working toward community betterment. If he works out at a gym or plays golf weekly, we assume that he believes exercise is good for his health or his business.

Group Memberships. The groups a person belongs to are usually reliable indicators of his beliefs. If a man belongs to the American Legion, the Knights of Columbus, the National Association for the Advancement of Colored People, or the Circus Fans Association of America, we know something about his previous experience, religious convictions, or avocational interests. Usually one joins a particular group because it has belief systems much like his own. In turn, each organization exerts strong pressures on its members to accept the values and goals of the group.

Public Statements. People often make public statements about their beliefs or express them in informal gatherings. Public-opinion polls usually reflect quite accurately the beliefs of large groups of people on current issues. The "Letters to the Editor" columns in newspapers, the book review sections of professional journals, and the radio and television interview programs are barometers of what people believe on selected subjects.

Cultural and Socioeconomic Backgrounds. Another indicator of beliefs is the cultural and socioeconomic milieu in which people live. Anthropological studies of different racial groups reveal widespread differences in beliefs about the roles of men and women in the household, marriage, sex matters, and care of the aged.

The Mennonites, Mormons, and Seventh-Day Adventists hold

varying beliefs about family life, religious training and worship, and participation in the affairs of citizenship. People from Bucks County, Pennsylvania, and the Watts area in Los Angeles County, California, have widely differing beliefs about public welfare, taxation, educational needs, and the role of peace officers in law enforcement.

Many studies have been made of the beliefs of people in almost all walks of life.[14] These give the speaker some information about the commonly held beliefs of American people. The speaker must also become familiar with the specific beliefs of his particular audience. Here is a list of some major value-orientations of Americans:[15]

1. Personal achievement as demonstrated by the "success story," expansion, mastery, and an ever higher standard of living.
2. Activity and work—the belief, largely inherited from our Puritan past, that idleness is evil.
3. Moral orientation—the tendency to view action in terms of ethical judgments. Often our moralizations become split between theory and necessity, resulting in hypocrisy and empty "lip service."
4. Humanitarianism—that complex of such values as charity, helping the underdog, and spontaneous aid in mass disasters. One could cite evidence to the contrary (wars, lynching, treatment of the American Indian), although there is a national norm of generosity.
5. Efficiency and practicality—reverence for getting things done, for quantity and standardization.
6. Progress—the concept of change and forward movement.
7. Material comfort—a desire for material success, ease, and effortless gratification of desires.
8. Equality—a belief in the inherent value of the individual, in equality of legal rights and responsibilities, and in equality of opportunity.
9. Freedom—the individual's independence from outside constraint, moral autonomy in decision making.
10. External conformity—sensitivity to group pressure.

Obviously many others could be added to this list. Obviously, too, not everyone would subscribe to all these beliefs. However, since most of them are part of the value systems of most people who live in the American culture, they are useful supporting material for almost any speech to an audience of Americans.

The Nature of Attitudes

Attitudes are closely related to beliefs. However, a separate consideration of their characteristics and the ways in which they may be modified can be helpful to the speaker.

The definition of attitude is generally agreed upon and has remained fairly constant through the years. In 1930 the social psychologist Kimball Young stated that attitudes may be described as learned and more or less generalized, stable, consistent tendencies to respond or act, with like or dislike, in reference to some situation, idea, value, norm, material object, class of objects, institution, person, or group of persons.[16] In 1969 the psychologists Krech, Crutchfield, and Livson defined attitude in much the same way:[17] "An attitude is a complex organization of evaluative beliefs, emotional feelings, and action orientation focused upon an object, predisposing the individual to respond to the object in certain ways." Briefly, we may say that an attitude is an energizing tendency to behave in a given way toward some object.

Characteristics of Attitudes

Both attitudes and beliefs are rooted in the individual's experience, emotional makeup, intellectual capacity, and cultural environment. Attitudes, are never neutral: they are always for or against something. Attitudes are sometimes latent: they may be formed without benefit of thinking. For example, we may have attitudes toward situations, persons, or objects that are almost reflexive. We frequently form our attitudes towards hot stoves, poor food, or crude manners on the basis of sensory experience or first impressions.

In discussing attitudes we are concerned with their intensity, clarity, persistence, and integration with other attitudes (energizing potential).

Intensity. This refers to the degree to which an attitude is for or against something. An attitude may be conceived of as lying at some point on a continuum ranging from "extremely favorable" to "extremely unfavorable." This "more or less" aspect is the basis of the scales for measuring attitudes toward political issues, merchandise, ethnic groups, action proposals, and so on.[18] The attitudes at the extremes are the hardest to change. Hence in a persuasive talk the speaker aims at those whose minds are not yet made up on an issue.

Clarity. The clarity of attitudes also concerns the speaker. Some persons know exactly why they hold a given attitude, they remember the experiences which caused it, they can cite evidence to support it, and they recognize its role in their lives. Other persons have vaguely formed attitudes; both the attitude itself and their reasons for holding it are unclear. The latter frequently are more susceptible to influences seeking to change their attitudes.

Persistence. Some attitudes, having been held over a long period of time, have a lasting quality which gives them strength. Attitudes that are recently formed can often be quickly changed.

Energizing Potential. Cutting across the characteristics of attitudes we have mentioned is their energizing potential. Because they are always related to life situations, attitudes both determine and reflect our daily behavior.

Modification of Attitudes

Frequently a person's beliefs about such feelings as justice, brotherhood, and tolerance conflict with his attitudes and actions. Thus he may believe that gambling is a vice but take a chance on the "wheel of fortune." He may believe in racial equality and yet refuse to sell his house to a minority-group member. A judge's belief in duty may be modified by his attitude of mercy. A storekeeper who believes that "honesty is the best policy" may make every effort to dispose of shopworn goods. In general, though, attitudes are closely related to action, playing an important role in causing people to act the way they do. It is definitely to the speaker's interest to understand how attitudes can be modified, since he may often wish to achieve this objective.

Enforced Changes in Behavior. External forces sometimes cause changes in behavior that in turn modify attitudes. Suppose that a change in government causes you to lose your job, or a street blocked off for repairs forces you to take a new route to work, or a school bond issue increases your taxes. If you have previously had favorable attitudes toward the government agencies involved in these actions, your attitudes might now become unfavorable.

An enforced change in behavior may just as easily result in the formation of favorable attitudes. A citizen who originally opposed the bond issue may discover that the new school makes it easier to get his children to and from school and, furthermore, that the school has summer playground activities. Thus, in spite of the increased expense, his attitude may become more favorable.

New Information. Attitudes result in part from information about objects, persons, events, and ideas. We constantly learn new facts about things of concern to us in our reading, conversation, experience, and the like. Some are hearsay and some we invent. You may have regarded someone as miserly and unfriendly; after his death you learn of his many charities and change your attitude toward him. A father's attitude toward a son may change with the discovery that a good part of the latter's allowance was put into a fast-growing savings account and not spent foolishly. The attitudes of many Americans toward Soviet Russia changed considerably when they put a Sputnik into space.

Changes in Individual Goals. The president of a large industrial corporation and the shop steward of a local union will certainly have different outlooks on life. Their economic and social situations are different, they see their roles in society differently, and they doubtless have divergent status values. But let their positions be reversed, and many of their attitudes will change. Some 25,000,000 investors had stock losses totaling about $50 billion during the two years after the stock market crash of 1929. Certainly their attitudes toward life, as well as their goals, underwent some change.

The changing interests and goals that accompany increasing maturity also result in changed attitudes, especially attitudes toward the opposite sex, health, social values, and esthetic experience. Attitudes toward savings, taxes, community improvement, property ownership, and participation in sports are also modified as a person grows older.

Changes in Internal States. Changes in one's mental, physical, or emotional states also result in changes in his attitudes. A man who has just discovered that he can stretch his salary check to pay all his monthly bills takes a somewhat more friendly attitude toward his creditors. Someone who has just listened to several long speeches does not look forward with enthusiasm to hearing the final speaker on the program. There is an old song that goes, "Sometimes I'm happy, sometimes I'm blue. . . ." With each change in disposition our outlook toward people, events, and life in general changes.

New Experiences. The person who has looked forward eagerly to a mountain-climbing trip may feel differently if the climb proves hazardous. In wartime attitudes toward persons of different color, race, and economic level have been known to change drastically under combat conditions.[19] After participating in such sports as sky-diving, skin-diving, aqua-skiing, or sports-car racing, many people no longer consider them dangerous, perhaps because they have learned the precautions necessary to avoid accidents.

Most of us have had experiences that resulted in changed attitudes—being stopped by a policeman and receiving a warning instead of a ticket, working with a minority-group member and discovering that our prejudices are unfounded, feeling that our work is unappreciated and then having an unexpected testimonial event given in our honor.

Extent of Personal Involvement. You have undoubtedly been at some time asked why you hold firmly to certain attitudes. If the matter is one that affects you deeply, you are likely to defend your attitude, even to the point of rationalizing it. For example, the attitude of labor toward wages, which amounts almost to a firm belief that workers are always underpaid, would be hard to change. Similarly, it is generally difficult to change the attitudes of parents toward their children; one's own children are usually right even when wrong.

On the other hand, if you have little personal involvement, you may be willing to change. The extent to which attitudes can be held because of personal involvement can be seen in the Marines, the submarine service of the Navy, and the élite of the Army, the paratroopers. The parents of high-school students performing in the Junior Class Play cannot stay at home the night of the performance; however, the parents of members of the stage crew do not feel it quite so urgent to attend.

Group Influences. Everyone is aware of the influence of the family on the personality development of its members: as the twig is bent, so grows the tree. The child from a broken home has attitudes toward parents that are different from those of a child whose parents have given him love, protection, and guidance.

In adult life, too, group pressures exert influences on attitudes. Books like William H. Whyte, Jr.'s *The Organization Man,* Sinclair Lewis' *Babbitt,* and David Riesman's *The Lonely Crowd* show the changes in attitudes that group pressures can bring about in individuals. America is a nation of pressure groups. Participation in any of them usually means some degree of conformity, a part of which is the acceptance of the values and attitudes held by the group.

The behavior of an individual acting alone is not the same as that of the individual acting as a part of an audience or other group. The individual's attitudes and behavior are influenced by the group.

A classic experiment made by Asch[20] indicates that majority opinion tends to change the attitudes, or at least the behavior, of individuals when they find themselves in a group. In 1956 Asch conducted a number of experiments to investigate what happens when (1) an individual trying to make a value judgment is faced with strong opposition from the group and (2) when the individual feels that his judgment is correct in spite of a unanimous contrary opinion. In this study the experimental subjects were asked to give a visual judgment as to which of three lines projected on a screen before a group of persons was equal in length to a standard line. All other persons participating in the experiment had been instructed beforehand to give identical wrong judgments at certain points. About one third of the subjects gave judgments distorted in the direction of the unanimously incorrect group judgment. The size of the opposing group consensus was also found to be a significant factor. When one person differed, the subject remained completely independent; when two were against him, he tended to conform to the group's opinion; when three were against him, conformity reached a high level.

A good speaker will attempt to achieve *audience polarization*—a strong cohesiveness and unity—in order to secure a concerted response. When an audience is polarized, the individual, as Stevens says,[21] "tends to relinquish his own set of values and to adopt the values of the audience. Instead of many diverse, individual reflective responses to a speech, we observe a unified group response. As the group reacts, so does each person conform."

Another phenomenon occurring in groups is *social facilitation*, which is the influence of others upon the individual because of physical proximity. We applaud a poor or mediocre performance, because others around us are applauding; we laugh at jokes we may not even understand, because others are laughing; we feel embarrassed when we laugh at some line in a play, because we realize that we are the only ones in the audience who have laughed. A notable and highly successful application of this principle is observed in the almost universal use of "canned" laughter on televised comedy shows.

Membership in organizations tends to influence the attitudes and behavior of individuals. When an individual is a member of a religious organization, service club, fraternity, political party, professional society, labor union, or street gang, he tends to identify himself with the group and accept its norms as his own. Individual members of any group take on the customs, loyalties, and coloring of their group.

The conscientious communicator will consider these phenomena when he analyzes his audience.

The Relation of Opinion to Attitude

Opinion polls are commonplace in America. We have polls on the popularity of our presidents, food-buying habits, political issues, new fashion creations—in fact, on almost everything in the public focus at a given moment. These polls seek to measure attitudes. An opinion is generally considered to be the expressed attitude of an individual or group. Opinions are verbalizations offered for public consumption. Because they are public, they frequently are watered down. The speech educators Winston L. Brembeck and William S. Howell comment on this difference between expressed and real attitudes:[22]

An opinion is considered an expressed or verbalized attitude which may or may not correspond to the attitude that is supposed to be expressed. An opinion might be called a public attitude. . . . Our opinions generally are subject to social pressures; they serve various social motives. Therefore, an opinion may not be a reliable index to a person's true attitude.

Although opinions are not always reliable yardsticks of true beliefs and attitudes, this does not mean that public-opinion polls have no value. Quite the contrary! People feel important when asked to give their opinions on matters of public interest; those who reply to polls know that their answers are anonymous; replying to a poll has little effect on the person polled; furthermore, the sampling procedures used counteract the effect of false answers. Therefore, opinion polls reflect a collective opinion, which is general enough to reconcile many "shades and hues" of attitudes. Despite their shortcomings, public-opinion polls seem to be the best indicators of public opinion we possess.

Knowing the nature of opinions and their relationship to attitudes and beliefs helps the speaker in numerous ways:

1. Public opinion is collective opinion; when it reflects majority opinion it can provide powerful support for a speaker's proposal.
2. Even though some may not give their true attitudes when responding to an opinion poll, if a poll is a good sample of the population it represents, its results usually indicate accurately the attitudes held. Such polls tell much about what the public thinks.
3. Sometimes one's action is a better indicator of his real attitudes than his expressed opinion. The effective speaker considers both in his preparation.
4. The speaker must study the attitudes and beliefs of an audience rather than its opinions alone, to determine its tendencies to action.
5. Every listener thinks that his own beliefs, attitudes, and opinions are rationally formed and are true. They are a part of what he calls reality. The speaker must respect this reality, even though he may seek to change it.

THE USE OF INDIVIDUAL DRIVES IN MOTIVATION

In this chapter we have considered the nature of needs, beliefs, attitudes, and opinions, which, taken collectively, we call the individual's value system. This is the gestalt of forces that arouses the individual to action. We have seen that these drives to action have varying degrees of intensity. We have described some of the sources of these drives:

Finally, we have considered some of the factors that serve to modify the attitudes an individual may have about the components of his value system.

The value system of an individual has great significance to that person in two ways: first, it represents the configuration of goals the individual seeks to achieve during his lifetime; second, it serves as a set of criteria by which the individual measures his progress toward these goals.

To illustrate: A young man who has beliefs and attitudes favorable to home ownership feels that he needs a certain type of home and an annual income of $11,000 to maintain a desired standard of living. If he is just beginning his career, the home and income probably represent long-time goals, though at the same time they serve as yardsticks by which he measures his progress.

The universe of every individual includes many different beliefs, needs, desires, and attitudes. Taken together they constitute both ends and means in the struggle to achieve what many consider to be man's basic need, a sense of *adequacy*. This unitary need is conceived of as encompassing the total configuration of beliefs, needs, and desires that provide the drives in human behavior. Combs and Snygg state the matter clearly:[23]

> . . . *we have seen: (1) that man, like the universe of which he is a part, characteristically seeks the maintenance of organization; (2) that the organization man seeks to maintain is the organization of which he is aware, namely, his phenomenal self; and (3) that, because man lives in a changing world and is aware of the future as well as the present, maintenance of the self requires, not simply maintenance of the status quo, but an active seeking for personal adequacy.*
>
> We can define man's basic need, then, as a need for adequacy. *It represents in man the expression of a universal tendency of all things. It is . . . that* great driving, striving force in each of us by which we are continually seeking to make ourselves ever more adequate to cope with life.

Other writers, discussing the unitary drive for ascendency, ego satisfaction, or self-realization, are referring to essentially the same concept: the need of the individual to handle life's problems, satisfy his present wants, and achieve his aspiration.

To accept the existence of a single, unitary human need certainly does not mean that understanding the effect of drives on the individual is a simple one, or that the speaker's task in motivation is easy. But it is useful in that it suggests the way in which beliefs, needs, and attitudes (all terms that refer to motivating factors in human behavior) serve the individual. Simply stated, this is the concept: because of the phenomenal nature of perception, the individual will accept only those beliefs, seek to satisfy only those wants, hold only those attitudes, and sustain only those desires which contribute to his concept of adequacy.

As students or practitioners of speech communication, we must now ask ourselves this: "How can I employ the existence of these drives—whether one posits this motivational force to be of a unitary nature or multifaceted—in getting my message accepted by my listeners?" No single answer to this question exists, although partial answers are found throughout this text. However, certain principles or conditions are related to a listener's belief-need pattern, explained in the following pages.

Immediacy of Needs

From one point of view the principle of immediacy of needs is obvious. First things should come first. The student in college, whether he has a family or not, is not primarily concerned with plans for retirement. The political candidate talks about farm prices to farmers, wages to workers, and adjusting to civilian life to returned war veterans. A sabbatical leave that is three years off is of less concern to the teacher than his teaching load for the ensuing semester. So the speaker must show his listeners how his message is related to what is uppermost in their minds at the time: their immediate needs.

To say that some needs or desires are of more concern to a person now than they will be later on is the same as saying that these drives have relative prepotency. Hunger, sex, thirst, and pain are assumed to be basic; writers call them instinctive. On the other hand, the drives to gain recognition, to exert influence over others, and to acquire property, developing as we mature, reflect the universal urge to move up the ladder of need satisfaction. This is one of the basic tenets of Packard's much-discussed book *The Status Seekers*.[24] He maintains that status consciousness (a higher-need-level manifestation) provides the urge that advertisers exploit through hidden persuasion. Once we have satisfied our need for the basic essentials, we become easy prey to appeals to status, prestige, acceptability, and power.

Fear Reduction

Feelings of fear, uncertainty, anxiety, and insecurity have marked effects on human behavior. Children are taught to fear hot stoves, bad dogs, and uncovered holes; adults learn to fear "not getting ahead on the job" and "not being able to provide for our family." There appears to be a close relationship between the tendency to be fearful and other so-called drives or needs. Psychologists tell us that fear as a motivator may keep us from acting or may goad us to action.

Fear seems to be a prime motivating force in almost every area of life. Public speakers make extensive use of appeals to fear.

In a speech given at the American Management Association's annual conference in New York City in February, 1971, an assistant Secretary of Labor sought first to develop in his listeners feelings of anxiety, concern, and fear about the conditions of the blue-collar workers in this country. Then he made suggestions about how the conditions of these workers could be improved. Excerpts from his speech follow:[25]

The fact is that millions of workers who earn between $5 and 10 thousand a year are getting increasingly frustrated. Despite steady labor they cannot attain the quality of life for themselves or their families that is expected to result from conscientious job performance.

. . . Their paychecks do not cover legitimate basic family needs.

. . . Their work life is unsatisfactory but they see no way of breaking out.

. . . Their total life pattern is discouraging.

In short they are caught in a 3-way squeeze: an economic squeeze, a work place squeeze and a socio-economic squeeze. . . .

The result is that after years of vigorous, dependable job performance, many find themselves worse off *economically than when they started their working lives. This is a sad situation—in stark contrast to the American dream and our world of rising expectations. . . .*

Economic rewards, personal job satisfaction and future opportunity are the three basic elements that turn people on. Failure and frustration turn them off.

Speaking in the United States Senate in February, 1972, on the subject of drug abuse, George McGovern stated:[26]

All statistics on narcotics addiction are questionable, but best current estimates—and they are admittedly understated—put the American drug addict population at about 350,000 persons. In New York City that may mean as many as 100,000 people. In one District of Columbia neighborhood it translates into a constant heroin craving for one in three males between the ages of 15 and 24.

The human tragedy involved in such statistics is bad enough. But the addicts themselves, although they are the most seriously damaged, constitute only a portion of the total problem. Narcotics addiction and crime are inseparable companions.

A heroin addict with a $35 daily habit . . . must somehow come up with that amount of cash each day, every day of his life. In 98 percent of the cases he steals to pay the pusher . . . On an annual basis he must steal nearly $64,000 worth of property. Countrywide . . . that translates into about $4.4 billion in crime. . . .

Considering their total costs to society and their infliction of virtually permanent damage on the user, the control of addictive drugs must be the main priority of overall national drug policy.

In the remainder of the speech McGovern gave further data on the costs of drug addiction, its effects on the user, and the extent of the use of nonaddictive drugs, such as marijuana. In the conclusion of his speech McGovern outlined a comprehensive list of things that should be done by the federal government and through education programs to solve the problem.

It is important to note that in using feelings of anxiety and fear as motivating drives the speaker must also give suggestions aimed at reducing the fear. The speaker is essentially saying: "This is the problem. It is a serious one! And here is what should be done to help solve the problem." Research has shown that fear arousal as a persuasive technique is only effective when assurance is also presented that the problem to which the fear has been related can somehow be resolved. A growing body of research data suggests that the overall effectiveness of a persuasive communication will be reduced by the use of a fear appeal that evokes high emotional tension, if the communication does not at the same time satisfy the need for assurance.

Cognitive Balance

The tendency of any organism to maintain a state of stability or balance has applications over the entire belief-need pattern. The term *homeostasis* usually is applied to the physiological results of this tendency, but it sometimes is applied to the intellectual results as well. One psychologist states that the maintenance of a relatively constant inner state is a primary task of the life processes of each individual. Whenever an imbalance occurs in this inner state, the individual seeks ways of restoring the balance. As a speaker you seek to show that your proposal will bring about cognitive balance.

The need of equilibrium is a potent human drive to action. Festinger comments as follows:[27]

I should like to postulate the existence of cognitive dissonance as a motivating state in human beings. . . . The word "dissonance" was not chosen arbitrarily to denote this motivating state. It was chosen because its ordinary meaning in the English language is so close to the technical meaning I want to give it. The synonyms which the dictionary gives for the word "dissonant" are "harsh," "jarring," "grating," "unmelodious," "inharmonious," "inconsistent," "contradictory," "disagreeing," "incongruous," "discrepant." The word, in this ordinary meaning specifies a relation between two things. In connection with musical tones, where it is usually used, the relation between the tones is such that they sound unpleasant together. In general, one might say that a dissonant relation exists between two things which occur together, if, in some way, they do not belong together or fit together.

Cognitive dissonance refers to this kind of relation between cognitions which exist simultaneously for a person. If a person knows two things, for example, something about himself and something about the world in which he lives, which somehow do not fit together, we will speak of this as cognitive dissonance. . . .

. . . Just as hunger is motivating, cognitive dissonance is motivating. Cognitive dissonance will give rise to activity oriented toward reducing or eliminating the dissonance. . . . In other words, if two cognitions are dissonant with each other there will be some tendency for the person to attempt to change one of them so that they fit together, thus reducing or eliminating the dissonance.

Let us look at two situations in which this cognitive conflict occurs. In this country the great majority of people believe that the Ten Commandments are meant to be obeyed. When patriotism requires a man to disobey the commandment "Thou shalt not kill," he is faced with a serious conflict and is likely to seek every possible means of evading it. At one extreme he may become a conscientious objector; at the other, he merely rationalizes, adopting an attitude that places the blame on the government or makes war an "act of God." In between, however, there are decisions regarding self-defense, to which there may be no easy answers.

We are usually willing to believe whatever will reconcile conflicting points of view that trouble us. In other words, the need to remove the imbalance has motivating effect.

A salesman with a sales quota to meet will take immediate steps, though a number of factors make increased sales in his territory doubtful. He may seek new markets, he may try to improve his sales methods, he may seek a quota revision, or he may even look for a new job. Each of these actions would be an effort to satisfy his need for equilibrium.

Some research data indicate some of the ways in which cognitive balance is achieved. For example, certain studies conducted at Yale University produced the following findings:[28]

1. *Individuals are more highly persuasible by messages arguing in a direction which increases consistency and are more resistant to those arguing in a direction that increases inconsistency.*
2. *The preferred solution to a temporary dilemma is one involving the least effortful path.*
3. *In resolving cognitive discrepancies, subjects seek not only the attainment of balance and consistency but also the solution that maximizes potential gain and minimizes potential loss.*

The existence of a strong drive to achieve cognitive balance is also supported by related psychological theories. Murray[29] talks about the "need to ascend," Combs and Snygg[29] speak of the "drive for adequacy," and Symonds says the human being has a "need for adjustment." Each of these men says, in effect, that the need to ascend, to deem oneself adequate, or to feel adjusted is of such compelling force that the individual will act to reduce or remove the perceived difference between two dissonant conditions. Festinger[30] adds that the basic background of this theory is "that the human organism tries to establish internal harmony, consistency or congruity among his opinions, attitudes, knowledge, and values. That is, there is a drive toward consonance among cognitions."

The meaning of this for the speaker should be clear. He must present his proposal so that it appears as a means of resolving the dissonance. A union member debating how to vote on a proposed strike is apt to act on the suggestion of a speaker who claims that a "yes" vote will give support to his union and at the same time insure greater take-home pay.

John N. Mitchell, then Attorney General of the United States, in a speech given before the Bar Association of the District of Columbia in May, 1970, attempted to resolve the dissonance that existed in the minds of the attorneys in his audience relative to certain judicial decisions. His listeners—all attorneys—held a firm belief in the sanctity of the law and, at the same time, may have been displeased with some of the judicial decisions made. He reasoned that the dissonance could be resolved by recognition of the fact that disagreements between what a given legal principle means and making the principle work lies in the application, not in a denial of the principle itself. He stated:[31]

The developments in Constitutional law over the recent decades have properly attempted to serve, as Mr. Justice Holmes said, "the felt necessities of the time."

I do not believe that any lawyer here, or any responsible citizen in this country, does not agree with the fundamental principles of Brown—that all citizens should be treated equally regardless of their race; or with the basic principles of Gideon *and* Miranda—*that all criminal defendants must be treated equally regardless of their financial status; or with the precepts of* Baker—*that all voters' ballots should be counted equally; or with the precepts of* Roth—*that obscenity is not protected by the First Amendment; or with the precepts of* Engel—*that the state may not involve itself in supporting religious activities.*

These cases stand for principles of our society—principles of equal protection, of the right to counsel and of freedom of speech and religion.

The disagreements arise over the application of these principles to particular cases. I think that critics should make it very clear that a disagreement over the application of a principle in a particular case only means a dedication to making the underlying idea work—it does not imply an abandonment of the principle itself.

The following excerpt from a speech by William J. Trent, Jr., Assistant Personnel Director, Time, Inc., attempts to resolve the dissonance a middle-class Negro may have when he feels guilty because of charges pressed upon him by the militant blacks. He spoke to the Biennial Banquet of Epsilon Omega Chapter of Omegi Psi Phi Fraternity, South Carolina State College, Orangeburg, South Carolina, on November 18, 1966.[32]

A man does his job well. A man provides as best he can for his family needs, physical as well as spiritual and mental. A man invests as much as he can or dares of his emotional involvement in his fellow man. A man finds time to enrich his life through his appreciation of the good, the true, the beautiful, the wonders of the ages. If this man happens to be a middle class Negro, he need have no fear of feeling "guilty" because he hasn't done what someone else tells him he ought to do. He is fulfilling his destiny. He has made his contribution. If this is not enough—so be it!

Positive Association

When an individual has a feeling of liking for an object, he will tend to associate the object in a positive way with his desires and beliefs. This is the principle of positive association. Conversely, if an object is associated in a positive way with a person's beliefs, that individual will tend to have a liking for the object. Action may follow the positive association or the liking. The most obvious application of this principle is in the field of merchandizing. If an object (a thing to be purchased) supports or enhances the beliefs a person has about himself, he is likely to like (want) that object. Objects the individual sees on the shelves or advertised on television or in newspapers are assessed according to standards, which he has established himself, of what is important or potentially important to him.

An examination of almost any popular magazine reveals many examples of how advertisers make positive associations between a product and some belief or value. The following are typical:

> An ad for office furniture describes it as "sleek, slim and beautiful." The picture includes a delectable secretary.
> A clothier offers suits that give the wearer a "youthful, dynamic look, but are consistent with the dignity of maturity."
> An automobile company describes one of its cars: "Its Clean Look of Action *looks* like success. Lean, low and uncluttered, it is a mark of a man's good taste."

Perhaps this principle also accounts for modern terminology describing jobs. Thus a dressmaker is an "apparel-design expert," a janitor is a "maintenance engineer," an undertaker is a "personal service consultant," and a mechanic is an "automotive specialist."

This same principle is at work in the field of institutional advertising, where it has been called "status contagion." It consists of associating an industrial firm with values considered eminently respectable in our society: the sanctity of the family, reverence toward religion, the right of free speech, the protection of our country, the heroism of our veterans, or the American Way of Life.

Potency of External Force

Although most people like new experiences, there is built into all of us the tendency to resist change. We tend to favor old friends, familiar eating places, and routine patterns of behavior, over strangers, untried restaurants, and unfamiliar behavior patterns. Sometimes this resistance is so great that only the strongest of external forces can effect a change. The potency of external force suggests that some external forces become strong enough to induce both attitudinal and behavioral changes. Among these forces are groups, authority, and prestige.

One of the major reasons we are willing to change our attitudes, and even our behavior, is to gain the approval of others—to become a member of what sociologists call an "in group." Our attitudes about thrift will seldom stand up against our desire to live in the best neighborhood, dress in the latest style, or own a late-model car. We change our attitudes toward political issues, minority groups, and avocational interests when this makes us appear liberal, tolerant, or knowledgeable.

A second powerful influence in shaping our attitudes is that of authority—as we might expect, in a culture in which specialization is so dominant. Few of us have enough knowledge to go it alone. We seek the advice of doctors, plumbers, architects, electricians, travel agents, body-conditioning experts, and countless other specialists. Americans are constantly listening to the voice of authority from some quarter. As a people we have almost a slavish regard for "experts" in any field. When a speaker uses the force of authority to attempt to change attitudes, he should remember that its effectiveness depends upon the extent to which his listeners accept that authority.

A third external influence operating in the process of motivation is that of intellectual prestige. This is best seen in our worship of scientific achievement. Few persons would wish to be without the necessities and luxuries that science has provided, yet we are at a point where scientific knowledge and achievement are almost fetishes. If a product is scientifically controlled, hermetically sealed, dynamically programmed, or electronically activated, it is immediately desirable. If an idea results from the application of the experimental method, electronic data processing, or inertial navigation theory, it is accepted without question by most people.

Prestige is the subject of Packard's *The Status Seekers*.[33] He reports that within and among occupational groups there are criteria which determine the "pecking order" or relative status. Near the top of the list are physicians, college professors, bankers, ministers, and architects.

Each of the external forces we have mentioned may be employed, if its potency is adequate, to enhance the motivating effect of the particular appeal made by a speaker.

Universal Acceptance

Some audiences are characterized by wide differences of age, education, social background, or vocational interests. A church congregation, for example, contains innumerable differences, which make it impractical for the speaker to attempt to deal with individual attitudes and needs. In such a situation communication usually is more productive when the speaker utilizes the fundamental beliefs of his listeners in planning his appeals.

When we discussed the general nature of beliefs, we described them as abstract and deeply rooted, reflecting for the most part ideal, universally accepted values. Such fundamental values as freedom of worship, belief in democratic procedures, and the dignity of the individual are accepted by persons of widely varying backgrounds. In this country most of us believe in a two-party political system, in universal education, and in the preeminence of baseball as a national pastime. We differ widely, however, about loyalty to a political party, what kind of an education we should get and who should pay for it, and the best team in our favorite league.

Appeals to universally held beliefs have pervaded the speeches of speakers from the age of Pericles to now. Woodrow Wilson's War Message, asking Congress to declare war on Germany, is an outstanding illustration of how a dramatic and vital issue can be related to the deep-seated beliefs of millions of people:[34]

It is a fearful thing to lead this great peaceful people into war. . . . But the right is more precious than peace, and we shall fight for the things which we have always carried nearest our hearts—for democracy, for the right of those who submit to authority to have a voice in their own governments, for the rights and liberties of small nations, for a universal dominion of right by such a concert of free people as shall bring peace and safety to all nations and make the world at last free.

This has no trace of the narrow attitudes of political party allegiance, nor does it utilize some transitory audience need; its appeal is to broad and permanent values.

Advertisers frequently appeal to widely held consumer beliefs. Insurance companies stress the need to protect our loved ones; banks and savings and loan companies emphasize the values of thrift and regular saving; health-food companies urge us to maintain a balanced diet. Most people accept these basic appeals, though they differ on the type of insurance they want, where they place their savings, and the food they eat.

Most great speeches employ the principle of universal acceptance—for example, Lincoln's Gettysburg Address, Churchill's "blood and tears" speech, and Roosevelt's "Declaration of War Against Japan."

Almost all speaking occasions offer some opportunity to make use of the principle of universal acceptance. For some types of speech it is practically a requirement: commemorative occasions, patriotic rallies, convocations, dedication ceremonies, installation programs, and the like.

The speaker who can establish a common bond between himself and his listeners by appealing to mutually held values has taken an important step toward securing desired goals.

IMPLICATIONS

1. Needs are related to deficiency and abundancy motivation, respectively. In his speech preparation the speaker must recognize that the former has a higher degree of urgency than the latter.

2. Beliefs are rooted deep in a person's character; they are developed over a long period of time. Because of this the speaker should not attempt to change most beliefs in a single speech.
3. Because of their basic character, the speaker should always seek to make his appeals conform to his listeners' beliefs and needs. Most people will regard an idea as sound, true, and acceptable if it conforms to what they believe and want.
4. Maslow's "hierarchy of needs" suggests that the speaker select forms of support that meet the level of his listeners' needs.
5. Needs, beliefs, and attitudes are an inherent part of each person's perceptual field. Taken together they constitute a gestalt or "configuration" of motivating forces. Because these configurations are of a highly personal nature they differ from one person to another. The speaker must, therefore, make his appeals consonant with the common denominator of motive orientations held by all members of the audience.
6. The supporting materials selected by a speaker should always relate to the belief-need systems of the listener. Appeals will have greater motivating effect if they also (1) relate to the immediate needs of the listeners, (2) cause a moderate degree of anxiety and fear that are allayed by the speaker's proposal, (3) resolve some cognitive imbalance in the minds of the listeners, (4) are in conformity with forces the listeners consider to be potent, and (5) conform to beliefs and attitudes that are universally held.

EXERCISES

1. Which of these two situations has more motivating force: (1) when you need an A in a course in order to enter law school or (2) when you desire an A to raise your grade-point average? Why?
2. Make a list of ten "needs" that are deficiencies. Make a similar list of needs that are related to abundancy motivation. What basic differences do you see in the two lists? Comment on this difference in class.
3. On pages 152–153 is Maslow's hierarchy of needs. Do you agree that the lower-level needs must be served before an individual will be concerned about the higher-level ones? Be prepared to give a three-minute talk in which you explain the reasons for your answer.
4. In this chapter we presented seven groups of basic motives. Assume that you are to give a speech to your classmates. Under each of the seven groups make a list of three forms of support that would motivate your classmates to some action you ask them to take.
5. Prepare to participate in a class discussion about the relative merits of choosing speech content in harmony with the listeners' beliefs and choosing materials that support the speaker's beliefs.
6. Make a list of three beliefs you have held throughout your life. Under what conditions would you change them?
7. What effect has your college training had on your beliefs, if any? Have you changed any of your beliefs since you started college? In what ways have these changes been beneficial to you?

8. Make a list of organizations that have different attitudes toward social service but avow the same goal. Try to determine the reasons for the differences in attitude.

9. Are your beliefs generally based on sound reasoning? If there is one that is not logically based, can you explain the reason for holding it?

10. Select a volume of American speeches and read one of the speeches making a list of the beliefs to which the speaker appeals. How effectively has the speaker employed the use of beliefs in his speech?

11. List three beliefs that you hold as a result of your family life, three that have resulted from the culture in which you live, and three that are rooted in logic and reasoning—exclusive of family and culture influences. Which beliefs would be hardest for you to change? Why?

12. Write down briefly your attitudes toward four of the following topics. To what extent do your attitudes form an integrated pattern?

    a. Russia
    b. Red China
    c. Cuba
    d. Charity
    e. Frugality
    f. Waste
    g. States' Rights
    h. Desegregation
    i. Pork Barrel
    j. Beauty Contests
    k. Horse racing
    l. Politics
    m. The Establishment
    n. The Vietnam War
    o. The Pill
    p. Abortion
    q. Mercy Killing
    r. The Death Penalty

13. Prepare to give a brief speech in which you explain the extent and manner in which each of the following sources of beliefs has been instrumental in the formation of one of your firmly held beliefs: Primary-group experiences, cultural influences, intellectual factors, and nonrational factors.

14. For a period of one week observe as many television commercials as you can. Note the ways in which the appeals in the ads employ the six principles presented in the latter part of this chapter. Which principle seems to predominate?

15. Prepare a two-minute speech in which you support the statement that "every individual acts only in ways that will enable him to attain a sense of adequacy."

16. On page 164 we presented a list of ten beliefs held in varying degrees of intensity by a majority of Americans. Which of these beliefs do you feel are not held by "a majority of Americans"? Make a list of beliefs held by a

majority of young liberal or conservative Americans. Compare your list with the lists of two of your classmates. Comment in class on differences and similarities among the items in the list.

17. Review the speeches given in several recent issues of *Vital Speeches of the Day*. Try to find at least two examples of the use of the six principles of motivation given on pages 172 to 180. Which principle seems to be used most frequently? Be prepared to comment on your findings in class.

ADDITIONAL READINGS

Abelson, Herbert I., *Persuasion: How Opinions And Attitudes Are Changed*, New York, Springer, 1959.

Asch, S. E., "Effects of group pressure upon the modification and distortion of judgments," in G. E. Swanson, T. M. Newcomb, and E. L. Hartley, eds., *Readings in Social Psychology*, rev. ed., New York, Holt, Rinehart & Winston, 1952, pp. 2–11.

Barnett, H. G., *Innovation: The Basis of Cultural Change*, New York, McGraw-Hill, 1953, chaps. 4, 5, 6, 10.

Bindra, Dalbir, *Motivation: A Systematic Reinterpretation*, New York, Ronald, 1959, chaps. 1, 2, 3, 5, 6.

Brembeck, Winston Lamont, and William Smiley Howell, *Persuasion: A Means of Social Control*, Englewood Cliffs, N.J., Prentice-Hall, 1952, chaps. 6, 7.

Cartwright, Dorwin, "Achieving change in people: Some applications of group dynamics theory," *Human Relations*, 4 (no. 4, 1951), 381–392.

Corey, Stephen N., "Attitudes, values, and aversions," *Teachers College Record*, 56 (no. 3, Dec. 1954), 121–128.

Festinger, Leon, "The motivating effect of cognitive dissonance," in Gardner Lindzey, ed., *Assessment of Human Motives*, New York, Holt, Rinehart & Winston, 1958, pp. 65–66.

Haiman, Franklyn S., "Democratic ethics and the hidden persuaders," *Quart. J. Speech*, 44 (no. 4, Dec. 1958), 385–392.

Hall, John F., *Psychology of Motivation*, Philadelphia, Lippincott, 1961, chaps. 3, 4.

Hilgard, Ernest R., "Success in relation to level of aspiration," in Chalmers L. Stacey and Manfred F. DeMartino, *Understanding Human Motivation*, Cleveland, Howard Allen, 1958, pp. 235–241.

Hovland, Carl I., ed., *The Order of Presentation in Persuasion*, New Haven, Yale Univ. Press, 1957.

Hovland, Carl I., Irving L. Janis, and Harold H. Kelley, *Communication and Persuasion*, New Haven, Yale Univ. Press, 1953.

Lindzey, Gardner, ed., *Assessment of Human Motives*, New York, Holt, Rinehart & Winston, 1958, chaps. 1, 3, 4, 7.

Mann, John, *Changing Human Behavior*, New York, Scribner, 1965, chaps. 1, 5, 7, 8, 12.

Maslow, A. H., *Motivation and Personality*, New York, Harper & Row, 1954, pp. 63–106.

Maslow, A. H., "Higher and lower needs," in Chalmers L. Stacey and Manfred F. DeMartino, eds., *Understanding Human Motivation*, Cleveland, Howard Allen, 1958, pp. 48–51.

Ruch, Floyd L., *Psychology and Life*, 5th ed., Chicago, Scott, Foresman, 1958, chaps. 5, 7, 12.

Stacey, Chalmers L., and Manfred F. DeMartino, eds., *Understanding Human Motivation*, Cleveland, Howard Allen, 1958, chaps. 2, 4, 5, 8, 25, 30.

NOTES

[1] David Krech, Richard S. Crutchfield, and Norman Livson, *Elements of Psychology*, 2nd rev. ed., Knopf, 1969, p. 497.

[2] See Clifford T. Morgan and Richard A. King, *Introduction to Psychology*, 4th ed., New York, McGraw-Hill, 1971, pp. 187–188.

[3]See *Ibid.*, p. 491. Some writers make only slight distinctions among these terms. We use them interchangeably to avoid excessive repetition.

[4]A. H. Maslow, *Motivation and Personality*, New York, Harper & Row, 1954, pp. 80–92.

[5]Whitney Young, in an address delivered at the 58th National Urban League Conference, New Orleans, Louisiana, July 29, 1968. By permission.

[6]J. L. Robertson, "The task ahead," *Vital Speeches*, 37 (no. 17, June 15, 1970), 523.

[7]H. E. Markley, "Survival in the seventies," *Vital Speeches*, 38 (no. 11, Mar. 15, 1972), 345.

[8]Douglas MacArthur, "The direction of our military policy," *Vital Speeches*, 18 (no. 2, Nov. 1, 1951), 36–37.

[9]James A. Farley, "Brand names: A basis for unity," *Vital Speeches*, 18 (no. 15, May 15, 1952), 474.

[10]Charles Evers, *The New Yorker*, June 14, 1969.

[11]Admiral E. R. Zumwalt, Jr., "Personal accountability," *Vital Speeches*, 37 (no. 19, July 15, 1971), 608.

[12]Martin Luther King, Jr., "The American Dream," in Roy L. Hill, ed., *Rhetoric of Racial Revolt*, Denver, Golden Bell Press, 1964, pp. 372–375.

[13]Morgan and King, *op. cit.*, p. 510.

[14]See for example, Richard Centers, "Attitude and belief in relation to occupational stratification," pp. 132–151, and Wesley and Beverly Allinsmith, "Religious affiliation and politico-economic attitude," in Daniel Katz, et al., eds., *Public Opinion and Propaganda*, New York, Holt, Rinehart & Winston, 1954; Bruno Bettelheim and Morris Janowitz, *The Dynamics of Prejudice*, New York, Harper & Row, 1950; and Siegfried Kracauer, "National types as Hollywood presents them," *Public Opinion Quart.*, 22 (no. 1, Spring 1949), 53–72.

[15]R. M. Williams, *American Society: A Sociological Interpretation*, New York, Knopf, 1951, pp. 388–426.

[16]Kimball Young, *Social Psychology*, New York, Appleton-Century-Crofts, 1930, pp. 137–141.

[17]Krech et al., *op. cit.*, p. 813.

[18]The work of Thurstone is basic in attitude scale construction. See L. L. Thurstone, "Rank order as a psychophysical method," *J. Exper. Psychol.*, 14 (no. 3, June 1931), 187–201.

[19]See Samuel A. Stouffer, et al., *The American Soldier*, Vol. II, in *Studies in Social Psychology in World War II*, Princeton, N.J., Princeton Univ. Press, 1949.

[20]S. E. Asch, "Studies of independence and conformity: A minority of one against a unanimous majority," *Psychological Monographs*, 52 (Whole no. 416, 1956), 1–70.

[21]Walter W. Stevens, "Polarization, social facilitation, and listening," *Western Speech*, 25 (no. 3, Summer 1961), 171.

[22]Winston L. Brembeck and William S. Howell, *Persuasion: A Means of Social Control*, Englewood Cliffs, N.J., Prentice-Hall, 1952, p. 99.

[23]Arthur W. Combs and Donald Snygg, *Individual Behavior: A Perceptual Approach to Behavior*, rev. ed., New York, Harper & Row, 1959, p. 46.

[24]Vance Packard, *The Status Seekers*, New York, McKay, 1959, pp. 307–319.

[25]Jerome M. Rosow, "Productivity: The blue collar blues," *Vital Speeches*, 37 (no. 16, June 1, 1971), 489–491.

[26]George McGovern, "Toward an end to drug abuse," *Vital Speeches*, 38 (no. 11, Mar. 15, 1972), 323–327.

[27]Leon Festinger, "The motivating effect of cognitive dissonance," in Gardner Lindzey, ed., *Assessment of Human Motives*, New York, Holt, Rinehart & Winston, 1958, pp. 69–70.

[28]Carl I. Hovland and Milton J. Rosenberg, eds., *Attitude Organization and Change*, Vol. 3, New Haven, Yale Univ. Press, 1960, pp. 204–209. Anyone interested in problems related to attitude change, persuasion and persuasibility should consult the extensive

and systematic studies conducted by Carl I. Hovland and his associates in the Yale Communication and Attitude Change Program.

[29]Henry A. Murray, "Drive, time strategy, measurement, and our way of life," in Gardner Lindzey, ed., *Assessment of Human Motives*, New York, Holt, Rinehart & Winston, 1958, pp. 192–196; Combs and Snygg, *op. cit.*, 23 pp. 37–58. See also Percival M. Symonds, "Human drives," *J. Educ. Psychol.*, 25 (no. 9, Dec. 1934), 681–694.

[30]Leon Festinger, *A Theory of Cognitive Dissonance*, New York, Harper & Row, 1957, p. 260.

[31]John N. Mitchell, "The Supreme Court," *Vital Speeches*, 37 (no. 17, June 15, 1970), 516.

[32]William J. Trent, Jr., by special permission.

[33]Packard, *op. cit.*, pp. 93–113.

[34]Woodrow Wilson, "Declaration of War," in Glenn R. Capp, ed., *Famous Speeches in American History*, Indianapolis, Bobbs-Merrill, 1963, p. 159.

CHAPTER SEVEN
STYLE: A LINK BETWEEN SPEAKER AND LISTENER

His speech was the lucid mirror of his mind and life.
Cardinal Newman

For 2300 years the term *style* as it refers to rhetoric has meant the speaker's or writer's use of language. Aristotle was among the first to establish this concept and, except for a few abortive attempts to view style in a larger sense, this concept has firmly gripped rhetoricians until now. For example, Mary G. McEdwards in her recent book writes of style:[1] "Because of the importance of *how* we use our language, we need to know what we are doing when we use words. That use, our individual management of language, we label *style.*" Blankenship corroborates McEdwards. Her definition follows:[2] "An individual's style is his characteristic way of using the resources of the English language."

These two examples are typical of the definitions of style found in current textbooks, whether they treat primarily of public speaking or writing. It appears, then, from traditional use and current acceptance, that style is related solely to the use of language. McEdwards, however, states:[1] "From Aristotle on, men have offered ideas, methods, and descriptions of style. Some of these ideas, methods and descriptions work better than others, but style is still not yet fully understood nor fully defined."

THE WHOLE MAN COMMUNICATING
We agree wholeheartedly that style has not been fully understood or defined. We believe that it is incumbent upon us as students of rhetoric to continue the age-old efforts to reach a more definitive understanding of the nature of style. We believe that style has a relationship to the use of language. We also believe that the word style has a broader meaning

than tradition has given us. Our first task in increasing our understanding is to examine the nature of style as it relates to the oral process.

Style is deeply involved, not only in the use of language, but also in every activity of the communicator. In our society it is no longer possible to confine style to a part-whole relationship. This concept was established in classic times by the canons of rhetoric: invention, arrangement, delivery, memory, and style. Retaining the concept that style is one of five factors involved in the speech process inhibits the possibility of a new vision of the nature of style. If style is to have a new context in the rhetorical process, we must determine what that context is and how it relates to the other processes of oral communication.

We view style in its relationship to every aspect of the process of oral communication. Its nature is that of an eloquent, often unidentified, catalyst that determines the meaning of the message perceived by the respondent and guides him in the particular response he makes to it. Such a view of style is found in Samuel Butler's comment on the relationship between style and respondent reaction. His statement follows:[3]

I have also taken much pains, with what success I know not, to correct impatience, irritability and other like faults in my own character—and this not because I care two straws about my own character, but because I find the correction of such faults as I have been able to correct makes life easier, and saves me from getting into scrapes, and attaches nice people to me more readily. But I suppose this really is attending to style after all.

Butler is suggesting a very important interpersonal relationship. Almost as an afterthought he suggests that he's talking about style.

Cardinal Newman,[4] in defining style, sets up an almost identical relationship. He said, "It concerns (1) the thought, (2) the personality of the speaker, and (3) the audience."

Lucas strikes the same note when he says,[5] "Style is a means by which a human being gains contact with others."

All three of these statements emphasize the role played by style in linking the communicator and the respondent. This link is not limited to language but relates to the entire operation of a man communicating.

The prolific French naturalist, George Louis Leclerc, Comte de Buffon, injected into his famous discourse before the French Academy in 1753 a profound definition of style, which is often quoted but seldom understood: "Style is the man." Buffon in this statement has said succinctly what Butler, Newman, Lucas, and others have taken many words to say. Some, however, have complained that the Comte de Buffon's definition is too generalized to be of value, and consequently writer after writer in the area of style has paid his respects to Buffon by quoting him, and immediately returned to the concept that style in rhetoric relates to the use of language only.

For after all, did not Jonathan Swift say, "Proper words in proper places make the true definition of a style"? And did not Aristotle say of style in rhetoric that it relates to the use of language? It certainly does relate to language, but we must remember that Aristotle was observing speeches that were made in the legislative halls, judicial courts, and formal occasions of tribute or blame. These speeches were written by professional speech writers who gave special attention to the language.

Largely because of Aristotle's definition of style, and because writers had need of a word that would describe their handling of language, style became entrenched in the minds of scholars as relating only to the use of language. Even scholars and literary critics, as well as those who have no particular pretensions in the area of language definition, have realized that style has always had another meaning, which is precisely the concept of Buffon: that style designates the entire process of a man communicating, not just his language.

The Oxford English Dictionary makes this clear in its third category of meanings attributed to the word *style,* where it defines style as relating to the whole man. We must realize that when we are dealing with formal public speaking, in which the manuscript is essential, then the word, in the neo-Aristotelian sense of relating to the use of language, is appropriate. However, when we think of communication in the interpersonal sense or of the speaker in an extemporaneous situation, another definition is not only appropriate but mandatory.

It is taken for granted that people have style. Richard Wilson, in a syndicated column, illustrates this very well as it affects the realm of political figures:[6]

Having no style in the current jargon of politics reduces down to not being like John F. Kennedy. Everybody agrees Jack Kennedy had style. Lyndon Johnson was anti-style, the less said about it the better. It irritated him that some people thought he was just a crude cornball and he never hesitated to speak wryly of such detractors.

In speaking of President Nixon in the same place Wilson quotes a monograph entitled "The Nixon Style":[6]

It is the style of a longheaded individual, no hail-fellow-well-met, who admired the reach for greatness and identification with a national spirit of De Gaulle and Churchill, who believes he can succeed where Wood-row Wilson failed.

It is the style of a borer-in rather than a counter-puncher, more Louis, Graziano or Frazier than Conn, Zale or Clay; switching sports, more of a Unitas than a Namath.

It is a style that will not be universally liked or admired because it places progress ahead of unity, a cool sense of purpose ahead of warm expressions of compassion, and an odd mixing of practicality and idealism ahead of a clearcut picture of one or the other.

Obviously, this assessment of President Nixon's style is based on more than an analysis of his use of language. It is, in fact, Buffon's concept of the whole man communicating.

We have made the statement that such a concept is mandatory in dealing with style as it relates to extemporaneous and impromptu speaking. For every formal speech delivered from manuscript, there are millions of words spoken without manuscript. We cannot fairly apply the same standard—that is, the standard of the literary critic—to those who communicate orally without checking the dictionary and indulging in lucid self-criticism before issuing their words. Criticism limited to the use of language has its place only when we are dealing with manuscript speaking.

In summation, then, we have shown the need for a nontraditional definition of style to meet the demands of oral communication. We believe that such a definition should be based on the concept of the whole man communicating and that the essence of this process is the expression of the perceptions of both the communicator and the respondent. Style, then, is a relationship that permeates all the specific processes involved in communicating. As such it is a catalyst that can bring the communicator and respondent into a more profitable relationship with each other.

The Functions of Style
Having shown the necessity of considering style to be related to the whole man, let us examine its functions in communication.

In Our Analysis
First of all, style tells us what the man thinks of himself as he moves, reacts, walks, holds and uses his head, focuses upon us or avoids us, speaks intensely or not, and sets forth his knowledge. All these and many more tell us about his self-esteem—whether he is confident, assertive, timid, congenial, overbearing, or what.

Our perceptions of the speaker are the result, not just of what he says or of the language he uses, but of his entire demeanor as manifested in the production of his message. It is from this perception of the speaker's style that we draw certain conclusions as respondents. One conclusion is whether or not we like the speaker's style as we perceive it.

If we like the speaker's style, it can become the catalytic agent that causes us to accept his message. If we have reservations about the speaker's style, we probably shall have reservations about his message and will attempt to nullify, rationalize, or waive it in some fashion. If this were not true, it would be very difficult to explain why identical messages delivered by different people do not elicit identical responses.

In Attitude Change

When we say that style is a catalyst, we mean that it effects an attitude change. Many important schemas, such as cognitive dissonance, have been introduced to explain why attitude change takes place. Such concepts are helpful, but many of them fail to identify the role of style in attitude change.

It has been demonstrated in a number of studies that the prestige of the speaker and the trust with which the respondent regards him have a strong effect upon the listener's response to the message. These experimental studies are usually made under circumstances in which the speaker's prestige or trustworthiness are conveyed through some medium other than the speaker himself. Consequently they do not demonstrate how style provides a basis for this kind of judgment by the listener.

In real life the listener must go through the process of determining for himself the speaker's trustworthiness, and although many may tell him of the speaker's trustworthiness and prestige, the final judgment that governs the listener's response, unless he abdicates his role, will be made by himself.

The question, then, is moot: How does style operate in the area of attitude change? To answer this question we must review our understanding of attitude and attitude change. The most important characteristic of any attitude is its salience—the degree of ego involvement of the holder of the attitude. Weakly held attitudes, then, are equivalent to attitudes that have little ego involvement.

Conversely, those attitudes and beliefs which we hold very strongly relate to those things which are personally most precious. Katz has asked the question, What function does attitude perform for the individual who holds it? His answer is that the functions of adjustment, ego defense, value expression, and the acquisition of knowledge may be performed by attitudes. It is obvious that Katz is dealing with factors specifically related to ego involvement.[7]

To illustrate, Martin Luther's view of his own ego involvement with doctrine was more important to him than his existence on this planet. The ego involvement of General Patton ultimately became a factor in his being relieved of command, for it was more important to him than national policy as that was reflected in the orders he received from his commander.

To bring the concept closer home, a mother's resistance to her son's desire to become a proficient scuba diver may help to illustrate the point. For the son there is strong ego involvement in his desire to have this proficiency. His mother believes firmly that it is dangerous, and anything which could be a threat to her son causes tremendous ego involvement. If his mother is to respond favorably to his involvement in scuba diving, the son will have to find some way of gratifying her, of making her more receptive to his desire. If any communication lines are to remain open and effective, the gratification of others is necessary. As a result, style comes into the picture, for it is only through our unique style that we are guided in our methods of approaching the respondent. We achieve the desired response in our listener, not only because we are aware of his needs, desires, and attitudes (insofar as that is possible), but also because we use our style as the catalyst that will displace the respondent's resistance or inertia and energize him.

The more salient an attitude becomes, the more vulnerable it is. We mean by this that an attitude tends to be supported more by emotional beliefs than by cognitions supportable by evidence and reasoning. Recognizing that our attitudes may have cognitive dissonance (conflict) does not necessarily move us along the road to better communication. The frustration of the situation may cause us to lash out in a spontaneous emotional fashion. All of us have different attitudes, but only with the most vulnerable (having a high degree of ego saturation) are we sufficiently concerned to make vigorous response. At that stage of ego involvement, however, we usually are very defensive and make emotional decisions.

Festinger tells us what the decisions may be: (1) we grasp at straws to gain a consensus or evidence that will support our own belief, (2) we derogate the communicator, who has revealed for us our communicative dissonance, and (3), last and probably least likely, we could change our attitude.

The communicator must recognize this vulnerability and assist the respondent by supplying the positive ingredients that will allow him to dispel his previous attitude. Otherwise his ego involvement will tend to close the door on any change.

When we speak of style, then, we are speaking of that which causes one individual's communication, though similar in subject matter, length, wisdom, language, and appeal, to be different from that of another individual. We are speaking also of utilizing this individual stimulus as a means of obtaining the goal we seek. Style is not method, nor is it purpose, nor is it motivation, though all of these things will have their effect upon style. As an individual process, style will affect all of the speaker's or communicator's activities in the determination of his purpose, the analysis of his audience, the selection of his materials, and the preparation and production of his message; for in each of these activities he will be guided by his own individual perceptions of the needs and desires of his audience as well as himself.

In Selection of Content

In that area of speech preparation traditionally referred to as *inventio,* or the evaluation and selection of materials for a particular audience, the speaker cannot help but be guided by his own tastes and preferences. His style is the expression of these tastes and preferences as he makes decisions among the choices he perceives.

For instance, an engineer is likely to resort to technical language to explain stresses and tolerances, which are difficult to distinguish in general terms. An artist might tend to select materials for their vividness or ability to attract the eye or for the nature of the lines and mass that his perceptions find acceptable. A student in a class will tend to draw his illustrations from experiences that are familiar to him and his friends.

Style, then, directs the expression of the individual in his choice of materials and his understanding of his audience, and it modifies his selection of materials so that his goal may be achieved.

In Organizing Materials

Style not only affects the selection of materials but has a great deal to do with the way they are organized. If the communicator perceives that there may be a great deal of resistance to the changes in attitudes or behavior forming the purpose of his speech, he will have a number of options regarding the order in which he presents his material. If he is formidable in his approach, he may believe that confrontation is the most effective way to alert an audience to his message. On the other hand, he may achieve his success because he perceives that people are more easily led than pushed and so may use his organizational method to induce rather than confront.

Often a speaker tends to follow procedures that resemble the steps in problem solving laid down by John Dewey. First he perceives a need; then he defines his need and establishes criteria that will enable him to satisfy that need; then he considers several solutions in the light of these criteria; finally he selects the solution that seems the most satisfactory.

Success or failure in the influence of our messages depends upon our use of style, particularly in what we elect to say, how we determine to organize it, and what modifications we make for our particular respondent.

To illustrate, let us refer to one of the many poignant but sometimes apocryphal stories about General Eisenhower. The story concerns the problem he had in handling the bold, courageous, but precipitate nature of General Patton, who often was the target of the complaint that he misused his troops or pushed them too hard. Even in the armed forces one may demand more than one's troops deem reasonable. The point General Eisenhower wished to make about leadership could have been made in a number of different ways. He could have given his subordinate a reprimand; he could have provided him with a lecture on leadership; he could have pointed out examples for his subordinate to follow. He did none of these things. Instead, by the use of a simple analogy he made his point clear. After a dinner-table discussion of General Patton's problems of command, Ike took a piece of limp spaghetti from the platter and laid it on the tablecloth and, with the look of quizzical affableness for which he became famous, said to his subordinate, "Can you push it?"

Eisenhower's style in this case was not only appropriate but concise and made the point obvious with considerable impact and without offense to a man whose abilities were needed.

In Delivery

The effect of style is much more easily observed as a determinant in delivery, for we as respondents tend to react very quickly to the personal attributes of the speaker. If we find his voice too low, someone at the rear of the room will shout "Louder!" If the attire of the communicator is not acceptable to the group, comments will be passed. If the speaker paces too much or makes gestures that appear gross in an intimate setting, reaction will set in.

The speaker must learn through careful observation of feedback the effect that his style is having upon the audience. The adjustments that he then makes will be the result of modifying the manner in which he expresses his new perceptions—a concept that can be traced precisely on the communication model.

Traditional Rhetorical Concepts of Style

Traditionally there have been three rhetorical concepts of style. As we have previously indicated, all of them view style as related to the use of language.

As a Means to an End

Aristotle viewed style as a means to an end—that is, as showing a relationship through clear, emphatic, coherent language. A pioneer in the development of the theory concerning language, he catalogued, described, and named many of the uses of language symbols. Thus we have *synecdoche*, the substitution of a part or attribute for the whole, such as "wheels" for "automobile," "pulpit" for "church," and "hull" for "boat." Another is *onomatopoeia*, a language symbol whose sound resembles its referent, such as "splash," "boom," "ping pong."

Aristotle was concerned with the utility of figures of speech in relating language symbols to their referents. He saw language as a functional process rather than a decorative one. In describing the metaphor, he emphasizes its importance in establishing relationships between the known and the yet unknown. As the metaphor crystallizes—that is, as the same words are used over and over to express a specific idea—users tend to forget the utilitarian aspect of the figure of speech and to see only its decorative quality. Words, then, are chosen because the user feels that this decorative quality is needed.

For Aristotle style was a means to an end:[8] "Metaphor, moreover, gives style clearness, charm, and distinction as nothing else can: and it is not a thing whose use can be taught by one man to another."

Tradition suggests that the attributes of style that we have listed—clarity, emphasis, and coherence—may be achieved by anyone who wishes to become competent in the use of language. This is true, but it does not answer the question we asked about style: What is it that makes one man different from another, even when they present their messages under a controlled situation?

Although Cicero's view of style was not greatly different from that of Aristotle, his speeches and his comments about style indicate that a penetrating elegance in the use of language was very important to him. He made it quite clear that, although he did not consider it the chief end of speaking, he did consider style to be the orator's predominant means of gaining his end. Cicero was most concerned about the orator's image before his audience and felt that it was necessary to act in such fashion and use such words as would elicit an excited, enlightened response.

Cicero says[9] of style in speaking that the greatest was he who shone "well in wisdom and penetration, grace and refinement as in eloquence, variety and copiousness of language on whatever subject he took in hand."

As Adornment

In many societies in different periods in history style has been considered a means of adorning a message. It has even been considered the prime mark of skill in speaking. Thonssen and Baird attribute these attitudes to a marked lack of interest in content:[10]

When schools of declamation held sway in Greece and Rome, style was practically everything. Style and delivery, linked indissolubly, marked the speaker of skill. The essential relation of manner to matter was lost sight of, with the result that the cogency of ideas figured for naught. Display was the keynote. Divorced from what Charles S. Baldwin called the "urgencies of subject," style moved toward decoration, exhibitionism, "virtuosity." During the eighteenth century in England, there was a resurgence of interest in the conception of rhetoric as style.

This movement inevitably led beyond the concept of style as adornment to the concept of style as an end in itself.

As an End in Itself

Probably in no period of history was the worship of style more flagrantly practiced by the rhetors of the time than in the eighteenth and nineteenth centuries. During this period important attributes of rhetoric, such as selection and organization of materials, audience analysis, and development of proof, were set aside, and *elocution*—the Roman term for style—held full sway. The term was a misnomer, however, for it was not style that was taught, but delivery; and perfection of style came to mean the proper pronunciation of words, the development of suitable inflection, and the practice of preconceived gestures. Such teachers as Rush, Mason, Sheridan, and Fulton developed schools of declamation and elocution, in which messages were memorized and rehearsal was designed to perfect the manner in which the speech was delivered. Style—that is, delivery—as an end in itself was never the intention of the great classical rhetoricians and orators such as Aristotle and Cicero; nor is it supported by the conclusions of present-day scholars.

Using Language

In recent years theory and research in mathematics, logic, linguistics, engineering, medicine, and human relations have helped to expand our horizons about speech and language. The significant fact that emerges from this wealth of data is that speech—this "wonder of words"—contributes to and draws from most areas of human knowledge. Our communicative skills are improved to the extent that we are aware of these relationships.

Throughout life a person is bombarded with all sorts of stimuli from three different worlds: the world of physical things, the world of people around him, and his own personal world. The last world comprises all the thinking, feeling, believing, dreaming, remembering, and perceiving that a person does about stimuli from the first two worlds. The small child first learns the words the people around him use to refer to things. After frequent enough association of a word with a given object or event, he learns to react to the word just as he first reacted to the object.

A child's experiences are obviously a direct function of the environment in which he lives. The rich child lives in a world of servants, private schools, and vacations in Europe. The poor child lives in a world of "all the kids work," public schools, and summer jobs. Their outlooks on life are bound to be different, frequently at great variance. Their work habits, schooling, recreational activities, and family relationships usually differ widely. This is an important fact for us to remember. The experiences of the members of an audience will affect their interest in and understanding of what we say as speakers.

Language As Symbolism

Words are symbols standing for objects and ideas. Our understanding of the meaning of symbol relationship can be enhanced by distinguishing the reactions of animals from those of humans. Animals usually get the meaning of a stimulus from the properties of the stimulus itself. Only in a situation of conditioned response do they react as if to a symbol, and even then they respond to the symbol as if it were the original stimulus.

Signal and Symbol Relationships

The semanticist S. I. Hayakawa describes the difference between animal and human reactions as follows:[11]

For animals the relationship in which one thing stands for something else does not appear to exist except in very rudimentary form. . . . For example, it appears likely that a chimpanzee can be taught to drive a simplified car, but there is one thing wrong with its driving: its reactions are such that if a red light shows when it is halfway across a street, it would stop in the middle of the crossing, while, if a green light shows while another car is stalled in its path, it would go ahead regardless of consequences. In other words, so far as such a chimpanzee is concerned, the red light could hardly be said to stand *for stop; it* is *stop.*

Just as the green light means a "clear street" to the chimpanzee, smoke and flames mean fire to wild animals; the cheese is food to the mouse, and it will ignore the trap to get it. In other words, the animal's signal-response is immediate, automatic, unvarying, and generally unperceptive.

By contrast, human language is symbolic. Words *stand for* an event or thing: they direct attention to specific differentiating aspects of the thing they symbolize. Symbols are autonomous, they are independent of external factors. You can demonstrate this by asking several persons to indicate reactions to the word *dog*. To one it will mean a terrier, to another a Great Dane, to another a poodle, and so on. To each person the meaning of the word is in the mind of that person, what the referent stands for to him, not the black marks on the paper.

What the referent of a word means, of course, depends on the individual's experience with that word. The word *home*, for example, means very different things to a sailor returning from a long tour of duty, to a juvenile delinquent, and to an aged person. *Religion* to one person means Catholicism, to another Science of the Mind, and to a third a Protestant denomination.

One aspect of the signal-symbol relationship is of utmost significance. At times people give signal responses to symbols. This is beneficial in situations of possible danger, when we act instantly upon the command "Stop!" or "Look out!" In other situations, when such expressions as "square," "stool pigeon," "slob" or "scab" are directed toward us, we tend to react too quickly with a signal response when, instead, we should be attempting to analyze the situation in order to respond symbolically.

Time-Binding

Another essential difference between the vocal signals of animals and the verbal symbols of human beings is that the number of animal sounds does not increase. By contrast, symbolic language in humans is constantly growing and keeping pace with changing needs. To us a symbol may refer to things present or to things past; to an animal a signal is of the present only. Hayakawa states it this way:[12]

Dogs and cats and chimpanzees do not, so far as we can tell, increase their wisdom, their information, or their control over their environment from one generation to the next. But human beings do. The cultural accomplishments of the ages, the invention of cooking, of weapons, of writing, of printing, of methods of building, of games and amusements, of means of transportation, and the discoveries of all the arts and sciences come to us as free gifts from the dead.

This is what is called the *time-binding* characteristic of language, by which man is able to relate to his own life the facts of the past and the probable happenings of the future and to pass on to succeeding generations the accumulated experience of his past. His symbols give him a place in recorded history; signals serve animals in their lifetimes only.[13]

The Principle of Nonidentity

If the meaning of a word could be found in the word itself, words and their referents would be identical, which is obviously impossible. Semanticists call this the principle of nonidentity. That is, the word is not the object it represents; one does not sleep on the *word* bed or eat the *word* steak. Furthermore, the same object or event usually is designated by different words in different languages. The "dog" in English becomes a "chien" in French and "hund" in German and Danish. One lives in a "house," a "maison," or a "hus." In each instance the meaning is in the referent, not the word.

The Map-Territory Relationship

Korzybski developed the principle of nonidentity in his use of the expression "map-territory."[14] A map bears the same relationship to the territory it represents as a word does to its referent. One does not travel *on* a map but, rather, on the territory the map represents.

Our words do not always accurately reflect the reality of the territory to which they refer. This has a direct effect on the individual, as Hayakawa states:[15]

> . . . this verbal world ought to stand in relation to the extensional world as a map does to the territory it is supposed to represent. If the child grows to adulthood with a verbal world in his head which corresponds fairly closely to the extensional world that he finds around him in his widening experience, he is in relatively small danger of being shocked or hurt by what he finds, because his verbal world has told him what, more or less, to expect. He is prepared for life. If, however, he grows up with a false map in his head—that is, with a head crammed with error and superstition—he will constantly be running into trouble, wasting his efforts, and acting like a fool. He will not be adjusted to the world as it is; he may, if the lack of adjustment is serious, end up in mental hospital.

Language as a Flexible Tool

That language is flexible is merely another way of saying that most words have many referents. This is in some ways a barrier to communication, but one that cannot be helped. If each word in a language represented only one separate and fixed meaning, the number of words would be staggering. Colin Cherry says:[16]

> Language cannot give precise representation of things or ideas because there are simply not enough different words to express the subtlety of every shade of thought. If we had words for everything, their numbers would be astronomically large and beyond our powers of memory or our skill to use them.

Various languages have limitations, depending upon their structures. One of the limitations of English, according to Kahlil Gibran, is its use of only one word to express the many nuances of the word *love*, there being, as he said,[17] "fifty words in Arabic to give expression to the many aspects of love."

Even though we are obliged, for economy's sake, to use one word in many different ways, that is not the only reason for multiple meanings. A word never stirs up quite the same mental picture in any two individuals, because words are tied up with entirely different sets of subconscious associations. The meanings of a given word, therefore, are almost as numerous as the number of persons who use it. The outstanding exceptions are scientific and technical terms, which have uniform meanings among most users.

The English language, as recorded by *The Oxford English Dictionary*, consists of approximately half a million words. The average person has a vocabulary amounting to 60,000 to 80,000 words (*Encyclopedia Americana*, 1969 ed., p. 202). The English language, however, may be communicated adequately through the use of only 800 words. These 800 carefully chosen words form what is known as Basic English.

You may well ask, then, how can a language numbering half a million individual words be spoken with so few? The secret lies in the flexibility of our language, which arises in a large part from our ability to handle context. Let us take, for instance, a very simple word such as "run," in its verb sense only. Let us check the dictionary and see how many different meanings are attributed to this one word. *Funk and Wagnalls Dictionary* (abridged) lists 54 different meanings. *Webster's New World Dictionary* (College Edition) also lists 54 meanings. *The Oxford English Dictionary* (abridged) lists 58. The meanings of this word include rapid moving of the legs, moving machinery, declaring oneself a candidate for office, and unraveling a stocking. These examples illustrate very well how we make our words do multiple duty, using them in different contexts, relieving the communicator of the necessity of having a different symbol for each context.

We must realize, however, that context does not always make clear the meaning of a word we have in mind. The following illustrates the danger of using a word that is subject to many connotations:[18]

Of all the terms in current usage, one of the most devastating, belittling, demeaning, stop-in-the-tracksing epithets that can be applied is "reactionary." It is a red-flag word and the mere pronouncement of it tends to conjure up a vision of a dangerous, unthinking, unyielding type. And that is a paradox, for if the word does produce that result, it is an unthinking, unyielding reaction. The word reactionary, used in a political or social context, properly describes one who favors a return to former political or social policies. Surely, thinking man does not want to rule out the possibility of reinstituting policies that have proven workable in the past when successor policies have proven ineffective. Thinking man doesn't, but contemporary man blinded by the supposed virtue of innovation seems to.

Consider the phrase "Black is beautiful." To a middle-class White in Trenton, New Jersey, it means something very different from what it does to his counterpart in Jackson, Mississippi; for a Black in the bayous of Louisiana it means something different from what it means to his brother in Chicago. The following illustration makes the point:[19]

And we might remember that the Black movement didn't really get started in this country until people began to believe that truly BLACK IS BEAUTIFUL and we see today beautiful black people with their heads held high. And as blacks truly believe black is beautiful, then there is no need for skin lighteners and hair straighteners to make them white. And, I would think that as OLD AGE BECOMES BEAUTIFUL, old people hold their heads high—and there is no need for rejuvenation skin creams and the other trappings of youth because OLD AGE IS BEAUTIFUL.

When there is no common experience between speaker and listener, bridges to understanding must be built. The metropolitan apartment dweller has few experiences in common with the wheat farmer on the plains of Montana, and the coal miner and the airplane pilot live in two entirely different worlds. Each has his own vocabulary, and each must add to his store of word meanings if he is to be understood by the other.

Specialization

Another reason that words can have many meanings is that certain words may have a highly restricted meaning within a group of persons, depending on occupation, age, geographical area, and avocational interests. In occupations with highly specialized vocabularies words in common use are sometimes given special meanings, new words are coined, and combinations of old words are common. In journalism, for example, a reporter is a "bloodhound," a critic is a "boogie man," and to rewrite is to "doctor." Professions, such as medicine, engineering, music, and law, have vocabularies familiar only to their members. University professors are guilty of giving many lectures not completely understood by all their hearers.

Slang expressions may consist of common words or newly invented words, the meanings of either of which are known only to the initiated. Examples of the first are *blast* (a thrill or kick), *blow the whistle* (to stop someone from doing something), *take a gander* (look over), and *think piece* (a thoughtful or provocative piece of journalistic writing as opposed to a news account). Examples of the second are *twerp* (objectionable person), *veep* (vice president), *icky* (overly sentimental, nonconforming), and *pizzazz* (power, pep, aggression).

It is important to realize that when you use words with restricted meanings or newly invented words you have entered the realm of the esoteric; you are speaking only to the initiated. Many will not be familiar with the words or the senses in which you are using them. Consequently, your use of these words will tend to draw a circle that may exclude the listener. If this is the case, a communication may take place that was not intended by the communicator; that is, the listener may assume that the communicator does not care whether he understands the word or not.

Denotation

Denotations are the meanings agreed upon by a large number of people who, through their observations, have determined that a certain name or word will be used to represent a specific object or idea. Such agreement becomes accepted when the term is included in a dictionary or some specialized inventory of words. It is generally agreed that large bodies of water should be called "oceans" and some use the term "sea." Both are officially recorded in the dictionary. If you wish to call the ocean something else, it is your privilege, but not everyone else will agree. In the same fashion new words are coined. *Cannon* was a word not needed until the invention of gunpowder. *Submarine* became a word, piecing together two Latin forms, when a practical submersible ship was developed. We now have also such terms as *astronaut*, *laser*, *sonic*, and *leukemia*.

When we deal with the denotative content of concrete words, qualities, or events, the meanings are usually identical or at least similar among persons of similar cultural, social, economic, or vocational background.

Abstract words such as *democracy, bravery, society, burden, politician, pride,* or *intolerance* also have denotativeness, though their connotative meanings are usually dominant. Thus, by dictionary definition, democracy is "a form of government in which the supreme power is vested in the people and exercised by them or their elected agents under a free electoral system." This denotative meaning suggests structural relationships and procedures without reference to the personal experiences that different individuals have had with the democratic process.

Connotation

Connotative meanings vary from person to person and are the result of the unique experiences each has had with these words. For example, *water* connotes entirely different things to a thirsty desert traveler, a flood victim, an artist, an ocean voyager, a gardener, a skin diver, and a guest at a health spa.

Abstract words usually have more connotative coloring than do concrete words. What the phrase "civil rights" connotes, for example, will be different for each individual. An election official, worker, congressman, student, historian, minority-group member, and soldier have each had different experiences with civil rights. In the following paragraph the late Whitney Young describes what racism meant to him:[20]

But what—in fact—is *racism?*

—*Racism is the assumption of superiority of white over black—and the arrogance that goes with such an assumption.*

—*Racism reduces the paycheck of a black worker to half that of a white worker.*

—*Racism puts one out of three black teenagers out of work this summer—while only one out of ten white teenagers is unemployed.*

—*Racism produces cities that are daily becoming blacker while the suburbs around them are 95% white.*

—*Racism causes deteriorating slums where overcrowding for black families increased by 20% in a decade—while overcrowding for white families declined.*

—*Racism tolerates welfare bureaucracies which keep half the people entitled to benefits off the rolls.*

—*Racism is reflected in the ghetto here in New Orleans, where, as in other cities, half the people are unemployed or underemployed, and despair and frustration have become the rule rather than the exception.*

Language as Abstraction

Whenever we respond to a situation, a stimulus, we abstract some of the details from the total situation and ignore others. Of the countless things that may be happening around us we necessarily leave out many and select those we want or are forced to attend to. At the beach, for example, though many things are going on, we may be aware only of the lifeguard plunging into the surf, the girl in the bikini, the helicopter overhead, or the two children (we call them something else) who are getting sand in our food. That is to say, abstraction is a selective process.

Similarly, of all the qualities we associate with a business friend we select one word and describe him as "fair-dealing." You describe a certain teacher as a "tough grader," although he is also a good teacher, an outstanding researcher, an effective counselor, and well liked by most of his students. The prices at a certain restaurant may be excessively high, the service mediocre, and the meals just fair, but the place is "popular."

Abstraction is a necessary convenience in all human communication, as a few examples will make clear. The word *house* as an abstraction refers to certain characteristics that a split-level house, a bungalow, a ranch house, a two-story house, and a mansion have in common. The word *food* as an abstraction covers innumerable items that would not be included if we were to talk about pizza, blintzes, tacos, hot dogs, clam chowder, or crêpes suzette.

Levels of Abstraction

Another aspect of abstracting important for both the speaker and his listeners is the level upon which it operates. First, of course, is the object or event itself, though below that is the submicroscopic level of electrons that compose it and that we do not need to consider for our purposes. As we move to higher levels, fewer details of the event or object are included in our concept, and the word symbol we use becomes more general. If we start with *Buick*, for example, a higher level of abstraction would give us, let us say, *automobile*, which is much less specific. As we move to still higher levels we might get *motor vehicles*, which is yet more inclusive, and then perhaps *transportation system*, possibly even *national economy*. In the case of food we might go from *cornflakes* to *cereals*, to *nutrition*, to *food*. Or we might go from *Paradise Lost* to *epic*, to *poem*, to *literature*, to *humanities*. The chief significance to the speaker of these levels of abstraction is this: the higher the level of abstraction the more difficult it is to make our language meaningful to our listeners.

Risks in Abstraction

The speaker also needs to be aware of the risk that he may abstract too much about an object, person, or event. For example, to describe a person as a "good father," a "B" student, a "religious person," a "drunkard," or a "successful businessman" may omit too many details to give an accurate picture of the person involved. Stuart Chase describes this risk vividly:[21]

. . . take the word "bad." It probably arose to express a vague feeling of dislike. Rather than go to the trouble of describing the characteristics one did not like in an animal or plot of soil, one said, "It is bad." All right, a useful short cut. Then the word was made into a substantive, "badness." At this abstraction level, it became something ominous and menacing in its own right. One had better not be associated with badness. Badness was incorporated into rigid standards of judgment, especially moral judgment. "This girl is bad." The statement implies that she is wholly bad, a veritable chunk of badness. But she may also be a charming girl, kind to children, kind to her parents, and perhaps overkind to her young man. To cast her out of society as "bad" is the result of a false, one-valued or two-valued appraisal. Adequately to judge this girl, we must . . . know her other characteristics, the circumstances of the environment in which she was brought up, the status of the moral code at the place and time of the alleged badness, and something about the economic and social prejudices of the judge who calls her "bad."

Our language is loaded with words that represent this type of abstraction (one-valued appraisal): *stubborn, radical, communist, careless, extravagant.* The effective speaker must be careful, in abstracting, to include enough details for his listeners to get the ideas he intends them to get.

Paul R. Beall, a management consultant, sums up the point in these words:[22]

The crux of the matter, at least as far as the problem of communicating is concerned, is that the meaning of a word resides in two places; in the mind of the speaker or writer and again in the mind of the hearer or reader. When the word is assigned the same meaning in both places, the speaker and hearer or writer and reader successfully communicate with each other.

Constructive and Destructive Uses

Attitudes have a tendency to fall somewhere on a continuum, half of which could be marked "plus" and half "minus." In most cases in which we use a word to describe a situation, person, or concept, the word we select tends to reflect the amount of our negative or positive feelings. For instance, if a salesman whose product has been rejected returns frequently to my door, I may express my negative attitude toward him by saying, "He's stubborn." He, on the other hand, may feel that "persistence" pays off, expressing a very positive attitude to justify his procedure.

We may review the English language and note that for every

positive modifier we can find we shall also be able to discover a suitable negative modifer. Consider the following pairs of words:

lazy—relaxed	aggressive—pushy
hyperactive—energetic	solicitous—ingratiating
nitpicking—thorough	clever—sly
discriminating—finicky	cautious—fearful

Except for inflection and bodily movement, the modifiers we use are the greatest instruments we have to express our feelings, which in turn affect our interpersonal relationships. Thus, style as we have defined it—the expression we give to our perceptions—is governed significantly by the modifiers we use. At times our disenchantment, irritation, or anger with another person becomes so great that we even choose words which, in terms of their referents, have no application whatsoever to the person or situation we wish to describe. The four-letter-word movement which issued several years ago from the Berkeley campus of the University of California provides an example of the use of words whose referents are inapplicable but reveal the distaste and bitterness pent up in the minds of those who use them. Such reactions are emotional expressions lacking logical bridges to their referents. The use of a four-letter word for excrement to describe a person or his activities is a release of an emotional reaction of intense dislike or contempt. As such it fits Aristotle's category of ways of slighting your respondent—considered by him to be unproductive in terms of persuasion. To respond that "everybody knows what I mean when I use that word" in no way answers the objection that it is unproductive in the sense that it solves no problem.

Two claims are made for the use of demeaning four-letter words in public discourse. First, it provides for the release of frustration through catharsis. Second, the shock value of the term is desirable, for it gains attention.

In regard to the release of frustration we have already indicated the lack of referent. John Condon, Jr., points this out:[23]

Because expressions of catharsis have no referential meanings, any word may serve the cathartic function. Probably each person has some favorite expressions for releasing anger . . . the meaning of any of these expressions is to be found in what they do for us, not in a dictionary or in what they do for anybody else. Through repetition we give our select swear words added significance, so that with each new experience and repeated expression we may recall the release of tension from past experiences.

McCroskey separates the use of "expressive communication" from persuasion. He calls the former nonrhetorical, that is, it is not designed to further the speaker's goal:[24]

The purpose of expressive communication is merely to represent as clearly as possible the meaning in the mind of the source. The effects of this expression upon the receiver are irrelevant to the source's purpose.

The use of demeaning terms is a negative practice and will tend to create more havoc than constructive solutions.

The second justification of four-letter words is shock value.[25] We are not concerned here with "expressive communication," but, rather, with the deliberate attempt to achieve a goal through shock. In some situations shock is a valuable factor. In practice, however, it is a precarious one, for it can have a kickback response. At the therapeutic level such practice is reserved for extreme cases under highly selective conditions and the close supervision of a psychiatrist. For untrained people to employ shock methods on an audience or respondent of whose stability or instability they are not fully apprised is dangerous.

We cannot, however, dismiss the fact that shock does create attention. It is this phenomenon that entices speakers to use it. With continuing use the shock value of four-letter words decreases, until such words degenerate into meaninglessness with little effect other than redundancy.

The discrimination with which we interpret and evaluate our perceptions gives rise to an expression of an individual attitude. To limit a rich storehouse of vocabulary, such as the English language represents, to a few four-letter words is to reduce interpersonal communication to its smallest fragment of effectiveness.

An excellent example of this occurred on a state college campus recently, when a meeting was initiated by a small number of so-called campus revolutionaries. The purpose of the meeting was to decide upon some form of violent, physical protest that would cause the "gutless" administration and "apathetical" student body to come to terms with this radical group, which had determined to take over the campus. The meeting started with a number of harangues presented by various leaders of the group, each blast being interspersed liberally with invectives, primarily of the four-letter category. Considerable lack of agreement about the means of carrying on the revolutionary enterprise was soon apparent. Some felt that calling a "goddam" strike was the best approach. Others felt that nothing less than burning down a "goddam" building would do. As the disagreement increased among the agitators, they began to apply their invectives not to the "stupid" administration, the "listless" student body, and the buildings that housed them, but to each other. All of the original purpose of the meeting was lost. As a result, the meeting ended in complete self-defeat for the agitators, a cleanup job for the custodians, and a smug attitude on the part of the "lethargic" students. The catastrophe in communication described here emphasizes the failure of a group to follow sound rhetorical practices.[26]

Asa T. Spaulding, former President, North Carolina Mutual Life Insurance Company, has contrasted the destructive approach with the constructive extremely well:[27]

Before the building of the new social order . . . before the Negro could begin, the walls of segregation had to be knocked down . . . the battering rams of Supreme Court decisions, the bulldozers of freedom walks, freedom rides . . . and the dynamite of peaceful marches . . . cracked the walls of segregation and the barriers of discrimination . . . Violence can take on many forms: physical, mental and moral; violence to one's person, property, personality, dignity, rights, etc. This is why avoidance of inflammatory statements is so important. It makes working together so much easier.

This example, even if we had no other, would be convincing evidence that we must be discriminating in our selection of words, realizing that negative implications are necessary as part of the process of preparing to replace the obsolete. Dynamic, stimulating language is necessary to build new structures or create new social attitudes.

USING NONVERBAL MESSAGES
The Speaker's Use
As far as nonverbal messages are concerned, the speaker has three elements with which he works: the clothes he wears and his personal grooming or lack of it, his conscious use of gestures, and the bodily movements he makes, of which he ordinarily is unaware. Each of these particular channels through which meaning is expressed may be considered from three points of view: literal, implicative, and distorted.

When the audience, whether it be formal or informal, first puts up its periscope to observe the communicator, it will tend to focus on his nonverbal messages; that is, the appearance of the communicator will be evaluated. If the judgment of the audience is that his appearance is suitable to the occasion, attention will move on to other types of nonverbal message. If his appearance is inappropriate, the audience will have some reservations. It will be incumbent upon the communicator to identify the cause of these reservations and make the audience see the relevance to them of his unusual appearance. If he cannot do this, he cannot expect the audience to proceed with him in the consideration of his message.

The audience will observe the other nonverbal messages: how he walks, stands, sits. Again the first focus will be on the literal happenings: if they seem to be suitable to the occasion, the audience will be in a position to listen to the message without distraction.

Innate in the audience is the knowledge that, besides having a literal quality, nonverbal symbols have an implicative quality, and as the speaker presents his message, his movements and gestures will be read to see whether he is saying anything with his body that conflicts with the word symbols he is using. As long as the implications they read are in tune with the verbal message, no dissonance will arise.

Through such observations of your style, your ethos is being built in the minds of your audience, whether it be in an interview, a small group, or a large audience. If the communication transaction means a great deal to you, you will see to it that your dress and manner of movement pave the way toward understanding.

The Listener's Use

The bare language symbols themselves are only a blueprint. It is the intonation, the change of pace, the volume, the voice quality, and movement that tend to make language symbols meaningful, especially when we realize that all words are ambiguous and that the sense in which they are used is indicated to us by the speaker's way of handling them. These indications are messages also and may be classified as *metacommunication*, or messages about messages.

We have stated already that what the speaker means is not necessarily what the listener perceives. Then, of course, we ask the question, How does the listener get his perceptions? The answer usually given is that the listener's perceptions are the sum total of his experiences as they focus on this particular message. Although this statement makes an important point and forces us to appreciate the unique identity of the listener, it is not really helpful as a diagnostic statement. We can only guess at the experiences an individual has had.

Whether or not we are conscious of it, we are exposed to the nonverbal language of our entire communicative environment. As the cultural anthropologist Edward T. Hall, states:[28]

Most Americans are only dimly aware of this silent language even though they use it every day. They are not conscious of the elaborate patterning of behavior which prescribes our handling of time, our spatial relationships, our attitudes toward work, play, and learning. In addition to what we say with our verbal language we are constantly com-

municating our real feelings in our silent language—the language of be-havior.

As Hall implies, nonverbal language permeates all our communication. It is a language that helps us understand our relations with other people, whether they occur at the level of conversation, in a one-to-one relationship, in a small group, or in a large audience. For the most part the importance of nonverbal language will be seen in the one-to-one and small-group situations, for they tend to more flexibility. Space does not permit us to explain all of the many nonverbal languages that exist. However, we feel that the three mentioned above are sufficiently important in our communication relationships for us to take at least a brief look at them.

The Language of Time

If we are to improve our relations with others, we shall soon become conscious of our messages relating to time and our respondent's attitude toward them. As Hall points out, the cultural attitudes that relate to time are deeply ingrained and complex. It may take a child until the age of twelve to attain a reasonable comprehension of the factors involved in his society's attitudes toward time. To assist us in our handling of the messages relating to time we must learn to distinguish among the three basic situations.

The first is the informal one, in which the measuring rod of lateness or earliness can be reasonably flexible. We are well aware, for example, that a friend may keep us waiting five or ten minutes for our luncheon engagement without undue censure, for this is a reasonably informal situation, and the time is flexible; but if he keeps us waiting beyond the period of acceptability, his action might be read as an affront.

The second situation is more formal, and the degree of tolerance is fine. How late can we be to an interview with a prospective employer? How late do you dare walk into a wedding ceremony?

The third involves a special sense of time, for which exceedingly accurate measuring is required. For example, when a discussion group or interview is to appear on a television broadcast, the particular time is fixed to the exact second.

One disregards these concepts of time as they relate to the communicative process at great risk to his ethos and his desired objective.

The Language of Space

Each man must have his space for living. For some it is large and comfortable; for others it is cramped, limiting and unsatisfactory. Each man carries a sense of space with him wherever he goes. Thus, as he walks down the sidewalk, the path immediately in front of him is his space, and if someone intrudes in it, there usually will be an exchange of apologetic remarks.

In the interests of improving our relations with others we learn to interpret varying attitudes toward messages relating to space. First there is the informal one, in which space is shared without a precise use of the measuring rod. A family's use of a home might well illustrate this, where use is adjusted for the most part to the needs of each member. The second situation, the reasonably flexible one, is that in which we know rather definitely who's going to use what room at what time. Such a situation should be understood by, and reasonably acceptable to, all concerned. Our third use of space is again a special and sometimes highly technical use. It may be represented by an area that has been considered by experts to be dangerous and is therefore restricted. Or it may be a matter of making reservations for space in a given restaurant or theatre or concert on a given night.

In considering the classifications illustrated above it is easy to see that most institutions have aspects of each, whether it be a family, an office, a school, or a hotel. The nature of a message and its occasion, and whether it will be presented in a dyad, a small discussion group, or a public address situation, will have something to do with the amount of space that will be needed if the people involved are to be comfortable as they regard the message. A room can be too large for a small group. The distance between two people can be far too great for efficient communication.

As in the case of time, the etiquette of space as it relates to the communicative process may be disregarded only at the peril of destroying both interrelationships and the possibility of obtaining your goal.

The Language of Sexuality

In the animal world sex is a basic factor that must be determined immediately in the meeting of two individuals of the same species, since subsequent behavior is dependent upon this. Among humans sex is also a significant physiological difference, but most anthropologists and psychologists are agreed that subsequent behavior depends upon customs and mores that are culturally centered rather than physiologically centered.

This is well borne out in the area of communication, for it is difficult, on the basis of present literature, to find a base for rhetorical communication that may be identified solely with the physiological aspects of sexuality. Consequently, we shall not attempt here to distinguish physiological causation from cultural. Our purpose is to determine what differences have been found to exist between men and women in Western culture and how those differences affect communication. That the differences are significant is established by McClelland:[29]

The differences between the sexes are sufficiently important to shape their reactions in many areas of life. Psychologists have found that they lump together men and women in their experiments at their peril since women are very apt to react differently from men. To cite a few examples, I found years ago that all I had to do to get college men to write imaginative stories full of achievement themes was to tell them their intelligence and leadership qualities were at stake. The same approach had no effect on the women's fantasies. They remained unmoved by all sorts of appeals of this kind which we tried in an attempt to generalize our finding to the female sex. No luck. Women were just "different."

Active Interest in the Opposite Sex. This is a trait of males that has been found to be consistent. It tends to operate over the years as a stable male characteristic. McClelland reports[30] that "the two characteristics which were much more stable or consistent over the years for boys than for girls were aggressiveness and active interest in the opposite sex." Active interest in the opposite sex is so stable an element for the male that it has become a basic factor in advertising, where an attractive female will frequently be shown regardless of the nature of the product.

Tendency To Aggression. It is clear from the studies of Kagan and Moss and a number of others that aggressiveness is a stable and consistent characteristic of men. In terms of communication, men tend to carry their aggressiveness into assertiveness. They make statements with little intent to support them unless it is demanded. They come to the point quickly and expect others to do the same.[31]

Tendency To Interrelationships. Woman's counterpart of man's aggression is a sense of being interrelated to what is going on about her. Because of her sense of relationships she tends to be more adjustable, more able to adapt herself to the demands of her environment.

In the area of communication women tend to confide more and are adept at expressing their concerns as they view the various interrelationships of people. McClelland distinguishes very well the ability of women to use speech as a means of interacting as opposed to their interest in language itself:[32]

One can argue that this·is because language is par excellence *the means of interacting with people, of communicating with people and re-*

sponding to them. Since girls care about people more, they learn the means of interacting with them better. That the interest is not in language per se *is shown by the fact that girls are not better at tests of verbal meanings.*

Tendency To Task or Context Orientation. Men tend to be more issue oriented, whereas women tend to be more context oriented. This is not to imply a superiority in either instance, but to register a means by which each uses his intellect to gain the ends to which he is oriented. Men tend to abstract from situations that which applies to the immediate task or has a utilitarian value. Women approach situations from a contextual point of view; they are concerned with the entire situation and its implications for the interrelations of people. In attributing these characteristics to women and men, authorities in the field are quick to point out that these generalizations do not apply in every case. There are many men who are poor at issue analysis and many women who are excellent analysts, but the separate tendencies are sufficiently strong to be evident in the gross behavior of most men and women.

This in turn suggests that sex differences create a style for men that is different from the style of women. McClelland sums it up quite succinctly:[33]

Running through these differences is another theme which contrasts the way men and women go about dealing with the world—their respective styles. *Again, the male style is easiest to describe. It is, very simply,* analytic and manipulative *[issue oriented] . . . [the female] style is* contextual. *. . [women] have a more complex interdependent relationship with the world than men do. They are more "open" to influence where men are "closed."*

We might ask, then, how does man's issue-oriented style apply to his communication? By "being issue oriented" we mean concentrating upon the completion of a specific task. The objective of his endeavor is a product of some kind, whether it be a material thing or an idea to be accepted. The feelings of those people who relate specifically to the end in view are not so much the subject of the man's concern as the accomplishment of the task. Therefore, if personal relations tend to sag a bit within a sales organization, it may be that a quota has been raised and less time is available for the improvement of the relations among personnel, for the men are employed to accomplish tasks, not make people feel better. Communication, then, will tend to be task oriented and terse and to deprecate failure more than reward success.

In general the female image tends to counter the picture we have given of the male. Where the male is task oriented, the female tends to be people oriented. McClelland's term "contextually oriented" tends to indicate that, although she has a job to do, she can do it only in the context of its effect on the people who may be related. In the home it may be a matter of getting the washing done, but whether the washing gets put into the washer depends to some extent on whether the baby is crying with penetrating significance at the same time. A woman is contextually oriented because she has to think not only of the immediate job but the added problem of meeting the needs of the associated people.

In our society men have tended to fill the issue-oriented role in part by virtue of characteristics mentioned above, such as aggression, and in part by the natural accident of not being confined by childbirth. Women have tended toward the contextual role, partly by accident and partly for reasons in opposition to those above. It is not our intent here to stress the superiority of either of these roles but, rather, to point out that both roles are absolutely necessary. Neither is the sole property of one of the sexes.

As these principles demonstrate themselves in decision-making groups and formal speaker-audience relationships, it is likely that the female, being the most contextually oriented, will tend to prepare the way, working to assuage personal feelings, hoping by this method to reach a satisfactory conclusion. On the other hand, the man will tend to be direct and aggressive, to let the chips fall where they may, and to be less inclined to smooth the way for a later result.

The Women's Liberation Movement emphasizes the rapid acceleration of a long transitional period in which attitudes toward women have been changing. Whereas in the past women were quite dependent upon men, they are less so now. The myth of chivalry has in the past placed women on a pedestal, a situation that affected communication specifically. Woman deferred to man in the sense of yielding to his will or opinion. Not being able to argue, she was forced to work behind the scenes. She could not then compete with man economically and therefore became his charge.

Because of the Women's Liberation Movement many women, and men for that matter, have been forced to reconsider women's role in our society. As a consequence many women have jumped off the pedestal, delighted to involve themselves in freedom. Others have been much more hesitant, and in many cases a woman will find herself with one foot on the pedestal and one off, a necessary transitional stance that must be understood if we are to draw reasonable conclusions about either sex. We say "either sex" because it is not conceivable that female behavior can change without affecting male behavior.

Lipman-Blumen in a recent study demonstrated the changing values among women with contemporary and traditional patterns.[34]

Interpersonal skill rated only slightly less than emotional maturity in the traditional value system, but it has rated much lower in the contemporary value system. Such findings have tremendous implications for communication in our rapidly changing social-sexual milieu. Women of a contemporary life style will tend not to be fulfilling the interpersonal needs of their relationships if they pursue this tendency to become more issue oriented and intellectually curious. This in itself is a partial abandonment of a significant role that women have played in dyadic and small-group situations. Whether or not there is a suitable way to replace woman in this role remains to be seen.

In sum, we may say that there is a characteristic male style and a characteristic female style. During the next few years observation of behavioral tendencies may suggest a change in these styles and a specific effect on communication. It should be apparent that we are dealing with background areas that are very important to understanding communication at the interpersonal level. Such understanding requires fairly acute perceptive ability, as do all facets of style.

STIMULATING THE AUDIENCE

As we have emphasized in the title of this chapter, style is the speaker's link to his audience. In the foregoing pages we have shown how style, defined as the individual's unique expression of his perceptions, plays a significant and frequently determining role in the stimulation of audience response. We have shown how style relates to the process of invention, organization, and delivery. Style is also a decisive factor in influencing people. In concluding this chapter we consider how style stimulates the audience in three different ways:

1. It helps to create a desirable speaker ethos, without which a bond of trust cannot exist.
2. It helps give messages meaning and impact to make possible accurate audience evaluation.
3. It assists in creating emotional satisfaction, without which an audience cannot act.

Creating a Desirable Speaker Image

In order that a speaker may create a completely satisfactory image of himself in the mind of his audience, he must be able to make his audience *recognize* his qualities. This fact is taken up in the following paragraphs.

The Speaker's Attitude Toward Himself

The appropriate amount of self-confidence, avoiding on the one side the boorishness of egocentricity and on the other side the image of self-abasement, is essential to the creation of a favorable self-image. It is necessary for the speaker to show that he respects himself before he can expect the audience to do the same.

The Speaker's Positive Physical Characteristics

You must assist your audience to recognize the positive physical characteristics that can contribute to your speech. This does not mean that to be a good speaker you must have a perfect masculine or feminine configuration. A paraplegic may attain great speaking heights, but only because he is able to focus the audience's attention on those physical qualities that he can control. No one who saw him speak will ever forget the tremendous arm, shoulder, and chest muscles of Franklin Delano Roosevelt nor his commanding voice and head movements.

You will influence your audience more favorably with your physical behavior as you learn what to accentuate and what to diminish. No two people will influence in quite the same way. At the same time you will realize that bodily movement of which you are largely unaware is the metacommunication which helps the audience read your character.

The Speaker's Mental Abilities

It is not enough that we appear physically able. We must also appear mentally able. We might ask ourselves the question, What are the characteristics that cause a speaker to appear mentally alert? A number of different answers can be given to this, and they will include:

1. An adequate vocabulary: The speaker, now understanding the ambiguity of language, gives enough time and attention to preparing his remarks to discover the words that most closely give the desired meaning.
2. Fluency: The speaker not only has chosen his words and materials well but has become sufficiently familiar with them to speak them easily.
3. Ability to adjust topic to audience: Realizing the need of a close analysis of his audience and their understanding of his purpose, he does not leave the audience wondering, "Why is he saying this?"
4. Reasonableness: Aware that the attitudes of an audience are not easy to change, the speaker makes his requests of the audience seem reasonable.

It is most important that the speaker realize that satisfying the audience's intellectual demands is not as overwhelming a factor as it might seem. Many students, in speaking to an audience, tend to play down their most attractive intellectual qualities, for they feel it is not in fashion to be very skilled with words. Unfortunately, their thoughts may never be known because of their unwillingness to be skilled in man's unique activity—handling language symbols.

The Speaker's Attitude Toward the Audience

Once a speaker has shown that he is in accord with himself, he must obtain recognition of his favorable attitude toward the audience. It is not always easy for the beginning student to understand that his speaking before an audience ought not to be considered a performance. Rather, he is speaking with a group of people, and the outcome of his speech depends upon the attitudes of this audience at the end of the speech. Once this concept is grasped, the speaker may realize that the best articulation in the world may not change the attitude of an audience, and that the best organized speech may not change it, either. It is only when the speaker grapples with the ever-present attitudes of this particular group of people that he will become an effective speaker. To do this he must demonstrate to the audience his ability to identify with them in such fashion that they do not think, that he is, on the one hand, condescending or, on the other, showing off. Identification with the audience means the bringing about of a real feeling of acceptance between speaker and audience. He must be continually delivering a message of metacommunication to his audience, one that is saying, "I am friendly with you. I have your best interests in mind." If he can do this, he will discover that even some of the more stubborn attitudes will tend to yield a bit.

The Speaker's Attitude Toward His Subject

The audience has now satisfied itself that the speaker has sufficient respect for himself, that he identifies with the audience, and looks upon it in a friendly fashion. The audience has one thing yet to learn—what kind of a view of his subject does the speaker have?

The audience is really asking two questions: "How expert is he?" and "How much should that expertness be allowed to affect us?"

First let us examine the problem of expertise. Obviously, we are not going to listen to any speaker unless we feel that he has some reasonable amount of expertise. It may not even be possible for us as an audience to determine the extent of the speaker's expertise. We shall probably have to take this matter on faith from his colleagues or those in a position to understand fully the nature of his expertise. If a tax expert should come before us to discuss the excise tax and business profits, most of us would not be in a position to judge his expertise.

A student speaking to his class frequently will not be a true expert. He should, however, when he has an area of competence or expertise, make use of it, although it may not necessarily form the topic of every speech. For instance, a student who is rated as one of the top intercollegiate tennis players or long-distance runners, a student who has qualified as theatre stage manager or costume mistress, or who sits in the chair of the first flutist in the orchestra, has expertise that may be applied to the speaking situations in which he finds himself. No student should make the plea that he has no expertise. Even though your own opinion of your expertise is limited, realize that it is unique and can be developed. Also realize that the audience must in some fashion become aware of it without your appearing egocentric in stating it.

As a speaker with a certain expertise you must be careful to indicate to the audience that your expertise is based on objectivity. Otherwise the enthusiasm you may need to influence people toward your point of view may be subject to disbelief. By assuring the members of the audience of your belief in yourself, of your good will toward them and, finally, of your ability to project your enthusiasm for your subject, you will find that your style will begin to stimulate the audience.

Making Messages Meaningful

In previous portions of this chapter we indicated some of the aspects through which style helps to make messages more meaningful. Our study of language as a symbol system and our introduction to non-verbal languages have provided a basis for achieving meaningful messages. It is our purpose here to consider an additional way in which style through language contributes to raising the perception level of the listener.

We have already pointed out the necessity of establishing new cognitions, attempting to change attitudes, and adapting to the needs and desires of the audience, but we have not considered the means by which our symbol system can stimulate a new concept in the mind of the hearer.

As long as we are dealing with terms for which we think the respondent has a definite referent in mind, whether it be exactly the same as ours or not, we can still carry on a conversation and, although some misunderstandings may occur, we shall probably come close enough to attaining our end to overlook what has been misunderstood. Suppose, on the other hand, that we are using words for which the respondent has no referent. It would be impossible to communicate with him, although we might "talk." Perhaps we get a response such as "What in the world are you talking about?" Such a response is a shock, for we have assumed that the respondent could identify referents for the words that we were using.

Consider these examples. How would you describe the color green to someone who had been blind from birth? Have you ever tried to explain the international monetary system to someone who has trouble balancing his checkbook? Have you ever tried to explain the differential in your car to your wife? Or have you ever attempted to explain to an uninitiated male how to make hollandaise sauce? The challenge presented to the communicator is to find words with referents that will enable the respondent to move from the known to the unknown. The most common means of doing this is through the use of the *metaphor.*

The function of the metaphor is to provide the respondent with a word picture or phrase that he is familiar with and that exhibits characteristics you wish him to apply to the new concept. For instance, the concept of God is very difficult to construct. Many prophets, teachers, and philosophers have attempted to explain it. The following metaphor gives one version of what God means: "A mighty fortress is our God." Here is another: "God is a shepherd bringing his sheep into the fold."

We all have been warned that we should not become angry in the midst of a crisis or difficult undertaking. Here are two metaphors that express this concept: "Anger is a wind which blows out the lamp of the mind" and "Don't lose your cool."

When whisky is called firewater and a stadium a bowl, when a mental process is referred to as a train of thought, when a former love is referred to as an old flame, or when unlikely people gathered together are referred to as strange bedfellows, we see metaphor operating as the very common process which it is in our language.

It is frequently a surprise to many individuals to learn for the first time that they use metaphors commonly in their everyday speech. Most of these, however, are not unique or original metaphors; they are picked up and used because they seem so apropos or pertinent or even a shortcut in expressing some idea. Those metaphors which have been in the language for a long time and are used with such familiarity that we do not recognize them as metaphors are called *dead metaphors.*

Many metaphors developed from the word *home* are in such common use that we no longer think of them as metaphors: home plate, a missile that homes in on its target, her words struck home.

It should be clear from these comments that the use of metaphor is not a decoration or frill added to the language to make it prettier. A metaphor has a functional contribution to make to the establishment of meaning in the mind of the respondent. An effective original metaphor probably is a stroke of genius rather than a method that can be learned. When we begin to explain a metaphor, citing the characteristics of the known and indicating how they relate to the unknown, we progress very quickly into *analogy,* which is an enlargement of the metaphor. We deal with analogy as a supporting material in Chapter Eleven.

We have not dealt with such figures of speech as *hyperbole,* an exaggeration of language used for effect, or *apostrophe,* direct address to an absent person or thing, or *personification,* a form of metaphor that attributes personal qualities to inanimate objects; for there is a danger of feeding the illusion that they are used for decorative purposes. Very often they are used for emphasis or to gain attention rather than for clarity or establishing meaning.

The function of style in the traditional sense is to provide clarity and impressiveness. Since in this chapter style has been considered the unique manner in which an individual expresses his perceptions, we deal here only with concepts that enable us to establish this unique individuality. Emphasis and clarity are factors in the selection and use of speech materials that do not identify the individual as much as they constitute standard ingredients of good speaking. Consequently it appears more logical to treat them in Chapter Eleven as part of the means of selecting and using speech materials.

Providing Emotional Satisfaction

We have seen how style can assist in the creation of a desirable speaker ethos and how it can assist in making messages meaningful. It assists in one additional important process: it can help provide an audience with the emotional satisfaction that it needs before it can respond to the speaker's request. Recognition by the audience of its own potential results in emotional satisfaction. Sometimes the style of the speaker is able to awaken an audience's desire for that recognition; it can be awakened when the audience recognizes that the speaker believes in its ability. The speaker's style should be continually telling the members of his audience to believe in themselves, either for their own satisfaction or for the recognition it will bring them.

The things that have been said in this chapter regarding the importance of metacommunication and the way meaning is established contribute to a speaker's style. That style will be effective if it is continually coherent, believable, and stimulating.

We have seen, then, how style contributes to two of the classic concepts of proof—*ethos* and *pathos.* Its relation to the third concept of proof—*logos*—is considered in Chapters Eleven and Twelve.

IMPLICATIONS
1. Since many more thousands of words are spoken in formal and informal situations, on an impromptu or extemporaneous basis, than are in writing, we

need a definition of style that is not confined to the traditional "use of language."

2. Since style is not a single element of a part-whole relationship but rather a catalyst which, when used effectively, brings together different elements to give the total configuration significance and meaning, your style should also serve as a catalyst for the audience.

3. If we expect attitude change as a result of our message, we must be sincere (trustworthy), or the nonverbal aspects of our style may betray us.

4. Because of ego involvement we can influence others favorably only when our style is able to gratify them.

5. When attempting to affect someone else's attitude, the selection of our content and method spells the difference between success and failure.

6. The importance of style is its relationship to the establishment of meaning. To use it as adornment or as an end in itself diverts it from its true purpose.

7. The semantic elements of our symbol system, through which we attempt to make meaning precise, are essential ingredients of style as a means of expressing what we perceive.

8. The sign-symbol relationship is significant because each of its aspects must have its own type of response.

9. The higher the level of our abstractions, the more difficulty in making language meaningful to listeners.

10. Since there are constructive and destructive uses of language, we should understand that the destructive use is designed to clear the way for the constructive use.

11. Nonverbal communication accounts for the saying, "What you are speaks so loud I cannot hear what you say."

12. Since sex differences create a style for men that is different from the style of women, we may assume that both speaker and audience will be affected.

13. A speaker's style can help to establish the bond of trust that must exist if there is to be a desirable speaker ethos.

14. A speaker's style gives meaning and impact to his messages, increasing the accuracy of audience evaluation.

15. The audience cannot act without sufficient emotional satisfaction, much of which is achieved through the speaker's style.

EXERCISES

1. Make a list of as many ways as you can think of in which men communicate with each other. Could any of these ways be used as our exclusive and only method of communication? If not, why not?

2. Give a number of illustrations showing the time-binding characteristics of our language.

3. Prepare a short speech on any of the following topics. In the preparation of your speech keep in mind what has been said in this chapter about time-binding.

   a. The last time I saw Paris (or Rome, London, etc.)

   b. When time flies it cannot be recalled

    c. Hope ever urges us on and tells us tomorrow will be better
    d. Lessons history teaches us
    e. What may tomorrow bring?
    f. I guess I forgot, that's all
    g. The birth of a nation
    h. Experience is the best teacher
    i. Where were you on the night of October 17 (or any other date)?
    j. Let's forget the past
    k. Why opinion polls sometimes go wrong

4. List a number of words to which you give signal responses. Try using some of these words in speeches and note the effect on the members of your audience.

5. What are the values of using language that is known "only to the initiated"? Select some code language with which you are familiar, such as the terminology used in sports, women's styles, trucking, jazz music, and the theater, and prepare a short speech in which you tell how the code is an aid to communication.

6. Make a list of words on your campus that have restricted meanings.

7. Make a list of ten words that have been added to the English vocabulary in the last ten years. What do these words tell you about the changing culture of the world in which we live? Prepare to comment on this in class.

8. List some ways of looking at things that are peculiar to your own family. How do they color the language you use in talking about them?

9. Be prepared to comment on the following statements in class discussion.
    a. All children must go through this infuriating stage of accumulating words by asking questions, or be handicapped for life. *(Stuart Chase)*
    b. It is absurd, therefore, to imagine that we ever perceive anything "as it really is." *(S. I. Hayakawa)*
    c. Speech is the index of the mind. *(Seneca)*
    d. England and America are two countries separated by the same language. *(G. B. Shaw)*
    e. A word or sentence is not merely a bundle of sounds; it is also a bundle of associations. These associations are not quite identical for any two speakers; neither will the words or sentences hold for them exactly the same semantic content. *(Mario Pei)*
    f. The standard meaning of *abstracting*, implies selecting, picking out, separating, summarizing, deducting, removing, omitting, disengaging, taking away, and stripping; the adjective *abstract* implies "not concrete." *(Alfred Korzybski)*

10. Make a list of a series of words that indicate various levels of abstraction, as in the examples below, going from low levels to high levels.

Dior creation	Papermate Pen
Paris gown	ballpoint pen
dress	pen
women's apparel	writing instrument
clothing	desk accessory
personal property	office equipment

Give a short speech in which you point out the details left out as you moved from the lowest to the highest levels.

11. Criticize this statement: "Proper words in proper places make the true definition of style."

12. Make a list of the factors that clue you in to what a speaker thinks of himself.

13. Your best friend is about to throw himself out of a twenty-story window. The police have asked you to come and talk him out of it. What would you use as your appeal?

14. Secure from the library a book on elocution as practiced in the last century. Demonstrate for your class some of the methods of oral expression described in the book.

ADDITIONAL READINGS

Bettinghaus, Erwin P., *Persuasive Communication*, New York, Holt, Rinehart & Winston, 1968, pp. 101–111.

Blankenship, Jane, *A Sense of Style*, Belmont, Calif., Dickenson, 1968, pp. 67–74.

Brown, Roger, *Words and Things, An Introduction to Language*, New York, Free Press, 1968, pp. 139–154.

Cicero on Oratory and Orators, trans. J. S. Watson, Carbondale, Southern Illinois Univ. Press, 1970, Book III.

Keltner, John W., *Interpersonal Speech-Communication, Elements and Structures*, Belmont, Calif., Wadsworth, 1970, chaps. 3 and 6.

Lucas, F. L., *Style*, London, Cassell, 1955, chap. 2.

Mackin, John H., *Classical Rhetoric for Modern Discourse*, New York, Free Press, 1969.

McEdwards, Mary G., *Introduction to Style*, Belmont, Calif., Dickenson, 1968, pp. 48–59.

Mudd, Charles S., and Malcolm O. Sillars, *Speech: Content and Communication*, 2nd ed., Scranton, Penn., Chandler, 1969, chap. 12.

Oliver, Robert T., *Making Your Meaning Effective*, Boston, Holbrook, 1971, chap. 7.

Rein, Irving J., *The Relevant Rhetoric*, New York, Free Press, 1969, chap. 6.

Smith, Donald K., *Man Speaking*, New York, Dodd Mead, 1969, chap. 6.

NOTES

[1] Mary G. McEdwards, *Introduction to Style*, Belmont, Calif., Dickenson, 1968, pref., n. p.

[2] Jane Blankenship, *A Sense of Style*, Belmont, Calif., Dickenson, 1968, p. 2.

[3] Samuel Butler, quoted in F. L. Lucas, *Style*, London, Cassell, 1955, p. 64.

[4] Quoted in William T. Brewster, *Representative Essays on the Theory of Style*, New York, Macmillan, 1911, p. xi.

[5] Lucas, *op. cit.*, p. 49.

[6] Richard Wilson, columnist, *Whittier Daily News*, Whittier, Calif., Sept. 14, 1971.

[7] Daniel Katz, "The functional approach to the study of attitudes," *Public Opinion Quart.*, 24 (no. 1, Spring 1960), 163–204.

[8] Aristotle, *Rhetoric and Poetics*, trans. Rhys Roberts, New York, Modern Library, 1954, p. 168.

[9] *Cicero on Oratory and Orators*, trans. J. S. Watson, Carbondale, Southern Illinois Univ. Press, 1970, p. 208.

[10] Lester Thonssen and A. Craig Baird, *Speech Criticism*, 2nd ed., New York, Ronald, 1970, p. 471.

[11] S. I. Hayakawa, *Language in Thought and Action*, New York, Harcourt, 1964, p. 23.

[12] *Ibid.*, p. 13.

[13] Alfred Korzybski, *Science and Sanity*, 3rd ed., Lakeville, Conn., International Non-Aristo-telian Library, 1948, pp. 231, 239, 376.

[14] *Ibid.*, p. 58.

[15] Hayakawa, *op. cit.*, p. 31

[16] Colin Cherry, *On Human Communication*, New York, Wiley, 1957, p. 69.

[17] Andrew Dib Sherfan, *Kahlil Gibran, The Nature of Love*, New York, Philosophical Library, 1971, p. 21.

[18] John A. Howard, "The innovation mirage," *Vital Speeches*, 36 (no. 24, Oct. 1, 1970), 744.

[19] Barbara A. Gunn, "Toward a national policy on aging," *Vital Speeches*, 37 (no. 19, July 15, 1971), 598.

[20] Whitney Young, "Building ghetto power," speech delivered at the 58th National Urban League Conference, New Orleans, July 28 to Aug. 1, 1968. By permission of National Urban League, Inc.

[21] Stuart Chase, *The Tyranny of Words*, New York, Harcourt, 1938, pp. 77–78.

[22] Paul R. Beall, "Pass the word along," *Vital Speeches*, 19 (no. 15, May 15, 1953), 465.

[23] John Condon, Jr., "When people talk with people," in James W. Gibson, *A Reader in Speech Communication*, New York, McGraw-Hill, 1971, p. 112.

[24] James C. McCroskey, *An Introduction to Rhetorical Communication*, Englewood Cliffs, N.J., Prentice-Hall, 1968, p. 31.

[25] See J. Dan Rothwell, "Verbal obscenity: Time for second thoughts," *Western Speech*, 35 (no. 4, Fall 1971), 233.

[26] For a discussion of the diatribe see Theodore Otto Windt, Jr., "The diatribe: Last resort for protest," *Quart. J. Speech*, 58 (no. 1, Feb. 1972), 1–14.

[27] Asa T. Spaulding, in speeches delivered to a regional meeting of the National Urban League in Arkansas, July 20, 1963 and to the Woman-in-Action Coalition for the Reduction of Violence, Sept. 4, 1968. By special permission of Mr. Spaulding. Besides being a leader in the black community, he is a consultant for the Ford Foundation and the General Electric Company.

[28] Edward T. Hall, *The Silent Language*, Greenwich, Conn., Fawcett, 1959, p. 10.

[29] David C. McClelland, "Wanted: A new self-image for Woman," in Robert Theobald, ed., *Dialogue on Woman*, New York, Bobbs-Merrill, 1967, pp. 44–45.

[30] *Ibid.*, p. 38.

[31] *Ibid.*, p. 37.

[32] *Ibid.*, p. 41.

[33] *Ibid.*, pp. 42–43.

[34] Jean Lipman-Blumen, "How ideology shapes women's lives," *Scient. Amer.*, 226 (no. 1, Jan. 1972), 34.

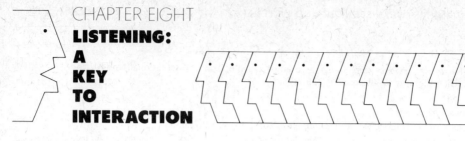

CHAPTER EIGHT
LISTENING: A KEY TO INTERACTION

Nature has given to man one tongue, but two ears, that we may hear from others twice as much as we speak.
Epictetus

We believe that effective communication depends more upon a thorough understanding of all aspects of the communicative situation than it does upon the strict adherence to a prescribed set of rules. We avoid rules here, although we list what we call implications at the ends of chapter texts. Unless you understand your own and your listeners' behavior in a communicative transaction and the nature of the transaction itself, your speech preparation and presentation will not be maximally effective. For this reason we have considered the values and reciprocal roles of the participants in communication, how communication has affected the development of society's institutions, the purposes and nature of the speech communication process, factors contributing to speaker attention and motivation, and the functions of language and style. A final consideration before the actual speech preparation is the role of listening, a frequently ignored aspect of the communication process. Unless listeners attend to, perceive, and comprehend (all dimensions of listening) what has been said and react in some way, there is no communication.

THE IMPORTANCE OF LISTENING
We stress throughout this text that communication is a two-way process—a transaction between two parties—in which the reciprocal interaction affects both the speech and the response. If speech communication is to be effective, then, both speaker and respondent must have rhetorical skills appropriate to the role they play in a communicative act. In this chapter we concern ourselves with the skill of listening and look first at its importance.

The study of listening is important for at least five reasons: the large amount of time each individual spends in listening, the relative lack of listening skill, the value of listening in promoting better human relations, the influence of listening ability on other language arts, and the values that a knowledge of listening can have for both speaker and listener.

Time Spent in Listening

If the communicative situation involves only two persons, about half the time spent is devoted to listening. As more persons are involved, as in a group discussion, the ratio of total listening time to total speaking time increases. Unless one is a complete extrovert and has a job that requires much talking, it is likely that he spends more time in listening than in talking. We can get some indication of the time we spend in listening from two studies conducted at the University of Michigan.

The first study, conducted by Paul T. Rankin,[1] a pioneer in communication-skills research, was completed in 1926 and has been supported by many studies conducted since. In fact, one writer says that the data from the study might well have been written in 1965. In an analysis of the listening habits of a selected group of persons, Rankin discovered that 70 percent of our waking hours is spent in verbal communication; of this time, 42 percent is spent in listening, 32 percent in speaking, 15 percent in reading, and 11 percent in writing. In other words, almost one-half of our communicating time is devoted to listening. Since much of what we learn comes through the auditory sense, it behooves us to make that listening effective.

The second study was of a different nature. The Survey Research Center at the University of Michigan sampled audiences after the 1952 and 1956 presidential campaigns.[2] One question was asked: "Of all these ways of following the campaign which one would you say you got the most information from—newspapers, radio, television, or magazines?" In 1952 a total of 59 percent reported that they got the most information from radio and television, in contrast to the 27 percent who got the most information from newspapers and magazines. The remaining 14 percent reported a combination of media, said they didn't follow the campaign, or didn't know. In 1956 the comparable figures were 59 percent getting the most information from the listening media, 29 percent from written materials, and 12 percent from the miscellaneous media. During both years people reported that they got approximately twice as much information from listening as from reading. With the growth of the radio and television media we may safely assume that the percentages were greater in 1972.

In all areas of public and private life skill in listening is of utmost importance. Judge and jury say little but must be good listeners.

The defense and prosecuting attorneys, too, must listen well, to know when to raise objections. The psychiatrist and psychological counselor speak little but listen much. Criminal and insurance investigators spend much of their time listening. Justice frequently depends on the court reporter's ability to listen and record accurately. The accuracy of a news release, the consummation of a business deal, and the success of a military air mission frequently depend on the listening ability of a reporter, an office secretary, or bomber pilot. The number of types of work in which listening ability is a major tool is so great that most students can anticipate this important skill as indispensable in their future positions.

Listening also plays a part in one's intellectual and emotional growth. Much of what an individual learns comes through aural stimuli. Education is largely a matter of listening. The student in a typical speech class may give seven to ten speeches during a semester, varying in length from one to fifteen minutes. If he "speaks" to his classmates a total of two hours—a high estimate—out of approximately fifty hours of class time, what does he do the remainder of the time? He listens, part of the time to the instructor but most of the time to other students.

Skill in Listening

A second important reason for the study of listening, in view of the fact that we do so much of it, is the relative lack of skill in listening among most people. Over the past fifteen years one of us has been involved as a staff member in a large number of training programs in communication skills for adults. Training in listening has been a part of the agenda. A standardized listening-comprehension test has been administered to more than 600 persons. On the basis of the norms for college freshmen it was discovered that only about 15 percent of the adults scored in the upper quartile, 20 percent in the third quartile, another 20 percent in the second quartile, and the remaining 45 percent in the first quartile, scoring no better than the lowest 25 percent of college freshmen. About 12 percent got scores in the bottom decile, suggesting almost a complete lack of listening skill.

Purposes of Listening

Knowledge about—or at least sensitivity to—listening has value in improving human relations. Almost every book on the subject of human relations suggests that, in order to know people, get along with them, and get them to work cooperatively on mutual projects, it is more important to listen than to talk. Webb and Morgan, in one of the first popularly written books of the how-to-influence type say:[3]

The easiest way to influence people and impress them favorably is to induce them to talk about their own affairs and problems. . . . Show your interest in these things by your manner of listening. Make it a definite part of your program to listen attentively when others speak to you.

More recent books place less emphasis on the manipulative value of listening and more on its value in creating a permissive atmosphere for work, play, or therapy.[4] The psychiatrist Dominick A. Barbara[5] says that "the more able he is to listen on a rational, responsible and humanistic basis, the more readily will Man ultimately realize himself and discover his most constructive possibilities."

Grievances in work situations come about largely as a result of poor interpersonal relations and frequently can be solved when a supervisor is willing to "hear out" the complaints. Family squabbles between children are usually resolved when a parent listens with an understanding ear. Professional family counselors must be skilled in the art of listening in order to help the many maladjusted couples who come to them.

The human-relations values of listening are summarized quite well in the following suggestions:

We learn by listening, not by talking.
We bolster the other person's ego by listening.
When a situation is tense, listen.
When someone is angry, let him talk.
When someone is unhappy, listen.
When someone needs encouragement, listen.
When someone brings you a problem, listen.
When someone accuses you, listen before you answer.
When two people come to you with a problem, listen to both.

Besides improved human relations resulting from skilled listening, there are other practical reasons for improving our listening skills. At times it keeps us out of trouble. Failure to get needed information on a term paper, a class assignment, or a final examination may result from careless listening. Many a business deal has been lost because a person did not listen. Hasty judgments, emotionally loaded statements, and false allegations often can be avoided when a speaker listens before he speaks.

Listening in the Language Arts
Listening is important because of its close relationship to the other language arts. Writing on the importance of listening Petrie states:[6]

Because listening, speaking, reading, and writing have many factors in common (such as vocabulary, sentence patterns, organization, etc.), and since . . . other language skills are learned through listening, it is not surprising that research has revealed a rather close relationship among the language abilities. Correlations between listening and reading abilities, for example, have been estimated to average as high as .70 and .75.

An analysis of research studies reported by Duker[7] reveals these rather significant generalizations:

1. Helping children to understand and interpret oral language may contribute to reading success.
2. In the prediction or evaluation of how much children will be able to interpret from reading, an evaluation of auding (listening) ability seems to be valuable.
3. The analysis of relationships between scores on listening tests and measures of general mental ability reveal positive correlations often in the 0.50's and 0.60's.
4. Studies of reading and listening comprehension show them to be closely related skills.
5. The factors that appear to be most important to listening comprehension are motivation to listen, intelligence, linguistic ability (including vocabulary and other skills related to the recognition, use, and assimilation of language), and the ability to separate and retain and subordinate ideas and concepts (to organize).

An Aid to Speaker and Listener

Finally, listening skills are important to both speaker and listener because of the improved communication that results. To know what listening involves, which elements block and which contribute to effective listening, what can be done by listeners themselves to improve their listening comprehension—in a word, to become a good listener—enables a speaker to communicate more effectively. The same is true for the listener: the more he knows about the physical and neurological aspects of hearing, about the functions of listening, about possible breakdown in listening, and methods of improving listening, the more will he contribute to the communicative transaction and the greater will be his comprehension of the speaker's message.

THE NATURE OF LISTENING

The two sides of the coin of speech communication are speaking and listening; the two are inseparable if communication has occurred. In situations such as interviews and small group discussions where the speaker and listener roles alternate frequently, we can communicate effectively "when our turn comes up" only if we first do an effective job of listening. Hence, we surely need to know what constitutes the process of listening.

Its Variety

Research data on many aspects of listening have been accumulating at a rapid rate over the past twenty years. Still, there is only general agreement on the nature of the process, on what is actually involved when a person listens. Common sense tells us something about it. We know that the physics of sound waves is involved, the various mechanisms of the ear operate on these audible stimuli, and the central nervous system interprets the nerve impulses so that what is heard has meaning. Attention, selective aural perception, memory, and cognition are involved. Sociopsychological, cultural, and experiential forces modify the process—many of us hear better under certain conditions than others. The physical aspects of the room in which the communication takes place, the acoustics, and the size of the audience have an effect on listening. Finally, listening is related to the intellectual and physical characteristics of the person listening.

Its Complexity

Listening is a broader concept than hearing. When we hear, we perceive a pattern of sounds only. Our ears report the pattern to the central nervous system, where meanings are assigned. However, when the sound signal is weak, when the message is dampened through noise, or when the channel is overloaded, the central nervous system may have insufficient data to assign a meaning. When only a portion of a signal is noted by the ear, the meaning assigned to a message may not be the same as when the total signal is received. Listening thus goes beyond hearing. When we listen, we attach meaning to aural symbols and to all other elements of the total situation in which words are uttered. Nichols and Lewis, two leaders in listening research, comment as follows:[8]

(a) Since much listening is done in intervals of quiet, and since silence frequently carries meaning, silence itself must be accepted as an aural symbol. (b) Since the assimilation of meaning sometimes starts before a speaker says a word, and since it very frequently continues long after he has said his final one, listening is not necessarily limited to the immediate speaking situation. (c) Although meaning may be attached to aural symbols with or without the presence of visual cues, listening as a medium of learning usually implies the presence of speakers in person, in "live" situations in which visual and aural cues complement each other in the mode of presentation.

The implication seems to be that meaning—the desired end result of listening—is attributed to a message by a listener prior to, during, and after a communicative act has occurred, and that meaning is assigned to both verbal and nonverbal stimuli.

An interesting facet of the process of listening is that frequently the mind-set of the listener, prior to his participation in a communicative act, determines how much listening takes place. You have undoubtedly participated in situations in which you were disposed to listen: a banquet at which you were named "athlete of the year" or "best debater" for your school, some event in which you heard a controversial or noteworthy figure such as Eldridge Cleaver, David Ellsberg, Jane Fonda, Ralph Nader, David R. Scott, Huey P. Newton, Golda Meir, or U Thant, or at a meeting at which a close friend is the speaker. On such occasions you began the "assimilation of meaning" before the speech was given and continued to attach meaning to what was said long after it was over. Research shows that the more our psychological "set" or state of expectancy coincides with the actual content of a speech, the more effective is our listening.

If we accept the implication stated, then we must define listening in such a way that it includes the understanding of—the attachment of meaning to—verbal, visual, and mechanical sounds, such as the opening of a squeaking door and the closing of a stuck window. Definitions of listening reflect a division of opinion on this point.[9] Nichols defines listening as "the attachment of meaning to aural symbols," a definition that seems to contradict the point of view in the quotation from Nichols and Lewis. By contrast, Jones defines listening as "a selective process by which sounds communicated by some source are received, critically interpreted, and acted upon by a purposeful listener."

When the definition of listening is limited to the hearing and assigning of meaning to oral language only, some writers prefer to describe the process as *auding*, rather than listening. One such writer is Petrie, who states:[10]

. . . unless otherwise specifically designated, the term "listening" or "listening comprehension" will be used synonymously with "auding" to mean the composite process by which oral language communicated by some source is received, critically and purposefully attended to, and interpreted (or comprehended) in terms of past experience and future expectancies.

Since a pragmatic definition is desirable, we define listening as the perceptual process by which verbal and nonverbal communications (including mechanical sounds) from some source or sources are selectively received, recognized, and interpreted by a receiver or receivers in relation to the perceptual fields of the parties to the process. Listening thus becomes a part of a total communicative transaction.

It is apparent that the comprehension of the nonverbal aspects of a communicative act must be a part of listening. Our interpretation of how firmly a conviction is held, how cordial a greeting actually is, or how beneficial to us will be the results of a proposed action results as much from what we see as from what we hear. That is, we interpret all the stimuli that come to us, to determine the meaning intended. Barbara says in this respect:[11]

What reaches us through words is only one side of the picture. There is also a nonverbal communication, expressed in the interplay of hidden gestures, feelings, bodily reactions, glances, and so forth, which is constantly going on among human beings. An awareness of both verbal and nonverbal facts is essential if we are to arrive at a more complete understanding of human behavior.

A final and significant dimension of listening—implied in what we have already said—is that listening is a sequential process. This facet of listening is well stated by Fessenden in an article dealing with "levels" of listening. He states:[12]

One basic assumption in the development of the present discussion of the levels of listening is that regardless of the apparent speed or spontaneity of an event involving sound, there is a time factor which must be recognized. . . .

. . . We do not hear words or phrases; rather we collect in our memory the several patterns of sounds as they come to us and then, as each recognized unit is completed, we let it discharge into our mental stream to mingle with present impulses in the building of concepts and ideas. . . .

The third and final assumption . . . is fundamentally that listening is not a single activity but rather a group of activities.

We believe listening is much more than the mere hearing of sounds, be they verbal or mechanical. It must include the concept of comprehension, which is attached to the total communicative act, from the listener's viewpoint. Visual as well as auditory perception is a part of the process.

Its Relation to Speaking
It is generally agreed that there is a positive correlation between effective speaking and good listening. Those who are good listeners are usually good speakers. Nichols and Lewis, quoted earlier in this chapter, state:[13] "When we spot the best speakers in a class, we have at the

same time spotted those who are most successfully improving their speech listening attentively to their mates."

Research on the effects of "delayed speech feedback" seems to support the belief that normal speech is in some way dependent upon or related to normal hearing. Subjects wearing earphones as they speak listen to the delayed feedback of their own speech; what they hear at any given moment is not, therefore, what is being spoken. The usual time sequence of hearing and perception is thus destroyed, and the resultant speech takes on characteristics of stuttering, drawling, and slurring, almost like drunken speech.

Some speakers seem to assume that if a person has heard he will understand. In a well-known study of public-speaking classes Lee[14] reported that only 25 percent of the audience "got" the central idea of the speeches given: "If the audience heard they did not seem to listen. Or if they listened, it seemed with only half an ear." Consideration of your own listening habits may perhaps bring to mind times you heard but did not listen.

Contrary to reality, speakers often act as if all members of the audience listen equally well. An early study made by Jones[15] showed that in the immediate recall of content of class lectures the highest performer did about six times as well as the poorest, with an average score for all of about 60 percent. On delayed recall, learning through listening usually drops to about 25 percent.[16] Not only is there a wide range in listening ability, but the best listening ability is found at the lower age levels.

The fact that all persons do not listen equally well is, of course, due partly to the fact that a listener brings many varied personal factors to bear on his interpretation of what he hears or "listens to":[17]

When attending to a speaker, a listener may operate upon the speech he hears in a great variety of ways; the significant attributes of the speech may be microscopic acoustic clues, broader acoustic qualities, syllabic rhythms, et cetera, or he may be guided by syntactic structure, or by knowledge of subject matter and of the speaker's interests, of seasonable topics—a whole hierarchy. The speaker's utterances play upon the entire past experience of the listener, stimulating him into response at all these levels. If addressed by a stranger, the listener may change his mode of operation, as the conversation proceeds, and while he is learning something of the speaker's accent, speech habits, phrasing, and interests.

THE FUNCTIONS OF LISTENING
There are at least four functions of listening: appreciative, therapeutic, critical, and informative.

Appreciating

Appreciative listening seeks emotional and intellectual satisfaction and enjoyment. This is our aim when we listen to the oral interpretation of literature, humorous speeches, and theatrical performances. The great increase in the sale of recorded readings and speeches in recent years testifies to the fact that people do like to listen for appreciation only. The recorded readings of Raymond Massey, Charles Laughton, Laurence Olivier and, more recently, of Burl Ives, Robert Frost, Ogden Nash, and Orson Welles have sold in the thousands. Play reading has become popular in this country in the last twenty years. To listen to the humorous recordings of such comedians as Woody Allen, Phyllis Diller, Dick Gregory, and Mort Sahl indicates that listening can be fun. There are even some radio and television programs worth listening to.

Nichols and Lewis have this to say about appreciative listening:[18]

The most important single fact about appreciative listening is this: The better we understand the thing we are hearing, the greater becomes our potential satisfaction and pleasure.

Appreciative listening can make very significant contributions to our lives. Let us briefly consider some of them.

1. It can increase our enjoyment of life.
2. It can enlarge our experience.
3. It can improve our use of language.
4. It can expand the range of what we enjoy.
5. It can decrease the tension of daily living.

As Nichols and Lewis imply, many of us deny ourselves much cultural, educational, and recreational enjoyment because we are not very appreciative listeners.

Improving Relationships

We commented earlier on the value of listening in building good interpersonal relations. This is another function of listening, used in therapy by both professional counselors and laymen alike. Ruesch comments as follows on what he calls "cathartic listening" in a therapist-patient relationship:[19]

The expression "cathartic listening" refers to an attitude of the therapist that implies the doctor's readiness to listen to the patient's concerns, his emotional qualms, and other expressions in an attempt to understand without interrupting, guiding, advising, or refuting whatever the patient has to say. In daily life, many of the father and mother confessors to whom people turn to tell their troubles have mastered the art of cathartic listening. It is their non-interference and their non-evalua-tive attitude which inspires confidence and induces the patient to tell.

Johnson makes this observation, which should be added as a qualification of cathartic listening:[20]

There is more to the art of listening, however, than merely keeping still and expressing no moral judgments. A good listener is one who seems alive. . . .
. . . If there is a place that needs an atmosphere of hope and chins-up cheer it is a place where people go for personality re-education.
In other words, a clinician must have a way of listening with his face and eyes, so to speak. Keeping discreetly quiet, he must nevertheless be alert and responsive.

One of the most helpful friends a person can have is one who listens well.

The relationship between appreciative and therapeutic listening is indicated in this statement of Nichols and Stevens:[21]

In the adult world the therapeutic value of listening has been associated mostly with music. However, appreciative listening to stories, poetry, drama, good conversation and the like can also help us to relax, to put aside personal worries and cares. This is not to intimate that good lis-tening is a panacea for deep-seated psychological disturbances, but it can serve as a relaxing agent against our lesser worries.

Evaluating

Critical listening seeks to evaluate; its goals are analysis and judgment. When a person listens critically, he weighs the evidence presented, looks for fallacies in reasoning, notes the denotative and connotative mean-ings of words and their levels of abstraction, and tries to determine the feasibility of any action suggested. This type of listening has its roots in critical thinking and is an essential in a democratic society. It provides a defense against political demagoguery, slick sales propaganda, and hasty or poorly thought-out pleas for social action. Critical listening, further-more, provides a useful tool in planning needed social action.

The critical listener concerns himself with both the substance and the purpose. He is aware of and applies accepted tests of the validity of the data and reasoning the speakers use and the reliability of the speaker himself.

The extent to which people refuse to accept specious argument, emotionally loaded words, and questionable motives is a measure of their critical listening skills.

Learning

A fourth type of listening is called informative. The purpose of this type seems obvious: we listen to gain information, to increase our comprehension of some subject. Informative listening is concerned primarily with cognitions; evaluative judgments of the message are minimized.

Every student knows the need for this type of listening, through which he learns essential facts, relationships, and processes. How ineffective your listening has been is frequently revealed, to your dismay, at examination time.

Note that these four types of listening are not necessarily mutually exclusive. You can listen critically when you are concerned primarily with comprehension; certainly you should not accept alleged statements of fact that you know to be contrary to reality. Esthetic satisfaction can also come from critical and informative listening. You should derive some pleasure from appropriate and clear patterns of organization, finely turned language, apt illustrations, and effective vocal patterns in a persuasive speech, quite apart from its logical appeal.

BREAKDOWNS IN LISTENING

We might, had we so desired, have asked and answered two questions in each part of the section, namely "What listening problem is involved?" and "What can be done to resolve or mitigate the problem?" Because the problems involved in ineffective listening relate to many physical and psychological factors, and because many methods of improvement apply equally to several listening inadequacies, we have chosen to look at the general nature of listening breakdowns in this section. You will easily be able to determine which improvement methods apply.

One large category of communication breakdowns may be described as simply auditory and includes the structural and functional speaking and hearing anomalies of the sender and of the receiver, channel interferences and malfunctions, and all the physical factors of the room in which the communication takes place.

Anatomical Dysfunctions

The first type of listening breakdown comes from structural defects or malfunctioning of the human speech and hearing mechanisms.

The number of persons who are hard of hearing is continuously on the increase. In part this increase results from better devices to detect hearing losses—we know now that there are more young children with hearing dysfunctions than we had thought possible ten years ago—and in part because we have more older people around now than we did years ago, and we find the majority of the hard-of-hearing among them.

We frequently conduct training programs in communication, conference methods, and listening for various adult groups. Earlier in this chapter we cited figures on the listening comprehension of six hundred persons who had taken the Brown-Carlson Listening Comprehension Test in these training programs. The large number of low scores has suggested to us that many adults are unaware of their hearing problems. To check on this assumption, we have frequently asked audiences to indicate how many were aware of a hearing problem. The results were shocking. In one audience of 130 persons, 8 indicated they had a series of minor hearing problems. In another audience of 60 there were 5 who indicated some problem. In the two groups 7 percent had a hearing problem that caused some decrease in listening effectiveness. In other words, if you are talking to a cross section of adults aged twenty-five to seventy, 1 out of about 14 will have a hearing loss.

A booklet published under a grant from the U.S. Department of Health, Education and Welfare in 1969 included reports on surveys on hearing impairments conducted during the 1960s by the National Center for Health Statistics. Of interest to us is the following summary statement:[22]

Thus, in summary, although contemporary data remain incomplete in important ways, it is reasonable to estimate that about 8,500,000 Americans have auditory problems of one type or another which are less severe than deafness but which impair communication and hence social efficiency. The majority of these individuals are in the older age groups, but about 4.5 percent (circa 360,000) are under 17 years.

The lesson to be learned from these data should be obvious. In speaking to a group of any size, speak slightly louder than you feel may be necessary; check to determine whether you can be heard in all parts of the room; test the public address system before you start speaking, and then talk directly into the microphone; and remember, if you can't be heard, there is little reason to speak.

Electronic Channels

Breakdowns in communication can occur in the channels used. We become acutely aware of this problem when we happen to be watching a well-liked newscaster or a special show on television and suddenly the sound or the picture is lost. We see streaks across the television screen or a sign reading "One moment please, we have temporarily lost our sound," or we hear a voice that asks us to "Please stand by, we have temporarily lost our picture." A somewhat similar situation can occur when you are speaking over a public-address system. The more typical problem, however, occurs when feedback into the system sets up a mechanical whine that drowns out your voice.

A form of "overloading" of the channels also can result in interference with the communication. Excessive repetition can cause a listener to turn you off. Poor timing of your aural message when you are using slides or strip films can be confusing to the listener. Speakers inept in using visual aids frequently leave one of them uncovered for a while before it is to be used. Most listeners try to attend to both the aural and the visual stimuli without actually getting the message you want them to have.

Overloading has still another aspect. Let us assume that you wish to talk to your speech classmates on some topic of current interest. But the same topic has been the subject of debate in the student senate, has appeared in editorials and news articles in your college paper, has been talked about by the college president before the entire student body, and has even reached the local community newspapers and been the subject of several television newscasts. The channels of communication have been overloaded; there is some question whether you could get through.

Physical Conditions

Finally, breakdowns in communication can occur as the result of physical factors in the speaking room. If you are far from your audience but could stand closer, if the room is overheated but windows could be opened, if outside noises distract but could be lessened, if seats are uncomfortable and you are to talk for an hour but a standing "stretch" period or two would not be out of order, if there are minor interruptions during your speech and you could stop talking momentarily but do not do so—if any of these things happen and you do not take the suggested precautions, then you can be certain that communication will be partially or totally ineffective.

IMPROVING LISTENING

Listening can be improved by either the person receiving or the person sending the message. We look first at what the receiver can do.

The Listener

Motivation

The effective listener has a purpose in listening, prepares himself for listening, and maintains an active interest in any speech while he is listening to it. This applies to all situations in which you are a member of the audience voluntarily, but when you are a member of a captive audience, you should double your motivation in order to gain something from the situation. Your purpose in listening, whether it be to gain specific facts, learn the speaker's general point of view, get reinforcement of your own attitudes, or become sensitive to a mood, should be considered in advance.

You can do a number of things to prepare yourself for purposeful listening. For one thing, give as much prior consideration to the topic as circumstances permit: think through what you know about the subject, seek out new information and points of view, discuss the topic with others, and try to discover as much as you can about the speaker's point of view and what he may already have said about the topic. Try to determine the speaker's purpose and its relation to the audience and occasion. Make some selective evaluation of what you might gain by listening: that is, establish goals for listening. Finally, prepare yourself physically for effective listening: get to the meeting place in good time, come prepared to take notes and to participate in any forum period, and try to satisfy the requirements of comfort, clear vision, and audibility. Don't sit in the back of the room and then condemn the speaker for not "speaking up." Effective listeners try to be ready to listen before, not after, the speaker starts.

Purposeful listening also means that hearers should have some interest in the topic. Most speeches have elements that relate to some self-interest, and you can be constantly alert for new ideas, relationships, and facts. Even if your interest is not aroused at first, recognize that alertness usually pays dividends. There are few speakers from whom one cannot learn something.

Listener interest is, of course, related to the impelling motives discussed in Chapter Six. Many writers insist that if a listener has no interest in a speech or is losing interest, he should adopt a pragmatic point of view and seek all possible reasons for listening. There are many completely utilitarian reasons for listening to speeches. Irvin suggests that the prime reason is self-interest.[23]

Motivated listening is creative listening. It requires a desire and willingness on the part of the listener to develop a feeling of empathy with the purpose and feeling of the speaker. Barbara has this to say about purposeful listening:[24]

To listen with purpose requires an inner strength and the courage to open our minds to other people's ideas, while at the same time we must face up to the fact that some of our own beliefs may be wrong. Lack of courage on the other hand results in a tenacity and stubborn resistance to change and an unwillingness to acknowledge defeat. It also prevents us from being flexible in most situations and from being sympathetic and opening our ears to whatever may be said.

We believe the world and our times need more people who are willing to listen in the manner which Barbara implies.

Practice
Nichols and Lewis, whose study of the characteristics of "best" and "poorest" listeners in a college population was quoted early in this chapter, found that the best listeners are experienced in listening: [25] they "had apparently developed an appetite for hearing a variety of expository presentations difficult enough to challenge their mental capacities." This observation has special significance for all students of speech, since, as we have seen, the greatest amount of time in a speech class is spent in listening. To make this time of value the student must participate as actively and intelligently when listening as when he himself is speaking.

Let us say that you are in a speech class of twenty-one students, and each student gives five speeches during the course. One hundred speeches! Think, for a moment, of the information you can gain by practicing listening. Besides the notes you will be required to make by your instructor on your colleagues' presentation, we suggest you also take substantive notes. Many of our students have stated they got valuable information for term papers by listening to speeches of their classmates. Others have stated that practice in listening in a speech class improved their listening and note-taking in other courses.

Americans are especially fortunate in having a wide variety of highly profitable listening experiences available. In spite of the highly commercialized and popularized nature of radio and television there is still much of quality to be heard. In most cities and in practically all college towns there are the fine programs of educational radio and television stations. Cultural, educational, and inspirational public lectures provide an almost continuous parade of good listening. At meetings of service clubs, community organizations, professional associations, and government groups this parade continues. The unpracticed listener need not lack for opportunities to practice.

In taking advantage of such opportunities, don't yield to the temptation to avoid difficult listening. Rather, let the things to which you listen give you successive experiences in which the demands on your listening skill will increase. Accept the challenge of listening to difficult material, and practice will make the ordeal much easier.

Objectivity
You can also improve your listening by maintaining an objectivity toward both what the speaker says and how he says it. The best listeners are those who do not prejudge the speaker's message, in spite of prior biases they may have.

Prior evaluation of a speech is like closing the door to new opportunities: it will block off whatever value there might be in the speech. Everyone has a natural tendency to hear only what he is set to hear, and often to interpret what he hears as reflecting his own point of view. The social psychologist Gardner Murphy has said:[26] "We pick out what is related to our needs, and give it emphasis . . . we hear what is important for us, what fits into our needs." This psychological fact makes it doubly important to maintain objectivity in listening. Wait until a speaker has developed an idea, before you judge its value. There is educational value in this, as Nichols and Stevens tell us:[27]

Withhold evaluation. *This is one of the most important principles of learning, especially learning through the ear. It requires self-control, sometimes more than many of us can muster, but with persistent practice it can often be turned into a valuable habit. While listening, the main object is to comprehend each point made by the talker. Judgments and decisions should be reserved until after the talker has finished. At that time, and only then, review his main ideas and make your assessment of them.*

The advice to withhold evaluation of a speech is easy to give but hard to carry out. You should try, however. Become aware of your biases before listening to a speaker; accept momentarily, at least, the legitimacy of his viewpoint; then try to discover the reasons he believes as he does. Perhaps you will discover some facts and inferences which you, too, can accept.

You should also try to be objective about the way in which the speaker makes his presentation. Almost every speaker has some peculiar mannerisms in his presentation: constant pacing back and forth on the platform—typical of some teachers—poor eye contact, constant adjusting of clothing, and repetition of meaningless phrases, such as "You see," "Let me make this clear," and "Well, anyway." It is only natural for a listener to divert his attention, at least occasionally, from what the speaker is saying to these distracting mannerisms. The more speech training you receive, the more flaws you will find in a speaker's delivery.

Many speakers have distracting mannerisms, but to gain anything from their message you must go beyond the barrier of relatively poor delivery and flaws of expression to the real content, to what they are saying.

Emotional Control

In Chapter Five we indicated that human beings often act in an emotional manner. The stimulus to emotional listening may be a word, phrase, sentence, or longer statement that contradicts some cherished belief, attitude, or value we hold. The listener at once becomes mentally incapable of hearing, and even less comprehending of what is being said. Some of the following words may be laden with emotion for you: *kike, fuzz, Black, Establishment, tax-collector, nigger, up yours, the Man, yeah, man, crap, Hippie, Jesus Christ Superstar, dove, hawk, homosexual, pervert,* and names of such people as Ronald Reagan, Spiro Agnew, and George Wallace.

At times your emotionality comes from sources other than the language used, but they still blur the ability and willingness to listen. You may have come to a meeting because your wife insisted on it; friends may have prevailed upon you to attend; you may think you should be seen at the meeting. In each case you are a captive auditor, and you resent it. Perhaps the occasion is distasteful: you may dislike huge gatherings, feel an aversion to after-dinner speaking, or lack the stamina to sit through several talks. Maybe you paid to attend the meeting and are sure that the speech will not give value received. Sometimes your reactions may be something like: "Why doesn't someone keep that kid quiet?" and "A fine thing, a travel talk and the projector doesn't work!" and your willingness and ability to listen are lessened because of your irritation. Emotions that get in the way of effective listening are like filters that interfere with reception.

The skillful listener, however, does not permit his emotions to divert him from his real purpose in listening. Rather, he seeks to eliminate or reduce physical barriers to effective listening by keeping his own attitudes and beliefs under control as he listens. Moreover, he tries to discern the denotation of the speaker's words rather than let himself be influenced unduly by their connotations, and he accepts his presence at the meeting willingly, even though he may be a captive listener.

The Thought-to-Speech Ratio

Another aspect of control in listening has to do with a rate differential between thought and speech. It is estimated that the typical lecture is given at 100 to 125 words per minute, whereas speed in thinking is at least four or five times faster.[28] In other words, the speaker needs five times more time to talk than the listener needs to think about what is being said. In effect, this gives the listener a lot of free time, which he can use either profitably or unprofitably. The poor listener usually wastes this time by going off on all sorts of mental tangents unrelated to the speaker's topic. A good listener tries to use this time constructively. Weaver and Ness make the following suggestions for constructive listening practice:[29]

The good listener talks to himself in amplification and support of what he hears and thus extends and enriches the meanings.

Specifically, here are some questions a listener can mull over in his mind as he "waits for" the speaker to get on with his next idea:

1. *What have been the speaker's main points up to now?*
2. *How does the idea he is elaborating at this point fit in with the previous idea?*
3. *Where will he go next? What might his next main idea be?*
4. *Is the statement he just made a matter of fact or of opinion?*
5. *Are the speaker's personal prejudices creeping into his speech at this point?*
6. *What is the relationship of this specific statement to the main purpose or theme of the speech? Is this an item of proof? Or an elaboration and amplification only?*
7. *How does what I am hearing fit in with what I heard about the same subject three nights ago?*

To these we add the following:

8. What conclusions will he draw from his statements?
9. What meaning is he trying to convey but not putting into words?
10. Do his ideas conform to the reality of the situation as I perceive it?

Proper Perspective

To say that listening should be in proper perspective means that the listener should try to relate what is said to his purpose in listening. He knows that listening is not a simple task and therefore tries to comprehend the significant aspects of the message received. He does not oversimplify; neither does he become bewildered if the message is complex. He recognizes the validity of different frames of reference and adjusts his interpretation and evaluation of what he hears accordingly.

The effective listener also tries to relate what is being said to the specific occasion and to the speaker's purpose and its relation to the occasion. He regards the occasion as a meaningful event from which he seeks to profit. He puts aside unrelated personal problems but recalls related personal experiences that amplify or add meaning to the speaker's message. He considers what the speaker says more than whom or what he represents.

The Speaker

Obviously the speaker cannot control conditions that are completely personal to the listener, such as his hearing acuity, motivation, and level of listening skill; however, he can anticipate and adjust to these factors to the extent that he knows or is able to conjecture about them. In addition, certain things within the control of the speaker himself will contribute to more effective listening by the members of an audience.

Adjusting to the Physical Situation

First, effective listening occurs when the physical conditions are conducive to listening. The position of the speaker's stand, the size of the audience and auditorium, physical distractions, and the physical comfort of the hearers are factors that a speaker can adjust to, modify, and sometimes completely control.

The speaker obviously can control his own audibility. When a public-address system is being used, he should always test it before speaking. When there is no amplifying system, he must judge his listeners' reactions by the many cues they give him. Although he cannot know his listeners' susceptibility to distractions, it may be indicated by their behavior. The alert speaker, when possible, makes adjustments in vocal force, rate, timing, position on the platform, and even content, in order to improve his listeners' comprehension.

Creating a Favorable Impression

Effective listening is most likely to occur when the speaker's general effect on the listener is positive. Nichols found that listening comprehension is improved when the hearer sees the speaker as generally effective, when there is admiration for him, and when the listener is emotionally adjusted to the subject.[30] Thus, whatever the speaker can do to create a favorable impression before he begins will enhance the listener's readiness to listen.

The favorable impression you create will result partly from your physical appearance, partly from psychological factors, such as identification with the audience, and partly from what the person introducing you says about you.

Content and Organization

Effective listening may occur when the speech content makes a positive impression on the listener. Listeners are impressed positively when the opening, organization, supporting materials, and closing of a speech contribute to an accepted identification of the speaker with the audience, an immediate understanding of the plan for the speech, a reasoned approval of the content, a perception of the speaker's proposal as contributing to the listeners' needs and values, and a willing commitment to the proposed action. In other words, careful preparation for every speaking situation will contribute to improved listening comprehension.

Adjusting to Feedback

A final way in which the speaker can contribute to more effective listening by the audience members is to adjust immediately to the feedback he gets from them. Skill in doing this comes with practice, but even the student can recognize the meaning of some overt audience reactions. Favorable reaction and undivided attention are easily recognized; the speaker may safely continue in the same vein. Inattention and disinterest usually are easily spotted; the speaker then needs to choose from a variety of techniques at his command to regain attention: silence, repetition, the use of visual aids, appropriate humor, some form of audience participation, modification of mode of delivery, or attention-getting physical action, to mention a few.

An anticipation of possible audience inattention will help you to plan preventives or countermeasures; practice makes perfect.

IMPLICATIONS

We present below two lists of implications, one for the listener and one for the speaker. They are in the form of suggestions that can be implemented in every communication situation. Do not consider them definitive rules to be followed in detail but, rather, a collection of useful listening patterns.

For the Listener

1. Throughout your study of speech consider the following:
   a. Recognize that speech communication is a transaction and that you have a responsibility for its success.
   b. Keep in mind the large amount of time you spend in listening; plan to spend time listening to a speech profitably.
   c. Think about the time you will spend listening in your job after graduation. Plan now to use that time profitably.
   d. Analyze, with the help of your instructor, your own listening skills and faults. Initiate a training program for improvement.
   e. By better listening on your part, try to improve the interpersonal relations in the groups in which you participate.
   f. Recognize and act on the knowledge that an improvement in your listening skill may improve your reading ability.
   g. Sensitize yourself to the fact that listening is more than hearing. Remember, to be heard does not mean that you are understood.
   h. Practice whenever you can the four types of listening: appreciative, therapeutic, critical, and informative.
   i. Recognize that breakdowns in communication may result from structural and functional anomalies in the speech and hearing mechanisms, from channel interferences and malfunctions, and from physical factors related to the speaking room. Do whatever you can to mitigate the seriousness of these breakdowns.
2. Before hearing a speech do the following:

    a. Make a listener's prespeech analysis of the speaking situation.

    b. Try to increase your personal motivation for listening.

    c. Establish firmly in mind your purpose for listening. Find some purpose, if none seems evident.

    d. To the extent circumstances permit, learn as much as possible about the subject.

    e. To the extent circumstances permit, learn as much as possible about the speaker.

    f. Set up standards for judging the speaker's content and delivery. Select standards that conform more to artistic and intellectual levels than to personal bias. Do not make these standards impossible to achieve.

    g. Try to be physically and emotionally fit for listening.

    h. Arrange personal schedules to permit arrival at the meeting place before a speech starts.

    i. Try to arrange the physical conditions so that effective listening is possible.

    j. Do not judge the speaker for any reason before you have heard him.

    k. Think of yourself as a partner in the communication transaction, and try to assume your fair share of the responsibility for effective communication.

    l. Determine in advance the values you want from listening: information, therapeutic help, esthetic enjoyment, or critical understanding. Plan your listening strategies accordingly.

    m. Determine in advance what listening breakdowns might be the direct result of some fault within yourself. Plan to minimize the listening loss that might result.

3. While hearing the speech do the following:

    a. Determine, as soon as possible, the purpose of the speech.

    b. Relate the purpose of the speech to your experience.

    c. Seek to discover main points and their relationships.

    d. Analyze supporting evidence and reasoning. Test their validity.

    e. Test the adequacy of the supporting material in proving the assertions made.

    f. Relate what the speaker says to other known information on the same topic. Consider the reasons for inconsistencies.

    g. Avoid emotional reactions to the speech; maintain objectivity.

    h. Try to determine any assumptions that are being made.

    i. Do not let attention wander; avoid distractions and try not to create any.

    j. Watch the speaker. Get as much meaning as possible from facial expression, gestures, and physical action.

    k. Frequently summarize what is being said as a means of reinforcing the ideas presented; check the speaker's summaries to see whether they are accurate or distort what has been said.

    l. Cooperate with the speaker by overt action; show indication of approval.

    m. If the speaker does not talk loudly enough, tell him so.

    n. Be close enough to the podium to hear well.

    o. Ask the ushers to try to eliminate distracting noises.

    p. Take needed notes on what is being said. Try to be unobtrusive in your note taking.

    q. Try to make value judgments of the speech and speaker on an objective, rather than subjective, basis.

r. Utilize the advantage of the thought-speech ratio.
4. After hearing a speech do the following:
   a. Express appreciation to the speaker. This is a part of the sharing experience.
   b. Ask questions, to clear up uncertain points.
   c. Review any notes you may have been taking as soon as possible.
   d. Discuss the speech with friends; try to crystallize its implications.
   e. Read other material relating to the same topic. Synthesize accumulated information for greater personal understanding.
   f. Relate what has been said to the purpose in listening.
   g. Use the speech as a step for other goals.

For the Speaker
1. Before giving a speech do the following:
   a. Plan the organization of your speech, the supporting materials, and the language, so it will be easy for the audience to listen and so they will want to listen.
   b. Consider all possible factors that might interfere with effective listening. Remove or mitigate as many as you can.
   c. If a public-address system is to be used, check in advance to see whether it is in working order.
   d. If a public-address system is not to be used, check in advance to determine how loudly you must speak to be heard in the far corners of the room.
2. While giving the speech do the following:
   a. If you have not had the opportunity to examine the speaking room in advance, make whatever adjustments you feel will aid listening.
   b. Check occasionally to be sure you can be heard. Watch for feedback, or ask the audience directly, "Can you hear me?" Talk louder if necessary.
   c. Check for feedback showing inattention. Take whatever steps you can to overcome it. If the audience is fatigued, cut your speech if need be.
3. After giving the speech do the following:
   a. If it is possible, do not leave immediately, so that members of the audience may ask you questions.
   b. Make an analysis of how well you accomplished your goal, including how effective you feel the listening was.

EXERCISES
1. Keep an account of the time you spend in listening and speaking during the period of a week. How do the percentages compare with those given in this chapter? Can you suggest types of work or activity in which a person would have to listen more than the average amount of time?
2. If your instructor gives all the members of your class a listening-comprehension test, be sure to discuss the results with your instructor and plan a remedial program if that is necessary.
3. Consider the members of the group with which you associate. Are there some who are shy, talk little, lack aggressiveness? Try to draw them out by questions and by listening. Do this over a period of weeks. Have you helped their relations with the total group?

4. Make a list of physical distractions to listening. Which ones can the speaker do something about? Which ones can the listener do something about? What are the physical distractions to effective listening?

5. What types of emotional factors affect your listening? In what ways have you prejudged speakers? In your next few listening experiences try to avoid these prejudgments.

6. Select and read three or four of the additional readings given at the end of this chapter. Pay particular attention to what is said about the nature of the listening process. Then prepare your own definition of listening. Compare it with the definitions of other members of your class. How do they differ? Why?

7. Make an educated estimate of how much you get from listening to your instructors lecture in other classes. Over a period of weeks try to apply some of the suggestions for effective listening given in this chapter. Does your listening in those classes improve? Do you get more out of the lectures?

8. Make an analysis of the next discussion in which you participate by answering these questions about it:
   a. In what ways do good and poor listeners differ?
   b. What are some specific evidences of effective listening?
   c. Note any emotional blocks to effective listening. What are they?
   d. In what ways do the good listeners adjust for even better listening?
   e. What evidence do you find of objectivity in listening?
   f. Are there any indications that members of the group themselves create listening distractions? What are these distractions?

9. Try to attend at least one campus lecture a week for four weeks. Keep a content record of the speeches. Make an analysis of your reactions to the speeches, based on the following questions.
   a. Were the lectures profitable as a learning experience? If not, was it because of the way in which you listened?
   b. Did the lectures stimulate your interest in this type of extracurricular activity? If not, why not?
   c. Have you followed up on the topic of any of the lectures by related readings, discussions with friends, special alertness to related newspaper stories, or attendance at other public lectures on the same topics?

10. Make a list of events, such as lectures, sermons, newscasts or programs on radio and television, dramatic performances, and student or student-faculty meetings, to which you listen regularly. Is the pattern of listening easy or difficult? What events would you add to the list to get practice in more difficult listening?

11. Pick some listening event that you can attend for enjoyment and relaxation only. Report to the class on the pattern of your listening. What were the enjoyable features of the event?

12. Select another listening event, and make the same sort of listening analysis after you have attended. How did the listening pattern differ from that reported in Exercise 11?

13. What are your usual motives in listening? Do they contribute to effective listening? Prepare a four-minute speech in which you comment on the things that motivate you to listen.

14. Attend a public lecture and pay particular attention to the listening habits of

those around you. Secure a seat at one side of the meeting-hall in order to do this. How can the listeners be classified? What overt actions do you note? How does the speaker react to such actions? If you know some of the members of the audience, can you establish a relationship between what they do and their known interests and attitudes about the speech purpose?

15. Think of some communication situation in which listening seemed to be completely ineffective—the speaker could not be heard, outside noises interfered, or the audience was inattentive. Analyze the situation to determine what caused the ineffective listening. Make a report to the class on your findings. What could have been done to improve the situation?

ADDITIONAL READINGS

Barbara, Dominick A., *The Art of Listening*, Springfield, Ill., C. C. Thomas, 1958, chaps. 1, 3, 4, 5, 7.

Briggs, Bernice Prince, "Testing listening effectiveness," *Speech Monographs*, 23 (no. 1, Mar. 1956), 9–13.

Dow, Clyde W., "Integrating the teaching of reading and listening comprehension," *J. Commun.*, 8 (no. 3, Autumn 1958), 118–126.

Duker, Sam, "In an age of communication, are we listening?", *Educ. Forum*, 18 (May 1954), 405–409.

Duker, Sam, ed., *Listening: Readings*, New York, Scarecrow, 1966.

Education, 75 (Jan. 1955). The entire issue is devoted to listening.

Irvin, Charles E., "Motivation in listening training," *J. Commun.*, 4 (no. 2, Summer 1954), 42–44.

Johnson, Wendell, *Your Most Enchanted Listener*, New York, Harper & Row, 1956.

Keller, Paul W., "Major findings in listening in the past ten years," *J. Commun.*, 10 (no. 1, Mar. 1960), 29–38.

Nichols, Ralph G., and Leonard A. Stevens, *Are You Listening?* New York, McGraw-Hill, 1957. 1957.

Nichols, Ralph G., and Thomas R. Lewis, *Listening and Speaking*, Dubuque, Brown, 1954, chaps. 1, 2, 4, 6.

Nichols, Ralph G., "Do we know how to listen? Practical helps in a modern age," *Speech Teacher*, 10 (no. 2, Mar. 1961), 118–124.

Robinson, Karl F., and E. J. Kerikas, *Teaching Speech: Methods and Materials*, New York, McKay, 1963, chap. 13.

Stevens, Walter W., "How well do you listen?" *Adult Educ.*, 12 (no. 1, Autumn 1961), 42–46.

NOTES

[1]Paul T. Rankin, "The importance of listening ability," *English J.*, 17 (Oct. 1928), 623–630.

[2]Reported by V. O. Key, Jr., "Media: Specter and reality," in Howard H. Martin and Kenneth E. Andersen, eds., *Speech Communication: Analysis and Readings*, Boston, Allyn & Bacon, 1968, pp. 108–109.

[3]Ewing T. Webb and John B. Morgan, *Strategy in Handling People*, Garden City, N.Y., Garden City Publishing, 1930, p. 92.

[4]See Norman R. F. Maier, *Principles of Human Relations*, New York, Wiley, 1952; Carl A. Rogers, *Client-Centered Therapy*, Boston, Houghton Mifflin, 1951; and Donald A. Laird and Eleanor C. Laird, *The Technique of Handling People*, New York, McGraw-Hill, 1954.

[5]Dominick A. Barbara, *The Art of Listening*, Springfield, Ill., C. C. Thomas, 1958, p. 191.

[6]Charles R. Petrie, Jr., "What is listening?" in Sam Duker, ed., *Listening: Readings*, New York, Scarecrow, 1966, p. 330.

[7]Duker, *Ibid.*, pp. 122, 197, 244, 345.

[8]Ralph G. Nichols and Thomas R. Lewis, *Listening and Speaking*, Dubuque, Ia., Brown, 1954, p. 1.

[9]See Petrie, *op. cit.*, p. 326.

[10]*Ibid.*, p. 329.

[11]Barbara, *op. cit.*, p. 59.

[12]Seth A. Fessenden, "Levels of listening—A theory," in Duker, *op. cit.*, pp. 28–33.

[13]Nichols and Lewis, *op. cit.*, pp. 6–7.

[14]Irvin J. Lee, *How to Talk With People*, New York, Harper & Row, 1952. p. x.

[15]Harold E. Jones, "Experimental studies of college teaching," *Archives of Psychology*, Columbia Univ., November, 1923, p. 62.

[16]Nichols and Lewis, *op. cit.*, p. 4.

[17]Colin Cherry, *On Human Communication*, New York, Wiley, 1957, pp. 158–159.

[18]Nichols and Lewis *op. cit.*, pp. 68–69. The authors have listed only the values cited; the explanations given have been excluded.

[19]Jurgen Ruesch, *Therapeutic Communication*, New York, Norton, 1961, p. 128.

[20]Wendell Johnson, *People in Quandaries*, New York, Harper & Row, 1946, p. 395.

[21]Ralph G. Nichols and Leonard A. Stevens, *Are You Listening?*, New York, McGraw-Hill, 1957, p. 32.

[22]*Human Communication and Its Disorders—An Overview*, a report prepared and published by the Subcommittee on Human Communication and Its Disorders, of the National Advisory Neurological Diseases and Stroke Council, under a grant from the U.S. Department of Health, Education and Welfare, Bethesda, Md., 1969, p. 13.

[23]Charles E. Irvin, "Motivation in listening training," *J. Commun.*, 4 (no. 2, Summer 1954), 42–44.

[24]Barbara, *op. cit.*, p. 95.

[25]Nichols and Lewis, *op. cit.*, p. 12.

[26]Gardner Murphy, *An Introduction to Psychology*, New York, Harper & Row, 1951, p. 189.

[27]Nichols and Stevens, *op. cit.*, pp. 102–103.

[28]Ralph G. Nichols, "Listening instruction in the secondary school," *Bull. Nat. Assoc. Secondary School Principals*, Department of Secondary School Administration of the National Education Association, 36 (May 1952), p. 169.

[29]Andrew Thomas Weaver and Ordean Gerhard Ness, *The Fundamentals and Forms of Speech*, New York, Odyssey, 1957, p. 97.

[30]Ralph G. Nichols, "Factors in listening comprehension," *Speech Monographs*, 15 (no. 2, 1948), p. 162.

PREPARING FOR THE COMMUNICATIVE SITUATION

It is somewhat difficult for us to attempt to separate *understanding* the communicative situation from *preparing* for the communicative act, for obviously one is interrelated with the other. Separating them serves a purpose, however, in enabling us first to consider a number of principles as background, as we did in Part One, and then, having digested them, to build upon them in preparation for a specific speech act, as we shall now do in Part Two.

We move, then, in this section to chapters specifically designed for those who are now preparing for oral discourse, whether it be for class or some other audience. Some of the principles identified and explained here are also applicable in the one-to-one or small-group situation, although traditionally they have been created and organized for the public speaker. Much of what is said here will be designed for this traditional purpose, for the speaker must make a creditable showing before his audience. This does not mean, however, that when he steps off the platform into the small group or is in an interview he necessarily stops using these principles. That which identifies "the good man speaking well" also identifies the effective man or woman in a position of leadership anywhere.

Having generated an understanding of certain basics, such as the individual's relationship to communication and society, the purpose of speech communication, and the nature of the communicative transaction, including how one handles himself in order to motivate someone else, we should be ready to take these principles and see how they work in terms of specific speakers, specific topics, and specific audiences.

It is suggested, then, that the student, as he proceeds through Part Two, read with a view to these specifics, continually asking himself,

"How do they apply to me, my message, and my respondent?" If the student can achieve this state of mind, the principles previously digested will begin to be seen as dynamic constructs which, in operation, take on real meaning and elicit real effect.

CHAPTER NINE

ANALYZING THE AUDIENCE AND OCCASION

Aristotle believed, and practically all writers since his time have concurred, that the audience determines the speech's end and object. In other words, the important aspect of the speech situation is the speaker-audience relationship. . . .

Consequently, to know and evaluate the outcome of a speech necessitates knowing as much as can be determined about each of the constituents of the speech situation. So canons of oratorical criticism cannot properly be divorced from considerations relating to speaker, audience, subject, and occasion. These are indispensable to critical inquiry.

Thonssen and Baird

This chapter deals with one of the first, and perhaps most important, steps in speech preparation, namely, the gathering and analyzing of essential knowledge about the audience, occasion, and setting. Such an analysis will help the speaker determine his exact speech purpose, aid in the selection of supporting materials, and guide him in the choice of language and delivery to be used. As a corollary to this it will also help to ensure the speaker against failure resulting from inadequate preparation, unforeseen contingencies, inappropriateness of substantive content, inadvertent slips of the tongue, and difficulties in making on-the-spot adaptations. We also include in prespeech analysis the speaker's view of himself as he faces the prospect of appearing before an audience. Emphasis is placed on understanding and controlling stage fright.

THE IMPORTANCE OF PRESPEECH ANALYSIS
In this book we have thus far directed our attention primarily to the individual in the speech communication situation. We have stressed that you—and every other individual—are a part of many communication networks in which the success of your goal seeking depends on your communication skills. We have indicated the role you can play in

influencing society through communication. We have outlined the nature of speech purposes and the process of speech communication, and we have considered what motivates the individual and how he acts, listens, and uses language for effective communication. We have repeatedly talked about how the intimate relationship must be maintained between speaker and respondent for communication to be effective.

Throughout this first section we have stressed the transactional nature of speech communication and the importance of the listeners and the speech occasion in which they are participating as starting points for good speech preparation. In this chapter we consider what you should try to find out about your audience and give some suggestions about securing this information.

The importance of prespeech analysis for the speaker is fourfold. All the reasons that we study an audience before speaking are essentially pragmatic, but we like to refine this broad statement and suggest that the values of prespeech analysis are practical, predictive, associative, and evaluative.

Prespeech analysis has a *practical* value. It provides an inventory of where the audience is at any given time: what they know about the subject, purpose, and speaker; what their attitudes and needs are (how they can be motivated); what their educational, cultural, and vocational backgrounds are; and something about their ages, sex, travel experience, and avocations. Obviously, you will also be concerned about the nature of the occasion and the speech setting. For the speaker this information establishes the data that are needed to take his next steps. Prespeech analysis for the speaker serves somewhat as does a benchmark for the surveyer: a mark or symbol of some fixed and permanent landmark that has a known position and altitude and can therefore be used in determining other altitudes, distances, and angles. Once the speaker's "benchmark" has been determined, he can then move on to the necessary steps in rhetorical preparation and presentation. The pragmatic value of prespeech analysis is clear. The writers of a popular speech text put it as follows.[1]

Since practical effect is the chief measure of success in speaking, your degree of achievement will depend heavily on your understanding of how men and women listen and respond. And in that fact lies a problem. It is not easy to regulate one's speech making according to the dictates of what is known about the listeners. . . . Just as you prefer your own ways of thinking about any question, every other person—every listener—prefers his way. Therefore, if the speaker is to reach the minds of listeners, he must forget himself enough to fit his thought to their preferences, understandings, and interests.

The value of prespeech analysis is that it tells the speaker something about the preferences, understandings, and interests of the listeners.

The *predictive* value of preparation lies in knowing as much as you can about your listeners. Knowing that an individual is a Democrat or a Republican will tell you much about how he will act on certain issues. Knowing that an audience is composed mainly of youth or of senior citizens will again give some indication of possible future action. But these are gross differences and may reflect gross polar differences in action. Much of what you will learn—or should try to learn—about an audience is subtler in nature and calls for a more delicate handling of rhetorical devices and materials. Whether the audience has conservative, neutral, or liberal attitudes, the nature of their prejudices, the reference groups that reflect their actions, their degree of participation in public affairs, and other data besides are sometimes hard to determine; but they aid in predicting the extent to which an audience will respond favorably to your message.

The *associative* value of prespeech analysis lies in the knowledge the speaker gains of his audience, which increases the number of connections among the partners in the transaction. Psychologically, it creates within the speaker an urge to communicate effectively. No speaker makes an effort to fail; some degree of success is always the goal. The more you know about your listeners, the more you will be compelled to be effective. Your associational bonds with your listeners have been increased in number and strengthened by what you have learned about them.

Finally, knowledge of an audience has *evaluative* benefits. If you assess your success in a given speech after it is over—and you always should—then your prespeech analysis will serve as a set of criteria by which to measure your success. Did you make effective use of local illustrations? Did you identify yourself with the audience? Did your motive appeals touch the interests and needs of the listeners? Did you move the listeners part of the way toward the acceptance of your proposal; These are the sorts of question you should ask yourself, and they can be answered more surely if you know something about the audience before you start speaking.

THE NATURE OF PRESPEECH ANALYSIS

In our introduction to Chapter Five we quoted George Campbell, one of the most important rhetoricians since the classical period: "The hearers must be considered in a two-fold view, as men in general, and as men in particular." In every speaking situation the speech must be tailored to a specific audience. A modern rhetorician stresses the need for and nature of audience analysis as follows:[2]

> . . . the speech-maker must compose his speech from the available potentials in his audience. He aims to link his propositions to their value systems, and the value systems differ with age, sex, educational development, economic class, social strata, political heritage, specialized interest, and so on. The speaker is a selector. He must exclude certain arguments and include others. . . . All this is determined by the audience for which the speech is designed.

In his prespeech analysis the speaker must study all facets of the audience he plans to address. As Campbell said, all audiences have certain general characteristics, but at the same time each one is a specific group, unique and different from every other audience: the Black Panthers, the League of United Latin American Citizens, the NAACP, Mexican-American Policy Association, the Student Nonviolent Coordinating Committee, and the El Modeno Community Center of Orange, California, are all organizations of minority groups. They have much in common, but the same speech could hardly be given to each group. The legislatures of the states of Nevada, Alaska, California, Alabama, New Jersey, and Ohio have many common interests in problems of taxation, minority group needs and demands, and budgets; but each legislature is unique in makeup, represents constituencies with widely differing characteristics, and differs in its approaches to its state's problems. Audiences are composed of individuals who have met together at a specific time, in a real place, to listen to a particular speech, and this should have some effect on their knowledge, beliefs, or perhaps future actions. The essence of prespeech analysis is to obtain facts related to the common and diverse experiences and characteristics of the particular audience, those which determine its attitudes toward the subject and the speaker's purpose.

Take a look at the composition of the following three audiences.

The Lions Club in a Midwestern city of 6500 persons is composed of 62 members, representing 45 different vocational interests, 10 religious groups, an age range of 35 years with an average of 35, somewhat similar educational backgrounds, a medium income level, and similar cultural and social interests. The club supports many local welfare projects, it promotes in every way possible all the activities of the city high schools and the nearby university, it participates, almost to a man, in certain types of hunting and fishing, and its civic pride knows few bounds. Although there are seven other luncheon clubs in the city, that of The Lions Club is the oldest and believes itself to be the best. Its longevity in the state Lions organization has enabled it to place many of its local members in state offices and a few in national offices. It has thus wielded some influence in policy making in the Lions International. The speaker addressing this audience should know these facts and other information about the club and its individual members, the club's current projects, and other information that might reveal its relations to the particular speech topic.

A group of young and middle aged people is meeting to consider rezoning—for the purpose of developing a community recreation facility—a large parcel of land near the newly developed tract in which the group lives. These facts are known about the group by the speaker who will speak in favor of rezoning:

1. The range in age is from 28-55, with one family over 64.
2. About 40 persons will be attending the meeting.
3. The members of the audience all live in relatively new homes in a tract where house prices range from $38,000 to $54,000.
4. Almost every family has one or more children, and several have five.

These facts are not known but should be discovered, if at all possible:

1. Whether this group is meeting for the first time or has met periodically.
2. Whether it has previously taken action relative to recreational projects.
3. Whether it holds common interests and convictions about the need for recreational facilities, zoning, cultural activities, or community beautification.
4. Whether it is well informed or only partially informed on the question of the need for a recreational area. Whether it has committees working on costs, tax liabilities, traffic problems, possible rezoning of nearby areas for commercial purposes, and so on.
5. Whether there are deeply held convictions about the need for the proposed recreational area.
6. What it would cost for the children of the families in the area to use the facilities.
7. Whether there are only a few active leaders in the group or whether leadership and concern about the problem are shared.
8. Whether the audience represents majority or minority inter-

ests in the community with respect to political beliefs, racial and religious attachments, and vocational pursuits.

9. Whether the attitudes about possible action are firm or weak.

10. Whether the County Land Planning Commission has contemplated, or committed itself to, other uses for the area.

Knowledge on all of these points would aid any speaker who talked before this group on some phase of community recreation.

A male Mexican-American student who is enrolled at a Community College of about 15,000 students in a city with a population of about 140,000 has been asked to talk to a local group of the League of Women Voters on the topic "The Mexican-American student in a bilingual world." The student knows these facts:

1. The audience will be composed of young and middle-aged women.
2. They are keenly interested in any problems that have educational, legislative, and community-wide implications.
3. The group has a leaning more toward liberal views than toward conservative.
4. The group is extremely aggressive in bringing before the total community the problems of civic interest.
5. They will be friendly to the speaker.
6. They view him as knowing the viewpoint of the Mexican-Americans and understand that he is the chairman of the local unit of the League of United Latin American Citizens.
7. The meeting at which he is to speak is a luncheon; his talk will be limited to 25 minutes.

He does not have information on these points:

1. Whether this unit of the League of Women Voters really understands the cultural and educational problems faced by Mexican-American children growing up in a predominantly Anglo culture.
2. Whether the group has any members that are Mexican-American.
3. Whether they would be willing to support programs designed to deal with such problems as drop-outs, to add a course called, say, "English as a second language" to the school curriculum, and to encourage the involvement of other community groups in the general problem.

4. Whether the club is more interested at this time in other pressing civic problems.
5. How many of the members of the group have had some first-hand experiences with Mexican-Americans, spent some time in a *barrio* area, speak Spanish, been in a Mexican-American home, participated in the activities of the eight Mexican-American community centers in the city, or participated in any discussions on these and related aspects of the problems of a Chicano student.
6. Whether the club has sufficient prestige and influence with the college school board and the city fathers to secure needed action, if any is called for.

About each of these audiences the speaker already has a varying amount of pertinent information. A member of The Lions Club speaking to his own group would know a great deal about the members and their interests; his needs for additional prespeech analysis would be minimal. In the second case, a speaker coming from outside the community would need to make a rather extensive analysis of the audience and occasion. In the third case, considerable information is already available. The student could probably get a lot of needed information from some college official such as the Dean of Special Services, from a member of the LWV, from one of the college speech-department teachers, or from some local Mexican-American businessman.

Whatever the speaking situation, probably no one will ever have *all* the information he needs in advance; further analysis will need to be made, and even then more information would be helpful. Of the rather detailed suggestions given in this chapter, therefore, not all will apply to every audience.

ASPECTS OF AUDIENCE ANALYSIS

Audience analysis has four aspects: the relation of the audience to the speaker, the relation of the audience to the subject and purpose of the speech, the basic beliefs and attitudes held in common by the audience, and the common and divergent characteristics of the members of the audience.

Audience and Speaker

Rhetoricians since Aristotle have stressed the significance of the speaker-listener relationship. Most audiences are by nature friendly and will accord a speaker the right to be heard, but there are exceptions. The reactions to certain topics—for example, political speeches, appeals for funds, requests necessitating some change in personal behavior—may range from indifference to outright antipathy. We need to know in advance, therefore, the extent to which the listeners are likely to be objective, unprejudiced, or friendly toward us. The following questions should help to analyze the speaker-audience relationship:

1. Will the audience respect the speaker? Must he establish himself as an authority? Is he an authority?
2. Does the audience hold widely differing opinions of the speaker?
3. Does the audience view the speaker as knowing the nature of its problems and interests?
4. Does the audience view the speaker as closely allied with its interests? Opposed or indifferent toward its interests?
5. Is the speaker respected because of what he knows or accepted because of his status?
6. Has the speaker only recently identified himself with the audience, as when Mayor John Lindsay of New York City switched from the Republican to the Democratic party? What effect will this have on the speaker's message?
7. Has the audience heard the speaker talk on the same subject before? Many times?

If you know that your listeners hold a favorable image of you, your task in adaptation will be relatively easy. An Eagle Scout will find a pack of Cub Scouts a friendly audience. A person who has kicked the drug habit will find an attentive audience among some teen-age groups, especially in a school where drug use is commonplace. Jane Fonda would be well accepted by some college audiences. These speakers would not have the initial task of trying to win the audience to a friendly position, but each would have the task of maintaining the friendly relationship. The test of a speaker's ability to do this comes when he presents ideas that are not entirely acceptable or may be contrary to the prevailing beliefs of his listeners. In such cases a goodly measure of tact is needed, but in any case the speaker should stand by his convictions. The purpose of the search for speaker-listener common denominators is not to enable the speaker to be "all things to all people" but to try to reconcile his listeners to views that may be counter to those they already hold. Competent speakers do not hesitate to express opinions that do not agree with those held by their listeners or call for some sacrifice from them. Certainly this is true of great speakers like John Wesley, Winston Churchill, Mohandas Gandhi, John Kennedy, and Rev. Martin Luther King, Jr.

If your listeners view you as a person of prestige—as they view high governmental officials, the clergy, successful industrialists, and professional persons in general—their attitude will be at least respectful. Many people will have come to hear a distinguished person, to gain authoritative information, to receive inspiration, or perhaps to judge whether a reputation is deserved. Nevertheless, even though they are favorably disposed, they will expect to hear a well-informed, convincing speaker.

Some people withhold judgment until they have heard a speaker: they will be friendly, but expect to evaluate critically the speaker's sincerity, reasoning, evidence, and apparent motivations. Some audiences are unfriendly, and then the speaker has a real challenge. Since the minds of such listeners are likely to be closed and unreceptive, his primary task will be to gain at least a fair hearing and earn their respect.

When an audience knows little of a speaker's background, it is usually necessary for him to establish his right to speak and to be viewed as an authority. Sometimes this is done for him by the person who introduces him. If not, the speaker must do it for himself, tactfully, by the force of his reasoning, the weight of his evidence, his depth of knowledge, and the conviction with which he speaks. Any speaker viewed as a member of an "out group" must first of all establish bonds of common experience and interest. A person's right to speak can sometimes be established by the quality of his speaking. At other times, as illustrated in the following excerpt from a speech before the House Committee on Interstate and Foreign Commerce, a speaker may find it necessary to state his qualifications at the outset:[3]

Mr. Chairman, my name is Robert J. McEwen. I am an associate professor of economics and chairman of the department in the university at Boston College. In addition, I am the chairman of the advisory consumer council to the attorney general of Massachusetts, the Honorable Edward J. McCormack, Jr. For the record, the membership of this advisory council is as follows: Mr. John Cort, Newspaper Guild; Dr. Virginia Galbraith, Mount Holyoke College; Prof. Phillip Gamble, University of Massachusetts; . . . Prof. Colston Warne, Amherst College. I may say that our position on the question of fair trade is a unanimous one.

I myself have specialized in teaching courses in social responsibilities of business, in socioeconomic teaching of the churches, and in business ethics. On the subject of fair trade legislation, I have been doing research and writing for the past years.

It is not always easy to determine how an audience will react to you as a speaker. As you give more speeches, you will learn more about how to make an audience accept you. At the outset of your speaking career much of the information you need about effective speaker-audience relationships must come from a self-analysis of your own rhetorical skills and personal ethos and from what you know and can learn about the speaking situation. You may be assured of an audience "willing" to listen if you appear sincere, understand the subject, can identify with the audience, and conform reasonably well to the audience's expectations of manner, delivery, and audience relationships. Other suggestions for securing helpful information are given in the last section of this chapter.

Audience and Speech Subject

Information about listeners' knowledge of the speech subject and their attitudes toward the speech purpose is of value to the speaker. The following questions focus on this matter:

1. Will the listeners be specialists in the subject, be partially informed, or have little or no knowledge of it?
2. Are they actively interested in learning more about the subject?
3. Will the text of the speech be available for later study by members of the audience? Will the speech be reported in news releases? Reprinted in other publications?
4. Has the audience heard the same or other speakers talk on this same topic?
5. Has the topic of the speech been acted upon in any way by the audience recently?

Obviously no audience is ever completely homogeneous in its knowledge about any subject, though many meetings—conferences on specialized topics such as arson detection, tax assessing, or prestressed concrete—are attended only by persons intensely interested in the subject matter and with some knowledge about it. In such cases you are assured of at least initial interest. This interest is apt to wane if your talk is either too elementary or too technical. However, the audience will give sustained consideration to a substantial, well-prepared, carefully documented and supported, understandable speech. But a technical presentation to uninformed hearers will encounter lack of understanding and waning interest. As a speaker, therefore, you must discover your listeners' approximate level of sophistication, and adapt your content and manner of presentation accordingly.

Audience and Speech Purpose

Both speaker and listener have some purpose in attending a speech occasion. The speaker's purpose often follows from his reputation or from the occasion. We expect a Fourth of July speaker to reinforce our concepts of freedom and independence. The general aim of a commencement address is sure to be inspiration and help in adjusting to the future. A pep rally whips up enthusiasm for some athletic event. Speakers on such occasions can safely assume that their listeners will be favorably disposed toward these purposes.

When a speech is listed in a printed program or included in an advance news story, the speech may be given a title. The speaker's specific goal is often obvious from such titles as these: "The Demise of Rural Medicine," "Toward a National Policy on Aging," "Ethical Consideration in Public Relations," and "The Nixon Doctrine: Divergencies, Digressions, Dodges, and Delays" or, as another viewer might respond, "The Nixon Doctrine: Development and Direction, but not Dependence." Other titles suggest the immediate purpose of the speaker with some degree of accuracy but not his viewpoint or exact boundaries, such as "Legal Services: Reform in the Seventies," "Business Leadership: The New Breed," "The Competitive System: To Work, To Preserve, To Protect," and "Public Employee Relations." In speaking on the topics indicated in some of the titles above, the speaker can safely assume also that his audience will be receptive, as, for example, "The Demise of Rural Medicine." In other instances, if the speaker is to change the attitudes of the audience, he must know all he can about his listeners. To give an acceptable speech on the competitive system, it would help the speaker to know the audience's political and vocational interests and affiliations and perhaps something about their ethnic characteristics and past job experiences. If speaking on public-employee relations, it would help him to have information on whether the audience represented largely management or labor, on state laws affecting employee strike restrictions, and on the results of recent attempts to secure pay increases for the employees.

Whether the speaker indicates his purpose in the title of his speech or it is obvious because of the occasion, it must always be definite in the speaker's mind. The following questions should prove helpful in deciding the speech purpose:

1. Will the listeners be generally favorable to the speaker's specific goal? Neutral? Opposed?
2. Are the opinions about the purpose deep-seated or superficial?
3. Do the opinions about purpose reflect individual points of view or group standards and beliefs?
4. Will the individual members of the audience be affected greatly by the norms of the listening group, if the speaker's proposal is accepted?
5. Will the audience be disposed to act, either immediately or later, on the speaker's proposals?

6. Is the audience in a position to act on the speaker's proposals?
7. What is the specific purpose of the speech as viewed by the listeners?
8. Does the purpose coincide with, or is it opposed to, general public opinion?

The listeners' attitudes toward the specific speech purpose can often be surmised from the nature of the expected audience. The special interests of certain groups suggest the kind of information and speech organization most in harmony with their needs: for example, scoutmasters, the board of directors of Dow Chemical or the Bank of America, the members of the Sigma Alpha Epsilon fraternity attending a summer convention at the Levere Memorial headquarters of the fraternity at Evanston, Illinois, the members of the United Farm Workers Organizing Committee meeting to consider the possibility of strike action against the grape growers in the San Joaquin Valley in California, the education committee of the Black Panthers, or a group of Black Muslims.

When possible the speaker should discover in advance the listeners' views toward his speech purpose. A favorable audience needs to have its views intensified, a neutral audience must be induced to move in the direction desired, and an unfavorable audience must first have its existing views weakened and then be moved gradually to an acceptance of the speech goal. If a speaker wants to make a proposal for action by his listeners, he should be aware of their capacity to act on it. Thus, a political speech early in a political campaign would have a different purpose from that on the eve of election day, a speech urging an increase in salaries of state employees would be developed differently if it were given before the state legislature or before a state employees' association. An orientation talk by a college official to a group of Upward Bound students entering college for the first time would have an entirely different purpose from that of an orientation talk to returning sophomores. The authority and disposition to act, the immediacy of needs, the estimated value placed on the proposal, and the commonality of interest in the audience vary from one situation to another and hence affect the speaker's selection of his speech purpose and content.

Audience Beliefs

In spite of our varied modes of living, certain fundamental beliefs are held in common by most Americans. In any given cultural, racial, or geographical group, one is likely to find certain behavior patterns and beliefs and customs. For example, bullfighting, considered a high art in

Spain and Mexico, is looked on with something akin to horror in many other countries. Women are held in high respect in most cultures, though in some they are still treated as chattel. One may pray to God, an ancestor, nature, Allah, or an animal, depending on where one lives; but at least most people pray to some symbol of higher authority. The rights of individuals are allegedly protected by law in most countries, but in totalitarian states the individual is useful only as long as he serves the state. In America we express our basic beliefs in such abstract phrases as "justice for all," "healthy economy," "the United States has the destiny to play a great role," "devotion to duty," "telling it as it is," "right will win out over wrong," "racial and economic justice," "brotherly love," and "peace for the generations to come." If a speaker is sincere and honest, lacking deceit in his use of these highly abstract and sometimes meaningless phrases, then we commend him in his appeals to the beliefs to which Americans at least give lip service. However, sometimes his phrases and the knowledge we have about a speaker reveal him as a charlatan, opportunist, agitator, or egotist.

By contrast, many great Americans have effectively and sincerely employed appeals to abstract and universally held beliefs. According to Horace G. Rahskopf, who made a study of the speaking of Clarence Darrow, Darrow's most frequent appeals were to "the common humanity of all men" and "man's love of liberty." Franklin D. Roosevelt, though a master in the use of specific illustrations, frequently employed appeals to such commonly held beliefs as human decency, self-preservation, security, equality of opportunity, and social justice. Great Black statesmen and leaders, such as Ralph Bunche, Edward W. Brooke, Rev. Martin Luther King, Jr., and Robert C. Weaver, have called for better race relations, equality of opportunity for Blacks, elimination of *de facto* segregation, nonviolence in race relations, and greater educational opportunities for all Blacks at all levels.[4]

Because of the serious nature of the problems of Blacks in America, because of the sincere desire on the part of white leaders to do something about these problems, and because of pressure, both nonviolent and violent, from many sources to speed up action on civil rights, desegregation, economic opportunity, and to lessen harassment of Blacks, many speeches by Whites have made broad appeals to human decency, social justice, and equal opportunity for all.[5]

An appeal on a broad scale was made by Ralph J. Bunche at a Lincoln's birthday dinner in Springfield, Illinois. His speech, "The International Significance of Human Relations," is an eloquent appeal for broad concepts of justice and brotherly love, a condemnation of bigotry, and a request for more applied democracy:[6]

For what is the situation? The relations among peoples are broadly characterized by dangerous animosities, hatreds, mutual recriminations, suspicions, bigotries, and intolerances. Man has made spectacular progress in science, in transportation and communication, in the arts, in all things material. Yet, it is a matter of colossal and tragic irony that man, in all his genius, having learned to harness nature, to control the relations among the elements and to mold them to his will—even to the point where he now has the means readily at hand for his own virtual self-destruction—has never yet learned how to live with himself; he has not mastered the art of human relations. In the realm of understanding the peoples of the world he remains shockingly illiterate. This has always been and today remains man's greatest challenge: how to teach the peoples of the world the elemental lesson of the essential kinship of mankind and man's identity of interest.

In a high school commencement address at East High School in Akron, Ohio, in 1950, E. J. Thomas, then president of the Goodyear Tire Company, appealed to broad beliefs concerning the value of individual freedom:[7]

The protection and preservation of these principles is not a new burden peculiar to tonight's graduating class. It is the quid pro quo *of the heritage of every American generation since Washington. It is the obligation placed upon you by the older generations who, themselves assuming obligations to the future, thus discharged their obligations to the past.*

Now please do not misunderstand my meaning. I am talking about the real substance of our way of life, the changeless principles of individual freedom and dignity. The forms which gave expression to these principles are not fixed, cannot be fixed, and should not be fixed. The forms are always subject to enlightened change and improvement—that is progress. Because we have held fast to the basic principles of personal freedom and dignity, while improving the forms of their application, the material and cultural advantages occurring to your generation are, on the whole, superior to those of past generations.

Although such broad appeals are usually effective with most large heterogeneous audiences, narrower appeals should be used whenever possible, focused directly upon the personal interests of individuals and small groups. Thus appeals may be made to the group loyalties of farmers, merchants, bankers, teachers, students, scientists, missionaries, union members, Blacks, Japanese, or Mexican-Americans. One might appeal to the common cultural heritage, language, living conditions, and difficulty in achieving human dignity in an Anglo society as reasons for working together on some beneficial project. Acceptance of the proposal made will not occur, however, when the speaker has no means of identification with his Mexican-American audience. If he does not speak the Spanish language, does not have a Spanish surname, has not associated with Mexican-Americans in their home *barrio* environment, and never has been identified with one of their action programs, his appeal will most very probably be unsuccessful. To appeal to group loyalties the speaker should be a member of the "in" group or at least be able to identify with it truly, not superficially.

In a speech delivered to the student body of Western Illinois University on June 3, 1971, Arvonne S. Fraser, chairman of the Washington, D.C., Chapter of Womens Equity Action League, made a realistic yet impassioned plea for the establishment of a new image for women. She said, in part:[8]

I come to Illinois tonight to talk about a very serious subject—one that all Americans are going to have to be concerned about—and one that will affect your lives profoundly. The subject is the new image of women in the United States.

. . . The new image of women is part of a social revolution that is shaking this country to the core. It is part of the technological revolution and what it means to society. It is part of the new quest for quality in life.

One can come to this new image of women in two ways: as an ideological view—on the idea that all men and women are created equal and it's about time we started acting like it—or one can come to the necessity for a new image of women on a functional basis—simply because society must change in order to function more efficiently.

I base my arguments both on ideology—on my beliefs—and on a pragmatic basis.

First, I see no reason for tolerating a society in which the white male minority runs everything—our universities, or businesses, our legal system, our military, our school systems, and our government. You name it . . . men run it.

So, I think we ought to change things. I believe in majority rule—and the majority of us in this country are not white male—53 per cent of us are female—a lot of us are black, red, or yellow.

The audience to which Mrs. Fraser was speaking was composed largely of students, a majority of whom were young women. They were likely to hold views similar to those of the speaker, and the speaker could safely assume that most young men nowadays treat their feminine school colleagues in the manner the speaker advised:[9] "So let me ask you to try a new experiment. The next young woman that comes to you—look at her with new eyes. Treat her first as a person, not as a young woman. For that, I think, is essentially what the new image of woman is: a person first, a woman second."

Audience Characteristics

Early in this chapter we indicated that the speaker's basic concern in prespeech analysis is to determine similarities and differences among his listeners. The more he knows about their common characteristics, the easier it will be for him to draw inferences about their opinions and attitudes. In fact, one writer says[10] that "systematic analysis of audience composition is a two-part process. First, you gather essential data about your audience; and second, you draw generalizations about the data that will affect your preparation."

The speaker must therefore seek information about those common characteristics which are the most influential determinants of belief and behavior. Selecting them is not a simple matter. Even among pollsters there is little agreement on which are the "significant" determinants of opinion. Berelson and Janowitz, writing on opinion formation,[11] say that "the field has yet to produce a rigorous investigation of the determinative influence of several factors upon opinion formation—personal characteristics, external events, communication content, personal associations, formal group membership—simultaneously and in combination, as they occur in reality." However many, varied, and complex the factors that determine beliefs and attitudes, we can be sure that they are in part affected by some combination of the following: income and occupation; geographic location; accepted stereotypes; broad social influence such as nationality, size of community, religion, racial stock, and group norms; and personal variables including sex, age, education, temperament, personal motivations, and feelings of adjustment.

In a later study Berelson and Steiner stated[12] that "at present, at least in the United States, differences in OAB's (opinions, attitudes, and beliefs) stem from three major and two minor ones. The major ones are residence, ethnic status, and class; the minor ones are age and sex."

Economic Status

Knowing something about the economic status of listeners will help in speech preparation. In speaking to a group of people in a ghetto area, a major objective might be merely to outline how to become eligible for food stamps and how to get them, or how to apply for some job-training program. The people in the Watts area in Los Angeles are concerned about lack of buses to get to and from work, the possibility of a small government loan to start or rebuild a business, or the need for available hospital and medical care. Persons of more moderate means might be more concerned with learning about insurance for their childrens' education, buying a home in a "respectable" neighborhood, or starting a nest egg of savings. People in higher income brackets would find matters of business prospects, the stock market, and financial security of primary interest. The supporting materials for each group would differ widely.

The economic status of a person is related to where he lives, his profession or vocation, his hobbies, his reference and membership groups (see below), his education, and his status positions. Find out what you can about these factors.

Membership and Reference Groups

It is sometimes easy and often quite difficult to determine the membership and reference groups to which a person belongs. Both affect an individual's beliefs and attitudes. By *membership group* we refer to any organized group having a membership roll, officers, regular meetings, and so on. It is an organization or group to which you belong by virtue of election, initiation, occupation, residence, or invitation. The definitions of *reference group* vary, but they are generally considered to be informal, nonstructured groups of people with whom you identify in some way. The members of some of your reference groups may never meet together, may live in different parts of the country, and may have little psychological awareness of the influence they have on you. For example, all your college teachers constitute one of your reference groups, for better or worse, as do your relatives, casual friends and golf partners (unless you play with the same group all the time), all the persons you have dated and the persons with whom you associate in school.

Social scientists call a reference group that group to which an individual looks for norms of behavior. In this sense a membership group is also a reference group. However, the pressure to conform to the norms of a membership group are greater because of the proximity of the members, the established or accepted rules of procedure, and the greater commonality of goals.

The degree to which you are associated with or affected by such organizations as the Brown Berets, the American Legion, the Veterans of Foreign Wars, the Green Berets, the Boy Scouts of America, or the Black Muslims probably affected your attitudes toward the Vietnam War. If your college teachers have been capable, helpful, and considerate and gave you good grades, you would probably support many of the causes for which teachers are struggling. If you have a staunch liberal view, you do as the liberals do; if you have conservative political views, you probably find few liberal causes you can support.

Occupation

One's occupation is closely related to membership groups as a factor in affecting the attitudes and beliefs of people. The groups with which you work affect you greatly. One writer states that there can be little question that the attitudes of people stem in part from their primary group affiliations, of which a work group is one.[13] It must be recognized that not all occupational groups are primary groups. For example, farmers, some professional workers, artists, newspaper editors or writers, and truck drivers have contacts with their fellow workers only occasionally. However, information about the occupation of one's audience does enable you to predict something about their beliefs and attitudes. Occupation does tell something about income level, amount and type of education, type of leisure activities, possible place of residence, and group affiliations. Doctors usually belong to the American Medical Association and state and local associations, truck-drivers usually belong to the International Brotherhood of Teamsters, Chauffeurs, Warehousemen, and Helpers of America or to the Transport Workers Union of America. Administrators have different interests, even on the job, from those of their employees; jewelers have few, if any, occupational interests in common with professional football players. Each group must be addressed in terms of its own vocational interests.

A frequent problem in speech preparation is to adapt to the high degree of specialization that may occur within a given audience of the same occupational group. Two generations ago farmers were, in a sense, generalists; today farming is highly specialized. The produce farmer in north central Indiana has little in common with the wheat farmer in Montana or the potato grower in Idaho, though all three carry on highly mechanized operations. Twenty-five years ago one man and helper might build a house; today at least a dozen different trades are involved. In science, literature, and the arts the ranges of knowledge and, hence, specialization are constantly increasing.

Geographical Backgrounds and Travel Experience

Whenever possible it is helpful to have some knowledge of the geographical and travel backgrounds of your listeners. In speaking to the foreign born or to Americans with foreign backgrounds, such as the Chicanos or Nisei, it is important to understand the differences between their cultural backgrounds and those of native Whites. In such cities as Boston, New Orleans, Salt Lake City, Washington, San Francisco, New Hope in Bucks County, Pennsylvania, and Kotzebue in Alaska the natives and the newcomers have entirely different standards by which they organize many facts of their lives and perceive those cities. Knowing about the geographical origins of your listeners will enable you to use supporting materials falling within their ken and thus establish a common ground.

Knowledge of the travel experiences of your audiences also aids in speech preparation. In this jet age more people travel more than at any previous time in our history. Try to discover whether your listeners are cosmopolitan or provincial. Because some people have traveled little, to mention such places and sights as the Mendenhall Glacier, Machupicchu, Capri, Matterhorn, the Inland Passage, Taxco, the Taj Mahal, or the Mayan ruins at Chichén-Itza would be meaningless. Your illustrations would have to be closer to home.

Age
Both average age and age span are important aspects of audience analysis. If you know that you will speak to a definite age group, as teenagers, the middle-aged, or the elderly, you can readily focus your material in their direction. On the other hand, if the audience is heterogeneous in age, the subject materials must be more general. A severe test of the speaker's adaptability is the universal father-son or mother-daughter banquet, where illustrations must appeal to both, simple expression is necessary, and careful, uninvolved organization is essential.

Sex and Marital Status
The predominant sex of an audience is another factor affecting speech preparation. The Lions International, League of Women Voters, Planned Parenthood Federation of America, Boys Clubs of America, and B'nai B'rith would require different considerations.

If you can, you should determine the marital status of your listeners. Young married women with families have interests entirely different from those of divorcées whose children are grown or who have no children. Single young men have their future lives to plan and live; married senior citizens look forward to fewer years of retired comfort or work.

Cultural, Educational, and Religious Backgrounds
Some knowledge of the cultural, ethnic, and racial backgrounds is certainly essential. Naturalized citizens have a tendency to retain some of the ties with their native home; second and third generations are somewhat more Americanized. When a particular background predominates among the listeners, understanding and acceptance by the speaker of their heritage and use of the language will increase his comprehension of that audience. A speaker talking about wartime sacrifices to Japanese Americans in the Los Angeles area certainly should be aware of the injustices to these people when they were relocated during World

War II. One appearing before a local cooperative near Superior, Wisconsin, would need to know something of the influence of the Finns in the development of cooperatives in that area. The Puerto Ricans living in New York City have unique problems with which the speaker should be familiar.

Educational and religious backgrounds also should be studied. A talk before the American Association of University Professors demands an entirely different treatment from one before a group of school drop-outs. Freshmen and graduates in college do not view their educational careers in the same ways. Probably you cannot discover the individual religious preferences and affiliations of your listeners. Nor would that be important: instead discover the predominant religion, if any. Members of the Church of Jesus Christ of the Latter-Day Saints, Jehovah's Witnesses, the Evangelical Mennonite Brethren, the Roman Catholic Church, and the Unitarian Universalist Association differ widely in religious beliefs and practices.

In each of these background areas—cultural, educational, and religious—homogeneity simplifies adaptation, and heterogeneity makes it somewhat more difficult. Try to discover how the backgrounds create different interests in such things as literature, food, art, folklore, the theatre, music, and sports. Knowing what listeners know about a given subject is essential if we would adapt our remarks to their level.

General Experience

The general knowledge possessed by your listeners usually will affect your speech preparation. Are they likely to be well read? Are forum, discussion, and lecture programs available in the community? Do they attend? Is there a legitimate theatre? Amateur theatres? Are the listeners sports-minded? Are both amateur and professional sports available? Do your listeners support some sports' boosters clubs? Do your listeners have the opportunity to participate in civic projects, and do they do so? Do they concern themselves with local municipal problems?

Information in most of the foregoing areas may be acquired by a few carefully phrased questions to the program planners or even to potential audience members. Many specific suggestions are given in the last section of this chapter.

ASPECTS OF OCCASION ANALYSIS

Most speech occasions are planned for definite and ascertainable reasons. Our gregariousness and the fact that we must meet to carry on mutually satisfying activities make speaking occasions an integral part of our lives. Analysis of these occasions is primarily concerned with background, group goals, and procedures.

Backgrounds

Many speech occasions are deeply rooted in the events precipitating the occasion or in the history of the people composing the audience. Lincoln's First Inaugural was delivered before 25,000 persons in Washington in 1861, when differences between the South and North were approaching a crisis. Booker T. Washington's speech at the opening of the Cotton States Exposition in Atlanta in 1895 was given on a memorable occasion, which had extensive historical backgrounds. The speech given by President John F. Kennedy, announcing his decision on the Cuban missile crisis, had intense economic, political, and military backgrounds and widespread repercussions. In an analysis of the antecedents of any given occasion, such questions as the following should be considered:

1. What are the longtime backgrounds of the occasion?
   a. Social
   b. Political
   c. Cultural
   d. Economic
   e. Religious
   f. Scientific
   g. Racial
   h. Educational
2. What recent events have led up to the occasion?
   a. Is the audience acquainted with these events?
   b. Do the immediate causes affect many or only a few?
   c. Do the immediate causes relate to the particular audience only or to the general public?
   d. Are the immediate causes of greater significance than the historical antecedents?
3. How widespread are the ramifications of the occasion?
   a. Local interest only?
   b. Statewide concern?
   c. Regional concern?
   d. National concern?
   e. International concern?

Longtime and recent antecedents of the speech occasion often reveal much that is of help to a speaker. They suggest the best type of illustrations to use, generalizations that may safely be made, allusions that will be understood, the accepted beliefs and attitudes of the audience, language that should be appropriate, and the extent of any probable commitment to a proposed action.

The significance of the occasion is also a factor in analysis. A speech before the United Nations General Assembly has requirements different from one before the Organization of American States. A speech before a national meeting of the National Management Association differs in many respects from one before a Junior Chamber of Commerce in Dayton, Ohio. A talk at a national convention of the American Legion might deal with broader and more significant issues than one given at the American Legion Post 132 at Orange, California.

Purpose and Nature

Knowledge of the purpose and nature of the gathering may be fully as important as the background. Occasions for speeches vary widely, and the specific purpose of the present occasion will tell much about the listeners' reasons for attending. Answers to the following questions should help the speaker determine the purpose:

1. Is the purpose a commemorative one? Will it honor a person, event, institution, or accomplishment?
2. Is the purpose to secure or promote goodwill? Extend courtesy or gratitude? Give information? Initiate or direct some action?
3. Is the purpose to mediate, negotiate, or arbitrate?
4. Is the occasion a confrontation meeting designed to make demands or give an ultimatum to a group?
5. Is it religious in nature, such as a meeting of the Campus Crusade for Christ, the Billy Graham Crusade, the Salvation Army, or the International General Assembly of Spiritualists?
6. Is the meeting one that is controlled or that may get out of the control of those in charge?
7. Is the purpose to gain status by being seen?
8. Is there no apparent reason for the meeting?
9. Has the occasion arisen because of general public concern or limited special interest?
10. Are all the members aware of the purpose of the occasion, or are only a few?
11. Does the purpose contribute to some immediate or future goal of the sponsors?

In other words, what do listeners expect to gain from the speech? It may well be a combination of the purposes listed. In any event, the more one can learn about the specific purpose, the more effective will he be in adapting a talk to the requirements of the occasion.

Some speeches are regarded as entertainment, and the listeners neither expect nor wish to participate actively. At other times, because of the vital nature of the topic, they may wish to be actively involved. They may want to ask questions, and hence you should arrange a discussion period following the speech. Under such circumstances an attentive and cooperative audience may be expected.

Some speeches are given in an atmosphere of conviviality and spontaneity, as at a postseason football banquet. Sometimes people attend a speech because they are curious to hear and see noted speakers. Some people attend simply because they wish to participate in the occasion or to be able to say "I was there." The audience's activity in such cases will be at a minimum.

Most speaking occasions belong on a continuum ranging from formal to informal. At one extreme there will be little or no deviation from the prescribed program; at the other, one should be prepared to adapt to a flexible situation.

Sometimes the extras are the significant aspects of a speech occasion, often to the embarrassment of the speaker. People frequently attend meetings because of business to be completed, friends to be greeted, or food to be eaten, the speech being regarded as merely a necessary evil. If they attend a meeting because of outside compulsion, such as group pressure or family urging, their attitudes will be affected.

It is always a good idea—and not too difficult—to find out about other activities planned for the occasion. If there are several speakers, each may need to adapt his introduction and conclusion to the order of speaking, and each should know something about the others. Such information can be easily secured in advance from the program chairman. A speaker who sits in on a business meeting preceding a speech can learn much about the audience, since the amenities that are a part of a meeting reflect the audience's attitudes and purpose. Unfortunately, sometimes the "other business" may continue so long that the speaker is obliged either to cut much of what he had planned to say or to make his delivery dynamic enough to capture a tired audience. His adaptation in such a case must be made on the spot. In general, advance knowledge of local customs and procedures makes the speaker's task much easier.

Physical Setting

If at all possible, inspect the room in which you are later to speak. If unforeseen problems exist, you may be able to solve them or at least to adapt yourself to them. Here are some of the items to be checked:

1. Accommodations for listeners:
   a. Are the seats comfortable?

      b. Are the lighting and ventilation adequate?
      c. What is the relation of the size of the expected audience to the seating capacity?
      d. Will the physical setting contribute to the mood of the speech?
      e. Can the platform be seen from all the seats?
      f. Can the meeting place be adapted to any special requirements for audience participation?
  2. Physical facilities for the speaker:
      a. Will a lectern be available?
      b. If required, will projection equipment be available and ready for use? Will a projectionist be available?
      c. Are the acoustics satisfactory? Is a public-address system available and in working order? Will the speaker have an opportunity to test the public-address system before starting his speech?
      d. Where will the speaker stand in relation to the audience?
      e. If needed, is equipment available for showing two-dimensional visual aids?
      f. Will water and a glass be available?

Many program chairmen are unaware of the importance of the foregoing items for effective communication. Ten or fifteen minutes spent in checking them before speaking often pays high dividends, enabling a speaker to make himself and his listeners more comfortable. The result should be better listening and increased understanding.

The size of the meeting place in relation to the size of the audience is more important than many speakers realize. A crowded audience reacts differently from a scattered one. It is easier for a speaker to develop rapport with his listeners when they are close to him than when they are some distance away. If you are likely to have a small group of listeners in a large room, try to have them concentrated near the front. Move the speaker's stand to bring yourself as close as possible to them.

Be sure that everyone is going to be able to hear you easily, without strain. Easy listening leads to greater attention. In large rooms and with large audiences a public-address system should be used if available. Don't depend on your voice alone to carry to the far corners of a large room. If there is no public-address system, at least test your ability to project your voice by having some one listen to you from various points in the room. Keep in mind, too, the possibility of distracting noises, such as the clearing of tables after a banquet.

In recent years the existence of hecklers, and worse, in an audience has had to be considered by the speaker. Even presidents and vice-presidents are not safe from it. Plan in advance how you will try to handle persons who attempt to disrupt the meeting.

Although there is, of course, no way in which a speaker can alter the physical layout of a room, he should at least be aware of such things as pillars that may obstruct the view, acoustics that may decrease audibility, entrances that prevent latecomers from taking their seats quickly, and the probability of outside distractions. If poor conditions cannot possibly be remedied, the speaker must make up his mind to counteract them by increasing the vitality of his delivery.

THE SPEAKER'S ANALYSIS OF HIMSELF

An important object of prespeech analysis is that period just before the speech, when the speaker takes a final look at himself. This period may be very brief or may be fifteen to thirty minutes. It is a period of heightened emotional and physical activity that is experienced by most participants in the performing arts, including speakers. It is the anxiety or fear most people have of speaking; it is called stage fright.

Anxiety

Fear of speaking may manifest itself in many different ways: a distressed or sinking feeling in the pit of the stomach, muscular tension, a quickened heart beat, shaking, or a seeming increase in body temperature. The condition, however it may manifest itself, is not a disease, and it will not kill you, but there is no cure for it. Rather, it is a normal reaction, and everyone has it to some degree. Therefore, if you experience it, do not conclude that there is something wrong with you.

To say that there is no cure for stage fright means that, although you may develop self-assurance and through experience learn how to control or ignore some of its symptoms, you will never be able to allay them completely.

In rhetorical communication your object is to influence the audience, which means you must have concern for them as well as for yourself. If you are highly concerned, anxiety will be present at either the conscious or subconscious level. Absence of this concern or anxiety is not desirable in the rhetorical situation. Such absence is an indication of egocentricity, and it suggests you are indifferent to the audience's response to your message. Or, the absence of anxiety may indicate insensitivity to the real demands of the speaking situation.

Stage fright is a very normal response to an exacting situation that requires a speaker to reveal all of his rhetorical skills—thinking, organizing ability, knowledge of his audience, and so forth—to a group of people who may be critical. It is the kind of situation that stimulates a degree of anxiety far greater than many challenges to one's prowess. For example, Buzz Aldrin, in commenting on the stress aroused in him by his engagement to speak before the Congress of the United States, said, "The day I had to address Congress I was petrified. Landing on the moon was child's play compared to it."[14]

The symptoms of stage fright are highly aggravated because the speaker "stands alone"; that is, he succeeds solely on the basis of his own ability. No matter how great his desire, he cannot blame failure on anyone but himself.

During the period in which the speaker becomes aware of and identifies his manifestations of fear of speaking, he should also identify what he has done to prepare himself for speaking. He should gird himself with the knowledge that he has prepared well, that he has examined his audience carefully, and that the level at which he has set his purpose is not beyond his capacity to achieve.

The knowledge that many experienced speakers undergo feelings of anxiety and fear—in the moment of truth before speaking—is hard for the student speaker to accept. He is willing to accept, however, the idea that he himself may have stage fright.

Let us view some of the feelings expressed by well-known and highly experienced speakers. President Nixon's oft-quoted "Checkers Speech" was an address to the nation in his defense of accusations by the press that he had a "fund," implying dishonesty. Many of General Eishenhower's top advisors were in favor of dumping Nixon as a vice-presidential candidate. The following paragraph conveys in Nixon's own words what he was going through in the last few minutes before the nationwide telecast.[15]

In such periods of intense preparation for battle, most individuals experience all the physical symptoms of tension—they become edgy and short-tempered, some can't eat, others can't sleep. I had experienced all these symptoms in the days since our train left Pomona. I had had a similar experience during the Hiss case. But what I had learned was that feeling this way before a battle was not something to worry about—on the contrary, failing to feel this way would mean that I was not adequately keyed up, mentally and emotionally, for the conflict ahead. It is only when the individual worries about how he feels that such physical factors become signs of self-destruction rather than of creativity.

Not only has Mr. Nixon confirmed our assertion that anyone can get stage fright, no matter how experienced he is, but he has made it extremely clear that we should be worried when this is not the case. In his words,[15] "It is only when the individual worries about how he feels that such physical factors become signs of self-destruction rather than of creativity." His further comment also may be of value to the speaker. Referring to the prespeech feelings set forth above, he said:[15]

Selflessness is by far the most helpful attribute an individual can have at such a time. A man is at his best in a crisis when he is thinking not of himself but of the problem at hand. Then he forgets, or at least is not bothered by, how he "feels" physically.

Norman Vincent Peale also has done a great deal of speaking. His biographer[16] says of him that "preaching never became easy. He always had a certain amount of stage fright. Once on his feet, assurance and authority came to him. But waiting for that moment can be misery."

Another noted speaker of our times who has stimulated an appreciation of his intellectual adroitness in polemics, William F. Buckley, has conjured audiences from the opposition from one end of the country to the other. His suave approach to bearding the lion in its den would not indicate that his efforts were accompanied either by timorousness or anxiety, though they are.

Many well-known speakers could be cited to extend our examples on prespeech anxiety. Obviously, their own testimony indicates that experience is not a cure. Good practice indicates that if one cannot achieve a cure, the next best thing is to control the problem.

Control of Anxiety

The importance of control has been indicated, and the fact has been stressed that the anxiety is inescapable—and necessary. We must then raise and attempt to answer the question: How do we set about using our anxiety to our best advantage? Many people will tell you that the way to handle stage fright is to follow such and such a prescription, take a drink of water before you go on stage, and breathe deeply. If such tricks are helpful to you, there probably is no reason why you should not use them. However, they do not help much during the period of prespeech anxiety. This is the time that a person about to speak needs to be kept busy performing tasks that will occupy him both mentally and physically.

We can analyze the room and perhaps even make some subtle changes that will be helpful. If we are there early enough, we can test our the public-address system, find out where the cold drafts are coming from, or get the chairman or janitor to do something if the room is overheated. Without appearing to be too much of a busybody the speaker can reduce his tensions by performing constructive tasks.

The purpose of this activity is to take your mind off yourself during those last few minutes when there is nothing that you can do about your speech. It is already crystallized. Once you have got through this period and are on stage, the problem changes. You find, as you enter into communication with an audience, that you have another dimension. Mother Nature intervenes and provides your inadequate physical system with a chemical change that enables you to proceed not only adequately but sometimes even superbly.

Referring again to the Checkers speech, Nixon stated the following about his feelings as he began to speak. He quotes himself:[17]

"My fellow Americans, I come before you tonight as a candidate for the vice presidency and as a man whose honesty and integrity has been questioned." As I spoke, all the tension suddenly went out of me. I felt in complete control of myself and of my material. I was calm and confident. Despite the lack of sleep or even of rest over the past six days, despite the abuse to which I had subjected my nerves and body—some way, somehow in a moment of great crisis a man calls up resources of physical, mental, and emotional power he never realized he had. This I was now able to do, because the hours and days of preparation had been for this one moment and I put into it everything I had. I knew what I wanted to say, and I said it from the heart.

Despite anxiety, or perhaps we should say because of it, men like Norman Vincent Peale and Billy Graham have influenced millions of people. Mr. Nixon, Mr. Johnson, and Mr. Kennedy have faced the most critical of situations and made their decisions, which have come to us through a filter of anxiety despite the need of each to appear at his most confident.

There is no easy way out for the minister or the politician or the speaker in any area of public life. He can only face up to the fact that anxiety may help him do the job he has chosen to do and to do it better than anyone else.

If you have a speech to make to your class, think not of yourself alone. Try thinking what would happen if your audience really listened to you. For your class is a real audience, and if you face the situation as other than just an assignment, you may find that something has sparked which you never thought possible, giving your prespeech analysis and yourself a new dimension of reality.

INFORMATION FOR PRESPEECH ANALYSIS

The following are some items of advice for preparing your prespeech analysis.

1. Consult the chairman of the program. He should be eager enough to have a successful meeting that he will be glad to provide whatever information he can. Usually he arranges for a speech well in advance, giving the speaker ample time in which to gather the information he needs.

Don't rely completely on the program chairman to send you all the information you would like to have about the audience. Give him a specific list of questions you want answered. Don't ask him to complete a six-page questionnaire about the audience, but do get enough so that you can make generalizations about their attitudes, interests, and needs.

2. If it is an organization, the program members of the organization may be helpful. Older members and those involved in planning for the occasion usually are willing to cooperate.

3. Printed materials pertaining to the history, traditions, and activities of the group constituting the audience may be available. Old periodicals, past programs, newspaper clippings, and other such data should prove helpful.

4. Community resources will be a fruitful source of information. Libraries provide information on national organizations as well as on local groups. Public and private agencies in the community sometimes can be helpful. A short visit to the local Chamber of Commerce may pay great dividends.

An excellent illustration of how useful information was obtained was actually reported in a speech given by D. A. Hulcy, then president of the Chamber of Commerce of the United States, before the Salt Lake City Chamber of Commerce. In opening his speech Mr. Hulcy called attention to events and conditions in the early days of Salt Lake City: the founding of the local Chamber of Commerce, the low cost of building lots, the cost of food, and the up-to-date nature of certain public utilities. He then added:[18] "Now I want you to know that I wasn't tipped off to these anecdotes from Salt Lake City's past by Gus Backman or anybody else. I found them for myself in the magic looking glass of your old newspaper files."

5. Frequently useful information can be secured from persons who have no connection with the event. A colleague of the authors, famed for his public lectures, makes it a policy to arrive in a city at least three hours before he is scheduled to lecture. He then uses this time to secure varied information from people he meets casually at hotels, in restaurants, in stores, or on the streets.

6. If possible, discover and study the publicly acknowledged goals and principal activities of the group you are to address: social reforms they have supported, special organizational interests, efforts to promote the general good, and the like. For example, some organizations, such as the National

Legion for Decency, the Family Service Association of America, the Probation and Parole Association, and the United World Federalists exist primarily to work for specific types of social reform.

The amount of information you can obtain about different audiences obviously will vary greatly. Occasionally you will not be able to find any fruitful source of information. Then you will have to rely on your own general experience and what you know about listeners in general. Fortunately, one is seldom asked to address an audience about which he can get no advance information at all. Nor is one often invited to speak before a group whose experiences and backgrounds differ in all respects from his own. Whatever the situation, however, you can be sure that prespeech analysis will provide some information to increase your effectiveness in communication.

To be sure, there are occasions on which prespeech analysis for a specific audience is virtually impossible. The political candidate who gives several speeches a day to different audiences in different areas has no time to analyze each audience. He can, however, study in advance the types of listener that will predominate in his audience in certain places: farmers, laborers, housewives, small-town dwellers, and so forth. His associates should assume responsibility for alerting him to unique local situations.

This chapter should at least make you realize that audiences are not alike and that you cannot safely trust to your common sense and native ability to make on-the-spot adaptations. The more skilled the speaker, the more likely is he to prepare his speeches with his specific audience in mind. The corollary to that is that the less he knows or can learn about a particular audience, the greater should be his effort in making a thorough prespeech analysis.

The principles we have presented in this chapter are not presented merely as guides for you to use "after graduation," "outside class," or "when you are working on your life's vocation." They can and should be used in preparation for the speeches you will give in the speech communication course you are now taking. We suggest that you begin early in the semester to learn as much as you can about your classmates. Listen carefully to the views expressed in their early speeches; talk to as many as you can outside your class, to discover their hobbies, majors, after-graduation plans, and other items suggested in this chapter. Finally, cooperate with your instructor and classmates in the completion of the first exercise in the items of advice; it should give you a wealth of data to guide you in making speeches adapted to your class colleagues.

IMPLICATIONS

1. Prespeech analysis of the audience, occasion, and setting is a first step in speech preparation.
2. Since communication is a transactional process, the listener being involved as a partner, the understanding between speaker and respondent must always be at a maximum. The understanding on the part of the speaker is achieved through prespeech analysis.
3. Prespeech analysis has four values: practical, predictive, associative, and evaluative. That is, prespeech analysis helps get the information needed in speech preparation, enables the speaker to make generalizations about his audience, builds satisfying ties between speaker and listeners, and establishes criteria by which to measure the effectiveness of a speech.
4. In general the essence of a prespeech analysis of the audience is the determination of the common and diverse experiences and characteristics, those which influence the audience's attitudes toward the subject and the speaker's purpose.
5. It is advisable to survey, at some time well in advance of the speaking date, what you know about the audience and to make a list of needed information.
6. The specific aspects of prespeech audience analysis are as follows: (1) the relation of the audience to the speaker, (2) the relation of the audience to the speech subject, (3) the relation of the audience to the speech purpose, (4) the basic beliefs of the audience, and (5) special characteristics of the audience, such as economic status, membership and reference groups, occupation, geographic backgrounds, travel experience, sex and marital status, cultural, educational, and religious backgrounds, and general experience.
7. Aspects of the analysis of the occasion include its longtime and recent backgrounds and the purpose and nature of the speech occasion.
8. Aspects of the analysis of the speech setting include the accommodations for the listeners, physical facilities for the speaker, the size of the meeting place in relation to the potential size of the audience, and the possibility of hecklers in the audience.
9. Sources of information for prespeech analysis include the program chairman of the meeting, actual members of the listening group, persons from outside the listening group, printed materials about the organization or group, the publicly stated goals of the listening audience, and other persons known to have talked to the same audience.

EXERCISES

1. Work in subgroups of four or five to complete this exercise. Together with the other members of your subgroup draw up a questionnaire that contains all the information about your classmates you believe would be desirable to have when you prepare speeches to be given in class. Select one member of your subgroup to work with a representative from each of the other subgroups. This class committee should then combine the ideas included in each subgroup's questionnaire into a master questionnaire, which your instructor will print

copies of and have completed by each class member. Your instructor will summarize the data and return a master information sheet about your class members. The master questionnaire should give you information about political affiliation, religious-group membership, outside jobs, hobbies, and such other items as may be included in the questionnaire.

2. Make a list of eight or ten different types of groups on your campus. Select the two with which you are the most familiar and the least familiar. Write an audience analysis of each, giving answers to these questions:

   a. What are its chief physical and social needs and values?

   b. What are the special customs, mores, or rules that affect the group's operation and that might affect its attitude toward you, the speech subject, and the speech purpose?

   c. What are the special characteristics of age, occupation, membership, reference groups, and so on?

   d. What recent activities has the group engaged in that might affect its response to your speech?

3. Interview some person on or off your campus who is known for his speaking ability and who speaks a lot, such as a preacher, trial lawyer, college staff member, student, or public relations expert in a large firm. Give a three-minute talk in class on how this person makes his prespeech analysis.

4. Assume that you have been asked to speak before a luncheon club, such as the Lions or Rotarians. Obtain information concerning these items:

   a. The nature of the speaking occasion.

   b. The relationship of the listeners to the speech situation.

   c. Their relationship to the speech subject.

   d. Their attitudes toward you.

   e. Their common characteristics.

5. What would be the most significant items of information to be determined in your prespeech analysis of a men's club? A women's club? A mixed group? A youth group?

6. From your local newspaper select an editorial dealing with some local issue. Plan a three-minute speech that might be given before your local city council or some other civic body and that would support the point of view expressed in the editorial. Now revise your speech and give it before your class. Submit a report to your instructor on the changes you made to adapt the speech to the classroom situation.

7. Using one of the following books as a source, investigate the ways in which some American speaker has gained information about his audience before speaking.

   William Norwood Brigance, ed., *A History and Criticism of American Public Address,* New York, McGraw-Hill, 1943, vols. 1 and 2.

   Marie Kathryn Hochmuth, ed., *A History and Criticism of American Public Address,* New York, Longmans, Green, Co., 1955, vol. 3.

   Loren Reid, ed., *American Public Address,* Univ. Missouri Press, 1961.

   John Graham, ed., *Great American Speeches,* New York, Appleton Century-Crofts, 1970.

8. Interview the chairman or president of some local community group, or the

head of a college campus department that frequently sponsors outside speakers, or the head of your students' speakers bureau, to discover the kind of information usually given to a person who is scheduled to make a speech. Is it adequate according to the standards established in this chapter?

9. Plan to take four to six weeks in the preparation of this exercise. Select some important speech by a famous American, and secure all the information you can about the circumstances under which it was given. Some helpful references are given in Exercise 5. Find out what the speaker knew about the factors that contributed to the development of the speaking situation, about the audience, and about the physical setting in which the speech was given.

Plan to give a six-minute speech in which you indicate the manner and effectiveness of the speaker's adaptation to the audience and occasion.

10. Assume that you are to give a talk on some subject that might be of interest to men, to women, or to teenagers, such as drug abuse, curfews, or the generation gap. Give a brief talk in class on what changes you would make in the speech to adapt to each of the three audiences.

11. Select three real audiences (existing organizations or groups), and for each make a list of the ten major factors that would influence their reactions to a speech on some current social or political issue.

ADDITIONAL READINGS

Braden, Waldo W., and Mary Louise Gehring, *Speech Practices: A Resource Book for the Student of Public Speaking*, New York, Harper & Row, 1958, chaps. 2, 4.

Capp, Glenn R., *How to Communicate Orally*, 2nd ed., Englewood Cliffs, N.J., Prentice-Hall, 1966, chap. 4.

Clevenger, Theodore, Jr., *Audience Analysis*, Indianapolis, Bobbs-Merrill, 1966.

Gerber, Philip L., *Effective English*, New York, Random House/Singer, 1959, chap. 2.

Hochmuth, Marie K., "The criticism of rhetoric," in Marie K. Hochmuth, ed., *A History and Criticism of American Public Address*, New York, Longmans, Green, 1955, vol. 13, pp. 1–23.

Hollingworth, Harry L., *The Psychology of the Audience*, New York, American Books, 1935, chaps. 3, 8, 10.

Holtzman, Paul D., *The Psychology of Speakers' Audiences*, Glenview, Ill., Scott, Foresman, 1970, chaps. 4, 5, 6, 7, 8, 9, 10.

Monroe, Alan H., and Douglas Ehninger, *Principles and Types of Speech*, 6th ed., Glenview, Ill., Scott, Foresman, 1967, chap. 8.

Oliver, Robert T., *The Psychology of Persuasive Speech*, New York, Longmans, Green, 1942, chap. 4.

Rogge, Edward, and James C. Ching, *Advanced Public Speaking*, New York, Holt, Rinehart & Winston, 1966, chap. 9.

St. Onge, Keith R., *Creative Speech*, Belmont, Calif., Wadsworth, 1964, chap. 12.

Sandford, William Phillips, and Willard Hayes Yeager, *Effective Business Speech*, 4th ed., New York, McGraw-Hill, 1960, chap. 5.

Smith, Donald K., *Man Speaking: A Rhetoric of Public Speech*, New York, Dodd, Mead, 1969, chap. 7.

Thayer, Lee O., *Administrative Communication*, Homewood, Ill., Irwin, 1961, chap. 2.

Windes, Russell, Jr., "Adlai E. Stevenson's speech staff in the 1956 campaign," *Quart. J. Speech*, 46 (no. 1, Feb. 1960), 32–43.

Zimbardo, Phillip, and Ebbe B. Ebbesen, *Influencing Attitudes and Changing Behavior*, Reading, Mass., Addison-Wesley, 1969, chaps. 1, 2, 3, 6.

NOTES

[1] John F. Wilson and Carroll C. Arnold, *Public Speaking as a Liberal Art*, 2nd ed., Boston, Allyn & Bacon, 1968, p. 74.

[2] Marie K. Hochmuth, ed., *A History and Criticism of American Public Address*, New York, Longmans, Green, 1955, vol. 3, p. 10.

[3] Robert J. McEwen, "Fair trade legislation," *Vital Speeches*, 25 (no. 18, July 1, 1959), 559.

[4] See Floyd W. Matson, ed., *Voices of Crisis*, New York, Odyssey, 1967, pp. 156–161, 162–174; Richard N. Current and John A. Garraty, eds., *Words That Made American History: The 1870's to the Present*, Boston, Little, Brown, 1962, pp. 508–520; and Loren Reid, ed., *American Public Address*, Columbia, Mo., Univ. Missouri Press, 1961, pp. 193–308.

[5] See Richard M. Nixon, "Bridges to human dignity," in Wil A. Linkugel, R. R. Allen, and Richard L. Johannesen, eds., *Contemporary American Speeches*, 2nd ed., Belmont, Calif., Wadsworth, 1969, pp. 255–261; Lyndon B. Johnson, "We shall overcome," in Floyd W. Matson, *op. cit.*,[4] pp. 146–155; and Robert F. Kennedy, "For a comprehensive Civil Rights Bill," in Thomas A. Hopkins, ed., *Rights for Americans: The Speeches of Robert F. Kennedy*, Indianapolis, Bobbs-Merrill, pp. 164–169.

[6] In Harold F. Harding, ed., *The Age of Danger*, New York, Random House/Singer, 1952, p. 453.

[7] *Ibid.*, p. 387.

[8] Arvonne S. Fraser, "Women: The new image," *Vital Speeches*, 37 (no. 19, July 15, 1971), 599–600.

[9] *Ibid.*, p. 605.

[10] Rudolph F. Verderber, *The Challenge of Effective Speaking*, Belmont, Calif., Wadsworth, 1970, p. 14.

[11] Bernard Berelson and Morris Janowitz, eds., *Reader in Public Opinion and Propaganda*, enl. ed., Glencoe, Ill., Free Press, 1953, p. 60.

[12] Bernard Berelson and Gary A. Steiner, *An Inventory of Scientific Findings*, New York, Harcourt, 1964, p. 570.

[13] See the report in David Krech and Richard S. Crutchfield, *Individual in Society: A Text Book of Social Psychology*, New York, McGraw-Hill, 1962, pp. 196–197.

[14] *The Los Angeles Times*, Los Angeles, California, Feb. 27, 1972.

[15] Richard M. Nixon, *Six Crises*, New York, Doubleday, 1962, pp. 108–109.

[16] Arthur Gordon, *Norman Vincent Peale*, Englewood Cliffs, N.J., Prentice-Hall, 1958, p. 181.

[17] Nixon, *op. cit.*, p. 113.

[18] Mr. Gus Backman was Executive Secretary of the Salt Lake City Chamber of Commerce.

CHAPTER TEN
DETERMINING THE SUBJECT AND THESIS STATEMENT

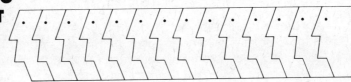

No wind makes for him that hath no intended port to sail into.
> Montaigne

A simple cause, though it may be defended in various ways, cannot contain more than one point on which a decision is to be pronounced.
> Quintilian

When a thought is too weak to be expressed simply, it is a proof that it should be rejected.
> Vauvenargues

"What shall I talk about?" This is a perennial problem for both experienced and inexperienced speakers. In this chapter we shall be concerned with the principles of selecting a suitable subject, limiting the subject to one central idea, dividing the central theme into its related parts, and connecting these parts in order that unity may be achieved, thereby increasing the impact of the message and helping the listeners make more intelligent decisions.

SELECTING THE SUBJECT

Selecting a subject suitable to a particular speaking situation seems to be a matter of considerable concern to the classroom student. In the "real world" the speech subject is normally determined by one of three types of circumstance. The first circumstance is that in which the speaker has no prior warning—a spontaneous conversation or discussion that arises out of the situation and is not determined by the communicator. The second is that in which the speaker is asked, perhaps a few days or a few weeks in advance, to speak to a particular club or organization; normally the group or person requesting the speech suggests the topic to be presented. The third is that in which an individual has an idea he wishes to communicate (perhaps some "axe to grind") and seeks an audience for his communication.

These three circumstances, in which most public speaking occurs outside the classroom, indicate that the selection of a subject is not a major problem in the "real world." However, the first two circumstances do not generally occur in the classroom. The student should consider the classroom situation to fall into the third circumstance, the situation in which the student has something to communicate to his fellow students. The most successful speeches a beginning student in speech communication will present will be on those subjects that interest him and that he desires to share with others.

We realize, however, that most beginning students view the selection of a suitable subject as a challenging task; therefore, some general principles to be kept in mind will be considered in this chapter. Since no two situations are ever identical, the selection and treatment of a subject present a continuously changing combination of variables. The variables must be adapted to the specific situation and must consider both the needs of the listeners and the qualifications and interests of the communicator.

The task of subject selection will be more realistic and will provide a training situation coinciding more nearly with that of real life, if you recognize that in the classroom you are speaking to an audience made up of real people. Many students are lulled into the belief that, since the speaking situation is forced upon them by the very nature of the class, they can pretend their audience to be anything they choose. When this is the attitude, the communication becomes nothing more than an exercise in delivery. Remember that the purpose of speech communication is to effect some sort of desired behavioral change in the receivers. To do this there must be a real audience and a suitable subject. The student speaker should keep in mind that his classmates constitute a real audience and should be treated as such.

Suiting Your Interest

The subject selected should be one in which the communicator is genuinely interested. Even the most informed speaker may seem dull when speaking on a subject in which he has little interest. The successful communicator "sparks" his information and ideas; genuine, motivated interest in a subject almost always vitalizes his physical expression.

Many speakers ignore the fact that audience interest in a subject can be aroused only if the speaker himself has, and makes evident, an interest in it. The successful salesman, the effective politician, the influential evangelist, the lively conversationalist, all manifest deep interest in what they are saying. Call to mind for a moment some of the great speakers of recent times: Franklin D. Roosevelt, Winston Churchill, Billy Graham, Adlai Stevenson, Norman Vincent Peale, and John F. Kennedy. You may not agree with their points of view, but it is impossible to deny their intense interest in their subjects. To be stimulating and challenging in the speaking situation the speaker needs the impetus that comes from the assurance that his subject is vital, alive with meaning, and of mutual concern.

Suiting Your Knowledge

One must understand a subject himself before he reasonably can expect to tell others about it. Too many speech students become overnight specialists on foreign trade or international relations or similar complex matters, assuming that reading an article in some magazine qualifies them to speak with authority.

Many subjects fall within any individual's area of competence, especially those derived from personal experiences. Consider the great number of topics that could come out of your own experiences, such as part-time or full-time jobs, reserve or active military service, watching or taking part in sports, travel, religious activities, organizations to which you have belonged, campus activities, various types of people you have met, and so on. It would be difficult, indeed, to conceive of any college or university student so young or with so few experiences that he could not find areas of competence in selecting subjects.

We do not intend to imply that a student might not find it necessary and desirable to supplement his own knowledge with additional research. His message might well have greater impact by adding the experiences of others to his own, by including the opinions of others, and by using additional facts and statistics that will support his views and add to his own body of knowledge on the subject. He might discover that there are facets of his subject that he had not considered.

When we restrict ourselves, especially in our first speaking attempts, to areas that are in harmony with our abilities, knowledge, and experience, we will have greater confidence; and confidence is contagious in an audience. Listeners involuntarily respond to the confidence that is apparent when a speaker is knowledgeable in his subject area.

Suiting the Listeners' Needs and Interests

In Chapter Nine we stressed the importance of analyzing the audience in terms of its demographics, its attitudes, and its interests. We can seldom know an audience completely, but the more we can analyze it in advance, the better able we are to secure from it the response we desire. The communicator should attempt to discover the audience's age level, educational background, common experiences, interests, knowledge, attitudes, and needs. Only when this is done is two-way communication possible. You may be well qualified to speak on a given subject, but unless that subject can be made of interest to your listeners, you will find success difficult to achieve. However, almost any topic that interests you can be made interesting to your respondents if you have made a careful audience preanalysis. If you have found the subject interesting, discover the reasons for your interest; they may be the same as those of your audience.

The subject should be significant to the respondents. It may be a subject that is already important to them or a subject about which you can generate interest and make important to them. Students often have the mistaken idea that a significant subject must be one that is "earth shattering," one about which volumes have been written, or one that deals with deep philosophical, political, or religious matters. Significance simply means a relationship to the needs and interests of the listeners. Your talk on the inspiration you received upon seeing the Grand Canyon for the first time can be significant to most audiences, because it parallels their impressions upon seeing the same sight or some other awe-inspiring work of Nature. Speeches on the heroic action of your dog, the thrill you experienced in some adventure, or the loneliness you felt when you spent Christmas far from home can be significant because they "touch" basic human emotions experienced in some degree by all members of your audience. Significant subjects relate to universal needs, values, and aspirations.

After a careful analysis of your audience you will probably realize that there are some subjects that would be too difficult for them to comprehend or would be unsuitable because of the nature of the content. Technical subjects requiring a knowledge of complicated processes and a specialized vocabulary beyond the range of your audience, subjects dealing with intimate or personal matters that would be embarrassing for them to listen to in a group, and subjects that require a quantity of highly statistical material—these you probably would consider unsuitable for your listening audience.

Barring the kinds of topic that we have just treated, perhaps the best rule of thumb would be that, if the subject is of interest to you, and if you are genuinely enthusiastic about it and want to share your enthusiasm with your listeners, then your respondents probably will be interested too.

Suiting the Listeners' Image of You

An important factor in almost every speaking situation is the image the audience has of the speaker, of his ethos. The speaker should ask himself whether or not he is viewed as experienced, sincere, and understanding of the listeners' needs and interests. Most audiences have some advance knowledge of the speaker's age, training, experience, and status; on this basis they draw conclusions about his ability to treat a given subject. The speaker therefore should select a subject in line with their perception of his ability to treat it adequately—assuming, of course, that he is free to choose his own subject. In the classroom, for example, a member of the college football team normally would be accepted as an authority on football; a class officer on campus politics or a returned war veteran, on his branch of the service. When a speaker is perceived as knowing his subject, the audience is usually interested in listening to him.

An audience should not be put in the position of questioning the speaker's judgment in the choice of a topic. Certainly no mature audience is impressed by some immature youth's attempt at solving world-shattering problems, as sometimes happens when a speech class is invited to send a student speaker to the local Rotary, Kiwanis, Lions, or other luncheon clubs. Nor is an authority accepted in one field necessarily accepted in another. However, individuals in certain fields, such as the ministry, public administration, teaching, or social work, are assumed to have considerable knowledge on many topics.

In some instances listeners have no advance image of a particular speaker, as when an organization sends out speakers to make appeals for funds. These speakers must talk on the assigned topic; they have no choice in subject selection. The listeners have no image of the speaker, but they have an attitude toward the cause he supports. Hence, the speaker must plan the content of his remarks in keeping with the listeners' image of the cause being promoted.

Suiting the Occasion and the Time Available

It is obvious that there are many subjects suitable for a particular audience on some occasions that would not be suitable for the same audience on other occasions. When you attend a dinner given for a friend who has just received a substantial promotion in his work, your subjects of conversation suitable for that occasion would not be suitable in comforting the same friend over the loss of his job, the death of his father, or the wisdom of returning to the United States from Canada, where he had chosen to go to avoid the military draft. So it is with subjects communicated to larger audiences. Analyze the speaking occasion carefully before deciding on your subject.

The speaker who does not respect the time limits specified for his speech is in real danger of failure. Few faults of the communicator are as sure to alienate his listeners as failure to stop near the expected time. Therefore, it is imperative that he consider the time allotted to him and that he select a topic that may be adequately treated in the time at his disposal. Some subjects are not suited to a short speech, and others are not suited to a long one.

Students especially should observe this caution. Problems of international relations, the training of children, or a year's trip through Europe cannot be adequately treated in the few minutes available for a practice speech in a classroom. Either select a different subject, or drastically limit the one you choose. The process of limiting your subject matter to keep within the allowed time limits is dealt with in the next section.

The following lists suggest many possible subjects that should satisfy the criteria mentioned and are within the interests and experiences of most college students. For very short talks even many of these need to be limited.

1. College life and activities:

Life in a college fraternity	Working in the bookstore
Running for a campus office	Selecting a vacation job
Values of military training	Acting in a school play
An extracurricular activity	A way to get good grades
Bane of college life: tests	How to relax on weekends
The veteran goes to college	Living in a college dorm
What teaching assistants do	Values of college debating
Editing a college newspaper	Getting off probation

2. Public issues (*all to be limited*):

Universal military training	Government management
Causes of juvenile	of news
delinquency	Race relations
The welfare state: good	Narcotics control
or evil?	Costs of a college
Conserving our natural	education
resources	Capital punishment
Industry's role in our	Marriage and divorce
economy	Veterans' legislation
Readjusting our tax structure	Medicare

3. Professions and jobs:

Accounting	Journalism	Banking
Music	Mechanical engineering	Librarianship
Medicine	Commercial art	Dress designing
Acting	Professional tennis	Movie production
Law	Gas station operation	Dietetics
Architecture	Landscape architecture	Auto mechanics
Insurance	Camp counseling	Dental technology
Real estate	Television announcing	Teaching

Several exercises at the end of this chapter give additional speech topics.

Meeting the Tests of Suitability

Before you proceed further in your preparation for a speaking situation, make certain that your subject meets the tests of suitability. Ask yourself the following questions:

1. Do I have an enthusiastic interest in the subject?
2. Do I have sufficient knowledge of the subject?
3. Is it suitable to the image my respondents have of me?
4. Is it a subject that will meet the needs, interests, attitudes, and knowledge of my respondents?
5. Does it add to my respondents' knowledge?
6. Is it appropriate to the occasion?
7. Can it be treated in the time allotted to me?

LIMITING THE SUBJECT

Such broad subjects as "Crime," "Education," "The Bible," "War," "Architecture," or "Recreation" are impossible to cover in one speech and should always be severely narrowed in scope. Even "The Causes, Kinds, and Cures of Crime," "Prophecy and Fulfillment in the Old and New Testaments," "The Major Wars of the United States," and "Noncompetitive Sports for Adults" are far too broad for a short speech. They must be further limited. Speakers seldom narrow their subject too much; most err in the opposite direction.

Three primary criteria of subject limitations are time limits, audience considerations, and specific response desired.

Adjusting to Time Limits

There are no rules to help determine exactly how to limit a subject to fit the time available. Common sense suggests, however, that you cannot treat adequately in two or three minutes subjects on which volumes have been written. Keep in mind that in a four-minute speech about one minute might be used for the introduction and the conclusion, leaving only three minutes for the body. At best, only two or three major points can be made in that time. In each case the subject must be narrowed accordingly.

Narrowing the Topic to Audience Interests

The nature of the audience often indicates how a subject might be limited. Do listeners know much about certain aspects of the subject and little about others? Are they interested only in certain phases of the subject? How does its homogeneity or lack of it affect the subject limitation? How do age, sex, physical condition, status, education, and attitude toward the subject affect its scope?

Consider the following examples. Many Minneapolis business-men are interested in the general subject of sports, and they usually become excited about "Minnesota's Football Prospects for Next Year." Young boys are interested in plans for the new Pony League ball diamond. The laborer probably attends a union meeting at which information about next year's contract is given, but he might not attend a lecture at the local college on problems affecting the American economy. Many of the aspects of audience analysis considered in Chapter Nine also apply to narrowing the subject.

Adapting the Topic to the Response Desired

What is the specific response you desire from the speech? Will any action be taken by your respondents or by others? Is the desired action to be immediate or delayed? Is the desired response related to vital needs or to peripheral interests of the listeners? Will this communication affect the listeners only, those close to them, or others to whom they have no personal ties? Each communicator needs to consider such questions and to limit or change his subject accordingly. For example, people who live through a disaster seek information on what they can do now to prevent repeated loss and to speed recovery. Many persons living in Southern California had their homes and businesses destroyed or damaged in the earthquake of February 9, 1971. Many thousands of school children and their parents were affected by having schools closed after being declared unsafe. Group meetings were held, public lectures were attended, and individual help was sought. The people listened to speakers who dealt with those immediate, vital problems. A speech correctionist talking to parents of children with speech defects will certainly present a different content and will seek a different response from one speaking before a group of professional colleagues. You should adapt your topic to the specific response you hope to obtain.

The best speeches are almost always those in which some part of a whole is presented with penetration and completeness. You cannot take your listeners "Around the World in Eighty Days" when you have only eight breathless minutes in which to speak—much less if you have only two or three. You can, however, make them see a little of the glamour and romance of the Hawaiian Islands, some bit of the scenery of Scotland, or perhaps the grandeur and majesty of Fujiyama.

Applying Methods of Limitation

A subject can almost always be narrowed through a selection of only part of it. Thus, a topic dealing with a particular automobile might be limited to its design, economy, ease of handling, motor features, or popularity. "Farming in California" could be limited to "The Value of

Cotton Crops." "Elementary Education" might be narrowed to "The Free Lunch Program" or "Readiness as a Factor in Learning."

A subject notable for its problems could be limited by considering a single problem and its solution, by presenting only the causes of the problem, or by showing only the ramifications of a single solution. Thus, the broad subject of problems in higher education might be narrowed by the taking of a single phase, such as "Participation of Students in Academic Planning" or "The Benefits of a No-Grade System." The subject of drug use could be restricted by a consideration in depth of a single cause or a single proposal for meeting the problem.

Here are a number of examples of reducing broad subjects to manageable size. Further limitations of most of them could be made.

1. General subject: The Natural Beauty of Colorado
   Limited subject: Close to the Sky: 54 peaks above 14,000 feet
2. General subject: Automation
   Limited subject: Uses of the IBM 370
3. General subject: Love
   Limited subject: The Sacrifice of Sidney Carton
4. General subject: Railroads in the United States
   Limited subject: The First Railroad West of Kansas City
5. General subject: Airplane Travel
   Limited subject: Why the Sign "Fasten Your Safety Belts"
6. General subject: Shopping
   Limited subject: The Economy of "Buying the Best"

Successive steps in narrowing make an effective way of limiting a speech subject. The following examples illustrate this technique:

1. Travel
   Traveling abroad
   Traveling in Europe
   Traveling in France
   Traveling by bicycle in France
2. Animals
   Household pets
   Dogs as household pets
   French Poodles as household pets
   My pet French Poodle "Fifi"
3. Education
   College education
   Attending a small college

School costs at a small college
Why tuition is so high at a small college
4. Food
American food
Inexpensive American food
Easily prepared inexpensive American food
The hot dog as a national institution

PLANNING THE THESIS STATEMENT

After the general subject has been determined and narrowed to work-able, suitable dimensions, the communicator is ready for the next step: formulating a specific, precise, brief statement of the central idea of the speech, the one main thought he wants to leave with his audience. Although this statement has been called by various names, we shall refer to it as the *thesis statement*.

Its Definition and Function

A thesis statement is a single, brief, precisely worded statement of the central idea of a speech. It must present only one idea; therefore, it must not be a compound sentence (which would represent two or more ideas for two or more speeches), although it might be a complex sentence (having one or more dependent clauses). However, the simple sentence (one subject, one predicate) should generally suffice and is preferred, since it indicates a single, uncluttered, concrete idea. It should be a declarative sentence, not interrogative, imperative, or ex-clamatory. It is an assertion, one that can be judged either true or false. It is the point you want your respondents to understand, the opinion you hope they will accept, or the action you desire them to take. Many speeches fail because the thesis statement has not been clearly thought out by the speaker, causing the listeners to become confused about what the central idea really is. If the speaker himself knows what his thesis statement is, he is likely to be able to communicate the idea to his audience.

A thesis statement, then, is a clear, concise, concrete, declarative sentence embodying the one central idea of the speech. Its preparation is one of the most important steps in preparing for the entire speaking situation.

Its Forms

There are many forms that the thesis statement can take. First, it may consist of a brief definition of the subject, describing or identifying the unique characteristic or characteristics of the subject. Such a thesis statement would be "California Institute of Technology is primarily an institution for the training of scientists and engineers." Or it may indicate the basic principle or principles involved in the subject.

The thesis statement may evaluate the subject, indicating the communicator's viewpoint on a problem, a situation, a concept, an object, or a person. It may deal with a solution to a problem of which the respondents are aware or to one that it will be necessary to explain before the solution is offered. It may be in the form of a statement of policy or value. "John Brown is the most qualified candidate for the office of President" and "The Federal Government should place further restrictions on the sale of firearms" are examples of this form of thesis statement.

A desired action on the part of the respondents may be indicated (although not necessarily directly stated) in the thesis statement. Such statements as "Pete Jones should be elected Social Chairman" or "Our church needs volunteer carpenters immediately" would indicate a definite call for action.

A thesis statement might suggest the divisions of a topic as, for example, "This university excels in scholarship, research, and community service" and "The operation of the XYZ camera is a four-step process." We shall deal with dividing or partitioning topics in a later section.

Its Placement in the Speech

Where in the speech should the thesis statement come? In most instances it would be stated in the introduction and probably again in the conclusion (introductions and conclusions are dealt with in detail in the next chapter). However, there may be occasions on which the thesis statement should not be revealed until the conclusion. Let us assume that you are going to ask for contributions to a worthwhile fund. You may feel that stating the central idea (collecting money from the audience) at the beginning of the speech might set up a barrier of resistance too difficult to overcome. By leading the audience through the major points you intend to cover—the worth of the charity, the quality of the activities conducted, and the need for financial assistance, for example—you hope to guide them logically and emotionally to your conclusion without any barrier's being raised. In the instance just cited the best placement for the thesis statement would undoubtedly be in the conclusion.

There may be occasions on which the thesis statement as you have worded it in your preparation may never be stated as such anywhere in the speech. Perhaps you might feel that more effectiveness could be achieved by phrasing the central idea dramatically so as to arouse the emotions of the respondents. Although you have planned your thesis statement as a declarative sentence, you might choose to say it in the form of a rhetorical question in the delivery of the conclusion, to stimulate further thinking on the part of your listeners. A question such as "What are you going to do to help these crippled children?" might be more effective than your thesis statement, which would be worded something like this: "The Crippled Children's Society needs your financial support now." By preparing a thesis statement as a declarative sentence you have formulated in your mind a concrete idea. If you have kept this thesis statement uppermost in your mind throughout the planning and delivery of the speech, whether you actually say the words or not during the speech, your respondents will be more likely to respond to the concluding question in the way you desire.

You may choose to conclude with an imperative, such as "Vote for John Brown for President," but your thesis statement for preparation and planning would be a declarative sentence: "John Brown is the best qualified candidate for President."

Regardless of the words used in the actual presentation of the speech, your central theme must be clear both to you and to your respondents. If any member of the audience should be asked, after the speech is over, "What did the speaker say?" he should be able to answer in words very similar to those the speaker had put together for the thesis statement. If your respondents are unable to do this after your speech, you have been guilty of one of three faults: (1) you did not formulate a thesis statement according to the criteria considered in this chapter, (2) you did not keep the thesis statement in mind as you were partitioning the topic and gathering supporting materials, or (3) you did not use the most effective placement of it.

Writing It Out

All of us have had the experience of having an idea that seemed to us to be definite and concrete, only to realize, when we attempted to write it out, that we were having trouble in doing so. The thesis statement must be concrete, it must say exactly what you intend it to say, and it must follow all the principles we have previously considered, for it is the focal point of your speech and the statement to which all your other statements have a direct relationship. Before you proceed further in your planning of a speech, try the thesis statement out on paper. Edit it, delete tangential material, make certain it expresses only one idea, remove any ambiguous words or phrases, and test it against the criteria of a good thesis statement. Only when this is done are you ready to proceed to the next step in your preparation.

The Speech Title

A word concerning speech titles is warranted at this point. A speech title is not necessarily a good thesis statement. Normally those who affix a title to a speech attempt to formulate a dramatic title, one that will capture attention readily. Often the titles are rather obscure in meaning, frequently borrowed from a metaphor or analogy that might be a part of the speech. Examples are "The Cross of Gold" and "Acres of Diamonds," the meanings of which become apparent only after the speech is heard. Titles, generally, do not make the statement of assertion that is necessary for a thesis statement.

For a great number of speeches titles are not necessary. A title might be needed when the speaker is introduced by another person or when a printed program, a poster, a bulletin board, or a press release announces the speech. The main function of a title is to attract advance favorable attention; its function is not that of a thesis statement. Our advice to you is, to avoid the temptation of falling into the trap of substituting a title for a good, sound thesis statement, do *not* give your speech a title. If, however, your classroom procedure calls for introductions by other members of the class, it will be necessary that you provide a title. But keep in mind that a speech title is *not* a thesis statement.

PARTITIONING THE THESIS STATEMENT
The thesis statement is the central idea of the speech. The speaker must now prepare his development of that idea, the points or issues that will prove, explain, or amplify the assertion made in the thesis statement.

Main Headings
Except for the very short one-point speech, for which the thesis statement would have only one supporting point, the speaker now turns his attention to the major divisions of his speech. These divisions are the major issues, or main heads, that will support the assertion he intends to make. In determining the main heads one must adhere to a number of standards or principles, which we shall now consider.

Support of Statement
All main heads must be in direct support of the thesis, proving, explaining, or amplifying the thesis statement. There may be many major issues a speaker could think of to support any one thesis, but limitations of time, audience, and occasion will dictate which ones he should employ. For example, if the thesis statement were "Crested Butte, Colorado, offers many advantages," the type of audience might influence the communicator's selection of major points. If he were speaking to a ski club, he would probably have as his main heads "Excellent skiing facilities," "Beautiful scenery," and "Modern lodges." If, however, he were speaking to a group of businessmen who were in the habit of taking summer vacations with their families, he might

develop his thesis with these main heads: "Excellent fishing," "Beautiful scenery," "Reasonable housing," and "Profitable investment opportunities."

Maybe a dozen partitions could be made, but the speaker must select from them only the ones that will best suit the audience, the occasion, the speaker's competence, and the time allotted. Moreover, he must ask himself this question: Does each of the main heads selected support my thesis statement? In the example just presented each of the main heads must indicate an advantage offered by the resort area. Such main heads as "The Town was incorporated in 1882" and "The first ski tow was built in 1963" would be inappropriate, although perhaps interesting, because they do not indicate advantages offered by Crested Butte and therefore do not directly support the thesis statement.

Coherence

Coherence is simply that quality of having a clear and logical relationship of ideas. It is not enough that a speech have a central theme and that all divisions of that theme support it directly; each division must bear the same relationship to the thesis statement as the others, and the order of arrangement must have some pattern—some consistent principle of organization that applies throughout.

Coherence is achieved, first, by having the partitions of the topic identical in their relationships to the topic. As an illustration, a coherent speech about "Causes of Traffic Accidents" might consider the condition of the road, condition of the car, and condition of the driver. If the sequence of causes was presented as slippery pavement, driving while drunk, faulty brakes, excessive speed, failure to heed road signs, loose sand, driving while tired, and poor tires, the speech would have little coherence. A talk about "Our Fighting Forces—Army, Navy, and Air Force" would be coherent if all content about the first branch were considered as a unit, the second branch were, too, and finally the third. There should be no overlapping, and the relationships among the three should be clear. To speak in sequence of the Marines, the Strategic Air Command, the Quartermaster Corps, the Navy submarine service, the Navy, the Militia, and the three service academies, would suggest an incoherent relationship among the major points in the speech. The table of contents of this text reveals our efforts to be coherent in arranging its content. We have been concerned first with developing an understanding of the communicative situation, next with the preparation for the communicative situation, and finally with participation in the communicative situation.

Not only must the major divisions bear the same relationships to the topic, but the relationships among them must be reasoned and logical. The order in which one unit of thought follows another must have some basis in tradition, logic, or purpose, or it must be inherent in the material itself.

In a speech on "Great Cities of the United States," for example, the sequence of Chicago, San Francisco, New York, Los Angeles, Miami, and Seattle would not be coherent geographically. However, it might be coherent in some other principle of organization, as the crime rate or the proportion of Boy Scouts to population. Various patterns of arrangement and examples are presented in the next chapter.

To ensure parallelism of relationship among the divisions we suggest the following rule. Make all main heads (and all subheads dividing the main heads) parallel in parts of speech and grammatical construction. If you begin with nouns (whether modified or not), make all the divisions on the same level nouns: for example, Hockey, Water Polo, Basketball, Football. A main head such as "Interesting" in combination with those just listed would be incorrect, because it is an adjective and does not bear the same relationship to the thesis as the others. Whether the partitions are words, phrases, clauses, or sentences, they must be parallel in construction. Following are some examples of partitions of thesis statements in the form of various parts of speech and grammatical constructions.

1. Nouns (modified)
   Thesis statement:
       Neighborhood pests can be infuriating.
   Partitions:
       Noisy party-givers
       Back-fence gossips
       Hot-rod and motorcycle drivers
       Brattish children
2. Adverbs
   Thesis statement:
       Center City's development has been phenomenal.
   Partitions:
       Yesteryear
       Today
3. Adjectives
   Thesis statement:
       Everyone should take up swimming
   Partitions:
       It is healthful.
       It is utilitarian.
       It is fun.
4. Present participle (gerund)
   Thesis statement:

Failure in school can easily be accomplished.
Partitions:
By turning in assignments late
By not asking questions about points that are unclear
By not taking effective notes in class
By not planning specific study-period times
5. Imperative form of the verb
Thesis statement:
Making a braided rug is a four-step process.
Partitions:
Cut the material into strips.
Sew the strips into long pieces.
Braid the long pieces.
Sew the braids together.
6. Infinitive form of the verb
Thesis statement:
My candidate pledges himself to improve the lot of the low-income working man.
Partitions:
To reduce sales taxes
To provide more substantial financial assistance in building low-cost housing.
To increase welfare assistance to the needy.
7. Present tense of the verb
Thesis statement:
A good discussion leader strives for good interpersonal relations within his group.
Partitions:
Establishes an informal "climate"
Encourages general participation
Instigates self-analysis of the group

Mutual Exclusiveness

Some speakers find that their communication is confusing to their listeners, even though they have been careful that all partitions directly support the thesis statement. Perhaps the fault lies in the fact that the partitions are not mutually independent of each other. Perhaps there is overlapping of the divisions, one being a part of the other, in which case the one should have been a main head and the other a subhead. Perhaps one of them is just a repetition, clothed in other words, of the other. Let us look at some examples. To describe various kinds of contemporary fiction the inclusion of the following as two of the main heads would be incorrect.

Detective stories
Works of Erle Stanley Gardner

Although both would be in support of the thesis, the second one is a part of the first and would properly be one of the subheads rather than a main head.

In preparing a speech to explain the component parts of a social fraternity, the major partitions could be:

Main head I: Pledges
Main head II: Actives
Main head III: Alumni

The inclusion of "Students" as one of the main heads would be incorrect, since the first two already include students. If, however, the speaker chose to differentiate between current students and alumni, his main heads and subheads might have been these:

Main head I: Students
   Subhead: Pledges
   Subhead: Actives
Main head II: Alumni

Another common fault, as suggested earlier, is repetition of the main heads or partitions. The following two partitions are, in fact, not partitions at all but merely the same main head said in different words:

Select a desired response from your audience.
Determine what you want from your audience.

Equally incorrect is the repetition of the thesis statement as one of the partitions. If the thesis statement were "The Federal Government should enact stricter legislation concerning sale and use of firearms," a main head such as "Congress should pass more rigid laws" would only be a restatement of the thesis statement, not a major division of the thesis.

Audiences can follow a speaker through the development of a speech if there are logical divisions. Whenever there is an overlapping of partitions or any repetition the audience becomes confused, and the unity and coherence and, therefore, the total effectiveness of the communication is destroyed.

More will be said on these points in the following chapter, where principles of outlining are considered.

Limited Number

There is no rigid rule concerning the number of main points or issues a speech should have. Despite the common-sense rule that something cannot be divided into only one part, there may be times that the speaker would deem it desirable to speak on only one point in support of his thesis. Usually, however, there will be two, three, four, or more, depending on the type of subject, the nature of the audience, the competence of the speaker, the occasion, and the time limits imposed. A six-minute speech with four or five major divisions would hardly allow much time for explanation or amplification of any one of them. The speech would probably appear "watered down" to the point that it would be highly ineffective. In addition, the audience can remember two or three main issues much better than it can five or six or more. The temptation of many inexperienced students is to attempt to speak on five or six divisions of a topic simply because they recognize them as being natural partitions of the thesis. One must be highly selective in his choice of divisions, determining which ones will have the greatest success in securing the desired response from the listeners. Difficult as it is for a student to discard a "good" idea he has thought of or material he has gathered from diligent research, he must do it, if he is to achieve effective communication. Further treatment of the number of main points and subpoints will be found in the section on outlining in the next chapter.

Subheadings

Little more needs to be said about subheads at this point. The same principles that apply in the relationship of main heads to thesis statement apply in the relationship of subheads to main heads. Further consideration of subheads will be presented in the next chapter in connection with outlining.

DETERMINING TRANSITIONS

We have stressed the importance of determining logical divisions of the thesis statement in securing the desired response of the auditors. However logical these divisions might be, they will not be effective, and coherence will not be achieved, unless the audience is aware of them. One of the techniques of creating this awareness is the use of transitions, or connecting words, phrases, clauses, or sentences, that clearly and smoothly indicate the partitioning of the thesis.

When a person reads a communication from the printed page, he is able to assimilate the information at his own pace; he may reread passages to understand relationships that may not have been clear on the first reading; he has the physical appearance of paragraphing and indentation to aid his understanding. The speaker has one time only to make his message clear to his listeners. The effective use of transitions will help achieve this goal.

Their Characteristics

Transitions show the relationship of one unit to another. Any transition, therefore, must perform three characteristic functions: (1) it must refer to the preceding point, (2) it must show the relationship between the preceding point and the following point, and (3) it must preview the following point. Often even single words can fulfill these three requirements, such as the word *consequently.* This transitional word (1) refers to the preceding point, (2) indicates a causal relationship, and (3) prepares the listener for the result or effect to be explained in the next point.

A speaker has at his disposal a vast variety of words and phrases that indicate specific relationships between two elements of the speech. A few examples are these: to indicate additional points, the words *and, furthermore, moreover, besides, likewise;* to indicate cause, *because, for, inasmuch as;* to indicate result, *hence, thus, consequently, therefore;* to indicate contrast, *but, nevertheless, despite, on the other hand, yet, however, in spite of;* to indicate alternatives, *either . . . or, otherwise, or;* to indicate restatement or expansion of an idea, *in fact, in other words, that is to say, namely.* Each of these, and many more that could be included, can perform the three functions of transitions, when used properly. To enumerate items the speaker could use any of several sets of transitions: *first, second, third, finally; primarily, secondarily;* etc. Do not mix these sets, however, within the same level of partitions.

The speaker may choose to employ entire sentences (sometimes several sentences, if necessary) to indicate transitions. Consider such statements as these:

> This basic problem can be traced to two principal causes. (The speaker has just described the problem and is now ready to take up the matter of its causes.)
>
> In addition to . . . there is . . . (The respondents are being alerted that another parallel and coordinate point is going to be made.)
>
> Let us now consider. . . . (The speaker is turning to another point or piece of supporting evidence, having completed consideration of the previous one.)
>
> So we see that this problem does exist. But what are the possible solutions? (Rhetorical questions are often very effective transitions.)
>
> But this is only one aspect. Equally important is. . . . (The speaker now will take up another coordinate point.)

Now let us look at this in a different way. (This indicates that a contrast is about to be made or an alternative is to be suggested.)

Another form that transitions may take, adding to the coherence of a speech, is the use of repetition of key words and phrases in parallel construction. Such a technique clearly indicates to the audience the coordination of points and at the same time adds force with each successive point. Lincoln used this device in closing his Gettysburg Address with the words, "Of the people, by the people, and for the people." Note how effectively Churchill used this kind of repetition in his famous Dunkirk speech:[1]

We shall fight in France, we shall fight on the seas and the oceans, we shall fight with growing confidence and growing strength in the air, we shall defend our island, whatever the cost may be, we shall fight on the beaches, we shall fight on the landing-grounds, we shall fight in the fields and in the streets, we shall fight in the hills; we shall never surrender.

Franklin D. Roosevelt used a similar parallel construction and repetition with dramatic effect in his call for a declaration of war against Japan. Note how this achieves a sense of coherence:[2]

Yesterday, December 7, 1941—a date which will live in infamy—the United States of America was suddenly and deliberately attacked by naval and air forces of the Empire of Japan. . . .
    Yesterday the Japanese government also launched an attack against Malaya.
    Last night Japanese forces attacked Hong Kong.
    Last night Japanese forces attacked Guam.
    Last night Japanese forces attacked the Philippine Islands.
    Last night the Japanese attacked Wake Island.
    This morning the Japanese attacked Midway Island.
    Japan has, therefore, undertaken a surprise offensive extending throughout the Pacific area.

Martin Luther King, Jr. demonstrated the effectiveness of this same form of repetition in two portions of his speech "I Have a Dream":[3]

I still have a dream. It is a dream deeply rooted in the American dream that one day this nation will rise up and live out the true meaning of its creed—we hold these truths to be self-evident, that all men are created equal.

I have a dream that one day on the red hills of Georgia, sons of former slaves and sons of former slave-owners will be able to sit down together at the table of brotherhood.

I have a dream that one day, even the state of Mississippi . . . will be transformed into an oasis of freedom and justice.

I have a dream my four little children will one day live in a nation where they will not be judged by the color of their skin but by the content of their character. I have a dream today!

I have a dream that one day, down in Alabama . . . little black boys and black girls will be able to join hands with little white boys and white girls as sisters and brothers. I have a dream today!

I have a dream that one day every valley shall be exalted, every hill and mountain shall be made low, the rough places shall be made plain, and the crooked places shall be made straight and the glory of the Lord shall be revealed and all flesh shall see it together. . . .

So let freedom ring from the prodigious hilltops of New Hampshire.

Let freedom ring from the mighty mountains of New York.

Let freedom ring from the heightening Alleghenies of Pennsylvania.

Let freedom ring from the snow-capped Rockies of Colorado.

Let freedom ring from the curvaceous slopes of California.

But not only that.

Let freedom ring from Stone Mountain of Georgia.

Let freedom ring from Lookout Mountain of Tennessee.

Let freedom ring from every hill and molehill of Mississippi, from every mountainside, let freedom ring.

Transitions indicate the relationship of one idea to another. Because they point out these relationships, they help the listener to "see" the organization of the speech and to follow intellectually the progression of main points and subpoints that support the speaker's thesis.

Their Placement

Transitions should be used wherever the listener should be made aware of a change from one unit of the speech to another or from one basic idea to another. Although they may be necessary and desirable in other instances, transitions are used to bridge the following obvious gaps:

From the introduction to the first main point
From subpoint to subpoint
From main point to main point

From the last main point to the conclusion

No more transitions than are needed should be used. If you feel that your audience, by the very nature of the content, will move with you from a particular point to another point, a transition probably is not necessary. In any event, make the transitions flow as smoothly as possible into the next point. They should not be made so consistently noticeable throughout a speech that they become mechanical and abrupt. McCall and Cohen say:[4] "Actual transition in thought is psychological rather than mechanical. It is something to be *felt* by both speaker and listener rather than merely observed."

Cautions

We have spent some time on the importance of transitions and their aid in achieving coherence in a speech. They are extremely important because they "outline" the speech for the listener. An auditor cannot possibly remember everything that he hears in a speech, nor should he be expected to, but he can remember the main points, the important subpoints, and their relationships to each other and the thesis. Effective transitions will guide him to this end.

Important as transitions are, they must be used carefully, for poor transitions—those which suggest relationships not intended by the communicator—confuse rather than clarify. If the listener is guided to false relationships or is not made aware of any relationship at all, the effectiveness of the communication may be lost entirely.

Almost as important to remember is the fact that overuse of transitions may interrupt the smooth flow of ideas. When there is an excessive amount of transitional material, the speech may appear to the respondents as a long series of separate items rather than a smooth and logical progression of ideas. When transitions begin to stand out so much that they call attention to themselves, they break the continuity of the speech. As we said previously, progress of thought during a speech should be psychological rather than mechanical. Use transitions to "smooth out" the speech rather than to "break it up."

Another caution is to avoid using the same set of transitions for different levels of points in a speech. For example, if you are using "first," "second," and "finally" for the main heads, do not use the same set for any of the subheads. To do so would confuse the listener.

IMPLICATIONS

1. In the world outside the classroom the selection of a subject is seldom a problem. The subject usually (1) arises spontaneously, (2) is chosen for you, or (3) is one that you feel a need or desire to communicate.

2. Your classmates should be recognized as a real audience and should be treated as any other audience.
3. The subject chosen should be one in which you have a real interest.
4. If you have found something in a subject area that fascinates you, it is likely that you can find something in that subject that will interest your listeners.
5. The subject chosen should be one about which you have had some knowledge or experience.
6. Additional research on a subject that suits your knowledge and experience is advisable; it will inform you of the opinions and experiences of others, may provide supporting material for your claims, and may suggest approaches to the subject that you had not considered.
7. We speak with greater confidence when our subjects are within the scope of our knowledge, experience, and interest.
8. The selected subject must suit the interests and needs of your listeners; it must have some significance for them.
9. The selected subject should suit the respondents' image of you.
10. The selected subject must be suitable to the occasion.
11. A major fault of beginning speakers is the attempt to cover subject areas too broadly.
12. The selected subject area must be narrowed to fit the time allotted, suit the interests of the audience, and effect the specific response desired.
13. A thesis statement—a single, brief, precisely worded statement of the central idea—must be well thought out by the communicator.
14. The thesis statement may (1) describe the unique characteristic or characteristics of the subject, (2) state the basic principle or principles involved in the subject, (3) evaluate the subject, (4) suggest a solution to the problem, (5) state a specific desired action to be taken by the audience, (6) suggest the divisions of a topic; and so forth.
15. There is no one proper placement of the thesis statement in a speech; you must make a careful analysis to discover the proper placement.
16. A thesis statement may sometimes never be stated as such in any part of the speech.
17. If you use a speech title, remember that the title does not substitute for a thesis statement.
18. The thesis statement must be divided into the major points or issues (main heads) that will prove, explain, or amplify it.
19. The partitioning of the thesis is not to be confused with the preparation of an outline.
20. Main heads must directly support, and bear the same relationships to, the thesis statement.
21. Main heads must be mutually exclusive and few in number.
22. The divisions or main points are not to be confused with evidence and other supporting materials.
23. Transitions aid the listeners' understanding by indicating the relationship of one unit to another.
24. Our treatment of the thesis statement does not generally apply to interviews (Chapter 15) and discussion (Chapter 16), since they are approached with an attitude of inquiry rather than of advocacy. However, our treatment of

transitions may well be applied to both interviewing and discussion situations.

EXERCISES

1. List five subjects on which you feel capable of speaking without further study. List five subjects in which you are interested, but which would require further study before you would feel competent to speak on them. Submit these lists to your instructor for review. When they are returned, keep them for later use.
2. List five different speech occasions on which a current public issue would be suitable for a speech subject. Phrase a good thesis statement for a seven-minute speech for each of these occasions.
3. Using the method suggested in this chapter, make five successive delimitations of each of the following general topic areas: sports, agriculture, business, literature, medicine. Write a good thesis statement for a four-minute speech for each topic.
4. The following do not meet the criteria of thesis statements. Rewrite each so it would be appropriate for a thesis statement for a five-minute speech to this class:
   a. What poetry means to me
   b. Rules for success in school
   c. Too much extracurricular work
   d. Needed improvement in this school
   e. Values of student government
5. Partition each of the thesis statements you have formulated for Exercise 4 into two to four major divisions suitable for a six-minute speech to your class.
6. Using the words and phrases listed in this chapter as a "starter," make a list of all transitional words and phrases that you can muster that indicate each of the following: additional points, result, contrast, alternatives, restatement or expansion of an idea.
7. Select one of the speeches in the Appendix and determine the thesis statement and the major points or issues. (Remember that the thesis statement may not be worded as such anywhere in the speech.)
8. For the speech in Exercise 7 determine the transitional devices used.
9. From the list below select three of the topic areas. For each write (1) a good thesis statement, (2) major divisions, and (3) whatever subdivisions you feel would be appropriate for a five-minute speech to your class.

The importance of the minority	Classical versus popular music
Television versus movies	My favorite fictional character
Movies in the classroom	How to be unpopular
Education by television	The ideal instructor
Good sportsmanship	The school's grading system
How to vote intelligently	Characteristics of a good citizen
The importance of a free press	The disappearance of chivalry
Mistakes parents make	Considerations in buying a car

ADDITIONAL READINGS

Abernathy, Elton, *Fundamentals of Speech Communication*, 3rd ed., Dubuque, Ia., Brown, 1970, chap. 15.

Baird, A. Craig, and Franklin H. Knower, *General Speech: An Introduction*, 3rd ed., New York, McGraw-Hill, 1963, chap. 3.

Blankenship, Jane, *Public Speaking: A Rhetorical Perspective*, 2nd ed., Englewood Cliffs, N.J., Prentice-Hall, 1972, pp. 185–200.

Bryant, Donald C., and Karl R. Wallace, *Fundamentals of Public Speaking*, 4th ed., New York, Appleton-Century-Crofts, 1969, chaps. 5, 9.

Grasty, William K., and Mary T. Newman, *Introduction to Basic Speech*, Beverly Hills, Calif., Glencoe Press, 1969, chap. 3.

Gray, Giles W., and Waldo W. Braden, *Public Speaking: Principles and Practice*, 2nd ed., New York, Harper & Row, 1963, chaps. 8, 9, 12, 13.

Henning, James H., *Improving Oral Communication*, New York, McGraw-Hill, 1966, chap. 7.

Kruger, Arthur N., *Effective Speaking: A Complete Course*, New York, Van Nostrand Reinhold, 1970, chap. 8.

La Russo, Dominic A., *Basic Skills of Oral Communication*, Dubuque, Ia., Brown, 1967, chaps. 4, 8.

McCall, Roy C., and Herman Cohen, *Fundamentals of Speech*, 2nd ed., New York, Macmillan, 1963, chaps. 3, 4.

McCroskey, James C., *An Introduction to Rhetorical Communication*, 2nd ed., Englewood Cliffs, N.J., Prentice-Hall, 1972, chap. 7.

Mills, Glen E., *Message Preparation: Analysis and Structure*, Indianapolis, Bobbs-Merrill, 1966, chaps. 1, 2, 6.

Nadeau, Ray E., *A Modern Rhetoric of Speech-Communication*, 2nd ed., Reading, Mass., Addison-Wesley, 1972, chap. 6.

Terris, Walter F., *Content and Organization of Speeches*, Dubuque, Ia., Brown, 1968, chaps. 2, 7.

Wilson, John F., and Carroll C. Arnold, *Public Speaking as a Liberal Art*, Boston, Allyn & Bacon, 1964, chaps. 5, 6.

NOTES

[1] Winston S. Churchill, *Their Finest Hour*, Boston, Houghton Mifflin, 1949, p. 118.

[2] Franklin D. Roosevelt, "War Message," in Wayland Maxfield Parrish and Marie Hochmuth, eds., *American Speeches*, New York, Longmans, Green, 1954, pp. 507–508.

[3] Martin Luther King, Jr., "I Have a Dream," in Roy L. Hill, *Rhetoric of Racial Revolt*, Denver, Golden Bell Press, 1964, pp. 373–375.

[4] Roy C. McCall and Herman Cohen, *Fundamentals of Speech*, 2nd ed., New York, Macmillan, 1963, p. 58.

CHAPTER ELEVEN
SELECTING AND ORGANIZING MATERIALS

But this at least I think you will allow, that every speech ought to be put together like a living creature, with a body of its own, so as to be neither without head, nor without feet, but to have both a middle and extremities, described proportionately to each other and to the whole.
    Plato

What do these Gestalt principles of organization mean? Perhaps what they emphasize the most is the importance of our need and search for order, regularity, and correlation in what we perceive. We perceive more easily (and remember, for similar reasons) those things that are simple and well organized.
    James Deese

In the previous chapter you learned the procedures to follow in planning a clearly stated thesis sentence. You are now ready to begin the task of selecting and organizing materials for the speech.

SOURCES OF SPEECH MATERIALS

When we talk about speech materials we refer to the illustrations, examples, analogies, facts, reasoning, narration, quotations, and language which give your speech its unique character.

There are two main sources of materials for speeches; the first is of a general nature, and the second includes all the specific references that are to be found in almost every college, community, county, private, or national library. We shall look at some of the courses of a general nature in this chapter.

Observation and Personal Experience

Although you may be unaware of the fact, you have every day personal experiences that are valuable source materials for speeches or for conversation with friends or for use in more formal discussions. Your first task, then, is to review your past experiences, to determine what bears on the topic for communication. What do you now know about the subject? Once this has been reviewed and recorded, you are ready to look to other general sources for materials.

The value of past and present experiences and observation—what you see happening to other people, the physical objects surrounding you, and events involving persons and objects—should be considered an invaluable source of materials.

Let us look briefly at the sort of direct personal experiences that make usable source materials. If you find it difficult to prepare one speech a week, or one every two weeks, during a semester, you probably are overlooking the rich mine of personal experience. You may have served in the Vietnam War or have a relative or friend who has; you may have been active in some political campaign—for Eugene McCarthy, Edmund Muskie, Richard Nixon, or Nelson Rockefeller; you may have helped in the fights against pollution, racial discrimination, drug use and abuse by teenagers, our country's involvement in Indo-China; you may have taken part in the Womens' Liberation Movement, the Campus Crusade for Christ, a May Day March on Washington, the Peace Corps, or VISTA.

Let us consider the possibility that you feel your life has been prosaic, uneventful, unusual, and perhaps even dull. You have traveled only a little, have no real hobbies, do not socialize much, and read mainly what is assigned in your school work. You still have had experiences worth sharing.

Have you been successfully interviewed for a job? Have you gotten a date through an agency such as "Computer Matching"? Have you won some scholastic award? Certainly such experience has given you ideas about how to get along with people, the value of work, and problems in growing up, all of which are of interest to your classmates. Sometimes the really significant experiences that we forget too quickly provide excellent material for speeches.

Observation, too, is a fruitful source of speech material. Most listeners appreciate personal observations that are interestingly, accurately, and vividly recounted. The range of information to be gained is wide indeed: places of scenic interest, personal do-it-yourself projects, athletic events, parades, newspaper and TV interviews with important or unusual personages, and the simple, homely things of everyday life. It is from these and the occurrences of our daily lives that we form our most accurate judgments of men, women, and events, judgments that should be part of our speeches. Listeners are impressed when the speaker is able to say, "I was there." It gives them a sense of nearness and familiarity and lets them enjoy vicariously the things the speaker describes.

Interviewing

After direct personal experience and observation, interviewing is perhaps the best source of speech materials. Interviewing provides on-the-
spot information about the topic of the interview, and a clarification of
answers is possible. It enables the interviewer to make comparisons of
answers, when several interviews are held. If needed—for example, when
respondents are to be quoted on a controversial topic—interviews can
be held immediately before a speech is to be given, assuring the latest
views; and it gives the interviewer—the speaker—the chance to test his
ideas in the crucible of public opinion. He will know in advance, to
some degree at least, the possible reactions to his ideas.

In Chapter Fifteen we shall give instructions about the preparation for and conduct of an interview. Let us give a few simple instructions for the conduct of a successful interview at this point:

1. Be discriminating in requesting interviews of busy people.
2. Don't ask for an interview on a trivial subject.
3. Plan carefully the sequence and content of questions to be
   asked.
4. Avoid asking leading, argumentative, unclear, or patronizing
   questions.
5. Explain the importance of the interview at the outset, keep
   the interview brief, and express thanks at the close.
6. Make your note taking unobtrusive.

Use the interview frequently as a source of speech materials;
you will find it invaluable. Your practice in college will help you later
toward perfection.

Oral and Written Exchanges

We have already commented on the interview as a means of gaining
source materials for a speech. There are other oral forms of exchange:
casual conversations, lectures, television and radio broadcasts, and informal or formal discussions. Informal conversations, either business or
social, are often a fruitful source of information, especially as a means
of testing ideas. They can also serve as a sounding board, giving some
indication of possible listener response. Conversation is good practice
for increasing your effectiveness in more formal speaking situations.
Conversation can often help to work out effective patterns of both
thought and language for larger audience occasions.

Lectures, when carefully selected in relation to your speech
topic, and radio and television broadcasts are other forms of oral
exchange of ideas, albeit usually one-way. Most readers have access to
three, four, or more radio and television broadcasts per evening and can

certainly keep up on the current news. The menu for radio and television listening is varied and up to date and provides information on almost every subject. Television and radio programs provide information on matters of local, national, and international news and on special events, sports, drama, music, economic issues, and travel.

Group discussion, which is a learning experience in its own right, is detailed in Chapter Sixteen and needs only mention here. It, too, is a means of gathering data for many speech subjects. New information may be gained, unsound or weak arguments exposed, hypotheses tested, suggestions for the limitation of a subject secured, or tentative proposals for action modified and improved. The discussion may also be used as a yardstick to measure possible audience reaction to a proposed topic. If a number of individuals with a variety of backgrounds can find common ground for agreement, it is reasonable to expect a similar reaction in a larger audience. Comparing notes with others in discussion before making a speech provides a test of effective speaker-listener relationships.

Correspondence is another way to secure source materials for a speech. The person from whom you wish to secure information may be too busy to reply to your letter, may not give the exact information you wish, or may give information you cannot use. However, correspondence and questionnaires should not be overlooked as source materials. Do not ask for very much information in a letter, make your questionnaires brief—if possible test them in advance—always explain the reason for your request, and make it easy for the respondent to reply by enclosing a stamped, self-addressed envelope for his use.

Reading

Reading is perhaps the most common method of gaining information, either for general knowledge or for specific speaking occasions. Written materials are generally readily available, can be referred to as often as necessary, can be secured at little cost, and usually provide opportunity for as extensive or intensive study as the speaker considers desirable.

Just as there are basic rules to follow in conducting an interview as a means of getting source materials, so are there certain simple techniques in getting the most out of your reading:

1. Read for a purpose. Decide in advance what you seek from what you read.
2. Scan the index and table of contents first to find relevant material, if the source is a book.
3. If your topic is a controversial one, be sure to read from sources representing different points of view. Your speech

may be persuasive, but you need to know what the other side believes.

4. Be selective in your reading.
5. Take notes as needed. Be systematic in note taking.

Experimentation

The research scientist gains much of his information through experimentation; this is his life work. Few people have time for controlled experiments to gain speech materials, nor do most speech topics lend themselves to scientific experimentation. Informal experimentation, however, may be conducted on many topics. Our own personal experiences are a type of informal experimentation. If you have experimented with different ways of cooking, you might talk about how to make gazpacho, flageolet, truffled cheese, potato ball, or caesar or corn salads. If you have grown different types of flower, refinished old furniture, worked needlepoint, painted landscapes or still life, or designed sets for some of the college plays, you can give advice on these matters.

Libraries

We listed reading as one important source of speech materials. Obviously, before you can do any reading you must know where to find the materials to be read. Maybe you have a large personal library in your home or have access to the library where you work. Most of you, however, will have to use your college or city library or other libraries near your home.

Don't overlook the many library sources available to you. By now you are acquainted with your college library and are sometimes frustrated because the book you want is always out. Try other libraries. In the cities within ten miles of the city in which we live, there are fifteen city libraries and eight junior colleges with excellent libraries, all of which are available for use. Many governmental libraries, such as county and city law libraries, libraries of special governmental agencies, state libraries, and others in Washington, D.C., are accessible to serious students. Use the resources of these libraries if they are located in your city. A few brief comments should be made here about using library resources effectively.

Library resources are now of three general types: (1) magazine, newspaper, and pamphlet indexes, (2) reference books of all types, and (3) nonbook materials, including such things as microfilms, microcards, and some musical materials.

First, consider the various types of indexes. Some are broad in scope, and others are limited to articles dealing with relatively specialized subjects. The *Reader's Guide to Periodical Literature*, published monthly in paper covers and bound annually in volumes, includes references to more than one hundred well-known general publications. The *International Index to Periodicals* includes articles from more than 250 foreign and specialized scholarly journals. *Poole's Index to Periodical Literature* covers the period of 1802 to 1906 and is indexed by subject only. Specialized guides include the *Agricultural Index, Applied Science and Technology Index, Art Index, Book Review Digest, Business Periodicals Index, Education Index, Engineering Index, Experimental Station Record* (digests of articles and literature on agriculture), *Facts on File* (weekly digest of world events), *Index Medicus, Index to Legal Periodicals, Industrial Arts Index, Music Index, Occupational Index, Psychological Index,* and *Song Index.* Other types of specialized guide include the *Monthly New York Times Index of United States Government Publications* (which includes material appearing in the *New York Times*), *United States Government Publications Monthly Catalogue,* which classifies pamphlets, documents, books, and articles in the fields of economics, political science, sociology, commerce, and finance, and the *Vertical File Service Catalog,* which is issued monthly as an annotated subject catalog of pamphlet materials.

A daily record of speeches and "extension of remarks," (the additional comments Congressmen wish to have included) are to be found in the *Congressional Record.* Check to see whether your library has copies.

Besides the index guides to books, magazines, newspapers, and pamphlets, many types of reference book may be found in the main reading room of a library and may be consulted without completing a call card.

Free Materials

Another source of reference material is readily available: the large amount of material published and distributed free of charge by public and private organizations. You do not need to return this material, it is seldom found in libraries, and is usually very well written, though it often represents a decidedly partisan point of view, which you should be aware of.

The 1971 issue of *The World Almanac and Book of Facts* lists more than 1150 national organizations ranging from the *Aaron Burr Association* to the *American Society of Zoologists.* It is safe to say there is not a special interest in this country without an organization supporting it. Many of the organizations are avowed pressure groups, and this must be kept in mind. The thousands of local, state, and regional groups are not included in the *World Almanac* list. There are several different ways of tapping this resource. The *World Almanac* gives addresses, and you may write directly to an organization at its national office, indicating the nature of the subject in which you are interested, and request such free material as may be available. Another way is to find the local office of the national organization in the telephone directory and make a similar request.

Good sources of materials in special fields are organizations and agencies that have something to do with international trade, international transportation, or international relations. This includes foreign consulates, many airlines, some industrial concerns, and many racial organizations. Most of these welcome the opportunity to aid in research or study in their fields of interest.

Effective speaking is in large part the outgrowth of the knowledge that comes from direct personal experience and observation, interviewing others, oral and written exchange of ideas, reading, experimentation, using available library resources, the many sources of free materials, and thinking constantly about the materials you secure. Listeners react favorably when they feel the speaker's content is substantial and his resources rich enough to let him select materials pertinent to the subject and of interest to the particular audience.

EFFECTIVE USE OF RESOURCE MATERIALS

Most adults, including college students, have had at least some practice in directed reading and study. By the time one is in college, his habits of study are fairly firmly established, sometimes ineffectively. If your college has a course on "Effective Study Habits" or has guides to "Effective Library Use," be sure to avail yourself of these aids. In any event, certain procedures should be followed, and we present them here as a trilogy for securing speech source materials.

Worthwhile Sources

Professional journals usually can be relied on to give reliable information. The works of reputable authorities can be counted on to provide accurate and well-grounded, though sometimes biased, materials. Standard reference works of the types mentioned in this chapter are generally worth investigating. When you make use of some of the other techniques we have suggested for securing source materials, seek the best sources available. Interview persons with considerable experience; get your written information from a cross section so that you may generalize about your data. Ask for help in selecting the best library resources, and remember, the house journals—although published by reputable firms—can be biased. You can develop a sense of the quality of a source, providing you can recognize its bias.

Materials Reflecting Various Viewpoints

The wise student will be objective and critical. He will consult sources representing different points of view. Reading from a single source or from sources presenting only one point of view definitely will limit one's effectiveness in analyzing and evaluating and, thus, in speaking. Read from opposing viewpoints, check the experiences others have had, try to balance your lecture, radio, and television listening to test your own ideas. Perhaps you may learn where opposing thought may be weak.

Systematic Note Taking

Most college students know how to take notes; a few do not. We give some suggestions for the latter group:

1. Always use cards or slips of paper of uniform size. A convenient size is four by six inches.
2. Always record only one item, idea, quotation, or statistic on a card.
3. Record quotations, sources, and statistics with absolute accuracy.
4. Summarize long but valuable ideas in precise form. Aim for honest reporting of the author's ideas.
5. Be discriminating in note taking. Don't copy everything, but don't be too brief.
6. Use headings to indicate the central idea of the card. Choose these headings carefully.
7. Include any evaluative statement that may aid in the use of the content of a card.

EVIDENCE SUPPORTING THE THESIS

The thesis statement for a speech may deal with any specific goal the speaker may have within the general purpose of influencing behavior. To reach a specific goal he may need to increase understanding, neutralize hostile attitudes, or demonstrate that the listener's needs or desires may be fulfilled. To accomplish these things he has several resources upon which he can rely: (1) his own expertness, character, and good will (ethos), (2) his ability to use effectively the emotional responses of his audience (pathos), and (3) his ability to set forth evidence and reasoning that will be recognized by his audience as credible (logos). These three elements, when handled effectively, compose proof. The first two, ethos and pathos, have already been discussed. Reasoning will be considered subsequently. In the remainder of this chapter it is our purpose to establish the nature and uses of evidence as a form of supporting material.

Facts and Opinions

Evidence may consist of facts or opinions. *Facts* are data, such as specific instances, cases, objects, events, or statistics that have been perceived and objectively verified and may be rechecked by another person. They are considered true or are known to have happened. They are reported to us directly by our senses. *Opinions* are personal judgments or evaluations of some topic under consideration. They are statements of one's attitude about that topic, which have been recorded and are available for reference. Opinions are not objectively verifiable.

Facts and opinions are called collectively *information* when they appear in informative communications, and they are called evidence when they are used as proof. To be accepted as proof, however, they must be credible to the listener. They become credible when they pass certain tests or criteria, which we will consider later in this chapter.

Facts as Evidence

As we have already stated, a fact is something that has actually happened or is true; it is a reality. It is an objective statement of an event, not an interpretation of that event. For example, in a radio speech from Washington, D.C., a speaker discussing the moral training of young people made the following statement:[1]

A number of years ago (April 28, 1952), the U.S. Supreme Court issued a judgment concerning the released time program. . . . This statement of the Court was greeted as a welcome relief by those who have been terrified by the inroads of Godlessness into our national way of life.

The first sentence here states a fact. Anyone who checks the Court records in the case of *Zorach v. Clauson,* April 28, 1952, will discover that such a decree was handed down. The second sentence, however, is an interpretation of a fact and is therefore an opinion.

Here are some other facts:

France exploded her first atomic bomb in the Sahara on February 13, 1960.

Great Britain set off her first hydrogen bomb in a Pacific test on May 18, 1967.

For his acting in *Ben-Hur* Charlton Heston won an Academy Award for the best performance of 1959.

For his acting in *True Grit* John Wayne won an Academy Award for the best performance of 1969.

Alaska and Hawaii were the forty-ninth and fiftieth states to be admitted to the Union.

Alaska has an area of 586,412 square miles and ranks first in size in the nation; Texas has an area of 267,339 square miles and ranks second in size in the nation.

There are important differences among the facts listed above. Few Americans could verify whether the first and second occurred; we should need to rely on others who could testify that the events actually did take place. The third and fourth facts may be verified by checking the records. The fifth and sixth facts are in the realm of common knowledge—except for the fact of the actual number of square miles in each state—although some Texans might argue that size is not important.

Opinions as Evidence

Opinions used as evidence are either expert or lay. An expert is one who is qualified to speak with some degree of authority. Most of us probably are expert in at least one area, and our opinion on matters in this area probably is regarded as competent. A layman, on the other hand, is one who has no specialized training or experience in the subject under discussion. Nevertheless, lay opinions may at times be considered good evidence. The farmer who has rotated his crops can give a useful personal opinion on the results, although he certainly cannot be considered an expert in agronomy. A student can give an opinion on true-false tests that may in certain circumstances be useful, but he cannot be considered an expert on test construction.

Actually we test opinions by evaluating the person who has expressed the opinion. If he is considered credible, his views will be accepted although, unless he is an expert, they may not carry much weight.

Validated Evidence

Another dimension of evidence is the manner in which it is validated: whether by the audience, the speaker, or external sources.

Audience-Validated Evidence

Audience-validated evidence is that of which the audience is aware and to which its members respond affirmatively. This type of evidence often is referred to as "common knowledge." It is our most valuable form of evidence, for it needs no further form of support. It is therefore most useful as a basis upon which to construct further argument. In making use of this type of evidence we must be fully aware that what is common knowledge to one audience may not be to another, and allowances must be made to tolerate these differences.

Examples of this type of evidence include such statements as "President Kennedy's term of office was ended by his assassination in

Dallas, Texas" and "Income-tax returns must be filed with the Internal Revenue Service by April 15" and "President Nixon has reduced the number of United States combat soldiers in Vietnam "

Speaker-Validated Evidence

Speaker-validated evidence is that which may not be known to the audience but which will be acceptable because the speaker's credibility is sufficient for the audience. Ordinarily such a speaker will have expertise and character that the audience recognizes as justification for accepting his assertion. If the superintendent of education makes the statement that it costs $2000 per year to educate a student in his district, the statement probably will be accepted. If a student asserts that he made a B in each of his courses, it probably will be accepted. If an anthropologist asserts that in some primitive cultures women fulfill many of the roles usually occupied by men in European cultures, the statement probably will be accepted. Conversely, however, the superintendent's credibility would not extend to his judgments about primitive cultures, nor would the anthropologist be thought expert in per-capita costs for education.

Externally Validated Evidence

A third type of evidence is that which must be made acceptable to the audience through the use of additional support obtained by the speaker from external sources. When we refer to external sources, we shall be dealing with three types of evidence:

1. That presented by a trained observer. We mean by this a person who is expert in the field, one qualified to observe and evaluate, and one who has actually witnessed the event in question.
2. That presented by an authority who is an expert in the field but not necessarily an observer of the specific event.
3. That presented by an ordinary observer. We mean by this a person not particularly trained to observe or evaluate matters pertaining to the question at issue.

Most speakers are faced with the need to compile documented data and opinions from qualified sources to support their assertions. An example of evidence from a trained observer is as follows:

"The commanding officer of the Coast Guard vessel which investigated the seizure of a cargo vessel by a Cuban naval vessel reported its position to be more than fifty miles beyond the territorial waters of Cuba at the time of the incident."

Examples of evidence from experts are as follows.

"The Bureau of Labor Statistics states that during the period January to June 1971, unemployment rose by 0.6 of 1%."

"The Registrar of Voters reports that only 56% of the voters exercised their franchise at the primary election."

An example of the observer who is not an expert would be a beauty shop operator waiting to cross the street at the time of an accident, who testified that Driver X was going 40 miles an hour when he struck the car of Driver Y.

Criteria for Acceptance of Evidence

We have established the nature of evidence as those facts and opinions that are credible to the audience. Because of the complications involved in determining the acceptability of evidence to an audience it becomes necessary to set up criteria by which we can judge this acceptability. We divide our criteria into two major parts, the first relating to how evidence supports the proposition; the second, to how sources make the evidence more credible:

How evidence supports the proposition

1. Is its date of significance?
2. Is it consistent within its context?
3. Is it consistent with other evidence?
4. Is it available for verification?

How the source meets audience acceptability

1. Is the observer or expert competent? (Is he in a position to know the facts?)
2. Is the observer or expert prejudiced? (Will he distort the facts?)
3. Is the observer or expert consistent? (Are errors apparent in his past record?)

FORMS OF SUPPORTING MATERIALS

It is not enough to know the sources of speech materials; you must also know about the kinds of material you can find and can use. The extent of understanding and acceptability of a speech by an audience depends to a large extent upon the speaker's ability to handle evidence in such fashion that the audience will find it credible. We shall consider nine types of supporting materials that the speaker may use.

Definition

To define, according to popular dictionaries, is to "determine and state the limits and nature of," "to describe exactly," or "to give the distinguishing characteristics of." Because words are symbols, not referents, and are perceived differently by different people, listeners may become confused about the meanings intended by a speaker. One way the speaker may help reduce this confusion in the mind of the respondent is to define as carefully as possible.

A word may be defined in many ways. One way is through classification. First we designate the general class to which a term belongs and then point out the characteristics that distinguish the term from other members of the class. For example:

Football—*The ball used in this game, an inflated oval with a bladder contained in a casing usually made of leather.*

The dictionary has indicated the class of things—a ball. It has specified the type of ball in two ways: first, how it relates to the game in which it is used and, second, that it is oval in shape. Otherwise its construction is similar to balls used in other sports.

Sometimes we define by the use of synonyms, frequently a single word but sometimes a phrase. For example, the common people may be described as "the masses," "the populace," "hoi polloi," or "the multitude." We may state that worship means to adore, deify, glorify, idolize, idolatrize, revere, or venerate.

Stating either the functions or the parts of an object is still another method of definition. Thus a "computer" is defined as "Any of various machines equipped with keyboards, electronic and electrical circuits, storage units, and recording devices for the high-speed performance of mathematical and logical operations, or for the processing of masses of coded information." In space technology, "hardware" is defined (in the *Aerospace Dictionary*) as follows: "A colloquial term for guided missiles, rockets, and weapons in general, their components and machinery. In a missile, the hardware covers the airframe, the metallic or ceramic parts of the motor, and the instruments. It does not include the fuel."

A term may be defined by giving its roots and origins:

Barbecue: *From the Spanish* barbacoa, *derived from the Haitian* barbacoa, *meaning framework of sticks, originally a raised framework for smoking, drying, or broiling meat.*

Counterfeit: *From the Old French* contrefait, *the past participle of* contrefaire, *to make in opposition, imitate; from* contre-, *counter, plus* faire, *derived from the Latin* facere, *to make; thus, made in imitation of something genuine with intention to deceive or defraud.*

Radical: *Used as an adjective,* radical, *derived from the Latin* radix, *root, means fundamental, basic, going to the root or origin, thoroughgoing, or extreme.*

Some words must be placed in context before they are understood, as in these examples:

Strike: *As in bowling, labor relations, a fight, baseball, mining, sailing (when used to mean lowering a sail or flag), the theater, or in minting.*

Run: *As in racing, music, transportation, campaigning, card playing, billiards, baseball, the movement of liquids, or the passage of time.*

Study: *As in the process of review of a subject, that which is studied, a place for study or reading, a musical étude, a product resulting from serious intellectual application, a curriculum, or a moral.*

Examples and Illustrations

A word, concept, or object is sometimes clarified or defined by the use of examples and illustrations, which may also be used for gaining attention, and to explain and substantiate.

The *example* cites a particular case or circumstance to support a generalization. In a speech presenting the idea that our nation is presently in a state of scientific starvation, the speaker first referred to the many scientific accomplishments of the last quarter-century, approximately the years 1945 to 1970. He then contrasted these achievements with current happenings and trends which indicated that this country was in danger of scientific starvation. On the positive side he cited these examples:[2]

Over the past quarter century . . . science and the U.S. economy have had the longest period of sustained growth, discovery, innovation and new industry development in history.

We have landed six men on the moon and returned them safely to Earth—a feat without parallel in human endeavor.

Our Earth-orbiting satellite systems are opening new eras in communication, weather forecasting, and resource analysis.

Our commercial aircraft dominate the air lanes of the world. . . .

Our military ships, missiles and aircraft . . . form a strong shield under which this nation is able, not only to exist, but to plan for the future in a less tranquil world.

We have developed in those years a technological momentum which carried us from one triumph to another. These included:

the world's first operational supersonic aircraft,
multi-purpose radar,
automatic guidance systems,
660-mile-per-hour passenger jets,
airborne computers,
high thrust rocket engines,

reliable spacecraft,
and work-horse satellites.

Examples are almost always brief; at times only the mere mention of a specific instance is all that is needed. Thus, to amplify the generalization that many cities get part of their characters from single streets, one might mention Market Street in San Francisco, the Champs-Elysées in Paris, Meridian Street in Indianapolis, Rossio Square in Lisbon, Wall Street in New York, and Paseo de la Reforma in Mexico City. To show the early concern of religious bodies with collegiate education in this country, it could be mentioned that St. John's College in Annapolis was chartered in 1784 under Episcopalian auspices, Bowdoin College in 1794 under Congregational auspices, the University of Notre Dame in 1844 under Catholic auspices, and Baylor University in 1845 under Baptist auspices.

Sometimes we define by illustration, which is an extended example. The illustration not only mentions the specific instance but gives details that amplify the general point to be made. Illustrations may be either real or hypothetical. Following is an illustration composed of a number of specific instances:[3]

An old Sanskrit proverb says: "Meet thy neighbor, talk with him, and there will be peace."

We believe this—or at least most of us want *to believe it. That's why we are encouraged to learn that more than 150,000 students cross national boundaries to study in another country each year; that's why there's so much interest in the exchange of books, pictures, magazines, tape recordings and movies; that's why our governments are encouraging cultural exchanges of various kinds; that's why we think it's good that there is a growing number of tourists going from one country to another. . . . If we can only get to meet our neighbors and talk with them, there will be peace—we hope.*

There are many different types of illustration. Generally, they are used as comparisons. The *analogy,* either literal or figurative, is one (treated in Chapter Twelve). The brief *narrative story* is another. The *simile* and *metaphor* also are forms of illustrations. The *fable* is a fictitious story (whose characters are usually animals) to teach a moral lesson; the *allegory* is a story in which people, things, and happenings have symbolic meanings; the *parable* is a short, simple story from which a moral lesson may be drawn. *Anecdotes* and *biographical sketches* are other forms of illustrations.

Sometimes an illustration is used to explain, as in this speech on economic growth and the "now generation," delivered before the Idaho Bankers Association in June, 1971.[4]

But the most deplorable trend which has developed . . . is a totalitarian philosophy, and intolerance which is the antithesis of democracy and which has the potential to destroy it. Intolerance is closely related to impatience; it is the desire to impose one's own solutions without adequate regard for other's opinions. How ironic it is that many of those today who are most outspoken in their criticism of our nation's social ills are so quick to shout down others' attempts to express a differing point of view; so eager to mock or otherwise denigrate the religious ideals of others; so willing to substitute violence for the ballot box!

Comparisons and Contrasts

Clarity may be gained through the use of comparison and contrast. The first shows how two things are alike and the second shows the ways in which they differ. Both may be used to lead the listener from something that is known to something that is unknown. In either we need to keep certain cautions in mind. The relationship between the two objects or ideas should be logical, meaningful likenesses or differences should be presented, and the relationship should be original, not commonplace or trite.

Paul-Henri Spaak uses the method of *comparison* in the following statement:[5]

We Europeans look towards the United States of America and admire her might, the prodigious development of her economy, the standard of living of her population, but if we count up our own resources, our own assets we have no cause for jealousy. . . .

Let us make a few comparisons. The United States covers an area of three million and twenty-seven thousand square miles. Western Europe has an area of one million five hundred and fifty-one square miles. . . .

There are 150 million Americans; there are 290 million Europeans in Western Europe.

On this basis Europe produces 441 million tons of coal and the United States of America 570 million. Europe produces 55 million tons of steel and the United States 100.

Contrast may be used to point out extreme or minor, yet distinct, differences. For example, the difference between a city-manager and a mayor-councilman form of city government is extreme, as would be the differences between Newfoundland and Chihuahua dogs, between certain aspects of the American form of government and that of Red China, between the samba and the highland fling, or between a hostel in Switzerland and the Hotel Malaga Palacio in Malaga, Spain.

Minor but distinct differences would be involved if the speaker were to contrast snow skis with water skis, Indian canoes and kayaks, snare drums and tabors, berets and tam-o'shanters, pointers and setters. The *contrast* in the following statement gives the argument for the realities of American agricultural production greater credence:[6]

Look at these facts of American life—these facts of the productivity of American life.

Largely because of the mechanization of agriculture, the American farmer is the most productive in the world. Each American farm worker produces enough to feed himself and 42 others. In China, one farm worker can feed himself and only one other person. Moreover, productivity on our farms has tripled in the last twenty years.

Last year, we produced as much in goods and services as all of Russia, Japan, West Germany, France, and the United Kingdom combined, although their population is two-and-a-half times ours—because of our productivity.

The average man in Moscow must work an average of seven times as long as the average man in New York City to buy basic consumer goods—because of our productivity.

To buy a good suit of clothes in the Soviet Union takes 183 hours of work; in France, 75 hours; in the United States, only 24 hours—because of productivity.

An analogy is also a comparison. In the analogy, similarities are pointed out between something already known or accepted by the audience and something of a similar class that is not known or accepted.

Explanation or Analysis

Analysis or explanation involve dividing a large unit of thought, a system, or process, or an event into its various parts, considering each part as a unit, and showing the relationship of the parts to the whole. We hear much these days about missiles—ICBM, CBM, SRBM, SAM, Poseidon, Minutemen III, Chaparral, Shilelagh—without knowing much about what a missile is or how it works. When we learn that a missile is any object thrown, dropped, hurled, projected, or propelled for the purpose of making it strike a target, the essential parts of a missile being the structure or frame, the propulsion system, and the guidance and control systems, we begin to get at least a glimmer of what a missile is. We gain some understanding of all types of naval guns when we learn that a gun's principal parts are the barrel or tube through which the projectile is fired, the breech assembly or the loading and firing mechanism, the sighting mechanism, and the mount, including all the supports necessary to point the gun in the proper direction. Any complicated process, organization, object, concept, historical event, or effect can be made clearer through analysis.

We use the process of explanation in numerous instances in this text: in the analysis of the communication process in Chapter Four, in the development of different patterns of speech organization given later in this chapter, in all of Chapter Nine, and in our comments on the duties of the discussion-group chairman on pages 537–543. In each case parts and their relationships were considered.

Description and Narration

Description is a useful type of supporting material when understanding is the goal. It is the process of picturing or portraying an object, event, person, mood or feeling, or attitude. Description concerns itself with the individual character of the thing described. Hence it deals with form, time, dimension, quality, color, sound, texture, order, intensity, or relative position. It may deal with both animate and inanimate objects, psychological and mechanical processes, and intellectual concepts and historical events. Its objects may be immediately present, remembered, or imaginary.

One of the characteristics of some description is order. In describing a landscape you go from foreground to background, or from one side to another. A description of the principal types of instruments in an orchestra would deal with the strings, brasses, woodwinds, and percussion instruments in their relation to the director. The description of some physical pain might consider first its overall effect, its location, and its specific symptoms. When the listener's sense of sight, sound, smell, taste, or feeling is stimulated, he is made to perceive a sensory image that carries the meaning intended.

Description always proceeds with some focus in mind. This center of interest becomes the criterion in the selection of details. We hear much these days about pollution. In California—as in Texas, Louisiana, and other states—we are especially concerned about oil spills from offshore oil drilling. In 1969 the citizens of the coast city of Santa Barbara were aroused because of the gigantic oil spill from one of the Union Oil Company's offshore oil wells. What was included in the many descriptions of the spill in speeches and articles depended on the purpose to be served by the description. Stress was placed variously on descriptive factors that emphasized costs of cleaning the beaches, the effect on fish and birds in the area, the decrease in tourism, and the damage to the beauty of the coast. Union Oil explained the situation so as to show "it can never happen again" and "our national economy needs this natural resource."

The language of description should stimulate vivid pictures in the minds of the listeners. Note the effective use of language in this speech excerpt:[7]

But Scouting and Cubbing is a business too, the business of dealing with that squirming, jumping, eager, active, unpredictable, stubborn, inquisitive, laughing, quarreling, wrestling, fighting, dirty, smelly, lovable, small edition of manhood, known as a boy. He has an affinity for whooping cough, measles, mumps, freckles, pimples, missing teeth, split tones of voice. He is a master at tearing up a room, churning up a family, being absent or present at the wrong moments. He frequently abjures the association of the human race for the companionship of chickens, dogs, turtles, snakes, rabbits, alligators, skunks. His questions are beyond the reach of Einstein, his answers vague, evasive, unintelligible. The sounds that emanate from his throat have no limit—and no predictability. He can be as artful as a fox, as talkative as a parrot, as irritating as a flea, as stubborn as a mule with its ears set back. And then—at some sacred moment—you look into his lighted eyes and see soul in unlimited dimensions—and you know that here in the eyes of a boy is the beginning shape of man to come.

Narration frequently serves a useful purpose. Narration tells a story; it places people, objects, scenes and other phenomena into a living, moving relationship with their environment. Narration deals with happenings, usually on the basis of their time sequence. Amplification of a point by narration may be brief or extended; at times an entire speech may be of the narrative type. Louis E. Lomax uses a short narrative story with extreme effectiveness in making a final point in a speech delivered in 1963 to a predominantly Negro audience in Pacoima, a Negro community in the San Fernando Valley area of Los Angeles. Because of the significance of the speech we begin at the point of the story at which the narration begins and cite the remainder of his speech:[8]

Just outside my home in Valdosta, some 30 miles I drove down the road one day, one comes to an old rickety bridge, way out in the woods all by itself. And there's a sign at the entrance as you come to that bridge. And the sign says, "Capacity load 5,000 pounds, law rigidly enforced." And I remember driving up to this bridge, and I read the sign, and I chuckled to myself. I said, "Now here I am 30 miles from nowhere. Who in the world is going to enforce the law on this bridge?" Then I drove on the bridge. I got the answer. The bridge began to sway, began to rock, began to reel. And it became clear to me that that bridge didn't need a policeman standing there. (slight laughter) The bridge was its own law. And if you got on that bridge with more than 5,000 pounds you'd wind up in the river. In a very real sense the American Negro is the bridge Western civilization must cross if it is to save itself and set up a firm communication with the rest of the world. And at the entrance to that bridge, which is my body and that of my son, your body and that of your daughter, there is a sign saying, "Justice, freedom, now! Law rigidly enforced."

*We don't have any guns. We don't have any ammunition. Despite the lies you tell, we don't even have any razors. (*slight laughter*) We don't have any money. You have the hydrogen bomb, the atomic bomb; all the artillery is on your side, and we have nothing; but here we are. I'm the bridge you must cross, Western civilization, before you can win back Asia. And there's no point in trying to stop Madame Nhu until you do something about Barry Goldwater. And there's no point in trying to invade Havana until you invade Birmingham. And there's no point in blowing down the Berlin Wall until you get Negroes across the railroad tracks in Pacoima, because they're all tied together. (*applause*) And so it is—my body—it stretches out, and this man must cross it, and the law is rigidly enforced. If he gets on me and he tramples me, I'm going to shake, and I'm going to rattle, and I'm going to make noise, and this whole thing is going to go plunging down into the sea.*

*But by the same token this which makes me the bridge makes me the salvation. For history hath brought me forth then for this hour. So then up ye mighty race. Join hands of one accord. Let us then, who love freedom, forget our ethnic and our religious origins. And let us commit ourselves to the task of liberating our sons and our daughters and ourselves from second-class citizenship. Let us kneel in, stand in, vote in, study in, do what we must, but make our world that which it must be. And it's only after we will have done this that we can link arms— Catholic and Protestant, Jew and Gentile, black and white—and march through the San Fernando Valley singing, "Free at last, Free at last, Thank God Almighty, Free at last." (*long applause*)*

As has been indicated, the personal experience makes excellent subject matter for a narrative. At other times the narrative relates what others have told us. Because narration can build to a climax, it serves well as a means of maintaining interest. It can be used to emphasize, to provide background, to illustrate and to summarize.

Statistics
Statistics are groups of figures or facts that are classified, tabulated, and presented in a manner to give significant information. The census data, stock market reports, election returns, weather bureau records, and cost-of-living data are but a few of the statistical data with which most of us are familiar.

There are cautions to be observed when we use statistics, however. First, figures alone are neither interesting nor meaningful. They must show something. It is usually necessary to use analogies, comparisons, or contrasts with the statistical information to get the listener's attention and to make the meaning of the figures understood. Statistics must be clear, accurate, relevant and, hopefully, not belabored. Note the effective use of statistics in these two brief speech excerpts:[9]

Ten years ago our passport agencies in this country and our foreign service posts abroad issued 800,000 passports. In 1970 the figure topped 2 million, an increase of almost 300 percent. And in 1970, in contrast to the usual 10 to 12 percent annual increase, passport issuances increased some 20 percent over 1969.

The speaker from whose speech the following excerpt is cited is making the point that "there are countries that surpass us in many important respects":[10]

Let me say parenthetically here that Americans do not live as long as other people. American males have a life expectancy of about 67 years at birth—and that's 26th in the United Nations longevity table compiled by the World Health Organization. American females are 12th down the list. Ahead of us are Sweden, Norway, Holland, Iceland, Denmark—also Israel, Britain, France, Australia, Russia, and many others.

A second caution is that listeners cannot remember much statistical data. Large doses of figures tend to confuse rather than clarify. Furthermore, when the figures are large they become confusing. The amounts our government spends for defense, farm subsidies, social security, and other costs are almost beyond comprehension unless they can be made meaningful. It is really hard to conceive how much is spent on national defense. Let us say it is $50 billion annually, a low estimate. What does this actually mean? It means that every man, woman, and child in this country contributes about $312 each year toward national defense. The total is thus made meaningful by breaking it down in terms of the individual.

Another point about statistics: round numbers are always easier to remember and therefore mean more than exact amounts, especially when the figures are large. This does not apply, of course, in highly technical or scientific talks.

Testimony and Quotations

In a previous section of this chapter we explained the use of evidence, including both facts and opinions. When you are not an authority on a given topic yourself, it is well to rely on the testimony of those who are. *Testimony* usually is considered an affirmation of a fact; it is usually oral, as by a witness in a court. A *quotation* is a direct citation from an authority.

We have made frequent use of quotations in this text. Whenever it seemed advisable and when we have used long quotations, we have told something about the speaker, the occasion, and the purpose of the quotation. A carefully selected quotation can add vitality, humor, vividness, and convincingness to most generalizations.

Questions

We recommend sparing use of questions in a speech, except perhaps for the rhetorical question (see Chapter Seven). Their use is primarily one of involvement, of getting the audience to think "along with you" on the subject. The questions that may be used are of five kinds: the rhetorical, hypothetical, direct and directed, overhead, and open-ended or closed-ended.

The rhetorical question seeks only a mental response from the listener. The desired reply is implied in the question. The question is worded so that the reaction will be in accordance with the speaker's viewpoint. A series of rhetorical questions was used in the introduction to a speech given by Senator Peter Dominick of Colorado to the United States Senate on June 10, 1971:[11]

Mr. President, which is the real *Communist China? The smiling welcome of Chou En-Lai to an American table tennis team visiting mainland China in mid-April? Or anti-Americans slogans shouted in the streets of dozens of Chinese cities on May Day, only two weeks later?*

A hint by Mao Tse-tung to journalist Edgar Snow last December that he favored a visit by President Nixon to mainland China? Or an editorial in the Peking Review *on April 16, 1971, vilifying President Nixon as an "arch-criminal," "arch-murderer," and "chief butcher?"*

Suggestions from Peking that it wants to negotiate its differences with the United States? Or its insistence in every Chinese Communist propaganda organ that "U. S. imperialism is the common enemy?"

Interpretations by various so-called "experts" in this country that the People's Republic of China is ready and willing to enter the United Nations? Or Peking's own declaration that it will reject a seat in the U. N. unless the Republic of China is expelled?

The hypothetical question is based on supposition, not on a real situation. It directs the listeners' attention to a situation that has not yet developed but that may develop. An example might be:

Suppose we test the strength of your racial bias. Suppose you now live

*in a suburban community, your house is worth $45,000 and you are
asking $49,000, you have been transferred by your company to a city
2,000 miles away, and have been given an offer to sell to a member of a
minority group for $52,750. What would you do? Many of your neigh-
bors have expressed the opinion that they would not want minority
groups moving into the neighborhood. What would you do?*

Restatement and Repetition

Because of their short spans of attention listeners cannot be expected
to give complete attention throughout a speech; there are bound to be
moments when they do not listen intently. Therefore, we use restatement to give a broader meaning to an idea, to ensure that more people
will understand it, because some may not perceive the first meaning
presented, to give emphasis, and to lend variety to a speech. Frank
Knox, Secretary of the Navy under Franklin D. Roosevelt, in a speech
before an American Legion audience, makes use of *restatement* to
emphasize his belief that to enjoy peace a country must be willing to
fight for it:[12]

*The only peace in which the world can put any confidence, for at least
one hundred years to come, is the kind of peace that can be enforced
by the peace-loving nations of the world. . . .*

    *You cannot preserve liberties such as we enjoy, save by willingness to
fight for them if need be.*

    *The currency with which you pay for peace is made up of manly
courage, fearless virility, readiness to serve justice and honor at any
cost, and a mind and a heart attuned to sacrifice.*

    *We must also remember that it is only the strong who can promote
and preserve a righteous peace. . . .*

    *A powerful national defense, especially on the high seas, is a pre-
requisite of a peace-promoting, justice-loving America.*

    For a contrast, note the use of *repetition* in Churchill's Dunkirk
speech:[13]

*We shall fight in France, we shall fight on the seas and oceans, we shall
fight with growing confidence and growing strength in the air, we shall
defend our island, whatever the cost may be, we shall fight on the
beaches, we shall fight on the landing grounds, we shall fight in the
fields and in the streets, we shall fight in the hills.*

    Because of their proven psychological value, restatement and
repetition should be used frequently. Their use in modern advertising
certainly gives evidence of their effectiveness.

ARRANGEMENT OF SUPPORTING MATERIALS

In large measure our mental processes consist of activities that *classify, rank, show relationships, contrast or compare, evaluate, arrange or rearrange, test reality, generalize, arouse feelings or emotions,* or in some other way deal with experiences so as to place them in meaningful order or satisfy our ego needs. In this section we shall be concerned with ways of arranging speech content to make its meaning clear and readily evident.

The Importance of Organization

The order of materials in a speech is important because it (1) enhances listener perception, (2) ensures adequate coverage of a subject, and (3) aids in the elimination of nonessentials.

For Listener Perception

That a speech should be effectively organized means that its parts should be arranged in some systematic, purposeful way. There should be a meaningful sequence among the major divisions, and the supporting details should relate appropriately to the more important points. This gives *order* to the speech.

Our perceptions have meanings largely as parts of a pattern of relationships associated with the object, event, person, or world perceived. As Krech and Crutchfield state in *Elements of Psychology:*[14] "Objects are perceived not in isolation but in relation to other objects. And the very perception of an object depends itself in part upon seeing certain relations among the parts that form the whole; thus the perceived *structure* of an object is the manner in which the parts combine to make up the whole." The "other objects" referred to here are frequently perceptions from some previous time. In other words, many perceptions are dependent for their meaning on previous perceptions. This can be readily illustrated. When a child touches a hot stove he instantly experiences discomfort. The next time he approaches a hot stove he is likely to recall the earlier unpleasantness and be a little more cautious. You may anticipate an injection of vaccine with either anxiety or unconcern, depending upon your previous experiences with hypodermic needles. You recommend to your friends the dentist whose extractions are painless. Students are likely to estimate the toughness of the final examination by the nature of the midterm test. We tend to stay away from speakers known to be dull and uninteresting, and we seek to hear those reported to be dynamic and entertaining.

The perception of abstract concepts similarly is a matter of relationships. The sense of distance, for example, is the result of countless experiences with objects that are at arm's length, two blocks long, or on the horizon. The perceived size of an object is affected by both its immediate surroundings and its relation to other familiar objects. An object may be as big as a barn or no bigger than the head of a pin. A person may be weak as a kitten or as strong as an ox. In other words, to make an abstract concept meaningful we try to relate it to images we have accumulated in past experiences. By thus relating an object in some way to other objects it becomes "ordered."

Our understanding of the physical world around us also comes largely from understanding the order in it. Discovering the patterns and relations surrounding us helps to make the mysteries of the world a little less perplexing. We then begin to see what things mean.

For Coverage of the Subject
Good organization obviously serves both listener and speaker. The speaker needs to know that the listener has perceived (understood) what has been said, and he also needs some assurance that he has adequately covered the subject.

In the last section of this chapter we deal with the rules for outlining a speech. Your outline will show the main headings of the speech, their relationships to each other and to the subordinate supporting materials, and whether each is adequately balanced and established. Several rules of thumb aid in determining whether the subject is adequately covered: "Have I touched on what seem to be the important aspects of the topics in the time permitted?" "Have I answered most of the objections or questions a listener might raise?" "Do the major and second-level points carry the speech to a reasonable progression and conclusion in relation to its purpose?" "Have I followed a reasonable pattern of progression: from simple to complex, known to unknown, or from ideas accepted to those less accepted?" Finally, a very practical question: "Have I devoted about the same amount of space in the outline to each major point?" If the pattern of the speech has been well worked out and "bare spots" have been filled in, your speech should gain attention, maintain interest, show the general importance and progression of ideas (which is important for perception), contribute to its acceptance, and aid the listener in remembering what you have said.

There is no rhetorical rule which says that exactly the same amount of time (space) should be devoted to each major point. However, the concept of major points is that they are equal in importance and that they deserve equal treatment. Your speech outline will indicate what parts have been slighted.

For Elimination of Nonessentials
The elimination of nonessentials is essentially the converse of the point made just above. After you have completed a first draft of the outline of your speech—and you may make several—you will be able to deter-

mine whether unimportant or less important major points can be eliminated, whether you have developed a point in depth when, perhaps, the point has already been accepted by the audience, whether you have excessive detail or have included points that take the listener—and you—off on some insignificant or irrelevant tangent. If your speech pattern is clear, has coherence, covers the subject adequately but without excessive nonessentials, progresses acceptably toward a goal, and deals with reasonable supporting materials in terms of the needs and values of the listeners, you can be reasonably sure that you will be understood and that your speech will have persuasive quality.

The general rhetorical structure of a speech laid down by the early rhetoricians is still followed today. A speech has an introduction, a body, and a conclusion. The relationships among them and the internal construction of each create the organizational pattern of the speech. We shall devote the remainder of this chapter to the consideration of these conventional divisions.

Patterns of Organizing Materials

There are many different ways of organizing the body of a speech. The choice must be made on the basis of what is most likely to aid the speaker in achieving his purpose and adapting to the other elements of the speaking situation. This section will therefore present the most frequently used patterns of speech organization.

Chronological Order

Chronological order implies the sequence in which events occur. A time order follows many patterns, such as "yesterday, today, and tomorrow," "morning, noon, and night," "childhood, adolescence, maturity, and old age," "preparing for a trip, taking it, recovering from it, and showing your friends all the slides you took." Some subjects lend themselves easily to a sequential historical development as, for example, our involvement in the Vietnam War, the steps taken in securing statehood for Hawaii, and the political careers of such persons as Joe McCarthy, Spiro Agnew, Harry S. Truman, and Wayne Morse. Processes can often be developed on a time basis; how-to-do-it speeches usually follow a step-by-step sequence.

Other types of subject that lend themselves to time-sequence development include sports events, biographical sketches, narratives, travel talks, eulogies, directions, and sometimes problem-solution.

Although chronological arrangement provides a natural pattern for many subjects, there is always the danger of including too many details. Thus long-drawn-out descriptions of trips handled strictly according to time order can easily lull rather than entertain. Student speakers held to strict time limits are sometimes obliged to stop when a trip is only half completed. Other speakers err in the opposite direction, making breathless attempts to travel around the world in eight minutes, never allowing their listeners to linger anywhere long enough to savor the sights or experiences presented. Speeches of introduction that present biographical data about a person are also frequently boring because of excessive and unimportant detail. Narrative accounts, too, are often marred in the same way.

When you use the time pattern, you must decide how much supporting detail is important. Work out a meaningful sequence of main points first, and then fill in with significant highlights and details that really add to the effectiveness of the treatment.

Spatial Order of Development

Sometimes speech subjects are most effectively presented according to their spatial or geographical relationships. In describing a ship, for example, you might move from bow to stern; your home town might be a point of reference in describing a trip throughout the United States. Another type of travel talk might make use of spatial relations by pointing out little known facts about cities in the United States and the world: that Nome, Alaska, is west of Honolulu, that Boston is east of Lima, Peru, or that Miami is west of the Canal Zone. Subjects lending themselves well to a spatial development include almost all descriptions—of pictures, outdoor scenes, military maneuvers, prominent buildings or sites, machinery, some art objects, fashions, some processes, and even our body ailments.

In using the spatial pattern, you might well begin by giving an overall picture and then considering the parts in their relationships to each other. In an effective speech on California's Disneyland a student began by effectively likening Disneyland to a huge fourleaf clover, in which the stem represented Main Street and each leaf represented one of the "lands"—Tomorrowland, Fantasyland, Adventureland, and Frontierland. Washington, D.C., is sometimes likened to a wagon wheel, the streets radiating like spokes from the central hub of the city; Michigan is often compared to a mitten, Italy to a boot, Chile to a string bean more than 2600 miles long, and North Dakota looks like an almost perfect rectangle.

The appropriateness of the spatial pattern of organization used in the development of the following speeches is evident from their titles:

The Islands of Hawaii	Hyde Park in London
38-24-37	The Dagwood Sandwich
The Vatican	What the Bagboy Must Know
The Florida Keys	About Packing Groceries

What Is a Three-Stage
   Rocket?
De Facto Segregation
The Amtrak Passenger Rail
   Service
San Quentin from the Inside

Why Bussing Won't Work
Rio from the Air
The Lands South of the
   Equator
The Indianapolis Speedway
The Coastline of Alaska

Topical Organization

The topical organization arranges material on the basis of some system of classification arising from the subject matter itself. The particular pattern is selected because it offers a natural division of the subject matter, is easy to remember, or provides meaningful and mutually exclusive categories of the content.

Component Parts. There are many different ways of shaping speech content into a topical pattern. Component parts form one basis of division. Thus, a talk dealing with the construction of an automobile might consider chassis, motor, and body; a talk on the human body probably would include at least the skeleton and internal organs; a description of a gun might treat the barrel, stock, and firing mechanism.

Parties Involved. A talk describing a campus population might have any of these series of main headings: freshmen, sophomores, juniors, and seniors; undergraduates and graduates; students, faculty, and nonacademic personnel. A speech on our military forces would certainly consider Army, Navy, and Air Force.

Fields of Activity. Fields of activity form another type of topical organization, as in talks on occupations, sports, racial customs, leisure-time interests, community projects, scientific research, and mass media.

Criteria for Evaluation. Various methods of evaluation may be used as bases for dividing a speech into its major parts: quality, quantity, requirements, characteristics, advantages, rank order, status, degree of complexity, rate of progress, and so on. For example, the benefits attainable might be used in this way in a speech on "The Importance of Reading." One might point out that reading helps to increase knowledge, provide entertainment, develop personality, and improve thought processes. A campaign speech about the qualities of a political candidate might be concerned about whether he is loyal to his party, knowledgeable in local, national, or world affairs, experienced in politics, acceptable to party leaders, and close to the people.

Rank Order. Rank order places each class or item of a series in the order of its priority as determined by some criterion. Thus, any speech in which the main parts can be arranged in a sequence from one extreme to its opposite—favorable to unfavorable, most to least, highest to lowest—follows the rank-order topical pattern.

When the topical pattern is used, all headings deal, in the main, with parts of a whole. Each major heading is on the same level as the other major headings, and all bear the same relation to the overall theme. Together they cover the total scope to be covered by the speech subject.

You will probably note a relationship between the topical pattern and the spatial and chronological patterns. Actually, the latter two are also topical patterns. In the usual topical arrangement, however, with the possible exception of rank order, there is no reason inherent in the content itself why one heading should precede another. You could use the topical sequence of Army, Navy, and Air Force just as effectively as Navy, Air Force, and Army, or Air Force, Army, and Navy. Many speakers would begin with the branch of service in which they have served. The nature of the content treated would rarely affect the order in which the various branches are treated. In time and space patterns, on the other hand, a "best" order usually is inherent in the subject matter and should be planned for a good psychological effect.

Logical Patterns

All logical patterns of speech organization have one element in common: a necessary and reasoned relationship among the parts of the speech. There is a rational basis for the order of the main points and also for the order of subordinate points, which provide proof, application, or inferences drawn from the major points. A logical pattern leads toward conviction and is usually used in persuasive speeches.

Inductive Order. There are four major kinds of logical patterns. The inductive order uses a number of specific illustrations, similar instances, related events, or supporting details as a basis for inferring a general principle or truth. The various main points support the conclusion or generalization the speaker wishes to establish.

This method is especially useful in talks before scientific groups, business reports, appeals for community action, pleas to a jury—in fact, in any speech in which the conclusion can be inferred from the supporting details.

Deductive Order. The deductive order begins with a generalization and then makes applications to specific situations. It asserts that any member of a class will have characteristics belonging to that class. In deduction apply a "general rule" to specifics that seem to fall within that rule. This method is useful in the field of criminal investigation, in scientific research in which generalized principles have already been established, in certain theological doctrines, and in practical pedagogy.

Cause-Effect Order. A cause-to-effect or effect-to-cause relationship is another logical pattern. Here we start with known causes of some social or economic problem and then consider the effects, or we start with the reverse, arguing from the effect back to the cause. Both patterns are illustrated in the following outlines.[15]

The Problem of Juvenile Delinquency (cause to effect)
  I. Juvenile delinquency results from many causes.
      A. Needed recreational facilities frequently are lacking.
      B. Parental control is often ineffective.
      C. Teenage gangs contribute to delinquency.
      D. The use of narcotics is increasing.
  II. The effects of juvenile delinquency give cause for public concern.
      A. Vandalism has been on the increase.
      B. Juvenile crimes have increased.
      C. The scope of both public and private rehabilitation services has been enlarged.
      D. Public costs and tax rates have risen.

Modern Food Distribution (effect to cause)
  I. What the effects of modern food distribution have been on the nation:
      A. Consumer services have been greatly improved.
      B. Savings to the consumer in food costs has increased.
      C. Opportunities for careers in food distribution have expanded.
      D. Farm production and distribution practices have improved.
  II. Why modern food distribution methods have developed in America:
      A. Increased production has required more outlets for farm products.
      B. Consumers have demanded simplified systems of food distribution.
      C. Population growth has necessitated improved distribution methods.
      D. The demand for a higher standard of living has forced food distributors to keep pace with advances in technology.

Problem-Solution Order. The problem-solution sequence, sometimes called the *disease-remedy plan,* is a logical organization that begins with a description of the problem and its importance and is followed by a presentation of a solution or of solutions. This development is almost essential in many kinds of argument, especially when action is called for, decisions are required and, sometimes, differences are to be reconciled, as when the speaker is concerned with social problems calling for solution. Most debate speeches follow this type of organization. The speaker takes his listeners by logical steps to the desired conclusions. Usually he raises and answers the following stock questions, phrasing them in terms of his specific subject:

1. Is the problem so serious that some action must be taken?
2. Would the proposed solution remedy the situation?
3. Would the proposed solution result in new problems?
4. Is the proposed solution the best possible way to solve the problem?

Other Patterns
A few other patterns are described below: the motivated sequence, the text pattern, Borden's formula, and the "string of beads."

The Motivated Sequence. Monroe's motivated sequence[16] pattern of organization is based on both logical and psychological principles and combines features of several of the types of development just described. Note, however, that, except for the first step, this plan, like the problem-solution plan, is well adapted only to speeches calling for action of some sort. The motivated sequence development calls for the following steps:

1. *The attention step* seeks to get the listener to say, "I want to listen," and is, of course, essential in every speech, regardless of the type of development to be followed.
2. *The need step* gives the causes of the proposed action and seeks to create in the listener a feeling of dissatisfaction with the existing state of affairs.
3. *The satisfaction step* suggests a remedy and shows how it is the best way of meeting the problem.
4. *The visualization step* dramatizes the remedy in action and shows how the listener may enjoy the proposed action.
5. *The action step* points out what the audience should do and urges listener action.

The "Text" Pattern. What might be called the text pattern of developing a speech is built around a proverb, axiom, adage, Biblical text, or literary excerpt, which is broken into a number of parts, each becoming a major point in the speech. Here are some typical texts that could be developed in this way:

> Write injuries in sand, but benefits in marble.
> A soft answer turneth away wrath: but grievous words stir up anger.
> Government of the people, by the people, and for the people.
> Mercy and truth preserve the king; and his throne is upholden by mercy.

Borden's Formula. This is a four-step plan for a speech based on assumed audience reaction. The sequence is as follows:[17]

1. "Ho hum!" This step aims to "build a fire."
2. "Why bring that up?" This step builds a bridge between listener needs and the speaker's proposition.
3. "For instance." Specific cases are cited in this step.
4. "So what?" Here appeals for the desired action are given.

The "String of Beads." In the string-of-beads pattern of speech development, the speaker illustrates his main theme by developing a series of examples. This is a highly flexible method, since he can readily shorten or lengthen his speech according to the time available or to other aspects of the occasion. A famous speech of this type is Dr. Russell H. Conwell's "Acres of Diamonds." Reputedly given more than 6,000 times,[18] this speech stressed the theme that wealth and happiness can be found close to home if we but look around us. For each presentation the speech was adapted, both in length and in illustrations, to the local situation.

THE SPEECH INTRODUCTION
The content presented in the previous section on the organization of materials applies primarily to the body of the speech. There are, in addition, two speech segments that deserve special treatment, namely the introduction and the conclusion. We consider these parts of the speech now.

Having Purpose
The introduction to a speech has six possible functions, though they are not necessarily all present in the same speech: (1) to capture the immediate attention of the audience, (2) to arouse interest in the subject, (3) to preview the nature and scope of the subject and the speaker's point of view, (4) to establish goodwill between speaker and audience, (5) to indicate the speaker's qualifications for speaking, and

(6) to contribute to the overall goal of the speech. Some of these functions may be omitted on occasion, as when the chairman of a meeting describes the speaker's qualifications or they are already known to the listeners, or when it might prejudice the audience for the speaker to reveal prematurely his point of view, or when the composition of the audience or the nature of the occasion ensures interest in the subject.

A good rule of thumb to follow in determining which functions are necessary is their adaptability to the demands of the occasion. You should always prepare your introduction in advance on the basis of the best possible prespeech analysis of the audience. However, at times you may wish to make changes in your introduction, and common sense and alertness to the speaking situation will suggest the modifications to be made.

Capturing Attention

The beginning of any speech is important, because listeners usually pay close attention at the outset; if the introduction is stimulating or provocative, the speaker usually can maintain their interest. The introduction must arouse the audience and make it want to listen. As Cicero put it, the aim of the introduction is "to render hearers well disposed toward the speaker, attentive to his speech, and open to conviction."

Arousing Interest

The introduction serves somewhat the same purpose for the speech that the table of contents, the preface, or the blurbs on the inside of the dust cover do for a book. A favorable impression made by the speaker in his introduction is the entering wedge in creating the desire to hear more. The introduction should make the listener say "I believe there is something in this speech for me."

Previewing the Subject

The introduction may acquaint the listeners with the nature and scope of the subject and the point of view of the speaker. The specific nature of coverage may be indicated. If the topic is controversial, the point of view of the speaker might be frequently stated.

Establishing Goodwill

The introduction to any speech, except under the most unusual conditions, should establish goodwill between the speaker and audience. A feeling of friendly rapport is conducive to attentive listening. This friendly atmosphere can be secured by the speaker's manner, by references to experiences he has in common with the audience, to similar background or training, or possibly to his interest in the welfare of the audience—sometimes by indicating that he is speaking at the request of the organization the audience represents. The speaker needs to be perceived as friendly, understanding, sincere, and competent.

Establishing the Speaker's Qualifications

Often the introduction must establish the qualifications the speaker has for discussing a particular subject, if this is not done by the person who introduces him. If the speaker is a recognized authority on the subject or is known to have had first-hand experience with it, his listeners usually will assume he is qualified. He might also be qualified by virtue of the fact that he is a member of the group to which he is speaking, closely associated with it, or known to support the principles endorsed by it. Sometimes a speaker is invited because of his character, special skills, or position. If you are not known to the audience, it is not out of order to state your qualifications in a modest manner.

Contribute to the Goal

At times the introduction can contribute to the achievement of the specific goal of the speech in other ways than those already mentioned. This happens when the content of the introduction is related more or less directly to the specific subject matter of the speech, serving as a transition into it. This is most obvious when the speaker lists the major points of the speech in his introduction.

Fitting the Situation

As we have seen, the speaking situation includes the physical setting, the speech purpose, the audience, and any customs or rituals to be followed. The speaker may use his introduction to adapt his speech to the occasion by (1) references to the occasion, (2) references to the speech purpose, (3) references to the audience, (4) appropriate personal references, (5) a narrative related to the occasion, (6) a startling or challenging statement, (7) an appropriate quotation or text, (8) a question or series of questions, (9) a brief statement of the theme of the speech, if it is related to the occasion, and (10) appropriate humor. These techniques may be used in any combination necessary to achieve the various purposes of the introduction. Examples of their use are given below.

Reference to the Occasion

This is a day of national consecration. (Franklin D. Roosevelt, in his First Inaugural Address.)

We come now to lay this man's case in the hands of a jury of our peers—the first defense and the last defense in the protection of home and life as provided by law. (Clarence Darrow, in his final plea in defense of a Negro, Henry Sweet, in Detroit in 1926.)

I am happy to join with you today in what will go down in history as the greatest demonstration for freedom in the history of the Nation. (Dr. Martin Luther King, Jr., speaking before 200,000 at the "walk for freedom" meeting in Washington, D.C., August 28, 1963.)

We welcome to the membership of Phi Kappa Phi the new members. (Dr. Waldo W. Braden, Professor of Speech at the Louisiana State University, speaking at the 1971 Recognition Banquet of Phi Kappa Phi.)

Reference to the Purpose of the Speech

I come to Illinois tonight to talk about a very serious subject—one that all Americans are going to have to be concerned about—and one that will affect your lives profoundly. This subject is the new image of women in the United States. (Arvonne S. Fraser, Chairman of the Washington, D.C., Chapter of Women's Equity Action League, before the student body of Western Illinois University, June 3, 1971.)

I have called the Congress into extraordinary session because there are serious, very serious, choices of policy to be made, and made immediately, which it is neither right nor constitutionally permissible that I should assume the responsibility of making. (Woodrow Wilson, President of the United States, in his War Message to the nation on April 2, 1917.)

Reference to the Audience

This uncounted multitude before me . . . these thousands of human faces . . . the purpose of our assembling. . . . (Daniel Webster, in speaking before an audience estimated at nearly a hundred thousand, at the fiftieth anniversary of the Battle of Bunker Hill.)

I was very pleased to receive Bill Clark's invitation to address the Executive Club of Chicago. It is always pleasant to return to where I have had so many fond memories and pleasant associations. Your Club has a well-earned reputation. Your membership reflects a great diversity of interests and a fine record of accomplishments. The Club is known as an excellent forum for frank and thoughtful discussion. Here is the place to raise issues that should concern all of us who care about the well-being of our country and its economy. (James

M. Roche, Chairman, General Motors Company, before the Executive Club of Chicago, March 25, 1971.)

A Personal Reference

I have not come here to make a political speech. Spring is not the season for politics, unless you are a young man running for the Presidency. Or unless you are a President in your first term. I am no longer that young. I am in my fourth term in the Senate. I run for office only in Montana and I have only recently been re-elected. (Mike Mansfield speaking on "The Nixon Doctrine" before the student body at Olivet College in Olivet, Michigan, on March 29, 1971.)

It is a great pleasure to return to the campus of St. John's University where I spent four of the most peaceful and satisfying years of my life. (Dr. John E. Reilly, Senior Fellow of the Overseas Development Council, speaking at a Conference on International Justice, at St. John's University, Collegeville, Minnesota, on March 15, 1971.)

Narrative

On February 1, 1960, lightning struck in Greensboro, N.C., but the storm had been brewing for years among restless students "tired of old answers," aspiring for "something better than what their parents had had." Four college freshmen at the Agricultural and Technical College, Greensboro, sat down at a Woolworth lunchroom counter in Greensboro, N.C., and asked for coffee. (Roy L. Hill, Department of Speech, Denver, Colorado, in a speech entitled "The 1960's: Rhetoric Becomes Resistance.")

A Startling or Challenging Statement

My propositions are simple. You have no assurance of a future. The views of man and nature which permeate the entire western culture are the reason. Our view of man and nature does not correspond to reality, has no survival value—indeed, it is the best guarantee of the extinction of man. (Ian McHarg, Professor of Regional Planning, University of Pennsylvania, in a speech delivered at the North American Wildlife and Natural Resources Conference at Portland, Oregon, March 10, 1971.)

In view of what has happened since 1940 in Southeast Asia the following speech introduction seems prophetic:

If you have a son of military age, you had better secure an atlas to find out where Malacca, Kedag, Panang, Johore or Rangoon are located. It is very likely that your son will be sent to any of those places if our present warlike policy in the Far East is continued. (Senator Rush D. Holt of West Virginia, in a broadcast over the National Broadcasting Company network on October 17, 1940.)

An Appropriate Quotation or Text

"And they that shall be of thee shall build the old waste places; thou shalt raise up the foundations of many generations, and thou shalt be called, The repairer of the breach, The restorer of paths to dwell in." (Isaiah, 58:12). Thus a prophet named Isaiah spoke over 2800 years ago words that should indeed challenge us to comprehend the need for pressing forward, ever broadening the horizons of our correctional programs and repairing the breaches that too often destroy our human potentials. (William H. Gray, Jr., a Black executive of the Pennsylvania Department of Labor and Industry, speaking before the annual meeting of the Pennsylvania Prison Society, May 23, 1952.)

A Single Question or Series of Questions

IS SUCCESS ILLEGAL? Ridiculous as this question seems it is one which businessmen are being forced to ask today. (Lee Loevinger, in a speech delivered before the Detroit Kiwanis Club on May 4, 1971, on the topic "How to Succeed in Business Without Being Tried.")

A student began a speech on student involvement in the administration of college academic and administration affairs in this manner. The speech was presented to the College Academic Senate:

Thank you for letting me speak before you. I shall try to give specific answers to some questions which are frequently asked by you faculty members and administrators:

What do students mean when they ask to have courses made more relevant?

What is the basis for the students' demands for minority group studies?

Why do students feel they are capable and should have the right to take part in the administration of college academic affairs?

And this may be the hardest question of all to answer to your satisfaction: "Why do students want the right to have a small part in the evaluation of a teacher's instructional abilities?"

Brief Statement of the Theme of the Speech

We are to consider today an important aspect of this year's Congress theme. "Technology and Society: A Challenge to Private Enterprise." Our concern is the use of the world's mineral and energy resources. (Ian K. MacGregor, Chief Executive Officer of the American Metal Climax, Inc., of New York City, speaking before the 23rd Congress of the ICC, at Vienna, in April, 1971.)

Today I want to talk to you about the great need in our society for a better understanding of unity. (This single sentence gives the theme of the Commencement address given by Arthur S. Adams, President of the American Council on Education, at Northeastern University, in 1952.)

Appropriate Humor

It is a great pleasure for me to be here in Las Vegas for your Ninth Annual Symposium on Reliability Physics in Electronics. When I consider how much progress your distinguished group has made over the past nine years in the study of the mechanisms of failure, I'm tempted to observe that, in your case at least, nothing succeeds like failure. Frankly, I cannot conceive of a more appropriate locale for exploring mechanisms of failure than Las Vegas. Has anybody ever designed a more efficient mechanism for failure than the roulette table? (Dr. James Hillier, Executive Vice President of Research and Engineering of the RCA Corporation, speaking before a conference on "Reliability Physics," in April, 1971.)

One reason for the big apples on the top of the basket is that there are always a lot of little apples holding them up. (The Vice-president of a large industrial concern, emphasizing the important contribution made by the salesmen of the company, at a meeting of salesmanagers.)

THE SPEECH CONCLUSION

Purposefulness

Whatever the purpose of your speech, its conclusion should always be forceful, providing a climactic last impression. The effect of a good speech can be almost completely nullified by a weak conclusion.

Since the conclusion provides the speaker's last opportunity to win the response he seeks from his listeners, its importance is obvious. Among the several functions a conclusion serves are the following: (1) it usually summarizes briefly the content of the speech, either by restating the speech purpose or by recapitulating its salient points, (2) it stresses again the specific response the speaker wants from his listeners, (3) it certainly reinforces any feeling of goodwill the speaker has created with his listeners, and (4) it seeks to heighten any emotional state the speaker desires to arouse in his listeners.

Forms

Simple Summary

Sometimes a simple summary of the speaker's main points is all that is necessary. This serves to reinforce what has been said: when couched in effective language, a summary can be forceful, and the final complete résumé helps the listener remember the main points longer.

Quotation or Story

A quotation or a story sometimes captures the essence of a speech and makes a fitting conclusion. This method holds attention, can have dramatic value, can build to a climax, and always serves to reinforce what the speaker may have said in another way.

Direct Challenge or Call for Action

Sometimes a fitting closure to a speech is to issue a direct challenge or call for action. This is the type of conclusion that ends with "We must do . . .," "It is your responsibility . . .," "Our destiny is in your hands." When action is called for, the speaker may wish to enumerate the specific tasks that must be done. Thus, this form of closure can also serve as a summary.

Restatement of the Theme

Restating the theme serves to give variety to the conclusion of a speech. It is essentially a restatement of the thesis statement, used for clarity when the purpose is understanding and given with added force when action is sought.

THE SPEECH OUTLINE

It is not enough that we know the different patterns of organization for a speech and the functions and types of introductions and conclusions. We must also be skilled in the use of the tool that enables us to incorporate in the introduction, body, and conclusion the order essential for meaningful communication. That tool is the outline. The primary function of the outline is to aid in the preparation and composition of the speech prior to its delivery. When completed, it reveals the total content of the speech, its unity and coherence, the internal relationships of the major points and subpoints, and the relevancy and adequacy of the materials included. Such an outline is usually detailed, although the preparation of some shorter speeches may require only properly arranged, brief notes.

When the outline has been completed, you can tell at a glance whether the major and minor points are arranged appropriately, additional materials need to be added, or some points are unnecessarily covered in too great detail.

The preparation of the outline for a speech requires skill. The following rules will aid in achieving logical arrangement and adequacy of coverage.

The Standard Symbols

The symbols indicate the relationships among the parts of the outline. You designate all main points by Roman numerals, all points that directly explain or support them by capital letters, the next degree of subordination by Arabic numerals, the next by lower case letters, and so on, each order of topics indented under that immediately superior to it. The skeleton form for such an outline looks like this:

Introduction

  I. First level
 II. First level

Body

  I. First level, or principal heading
    A. Second level subpoint
      1. Third level "
        a. Fourth level "
          (1) Fifth level "
            (a) Sixth level "
            (b) Sixth level "
          (2)
        b.
      2.
    B.
 II.

Conclusion

  I.
 II.

Note that the numbering of the main points in the Body and Conclusion begins over again with Roman numeral I. The primary reason for this is so that one may tell at a glance the number of major points in the body of the speech. If this numbering system is used, it is possible to tell at a glance the relative importance of the points being made. As for detail, rarely would the outline for a brief classroom speech contain items below the fourth or fifth levels.

We have indicated that each outline has three parts: introduction, body (sometimes called the discussion), and conclusion. Some authors consider this threefold division another rule for outlining a speech. Please note that no symbols are needed to indicate these divisions.

The Single Idea

Each heading should contain a single, separate, and distinct idea. The rule is violated when a series of details is combined in one heading, when two coordinate (equal in generality), overlapping, or nonrelated points are included in one heading, or when there is overlapping of ideas between headings. Note the improvement in the examples given below, when the headings are reduced to single ideas:

Incorrect	Correct

"See California First"

Incorrect	Correct

I. Mission Dolores, Santa Barbara Mission, and San Juan Capistrano	I. Historic Missions
	   A. Mission Dolores
	   B. Santa Barbara Mission
	   C. San Juan Capistrano

II. Yosemite, Sequoia, and Kings Canyon National Parks	II. National Parks
	   A. Yosemite
	   B. Sequoia
	   C. Kings Canyon

III. The Pacific Ocean, Sierra Mountains, and Death Valley	III. Variety of Scenery
	   A. Pacific Ocean
	   B. Sierra Mountains
	   C. Death Valley

"See California First"

Incorrect	Correct
I. California has beautiful scenery and has many interesting historic sites.	I. California has beautiful scenery. II. California has many interesting sites.

"See New York First"

Incorrect	Correct
I. The historic sites, scenery, and people make New York famous.	I. The historic sites in New York make it prominent in American history. II. New York's varied scenery makes it a tourist attraction. III. Many of the nation's leaders make New York their home.

Coordination

Coordination in an outline means that the major divisions of the body of the speech are of the same relative importance and are indicated by Roman numerals. Similarly, all subpoints on the same level must be of the same relative importance. This coordination should extend down to the smallest division of the outline.

Coordination deals with the level of generality of the ideas in an outline. That is, the ideas are equally important in the development of the speech with other items on the same level (having the same symbol type and indentation). Confusion and unintentional emphasis on less important details can result when the points are not coordinate. In a skeleton outline point B is of the same importance as point A, point 2 is of the same importance as point 1, and so on. In the following partial outline of the topic, item D is clearly not of the same character as A, B, and C:

I. Important modes of transportation
   A. Trains
   B. Airplanes
   C. Ocean liners
   D. Station wagons

Now, if we change D to Automobiles, the four subheads are equivalent. Station wagons can be made a subhead of D. In each of the following series pick out the one item not of coordinate rank with the other three:

Sports:
   Basketball, football, golf, hockey
National parks:
   Yosemite, Yellowstone, Gettysburg, Rocky Mountain
Mass communication media:
   Newspapers, books, television, radio

Subordination

Subordination is really just a corollary of coordination. In outlining it means that all coordinate subpoints under a given heading must be less important and contributory to the point to which they are subordinated. Subpoints may consist of illustrations of a main point, details that amplify a generalization, or some form of proof of a proposition. The partial outline below shows a series of subpoints arranged both incorrectly and correctly.

"The High Cost of Living"

I. Household expenses	I. Household expenses
A. Food	A. Food
B. Maintenance	B. Maintenance
C. Utilities	C. Utilities
D. Car expenses	II. Other living costs
E. Entertainment	A. Car Expenses
	B. Entertainment

The Number of Major Divisions

Use only a few—in no case more than four or five—major divisions in your speech and, hence, in your outline. Few listeners can remember a greater number of major ideas. To develop a larger number of main points adequately would take more time than is usually available.

The Sentence Outline

The two common types of outlines are the *sentence* and the *key-phrase*. In the former, each point is phrased in a complete sentence, whereas in the latter, key phrases or words are used to suggest the ideas to be conveyed. The sentence form is preferable, at least for beginning students. This method ensures that each idea is thought through carefully, it shows the relationships among the major and subordinate points more clearly, and it is better adapted for use in classroom situations, where the teacher must diagnose a student's individual speech problems. With the key-phrase form it is sometimes difficult to determine precisely the ideas to be conveyed by the words or phrases. However, some experienced speakers use the key-phrase form, or writers may use this type for purposes of illustration, as we have done in this chapter. The sentence type is superior to the key-phrase outline and should be used consistently by students of speech. The differences between the sentence and the key-phrase form are seen in the two brief outlines below.

"Travel Can Be Fun for the Family"

I. Everyone in the family shares in getting ready.
  A. Planning the itinerary can be a pleasant learning experience.
  B. Decisions about what to take must be a cooperative endeavor.
  C. Last-minute preparations are sometimes hectic but always fun.

II. Our last summer's trip was a worthwhile experience.
  A. We followed the Mormon Trek from Denver to Salt Lake City.

       B. We discovered that Oregon scenery is a study in contrasts.

       C. We followed the Columbia River from the Pacific to Idaho's lakes.

       D. We viewed the glories of Nature's handiwork at Yellowstone Park.

"The Fun of Family Traveling"

  I. Getting ready a family venture

     A. Planning the itinerary

     B. Deciding what to take

     C. Making last-minute preparations

 II. Last summer's worthwhile trip

     A. Along the Mormon Trek from Denver to Salt Lake City

     B. Oregon scenery: a study in contrasts

     C. Along the Columbia from the Pacific to Idaho's lakes

     D. Nature's handiwork at Yellowstone

Parallel Structure

The use of parallel language structure—sentences or phrases—will contribute to the coherence of the outline and aid in planning the language to be used in the actual delivery of the speech. In the partial outline below the uniformity in sentence form adds emphasis to a point the speaker wishes to stress:

  V. There are many dangers in failing to vote.

     A. Failure to vote means forfeiting the privilege of being heard.

     B. Failure to vote means the rule of the many by the few.

     C. Failure to vote results in a decreasing interest in governmental affairs.

     D. Failure to vote leads to a breakdown in the democratic system.

Declarative Sentences

When questions are used in an outline, their relationship to subordinate and superior points usually is unclear. Questions do not make assertions about subordinate points, nor do they support a superior point. Since the outline represents the logical structure of the speech, it should make positive statements reflecting the point of view of the speaker rather than ask questions. This does not imply that questions may not be used in the actual delivery of the speech, when they may stimulate thought, provide transitions, give emphasis, and vary the language used.

Subheads for Amplification

If a heading is divided for amplification, it is customary to include at least two subheads. Logic suggests that if a point is divided, there must be at least two parts. While it is not essential that this rule be followed at all times, its use will ensure greater clarity, understandable relationships, and perhaps more complete coverage.

A carefully prepared outline is the first step in effective speaking. Study and application of the rules for outlining will aid materially in achieving this first step.

IMPLICATIONS

1. Effective selection and organization of speech supporting materials should aid in listener understanding and message acceptance.
2. The most usable supporting materials are those that are relevant to the subject, accurate and complete, related to the need-value systems of the listeners, and adapted to the speech purpose, occasion, and audience expectancies.
3. The most useful sources of speech materials are (1) direct experience and observation, interviews, oral and written exchanges of ideas, reading, experimentation, library sources, and commercial or professional free materials.
4. The selection of all speech materials should be purposeful. Get acquainted with what is in your college, community, and nearby private libraries, to save time in researching and studying for a speech.
5. Some guides to follow in using resource materials effectively are these:
   a. Seek worthwhile sources.
   b. Select materials that cover different points of view.
   c. Be objective and critical in reading.
   d. Time your study for maximal efficiency and learning.
   e. Employ some planned system of note taking.
   f. Employ all available shortcuts to the location of source materials: book indexes, tables of contents, etc.
6. A general form of supporting material is evidence, which may be either facts or opinions. Proper tests of the reliability and validity of evidence used should always be applied.
7. The most useful specific forms of supporting materials include definition, examples and illustrations, comparisons and contrast, explanation or analysis, description and narration, statistics, testimony and quotations, questions, and restatement and repetition.
8. The functions of supporting materials are to interest and impress, clarify and interpret, universalize and generalize, and to reinforce and prove.
9. Other patterns include Monroe's "motivated sequence," Borden's formula, the "text" and the "string of beads" arrangements.
10. Always plan your introduction to help achieve these aims: capture attention, arouse interest, preview the scope of the subject, establish the credibility of the speaker, and contribute in general to the goal of the speech.

11. Every introduction should be adapted to the particular speech purpose and occasion by using varied techniques, which include references to the occasion, to the speech purpose, or to the audience, appropriate personal references, narratives related to the occasion, a startling statement, an appropriate quotation, a question or series of questions, a brief statement of the theme, and appropriate humor.
12. Typical forms of conclusions are the simple summary, a story or quotation, a direct challenge to action, or a restatement of the theme.
13. For maximal effectiveness in speaking, an outline of every speech should be prepared in advance. Clarity, complete coverage, logical relationships among the parts of the speech, relative coordination and subordination, effective language use, and elimination of nonessentials will more nearly be assured when the rules outlined in the text are followed.

EXERCISES

1. Make a list of five subjects in which young people are now interested. Select two of the subjects, and make as complete lists as possible of where you would find source materials on those two topics.
2. Try to read your favorite newspaper with some degree of completeness for a week. Make cuttings of materials you might later use in a speech.
3. Keep a list of the experiences you have during a single day. Which ones would make suitable speech materials?
4. Select two subjects of current social, political, or economic interest. Select the one about which you know the least, and then try to get as much information about the topic as you can by oral exchange with your friends. Are they a good source of information? Where could you go to get more or better speech supporting materials, assuming you were to give a speech on the topic selected?
5. Following are the names of persons who are experts in their respective fields. Pick three, and plan a hypothetical interview to get needed information, for some speech you might give, that is related to the area of expertise of the three persons selected.

Steve Allen	Elmo Roper	George Meany
Eldridge Cleaver	Angela Davis	Cesar Chavez
J. W. Fulbright	Spiro Agnew	Edmund S. Muskie
Johnny Carson	David Frost	Merv Griffin
Roman Gabriel	Arthur Ashe, Jr.	Jack Nicklaus

6. On each of the subjects listed below find one general reference work (not a magazine article) in your college library:

Agriculture	Literature	Pollution
Airspace developments	Prison reform	Foreign aid
Ecology	Sports	Theatre
Stock transactions	National Parks	Fashions
Employment	Population information	Censorship
Racial problems	Problems of aging	Population movements

7. Make a diligent search of all the library and free commercial sources of material available to you in your area. Share your list with three of your classmates.
8. Select a news event that you anticipate may be reported in the papers for

several days. Follow the story in two different newspapers. Note the following:

a. What facts are included in one paper and left out of the other?

b. What space, position, and emphasis is given to the story in the different papers?

c. What editorial treatment has been given to the story?

d. What other differences are noted?

Be prepared to discuss in class your conclusions concerning the relative values of the two papers as sources of news events.

9. Nine different specific forms of supporting materials are listed in this chapter. Select some topic on which you plan to give a speech later in the semester. Locate and write out an illustration of each form of support that is applicable to the speech topic.

10. Select a single speech from a recent issue of *Vital Speeches* and do the following:

a. List the forms of support used.

b. Indicate the form of introduction and conclusion used.

c. Indicate the pattern of organization used for the entire speech.

11. List a number of ways in which you depend on order in nature and in your relations with people. In what ways does this order help you?

12. Make a list of professions and vocations in which order has predictive value. Examine your own sense of orderliness to see whether it aids you in picking your future occupation.

13. In the following speaking situations what devices for introductions would you use? Be specific.

    College Commencement

    Service club noon luncheon meeting

    Banquet beginning a drive for funds

    Ladies Aid Society meeting

    Meeting of a group of scientists

    A public meeting on the Fourth of July

    The anniversary of Franklin D. Roosevelt's birthday

14. For each of the following speech titles develop three or four major subdivisions:

Motivation and morale in industry	Racial discrimination
The unspoken word never does harm	Professional football
A team: management and the worker	Modern-day travel
Employee morale in a small business	Pornography
Confrontation: a modern phenomenon	Jet travel
Discount houses and supermarkets	The space age
The nature of the Black organizations	Jive talk
Business as usual in Washington, D.C.	Political strategies
The rights of the American Indian	New art forms
Pollution in Lake Erie	Integration
The plight of the Chicanos	Drugs and drug abuse
Integration	

15. What pattern of organization would you use for each of the following speech topics?

What makes togetherness so sticky?   Skiing
How to control high blood pressure   Coffee breaks
Tools, instruments, and methods   Old age
Esprit de corps, rapport, and harmony   The new African nations
I'd climb the highest mountain   Crime on the increase
Love is a many-splendored thing   Around Manhattan by boat
An outing in the Catskills   Death on the highway
Who attends theatrical premières?   Thrills of motorcycling
Student involvement in academic   Fewer jobs, less pay
    administration   Closing the generation gap
The Women's Liberation Movement   New developments in
Closing the credibility gap in   scientific medicine
    government   Statesmen versus politicians

16. For one of the topics listed in Exercise 1, write two different introductions and two different conclusions for a four-minute speech. Have these criticized by your instructor.

17. Prepare a five-minute speech in which you *explain how to do* any one of the following:

Apply paint with a roller   Make a king-size bed
Apply paint with a brush   Use a pressure cooker
Apply stage make-up   Wash a car
Double one's reading rate   Operate a bulldozer
Get into a sleeping bag   Lose weight
Equip a darkroom   Start a rumor
Multiply on a slide rule   Shoot a rifle

18. Prepare a three-minute speech in which you *describe* one of the following:

Alcatraz   Golden Gate Bridge
The Alcan Highway   Mount Rushmore
Death Valley   Everglades National Park
The Panama Canal   Crater Lake in Oregon
A three-ring circus   The Holland Tunnel in New York
Hoover Dam   Mesa Verde National Park
San Francisco Harbor   The American Flag

ADDITIONAL READINGS

Adler, Mortimer J., *How to Read a Book*, New York, Simon & Schuster, 1940, chaps. 2, 3, 6, 7, 9, 10, 11.

Baccus, J. H., "Building a stock of illustrations," *Quart. J. Speech*, 21 (no. 3, June, 1935), 373–375.

Baird, A. Craig, and Franklin H. Knower, *General Speech*, 3rd ed., New York, McGraw-Hill, 1963, chaps. 4, 5, 6.

Black, Edwin, and Harry P. Kerr, *American Issues: A Source-Book for Speech Topics*, New York, Harcourt, 1961.

Braden, Waldo W., and Mary Louise Gehrig, *Speech Practices*, New York, Harper & Row, 1958, chap. 3.

Brigance, William Norwood, *Speech: Its Techniques and Disciplines in a Free Society*, 2nd ed., New York, Appleton-Century-Crofts, 1961, chap. 11.

Cuomo, George, *Becoming a Better Reader*, New York, Holt, Rinehart & Winston, 1960.

Hackett, Herbert, et al., *Understanding and Being Understood*, New York, Longmans, Green, 1957, chap. 8.

Harwell, George C., *Technical Communication*, New York, Macmillan, 1960, chap. 2.

Judson, Horace, *The Techniques of Reading*, New York, Harcourt, 1954.

King, C. Harold, "The 'hobby' speech," *Quart. J. Speech*, 21 (no. 3, June, 1935), 370–373.

Leggett, Glen C., David Mead, and William Charvat, *Prentice-Hall Handbook for Writers*, 3rd ed., Englewood Cliffs, N.J., Prentice-Hall, 1960, sects. 12, 13, 14, 31, 32, 33, 47.

Lewis, Norman, *How to Read Better and Faster*, rev. ed., New York, T. Y. Crowell, 1951, chaps. 1, 2, 3, 4, 5, 10.

Macrorie, Ken, *The Perceptive Writer, Reader, and Speaker*, New York, Harcourt, 1959, chaps. 4, 5, 11, 13, 14, 15.

Maynard, Norma, "Poor reading, handmaiden of poor speech," *Speech Teacher*, 5 (no. 1, Jan. 1956), 40–46.

McPeek, James A. S., and Austin Wright, *Handbook of English*, New York, Ronald, chaps. 1, 2, 3, 4.

Mills, Glen E., *Composing the Speech*, Englewood Cliffs, N.J., Prentice-Hall, 1952, chaps. 11, 12, 13.

Oliver, Robert T., and Rupert L. Cortright, *Effective Speech*, 4th ed., New York, Holt, Rinehart & Winston, 1961, chap. 10.

Sanford, William P., "The problem of speech content," *Quart. J. Speech Educ.*, 8 (no. 3, Nov. 1922), 364–371.

Soper, Paul L., *Basic Public Speaking*, 3rd ed., New York, Oxford Univ. Press, 1963, chaps. 4, 5, 6.

Weaver, Carl H., *Speaking in Public*, New York, American Book, 1966, chaps. 6, 7, 9.

NOTES

[1] Rev. John L. Murphy, S.T.D., "Religious education and democracy," *Vital Speeches*, 26 (no. 1, Oct. 15, 1959), 30.

[2] Robert Anderson, "Scientific starvation today: A second-rate nation tomorrow," *Vital Speeches*, 37 (no. 16, June 1, 1971), 502.

[3] Harvey C. Jacobs, "News in search of new dimensions," *Vital Speeches*, 24 (no. 17, June 15, 1958), 541.

[4] George W. McKinney, Jr., "The Now Generation," *Vital Speeches*, 37 (no. 21, Aug. 15, 1971), 667.

[5] Paul-Henri Spaak, "The European tragedy," *Vital Speeches*, 17 (no. 11, Mar. 15, 1951), 324.

[6] F. N. Ikard, "Criticism, policy and reality: A national energy policy," *Vital Speeches*, 37 (no. 20, Aug. 1, 1971), 627.

[7] James W. Armstrong, "Foundations to manhood," *Vital Speeches*, 20 (no. 5, Dec. 15, 1953), 154.

[8] Louis E. Lomax, "I am somebody," in Charles W. Lomas, ed., *The Agitator in American Society*, Englewood Cliffs, N.J., Prentice-Hall, 1968, pp. 118–119.

[9] Barbara M. Watson, "International travel," *Vital Speeches*, 37 (no. 15, May 15, 1971), 463.

[10] Arvonne S. Fraser, "Toward a national policy on aging: Every person counts," *Vital Speeches*, 37 (no. 19, July 15, 1971), 599.

[11] Peter Dominick, "The real Communist China: The deed as well as the word," *Vital Speeches*, 37 (no. 19, July 15, 1971), 578.

[12] Frank Knox, "We must fight for our liberties," in Lewis Copeland and Lawrence Lamm, eds., *The World's Great Speeches*, 2nd rev. ed., New York, Dover, 1958, pp. 571–573.

[13] Winston Churchill, in Houston Peterson, ed., *The World's Great Speeches*, rev. ed., New York, Simon & Schuster, 1965, p. 780.

[14] David Krech and Richard S. Crutchfield, *Elements of Psychology*, New York, Knopf, 1958, p. 23.

[15] Adapted from a speech by the president of the National Association of Food Chains, John A.

Logan, before the Boston Conference of Distribution, October 20, 1958. From *Vital Speeches*, 25 (no. 3, Nov. 15, 1958), 84–87.

16Alan H. Monroe, *Principles and Types of Speech*, 4th ed., Glenview, Ill., Scott, Foresman, 1955, pp. 307–331.

17Richard C. Borden, *Public Speaking As Listeners Like It*, New York, Harper & Row, 1935, pp. 3–18.

18Dr. Conwell's income from this speech alone—well over one million dollars—along with other funds was devoted to the founding of Temple University.

CHAPTER TWELVE
INFLUENCING THE AUDIENCE THROUGH REASONING

Reason is a factor in experi-
ence which directs and criti-
cizes the urge towards the
attainment of an end realized
in imagination but not in fact.
Alfred North Whitehead

IDENTIFICATION OF THE PROCESS

It is frequently said that reason does not influence, that people do not respond to reason as a persuasive element in the rhetorical process. C. U. M. Smith, in introducing the concept of motivation, says:[1]

Aristotle defined man as the rational animal; since Freud we might more exactly describe him as the rationalizing animal. Many of the reasons we give when taxed with acting in such and such a manner are spurious. They are conscious or unconscious face-savers: justifications after the event. We all live in private worlds built of feeling or affect. The advertising industry has long realized this fact. Citizens are not induced to buy cigarettes or motor cars by appeals to their reason, but by appeals to their feeling, to their emotions. This is no new discovery . . . "reason is . . . the slave of the passions."

Having placed reason in chains, we stand back and in our greater wisdom pontificate concerning the "in" words of the moment. *They* are the concepts that indicate influence. *Relevance, concern, charisma, meaningful relationships, peace*—these are all words of inner importance, sealed with some charm, which will properly activate another individual.

Reason is not one of these words. For many people it is a word they could do without. It is a negative word. It tends to inhibit rather than thrust forward. It dulls the edge of emotional and creative living. In the midst of a round of champagne it asks whether you lighted the furnace or locked the garage. Without reason we undoubtedly can go on flights of fancy in our minds, but only in our minds. With reason our flights of fancy become real. No one born in the heritage of the jet age can successfully deny the real flights at the speed of sound and at even greater speeds.

Before we consider the proposition that reason has certain unique values, let us contrast it with accident, in order to distinguish the quality that makes reasoning essential to the process of influencing people. To attempt to drive two cars into the same space at the same time results in a collision. Our inferential term for this is *accident*. By this term we imply that the happening was outside the scope of reasoning—that is, neither driver intentionally or through reason decided to collide. Certain aspects of traffic control operate through reason to reduce the number of accidents to below a certain minimum. The true accidents—those that reason cannot find a means of preventing—will continue to happen. At this point reason suggests that if we cannot prevent all accidents, at least we may reduce the injuries that result; hence, seat belts and other safety devices.

How does reason do these things? It does them by seeking out and finding applicable patterns. Smith, in discussing perception, says,[2] "The important concept here is pattern. To perceive is to recognize a pattern, whether it is a pattern of properties which characterize a thing or a pattern of relationships between things."

Reason, the ability to relate perceptions—that is, to recognize patterns or create them—is an important function of the cerebral cortex, the highest level of the brain, which, Smith points out, acts also as the computer of a homeostat.[3]

Reason may be viewed, then, as a cerebral function by which we avoid accidents, solve problems, and satisfy our desires. Reason is impossible, however, without form of some kind. It demands form in time or space or the cerebral cortex. Our examples above have demonstrated form in time and space. Form in the brain is shown by the columnar organization of the visual cortex, indicating the extent to which cortical cells are organized. According to Smith:[4]

It can be shown that the cells of the striate cortex are arranged in functional columns. . . .

There is evidence that the simple, complex and hypercomplex cells concerned with the processing of information picked up by one area of the retina are all located in the same cortical column. In other words the column turns out to be the "unit of dynamic function" of the visual cortex.

Since we have conclusive evidence that functional patterning of cortical cells exists, it is not difficult to perceive that the groundwork is laid physiologically for the perception of patterns—the essence of reasoning. As far as speech is concerned, the adaptation of sensory information, its evaluation and preparation for an outgoing message, occurs, according to Smith, about like this:[5]

We may imagine that the interpretative cortex, like the speech cortex in the dominant hemisphere, is labile and uncommitted in the infant. Penfield and Perot suggest that whereas the speech cortex makes words and phrases available when speech is intended, so the interpretative cortex makes past experience available for comparison with incoming current experience. The interpretative cortex, in other words, holds a map or model of the world against which the world sensed by the sense organs is matched.

A meaningful message, then, proceeds from an organized cerebral cortex. It is responded to because the sensory organs of the audio system of the computer of another homeostat are able to sort these vibrations, translate them into meaning, compare them with a map of experience, and determine what kind of response to make to what they consider to be a reasoned or unreasoned stimulus. By contrast, accident is without form. It is whim. It is unpredictable. As such, man can deal with it only in an indirect fashion. He can react emotionally, but this is only a catharsis, which leaves the accident unaffected. He can give it a name as a substitute for explaining it. He can assume the role of soothsayer and allege that he is able to predict the unpredictable. But only reason can penetrate the fabrication.

There will always be a man to whom an accident is abhorrent; all his reason will be used in the attempt to explain or harness some accidental happening. There will always be a man to whom that accidental happening means profit; he is not opposed to reason but only to that reason which might eliminate his profit. Indeed, it may be the ability to harness this accident, at least in part, that makes it profitable (that is, the laws of chance are a partial effort to predict accident). Be he racetrack tout, blackjack dealer, insurance man or actuary, real-estate broker or investment counselor, he capitalizes upon accident because of reason.

There are some men who actually defy reason. Some of these are sick. If the sickness adversely affects other humans, they may be locked up. When a healthy person decides to defy reason, we say that he is taking a calculated risk. The amount of reward available rises in proportion to the amount of risk. Gambling is the attempt to harness available reason to the unpredictable, when the odds may be against you. Few people will not indulge occasionally, but those who are chronically addicted suggest that reason has little meaning for them other than as a "slave of the passions."

In reason, then, we discern a cognitive process shared with some competence by most people. As Kruger puts it:[6]

Reasoning is a process of the mind which begins with something known or believed to be true and reaches other supposed truths which cannot be, or have not been, directly determined by sense perception. We are reasoning when we give reasons or evidence for a particular conclusion. The French astronomer Leverrier was reasoning when he put certain facts together—Newton's Law of Gravitation (presumed to be true) and the regular deviation of the planet Uranus from its predicted orbit (observed)—and concluded that there must be a planet, theretofore undiscovered, which was causing Uranus to deviate. That his reasoning was sound is indicated by the discovery of the planet Neptune where Leverrier reasoned it should be.

Reason is characterized by its ability to bring order out of chaos or accident. Because of this function reason, though often unrecognized, is one of man's primary persuasive stimuli. When controversy arises, reason should be (though it is not always) used by both sides. Whatever solution is arrived at is not always a clearcut victory for the reasoning process of either side. Therefore, the assumption arises that reason was not effective. As a result it is very easy for one party, ordinarily the losing party, to assume or to allege that emotion alone has carried the day. We therefore often emphasize the stimulus to emotion inaccurately as being more persuasive than the stimulus to reason.

VALUES OF EFFECTIVE REASONING

We have emphasized that the one great value of reasoning is continually to find ways of bringing order out of chaos. Part of this process we call the solution of problems. Problems can include such diverse items as obtaining a satisfactory schedule of courses, finding a stolen automobile, and rehabilitating an economically impoverished urban center. Alfred North Whitehead describes the value of reason as follows:[7] "In this function Reason is the practical embodiment of the urge to transform mere existence into the good existence, and to transform the good existence into the better existence."

Reason also helps to explain or determine causes. Conditions for which we are trying to find causes may include cancer, for which the government has allotted millions of dollars, or a minor domestic problem such as why the linoleum is rotting under the kitchen sink. Or the problem may be one of ecology, such as the pouring of industrial waste into our lakes and rivers.

Reason helps to explain and predict effects. The seismological laboratory at the California Institute of Technology is in a position to advise us of the location of existing faults, explaining that destruction will be greater if we build on or near one, should a severe earthquake occur. If your professor is known to be a hard grader, reason may help you to see that the effect of turning in your paper late may be reflected in your grade. Reason might also tell one that, if he is to live successfully among Romans, it might be well to do as the Romans do.

Reason aids the communicator in checking the validity of his message. If my boss is a stickler for accuracy, and he depends upon me for information or advice, I would do well to use the principles of reasoning to validate my conclusions. A wife, in attempting to convince her husband that she needs a new dishwasher, should validate her conclusions before presenting her message.

The reverse situation is also true. The respondent must evaluate the message provided by the communicator. Again reason will be a chief tool in this process.

In addition to the set of values given above, which are fairly standard, it might also be suggested that reason helps to overcome certain blocks in communication. We have stressed in this book the fact that variations in perceptions are to a large extent responsible for people's not receiving the same meaning for messages. To the extent that reason distinguishes form and pattern in life, uncertainty is reduced. The increased perception of the familiar tends to be a strong stimulus toward less divergent views among people with similar routines and patterns. In other words, reason can help bring people together.

The use of reason increases the tendency to use words in the same rather than different senses, for reason insists that whenever a word shifts its meaning in our minds, we are no longer talking about the same thing. Therefore, careful definition or establishment of a referent for the word we use is part of the process of reasoning.

HISTORICAL DEVELOPMENT

It is only with the development of carbon dating that we are able to appreciate the number of thousands of years since the caveman applied reason to make his first tool. After that he left his cave and discovered how to build a house. A house made a town possible, and with that new environment a society or culture could be developed. Man learned to grow wheat and barley where he wanted them instead of where they occurred in nature. He domesticated animals so that he did not have to hunt them.

Once man had learned to live in towns, the rapidity with which his development took place was amazing. Because he needed to become an engineer and a navigator, he was forced to develop a science that would explain these two developments. Hence, geometry was born.

By the time Aristotle had established his Academy, many men had done a lot of reasoning, but no one had attempted to analyze reasoning itself. The Golden Age of Greece was important, for it was one of the few ancient civilizations in which men were rewarded for attempting to solve the philosophical and scientific problems they faced. Dialectic had already been developed. It was inherent in the dialogues of Plato. It was the instrument by which scholars of renown debated each other. In many cases it was a game in which the object was to put down your opponent. Thus the purpose of dialectic was to win your point. For this highly cerebral game Aristotle invented a method of testing reasoning, called the syllogism. The syllogism will be explained in detail later in this chapter.

THE NATURE OF REASONING
Identifying Relationships

Reasoning is a process of using words to emphasize the relationships between the objects or the ideas for which they stand. In reasoning we must keep firmly in mind that we are not dealing with words but with referents. It is possible, of course, that the referents may be present. If, for instance, we are discussing how the living-room furniture may be rearranged or what the effect of taking down the eucalyptus trees at the rear of the lot would be, we are discussing things that are present and tangible. As we deal with these objects and call them by their names, we are considering them in terms of their locations and possible changes that may be made.

In many cases we will not have actual objects as referents but, rather, ideas or hypothetical constructs, making the problem of identifying the referent much more difficult.

The process of reasoning is essentially a matter of seeing relationships. When the objects are before us, it is often difficult enough to recognize their forms. When we consider that many objects are not stable—that is, they change their form, and some objects are even highly volatile—the difficulty in dealing with them becomes apparent. Experiment repeated time after time tells us that the form of H_2O can be changed from a liquid to a gas at 100 degrees Centigrade. It also tells us that if this gas is confined too long it will explode. This chain of events can be established as a reliable construct and, hopefully, will be activated in our minds before we touch the radiator cap of an overheated car. Such a piece of reasoning appears to be simple enough, and as long as the relationship among the tangible elements is maintained, we can predict that we will get the same result.

When our reasoning involves relationships whose referents are neither objects nor constants but, rather, hypothetical constructs that may strengthen or fade, the problem involved in keeping our relationships in focus is much more difficult. The higher the level of abstraction, the more ambiguity involved in the terms we use to express our hypothetical constructs. It is necessary to examine the forms reasoning can take to assist us in keeping our relationships valid. Reasoning can help us to identify relationships, then, if we are willing to accept its forms.

Inductive Reasoning

The basic process of inductive reasoning occurs when we examine objects and ideas for similarities and dissimilarities. The goal of this process is to examine a sufficient number of instances of like objects or concepts in order that a generalization may be drawn. A generalization is simply a rule which states that certain objects or ideas are alike in all the critical aspects concerned. For a generalization to be conclusive it must examine all available instances. Induction proceeds, then, from the specific to the general, because it must examine many examples or instances before it can make a general claim of constant likeness or behavior. If our desire is to determine the minimal amount of time given to public-service telecasting, an examination of television stations operating in the United States may indicate that no less than 15 percent of broadcast time is made available for public service. This generalization is brought about by an examination of the program of each individual station, comparing each station's public-service time with every other, until that which is a minimum is discovered. This minimum may be stated as a generalization: no station provides less than 15 percent of public-service time.

Inductive reasoning is the method through which our knowledge is accumulated, but the generalizations drawn are always subject to revision, on the theory that new evidence may become available at any time.

Another inductive method, which depends upon the same process of comparison for similarities and dissimilarities, but which is less rigorous, is known as reasoning from example. A woman discovers that every so often her washing tends to come out pink. Disturbed by this phenomenon, she begins to inspect her washing. After she has examined several pink loads over a period of time, she has isolated one item—a red sock—which, when included in the wash, leaves a pink tinge. Reasoning inductively by example, she solves her problem by deciding that red dye runs.

A third method of reasoning inductively, which may be even less conclusive than reasoning from example, is the use of analogy. In analogy we conclude that, if certain characteristics are true of one instance of a phenomenon, they will be true of another like instance. Thus we might reason that if the characteristics of a Chevrolet were sufficiently similar to those of a Ford, we might expect similar performance from each automobile. In the summer of 1965 that area of Los Angeles called Watts was suffering from heat, an overcrowded black population, a feeling of neglect and frustration amounting to hopelessness, economic depression, and a sense of White oppression. This situation erupted in rioting. It could be reasoned by analogy that in any city where there was a Black ghetto with these characteristics, a riot was likely to ensue.

We see, then, that the essential method of reasoning in the inductive process is one of comparing specific instances for similarities and dissimilarities. As a result of this process we may draw a generalization which, if done properly, has the highest probability of truth. Second, we can apply the same processes of comparison to a number of examples and draw a conclusion that may very conveniently solve a problem, although it has a lesser probability of overall accuracy. Finally, we have the analogy in which only two objects are compared, but a conclusion may be drawn if the characteristics of each have sufficient similarity and no pertinent dissimilarity. Again a prediction may be made, which may solve a problem but not provide a valid, abiding rule.

Deductive Reasoning

Deductive reasoning is the reverse of the process of inductive reasoning. Instead of proceeding from the individual instance to the general law we take the generalization we have developed through induction and, using it as our measuring instrument, we inspect new instances that relate to this general rule. To be accepted as Grade A, frozen shrimp must meet certain qualifications. This generalization, or measuring instrument, will be specified by the Pure Food and Drug Administration once the characteristics of Grade A have been established. Then inspection of specific samples of frozen shrimp packed by various companies may be compared to these standards.

In the deductive situation the individual sample is being compared to the general law, whereas in inductive procedure individual samples are being compared to each other in order that a general law or standard may ultimately be formulated. We must realize, however, that whether we reason deductively or inductively, the same basic process of comparison for similarities and dissimilarities is being used. In solving problems we often use induction and deduction alternately and successfully without being aware of the difference. The terms, however, are helpful for instructive purposes.

The application of deductive reasoning forms a great part of our approach to everyday living. Many professional fields, organizations, and many governmental and private agencies have established, through inductive processes, generalizations that are widely circulated, not only in scholarly journals, but also through the media, and much of our existence is thereby directed. We tend to accept overall generalizations made by experts in their respective fields. For example, few people would contest the generalization that one should be vaccinated for smallpox. Most would agree that the Pill is effective, although some would urge that it has bad side effects.

Studies at Cornell University and the University of California at Los Angeles have demonstrated that fewer injuries occur to automobile passengers who wear seat belts than to those who do not. Although many people do not buckle up with them, few would be in a position to refute the generalization that the research has established.

Most of us tend to accept these generalizations and accommodate our ways of living to them; as a result the behavior of people within our culture tends to be more predictable. In fact, it is these accumulated beliefs, accepted over long periods of time, that cause a culture to develop.

Employing Classification
The Nature of Classification
We have indicated in the previous section that reasoning is a process of identifying relationships. It is our purpose now to show that classification is an integral part of discerning relationships.

Common Elements. If we are to examine various instances of a phenomenon, we must first determine which of its aspects are to be compared. For instance, if a poker player asserts that all one-eyed jacks are to be wild, he has quickly and efficiently limited the areas of comparison for determining wild cards. We have, then, a classification that consists of playing cards, a subclassification that consists of jacks, and another subclassification that consists of only those jacks seen in profile. The problem, for one who does not know, is to determine how many cards are in the last classification, so that he will know how the odds are affected by the wild cards announced. Thus the classification has established the basis of further assumptions about the number of wild cards.

A housewife is confronted with certain categories when she plans a meal or looks up a recipe. Let us assume that she is operating with five categories in mind, and they happen to be fruits, vegetables, cereals, meats, and dairy products. Let us assume that she is concerned also about the nutritional value of the contents of these different classifications. She may have determined that meats tend to be higher in protein and fat, cereals higher in starch, and so forth. She then plans her meal, taking certain items from each of these categories which in the combination served will provide the nutritional value she desires. Thus she relates what she knows about the protein in meat to what she knows about the starch in cereals, so that she may serve what she considers to be a nutritional diet.

The most important thing about classification is knowing the purpose for which we are classifying. Out of a possible thousand or more characteristics that might be inspected in any given example, we might be interested in only one. Therefore our classification would be built out of all examples having this one characteristic in common.

Let us observe a woman in the process of finding a scarf to go with a dress of a certain color. Color is her predominant motive: she is not interested in size, material, or price, but she must have that color. Let us consider, at a more abstract level, a person who wants to belong to what he considers an evangelical church. He is not concerned about how the church baptizes, he is not concerned about how and when Communion is served, and he is not concerned about the size of the church: he is concerned that the individuals in this congregation actually go into the community at large and present information concerning the Christian belief.

Most of our problems with classification come from a tendency to oversimplify or overcomplicate. The more items we decide to inspect when we set up our classification, the more problems we shall have in finding examples that meet our requirements. The semanticist warns us against one-valued judgments. For instance, if we have determined that drunken drivers should be confined until no longer inebriated, we have the problem of determining which drivers are drunk. Although many tests might be used, let us assume that we have selected a blood test and alcohol content above a certain level in the bloodstream as our criterion of drunkenness. This is a one-valued judgment, but essential to the purpose set forth.

On the other hand, other situations demand a many-valued approach. Let us assume that we are to select a new president for a university. It will immediately be seen that there are a number of qualifications this man should have. We should want to observe his leadership, his background, his understanding of student problems, his ability to build an exceptional faculty, among other things. Classification must be suited to the purpose we have in mind if it is to identify the pertinent relationships.

Class Name. We have a group of individuals, quite limited in number, called university presidents. If we can assume that in general they have been selected on the basis of somewhat similar criteria, we then have a group, roughly speaking, with certain common elements. The individuals in this group may show a great deal of variation, even though they are similar in certain selected respects. Our culture has numerous classifications of this kind. We may speak of stock-car racing teams, rock groups, country singers, municipal judges, journeyman plumbers, junior executives. If it were not possible to classify in this fashion, it would be very difficult to use our language. It is necessary to talk about groups of people, groups of animals, collected objects, but we must continually recall, when we do this, that we are talking about rather loosely woven characteristics.

Thus forewarned, we may proceed to use this verbal shorthand as a substitute for the impossible task of identifying every individual in a group we wanted to talk about.

The Problems in Classification

Unfortunately, a process as convenient as classification cannot exist without having certain problems connected with it.

Borderline Cases. A borderline case exists when those charged with distinguishing the difference cannot agree. Certain mechanical safeguards always can be taken when an outcome is significant in terms of money, prestige, and power. At the races photography is employed to reveal the winner in close finishes. Language is used to determine at what point on a scale something takes effect. That is, if we determine something should begin or conclude by March 26, what do we really mean? Do we mean at midnight of March 25 or noon of March 26 or midnight the beginning of March 27? We can modify the difficulty in determining borderline cases if we specify boundaries carefully. When we do this, we must acknowledge that in many cases we are being arbitrary, but arbitrariness is often justified, because it enables us to avoid later, insoluble, disputes.

Units of Classification. An example will show the importance of differences in the units of classification. We are used to thinking in terms of miles, inches, gallons, and acres. To think in terms of kilometers, liters, centimeters, and milligrams, if we are not familiar with them, is difficult. But the problems involved here are easily visualized. Many of us go along happily without understanding certain units of classification in many areas with which we are quite familiar. Perhaps the housewife knows better than anyone else the value of a dollar, for she measures it out in terms of the goods it will buy each week at the market. Inflation is a very difficult term to understand, and when it is presented to us in terms of percentage of increase in the wholesale commodity index for the third quarter of the year, our appreciation of the units involved is somewhat obscure. Those who are at this very moment computing the amount of retirement compensation upon which they may be able to exist fifteen to twenty years from now run the risk of missing the mark by a substantial sum, unless they are able to compute with some accuracy the inflation that may take place in that period.

Semantics. Additional difficulties in classification relate primarily to semantic problems. For instance, two observers do not see varied elements of an occurrence in the same fashion, nor do they necessarily perceive the same events at the same level of abstraction. Therefore, each tells a different story, because his mind has perceived a different picture. Thus, a lawyer happening to view an automobile accident would see the legalistic aspects, whereas a nurse standing by his side would tend to focus on the injuries that were being sustained.

Probabilities. We have already implied rather strongly that reasoning deals with probability. This is a very old concept, dating back to a man named Corax, who came to Athens from Sicily before Aristotle had begun his Academy. As a result of his teaching and that of many of the Sophists, probability was well established in Greek thought before Aristotle used it as a basis for reasoning in his *Analytics* and *Rhetoric.*

Probability means there is no absolute predictability—a thought that was philosophically abhorrent to Plato but one that Aristotle found necessary to the establishment of any logical system. When we deal with reasoning on the basis of probability, we are saying the prospects of a thing's having happened, being true as of now or coming about in the future, may be estimated somewhere on a scale of probability; for absolute certainty requires a superhuman view. Plato presents an excellent example of this kind of thought. When pressed to the fullest for his source of knowledge, he was forced to yield to the concept of superhuman knowledge. This takes us outside the reasoning process, where we deal with large problems such as life and death and meaning on a basis of faith, hope, or whatever attribute we wish to apply.

Aware that man had a faculty for using his reasoning powers, Aristotle concluded that, since there was sufficient need of reasoning in handling our everyday affairs, we should find a way to harness it and make it work for us. He was satisfied to formalize reasoning at this level and leave the grand questions, of life and death and their ultimate meaning, to the philosophers, such as Plato, who felt they could invoke information beyond the scope of human reasoning or, at least, through the skillful manipulation of dialectic, could put down those who disagreed with them.

As Aristotle recognized, if limited to absolutes, the power of reasoning is severely inhibited. In fact, for him the only absolutes were what he called infallible signs. In discussing the possibility of refuting infallible signs he said,[8] "All we can do is to show that the fact alleged does not exist. If there is no doubt that it does and that it is an infallible sign, refutation now becomes impossible, for this is equivalent to a demonstration which is clear in every respect."

One might then ask what the infallible signs are? Although Aristotle perfunctorily suggests a few, we are faced with a worldly situation in which it is not possible to produce infallible signs at will. At the operational level perhaps the best we can say is that no one has ever yet come up with two individuals who had like fingerprints. If this alleged fact is not true, its probability of truth is so high that few would argue it. If you put your mind to it, you can come up with other examples of this kind.

Much of our thinking, in terms which we might express as absolute, carries over from our training as children, when many situations of a probable nature were expressed by our parents to us in absolute terms. This was not done because of any failure to recognize the probable nature of the situation or, on the other hand, to deceive, but, rather, to take no chances with that which was considered precious. Therefore, a mother's ultimatum to her child about crossing the street was put in the form of an absolute. To do otherwise would have been folly. The child could not understand the nature of the probability involved, and the mother wished to make sure that her child was not going to be struck by some random automobile. As a result of many experiences of this kind, children grow up in a world of alleged absolutes. As they grow older and begin to perceive the probable nature of many happenings, they tend to discount the value of reason, not understanding that probability is its basis. They also tend to develop doubts about the wisdom of their elders, failing to realize that they will be forced to resort to similar strategems in the future. Mills emphasizes the importance of probability as follows:[9]

Some level of probability is all we can hope to achieve, because the human behavior about which we deliberate belongs in the class of uncertainties. We argue about matters which appear to admit of two possibilities: expedient or inexpedient, just or unjust, wise or foolish, etc. In each case we advocate a view which we think is true for the most part or as a general rule. The inherent reason is that probability statements cannot reliably predict a specific instance; they indicate a trend on a long-run basis. In practical affairs we must bet on the odds, as it were.

Credibility. Credibility as it relates to reasoning has two facets: on the one hand, acceptable, logical methods combined with reliable evidence;

on the other, an ability to fit our view of relationships to the experiential map of the receiver.

Validity requires that we follow processes of reasoning that have been demonstrated, that the method we use in coming to our conclusion is acceptable in the view of those qualified to make such judgments. Thus, if we are reasoning deductively and our structure is a syllogism, then the rules for the formulation of a syllogism should be followed accurately. We must realize, however, that structure or form as we have construed it guarantees only the method, not the evidence we have put into the method. Therefore, we must be concerned both with the reliability of evidence, which we have considered elsewhere, and the accuracy of the method of reasoning, which will be developed further in this chapter.

The second factor involved in credibility, that is, the acceptability to the audience of our conclusions, implies some knowledge and understanding of the respondent. We may in preliminary preparation have convinced ourselves of the accuracy of our conclusions, but if we have not examined the audience, and it does not join us in this acceptance, we have not established credibility. A statement or case may have the highest probability of truth, but if the audience does not believe it, it has not helped our argument.

The inverse may also occur; that is, an audience may accept faulty evidence and reasoning but, if it does, it is no credit to the speaker, except that he is a shrewd operator. When this is done with intent to deceive, we have what is known in common jargon as a con man.

Creativity. Attacks on reasoning have alleged that the syllogism does not provide new ideas, that the reasoning is all done before we put it into a formal mold. It is important to point out here that the syllogism was invented not primarily as a means of creating new ideas, but as a means of controlling ideas we already have. Nevertheless, forms of reasoning, usually, but not exclusively, inductive, are the keys to creative invention. When one has envisioned a goal worthy of achievement and perhaps somewhat imaginative, the creative energy to accomplish that end must be guided by the active use of reason. The imaginative concept or desire is not enough.

To illustrate, let us consider the ascent of the first balloon. Man has had the imaginative desire to fly as long as we have had written history. However, it was not until 1783 that Joseph Michel Montgolfier and his brother Jacques put together the hypothetical construct that, if one could enclose a cloud in a bag, that bag should float in the air, since such things as smoke and clouds seem to rise. This particular hypothetical construct in reasoning would be called an analogy. It was easy, then, to reason that if one could capture the smoke from a fire in a prepared bag, that bag would rise, as did the smoke. The Montgolfier brothers performed the experiment on June 5, 1783, and the bag rose as they had anticipated. It was only later that they discovered that the bag rose because of the heated air that entered it and not the particles that caused that heated air to appear as smoke. This, however, did not void the reasoning they used, for it was based on the tools and knowledge available. Before the summer was over they had hydrogen in the bag, and the great era of balloon ascensions had begun.

It should be clear from this that without reason there could be no creativity; although many people have insisted that because we cannot explain a flash of insight, reasoning has little to do with creativity. As we have pointed out previously, reasoning is a platform from which imaginative insight frequently takes off. The persistence to carry out the task is not enough. Without reason, definition of the purpose and completion of the task are impossible. As Alfred North Whitehead points out:[10]

Reason is the organ of emphasis upon novelty. It provides the judgment by which realization in idea obtains the emphasis by which it passes into realization in purpose, and thence its realization in fact.

As was pointed out in our illustration above, it took many centuries before reason was able to obtain the peculiar emphasis that enabled the brothers Montgolfier to define a purpose and translate that purpose through reason into fact.

Although we are familiar with the concept that the discovery of penicillin was an accidental byproduct of other research, reasoning was involved in the whole situation. Columbus's overall reasoning was accurate, even though he could not predict that a continental barrier would prevent him from carrying out his purpose of circumnavigating the globe and that he would discover America. Accidental discoveries are fairly commonplace. Ordinarily, however, a basis of reasoning is necessary to set up the creative situation. In the case of Columbus, he would never have discovered America had he not had a practical plan, based in reason, to circumnavigate the globe.

Although no one has been able to describe accurately such elements as imagination and insight, there is little doubt that creativity relies heavily upon reasoning.

THE NATURE OF RHETORICAL PROOF

In considering rhetorical proof we include three factors that cannot be separated in actual practice. For purposes of analysis we have treated them at various points throughout the text. We consider rhetorical proof to include (1) influencing the beliefs and attitudes of the audience, (2) establishing the speaker's trustworthiness and good will, and (3) obtaining audience acceptance of data and inferences.

In previous chapters we have given considerable attention to changing attitudes and beliefs and establishing through style the trustworthiness and competence of the speaker. We now consider the third element of proof, which is the acceptance of data and inferences. These three elements of proof may easily be recognized as the Aristotelian formula—logos, ethos, pathos. For academic purposes only we examine reasoning, or logos, separately from the other two, but not because we believe that proof for an audience can exist solely as a product of reasoning. As long as we accept communication as a two-way process, persuasion requires the inseparable functioning of all three modes of proof.

TYPES OF REASONING
When the effort is made to determine the types of reasoning, it quickly becomes apparent that there are almost as many arrangements as there are writers on the subject.[11] We have chosen to present only the simplest and most basic of these arrangements.

Since we have already explained the basic differences between deductive and inductive reasoning, we shall now take up the types and illustrate some of their uses. We must always keep in mind, however, that the structures of reasoning, when the rules are properly followed, will guarantee only that the method of reasoning is accurate. In most cases a continuum of probability serves as the measuring stick for materials introduced into the logical structure. If we can demonstrate high probability for the measures we advocate and the evidence we use to support them, we have done the most that can be expected of us.

Deductive Reasoning
Syllogisms and signs are the two types of deductive reasoning, and we shall examine them in the following paragraphs.

The Syllogism
Deductive reasoning presumes a generalization with a high probability of truth. This generalization is used in the formulation of a syllogism. It becomes the major premise. We may take such a generalization as "all foreign fishing vessels that violate American Territorial waters will be intercepted by the Coast Guard." We must realize that this premise, although stated as an absolute, must be considered as having only a high probability of truth, for some vessels may escape detection or for other reasons not be intercepted. Nevertheless, this is the general rule, and this is what any foreign fishing vessel may expect.

The major premise is divided into two parts, the first of which is called the middle term and, in our example, consists of "All foreign fishing vessels that violate American territorial waters." The predicate consists of "will be intercepted by the Coast Guard." The middle term sets up a classification. In this particular case it consists of all foreign fishing vessels, and the predicate tells us what will happen to them in one particular situation. We therefore may reason that what is true of all of the class will be true in this instance of any individual member of the class. We may have evidence enabling us to develop a minor premise, which may be stated as follows: "The *Petrov I. Nikolovich,* a Russian trawler, is a foreign fishing vessel, which violated American territorial waters." We have now established our minor premise by taking an individual case and showing how it is included within the general class, or middle term. We must realize that the middle term, to be accurate, must be used in the same sense in both the major and the minor premises. Otherwise we have a fallacy.

Having now set up a class and said what that class may expect under certain circumstances, we are able to predict with considerable accuracy what may happen to any individual unit in that class. We therefore conclude that the *Petrov I. Nikolovich,* a Russian trawler, will be intercepted by the Coast Guard.

We may see, then, that in the conclusion we repeat the particular term from the minor premise and the predicate from the major premise, in this way rounding out our conclusion in a form which, if always followed, provides validity in dealing with matters relating to classification. The entire syllogism will then appear as follows:

Major Premise

All foreign fishing vessels that violate American territorial waters (universal middle term)

will be intercepted by the Coast Guard (predicate)

Minor Premise

The *Petrov I. Nikolovich* (particular term)

is a foreign fishing vessel that violated American territorial waters (universal middle term)

Conclusion

The *Petrov I. Nikolovich* (particular term)

will be intercepted by the Coast Guard (predicate)

The actual process we have just gone through in analyzing the syllogism is one of classification. As such it can be illustrated graphically as in Figure 12-1.

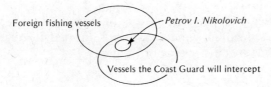

FIGURE 12-1. Deductive classification.

The syllogism that we have been considering is known as a *categorical syllogism.* There are other types of syllogisms, which we will not consider in this brief description. All are governed by specific rules, which we will not list here, believing that the sample presented above makes clear the essential form a syllogism must follow.

Having established what the syllogism is, we must make certain that its use is understood. For most of us its chief value will be in checking our own arguments to see whether they are valid and testing those of other people. The use of the syllogism, then, is in the preparation of the material or evidence, so that, if our argument is attacked, we are certain of its validity. Although we do not use the syllogism ordinarily in making a speech or in conversation, we frequently use a rhetorical version called the *enthymeme,* which will be discussed later. The entire syllogism is too stilted and too technical to be used in ordinary oral discourse.

The Sign

A generally accepted sign may be used to establish the occurrence of an unrelated but coexisting event. A flag flown at half mast provides an excellent example of a sign. According to custom, men of distinction are honored at death in this fashion. There is no causal link or actual relationship of any kind between the two events. However, if we see a flag at half mast we may state that someone of importance has died. Such is the proper use of sign. Much of our behavior is based on this type of reasoning. We look for written signs such as "The escalator is in this direction"; we distinguish the men's restroom from the women's by a sign.

Sign reasoning is included under deductive types because there must be general agreement on the meaning of the sign, which establishes a general rule, although it may exist only in custom or tradition. Those signs which participate also as partial cause or effect in the relationship between sign and event will be considered under causal explanation rather than as true types of sign reasoning. Such are clouds as an indication of rain and yellow leaves as an indication of fall weather.

Inductive Reasoning

In our consideration of the nature of inductive reasoning we have already suggested how a generalization is formed through the comparison of numerous specific events or items.

Generalizations

Generalizing, as was pointed out by Aristotle, is the chief means by which we accumulate knowledge. In primitive times, before many scientific experiments had been done and great libraries accumulated, the process of generalizing brought together the product of man's observations, and many conclusions were made and, in some cases, nailed down so tightly that erroneous generalizations were difficult to correct. Now we find that so much knowledge has been accumulated and catalogued that, although tremendous frontiers of knowledge still exist, the tools with which we make our observations and the methods involved have become highly sophisticated. Regardless of this fact, the making of generalizations is a process in which all of us indulge, frequently in too hasty a fashion, leaving ourselves open to the charge of overgeneralizing.

Examples

Under the nature of reasoning we have discussed the process by which examples may be used to solve specific problems. The processes involved here, as we previously pointed out, are similar to those of generalizing. However, the conclusions we derive are better adapted to solving specific problems than to drawing universal conclusions. Therefore reasoning from like characteristics in a series of examples can be of tremendous practical value. It enables us to react reasonably to many aspects of our environment when it is not possible for us to understand the totality.

Although the use of examples to solve problems has great practical value, it leaves a good deal wanting as an inductive process designed to provide substantial proof.

Analogies

We have not distinguished previously between the two types of analogy that are included as inductive processes. Analogies are divided into literal and figurative types.

That which is literal consists of two examples taken from the same class of objects or events. We mean "class" here in the same way we meant it in explaining the nature of classification. If an analogy is literal, then, we are comparing two cars, two countries, two riots or, possibly, two songs. We make a conclusion about one of the examples, and because the two things have like characteristics, we say that our conclusion about the first must also be true about the second. Thus, if a subway system works well in handling commuter traffic in New York City, we are likely to conclude that San Francisco, with its narrow, confined, and populous land areas, would benefit from a subway. If Chicago takes the neighborhood policeman out of the patrol car and puts him back on the beat, many might conclude that this would be an effective change for Los Angeles.

If we are to reason successfully with the analogy we must be certain that all factors that relate to the point we wish to prove are similar in both cases. Taking our second example, it could be pointed out that the geographical area that must be covered in Los Angeles is far greater than that in Chicago. Therefore, what might work efficiently and economically in Chicago would prove inefficient and expensive in Los Angeles.

The figurative analogy compares two examples from different classes, and there is really no limit on how remote these classes may be from each other. To say that we reason from a figurative analogy is true only in the sense that we see a relationship between two things. "It is bad practice to throw the baby out with the bath water" might be the figurative analogy used by those who oppose eliminating cars to get rid of smog. Through this analogy we have asserted a relationship which, although it may be true, is not valid in any directly comparable sense. The relationship is metaphorical.

The figurative analogy uses a graphic method of making a point without even stating the point. If the comparison is accepted as reasonable by an audience, it might be very difficult to dislodge. Such was the case when Clarence Darrow used this type of analogy in a speech delivered to the inmates of the Cook County jail in Chicago in 1902:[12]

Some of you people have lived in the country. It's prettier than it is here. And if you have ever lived on a farm you understand that if you put a lot of cattle in a field, when the pasture is short they will jump over the fence; but put them in a good field where there is plenty of pasture, and they will be law-abiding cattle to the end of time. The human animal is just like the rest of the animals, only a little more so. The same thing that governs in one governs in the other.

The audience was probably delighted to hear this analogy, because it brought into focus a concept they wanted to believe. But to support the reasonableness of the idea that what governs cattle is the same thing as governs men is not supportable. Put in any other fashion than an appealing figurative analogy, even the prisoners wouldn't have "bought" it. If it persuaded, it was only because the audience already believed, not because of any reasoning that existed in the example.

The figurative analogy frequently is a trap set by a speaker to snare the unthinking. Now we have just done this to you, dear reader, if you believe the last sentence. Whenever you hear a speaker indulge in this type of figurative analogy, you should raise warning signals of coming efforts to sweep you off your feet. This discourse is not designed to inhibit completely the use of the figurative analogy but, rather, to caution against accepting or making comparisons that use dramatic effect and imagery as a subterfuge for reason.

Such a metaphor as "Democracy is like a life raft; your feet are always wet but you never sink" can be used to excellent advantage. It is striking. It appears to suggest a tremendous basic value and also minor inconveniences. The metaphor has supplied this relationship, but in some cases the speaker may need to demonstrate how the aspects of the metaphor apply to the real situation. Then he will have founded his figurative analogy upon a reasonable basis rather than have invited criticism of an illogical comparison.

Causal Explanation

Argument from cause or effect is treated by some rhetoricians as an inductive process and by others as a deductive process. Here we will treat it independently, in part because it uses both processes in alternate fashion and in part to avoid oversimplification. For most of us it is easy to assume that an apparent effect has only one cause, or that an apparent cause has only one effect. Such thinking will appear simplistic to those who wish in every case to probe the deep scientific or psychological roots of any problem. This is, of course, the proper field of scientific investigation but not necessarily the field of rhetoric, which must deal with present problems and solutions, using what materials are available now.

Such simple problems as determining which can of tamales was contaminated we solve through the process of comparing for similarities and dissimilarities, which we described as the basic process both in formalizing a generalization and in reasoning from example.[13] We may find the contaminated can through such a process of comparison, but the chain of events by which this particular can became contaminated will not be revealed so easily, because it will be the result of a complex of causal relations. The problem of the speaker, then, in handling cause is to determine from the controversial situation what depth of causal explanation will be necessary to satisfy the parties involved.[14]

To say that because we have a cloud we are going to have rain is an excellent example of oversimplification. Whether or not the cloud will produce rain depends upon a number of complex aspects, which involve the moisture content of the air, wind direction, pressure, and temperature at any given elevation. How far we shall go into explaining any of these things will depend upon the situation.

We have often heard the simplistic charge that the ghetto is the effect of the white man's lack of concern for the black man. A more realistic appraisal of the situation involving both Black and White would involve the causal explanation of a number of factors that work together to produce the situation, such as the migration of many Blacks from the south after World War II in search of better conditions, the tendency of young people in the '50s to leave the city where they were raised and join each other in the suburbs, where the price was right, the tendency of housing in the central city to be available on a low-rental basis and of more job opportunities to be available in the central city, and the restrictions preventing Black settlement in the suburbs.

Since rhetoric is not designed to investigate all the complex aspects of causality nor, on the other hand, may it be satisfied with answers that are oversimplified, we must realize that a situational approach influenced by audience analysis is our only guide to how deeply we will have to probe in terms of causal explanation.

REASONING IN THE COMMUNICATIVE SITUATION

When Aristotle called a syllogism a process to be used in dialectic, he also used the term *enthymeme* to represent the kind of reasoning that would be usable in rhetoric. We have already indicated that the form of a syllogism is inappropriate in oral discourse.

Let us now examine the enthymeme. In doing so we may meet an unrecognized old friend, for all of us use enthymemes, whether we know it or not.

The Enthymeme

The enthymeme provides a less formal but still accurate method of conveying the argument to the audience. The following examples will illustrate what an enthymeme is like:

1. You should support busing, for it will break up de facto segregation of schools.
2. You should oppose busing, because it takes children too far from home.
3. Intelligent people use a fluoride toothpaste to prevent cavities.
4. Don't forget to lock your bicycle when you get to school.

The enthymeme in appearance is different from the syllogism, but basically it does the same thing. Its difference in appearance is due to the circumstance that the enthymeme is an informal syllogism. It does not follow the rigid pattern we outlined above. In addition, it may leave out some portion of what would have to be stated if it were a syllogism. The examples given, if formal syllogisms, would appear as follows:

1. All efforts to break up de facto segregation of schools should be supported. Busing is an effort to break up de facto segregation of schools. You should support busing.
2. Desegregation plans that take students too far from home should not be supported. Busing takes students too far from home. Busing should not be supported.
3. Intelligent people use a fluoride toothpaste to prevent cavities. You are intelligent. You use fluoride toothpaste to prevent cavities.
4. Children who have locked their bicycles at school are less likely to have them stolen. You lock your bicycle at school. Your bicycle is then less likely to be stolen.

In taking the enthymemes and transforming them into syllogisms we have demonstrated:

1. Why the syllogism is not as suitable to rhetoric as the enthymeme.
2. That, when we are concerned about the nature of the proof we use in the enthymeme, we can check it through the syllogism, for it is then easy to observe the basis of the argument and how high it may rate on our scale of probability.
3. The enthymeme not only must represent good reasoning but also must be acceptable to the audience, or it is of no value as argument.
4. Often we omit a portion of the syllogism when we state it as an enthymeme.

Although we have not demonstrated it here, the enthymeme serves not only as a means of stating our argument but as part of the invention process of discovering the argument, a matter which was considered in Chapter Eleven.

The Toulmin Sequence
Throughout the centuries the enthymeme has been the basic means of stating an argument. However, as we have previously indicated, another method has been developed recently for structuring an argument. We

do not offer the alternative method simply because it is new or necessarily better than the enthymeme. However, since it makes a different approach to the problem and uses a different form, some may find it easier to grasp. Before developing the method used by Stephen E. Toulmin in the model that bears his name, it might be well to suggest the following relationships to the syllogism-enthymeme sequence:

1. Instead of beginning with a universal, as the syllogism does, the Toulmin sequence transmits a claim together with supporting evidence and a reason for associating that evidence with the claim.
2. The structure of the Toulmin sequence is such that it can be used for either inductive or deductive processes.
3. When the Toulmin sequence is used deductively, it is quite similar to the enthymeme.
4. The Toulmin sequence seems to be more flexible than the syllogistic, because it includes concepts of reservation and qualification.

We have five elements in the Toulmin sequence. One of them is aptly named "the claim." This statement represents some factor in a controversy or a need situation that must be resolved. That is to say, not everyone believes the claim. We must find a way of bringing about belief in the claim. To show relationships better we shall use the same example that we used for the syllogism. Our claim, then, will be, "The *Petrov I. Nikolovich*, a Russian trawler, will be intercepted by the U.S. Coast Guard." The obvious question to be asked at this point is "Why?" In other words, whoever makes the claim must supply evidence why the Coast Guard should intercept this vessel.

This brings us to the stage of the Toulmin sequence called "datum." We provide the following evidence. "The *Petrov I. Nikolovich*, a Russian trawler, violated American territorial waters." Assuming this evidence to be accurate and supportable, one question remains unresolved: Why should this mean that the Coast Guard will take this action?

We now refer to the stage of the Toulmin sequence called "warrant." A warrant states why the evidence associates with the claim, or supports the claim. That is, it is a bridge between the data and the claim. In our example, the warrant is "The U.S. Coast Guard is under orders to intercept all foreign fishing vessels that violate American territorial waters."

As we have indicated previously, there is a fourth stage in the Toulmin process. This stage is called "reservation" and gives us an opportunity to list any exceptions to the general rule that we should like to make. The Coast Guard operates under a set of both general and specific orders, but that does not guarantee it will be able to carry out its mission in every instance. Although we have made the claim that the *Petrov I. Nikolovich* will be intercepted by the U.S. Coast Guard, it should be obvious that there are some possible reservations. Cases of bad weather and failure by the Coast Guard to detect or locate an offending vessel are two examples of possible reservations to our claim.

Once we have discovered that a pertinent reservation to our argument exists, we should do well to make use of Toulmin's concept of "qualification." Instead of making an absolute claim we now modify by using such "qualifying" words as "highly likely" or in "most cases."

Having described the stages of the sequence that make up the Toulmin model, it may be helpful to see it as a unified entity.

> Claim: The *Petrov I. Nikolovich*, a Russian trawler, probably will be intercepted by the U.S. Coast Guard.
> Datum: The *Petrov I. Nikolovich*, a Russian trawler, violated American territorial waters.
> Warrant: The U.S. Coast Guard is under orders to intercept all foreign fishing vessels that violate American territorial waters.
> Reservation: Cases of bad weather or failure by the Coast Guard to detect or locate an offending vessel may prevent interception.

Although we have indicated that the Toulmin method is not necessarily a better form than the Aristotelian syllogism-enthymeme, it has certain advantages that may tend to invite the interest of the modern student. To begin with, the label is less artificial and more pragmatic. We talk about "claim" and "datum," and these concepts are better understood than "major premise" and "minor premise." Although many people will use the Toulmin model in the sequential order presented, it is not necessary that this be done. One could present the evidence first or the warrant, depending upon the psychological reaction he wished to create in his audience.

Another important factor that may make this method appealing is the fact that reservations are suggested, and this calls attention to the fact that we are working with probabilities, and we can easily sort out the obvious exceptions, which are bound to arise. We probably should suggest here that the developments of both the enthymeme and the Toulmin model are the result of the observation of argument in action. As formulas they are suggesting to us the way in which claims are made, evidence is provided, and conclusions are drawn. We should indicate also that the Toulmin model, like the syllogism, is useful as a checking process. Thus, as respondents we may find it necessary to question the speaker about why he has not supplied data. Or it may be that the warrant has not been stated and cannot be supplied by the audience.

COMPARATIVE ANALYSIS

In the following comparative analysis we are comparing the Toulmin model with the Aristotelian syllogistic method. The notes in the margins refer to the organizational aspects of the speech, indicating what is happening as the speaker proceeds. At the end of each section of the speech, the reasoning process is illustrated by the Toulmin and Aristotelian methods.

Whether the enthymeme or the Toulmin method is used for structuring our reasoning, we cannot expect every speaker to use phrases and sentences that will easily conform to the models given. Therefore, in extracting the speaker's meaning for testing either in a syllogistic or Toulmin model, it may be necessary to paraphrase, as has been done in the following example. The models given here do not necessarily conform to or guarantee what the speaker had in mind.

The speech below was given by The Honorable Carl B. Stokes, Mayor of Cleveland, at the 32nd Annual Dinner of the Massachusetts Committee of Catholics, Protestants, and Jews, in Boston, Massachusetts, on May 15, 1969. The speech was provided by Mr. Stokes and is set forth here in the arrangement he desired for speaking.

The introduction answers some questions	*I am with you tonight to be honored, and while some degree of sophistication might reasonably be expected of a big-city mayor, I'm still new enough in the role to be surprised and delighted to find myself in such distinguished company on such an illustrious occasion.*
What kind of man am I?	
What kind of people do I think you are?	*In fact, as I look about me at the men and women of influence, power and of prestige and position gathered here, it strikes me as a perfect opportunity to demand reparations for my fellow Clevelanders.*
Do we have any common ground between us?	*We Clevelanders are still somewhat put out by the fact that our city's founder, General Moses Cleaveland, took one look at our place back in 1796, gave it his name, and left immediately for civilized home and hearth in his native New England, never to be seen again on the shores of Lake Erie.*
Uses humor to extend goodwill to his	*So we had to go it alone, and while we did make it, it has been pretty embarrassing to have had a founding father who barely stayed long enough for a cup of coffee.*
	But I suppose we can call it even, now. After all,

audience	*we captured the "Hawk" from the Red Sox. And now that I think about it, General Cleaveland was from Connecticut anyway.*
Transition to first point of body of speech	*I always enjoy visiting Boston. A great sense of history fills your city and your state, and it turns my thoughts to those who helped make that history, but how many of these names do you know?*
	—Crispus Attucks, first to fall in the American Revolution
Data	*—Peter Salem, who killed the British commander at Bunker Hill*
	—Phillis Wheatley, the second American woman to write a book
	—Cuff Whittemore, Cato Wood, Cambridge Moore, Caesar Prescott, Caesar Jones, who helped defend "The Bridge That Arched the Flood" at Concord on that April day nearly 200 years ago.
	—Lewis Temple, inventor of the "Temple Iron," the harpoon which led to vast wealth in the whaling industry—and who died in poverty.
Data culminate in conclusion and first point of speech	*—Paul Cuffee, spirited sailing captain who refused to pay his property tax because he was denied the full rights of citizenship, and who thereby became the first Negro to enjoy all the legal privileges granted to the white citizens of Massachusetts.*
	All were Black. All helped write the history of this great state, as my distinguished friend Senator Edward Brooke is doing today.

Toulmin Model

Data----------------*Crispus Attucks, an unhonored Black, was the first to fall in the American Revolution. (Peter Salem, Phillis Wheatley, Cuff Whittemore, et al.)*

Warrant-----------*Anyone, Black or White, honored or unhonored, who died for or otherwise helped to forge American liberty, contributed to the history of Massachusetts (unspoken but strongly implied).*

Claim--------------*Many unknown Blacks contributed to the history of Massachusetts.*

Aristotelian Model

Major Premise--*Anyone, Black or White, honored or unhonored, who died for or otherwise helped to forge American lib-*

ty, contributed to the history of Massachusetts (unspoken but strongly implied).

Minor Premise--*Crispus Attucks died for liberty in the American Revolution. (Peter Salem, Phillis Wheatley, Cuff Whittemore, et al.)*

Conclusion-------*Crispus Attucks et al. contributed to the history of Massachusetts.*

Transition to second point of speech

Every American boy and girl learns the dates, the names, the places of history. They learn that on April 6, 1909 Admiral Robert E. Peary discovered the North Pole.

Datum

But all of us would have to admit that the same school lesson did not tell us that Peary's dedicated Negro assistant, Matthew Henson, was the first man actually to reach the Pole. Peary, unable to walk, arrived by dogsled less than an hour later to confirm Henson's reading of their position.

Two items of the data culminate in conclusion and statement of second point of speech

Someone recently complained in a letter to a newspaper that he saw Negro cowboys depicted in a TV western, and everyone knew there were no Negro cowboys in the Old West. The sad thing is that our mind's eye—conditioned by gaps in our history—does see only White cowboys.

I don't expect to make headlines in this day and time by observing that the Black American has been erased from the pages of American history. You know that. You know what that sort of practice has contributed to.

Toulmin Model

Datum-------------*It is not taught in school that Peary's Negro assistant was the first to reach the North Pole.*

Warrant-----------*The man who first reached the North Pole should have been recognized in history books (unspoken but strongly implied).*

Claim --------------*The Black American has been erased from the pages of American history.*

Aristotelian Model

Major Premise --*All men who have performed significant deeds should be recognized in history books.*

Minor Premise--*Matthew Hensen, a Negro, achieved a significant deed as the first man to reach the North Pole.*

Conclusion-------	*Matthew Hensen should be recognized in the history books.*
Transition to third point of speech	*Now, after three centuries of his own personal dark ages, the American Negro is filling in the gaps of history. He is rediscovering his long-ago-lost heritage. He has weighed the words on America's deeds, and his anger, finally, at what has been done to him is echoing across our land.*
Data	*Black Power!*
	Black Studies!
	Reparations from the racist hands of White America!
Warrant	*Alexis de Tocqueville summed it up when he said, "A grievance patiently endured, so long as it seemed beyond redress, becomes intolerable once the possibility of remedy crosses men's minds."*
Conclusion and statement of third point of speech	*The cries of the rebels are going to have to be responded to; their genuine grievances must be redressed.*

Toulmin Model

Datum-------------	*Black Americans have grievances that have become intolerable because they see a possible remedy.*
Warrant-----------	*When men believe a remedy for their intolerable grievances is possible, these grievances must be redressed.*
Claim -------------	*Black Americans must have their grievances redressed.*

Aristotelian Model

Major Premise --	*All men whose grievances have become intolerable, because they see the possibility of remedy, must have their grievances redressed.*
Minor Premise--	*Black Americans have grievances that have become intolerable, because they see a possible remedy.*
Conclusion-------	*Black Americans must have their grievances redressed.*
Data presented as an appeal to audience	*Every American—that is, every American who understands this pluralistic society of ours—ought to be part of the Negroes' struggle to develop:*
	Black identity
	Black pride
	Black culture
	Black economic and political power

Reservation
to appeal

But none of these vital elements to one's sense of worth and peer-level in American society justifies or rationalizes the efficacy of a separate black nation within our nation.

Warrant

I believe with Winston Churchill that "Democracy is the worst form of government—except for every other kind." I believe in the system.

Conclusion and
statement of
fourth point
of speech

For the system can be made to work.

Not through anarchy. Not through nonnegotiable demands. Not through senseless destruction.

Second
reservation

On that point I agree with Bayard Rustin, who said recently, "I am very much opposed to violence as a means of protest—the appearance of youngsters on campuses carrying guns and attempting to get deci-

Data
supporting
second
reservation

sions while holding guns at the heads of administrators is first of all very bad for the students. Because they are being systematically taught in college that social change takes place at the point of a gun. This is not true. And they're going to be very much disabused."

Today's youth is too intelligent not to learn this eventually, hard though the lesson is, on them and on us.

Toulmin Model

Datum--------------*Every American who understands this system can help the Negro establish Black identity, Black pride, Black culture, Black economic and political power.*

Reservation------*As long as this does not lead to a Black state within our nation, these may be established.*

Warrant------------*Despite the faults of our democracy, it provides the means of helping the Negro (unspoken but strongly implied).*

Claim---------------*The system can be made to work*

Reservation------*So long as it is not done through anarchy*

Aristotelian Model

Major Premise--*Despite their faults, all democracies have the means of providing the Blacks with Black identity, Black pride, Black culture, Black economic and political power.*

Minor Premise--*All Americans are part of a democracy.*

Conclusion-------*All Americans are part of the means of providing the*

*Blacks with Black identity, Black pride, Black cul-
ture, Black economic and political power.*

**Fifth point
of speech**

*But I would warn: You cannot condemn the op-
pressed for the means by which they seek freedom
and justice and at the same time continue the denial
of freedom and justice! You cannot have it both
ways.*

Data

*Justice Oliver Wendell Holmes, that great Boston-
ian, said, "Life is action and passion. I think it is
required of a man that he should share the action and
passion of his time at peril of being judged not to
have lived."*

*There is the story told about Pericles of Ancient
Greece, who, in his later years, came across a young
lawyer of Athens who was involved in the actions and
passions of his time. Pericles upbraided the young
man for being too bold and brash, for concerning
himself with things better left to older men. Patroniz-
ingly, the older man said, "Of course, I understand,
for I too was overeager in my youth. But now that I
am older I have learned better. Take my advice and
do not become so involved." To which the young
man replied, "I regret, sir, I did not have the privilege
of knowing you when you were at your best."*

**Restatement,
reemphasis,
and expansion
of fourth
point**

*America, then, is in that very challenging and dan-
gerous stage of involvement. In the words of former
Health, Education and Welfare Secretary John W.
Gardner, "Extremists of the right and of the left
work with purposeful enthusiasm to deepen our suspicion and fear of one another and to loosen the
bonds that hold society [together]. And will anyone
really know how to put it together again?"*

*I believe that the fabric of America, weakened
though it may be, will hold; that those who seek to
pull our society apart will fail, although we may not
see it for a time and we may have doubts and good
reason for doubting.*

*For the first time in history a nation has almost
within its grasp the ability and the means to banish
the age-old terrors of hunger, disease, poverty, and
ignorance—but to implement that potential our society must reach an unprecendented level of political
and social awareness and of political and social activ-
ism.*

Transition

Thesis of
speech

In that fact lies the seed of the paradoxical hope I want to hold out to you this evening: That from today's unwanted crucible of dissent and unrest will emerge a nation more concerned about human values and more effective in caring for human needs than any the world has known.

You may ask, was it necessary to follow this badly built pathway to our goal, with its terrible strains on our nation? Leave the answer to history. We are on that pathway, and even if we did not choose it, never forget that it is here and that you and I helped build it.

Restates
faith in
America

I believe that America will emerge from the journey knowing in its collective conscience, for the first time, that this is not going to be a decent society for any of us until it is for all of us.

Finishes
with
emotional
appeal
in poem

I want to conclude with an epitaph on a Concord gravestone, marking the last resting place of one John Jack, a black slave who earned his freedom and became a successful farmer and respected citizen.

It was written by Daniel Bliss, a great-uncle of Ralph Waldo Emerson, and it reads:

God wills us free, man wills us slaves.
I will as God wills, God's will be done.
Here lies the body of
John Jack.
A native of Africa who died
March 1773, aged about sixty years.
Tho' born in a land of liberty
He lived a slave.
Till by his honest, tho' stolen labors,
He acquired the source of slavery,
Which gave him his freedom,
Tho' not long before
Death the great tyrant,
Gave him his final emancipation,
And set him on a footing with kings.
Tho' a slave to vice,
He practiced those virtues
Without which kings are but slaves.

John Jack: Born in a land of liberty, enslaved, freed again by his own labors.
John Jack made it, and so will America.

Toulmin Model
   Claim ------------- *I would warn: You cannot condemn the oppressed for the means by which they seek freedom and justice and at the same time continue the denial of freedom and justice:* You cannot have it both ways.
   Datum ------------- *"Life is action and passion. I think it is required of a man that he should share the action and passion of his time at peril of being judged not to have lived."*
   Warrant ----------- *If Americans enter the fray they will achieve their goal (unspoken but implied).*

Aristotelian Model
   Major Premise --*Americans who determine to enter the fray will achieve their goal of freedom and justice to the Black.*
   Minor Premise--*You as an American will enter the fray.*
   Conclusion-------*You as an American will achieve your goal of freedom and justice to the Black.*

Some speeches are more structured than others. The more unstructured the speech, the harder it is to detect the basic reasoning within the speech. To some extent Carl Stokes's speech is an example of phraseology used in such fashion as to make it difficult to pin down the exact reasoning used by the speaker. The fact that the use of either method of analysis has indicated logical relationships between the supporting evidence and the conclusions drawn does not mean that everyone will agree with the soundness of the reasoning. Some may tend even to set up opposing arguments based on refutative enthymemes or claims designed to counter Stokes's position. It is obvious that this could be done.

It is also obvious that we cannot be quite sure of the logic of Stokes's position unless we analyze each point in a logical framework. Indeed, there was a time when, if anyone suggested that historians left out the American Negro, eyebrows would have lifted, simply because the Whites had never heard of the Negroes who had been left out. Booker T. Washington and George Washington Carver certainly had been named in the history books. Who else was there? Carl Stokes has made his point.

Whether or not you as a student will be inclined to study Carl Stokes's speech for the ways in which he develops his reasoning or whether you will study it in the effort to locate fallacies, it will prove a profitable exercise.

FALLACIES IN THINKING
We can never be absolutely certain that some intelligent analyst will not be able to pick out the flaw in our reasoning. Because many of us fail to

recognize the errors we make—some of which we are able to cover gracefully, while others hang out in full view to embarrass us—it will be of value to study in the following section the fallacies we fall into.

Hasty Generalizations

All of us are familiar with hasty generalizations, because we have indulged in them so frequently. There are two ways of erring. The first is the failure to inspect enough examples—that is, the assumption that because five different kinds of detergent have phosphates in them, all do. The second is the failure to identify properly the similarities and dissimilarities among the examples. For instance, if we are concerned about whether Howard Hughes has really written his signature or not, considerable professional examination of the alleged signature will have to be made.

Elements of both errors are likely to be found in the following examples. If a teenager can't get along with his parents and knows two or three other teenagers who say that they also cannot get along with their parents, he concludes that no teenager can get along with his parents. Since investigation shows us that numerous teenagers are getting along with their parents, this reasoning, although it may relate to the experience of the teenager mentioned, is unsound.

The shy girl who decides that, because three or four of her classmates tend to ignore her, she is disliked by all, has made a hasty generalization. This kind of faulty reasoning has caused much grief for many teenagers, to whom it would never be plausible that logic could help them with such a personal problem. Do not let fallacious reasoning sell you down the river in your interpersonal relationships simply because you are unwilling to let your logical nature have a part in the judgment of a process that involves you. There are many examples of girls who, having received the proper counseling, have discovered that others did not dislike them but that, rather, they were creating their own problems through faulty logic. Hasty generalizations can do little for you except get you in trouble.

Disregard of Relevant Exceptions

Because rules are so often overdone or overemphasized, we get the feeling that in many cases they may be completely disregarded. For example, it has long been the custom of the school authorities of Reno, Nevada, to take students into the Sierra for skiing in the winter months. During the 1971–72 season an avalanche occurred at the ski site in an area that had been marked off-bounds to skiers. Two of the students who had violated the regulation in order to ski on what appeared to be much more appealing snow were rescued. It was impossible to save two others from the avalanche.

When the Weather Bureau puts up warnings from Point Arguella to the Mexican border, Coast Guard officers expect that some stupid fool will be out there and that they will have to go get him.

The remark that established religion is no longer relevant is quite familiar. However, people who are willing to join in such assumptions are forced to evade outstanding examples that indicate otherwise.

Why be the target of a relevant exception when some are so devastating?

Mistaken Causal Relationships

One of our biggest problems is sorting out things that happen at the same time. We are so strongly inclined to identify cause and effect, when we really have nothing more than coincidence. In previous pages we emphasized the concept of causal explanation, for it is infrequent that we can point to a single, simple cause of most effects.

It is highly unlikely that you came down with a cold because you went barefoot on a cold winter's day. However, this assertion probably will be made by someone in your family despite the fact that medical authorities insist that colds are caused by viruses.

One of our most prevalent questions is, "What caused your headache?" The answers run the gamut from "Oh, it's just a tension headache" (whatever that means) to "Well, if you had a boss like mine you would have a headache too," or "I always get a headache if I don't eat on time." Facetious as this may sound, people have a unique ability to label the causes of their headaches with seeming certainty despite their lack of scientific knowledge about the chemistry involved.

Frequently people who have something to gain from the venture will tend to make an event appear to have a cause-effect relationship when actually it does not. For instance, President Nixon announced his eight-point peace plan in January 1972 and revealed his numerous efforts secretly to negotiate an end to the war in Indo-China. Despite the fact that the President gave a number of justifications for presenting his information at that time, the charge was made that he released it when he did to take the public attention off wage and price controls, the pending dock strike, and unemployment. These disconnected assertions would be believed by those who readily accept negative information concerning Mr. Nixon.

Another example of a faulty conclusion is the assertion of an angry father to his son, "If you hadn't insisted on driving to that party, my car wouldn't have been hit by that drunk." Correlating the desire to go to a party with the inability of a drinker to control his car is, of course, absurd. Emotion-driven desires and needs are not good dictators of accurate causal explanation.

Argument From Ignorance

A number of fallacies may be considered under the heading "ignoring the point or avoiding the issue." One of the most frequently used methods is called *ad hominum* and simply means attacking the person who makes the argument rather than the argument itself. Therefore, we say, "Would you buy a used car from this man?" and transfer the argument from the issue to the man we dislike.

In the *ad populum* argument we appeal to the judgment of the people, as when we say, "Have you ever seen me other than honest? Would I ever do anything to make you distrust me?" Or we urge that a proposition not be passed, "for the people do not want it," whether the people's opinion has been registered or not. The *ad populum* argument may be carried to the point of stimulating the mob to make passionate decisions and take overt action without valid reason.

An additional argument of this type, the *ad ignorantiam,* avoids the issue when someone asserts a thing can exist because it cannot be proven that it does not exist. Therefore Scientist X says, "Our indications point to the likelihood that there is human life elsewhere in the universe." Certainly no one has proven there isn't.

Further argument from ignorance results when people with inadequate information make false conclusions with the assurance of ultimate authority. A number of recent examples are apropos, in which a recognized authority in one field attempts to carry his authority into an area where he has no expertise. For example, a nuclear physicist, expert in designing techniques for bombarding the nucleus of the atom, is not necessarily qualified to make judgments about the amount of money that should be allotted in the federal budget for national defense.

To be even more specific, a widely heralded pediatrician was hardly in a position through background and experience to determine how and when the United States Government should end the war in Vietnam and withdraw its soldiers.

We all believe that rewards and punishments are effective motivation. The student who makes the blanket assertion that all grades should be eliminated could just, possibly, be showing his ignorance of certain areas that might concern other students, such as the number of prelegal students that will be accepted by law schools with major reputations because of their grades. Without grades a whole new system would have to be set up for making this determination, which might not be as effective. A new system would also have to be set up for determining who should receive certain scholarships that require academic achievement.

It would be difficult to support the position that anyone who got hooked on heroin did it other than out of ignorance of the consequences. We all live under a code which says, "Ignorance of the law is no excuse." The argument from ignorance has led thousands of people into situations of humiliation, embarrassment, and pain.

Fallacies of Deduction

Fallacies of deduction, which relate largely to the proper structuring of the syllogism and the handling of the enthymeme, have already been considered in terms of errors of construction. They will not be reviewed here as fallacies.

REASONING—A PSYCHOLOGICAL PROCESS

It should now be fairly clear, as a result of this quick look at reasoning, that we have been dealing with a process which, contrary to general opinion, is more of a psychological than a logical nature. We are dealing with a symbol system, which evades the possibility of exactness of meaning between word and referent. As long as this is true, we are dependent more upon a psychological process than upon a purely logical one.

Aristotle recognized this difficulty in dealing with reasoning and consequently called the process *logos*, the Greek term for *word*, from which our word *logic* was developed. Reasoning, then, is the process of handling words consciously as symbols in order to obtain as near an exactness as possible in the communicator-respondent area of replication. Because it depends upon a symbol system, and because the six billion cells in the average brain do not have synapses that click in unison or according to very many specific and recognizable patterns, we never can be quite certain of the symbolic relationship we have established in another's mind. Reasoning can help us in the process, because it narrows the avenues of approach. It forces us to work within certain structures, in which it is easier to detect fallacies—that is, improper relationships. If we do not take this precaution in preparing our materials, the intermingling of ethos and pathos with logos may obscure in the audience's mind the full part that reasoning must play as a prime factor in proof.

IMPLICATIONS

1. Reason is a primary persuasive stimulus, for it is our only means of bringing order out of chaos and accident.
2. In the process of ordering chaos, reason enables the communicator-respondent to (1) solve problems, (2) explain or determine causes, (3) explain and predict effects, (4) check the validity of messages, and (5) help overcome blocks in communication.
3. Although man has been reasoning for many millenia, it is only in the last two

and a half that he has inquired about reason and discovered, identified, and developed the structures man uses.

4. Since we tend to see primarily those relationships which we are trained to recognize, it would be disastrous not to train ourselves in reasoning.

5. Although human knowledge is gathered through the inductive process of generalizing, that process has limited value as argument, for ordinarily it must be used in an incomplete stage. The deductive counterpart has greater value, for it usually has received more testing.

6. The deductive process not only enables us to classify, but also gives us a formula by which we may check individual instances against an established standard.

7. If we know the purpose for which we are classifying, it will be easier to determine whether our comparison should be based on one-valued or many-valued judgments.

8. Although few absolutes can be substantiated through reasoning, we as communicators and respondents can determine the probability of truth in a given argument and so aid the process of decision making.

9. Reasoning can provide you no more than a constant structure in which to mold your evidence. If the material you put in is false or unacceptable to your audience, reasoning is not going to guarantee your success with that audience.

10. For you the communicator, reasoning should be viewed, not as an inhibiting factor, but as the platform from which creativity can blast off.

11. In a reciprocally operating communication circuit the three modes of proof are not separable. Persuasion results from the intermingled operation of all three.

12. The syllogism and other such technical, logical structures are useful as checking devices as we prepare our own arguments or as we ponder the arguments of others. They are rarely useful in communication, either formal or informal.

13. The enthymeme and the Toulmin model, both the results of observation of argument in action, provide structures suitable for formal or informal discourse.

14. You should carefully inspect your arguments to be sure that you have avoided the common fallacies, for if the respondent's appraisal of you tends to go down instead of up, it may be that he has recognized your fallacies.

15. The thorough application of reasoning in formal or informal occasions does not change communication from a psychological to a logical process but substantially reinforces the speaker's chances of success with a critical audience.

EXERCISES

1. Give two examples of situations in which you have seen some kind of reasoning used to solve a problem or to avoid a danger.

2. Can you discover someone, other than the persons mentioned in the text, who contributed to the historical development of the principles of reasoning?

3. What comparisons would you have had to make if you had decided to use the term "stac" to represent a number of furry, clawed, and carnivorous animals (assuming the species had never before been named)? Bring your results to class for discussion.

4. Defend the proposition that classification does or does not employ a part-whole relationship. Write down a few arguments, and be prepared to present them in class.

5. Write a short essay in which you defend either the nature of probability or the nature of absolutes. Be prepared to read your views to the class.

6. Why is it that sometimes a valid argument will not be accepted by the audience? Be prepared to discuss your views in class.

7. Is there any situation or circumstance in which proof can be established only through the presentation of data and inferences? Be prepared to discuss your views in class.

8. Prepare a syllogism, an enthymeme, and a Toulmin model, using the same topic. Point out the differences that arise in adapting to the different forms. Be prepared to discuss your examples in class.

9. Using the same topic, develop a literal and a figurative analogy to support a point.

10. Make a list of five signs, not mentioned in the text, that could be used in sign reasoning.

11. Think of an example of why reasoning in rhetoric is a psychological rather than a logical process.

12. Prepare a short talk for your class, in which you reveal the flaw in the following example of reasoning by Bernard Shaw: "The reasonable man adapts himself to the world; the unreasonable one persists in trying to adapt the world to himself. Therefore all progress depends on the unreasonable man."

ADDITIONAL READINGS

Abernathy, Elton, *The Advocate: A Manual of Persuasion*, New York, McKay, 1964, chaps. 4 and 5.

Baird, A. Craig, Franklin H. Knower and Samuel L. Becker, *General Speech Communication*, New York, McGraw-Hill, 1971, pp. 303–315.

Brembeck, Winston Lamont, and William S. Howell, *Persuasion, A Means of Social Control*, Englewood Cliffs, N.J., Prentice-Hall, 1952, chaps. 11 and 12.

Ehninger, Douglas, and Wayne Brockriede, *Decision and Debate*, New York, Dodd, Mead, 1963, chap. 10.

Freeley, Austin J., *Argumentation and Debate, Rational Decision Making*, Belmont, Calif., Wadsworth, 1967, chap. 9.

Kruger, Arthur N., *Effective Speaking*, New York, Van Nostrand Reinhold, 1970, chap. 11.

Mills, Glen E., *Reason in Controversy*, Boston, Allyn & Bacon, 1968, chap. 8.

Mudd, Charles S., and Malcolm O. Sillars, *Speech: Content and Communication*, 2nd ed., San Francisco, Chandler, 1969, chap. 10.

Newman, Robert P., and Dale R., *Evidence*, Boston, Houghton Mifflin, 1969, chap. 3.

Nichols, Alan, *Discussion and Debate*, New York, Harcourt, 1941.

Smith, Donald K., *Man Speaking, A Rhetoric of Public Speech*, New York, Dodd, Mead, 1969, chap. 5.

Toulmin, Stephen Edelston, *The Uses of Argument*, London, Cambridge Univ. Press, 1958, pp. 97–135.

Whitehead, Alfred North, *The Function of Reason*, Princeton, Princeton Univ. Press, 1929.

NOTES

[1] C. U. M. Smith, *The Brain: Towards an Understanding*, New York, Putnam, 1970, pp. 233–234.

2*Ibid.*, p. 272.

3*Ibid.*, p. 234.

4*Ibid.*, p. 295.

5*Ibid.*, p. 270.

6Arthur N. Kruger, *Modern Debate, Its Logic and Strategy*, New York, McGraw-Hill, 1960, pp. 146–147.

7Alfred North Whitehead, *The Function of Reason*, Princeton, Princeton Univ. Press, 1929, p. 23.

8Aristotle, *Rhetoric and Poetics*, New York, Modern Library, 1954, p. 163.

9Glen E. Mills, *Reason in Controversy*, 2nd ed., Boston, Allyn & Bacon, 1968, p. 49.

10Whitehead, *op. cit.*, p. 15.

11*Ibid.*, pp. 185–197.

12Clarence Darrow, "Crime and criminals," in Carroll C. Arnold, Douglas Ehninger, and John C. Gerber, eds., *The Speaker's Resource Book*, New York, Scott, Foresman, 1961, p. 140.

13For anyone who wishes further explanations of the methods used in making such comparisons we refer you to John Stuart Mill, *A System of Logic*, London, Longmans, Green, 1935, pp. 133–134.

14Cf. Donald K. Smith, *Man Speaking, A Rhetoric of Public Speech*, New York, Dodd, Mead, 1969, p. 118.

CHAPTER THIRTEEN
COMMUNICATING THROUGH PHYSICAL BEHAVIOR

Suit the action to the word,
the word to the action; with
this special observance, that
you o'erstep not the modesty
of nature.

William Shakespeare

In Chapter Three we defined speech communication as "the purposeful, transactional process by which one person, through the use of audible and visible symbols, engenders meanings in the mind of one or more listeners." This may be interpreted as saying that the message the listener perceives comes to him through a code of auditory and visual symbols. The code is a complex pattern of three components: (1) the language used, which gives the content of the message, (2) the auditory aspect of the spoken language and any audio aids, which is what the listeners hear, and (3) the visual aspect of the code, which includes the speaker's bodily behavior, both intentional and unintentional, the physical surroundings, and the speaker's visual aids, all of which is what the listeners see.

The first of these three components, the content of the message, deals with such things as the actual language the speaker uses, his supporting materials, patterns of organization, and motive appeals. We are concerned in this chapter, however, with the second and third components, the auditory and visual aspects of the speaker's code, excluding audio and visual aids, which we shall consider in Chapter Fourteen. Let us look first at the visual aspects of the speaker's code.

THE VISUAL COMPONENT OF THE SPEAKER'S CODE
The classification of the three aspects of the visual component of the speaker's code that we have listed above—bodily action, physical surroundings, and visual aids—encompasses the classification of nonverbal communication suggested by Reusch and Kees. They state:[1]

In broad terms, nonverbal forms of codification fall into three distinct categories:

Sign language *includes all those forms of codification in which words, numbers, and punctuation signs have been supplanted by gestures; these vary from the "monosyllabic" gesture of the hitchhiker to such complete systems as the language of the deaf.*

Action language *embraces all movements that are not used exclusively as signals. Such acts as walking and drinking, for example, have a dual function: on one hand they serve personal needs, and on the other hand they constitute statements to those who may perceive them.*

Object language *comprises all intentional and nonintentional display of material things, such as implements, machines, art objects, architectural structures, and—last but not least—the human body and whatever clothes or covers it.*

While our classification of the forms of nonverbal communication differs from that given above, we believe that the Ruesch and Kees categories, and the stress these authors place on the importance of the nonverbal aspects of the language codes used by a speaker, emphasize the need for an understanding and skill in the use of nonverbal forms of communication.

Let us first consider some examples of the nonverbal language codification given above.

Sign language is gesture language. Ruesch and Kees say,[2] "Gestures are used to illustrate, to emphasize, to point, to explain, or to interrupt; therefore they cannot be isolated from the verbal components of speech." The V-for-victory sign, the downward stroke of the hand for emphasis, the pointed finger to indicate direction, the positioning of the hands to show the proper grip on a golf club, and the placing of a finger before the lips of the speaker to request silence, are all forms of sign or gesture language. One outstanding student of language reports that gestural language contains some seven hundred thousand distinctly different signals.[3] This suggests the widespread use of sign language as an auxiliary to the spoken word.

Action language includes those bodily movements which convey information about the persons who perform them. They may not be primarily intended to communicate, but to the observant audience member they usually indicate something of the state of mind, physical condition, attitudes, and purposes of the speaker. The "caged animal" pacing across the speaking platform, the incessant or occasional wiping of facial perspiration, the adjustment of clothing, and the constant adjustment of a speaker's notes tell much—or are usually interpreted as telling much—about the speaker. Quite frequently these movements—of which many speakers are unaware—detract from the message the speaker is trying to get across to his listeners.

Object language, as indicated above, includes the display of material things, those shown either intentionally or unintentionally. This category also includes the physical aspects of the meeting room, which the speaker may not be able to control completely, but of which he must be aware. We consider some of the things the speaker can do in this relation later in this chapter. Finally, object language includes the human body and whatever clothes or covers it. Certainly, the effective speaker gives consideration to this component of the visible code he uses.

At the risk of overstressing the inseparable relationships between the verbal and nonverbal components of language and the importance of gesture in speech, we quote Blackmur, from a book that deals primarily with essays in poetry but is entitled *Language as Gesture:*[4]

For gesture is native to language, and if you cut it out you cut roots and get a sapless and gradually a rotting if indeed not a petrifying language.

Our experience and common sense in observing speakers also tell us that the nonverbal aspects of speech communication are important. All the facets of bodily action, whether gesture or movement, whether intentional or not, and the physical objects which contribute to the speaker's general appearance and those which make up the physical surroundings, and also the pictorial and audiovisual aids, all carry meaning to the viewers. The way a speaker sits in his chair before speaking, his apparent awareness of, and interest or disinterest in, the physical setting and occasion, his manner of walking to the lectern, his posture and movement while speaking, the action of his arms, hands, and head, his facial expressions, the appropriateness of his dress, and the way he leaves the platform after speaking, all are noted and interpreted and contribute to or detract from the effectiveness of the content of the message. If any aspect of our nonverbal language is not suited to our words, we subject our listeners to conflicting impressions. What we do sometimes belies what we say.

BODILY ACTION
It is usually true that the first and last impression the audience gets of the speaker come from his physical actions. It is important, then, that bodily action be used only in ways that contribute to effective communication: that they gain attention, clarify, give emphasis, contribute to the speaker's personal adjustment, develop desirable audience empathy, and create appropriate moods.

The principles advocated in this chapter are designed to encourage the practice of those nonverbal forms of expression which contribute to the development of a direct and communicative physical personality. We discourage unmotivated, mechanical, or stereotyped movement and gesture. We believe that following a set of hard and fast rules results in artificial skills ill adapted to the speaker's personality, emotional attitudes, and use of subject matter, or to the demands of the occasion. To be adaptive, convincing, spontaneous, and sincere, speech delivery must reflect the speaker's own attitudes. But this is not to say that the speaker may not start with general principles and from them discover what applications are best suited to his individual needs. We urge flexible application of rules as the best way to develop each individual's communicative personality.

Man's natural tendency to use bodily action to supplement oral communication has been of concern to rhetoricians from antiquity to the present day. Both Cicero and Quintilian stressed its importance and gave suggestions for improving action in delivery. Cicero called action the eloquence of the body, and Quintilian insisted that attempts at persuasion must be ineffectual unless "enlivened by the voice of the speaker, by his looks, and by the action of almost his whole body." Today, too, rhetoricians recognize that effective physical behavior is a *sine qua non* of effective speaking. To speak well one must use both the visible and audible symbols of communication with skill. Two modern writers put it this way:[5]

Everything the speaker does should assist him in stirring up those meanings and only those meanings that will help him accomplish his purpose. There is very little possibility of a speaker's visible action being neutral; every posture he assumes and every motion he makes are almost certain either to increase or decrease his effectiveness. He cannot dodge the issue of visible action; if he tries to get along without it, the most obvious and significant aspect of his visible behavior will be his deficiency in this most fundamental part of the speech code.

Let the urge to communicate become a part of your physical being. When you feel the need to use bodily activity, do so, but let your reaction be controlled. Show by the dynamic quality, appropriateness, and variety of your physical action the urgency of your message.

Aspects of Bodily Action

Thus far we have been primarily concerned about the visual component of the speaker's code and the need for effective total bodily action. We now turn to the elements of bodily action: posture, movement, gesture, and facial expression. Next we shall consider how these elements should be adapted to the various needs of the speaking situation.

Posture

Posture may be described as the speaker's stance, how he stands when talking. There is no one posture that is best for all persons. However, certain guides help the appearance of the person who has cultivated poor posture habits. The bases of good posture are a reserve of physical energy and sufficient body control to ensure freedom of movement and comfortable erectness. The proper posture for the speaker is one that gives him the feeling of relaxation and makes him appear controlled, self-possessed, at ease, with reserve energy at his finger tips, and in command both of himself and the speaking situation. Such a posture provides a base for effective movement and gesture.

The body conformation should be distributed comfortably on both feet, not necessarily equally, with the hips straight, chest up, and shoulders back, and the head erect. The weight of the body should rest on the balls of your feet rather than on your heels or toes. You should avoid teetering and swaying caused by continuous shifting of the weight from heels to toes and from one foot to the other.

Not all effective speakers use the same posture, nor do all always have effective posture. Perhaps when you, too, gain prominence as a noted speaker you may indulge in some slight eccentricities of your posture. While a student you should try to practice until your bodily posture indicates poise, confidence, comfortable but appropriate adaptation to the speaking occasion, and a potential of reserve physical strength. The following suggestions may serve as guides:

1. *Avoid a military posture.* Almost always such a posture will be viewed as inappropriate. Avoid the stiffness and puppet-like character of the soldier at attention, but stand erect and alert.

2. *Avoid mechanical movements in changes of posture.* The speaker who is unduly precise, lacks animation, or appears overly conscious of changes of position on the platform will convey to his viewers the impression that he has little or no assurance that he can control his physical behavior. Avoid the stiff artificiality of mechanical movements. Rather, seek the spontaneity of the speaker who is alive with his ideas and feelings.

3. *Avoid extremes in posture.* An overrelaxed, slovenly, posture—described by some as the "athletic slouch"—is just as bad as a mechanical and completely rigid posture. The first

reflects indifference; the latter, the inability to control one's posture. The "middle ground" is always best.

4. *Avoid unnaturalness in posture.* Posture refers to body stance but is affected by arm and hand positions. Let the arms hang easily at the sides in a position to permit ready and effective gesture. To hold the arms and hands in any other position—folded behind the back, folded at the chest height in front, placed on hips—for any length of time will detract from what might otherwise be effective posture. Stooping forward, swaying, or bobbing up and down should be avoided.

5. *Avoid action that calls attention to posture.* The best posture is that which is unnoticed. Physical behavior that is unnecessary, uneconomical, unnatural, or extreme will call attention to itself and divert the listeners from the subject matter.

Posture is the result of good or bad habits formed outside the speaking situation. Good posture must be carefully cultivated in everyday living. It is difficult to affect the qualities of good posture only for a special occasion. The best posture is that which is ingrained and unstudied. But, again, for the student we recommend study and practice. Study the posture of capable speakers, and practice the suggestions we have made.

Movement

The successful display advertiser understands the effect of using motion to attract interest. Moving exhibits of objects often turn the innocent pedestrian into a motivated shopper. Everything else being equal, a store window displaying a moving model wearing the latest creation in dress, a miniature train running on a track, or a spinning object has more power to attract than has an exhibition of still objects. Currently there is an emphasis on mobiles and kinetic sculpture in art, and the galleries where these are shown are usually filled with viewers. The lesson for the speaker is to use well-timed movement to motivate audience interest.

Strictly speaking, bodily movement refers to total body movement as the speaker moves from one position to another. It includes walking from a sitting position to the lectern and back, movements toward or away from the audience or from one side to another on the platform, and the actual movement involved in changes in posture. Since the viewer's first impression of a speaker starts before he rises from his chair and is altered for better or worse as he walks to the speaking stand, the speaker should carry himself with dignity, move with ease, act unhurriedly, and appear confident. His return to his seat should convey the same impression.

When a platform speech is delivered, the speaker should stand a little in front of the center on a small platform and a few feet back from the edge of a platform of any size. The speaker should always determine in advance the position from which he will speak and walk directly to it.

No rule governs the amount and nature of a speaker's movement on the platform, except that both too much and too little movement should be avoided. The amount and variety of the speaker's movement should be determined by, and related to, his own physical personality, the ideas being conveyed, the emotional reactions he desires in the audience, the needs of emphasis and clarity, the nature of the occasion (whether solemn or festive), the urgency of the message and, frequently, the physical surroundings. Appropriate movement will aid in getting and holding attention and in reinforcing meaning.

The speaker's movements should be purposeful. Well-timed movements may be used to indicate transitions from one point in the speech to another. Purposeful movement also serves to indicate the relative importance of ideas, give emphasis, arouse emotional states, clarify meaning, and aid the speaker in relieving tension. Usually slight, well-timed movements are sufficient to indicate thought transitions and important concepts. Only a step or two to the right or left may serve the speaker's purpose. A few steps forward may suggest that the speaker is coming to a salient point, or a few steps backward may imply that the audience should relax and reflect upon the speaker's last remarks. For purposes of emphasis and the development of emotional states, movements may need to be vigorous and pronounced or restrained and barely discernible, depending on the nature of the feeling sought.

Effective movement is unobtrusive, appears spontaneous and natural, and is coordinated with the language, voice, and meaning of the speaker. Ineffective movement is often seen when the speaker walks aimlessly to and fro, repeatedly shifts his weight from one foot to the other, makes false starts to a blackboard or to visual aids, initiates some seemingly purposeful movement and then stops before it is completed, or starts some entirely different action. Complete immobility may also be a fault of ineffective movement. Purposeful, complete, and appropriate movement, when meaningful to the audience, will attract favorable attention and contribute to effective communication.

Gestures

A gesture is the movement of some part of the body rather than of the entire body. Gestures are made principally by movements of the arms, hands, head, shoulders and, occasionally, the feet. In speech as in many other activities where bodily coordination is important—golf, tennis, bowling, boxing, and swimming—"follow through" makes the difference between a good and a poor gesture. While we may speak of a gesture as a discrete action, as when referring to the movement of hands, an arm, or the shoulders, actually there is always some additional movement of other parts of the body; the head inclines, the upper torso moves slightly, and there is a shift in foot position and the total balance of weight changes. Gestures should flow, and not be jerky, stiff, and mechanical, unless the meaning calls for it. They should express physical energy when intense emotional content is being presented and physical control when logical content is under consideration. Gestures may be made rapidly or slowly, in sweeping arcs or close to the body, forcefully or with restraint, quickly or prolongedly, depending on the speech content. Gesture for its own sake should always be avoided.

Gestures may be classified in various ways. Some are *descriptive* and indicate meaning, either literally or by suggestion. They are analogous to word adjectives, indicating limitations or qualifications of things as to shape, movement, size, number, and so forth. *Symbolic* gestures are representative or figurative rather than literal. They are such conventional signs as the clenched fist to express force, determination, power, or anger. The open hand with the palm outward is a conventional gesture used to suggest "I am finished" with some object, person, or idea. Folded hands indicate reverence, a hand placed on to the brow suggests thoughtfulness, and a quick shrugging of the shoulders reflects hopelessness or indifference. A third type of gesture is the *locative*, which indicates place, position, or direction. *Emphatic* gestures are used when words or ideas need to be stressed or reinforced. Finally, "dramatic," or *imitative* gestures are those the speaker uses when he wishes to impersonate another's action or to "act out" part of a narrative. Imitative gestures may include any of the other four mentioned; but descriptive, symbolic, locative, and emphatic gestures have a function in themselves, apart from their use in impersonation.

Movements of the head itself, when combined with other forms of action, can be very expressive of meaning. Looking aside often suggests embarrassment; a lift of the head may suggest defiance or aggressiveness; shaking the head is interpreted as negation; and nodding confirms. Head movements and positions can express a wide variety of attitudes and feelings, such as self-confidence, courage, zest, pride, despair, or concern, and are effective in most speaking situations.

The qualities of effective gestures are appropriateness, coordination, completeness, variety, and expressiveness.

Facial Expression

Closely related to gesture is facial expression. Quintilian tells us that "from the face we understand numbers of things, and its expression is often equivalent to all the words we could use." Writers still stress the importance of facial expression as meaningful, visible symbols of speech. The mouth and jaws, brow and, especially, the eyes are important tools of visible communication. "Eye to eye" contact is an effective attention-getting device. It is through the eyes perhaps more than any other agency that contact with the audience is maintained.

Facial expression should reflect the speaker's thinking and emotional attitudes. The facial muscles should be flexible, permitting expressions that are animated, wistful, threatening, joyful, or natural, as the speaker indicates varying moods. Like everything else a speaker does, his facial expression can be a great aid in reinforcing and clarifying meaning, expressing moods, and giving emphasis. Fixed smiles, scowls, sneers, squinting, and gazing should be avoided; animated, friendly, sincere, or natural expression should be cultivated.

Because the immobile, or "poker," face is a frequent characteristic of many student speakers, we heartily recommend self-analysis and practice in this area. Has anyone ever said about you, "You never can tell what he's thinking," or "Relax, smile, don't be so serious!" If these comments have been made, you probably have an inexpressive face. Practice in front of a mirror, to see what your face does when you speak. Make up sentences that require extremes of facial expression, to complement the intended meaning. Read selections of prose or poetry that require expressions of anger, joy, surprise, disgust, or sympathy, to enhance their meaning. Finally, practice aloud, *before a mirror,* the speeches you will give in class, and try to use facial expressions effectively to enhance the meaning of your content.

Quintilian's advice of 1900 years ago about the use of facial expression in speaking is still valid today:[6]

But the chief part of the head is the face. With the face we show ourselves suppliant, menacing, soothing, sad, cheerful, proud, humble; on the face men hang as it were, and fix their gaze and entire attention on it, even before we begin to speak; by the face we express love and hate; from the face we understand numbers of things, and its expression is often equivalent to all the words that we could use.

But what is most expressive in the face is the eye, through which the mind chiefly manifests itself; insomuch that the eyes, even while they remain motionless, can sparkle with joy, or contract a gloomy look under sadness.

The problem of coordinating physical action—posture, movement, gesture, and facial expression—with the idea expressed will generally be made easier if a few simple guides are followed. First, think always of the message you are sending, its purpose, content, urgency, and relation to the audience. Ask, "Did the audience understand?" and not "Did I make a good appearance?" Second, think of the speaking occasion as a transaction in which involvement of the audience—at the physical, intellectual, and emotional levels—is important. Let your bodily action contribute to this involvement. Finally, try to concentrate on a mental image of the object, concept, event, or feeling that you are describing or expressing. Mental imagery is an essential part of thinking—sometimes called silent speaking. When our mental images are in clear focus, when our verbal and nonverbal languages are in tune, and when there is a sense of urgency in our desire to communicate, the expression of our thoughts is facilitated. Both concrete objects and abstract ideas are usually related to images involving some form of physical action or relationship. When the physical qualities of ideas or things are perceived, we usually may employ both bodily action and language more effectively in talking about them to others.

You must recognize that you cannot be trained or conditioned to make the *right* nonverbal action for a verbal message. You have been given generally accepted, useful suggestions in this text, your classmates and instructor will aid you, and you can learn much by watching effective speakers; but in the last analysis the way you relate the nonverbal and verbal aspects of a communicative act must be a part of you and so reflect your personality, the image you now know is desirable, and the sense of urgency you have to improve. That is, you must practice; there is no magic that will move you automatically from the ineffective end to the effective one on the continuum of meaningful use of nonverbal language.

Functions of Bodily Action

In our descriptions of the four types of bodily action we have frequently mentioned a specific use or function of a particular movement or facial expression. Let us now take a general view of the role of bodily activity in communication as it is related to both the communicator and the respondent. First, how does effective bodily action aid the speaker?

For the Communicator

Bodily action aids the speaker in fulfilling a number of communicative needs: to gain attention, to release excess physical energy, to create emphatic responses, and to enhance the meaning of the speech.

Gaining Attention. Appropriate physical action is basic to the process of communication because of the inherent ability of action to get and hold attention. Dynamic movements, directness in speaking, animated and appropriate facial expressions, dynamic and confident posture, and gestures that suggest to your listeners that you are talking to them personally, are some of the essential techniques of gaining attention. People will attend to total body movement on the platform. When you are not restricted to the immediate vicinity of a microphone, some movement on the platform may be desirable. If you perceive interest lagging in one part of the room, you may be able to get closer to that area by moving to the right or left of the lectern. To take the audience into your confidence, you may wish to move closer to those in the front row. Total bodily movement can also be used for transitions from one idea to another, for some types of emotional reactions and for emphasis.

Listeners will attend more readily to your message if they feel there is a close personal relationship between them and you. This type of rapport results in large measure from the speaker's ability to establish eye-to-eye contact, to make the members of the audience feel that he is talking to them as individuals and not merely as a part of a larger group.

In no case should the speaker neglect his audience by looking at the floor, out a window, or over its eye level. There are few faults of speaker action that will so surely lessen audience support and leave the speaker doing little more than talking to himself.

Releasing Physical Energy. Those speakers who are experienced, in control of most speaking situations, usually relaxed, well-prepared, and accepted by the audience, rarely need to be concerned about using bodily activity as a means of releasing tensions. Some speakers, on the other hand are tense, nervous, emotionally inhibited, and fearful of the total speaking situation—almost to the point of being inarticulate. It is the rare student speaker who does not have some of these manifestations of stage fright when he appears before an audience. Frequently body movements and activity help release some of this nervous physical energy. Once you become physically active, you are able to focus on the message and your audience and away from your personal tensions and fears.

Enhancing Meaning. This function of the use of bodily action hardly needs elaboration. We have stressed it and illustrated it frequently throughout this chapter. You can easily visualize physical action that indicates or suggests size, height, distance, position, various emotional states, speed of movement, negation or affirmation, emphasis, urgency, and the transition from one idea to another.

But it is not always the exactness or appropriateness of the physical action that carries your meaning. At times the relationship between the nonverbal and verbal languages used is more important. One complements and supplements the other. We mentioned the function of metacommunication in Chapter One. When the listener does not understand what you have said, your action gives him the meaning; when he does not understand or he misinterprets what you do physically, your words again give him the meaning. It is not only important that you use bodily action to communicate effectively; you must try to make your physical activity congruous with and supportive of the language conveying your message.

For the Respondent

The speaker's bodily action serves the respondent much as it does the speaker himself. First, as we have indicated, if the speaker's nonverbal behavior is in harmony with his verbal language—if they support each other—then the meaning of the message will be clearer.

Second, the physical action of the speaker may be made to point up the important parts of the speech. Transitions from one major point to another may be indicated by complete body movement, whereas subpoints and also major ideas may be given nonverbally with the fingers, as "In the first place . . . ," "Our second major point is . . . ," or "These three aspects are important." Such concepts as "the farthest," "the necessity for immediate action," "the responsibility of all of us," or "Listen carefully to this important idea!" can conceivably be shown through physical action.

Third, the speaker's physical action may easily heighten the listener's emotional involvement in the communicative transaction. Hate, anger, disgust, rejection, amazement, reverence, fright, or happiness as emotional states may be partially induced in listeners by what the speaker does and by the object language he uses as well as by what he says. We have only to recall any national party convention to realize that the listener's emotions may be aroused through nonverbal means.

Adaptation of Bodily Action

As we have said, the development of physical actions requires a somewhat flexible application of whatever specific rules may be established as guidelines. There is one basic principle, however, that we must always apply. In addition to the speech purpose and the physical abilities and limitations of the speaker the character of the speaking situation is the primary factor in determining appropriate action. The size and proximity of the audience to the speaker, the physical conditions of the meeting place, and what the audience considers appropriate for the particular speaking situation must all be considered.

To Size of Audience and Meeting Place

Consider the situation of a conversation, interview, or discussion group. Here it is usually better if the speaker adopts a more restrained bodily action than would be desirable if he were speaking to a larger audience. When the speaker and auditors are close together, broad sweeping gestures, gross movements of any sort, and exaggerated facial expressions are unnecessary. For these more intimate speaking occasions the need to make the speaker's action clearly visible does not present the same problem as when the listeners are many and the auditorium is large. Even in large rooms, when the audience is close to the speaker, the need for extremes in physical action is minimized.

In larger groups the speaker's movement and gestures should function in larger arcs, and posture changes necessarily involve more steps from one position to another. Where a few steps may serve the small audience to suggest emphasis or the partitioning of the speaker's subject matter, added movement may become necessary for the same purpose with a large audience. When there is considerable distance between the listeners and the speaker, it is necessary to make the descriptive and emphatic gestures sweeping, vigorous, and sustained. The action pattern in general is of longer duration than in small groups.

To Audience's Norms

Within the limitations and demands on physical activity in speaking, some consideration must also be given to the audience's standards of what is appropriate. Although some degree of physical animation and vigor is always essential, at some times these qualities must be held within bounds and at others they must be given free rein. Note the differences in the forcefulness and scope of physical action between the influential political or evangelistic speaker and the lecturer at the morning meeting of a women's club. Note also the differences between a speaker haranguing a small group of idlers in Pershing Square in Los Angeles or Washington Square in New York and one presenting a report to the board of directors of a large financial concern in either of those cities. Note the differences between the commencement speaker and the cheerleader at a pep rally or between the cleric at a prayer meeting and the football coach at a pep talk. If the physical action in any of these contrasting situations is not viewed by the audience as appropriate for the occasion, the speaker's action has become a barrier to communication.

Many speakers seemingly feel that the worth of their subject matter is all that is necessary for effective speech. Such an attitude is desirable only in one respect: it does recognize the value of a worthy topic and content. Rarely, however, is an audience so well informed and interested that it does not require appropriate physical and vocal expression to secure the response desired by the speaker. But the danger of going counter to the norms acceptable to the audience is also great and must constantly be kept in mind.

To Vocal Patterns. The degree of vigor and the scope of the speaker's action should also be in harmony with his vocal patterns. Increases in volume for emphasis and emotional effect should carry corresponding increases in physical action. Animated and forceful projection of the voice is not compatible with listless, inert physical behavior; quiet and restrained vocalization is inappropriate with dynamic, sweeping, and sustained gestures and movement. To adjust effectively to the size, expectations, and attitudes of his observing and listening audience, the speaker must integrate vocal delivery with his bodily action and the nature of the subject matter.

To Feedback from Audience

A final factor suggesting the degree of physical vigor and the nature of bodily action is the feedback the speaker receives from the audience. Restlessness, signs of disbelief, or apparent lack of perception may be the signal for the speaker to modify his action besides his voice and language. The speaker getting continuous signs of approval from his audience may take comfort in them. He should be assured that he has adapted his physical behavior to the reactions of his audience effectively.

To achieve successful adaptation of physical behavior to such varying situations as conversation, discussion, interviewing, and platform speaking cannot, we repeat, be encompassed in a specific set of rules. Such adaptation does, however, require thoughtful practice, keen observation of the success and failure of others, flexibility, and deep sensitivity to the reactions of the viewing audience.

Effective Bodily Action

The student of speech is, of course, primarily concerned with his own improvement in speech communication. There are no "ten easy steps" to effective physical behavior in speaking, but we believe the ideas presented in this chapter will be helpful. In addition, the following summary suggestions may serve you as a guide in developing your nonverbal language skills.

1. *Motivation for practice.* The student who uses little physical action in speaking situations will first need to motivate himself to use some form of bodily action, even though at first it is unnatural, random, awkward, and obtrusive. There must obviously be some action before training in what is

proper can begin. The individual who is not motivated to try
will never learn.

2. *Coordination of the elements of action.* When beginning
   your practice, try to develop some sensitivity to the four
   elements of action we have mentioned: posture, movement,
   gesture, and facial expression. Think of all four as you
   practice any one. Try to develop unity of bodily action, in
   which each of the elements is congruous with and supports
   the others.

3. *Elimination of nonessential action patterns.* If you habitually use movement and gesture when speaking, work to
   eliminate any repetitive, poorly timed, or awkward movement, overworked gestures, and ineffectual facial expressions.

4. *Integration with voice and content.* Assuming that your
   bodily activity is motivated, unified, and has no excesses,
   your next step is to integrate your action with the elements
   of voice, language, and meaning. What you do must support
   what you say.

5. *Establishment of standards.* As you practice, you should
   study effective and ineffective behavior in others. Note how
   action can aid and can lessen the effectiveness of communication. Seek constructive suggestions from your classmates
   for improving your physical behavior. Be guided by your
   instructor.

6. *Practice for flexibility.* Practice until you can adapt your
   physical behavior to different speaking situations, to needed
   variations in the elements of vocal delivery, and to your own
   physical personality. Bodily action should change to meet
   the changing demands of the speech occasions.

7. *Practice for economy.* Try to decrease excessive action;
   increase needed action.

8. *Practice for variety.* Seek to increase your repertoire of
   meaningful bodily activity. A wide range of action skills will
   insure appropriateness when you do act.

A final word for your personal-improvement program: Constructive advice from your speech instructor or some other knowledgeable person will be most valuable in pointing to physical behavior that is
undesirable or appears to block rather than aid communication. Bodily
action that is random, poorly timed, awkward, or excessive is destructive of desirable audience response. Conversely, bodily action that is
integrated with all aspects of the communicative act and is well-timed,
purposeful, smooth, and adequate is a great asset to any speaker.

VOCAL DELIVERY

Every speaker should realize that his voice influences his listeners, either favorably or unfavorably, in some degree. A poorly employed voice may seriously compromise what would otherwise be considered an effective message. Guidance and practice will usually improve vocal delivery. We shall now concern ourselves with the vocal mechanism and of the production of vocal sound, ways of developing vocal variety, and the essentials of clear articulation and acceptable pronunciation.

The Vocal Mechanism

In an earlier chapter we pointed out that we produce voice by using organs whose primary function is to keep the body alive and working properly. Speech is only a secondary or "overlaid" function of these organs, which also serve in breathing, chewing, and swallowing. In speech these organs provide the energy for speaking and serve as vibrators, resonators, and articulators.

The Motive Power

The source of energy for speech is provided by the air that is expelled from the lungs during the process of breathing. The organs involved are the lungs, bronchial tubes, trachea, ribs, and other bony structures of the chest cavity, and certain muscles, including the diaphragm, which control the size of the chest cavity.

The lungs, which play a passive role in the breathing process, are air sacs located in the upper region of the chest. They are connected with the outer air through the bronchial tubes, bronchi, trachea, larynx, pharynx, mouth, and nose. Below the lungs is the diaphragm, a dome-shaped muscle that separates the chest and abdominal cavities. In inhalation the diaphragm contracts or flattens, and the rib and abdominal muscles move the rib cage outward and upward. The increase in size of the chest cavity causes a partial vacuum in the lung region. Air rushes in to balance the inside and outside air pressure. When the diaphragm moves downard in inspiration, it presses on the viscera in the abdominal cavity and causes the abdominal muscles to distend in the area at the front of the body. In exhalation, the diaphragm relaxes and moves upward, pushing against the lungs from below. The ribs move generally downward, bringing horizontal pressure against the lungs. The air is thus forced out of the lungs and up through the trachea, the mouth, and the nose cavities.

The action in respiration is much like the action of a bellows. The size of the air cavity is increased when the bellows is opened. The air then rushes in to balance the pressure inside and outside the bellows. When the bellows are closed, air is forced out. See Figure 13-1.

In normal breathing the phases of inhalation and exhalation are

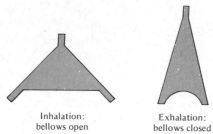

Inhalation: Exhalation:
bellows open   bellows closed

FIGURE 13-1. Action of the lungs in respiration.

about equal in length. When a person speaks, the rate of respiration increases, and more air is moved in and out of the lungs. Also in speaking the inspiration phase is shortened, and the expiration phase is lengthened and is under greater control. This control of the outgoing airstream is very important in the process of vocalization.

The Vibrators

The air compressed in the lungs is expelled through the trachea into the larynx, which houses the vocal cords. These cords, more properly called vocal folds, are two elastic membranes that extend from a single attachment to the thyroid cartilage (sometimes called the Adam's Apple) in front, to two attachments to the arytenoid cartilages at the back of the larynx. In a relaxed position in normal breathing these folds form a V-shaped opening called the glottis. In producing voice, we draw the folds together and momentarily block the escape of air from the lungs. The positions of the attachments of the vocal folds to the thyroid and arytenoid cartilages and the positions of the folds when open for breathing and for phonation are shown in a cross-section view from above in Figure 13-2.

When the pressure has built up sufficiently during phonation, the vocal folds are forced apart and a puff of air escapes. This process repeats itself, and successive puffs produce sound waves, which form the basic speech tone. The pitch of this tone is modified by variations in the tension of the vocal folds and the size of the glottis.

The Resonators

The sound originating in the larynx is weak and must be amplified to produce human speech. The main resonators are the pharynx, or throat cavity, the mouth, and the nasal cavities. These air chambers act in the same manner as the resonators and sounding boards of musical instruments: they amplify the tone, making it loud or soft, and modify its quality. Variations in tonal quality are essential in the communication of meaning and mood in speaking.

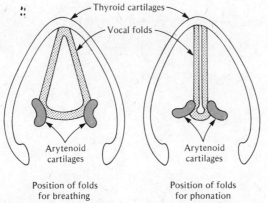

FIGURE 13-2. Positions of vocal folds for breathing and phonation.

The Articulators

Vocal sounds are formed into understandable phonetic symbols and words by the use of the articulators: the tongue, teeth, gum ridges, hard palate, lips, and soft palate. By manipulating these organs it is possible to interrupt the flow of the vowel tones to form consonant sounds such as "b," "k," "f," and "z." Active use of these articulating organs is necessary for precision and accuracy of tonal production. Figure 13-3 shows the total vocal mechanism.

To speak well you must have a sound and healthy vocal mechanism. You must also know how to use the speech organs properly. These brief suggestions will aid in developing a good speaking voice:

1. Keep the outgoing airstream for speech under your control at all times. This is especially important in producing changes in volume.
2. Keep the throat and neck muscles relaxed. Tension usually creates harshness and decreases flexibility of tone.
3. Employ diaphragmatic, or "abdominal," breathing in preference to clavicular breathing, in speech. In clavicular breathing the major expansion in the chest area on inspiration is vertical. The shoulders can be seen to rise perceptibly. In diaphragmatic breathing the expansion of the chest occurs at its base—laterally and in an anterior-posterior direction—as well as vertically. This increases the amount of air available for speech and avoids the throat and upper chest tensions, which often result from clavicular breathing.
4. Use the modifiers in an energetic and flexible manner. Poor resonance and articulation result when the tongue, lips, and jaw move in a sluggish manner or move but little.

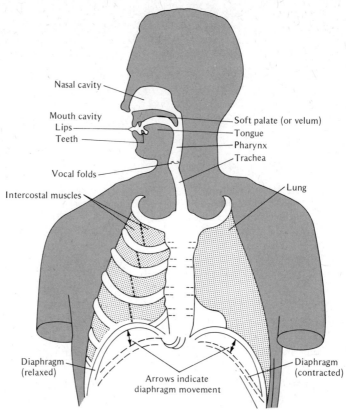

Nasal cavity

Mouth cavity
Lips
Teeth

Soft palate (or velum)
Tongue
Pharynx
Trachea

Vocal folds

Intercostal muscles

Lung

Diaphragm
(relaxed)

Diaphragm
(contracted)

Arrows indicate
diaphragm movement

FIGURE 13-3. The vocal mechanism.

Vocal Variety

Four factors in vocal delivery are controllable: force, timing, pitch, and quality. Variations in these four factors contribute to clarity and flexibility and an agreeable voice pattern. A monotonous or mechanical manner of delivery results from insufficient vocal variation.

Force

Force concerns loudness or volume. Variations in loudness are achieved by increasing or decreasing the force of impact of the air against the vocal folds. Thus, when the force of impact is greater—the tenseness of the folds remaining the same—the vocal folds vibrate through a greater distance (called the amplitude), and the intensity or loudness of sound is increased. As the force of impact is lessened, the sound becomes softer. Variations in force serve to get attention, give emphasis, convey meaning, and express feelings and emotions.

Force may vary in both degree and form. Changes in degree refer to variations in the amount of energy applied in speaking. Thus you may shout or whisper. Different occasions require different degrees of force. Less force is needed in a small room than in a large auditorium. The degree of force should also be appropriate to the meaning and purpose of the speech. The relative amount of force or emphasis within a word is called accent; thus, emphasis on the second syllable of the word *protest* makes it a verb; emphasis on the first syllable makes it a noun. We also make use of emphasis or stress to distinguish the relative importance of words in a sentence. Consider the changes in meaning when stress is placed on the various words in this sentence: "What are you doing?"

Changes in the form of force refer to the various ways in which force may be applied. Explosive force is applied abruptly, as when the sergeant shouts an order to a squad of soldiers. Expulsive force is that used in normal forceful conversation. Effusive force is applied gradually, resulting in a drawn-out tone; it indicates controlled but deep sentiment, contemplation, and grandeur. The three types of force are employed for different kinds of thought content and purposes.

Timing

This factor pertains to the time relationships of the sounds uttered in speaking. Timing has three aspects: pause, duration, and rate. Pause is the silence between words; duration is the length of the sounds in single words; rate is the number of words uttered for any unit of time and is the result of pause and duration.

Pauses serve many functions. They separate groups of words or ideas and indicate transitions from one thought to another. They are an attention-getting aid when combined with contrasting vocal techniques and serve as a medium of emphasis. Pauses also aid by giving the speaker time to breathe. They also give the listener time to react to what is said. There is one danger in the use of pauses: the tendency of the speaker to fill the time of a pause with such sounds as "uh" and "er." Speakers usually form this habit because they dread silence; they feel any silence is bad. Nothing could be further from the truth. Pauses may be used effectively, and the good speaker will avoid the meaningless sound connectives.

Duration, or quantity, varies according to the content, purpose, and mood of the speech. Long duration is needed when a speech deals with or is given in a background of reverence, solemnity, peacefulness, beauty, or grandeur. Short duration is used when gaiety, eagerness, joy, excitement, danger, or surprise is the keynote. The invocation at a commencement requires long duration; announcing at a sports event usually calls for short duration. Between these extremes, when a single duration is used throughout, ordinary speech should vary the duration of sounds to avoid monotony.

The overall rate of speaking is the result of combining the factors of pause and duration. Most speakers average 150 words a minute with a range of 120 to 180. It is usually unwise to maintain a steady rate at any one of these figures for an entire speech. The slow speaker may impress his audience as being dull, disinterested, lacking in confidence, unprepared, or apathetic. Likewise, the speaker who talks too fast does not impress his listeners favorably. The effective speaker talks in a lively, spirited, and crisp manner or in an emphatic, deliberate, and unhurried manner, as may be needed for the particular occasion. Meaningful changes in rate reflect a communicative personality.

Pitch

Pitch is the position of a sound on the musical scale. Pitch is determined by the number of vibrations made per second by the vocal folds. A sound that has 256 cycles per second is perceived as middle C. A tone one octave higher is produced by 512 vibrations per second. Most people have a usable pitch range of about two octaves, although few use this complete range effectively. Men's voices, because of the larger size and length of the vocal folds, are usually lower in pitch than women's voices. The best pitch for either sex is that which produces the most resonant tone. It is best for any speaker to use a pitch close to his optimal level and within his normal range.

Changes in pitch are secured by either steps or inflections. A step is an abrupt change in pitch, whereas an inflection, or glide, is a continuous and gradual change during a syllable. Changes may be either upward or downward. Thus, the following sentence might be spoken with a downward change by steps:

I

doubt

that.

Effective glide changes may be seen in this sentence:

                            w   I   u

           o   o   o   n

O   oh, n   der

                              sta

                                  nd.

Meaningful communication demands variations in pitch, for nothing can be as deadly as a monotonous voice. Appropriate variations, moreover, will improve communication. Rising inflections and steps usually suggest indecision, uncertainty, incompleteness of thought, suspense, or a question. Falling inflections suggest decisiveness, resolution, finality, confidence and, at times, annoyance.

Quality

Vocal quality may be defined in many different ways. One is in terms of the hearer's perception. For example, when we use such terms as "vibrant," "harsh," "shrill," "husky," "throaty," "weak," "hard," "falsetto," "feminine," or "dull" to describe a voice, we are merely telling how listeners perceive that particular voice. The quality of a voice may also refer to the peculiar character by which we distinguish one voice from another. Most of us have little difficulty in recognizing the voices of our acquaintances over the telephone. Quality may also be explained in terms of all the factors that create the unique voice of a given individual. All vibrators, including the vocal folds, vibrate over their entire length and, simultaneously, in parts, such as halves, thirds, and so on. The basic or overall vibration produces what is called the fundamental tone, and the partial vibrations produce overtones. The fundamentals and overtones combine to give each voice a personal timbre, or tone quality. As we speak, the tone quality is then subjected to changes of force, timing, and pitch, which are in turn determined by the unique characteristics of an individual's vocal mechanism. Consequently, while quality is a factor unique to each speaker, it can be improved.

Articulation and Pronunciation

As we have seen, the sounds of speech are started by the vibrations of the vocal folds. The resonating chambers amplify these sounds, and the articulating organs—mainly the teeth, lower jaw, tongue, palate, and soft palate—modify and refine the sound to produce syllables, words, and phrases. Thus, articulation is the process of forming, joining, and separating the basic sound to produce the vowels, diphthongs, and consonants that constitute the individual sounds of the oral pattern. For effective communication articulation must be precise and distinct. Thus, much flexibility in the use of the articulating organs is necessary.

The sounds of spoken English are made by delicate and complicated adjustments among many of the vocal organs. To produce vowels five actions must occur: the vocal folds must vibrate, the opening into the nasal cavity must be closed, the tongue tip must be in a position approximately in back of the lower front teeth, the throat and mouth cavities must be unobstructed to permit the escape of the sound, and the lower jaw, tongue and lips must take appropriate positions for each sound. Diphthongs are formed by the blending of two or more sounds. Consonants are formed by momentarily blocking, interrupting, or restricting the free flow of the breath stream. The vowels and diphthongs give strength and carrying power to the voice; the consonants give it clarity, liveliness, and distinctness.

Pronounciation also deals with the process of producing words and phrases, but it is concerned primarily with the syllabic emphasis, which is prescribed by the standards of common usage. Good pronounciation is that followed by the educated people in a given area. General standards may be determined by following the dictionary pronounciation. However, regional standards of what is considered correct may differ, and it is wise to be guided by local usage.

Effective Vocal Delivery

In this chapter we have stressed the close relationship between the verbal and nonverbal aspects of speech communication. Earlier we mentioned briefly the functions of body action in communication for both the communicator and the respondent. Effective vocal delivery serves essentially the same functions as the effective use of nonverbal language. We first consider the uses of effective vocal delivery for the communicator.

For the Communicator

First, effective vocal delivery helps to gain and hold attention. Variety and abrupt changes in pitch, timing, and force, the substitution of physical action for sequences of verbal language, at times the use of silence, the use of *object* language, and audience involvement, all contribute much to continued audience attention.

Second, vocal delivery can give emphasis to important parts of speech. Major ideas may be spoken more loudly, more slowly, or with greater duration than less important ideas. Impersonation of the vocal quality of a person quoted—if appropriately done—will make the citation stand out from the rest of the speech.

Finally, effective vocal delivery may be used to heighten the emotional involvement of the listeners. Vivid images meaningfully articulated, variations in pitch to reflect affective states such as contempt, fear, or indifference, and changes in rate and force to reflect the gaiety or solemnity of the occasion are techniques used.

For the Respondent

Again, effective vocal delivery serves the respondent in essentially the same ways that effective nonverbal activity does. Effective use of the voice can make meanings clearer, point up important parts of the speech—and minimize lesser ideas—and heighten the listener's emotional involvement in the communicative transaction.

One aspect of the *oral* delivery which has been of concern to researchers in recent years is "nonverbal vocalic communication," sometimes called "word-free" or "content-free" speech. This is essentially speech in which verbal intelligibility (the meaning of the language used) has been removed, but the major vocal characteristics of the speaker are retained. In a recent study on "content-free" speech two researchers make this statement based on a review of the literature in the area of nonverbal vocalic communication:[7]

These studies indicate that nonverbal voice sounds constitute an independent channel of information about the speaker. . . . Experienced public speakers develop characteristic manners of presentation that lead audiences to draw desired or undesired inferences about them which, whether accurate or not, affect the continuation and effectiveness of the communication. If a speaker is perceived as effeminate, arrogant, unscrupulous, or incompetent because of his vocal cues, the verbal content of his message or his actual personality and credibility may be superfluous.

. . . The fact that audiences will draw inferences about their [the speakers'] credibility, personality, and demographic characteristics from the nonverbal voice sounds in speech should not be ignored.

The points we wish to make are two: the way you use your voice in articulating the content aspects of your message will affect your audience in helpful or distracting ways, and the nonverbal vocalic aspects of your voice contribute to or detract from the audience's acceptance of you and your message.

Vocal Skills

Effective vocal delivery is a function of your vocal mechanism, what you know about effective use of your voice, your desire to better your vocal skills, and practice in improvement. We now consider briefly some suggestions for improving your vocal skills.

Essentials

A good speaking voice has five characteristics, as follows:

1. It is easily heard. Obviously, there will be no communication if the listeners do not hear what is spoken. Hence, adequate projection to all parts of the room is a basic requisite of good speech. For adequate projection speakers usually need

exercises that will aid in developing an adequate and controlled breath supply.

2. It is flexible. The effective speaker must be able to adapt his voice to varying occasions, purposes, subject matter, external distractions, and room sizes.

3. It is unobtrusive. A good speaking voice does not call attention to itself: it has no noticeable faults; force, pitch, timing, and quality are in balance and suited to the speech content and purpose; pronunciation follows accepted local standards.

4. It is pleasant. The good speaking voice is resonant, not shrill; it is lively, not dull; it is forceful, not muffled; it is variable, not monotonous.

5. It is meaningful. The audible element of delivery complements or enhances the word meanings. Changes in the meaning of words are reflected in appropriate tonal changes. Unnecessary vocalization, such as "ers" and "ahs," between sentences is minimal.

Exercises for Vocal Improvement
You can improve your voice through proper drill. Consult your instructor and work out a plan for regular drill suited to your special needs.

Improvement in Breathing. Before you begin any of the following vocal exercises, be sure that your body is relatively relaxed. Stand on your toes and reach upward; then bend forward from the waist, allowing the trunk, arms, and neck to hang down limply. Now straighten slowly. Repeat this several times.

As you straighten, inhale as you come to an upright position. Now exhale slowly as you again bend forward from the waist.

Standing erect, tighten and then relax the muscles of the neck. Let your head fall forward, then to one side, to the back, to the other side, and forward again.

1. Stand erect with your weight well balanced on both feet; avoid both tension and extreme relaxation. Place the open palms against your lower front ribs. Inhale slowly and deeply through both mouth and nose, feeling the lower rib wall push against your hands. Hold your breath for a count of five. Note that your ribs are pushed up and out. Exhale slowly, pushing in with your hands against your ribs. Now turn your hands so that the fingers point toward the back, and repeat the slow inhalation and exhalation. Note the movement of the side and back rib cage areas.

2. In the same standing position place your hands on your

lower front ribs and yawn as you inhale. Maintain the open, relaxed throat as you produce the sound "ah." Repeat several times, maintaining a steady flow of sounds. As most of the air escapes, try to keep the pressure for continued sound in the area of the lower ribs and diaphragm rather than in the throat.

3. Inhale in a standing, relaxed position. As you exhale slowly, count from one to five, keeping the tone steady. Now repeat a number of times, increasing your count to a larger number each time.

4. Sit comfortably, without slouching, in a straight-backed chair. Place your hands so that the thumbs are just under the lower ribs and the fingers extend inward over your abdomen. Inhale as much air as you can, noting the action of your hands as they are pushed outward by the action of the abdomen and lower rib cage. Exhale, noting how your hands move inward. Now place one hand on the upper chest region and repeat the inhalation-exhalation process. Continue until there is little movement in the chest area.

5. Breathe deeply. As you exhale produce the sound "ah" in a staccato manner as many times as possible in one breath. Do this several times. Now repeat, saying "ah! O! Oo!" as many times as you can with one breath. Note the changes in mouth position.

Characteristics of Breathing. A list of the characteristics of proper breathing for speech follows.

1. Inhalation and exhalation tend to be equal in normal breathing; but in speech inhalation is quick, and exhalation is governed by the ideas being expressed.

2. Inhalation is active and exhalation is passive, in normal breathing. In speech both are active processes.

3. Exhalation in speech should be controlled.

4. Inhalation should be silent and unnoticed.

5. Breathing for speech should be relaxed. There should be no tension in the throat area.

6. To ensure a sufficient supply of breath for speech, the major muscular activity should be centered in the lower rib and abdominal region.

Improvement in Vocal Variety. Appropriate vocal variety serves a number of purposes. It avoids monotony, gets attention, gives emphasis, creates a mood, conveys meaning, builds to a climax, shows contrast, or creates a lively sense of communication. To achieve these ends you should practice these exercises for fifteen or twenty minutes each day, until a proper variety of vocal production becomes a natural part of your everyday speech.

Changes in Force. The following exercises will help you learn to change the force of your voice.

1. Repeat the letters of the alphabet from A to G, as if G were the climax of an important idea.
2. Read the following sets of three sentences in this manner: (1) speak the first as if you were talking in casual tones to a friend sitting next to you; (2) speak the second as if you were talking to a group of fifty persons in a classroom; (3) speak the third in a manner suitable to a large auditorium.

First set:

At first I thought the problem would be easy to solve. Later I discovered it to be more difficult than I had thought. Now I am not sure it can ever be solved.

Second set:

The time it takes to solve social problems is well known. We have tried for years to achieve racial equality. It is apparent that we must now use more forceful methods.

Third set:

We hear much about the apathetic attitudes of American citizens. But many have grown tired of fighting bureaucratic red tape. What we need is more courageous leaders whom the people can follow.

3. Practice reading the following sentences, first reading the first word with extra loudness, then the second word, and then the third.

> Will she come?
> Why should I?
> Ask that man.
> Everyone is coming.

4. Count to ten on one breath, increasing in loudness with each number. Practice until you can count to fifteen or twenty.
5. Sing "ah" at a very soft level, then increase the force to a loud tone, and then decrease it again. Do this several times in one breath.
6. Read the following two groups of three passages at the three force levels of soft, medium, and loud.

First Group

In building a more secure and prosperous world, we must never lose sight of the basic motivation of our effort, the inherent worth of the individual.

While we are engaged in creating conditions of real peace in the world, we must always go forward under the banner of liberty. Our faith and our strength are rooted in free institutions and the rights of men everywhere.

We speak here as representatives of governments, but we must also speak from the hearts of our countrymen. We speak for people, whose deep concern is whether the children are well or sick, whether there is enough food, and whether there will be peace.

Second Group

In this place peace and quiet shall always be with you. The morning's dawn shall bring you the joy of solitude. Stillness, the beauty of vast expanses, the faint music of birds will bring you rest.

This is not the time to hold back. Action, immediate action, is imperative. Unless we combine our forces to withstand possible aggression, we may soon find ourselves under the domineering heel of the tyrant.

Rise! Rise, everyone, everywhere! The freedom of the common man, peace in the world, and security for our loved ones are the goals for which we fight. Today is the day to strike for our cause.

Changes in Pitch. The following exercises will help you learn to change the pitch of your voice.

1. Read the following with a rising step in pitch after the first and second words:

Here and there   I thought so   Don't stop now

You are going	Go in peace	The train's late
Here they are	The wind howled	Close the book
Once in a while	Mom and Dad	Away over there
On to victory	Come with me	Love me too

2. Read the following with a slight pause after the first word. Then make a step change in pitch, either up or down, for the second word. When you have done this, read the same expression with glide changes in pitch.

Don't stop	Over there	After him	Who's calling?
You would	Why not?	Page forty	We will?
Never more	Please don't	Oh, look	Follow me
Don't go	See here	Look out	Stop, thief

3. As you read the following, introduce all the pitch changes necessary for meaning:

The steady, slow beat of the tom-toms seemed to contrast with the high, weird, piercing cries of the natives.

What a parade! The comical clowns, beautiful bareback riders, high-stepping bandsmen, and hoarse barkers seemed to say, "Come with us for fun and excitement!" The animals, too—lions, elephants, horses—all added to the spectacle.

In addition to the original, three carbon copies should be made. The first goes to the business manager, the second to the superintendent, and the third is for our files.

It was a beautiful day! The sky was clear blue, flecked here and there with fleecy clouds. The sun was warm, and a light breeze was blowing. Toward night, though, the fog rolled in, filling the lowlands with a dense, opaque blanket.

4. Make up two different sentences to suit each of the following situations. Then read the sentences aloud with the appropriate pitch level and pitch changes.
   a. A sports announcer at a thrilling football game.
   b. A mother calling to a small child several houses away from home.
   c. A salesmanager telling a group of salesmen about a forthcoming sales drive.
   d. A television announcer introducing a mystery-thriller.

Changes in Timing. The following exercises will help you learn changes in timing.

1. Determine how pause is to be used for proper meaning in the following:

   Stop look listen.

   I came I saw I conquered.

   Ouch stop that's hurting me.

   As I mentioned before and I repeat once more the income tax must be lowered.

   These yes these are mine I say.

   And in the phrase which you are now reading it would not affect the meaning to pause slightly after reading.

   You should repeat whenever necessary the main points of your argument.

   That that is is and that that is not is not.

2. Select a number of short passages from some prose work. Try to find a passage that calls for a slow rate, as for grief, sorrow, and loneliness; select another passage that calls for a fast rate, as for gaiety, excitement, or nervousness. Now choose a passage requiring a variety of rates. Practice reading each passage with the appropriate rates.

3. Rate tends to vary with the meaning and emotional content of the material spoken. Conscious use of such variations helps to reinforce the ideas. Consider this as you read the following sentences. Read each at what you consider to be the proper rate.

   It was long, long ago.

   Can't you drive any faster?

   His clothes were tattered and torn.

   The golden fields of waving grain.

   He was a bitter, bitter man.

   He plodded slowly along.

   Well, now I'm not so sure.

   It's a very lazy day.

   Hurry, the train is about to leave.

   He hit the floor with a thud.

   It was a bitter pill to swallow.

   Get out of my sight.

4. Sometimes the meaning of words depends on the duration of sounds. Practice extending the vowel sounds in these words:

Go	Hole	Going	War	Rain	Song
Blue	Moon	Sun	Stray	Grew	Theme
Born	High	World	Sound	Two	Come
See	Dumb	Forth	Cage	Sleet	High

5. As you read the following words, vary the duration of the

vowel sounds, first making them short and staccato, next of long duration, and then of normal duration:

Get	Mud	Law	Peat	Lit	Hat	Set
Shoe	Lie	Jug	Dog	Hay	Same	Mike
Peat	Man	Wise	Red	Tie	Got	Camp
Hoot	Full	House	You	Go	Day	Eat
Kite	Bang	Shove	Sick	Sill	Green	Bum

6. Practice reading the following excerpts aloud with appropriate duration of sounds:

I never rightly knew why I was always dissatisfied, and yearning for the next hour, the next day, the next year, hoping that it would bring me that which I could not find in the present. It was not for love, for love does not satisfy. I desired to live in the passing moment, but could not. It always seemed as if something were waiting for me without the door, and calling me. What could it have been?

I know now; it was a desire to be at one with myself, to understand myself. Myself in the world, and the world in me. (Bethold Auerbach)

Life is a narrow vale between the cold and barren peaks of two eternities. We strive in vain to look beyond the heights. We cry aloud, and the only answer is the echo of our wailing cry. From the voiceless lips of the unreplying dead, there comes no word; but in the night of death, hope sees a star, and listening love can hear the rustle of a wing. (Robert Ingersoll)

Improvement in Articulation. Clear and distinct diction depends on how well you use the organs of articulation, especially the tongue, lips, and jaw. Flexibility is important.

1. Open your mouth as wide as possible; keep the neck and throat muscles from becoming completely tense. Now close it, relax for a moment, and then open it wide again.
2. Purse the lips and protrude them as far as possible. Relax, and repeat.
3. Open your mouth and thrust your tongue forward as far as it will go. Now raise it, and try to touch the tip of your nose and then your chin; then move it from side to side. Open your mouth slightly and run the tip of your tongue from the back of the lower front teeth back as far as it will go along the palate.
4. Speak the letters P through X in an exaggerated manner as

quickly as possible. Read the following in a loud tone as quickly as possible, exaggerating all movements of the articulators:

Pretty queens repeat small trivialities unless vigorously warned. Except in Yucatan and Zanzibar.

5. Practice a vigorous attack by stressing the initial consonants in these words:

But	Cat	Dab	Fat	Pat	Tan
Back	Kill	Dead	Five	Pent	Ten
Bed	Cut	Dint	Fun	Pull	Ton
Blunder	Cannon	Damage	Famous	Perish	Tonic

6. In polysyllable words sounds are often slurred or omitted completely. Give full value to each syllable in the following. Please note that some syllables should be unstressed.

Adequately	Dreariness	Minimal
Beforehand	Discipline	Paragraph
Devastating	Handkerchief	Primary Resolution
Civilization	Incomparable	Reverend
Comparable	Interesting	Utterance
Devotedly	Monumental	Vestibule
Dramatization	Percolator	

7. Practice stressing the consonants in these sentences:

Candid cameras challenge the concealment of characteristics.
Dutiful druggists dispense dosages desired by dedicated doctors.
Famous facades frequently feature flamboyant figures.
Merry minstrels make melodious music.
Neat nesteggs net numerable noteworthy notices.
Salty sailors and suntanned Shebas swarm seashores on sunny Saturdays
Wearisome women wait woefully at wishing wells.
Zany Zabus zig and zag zestfully.

8. Enunciate the final sounds distinctly in the following words, using a short humming sound:

Dying	Nagging	Rhyming
Giving	Naming	Roosting
Going	Nesting	Sewing
Haunting	Noting	Sifting

EXERCISES

Since we have included in the body of the chapter numerous drills for the improvement of vocal delivery, this set of exercises will deal solely with the improvement of physical action in speaking.

1. Make a detailed analysis of your "physical action pattern." Include your primary personality characteristics and the physical factors affecting your use of gestures and movements when speaking. Then make a list of ways in which you might improve your use of the visible symbols of speech. Practice these until you can incorporate them into the speaking situation.

2. Assume various postures until you discover one that seems comfortable and neither too stiff nor too relaxed. Observe the positions of your feet, arms, head, and body. Practice the position until you can assume it readily.

3. Observe speakers outside the classroom situation, and analyze their physical actions to determine what they do that reinforces their meaning. Analyze what they do physically that creates barriers to communication.

4. In watching television programs note the action of various personalities. Critically evaluate their postures, movements, and gestures.

5. Practice what you would consider appropriate arm and hand positions for a particular situation, as you say the following:
   a. Sitting over there is an old friend.
   b. Please note this point.
   c. Let us observe a moment of silence.
   d. Don't speak to me about it. I will not listen.
   e. The desert stretched out before me.
   f. Here, take this money if you really need it.
   g. See, there is nothing in my hand.
   h. Ouch! Stop! You're hurting me!
   i. He dragged one leg, something like this.
   j. I absolutely disagree, absolutely!
   k. You have given me the wrong change.
   l. Don't bother me, can't you see I'm busy!

6. Keep the elbows well out from the body and the wrists flexible, use a vigorous excess of energy, and do the following things in sequence:
   a. Shake your arms and hands vigorously as if trying to get something loose from your fingers. Do this with your arms far out at the sides, then up over your head, then out in front of you; continue until all stiffness is eliminated.
   b. While you are doing this, begin repeating the alphabet over and over—not in a monotonous rhythm, but as if you were actually talking in highly colored language. Continue this "talking" throughout the remainder of this series.
   c. Let one hand at a time fall to your side and continue shaking the other.
   d. Gradually change from mere shaking of the arm and hand into varied gestures: that is, shake your fist, point your finger, reject the idea, drive home a point, etc. During this change be sure to continue the vigor and complete abandon of the arm movement.

7. Prepare a speech in which you describe certain of the signs used in the following activities:
   a. Baseball
   b. Football

    c. The stock market
    d. Preaching
    e. Landing an airplane on a flattop
    f. Orchestral conducting
    g. Scouting
    h. Ushering
    i. Railroading
    j. Building construction

8. Study persons you may know who are of different racial or cultural backgrounds. How do their physical actions when speaking differ? Read pages 22 to 25 of the book *Nonverbal Communication* by Ruesch and Kees in this connection. How do your conclusions compare with their conclusions?

9. Make a study of a person whom you hear speak frequently. What physical action does he use to supplement the oral code of speech? Is the physical action effective? Why? Prepare a brief report on your findings for classroom presentation.

10. Using any of the following references as a source, prepare a speech in which you indicate the relationship between the visible and oral codes of speech, or the development of speech as it is related to physical action.

    a. Charles Morris, *Signs, Language and Behavior*, New York, George Braziller, 1955.

    b. Joshua Whatmough, *Language: A Modern Synthesis*, New York, St. Martin's Press, 1956.

    c. Issac Goldberg, *The Wonder of Words*, New York, Appleton-Century-Crofts, 1939.

    d. S. I. Hayakawa, *Language in Thought and Action*, 2nd ed., New York, Harcourt Brace Jovanovich, 1949.

    e. Edward T. Hall, *The Silent Language*, New York, Doubleday, 1959.

    f. Margaret Schlauch, *The Gift of Language*, New York, Dover, 1955.

    g. Jurgen Ruesch and Weldon Kees, *Nonverbal Communication*, Berkeley, Calif., Univ. of California Press, 1956.

    h. George N. Gordon, *The Languages of Communication*, New York, Hastings House, 1969.

ADDITIONAL READINGS

Blankenship, Jane, and Robert Wilhoit, *Selected Readings in Public Speaking*, Belmont, Calif., Dickenson, 1966, chap. 5.

Clevenger, Theodore, Jr., "A Synthesis of Experimental Research in Stage Fright," *Quart. J. Speech*, 45 (no. 2, April 1959), 134–145.

Fairbanks, Grant, *Voice and Articulation Drillbook*, 2nd ed., New York, Harper & Row, 1960.

Gordon, George N., *The Languages of Communication*, New York, Hastings House, 1969, chaps. 4, 5, 6, 16.

Hall, Edward T., *The Silent Language*, New York, Doubleday, 1959.

Hollingworth, H. L., *The Psychology of the Audience*, New York, American Book, 1935, chap. 6.

Kaplan, Harold M., *Anatomy and Physiology of Speech*, New York, McGraw-Hill, 1960.

Mead, George H., *Mind, Self and Society*, Chicago, Univ. Chicago Press, 1934, 248–249, 362–363.

Oliver, Robert T., Harold P. Zelko, and Paul D. Holtzman, *Communicative Speaking and Listening*, 4th ed., New York, Holt, Rinehart & Winston, 1968, chap. 9.
Ruesch, Jurgen, and Weldon Kees, *Nonverbal Communication*, Berkeley, Calif., Univ. California Press, 1956, chaps. 1, 2, 3.
Thonssen, Lester, *Selected Readings in Rhetoric and Public Speaking*, New York, Wilson, 1942, 215–217.
Weaver, Carl H., *Speaking in Public*, New York, American Book, 1966, chaps. 13, 14, 15, 16.

NOTES

[1] Jurgen Ruesch and Weldon Kees, *Nonverbal Communication*, Berkeley, Calif., Univ. California Press, 1956, p. 189.

[2] *Ibid.*, p. 37.

[3] Mario Pei, *The Story of Language*, Philadelphia, Lippincott, 1949, p. 13.

[4] R. P. Blackmur, *Language as Gesture*, New York, Harcourt, 1952, p. 4.

[5] Andrew T. Weaver and Ordean G. Ness, *An Introduction to Public Speaking*, New York, Odyssey, 1961, p. 215.

[6] Quintilian, *Institutes of Oratory*, Book XI, chap. 3, pars, 72, 75.

[7] W. Barnett Pearce and Forrest Conklin, "Nonverbal vocalic communication and perceptions of a speaker," *Speech Monographs*, 38 (no. 3, Aug. 1971), 236–237, 241.

CHAPTER FOURTEEN
USING AUDIOVISUAL RESOURCES

Sounds which address the ear
are lost and die
In one short hour; but that
which strikes the eye
Lives long upon the mind; the
faithful sight
Engraves the knowledge with a
beam of light
                    Anonymous

Face-to-face speech communication employs both verbal and nonverbal symbols. Sometimes what we do in speaking is as important as what we say. Sometimes our nonverbal symbols carry the complete or the essential part of our message, and the verbal language is the supplement. When we talk to a friend or to a stranger, much of the message he receives comes from our actions and facial expressions. A firm hand-shake, an engaging smile, and the appearance of willingness to listen can do much to build friendly relationships. When language needs greater clarity, heightened dramatic effect, or the demonstrations of manual skills, audiovisual tools are necessary to supplement verbal communication.

The inclusion of a separate chapter on audiovisual techniques is a moot point among writers of speech texts. Obviously, the inclusion of the present chapter makes it apparent that we believe that knowledge of modern audiovisual technology is needed by every speaker, but the use of audiovisual aids is not needed for every speech. In this, as in all applications of rhetorical principles, adaptability to the needs of the situation is the key. Audiovisual technology is now more scientific, innovative, and creative than ever before. The effective speaker can profit from these advances. Changing instructional patterns at all levels, with an increased use of "new" media, have attuned the youth and many adults of today to visual learning. Among many others, one singularly important reason speakers need to be well versed in the use of audiovisual resources is the rapid, almost phenomenal, growth of knowledge. At the present rate knowledge is doubled every ten years. What are the implications of this fact for the speaker? Simply this: in many communicative situations the time-binding aspect of verbal and *nonverbal* languages—the use of words or pictures to tell of the past or indicate the possible nature of the future and of events occurring in distant places—can be demonstrated most effectively through the use of visuals. To transmit from one generation to another in a single speech even a small bit of the heritage of the past requires the use of every medium possible. Consider the problems involved in transmitting knowledge about events that have occurred in our own generation—a single generation—without some use of visual communication. To "cover ground," lecturers and speakers who deal with such subjects as medical and dental technology, all scientific fields, most aspects of sports, solutions to the problems of the inner city, ecology, modern city planning, travel experiences, social reforms, the involvement of the United States in Southeast Asia, and the use and abuse of drugs, can expect to achieve their speech goals more readily through some use of audiovisual media.

VALUES OF AUDIOVISUAL TECHNIQUES
Audiovisual techniques serve the speaker in numerous ways. We consider the four that have the greatest significance.

Gaining and Holding Attention
The first value of audiovisual techniques is to gain and hold the listener's attention. In Chapter Five we considered the nature of attention in motivation, in explaining what psychologists call the figure-ground theory, and we indicated some of its characteristics: size, intensity, duration, and movement, for example. When you use at the start of a speech an audiovisual aid having some of these characteristics, you can generally be assured that all members of the audience will focus on what you want to appear the central idea at the moment. You frequently can regain lagging interest, since change always captures attention. Alternating audible and visible presentations heightens interest and thereby holds attention. The dramatic effects possible with some visual aids, the vivid details in others, the contrasts available, the direct impact achievable, and the stark realism of certain types, all contribute to sustain attention.

It should be pointed out that listeners have varying degrees of understanding and reaction to attention-getting devices. Thus, variety in using audiovisual aids ensures that you will gain and hold the attention of a greater number in your audience.

Audience Understanding
A second value of the use of audiovisual techniques is perhaps the most significant in terms of the achievement of the speaker's goals, namely the increase in the audience's understanding of his subject.

Psychologists tell us that the sources of learning, or understanding, in order of their effectiveness are (1) experiencing a thing directly, (2) seeing a picture or model of the object or event, (3) being told about it by someone who has experienced it directly, and (4) reading about it. Because we believe this concept of levels of learning is important for the speaker to understand and apply, we quote an audiovisual educator, Edgar Dale, on the same point. He says there are three levels at which experiences may be secured:[1]

1. *One meets the object or event directly with the use of all the senses. You see, hear, smell, taste, or feel it. The meaning is tied up with action. . . .*
2. *We meet the event less directly through a picture, a model, or a photograph. As noted above, it "bears some resemblance" to the object or event. This "compressed" reality may be enough to convey the idea.*
3. *The event or object is turned into a symbol—a printed word or formula—which bears no resemblance to the reality for which the symbol stands. . . .*

Jerome Bruner of Harvard has made a somewhat similar threefold analysis of experience. The first level he calls enactive. *Here doing is involved. You* actually *tie a knot. At the second level, labeled* iconic, *you may look at pictures or drawings and learn to tie knots you never tied before. The third level is* symbolic *as defined above. You read the word "knot" and its mental referent is now an image or picture, or your actual experience in tying one.*

Because we believe so sincerely that speech communication usually may be improved by the use of appropriate audiovisual aids, we list below the titles of some recent student speeches—the content of which may be inferred from the title—in which meanings were made clearer because audiovisual techniques were employed:

Playing the Double-Reed Woodwind: The Bassoon
How the Option Play Works in Football
The Amazing Amazon
Three Men in a Tub: How the Astronauts Live and Work
What Did the Kent State Debacle Prove?
The Rock Hound: A Paying Hobby
Our Withdrawal from Vietnam: Let's Look at the Facts
How Vice-Presidents Look Through the Cartoonist's Eye: Agnew, Humphrey, Johnson, and Nixon
Progress in Aviation: From the Spirit of St. Louis to the Modern Jet

Two Can't Live as Cheaply as One: Planning the Budget for a College Couple

In each of the speeches on these topics some form of audio-visual aid was used informatively, understandably, occasionally humorously; provided varied sensory experiences; and held the attention of the students throughout the speech. Since we frequently cannot bring a point to an audience through words alone, we must use some visual presentation. The beauty of Niagara Falls in North America, the Iguassu Falls in South America, the Taj Mahal in India, and the Parthenon in Athens; the stark brutality of Dachau and Auschwitz in Europe and of Attica and Watts in America; and the historical heritage of Chichén-Itza in Yucatan, Mexico, and of Pompeii in Italy, cannot be adequately described by words alone. You must have been there or at least seen pictures of these sights.

Audiovisual techniques increase the audience's understanding of a subject in a number of ways. We list some of them, not necessarily in the order of their importance.

Focusing and Intensifying

At times the only visual aid (sometimes called a "visual") available to a speaker is one filled with details, yet he wishes to focus on some specified aspect. We are all familiar with the techniques used: a part of the visual is encircled, an arrow points to the significant part, color highlights certain items, and parts of the visual are shown in sequence by the use of overlays. Duration, size, contrast in color, intensity of the stimulus, and movement will all aid in focusing the attention of the audience on a particular aspect of a visual aid. The visual aid or audio aid serves to reinforce the verbal message.

Providing a Uniform Stimulus

Visual and audio aids used in speeches provide stimuli that are identical and uniform for numbers of listeners. Further, the complete meaning in many instances is presented all at once. The essential and key aspects of a topic may be so highlighted that a single impression is perceived by the audience. For example, when visuals are used—a chart, a model, a photograph, or a diagram—all listeners see the same thing; when words alone are used, we can never be sure that all listeners get the same meaning from them, in fact, we may be pretty certain they will never all get the same meaning. Although it is usually true that, when an entire audience sees or hears the *same* visual or audible stimulus, its perception of it has some degree of commonality, we can never be sure, because of varied background experiences, that the interpretations will be the same. This is one reason for combining verbal with nonverbal language. What you say before or after using an audiovisual technique serves to lessen or eliminate extraneous meanings.

Giving Emphasis

Visual and audio aids can be used to give emphasis to important points in a speech. They aid in directing the thinking of listeners, in guiding it to the conclusion desired by the speaker. Pictures of highway accidents may point up the dangers of unposted street crossings, the color red invariably suggests danger, in a chalktalk (blackboard presentation) the underscoring—a single, double, or triple line—will suggest which idea is most important, and important ideas may be indicated by gestures. Besides underlining there are many techniques that may be used to emphasize major points. Some include indentation, capital letters, various sizes of numbers or letters, numbering of items to show priority, contrasting colors or sounds, arrows, and framing.

Reducing Complexity

To explain the parts and functioning of an internal combustion engine, a jet propulsion motor, the guidance system of a missile, or even the process of communication are just a few examples of speech topics whose complexity may be lessened by means of visuals. The parts may be shown separately or in sequence, unessential details may be omitted, or working relationships among the parts may be shown by mockups or cutaways (two types of visual that will be described later). The football coach always uses a blackboard to explain a complicated football play, the members of a scientific research team converse largely in symbols, diagrams, and formulae, and the teacher explaining the relationships of the planets in the universe uses a diagram or a model. If you ask someone to explain the concept "spiral" he usually will use his finger to show the rotating and converging nature of a spiral.

Some motor skills are complicated, and learning a particular skill is not always easy without some form of visual aid. In teaching the care and use of equipment it is common practice to diagram the layout of the equipment. Many projection machines are now threaded automatically, but most are not. It is difficult to teach a person who is not adept in the use of equipment to thread a projection machine without an instructional chart that serves as a visual demonstration. Figure 14-1 shows a threading chart for one type of projector. It is easy to see how errors in threading could be made without the use of such a chart. Further, when the chart is enlarged or projected on a screen, the teaching of this mechanical process to large numbers of persons is simplified. Many a speaker has failed to communicate effectively because he could not thread a movie-projection camera or operate a slide projector. A little study might have ensured greater success.

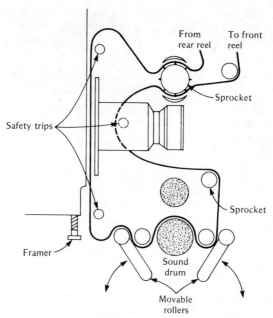

FIGURE 14-1. Threading chart for Victor motion-picture projector. (From Sidney C. Eboch, *Operating Audio-Visual Equipment*, 2nd ed., San Francisco, Chandler Publishing Company, Inc., 1968.)

Shortening the Time

That "one picture is worth a thousand words" is often literally true for explaining complicated processes or detailed relationships, for stressing dramatic impact—for example, with pictures of the Attica prison riots of 1971—or for showing relationships of size.

Before Alaska became a state in 1959, Texas was the largest state in the nation. It is the Alaskans who can now boast of their size. The two map overlays shown in Figures 14-2 and 14-3 indicate the comparative sizes of Texas and of Alaska and the comparative widths of the United States and of Alaska, Alaska here stretching from Seattle to Miami. As we look at the first overlay, it is obvious that less time is involved in showing size relationships than if we were to explain that Alaska is more than 586,000 square miles in size and Texas slightly more than 267,000, that Alaska has 33,000 miles of coast line and Texas 367, and that Alaska extends approximately 3,000 miles from the tip of the Aleutian Islands to the southernmost point of the Panhandle in a general westerly direction and Texas about 730 miles from El Paso near the western border of Texas to Port Arthur close to the eastern border in a generally easterly direction.

In practically every situation in which learning time is minimal and maximal learning is the goal, some type of audiovisual technique is

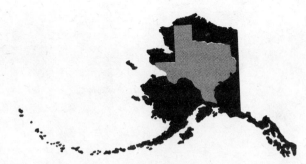

FIGURE 14-2. Overlay Showing relative sizes of Texas and Alaska. (From *How to See the Real Alaska,* Department of Economic Development, Travel Division, State of Alaska.)

used. The armed forces use all types of audiovisual aid, including scaled models, mockups, actual objects, maps, flannel boards, and pictures of equipment, for training in the use of equipment, in team problem-solving, in tactical maneuvers and deployment of troops, and even in personal hygiene. At all educational institutions hardly a class in a foreign language is taught without the use of foreign voice records or tapes for drill. Extensive use is made of visual aids in citizenship classes, where teaching time is one consideration, in developing an understanding and appreciation of American traditions, customs, and form of government, and the rights and privileges of citizenship.

In the past decade in the field of education the increase in the use of audiovisual techniques can almost be called a "communication explosion." Audiovisual communication techniques are at last coming into their own, in part because of the time saved in teaching a certain concept or skill and in part because of their learning values, adaptability to real-life situations, interest qualities, dramatic effects, the decrease in "wear and tear" on the teacher, and the freedom given the teacher to do the tasks he does best, once the aids are prepared or the field trip planned.

Aiding in Summarizing
Visuals are frequently used quite effectively to summarize the main points or the general message of a speech. Key words, which capture the main ideas of a speech, may be written on the blackboard as the speaker reviews his talk. Flip charts, the main idea lettered on each chart, may be used in the same way. Some speakers like the method of placing on the board a single word or phrase, each initial letter of which stands for one main idea in the speech. Thus, a student used the word *Self* to summarize a speech on "Developing Effective Interpersonal Relations".

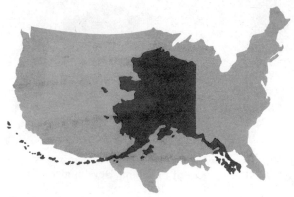

FIGURE 14-3. Overlay showing relative sizes of United States and Alaska. (From *How to See The Real Alaska,* Department of Economic Development, Travel Division, State of Alaska.)

S ensitivity to others at all times
E xpression of feelings
L ove shown by acts of kindness and courtesy
F rankness and fairness in dealing with others

A method of using visual aids to summarize with dramatic effect is illustrated by a speech given by a Housing Commission representative urging an urban redevelopment plan in a large eastern city. In his conclusion he showed several pictures of the existing slums in the redevelopment area. Then he quickly showed three drawings of models of what he caled the "Inner City of the Future": high-rise low-rent dwelling units, playground and park areas, easy entrance and exit routes, and well-planned location of business and industrial areas. The speaker's conclusion was truly effective.

Extending Vicarious Experiences
The goal of many speakers is to bring to listeners and viewers experiences they could not possibly have in their own localities. For those of us who must "stay at home," the slides, pictures, and movies of friends, lecturers, or travel movies bring to us vicariously experiences that frequently seem almost real. We can see and appreciate the grace and dexterity and beauty of the figure skating of Peggy Fleming of the United States, the ski jumping of Jiri Raska of Czechoslovakia, or the diving of Sue Gossick of the United States, all three of whom were Olympic champions in 1968. Visually we can experience the grandeur of Mount McKinley in Alaska, the new capital Brazilia of Brazil, or the Victoria Falls on the Zambesi in Africa. From visuals of many types we can become partially acquainted with the environs of the locales and

the panoramic vistas as seen from the Space Needle in Seattle, the Husky Tower in Calgary, Canada, or the Moana Loa Tower in Honolulu.

Only a few people have been inside a space capsule, seen the moon's surface, or ridden in a Moon Land Rover, but millions of us have had these experiences through visuals. In an entirely different area of our national life—the solution of some of our pressing social and economic problems—many of us, largely due to the exposure provided by many forms of audiovisual media, are becoming aware of, and are beginning to be willing to work toward, solutions of such problems as drug abuse, the use of wetback labor, slum clearance and urban renewal, pollution, and the national economy.

Serving the Speaker

Audiovisual communication techniques serve the speaker personally both physically and psychologically. We have talked about how stage fright affects the speaker: quickened heartbeat, muscular tension, excess perspiration, and uncontrolled bodily action. The excess nervous energy that often develops as a part of stage fright may be utilized positively in setting up, displaying, or moving a visual aid. Momentarily, at least, the speaker focuses on the content rather than his own fears.

The use of audiovisual aids also has psychological advantages. A visual may be made so that the complete outline of a speech is a part of the aid. Thus the speaker may feel secure that he will not forget. Visual aids, regardless of their type, always contain cues about "what comes next." The time factor in using a visual or audio technique also gives the speaker a chance to review the points coming up. Finally, the speaker who uses audiovisual aids effectively can be, and usually is, more assured of being an effective communicator.

KINDS OF VISUAL AID

A visual aid is a presentation, such as a graph, filmstrip, model, or photograph, directed to the visual senses of the listener and viewer, rather than to his ear. Visuals are communication tools or techniques; they are not always needed or advisable, but when effectively employed, they have many values to both speaker and listener. They save time, increase understanding, sometimes explain concepts that cannot be conveyed with words, create listener interest, and ease the task of the speaker.

Visual aids may be classified in several different ways:

1. Manner of construction (two or three dimensional)
2. Time of construction (prior to use or at the time of use, as a chalktalk)

3. Manner of showing (projected, as films or slides, or non-projectional, as specimens or pictures)
4. Type of content (symbolic or realistic)

No single class is exclusive of the others: a three-dimensional visual may be realistic or symbolic, a two-dimensional aid may be projected or nonprojected, and a symbolic visual may be offered prior to or at the time of showing. We believe the first class listed has the greatest value for the student.

Two-Dimensional Media

Two-dimensional media are all "flat" aids, those having only length and width, such as flipcharts, cartoons, maps, and graphs. Visuals of this category are the most frequently used.

Graphics

Graphics are representations of an idea by drawing, painting, words, figures, or any other art using lines and strokes; they include maps, charts, diagrams, graphs, cartoons, posters, and flashcards. Graphic representations are designed to present ideas and facts clearly and succinctly. They may be found in textbooks, wall displays, transparencies, filmstrip or slide frames, and in programmed self-instruction.

Maps. A common type of graphic is the map. Most maps are scaled representations of the earth's surface or of the heavens or of any part of either, in which certain characteristics or features are indicated. Maps may be drawn to show many different things, such as geographical, political, cultural, economic, recreational, social, astronomical, or other features of a given area. For example, the usual road map shows the relative positions of the various cities and towns, the densely and sparsely settled areas, distances, and sometimes the nature of the terrain. Depending on its purpose, a map can present an almost unlimited amount of detailed information, and a series of maps can show changes over a period of time. One caution should be observed in using maps in a speech: if they contain so much detail that they tend to confuse the viewer, or if they contain abbreviations that may not be understood, some other type of representation may be more useful, or a map should be made that will convey only the desired information. This may be done in different ways. For example, suppose you were to give a speech about the National Parks in the United States. You might have a map showing the locations and names only. If you wished to focus on one park, say Yellowstone, details of the park might be magnified, while the other parks would be shown only in smaller contours. Or, if you wished to say some things about the parks in the western part of the country only, you might show a partial map of the United States, indicating in some way the unique features of each: Old Faithful at Yellowstone, the Grand Canyon National Park, Half Dome at Yosemite, or the ruins of the prehistoric cliff dwellings at Mesa Verde. Sometimes only the outlines of areas are necessary, as indicated in Figures 14-2 and 14-3.

When appropriately prepared and used, maps may serve many uses: (1) show relative or exact positions, (2) provide specific data on characteristics of areas, events, and conditions, (3) show visual comparisons, (4) provide a basis for the study of regions, processes, distributions, cultures, and activities, and (5) serve in the design, for example, of recreational and housing development, or in the governmental reapportionment of areas.

Charts. The term *chart* is sometimes used in a broad sense, synonymous with diagram and map, to refer to schematic, pictorial, numerical (tabular), or alphabetical representations of data. Charts may be constructed to show relationships in processes, objects, institutions, events, abstract ideas, or sequences. They may also show classifications of data, structure, or operations. A chart may show a large or small amount of data; it may show sequences of time or space or show logical relationships. It may be constructed to deal with almost any subject matter that is not geographical, such as the schematic flow of parts in an assembly line, steps in registration at college, the line and staff relations in a large company, and a genealogical tree. Charts are of six major types.

Tabular charts are essentially data of a numerical nature, usually in large amounts, such as airline timetables. Usually these must be combined with verbal designations of what the data represent.

Language charts make use of single words, expressions, or some combination of them, written on large cards, strips of cardboard, or a blackboard. If single words are used, they may be shown singly or in sequence. In "To the Student" in the beginning of this book we give nine steps for speech preparation. A language chart of these suggestions would be a list, as follows. It probably would be framed by a heavy line.

Steps in speech preparation

1. Analyze the communicative situation.
2. Select the subject of the communication.
3. Determine the specific audience response desired.
4. Determine the central idea of the communication.
5. Gather needed speech materials.
6. Plan the organization of your speech.

7. Consider the style of the speech.
8. Plan the physical aspects of the presentation.
9. Rehearse the speech.

Organization charts, or *flowcharts,* sometimes called *developmental charts,* show functional relationships within an organization, process, or institution, by the use of lines, arrows, circles, rectangles, and other geometrical figures. Every large organization uses this type of chart to show its line and staff structures. They are commonly used to show the relationships among the legislative, judicial, and administrative branches of our government. Other common organization charts are those used to show the bodies within the United Nations, SEATO and NATO, the command relationships within the branches of our military forces, or the administrative and academic relationships within a collegiate institution. A *flowchart* also shows relationships, but in addition shows them in a time or sequential order. For example, a chart may show the steps or stages required to achieve a certain goal as the steps by which a bill becomes a law. Sometimes this type is called a *stream chart,* as a chart which shows all the raw materials needed to construct a product, such as a tractor, and the stages through which they pass in producing the finished product. The PERT chart (Program Evaluation and Review Technique) is a flowchart.[2] It is commonly used in governmental and civilian agencies in the development of program plans. When a group has decided on a solution to a problem, PERT portrays the overall plan of the solution and indicates progress to date on each activity within the program. The chart then shows direct comparisons between the planned schedule of activities and the actual progress made.

Another form of chart is the *flipchart,* or sequence chart. A sequence of charts, each showing a small amount of content, is shown quite rapidly. Sometimes they are called *flash cards* because of the speed of showing. They are used extensively in teaching situations when memorization is required. They are used in the military in teaching airplane recognition and Navy signal flags, in some aspects of foreign-language teaching, and in laboratory classes when the learning of sequential steps is the goal. Students have used flash cards effectively in speeches on such subjects as cell division, ship maneuvers, salesmanship, and period-furniture styles. Flipcharts are also helpful in summarizing the points made in a speech.

Diagrams. Diagrams are drawings, or a form of chart, composed of lines and geometrical forms only. They contain no pictorial elements. Diagrams are representative. They are designed to show interrelationships, the essence or the general idea of an event or process, or the key features of an area or object. In describing the diagram Wittich and Schuller, authors of a widely used text on audiovisual techniques, state:[3]

Although most graphic forms are condensed visual summaries, the diagram is the most condensed of all. The diagram relies heavily on symbols—a form of visual shorthand—to convey information and, because it has also stripped down the full concept to its barest essentials, the diagram tends to be highly abstract.

Thus, to understand diagrams, one must have some knowledge of the related subject matter. Blueprints, two-dimensional cutaways, floor plans of plant layouts, or the representations of objects found in some do-it-yourself assembly instructions are all diagrams.

Diagrams vary greatly in complexity, from simple sketches, like a plot of the stage movements in a play, to the extremely complex, like the schematic, or plan of wiring, for a television or radio set. When diagrams are used, it is usually important that they be drawn to scale so as to represent accurately the relationships and information involved.

Graphs. One of the most frequently used graphics is the graph, of which there are six major types: the line graph, the bar graph, the circle, or pie graph, the profile, or silhouette graph, the solid-figure graph, and the picture graph. Illustrations of the first four are shown in Figure 14-4 and of the last two in Figures 14-5 and 14-6. The primary use of graphs is to show trends and comparisons among quantitative data.

The *line graph* shows trends that may be represented by either a single or multiple lines. The *bar graph* shows a comparison of actual amounts. The axes of the graph may relate the amounts to time, area, group, or some other relevant factor. Bar graphs are modified in several ways. In one type a number of solid vertical or horizontal bars are shown, each representing 100 percent of the total. In a composite bar graph each bar is divided into different parts by the use of dots, crosses, cross lines, different intensities of color, and solid color. The multiple bar graph uses two or more bars in lieu of a single bar. The *circle graph*, frequently called a pie, or sector, graph, shows percentage comparisons. Each section represents a part or percentage of the whole, and all add up to one hundred percent. Wittich and Schuller report[4] that "circle graphs are the most accurately read of all common graph forms when used to compare parts of a whole."

The *profile graph*, or silhouette graph, is a line graph in which the area under the line or lines is shaded so as to emphasize a single feature or several features of the data represented. When a single feature

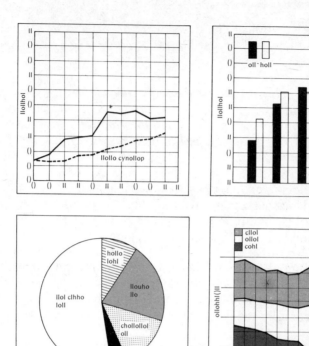

FIGURE 14-4. Line, bar, circle, and profile graphs.

is to be stressed, the area under a single line only is shaded; when two or more aspects of the data are to be indicated, the areas under two or more lines are shaded. The illustration in Figure 14-4 shows a multiple profile graph.

Figures 14-5 and 14-6 show a *solid-figure graph* and a *picture graph,* which represent hypothetical data. A solid-figure graph is composed of one or more cubes, spheres, cylinders, or other geometrical figures that present a three-dimensional effect. Usually a solid-figure graph is used for its striking or dramatic quality. A picture graph uses picture symbols primarily as an attention device. The symbols may be used alone or may be combined with any of the graph types we have described. Each symbol represents a given quantity of an item, such as a barrel to represent a daily production of 10,000 barrels, a house to represent the weekly completion of 5,000 housing units, and a person to represent, say, a percentage of a total population.

Cartoons. The cartoon, defined by Wittich and Schuller[5] as "a pictorial representation or caricature of a person, idea, or situation that is designed to influence public opinion," sometimes is used as a visual aid

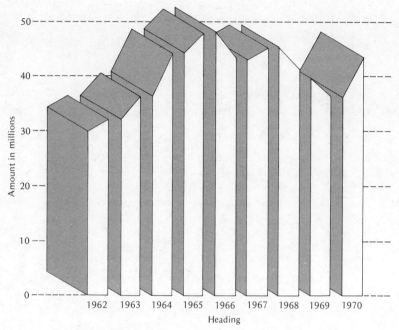

FIGURE 14-5. Solid-figure graph.

in speaking, though it is better suited to written materials. Although cartoons usually try to convey only a single idea, the viewer may require a minute or two to get the point. Cartoons should always be prepared in advance, unless the speaker has considerable skill in free-hand drawing. The value of a cartoon lies in its ability to focus attention on some aspect of an event, object, or person. Most are caricatures, which exaggerate, suggest contrasts, oversimplify, point up incongruities, and call attention to neglected issues, or merely provide humor.

Posters. Posters are drawings that are realistic or symbolic representations. They may depict places, events, persons, institutions, appeals of all sorts, processes, or the pleasures and joys of taking part in some activity. They are used to commemorate, promote, or advertise. Posters are usually found (posted) in public places. Although they are used extensively both indoors and out, they are not very effective as aids in speaking, except on special occasions, as when several are used to set a mood for a travel talk. The force of a poster lies in its immediate impact; it must be instantly intelligible to the observer. Effective posters are simple in design, have a single center of interest, employ eye-catching color contrasts and slogans, and, as a rule, have artistic qualities. A viewer will look twice at a good poster.

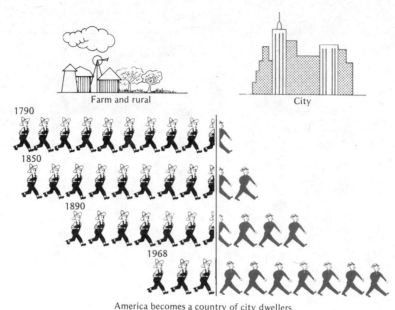

FIGURE 14-6. Picture graph. (From Pictograph Corporation, New York.)

Pictures and Pictorial Elements

Pictorial visual aids include photographs and various other kinds of pictures, which can be extremely effective in some speaking situations. In the courtroom, for example, lawyers use them to show details of accidents, results of fires, scenes of crimes, or reproductions of evidence that cannot be brought into court. In talks on safe driving pictures of automobile accidents show the disastrous results of careless driving. In travel talks photographs projected on a screen show the beauty, charm, grandeur, or challenge of faraway places. The speaker can use photographs effectively in talks on such subjects as art appreciation, architecture, anthropology, horticulture, and sports, to mention only a few. Because photographs are literal representations, they are more valuable than language alone in situations requiring realism and detail.

The speaker should be cautioned in the use of pictorial aids, however; they have certain weaknesses. Sometimes they are too small for showing to a large group, unless they are projected. We have seen student speakers use photographs as visual aids when only a few persons in the first row could see them. It is even worse when a speaker passes a picture among the audience members, who immediately stop listening to the speaker. When you use a pictorial aid, you should also make certain that the reproduction is good, that the purpose is clear, that the viewer may not be diverted from the intended message by the artistic quality, and that the multitude of detail does not also distract from the message.

Overlays

Overlays consist of a number of transparencies, which are the equivalent of slides of large dimensions, either 7 by 7 inches or 10 by 10 inches in size, arranged in sequence. Each overlay after the first transparency presents different or more detailed information. Thus, as each overlay is added, a more complete part of the total concept or process is revealed, sequential stages of development are seen, or additional data are presented.

Overlays are extensively used, partly because a speaker can control the amount of material shown and partly because they can be projected by an overhead projector, which permits the speaker to face the audience as he displays his successive overlays. The typical kinds of overlays are those which show, in succession, the essential parts of the human body (skeleton, circulation system, central nervous system, and so on), the growth of the United States, the corporate structure of a large organization, and the assemblage of some mechanical object.

Usually overlays are projected on a screen. However, they may also be used with charts or drawings. In our description of our model of the communication process (see Chapter Four), we followed the procedures used with overlays. We first showed the "total communication environment" and next the sender and receiver and how they function when acting as source and communicator and as listener and respondent, respectively. We used the same diagram to illustrate the concept of message replication. Finally, we put all components of the process of communication together in Figure 4-10 (p. 92).

Flannel Boards

Flannel boards are used because napped material, such as flannel, wool, felt, balsa wood, styrofoam, or wool, adheres to similar surfaces. Large pieces of plywood, masonite, or heavy cardboard are first covered with one of the napped materials. Each item—word, object, scaled diagram of a person, symbol, or whatever—to be displayed on the flannel board has the same type of material attached to its back. When the displayed item is pressed against the flannel board, it adheres as if glued.

Flannel boards have some of the values of overlays. The speaker can control the amount of material, the suspense of "what is to come" holds attention, its use is especially adapted to material that must be shown in sequence, and the board and display items are economical to prepare and flexible to use.

Blackboards

Blackboard presentations are talks during which the speaker uses a chalkboard on which to display sketches, drawings, symbols, letters, or numbers relating to the subject of the speech. This visual technique is sometimes called the *chalktalk*, which gives the impression that it is composed of casual, off-the-cuff, unplanned ideas that the speaker places on the blackboard in an improvised manner. It is regrettable that many teachers use—or, should we say, abuse—this technique in this manner.

Because of its widespread use, we make these suggestions for the use of the chalkboard in oral presentations:[6]

1. Plan in advance. Do not use the chalktalk technique without advance planning. Think about the size, content, position, sequence, and approximate drawing time of each diagram and the number to be made. Decide on how you will introduce each sketch or drawing, and relate it to what follows. Don't make the error suggested in the well-known sign shown in the accompanying cut.

2. Practice in advance. Freehand drawings presented as a part of a chalktalk should be neat, reasonably accurate, proportional to the object represented, and properly positioned on the blackboard; and letters and numbers should be large enough to be seen from all parts of the room. If possible, practice in the room in which you will give the talk. If that is not possible, use newsprint, and practice making your sketches the approximate size anticipated when you actually make them.

3. Be sure that the audience can see at all times. Because the speaker is so close to the blackboard, he has a tendency to make his sketches or writing too small to be seen by persons in the back of the room. Write large! Draw large! Try to avoid having part of your board work placed so that it is hidden from the viewers by the lectern or posts. Try also to avoid placing drawings where the glare from lights might prevent visibility.

4. Maintain continuous audience control during a chalktalk.

You should do several things to maintain audience control. Always face the audience while speaking; do not continue talking while writing on the board. This destroys direct audience eye contact. Further, if you talk while facing the board, you may not be heard, and audience interest will be lessened. Erase the board when you have finished a drawing and before you go on to the next point.

5. Maintain continuous audience attention and interest. You can do a number of things to maintain audience interest. Let us mention just a few at this point; we shall consider this matter again later in the chapter. Use a long pointer, so your drawings are not covered by your body. Draw only part of a sketch at one time, if possible; keep the suspense high. Use different chalk colors for contrast. Always prepare the audience in advance for what they will see; direct their attention to the first focal point of interest.

Three-Dimensional Media

In some situations three-dimensional visual materials are preferable to any kind of graphic. They are usually more like the real object; in some cases they may be the real object; they may be examined closely by the audience; some show actual operating processes; they frequently have greater flexibility than two-dimensional aids.

Actual Objects

An actual object is likely to be effective if everyone in the audience can see it. If it is large, it may have to be mounted in such a way that it can be rotated to show all sides, or the audience must be permitted to walk around it. However, to mount a large object may be both costly and time consuming, and it may be difficult to provide easy access to the object unless the audience is small. If the object is too small to be seen from a distance, and it can be handled, it is sometimes passed around in the audience; this, however, may be extremely distracting, unless each member of the audience can be given a sample. In our speech communication classes, for example, students have used the following real objects in speeches: a zither, a grass skirt used in the hula dance, the protective equipment worn by a football player, marijuana leaves, and an Eskimo harpoon.

Specimens

A specimen is a small sample of a real object, such as part of a rock—our astronauts brought back some of these from the Moon—various metals, cloth swatches or rug samples, certain solid or liquid foods, or some archeological artifacts. Specimens are useful in teaching situations, when there are enough of them to be studied by each member of the audience simultaneously, and when adequate time is available for complete examination and questions and answers.

Models

Models are exact replicas or scaled representations of real objects. Because they can be made on a larger or smaller scale than the real object and can be made of lightweight, transparent, and durable materials, they are generally more useful than the real object—probably more useful than any other three-dimensional aids. When made of lightweight materials, they can be easily moved; they are realistic; they can be made to show inner relationships and parts, as in the case of models of parts of the human body; different parts of a model can be colored for emphasis; and they ensure, in many instances, a comprehensive understanding of the total subject, as does a model of the Earth, a model city, or a relief map of parts of the earth's surface. Sometimes a model is essential; for example, a model of an Atlas missile could be used by a speaker, whereas the real object would be out of the question.

Mockups

Mockups are sometimes called *working models*. They are a type of visual aid used extensively in developing manual skills and in showing and analyzing mechanical procedures. A mockup is an exact replica or a scaled model of part or all of a real object, arranged to show movements, relationships, and technical principles. A well-known mockup is the Link Trainer, an enclosed, scaled model of the essential parts of the cockpit of an airplane used in training airplane pilots. Mockups are designed to focus on one important aspect of an object under consideration; nonessential aspects are not shown. The type of mockup with which most present-day students are familiar is the driver-trainer simulator. Students are seated in scaled models of the driver section of an auto—not the back seat—and view movies of real driving and traffic situations. The students' reactions are automatically recorded and can later be analyzed. The use of this type of trainer saves much actual "road" teaching.

Cutaways

Cutaways are either scaled models or exact replicas of parts of objects in which the outer covering has been cut away to show selected inner parts or processes. You undoubtedly have seen cutaways of organs of the human body. This type of visual aid is especially useful in certain teaching situations calling for explanations of spatial relationships.

Table Displays

Table displays are actual-sized or scaled three-dimensional representations. They are used to present a panoramic view of an event or process, a real or simulated life activity, an object, or some combination of these. Movement, color, lighting, and smells are often added to make the displays more realistic. Every male student probably had, when much younger, a display or one or more model trains, together with a railroad station, loading dock, tunnel, and bridges. The girls had somewhat the equivalent in the open-roof doll-house displays. Simulated war games employ table models to demonstrate ship or troop maneuvers. Some type of table display is to be seen at every elementary school's Parent Night: a model city, a country scene, a shopping center, or a model airport. Almost every relatively new collegiate institution, or one that has a long-range building program, will have, some place on the campus, a table display of what the school will look like twenty years ahead.

Projections

Students who have gone through high school in relatively recent years, persons who have served in the military forces, persons who attend professional or sales training conferences, engineers and technicians who work in any type of research and development, and the friends of persons who travel a lot and insist that "you must come over and see the slides of our latest trip," all these and more are well acquainted with most types and uses of projected visual aids. We merely wish to call them to your attention briefly at this point and suggest that they have advantages over nonprojected visuals: magnification is possible, more people can see them, they have greater attention values, they usually have greater flexibility in use, and they are easy to store.

Types

There are two types of projected visual: still-projection materials and movies. Still-projection materials are of two types: transparencies and opaque materials.

In the section earlier in the chapter dealing with overlays we mentioned the use of slides and transparencies. Transparencies are any surfaces on which may be placed a recorded image that can be projected (viewed) by having light passed through it. The major types of still-projected materials—all of which might be called transparencies— are the slide, transparency, filmstrip, and microfilm.

The *slide* is a piece of film or other transparent material on which a single image has been placed. Slides vary in size from 2 by 2 to 3¼ by 4 inches. A *transparency* is a large slide, usually 7 by 7 or 10 by

10 inches in size. The overhead projector is the type of equipment used to project transparencies. A *filmstrip* is a sequence of related photographic images on a strip of film, each frame of which presents a different visual picture. A *microfilm* is a filmstrip that has a special use. Pages of books, newspapers, periodicals, college dissertations, records of government agencies, legal documents, and many other printed materials are photographed and developed in sequence as filmstrips. Special viewing machines enlarge the successive frames for easy reading or viewing. Most college and university libraries are now enlarging their stock of microfilms. Your librarian will help you find what is available.

The four types of visuals mentioned above are still-projected materials. A *motion-picture,* sometimes called a movie or film, is a sequence of still pictures taken in rapid succession and, when projected through a motion-picture camera, giving the illusion of continuous movement. The film used usually is 8 or 16 mm in width. The advantages of movies are well known. They ensure sustained attention—if well produced and appropriate to the speech subject. They can be informative and dramatically stimulating. They heighten the sense of reality. They are useful in training in motor skills as well as in reinforcing or developing new attitudes. They usually add the dimension of sound.

We have three cautions for the speaker who wishes to use a movie as an audiovisual aid: be sure the movie deals with, and will supplement, your speech, preview the movie before its use, and tell the audience in advance what to look for in the movie. Remember that any visual or audiovisual technique is intended only as a supplement to your speech.

Equipment

Your school may have an audiovisual service department which provides needed help in setting up and servicing audio presentations, but you should at least know the names and uses of the basic projection equipment now available. There are two types of projector, for the still picture and for the motion picture. We shall consider the first type only, since it is the one most frequently used in audiovisual speech communication.

The *opaque projector* is a machine that reflects light from any type of opaque material, including pictures, tables, book illustrations, diagrams, printed material, and even some actual objects, by an arrangement of mirrors upon a screen. The original material is undamaged, colors reproduce well, and the machine can be used for enlarging small objects. The size of the material to be projected must be limited to 8½ by 11 or 10 by 10 inches, depending on the make of projector used. One of the key advantages of the opaque projector is that no prepara-

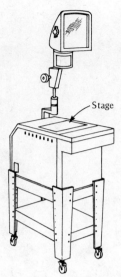

Stage

FIGURE 14-7. An overhead projector for showing large transparencies.

tion of the materials to be projected is necessary; they are projected "as is." The range of subject material that can be used thus covers the gamut of knowledge to be found on nontransparent material. A key disadvantage is that for a clear picture a well-darkened room is needed.

The *overhead projector* is increasingly popular and is found in almost every school and large business organization and in many governmental agencies. The machine is constructed so that when the image on a sheet of transparent acetate, which may be up to 10 by 12½ inches in size, is placed on an illuminated stage, the image is projected on a screen. Since the user is seated facing the audience and sees the image on the transparency exactly as it is seen on the screen by the viewers, he can point to parts of the diagram, write on it, or add to the projected image in any way, to make his meaning clear. The overhead projector has many advantages. We have mentioned the fact that the speaker faces the audience, enabling him to gauge the attention and understanding of the viewers. Although most transparencies are made in advance and can cover a wide range of subjects, the speaker can make his own visual as he speaks by writing or drawing on a piece of cellophane placed on the stage or platform of the projector. The acetate is easily cleaned with a dry cloth and may be reused.

Figure 14-7 shows a picture of a typical overhead projector, and Figure 14-8 shows its simulated use in a lecture situation.

Two other types of transparency projector should be mentioned: the *filmstrip* and the *automatic slide* projectors. Both operate on the basic principle of the overhead projector: a photograph, a

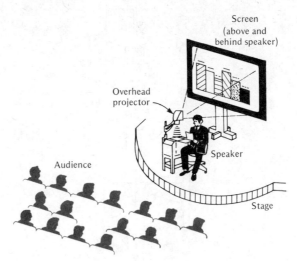

FIGURE 14-8. An overhead projector in operation. The speaker faces the audience.

drawing, or written material is placed on a transparency, and light from the machine projects the image on the screen. Both machines have similar advantages: the machines themselves as well as the filmstrips and slides are small and easy to store or carry; the rate of presentation can be controlled in both machines; depending on certain conditions, filmstrips and slides can be shown in a lighted room; both machines magnify considerably the images projected; neither machine is really difficult to operate. The modern automatic slide projectors are equipped with rotary automatic slide feeders and have control mechanisms permitting a reversal of the slide sequences besides a random selection of single slides. Remote control also is possible.

SELECTION AND CONSTRUCTION OF VISUAL AIDS

If you plan to use any type of visual as a part of a speech, you should have some familiarity with its selection and construction.

Selection

The criteria for selecting visual aids are listed in the following paragraphs.

1. The purpose for which a visual aid is to be used is the primary factor to be kept in mind. An aid should supplement the oral presentation, not supplant it. Is the aid to be used primarily to get attention, emphasize some selected aspect of a topic, show detail, give dramatic realism, develop an emotional atmosphere, show relationships

or processes, or condense a large amount of information into a relatively small pictorial or graphical representation?

2. Adaptability to the specific audience is a second criterion. Is the aid appropriate to the level of understanding and sophistication of the viewers? Will it get and hold attention, relate to their needs and attitudes, and have motivating effect? Does the visual meet any audience expectations? Has the audience been saturated with visual and audiovisual presentations? Are the aids flexible enough to meet the exigencies of varying audience situations? Will the aid be used once or on many occasions?

3. A number of technical questions relative to the audio or visual aid itself constitute a third criterion of selection. Is the aid itself of good enough technical quality to warrant its use? Is artistry important? Would a home-made aid be acceptable and adequate? Is expense a factor? Does the cost of purchase or construction warrant the expenditure in terms of potential results? Is the type of aid desired available? Will a substitute serve the purpose?

Remember that a visual aid is no aid at all unless it can be seen easily and handled effectively. This means that the size of the aid itself, the size of the lettering, and whether it gives only the needed information, must also be considered in its selection.

4. The matter of the availability and use of aids, called "software," and of the equipment, called "hardware," must also be considered. Will the aids be available when needed, whether made commercially or by the user? Is the needed projection equipment available? Can the equipment be used in the meeting room? Will you as the speaker have the opportunity to check out the equipment and practice with it before your speech? Do you have the needed expertise and confidence to use audiovisual aids effectively?

5. A final criterion for the selection of visual aids is perhaps the most important and relates to the viewer. This is the converse of the first criterion. We must ask not only whether the visual serves the purpose the speaker has in mind but whether it contributes to the viewers' needs for learning and development of motor skills or gives motivation to attitudinal and behavorial changes. That is, does the use of visuals contribute to the respondent's reasons for participating in the communicative situation?

Construction

If you can get commercially made visuals or have them made by your college audiovisual department, do so. If you make your own visuals, keep these suggestions in mind:

1. Make your visuals as neat as possible; avoid sloppy work.

Make straight lines with a ruler; make corners sharp and clean; use a compass or template for curved lines. Use a typewriter for letters and numbers, when possible. If the letters are hand drawn, make them all the same size.

2. Make lettering large enough for visibility. The following scale will ensure the visibility of nonprojectional aids:

Sight distance	Height of letters	Width of letters
15 feet	1/2 to 5/8 inch	3/32 inch
25 feet	3/4 to 1 inch	1/8 inch
50 feet	2 inches	3/16 inch
75 feet	3 inches	1/4 inch
100 feet	4 inches	5/16 inch

3. Use appropriate techniques for emphasis. The following techniques are valuable: vary the size of the letters and numbers; use indentation and capital letters to show relative importance of ideas; number the points to indicate priority; use underscoring, arrows, or boxing.

4. Limit the amount of content. Do not put more content on your visual than can be perceived at a single glance. You make an exception when you use special techniques to show parts of the content in sequence.

5. Try to make your visuals attractive and attention-getting. Colors can be used for contrast, variety, and visibility. Positioning of the material on the aid is important.

6. Finally, as in the selection of visuals, construct them so that they supplement, not replace, the oral part of your message.

KINDS OF AUDIO AID

The types of audio aid a speaker might frequently use are reproductions, including recorded sound, tapes and recordings, and *actual objects*, such as different kinds of musical instruments. Such aids may be employed only for a limited range of subjects and uses. Some indication of speech topics that have been made more effective by the use of audio aids is seen in the following list of titles of speeches given by college students:

The Music of Some American Birds
Making Sound Effects in the Movies
Learning to Play the Alto-Saxophone
The Sounds of Night Animals
The Importance of the Voice in Communication
Voice Samples of Speech Disorders

Some Home-Made Musical Instruments
Cultural Differences in Musical Preferences
Vocal Skills of the Professional Actor: Burton and Laughton

EFFECTIVE USE OF AUDIOVISUAL AIDS

The best audiovisual aids add nothing to a speech unless they are properly used. The following practical suggestions should serve as a summary to this chapter.

Points to Keep in Mind

The most important requirement of any audio or visual aid is that it serve the specific purpose for which it is intended. Audiovisual aids serve many purposes. For example, they get attention, show detail, show relationships, increase understanding, heighten emotional involvement, maintain interest, enlarge or broaden experience, and summarize. No one audiovisual aid can accomplish all these things. The specific aid selected must be adapted to the purpose intended. If an aid is to focus on a single concept or part of an object, it is unlikely that a wealth of detail should be shown. In fact, showing detail would detract from the intent of the speaker.

Each point that needs an aid must be recognized in advance. Each aid must be an integral part of the talk, giving needed support rather than merely serving as a means of livening the talk. Always plan the message—its *overall goal*—first, then the details, and then decide whether an audiovisual aid or technique will make the message clearer. The aid should be functional rather than decorative.

Keep your *audience* in mind, as you decide whether or not to use audiovisual aids. Different audiences require different aids and techniques. Knowledge about the subject, age level, background experience, including cultural differences, sex, needs, and values, and readiness to learn or act—these are a few of the audience factors to be considered.

Finally, give some advance consideration to the *facilities*, including the aids themselves, the equipment, and the meeting room. Be sure in advance that everything needed can be made available and will be in working order.

Selection and Practice Before Speaking

Once you have decided that audiovisual aids are needed—have done your general planning—you are ready to plan for—select or construct—the actual aids and to practice their use. Keep the following suggestions in mind:

1. Use visuals that are simple, direct, and accurate.

2. Vary the type of aids used.
3. Limit the number of aids used; frequently words alone carry the message.
4. All visuals, except drawings made during the speech, should be prepared in advance.
5. In advance of showing an aid tell the audience its importance, how it is related to what you have just said, and where to look on the visual. Focus the attention of the audience!
6. Know how much time you need for showing each aid, and be sure to allow for this time in the overall time schedule of the speech.
7. Know exactly the place in the speech at which each aid will be shown.
8. If an assistant is needed to help you show an aid properly, arrange for this help before starting to speak.
9. If several aids are to be shown, arrange them in proper sequence for showing. Do not show more than one at a time, unless they are aids you already have talked about.
10. If you intend to provide hand-out materials, be sure their distribution does not interfere with your presentation.
11. Be sure that the various auxiliary aids you will need, such as pointer, chalk, eraser, masking tape, or newsprint, are on the platform before you start to speak.
12. Plan the specific place on the platform where you will stand when showing an aid.
13. Plan the manner in which you will lay aside or cover the aids after they have been used.
14. Plan the manner in which you will collect any aids distributed to the audience after the speech.
15. If simple diagrams are to be placed on the blackboard, practice making them before the time of your speech.
16. Practice handling all aids before giving the speech.
17. If assistants are to help in your presentation, be sure they are instructed properly.

Handling the Aids

You have done your best in planning, selecting, or constructing the aids you wish to use and have practiced with them before giving your speech. Now comes the moment that you face your audience and will be using the aids. You should keep in mind a number of do's and don'ts at this time. The most important are the following:

1. When making a freehand drawing, make the letters and

numbers large enough to be seen from all parts of the room.

2. The viewing angle for an aid should be such that all members of the audience can see it with ease.
3. All labels and written material should be short and simple.
4. Visual aids should not be shown in the glare of a light.
5. Keep your visual aids close to the speaker's stand. If possible, avoid walking a great distance to and from a blackboard.
6. When attention is called to a visual aid, the aid always should be shown.
7. When drawings are placed on a blackboard during a speech, too many should not be put on the board at any one time.
8. Never talk facing the blackboard for an excessive amount of time. Maintain as much direct contact with the audience as possible while putting a drawing on the board.
9. In using maps or graphic aids always use a pointer to indicate details referred to.
10. Never reach across your body to point to items. Hold the pointer in the hand that is closer to the visual aid.
11. Always give the audience sufficient time in which to grasp the content of the aid.
12. After a visual aid has been shown, the content should be summarized, to emphasize the important points.
13. All visual aids should be put away, covered, or erased after showing.
14. Avoid possible distractions when using audio and visual aids. Remove all but needed materials and equipment from the speaking area before the presentation.
15. Never forget that you are the chief instrument of communication, and allow the exhibit to become the center of interest.

EXERCISES

1. Plan to give a three-minute talk in which you comment on the values of visual aids.
2. Plan to give a four-minute talk in which you use at least two different types of visual aid.
3. Observe the use of visual aids by teachers in your various classes (especially geology, astronomy, biology, economics, and engineering). Make a note of the ways in which they are used effectively or ineffectively. Be prepared to comment on your findings in class.
4. List six or eight types of subject matter that lend themselves to the use of visual aids. List some topics that could not be effectively presented visually.

5. List a number of types of subject matter that lend themselves to the use of audio aids. Make a note of the ways in which they could be used effectively or ineffectively. Be prepared to comment on your findings in class.

6. Bring to class two different types of three-dimensional visual aids, and tell how they might be used in a speech. Explain the problems you might encounter in their use.

7. Choose some subject that can best be developed by using an actual object. Prepare a five-minute speech on the subject.

8. Plan to give a five-minute speech in which you make use of any of the following types of equipment: a slide projector, an overhead projector, a recording of a speech by some public leader, an actual musical instrument, a flannel board, and a flipchart.

9. From any one of the following general areas select a topic for a four-minute informative talk. Plan to use a map or maps in your presentation.
   a. Nationwide Weather Conditions
   b. Seeing the United States First
   c. Hot Spots on College Campuses
   d. The Trail of the Mayans
   e. America's Push to the West
   f. The Shift of Population in the United States

10. Plan to give a talk on some campus-related topic. Construct a circle graph to use in connection with your talk.

11. Give a five-minute informative talk on some mechanical device. Use a visual aid in connection with the speech.

12. Select two topics that you could develop by each of these visual aids: cutaway, mockup, circle graph, actual object, map, and photograph. Comment in class on why a given visual aid is suited to your topics.

13. Plan to give a four-minute speech on any of the following topics:
   a. Line and Staff Functions in an Industrial Organization
   b. Modern Fashions for the Ladies
   c. Stages in the Passage of a Bill in Congress
   d. The Organization of the Common Market
   e. The Organization of Student Government on Your Campus
   f. What the Shortstop Does in a Ball Game
   g. Following a Candidate in the Hustings
   h. Getting the Oil from the North Slope to Valdez
   i. Changes in Dance Styles: from the Charleston to the Twist
   j. Who Sits Where and Why in a Symphony Orchestra
   k. Designs in Oriental Rugs
   l. How the Human Ear Operates
   m. Percussion Instruments' Differences in Africa, Asia, and America

14. Observe the audiovisual aids used in various types of television programs and commercials. Comment on the implications of their use in the light of the principles presented in this chapter.

ADDITIONAL READINGS

Brown, James W., Richard B. Lewis, and Fred F. Harcleroad, *AV Instruction Media and Methods*, 3rd ed., New York, McGraw-Hill, 1969.

Bryant, Donald C., and Karl R. Wallace, *Fundamentals of Speaking*, 4th ed., New York, Appleton-Century-Crofts, 1969, chap. 8.

Dale, Edgar, *Audio Visual Methods in Teaching*, 3rd ed., New York, Dryden Press, 1964.

Dietrich, John E., and Keith Brooks, *Practical Speaking for the Technical Man*, Englewood Cliffs, N.J., Prentice-Hall, 1958, chap. 7.

Eboch, Sidney C., and George W. Cochern, *Operating Audio-Visual Equipment*, 2d ed., San Francisco, Chandler, 1968.

Gerlach, Vernon S., and Donald P. Ely, *Teaching and Media: A Systematic Approach*, Englewood Cliffs, N.J., Prentice-Hall, 1971.

Haas, Kenneth B., and Harry Q. Packer, *Preparation and Use of Visual Aids*, Englewood Cliffs, N.J., Prentice-Hall, 1950, chaps. 5, 6, 7, 8, 10.

Hance, Kenneth G., David C. Ralph, and Milton J. Wiksell, *Principles of Speaking*, 2d ed., Belmont, Calif., Wadsworth, 1969, chap. 13.

Kinder, James S., and F. Dean McCluskey, *The Audio-Visual Reader*, Dubuque, Ia., Brown, 1954, chaps. 1, 2.

Ruesch, Jurgen, and Weldon Kees, *Nonverbal Communication*, Berkeley, Calif., Univ. California Press, 1956, chaps. 9, 10.

Weaver, Carl H., *Speaking in Public*, New York, American Book, 1966, chap. 18.

Wittich, Walter A., and Charles F. Schuller, *Audio-Visual Materials, Their Nature and Use*, 4th ed., New York, Harper & Row, 1967.

NOTES

[1] Edgar Dale, *Audiovisual Methods in Teaching*, 3rd ed., New York, Dryden Press, 1969, pp. 13–14.

[2] For an explanation of PERT-based small-group discussion see Gerald M. Phillips, *Communication and the Small Group*, Indianapolis, Bobbs-Merrill, 1966.

[3] Arno Wittich and Charles Francis Schuller, *Audiovisual Materials: Nature and Use*, 4th ed., New York, Harper & Row, 1967, p. 141.

[4] *Ibid.*, p. 136.

[5] *Ibid.*, p. 154.

[6] Adapted from material in Martin P. Andersen and Daniel R. De Chaine, *Visual Aids Handbook: Planning, Production, Presentation*, Santa Monica, Calif., System Development Corporation, 1966, pp. 51–54.

PARTICIPATING IN THE COMMUNICATIVE SITUATION

Communication cannot exist in a vacuum. Neither can it exist when only one party is involved. For communication to take place, whether it be verbal or nonverbal, there must be a communicator and at least one respondent—some human system that receives the message being communicated, interprets that message on the basis of the respondent's own perceptions, and responds or reacts in some overt or covert manner to the message so received and so interpreted. This respondent or group of respondents has long been referred to as the audience.

The material in Part One of this book applied to all types of human communication and to all types and sizes of audience. The principles set forth in those chapters are universally applicable to communication with one respondent, a few respondents, or many respondents.

Part Two dealt with special considerations associated with preparing for the communicative situation. Although many of the concepts treated in those chapters apply equally to all types and sizes of audience (such as analysis of audiences and occasions, reasoning, and the physical aspect of verbal and nonverbal communication), some of the material is expressly applicable to the public speaking situation. Material primarily concerning this type of speech communication, then, would not be directly applicable in the situations found in the interview or the small-group discussion.

Part Three of this book therefore considers concepts and suggestions applying specifically to situations in which there is a constant interchange of ideas, where the roles of communicator and respondent frequently change—in short, the communicative situation involving the interview and the small-group discussion.

CHAPTER FIFTEEN

COMMUNICATING IN THE INTERVIEW

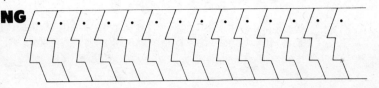

*It takes two to speak truth—
one to speak and another to
hear.*
       Thoreau

*Two heads are better than
one.*
       Heywood

Up to this point we have considered the theoretical bases and elements for understanding and preparing for the communicative situation. We shall now turn to helping the communicator apply the principles previously established to two kinds of speaking situations in which adults frequently participate. In this chapter we shall consider face-to-face communication involving two persons and, in Chapter Sixteen, communication in small groups.

Effective communication is always two-way communication. Perhaps nowhere is this more obvious than in the interview.

THE INTERVIEW IN TODAY'S SOCIETY
The number of interview situations is legion. In some fields interviewing is a major professional technique. Opinion pollsters keep us abreast of what the nation is thinking by reporting to the press the results of their interviews. Personnel workers in business and industry carry on a continuous round of interviewing new or potential employees or those with problems or grievances. Research workers use the interview as a technique for gathering data. Psychologists and psychiatrists, social caseworkers, employment-agency personnel, doctors, lawyers, clergymen, teachers, salesmen, journalists, and criminal investigators use the interview daily as a major tool of their professions.

The average individual interviews or is interviewed frequently, for various purposes. Much of the time spent in the doctor's office takes the form of an interview; the doctor seeks information that will enable him to make a diagnosis, and you as patient seek information you feel you need. You can hardly seek a position without having a job-application interview. Workers request interviews with their superiors to secure information, resolve an issue, or present a grievance. Students interview teachers to secure help on a project or even on how to study. Farmers interview county Agricultural Extension Agents to get help on specific farm problems. Representatives of management interview factory workers to secure information about worker attitudes. College graduate students often use the interview technique in gathering research data for theses and dissertations. Frequently an important decision or action you must make depends on the result of interviews.

Although much of the interviewing in which we participate is in connection with our work, a large part of each day is spent in interviewing in other situations. We interview our doctor, lawyer, and banker. We engage in interviews with the insurance salesman, the butcher, and the mechanic working on our car. Many of these conversations are, in fact, interviews, for the purpose of giving out information, seeking information, solving problems, or inducing some sort of change.

Interviews are not necessarily conducted with the participants seated face to face across a desk. They may be conducted almost anywhere and in almost any situation. Although we shall consider interviews in this chapter as face-to-face encounters, we recognize that many occur on the telephone and over the intercom.

Although the interview is used in many walks of life, the situations in which it is used are basically of three types: when the specific goal is to secure or give information, when it is to induce change, and when it is to solve problems. Many times, of course, these aims overlap. Typical of the first type of interview are those conducted by reporters, law-enforcement officers, census takers, persons engaged in marketing and consumer research, and insurance investigators. The second type occurs when supervision, social investigation, sales, certain forms of therapy, or changes in cultural mores are involved. Problem-solving interviews include consulting, counseling, and correction situations, among others.

Because all interview situations are purposeful, success is most likely when both parties are skilled in the techniques involved. An interview is more than a mere conversation, as we shall see later; it involves techniques to be learned. Keith Davis says,[1] "It is one of the most difficult communication acts because of the close personal relationship it develops. Interviewing skill does not come naturally. It requires training and experience plus a genuine desire to communicate with others." There is, however, no fixed formula for all interviewing situations, since any two people involved will not have the same backgrounds and personalities. There are, however, some basic principles that must be understood before one can become skilled in inter-viewing techniques. It is the aim of this chapter to treat these funda-mental principles and provide suggestions of their application in various interviewing situations. First, however, let us take an analytical look at the speech-communication act we are considering.

CHARACTERISTICS OF THE INTERVIEW

Interview has often been defined as *a planned conversation.* Although we cannot disagree with the fact that an interview is planned and that it involves conversation, there are other characteristics that should be considered. For our purposes let us define an interview as *a prear-ranged, face-to-face conversation between two people, the purpose and content area of which is known by at least one of the participants.*

Conversation

An interview is a conversation between two people; it involves both speaking and listening on the part of both. A substantial part of most interviews is questions and answers, although, as we shall see later, the interviewer who approaches the situation with the philosophy that it is merely a question-answer session will realize that important relevant information may not come out of the meeting. It is, rather, a conversa-tion:[2]

... *a "constant two-way interaction that must take place between the parties. ... If one person does all—or almost all—of the talking, and the other person does all—or almost all—of the listening, what is probably taking place is not an interview at all, but a public speech to an audi-ence of one. The "high-pressure" salesman who rattles off a memorized "pitch" to the captive housewife at the door is not really engaging in an interview, but in a public speech.*

Despite the fact that an interview is a conversation, it is some-what more formal than the casual, unplanned conversation. A look at some of the other characteristics considered later will suggest the differences between such a conversation and an interview.

The Two Persons

Although "group" interviewing procedures are sometimes used in such situations as therapy sessions and employee selection, they are of a highly specialized nature. Only the two-person interview will be con-sidered here. The two parties are usually called the *interviewer* and the *respondent,* or *interviewee.* The term *respondent* is used here because it implies that the second party to the interview is also active in the exchange, being influenced by, and in turn influencing, the interviewer. An interview actually is a continuous chain of stimuli and responses which, if effective, establishes a communicative partnership.

In modern broadcasting the televised interview has become commonplace. Here there is often a studio audience, but the listeners are merely eavesdropppers and seldom have an effect on the interview. The flow of communication depends upon the situation giving rise to the interview, its content, and the manner of speaking, and these three factors relate to the interviewer and respondent only.

The interviewer usually is the one who has initiated and arranged for the interview. He is aware of the purpose of the interview and usually plans its structure. He is generally the one who opens the interview, terminates it, and asks most of the questions. The respondent may or may not be aware of the specific purpose. He usually spends more time during the interview answering questions than asking them. He usually has not structured the interview but follows the lead of the interviewer. These roles, however, may change during the course of the meeting. Even in an employment-application interview, which has been structured by the representative of the employer who is seeking information concerning the qualifications and personality of the applicant, the role may be reversed when the applicant seeks information concerning the organization, wages, vacations, and other matters.

Purpose

One of the distinguishing differences between casual conversation and the interview is that the latter is purposeful. The three general goals, as suggested earlier, are to seek or give information, to induce change, and to solve problems. These aims often overlap, and any one interview may well be planned to satisfy all three of these goals. However, each interview usually has one of these as the ultimate purpose, usually determined by the interviewer. The respondent may or may not be aware of the specific purpose of the interview in advance. We shall consider the three general goals at greater length later in this chapter.

Arrangement and Planning

Unlike the casual conversation, an interview is prearranged, and its basic structure is carefully planned by at least one of the participants. In speaking of planning we do not mean preparing a script to be followed. Although the interview cannot and should not be rigidly planned in advance, certain aspects of it should be carefully thought out ahead of time by at least one of the parties. The interviewer probably will consider the best way to open the interview, the areas to be covered in the interview, the materials necessary to be on hand during the interview, and even possible ways of terminating the interview.

Although there should be advance planning for a successful interview, there must be a great amount of flexibility. Under no circumstances should the interview be considered simply a mechanical process in which questions are asked and answers given. At times the respondent may withhold information or give incomplete or incorrect information; sometimes he is not even aware that he has the desired information. He may reply as he thinks the interviewer wants him to, even if his answer does not represent his true opinion. An interviewer may have planned the questions he feels he must ask, and the sequence for them, before the interview takes place. However, a segment of one of the remarks by the respondent might call his attention to a facet of the content of which he was totally unaware. If he rigidly follows his initial plan, this important information will never be pursued. To all of these situations the interviewer must make some adjustments, and he can seldom foresee them. He must be flexible; he must adapt to any changes in the situation; he must be alert to bits of information dropped either intentionally or unintentionally by the respondent. Yet without an initial plan the interview is likely to get "off the track," to wander aimlessly, resulting in a waste of valuable time and the failure to fulfill the specific purpose of the interview.

The best time to decide on the limitations of the content area is before the interview takes place. Thought should be given to which facets of the area are necessary to pursue and which should be eliminated. By advance planning the interview will be more likely to stay within the boundaries that will result in accomplishment of the purpose in the minimal amount of time.

Even though the purpose of the interview may not be known to the respondent in advance, the time and the place of the interview should be mutually arranged. Careful planning of time and place can make the difference between a successful and an unsuccessful interview. We shall discuss more fully some principles concerning time and place later in this chapter.

Informality
Although it is more formal than the casual conversation, the informality of the usual interview is in striking contrast to the formal procedures of most public-speech situations. Comfortable physical surroundings, a friendly relationship between interviewer and respondent, and lack of tension usually characterize the interview, if both parties are cooperating to make it a success. Note, however, that informality should never extend to casualness in dress, indifference to social courtesies, or careless language. Furthermore, all interviews are expected to follow certain ground rules, such as adhering to predetermined time limits, following some semblance of order, staying within agreed-upon

content boundaries, and respecting the nature of possible confidential remarks.

Verbal and Nonverbal Communication

As in all speaking situations, a good deal of nonverbal communication goes on in the interview and should not be ignored.

Since two parties to an interview usually sit face to face and quite close together, both will be more affected by nonverbal communicative clues than they would be in speaker-audience situations. Visual symbols are more noticeable, and their meaning is accentuated. There may even be moments when communication is completely nonverbal. Since at any given moment in an interview there is only one listener, all cues to the speaker indicating approval, understanding, friendliness, interest, or their opposites, come from that one person. However, the two parties to the interview alternate as speaker and listener. If these cues are not seen or are ignored or misinterpreted, the interview may miss its goal.

Because the exact nature and sequence of questions in an interview cannot be predetermined, some questions may, momentarily at least, create blocks to communication. Such signs as the wrinkled brow, puzzled expression, shaking of the head, sudden silences, or slight stiffening of the body, carry as important messages as the words uttered.

Other nonverbal elements in the situation can affect communication, possibly by serving as cues. An array of books, framed college diplomas, trophies, or an Elks lapel pin can sometimes tell a respondent a great deal about his partner in the interview. Holm suggests the importance of the nonverbal communication of personal appearance:[3]

Few treatments of interviewing fail to give attention to matters of dress and grooming, and certainly these items can often be vital, especially when seeking employment, when selling, or when interviewing for information. What your respondent sees conditions to a large extent his reception of what he hears, and therefore it can be important that you make a good visual impression.

In sum, the interview has the following characteristics: it is a conversation, it involves two persons, it is purposeful, it is prearranged, its basic structure is planned, it is usually informal, and it involves both verbal and nonverbal communication. Now we are ready to consider its goals, its types, and the techniques employed.

THE GOALS OF INTERVIEWS

The three general goals of interviews are to secure or give information, to create change, and to solve problems. Although these may overlap, one of them usually will be the dominant or ultimate aim. Let us consider each separately.

To Secure or Give Information

The types of interview having as the goal either getting or giving information probably come closest to being question-answer meetings, although in many successful interviews few questions are asked and answered, and there is free interchange of facts, opinions, and ideas. Employment interviews, however, are based primarily on questions and answers. In most cases the information exchanged in an interview is not an end in itself but a means to an end. The information may be used eventually to solve a problem, to formulate a new policy, to cause some change to occur, or to make a decision.

An error that interviewers frequently make is the assumption that factual or objective data are synonymous with information. Factual and objective data may be part of information, but there are other data—subjective data—that may provide information just as important, if not more so. Fact finding, then, is not necessarily the same as information getting. When interviewing an applicant for a job position, for example, a prospective employer should be as concerned with attitudes, values, feelings, aspirations, and the self-image of the applicant as with factual biographical information. Garrett considers the objective and subjective aspects of every situation as follows:[4]

A man loses his job. That is an objective fact. His feelings about this event constitute a subjective fact. A man is ill with tuberculosis. That is a medical fact. But every person who has any sort of illness has accompanying it certain feelings about the illness. There are variations in the physical aspects of tuberculosis, but there are many more variations in human reactions to that disease. So we could run the gamut of human experiences and note that every objective experience—marriage, hunger, getting a job, leaving one's children in a day nursery—has its accompanying subjective counterpart of emotional attitudes.

A mile can be measured; this is an objective fact, yet attitudes concerning this fact vary with the individual. To the teenager who wants to go to a rock festival a mile away, walking the distance might be very pleasant. To a woman who has spent all day shopping, however, walking another mile might be quite different.

Objective facts alone cannot provide all the information; even verbal expressions, supposedly revealing one's attitudes, may not provide the true information. We are reminded of Owen Wister's Virginian, who responded to an unsavory epithet, "When you call me that, smile!" Many times it is not the words that express the true meaning or give the accurate information, but the attitude behind the words. The keen observer, one who is alert to nonverbal cues, will be able to secure an abundance of information.

To Induce Change

Interviews whose ultimate goal is to induce change or bring about a specific course of action will undoubtedly involve much interchange of information. However, what information is exchanged is for the purpose of effecting some predetermined change in behavior of one or both of the participants.

The guidance counselor or probation officer may attempt through interviews to change the attitudes and, consequently, the behavior of his clients. The supervisor conducting a disciplinary interview will not only reprimand the worker but anticipate a change of behavior. In a sales interview the respondent will be persuaded to take a specific course of action. The teacher who interviews a student with low grades will hope to bring about a change in study habits.

What we said earlier concerning "reading" nonverbal cues is of prime importance in effecting change. If we hope to induce a change of attitudes, we must make every effort to identify and understand the attitudes held by the respondent. We cannot do this unless we are alert to the nonverbal cues.

To Solve Problems

The third goal to be considered is problem solving or decision making. Many types of interview fall into this category. Guidance-counseling interviews usually involve problems that must be solved. Consulting interviews are normally conducted with the aim of solving problems or making decisions. The grievance interview obviously presents a problem that calls for a solution. Correction, or disciplinary, interviews usually involve problems for which solutions are sought. Employment interviews pose a problem to be solved and a decision to be made: the selection of one of several applicants for the job vacancy.

As we have stated previously, the three goals often overlap. Furthermore, the dominant aim may change during the course of any one interview. An example might be found in the correction, or disciplinary, interview. The initial aim of such an interview is to secure information concerning the situation the supervisor feels needs correcting. Perhaps information that is forthcoming will present data that indicate no discipline or correction is necessary. It becomes, then, only an information-gathering interview. If, however, after the information is secured, the supervisor feels that some change of attitude is called for, the major goal of the interview at this point is to induce that change.

The specific aim may later shift to problem solving: which of several alternate courses should the modified behavior take.

The problem-solving interview or the problem-solving phase of an interview presupposes that the participants enter the interacting situation with an open mind to the problem, seeking a mutually beneficial solution. Holm states in this connection:[5]

Unlike either of the other two purposes, problem solving is creative in the sense that the outcome develops from the interaction of the two participants in a way which neither had specifically foreseen nor planned. When other purposes govern, one or both of those involved is hoping for a specific predicted outcome, whereas problem solving requires neither to be committed before the conversation begins. . . . When an interview is problem solving, each must be open enough to strive for a mutually satisfying conclusion. . . . Many problem solving interviews are organized on the basis of the reflective-thought sequence. . . . They are, in effect, conferences involving two people only, usually structured by the interviewer in the conventional pattern of creative thinking.

TYPES OF INTERVIEW

In the preceding sections of this chapter many types of interviews have been mentioned. At this point let us consider a few of these types and how they differ from each other.

Employment Interview

When a student thinks of an interview, perhaps the first type that comes to mind is the employment-application interview. No doubt many of you have already engaged in several interviews of this type, for it is an almost universally used technique in the selection of personnel by employers, whether the job is that of a box-boy in a super market, a teller in a bank, or an executive of a corporation. In a recent publication of the American Management Association we are told:[6]

Without exception, interviewing is the one technique universally used to help make decisions about job applicants and promotees. Even when interviewing is practiced in conjunction with other screening methods, it emerges as the most critical, pivotal, and potentially powerful technique.

The important place employment interviews hold in modern business and industry has not changed significantly in recent decades. Nearly twenty years earlier than the date of the quotation just cited, a professor of industrial psychology had this to say:[7]

The interview occupies a major position in the employment procedure of nearly all industrial concerns. More than any other selection device, interviews are relied upon for hiring decisions. These interviews vary from a short, cursory conversation to an exhaustive analysis of the applicant's qualifications. Regardless of the nature and extent of the procedure, few applicants are hired in American industry without an interview.

In the employment interview the burden of persuasion is usually placed upon the applicant. Since this is the case, the applicant must make every effort to influence the prospective employer in his behalf. One of the most important considerations is appearance. The applicant should be neatly and conservatively dressed and well groomed. He should present himself as favorably as he can; he is the one who must do the persuading, and a great part of his persuasion will result from his personal appearance and behavior during the interview. Remember the old saying: "Your actions speak so loudly I can't hear what you are saying."

The applicant who is serious about getting a job will learn as much as possible about the firm and the job before going to the interview. By so doing he can respond much more intelligently in the light of his qualifications for the job, and he can ask more relevant questions concerning the job and the company.

The interviewer in an employment-interview situation has certain specific responsibilities. He must know as much about the applicant and the job to be filled as time and feasibility permit before the interview begins. One of the most common sources of background information concerning an applicant is his completed application form. The interviewer should read this carefully, taking notes on areas he would like to pursue further during the interview. The interviewer should not ask questions that are already answered on the application form; such a practice, although it is often done, provides little or no new information and turns the interview into an examination period testing the applicant's memory of what he has previously written. The interviewer, if he really wants to learn as much as he can about the applicant during the interview session, will be neither patronizing nor domineering. The interviewer must be truthful about the job and the company and should give no false impressions of his appraisal of the applicant. A final decision concerning the applicant is, of course, not necessarily revealed to the respondent at the close of the interview. However, do not mislead him or give him false hopes if, in fact, there is no hope of his getting the job at all.

Appraisal Interview

The appraisal interview, or performance-review interview, is widely used in business and industry today. Employment selection is not infallible and occasionally results in the hiring of persons who are not equipped with the technical skills or mental attitudes and motivations to do a job well. Successful executives are forever concerned with improvement within their organizations. By frequent reviews of the performances of their employees, managers hope to achieve improvement. One industrial communication expert suggests the objectives of this type of interview:[8]

At the present time management supervisors conduct appraisal interviews with subordinates to (a) let them know where they stand; (b) recognize their good work; (c) communicate to them the directions in which they should improve; (d) develop them on their present jobs; (e) develop and train them for higher jobs; (f) let them know the direction in which they may make progress in the company; (g) serve as a record for assessment of the department or unit as a whole and show where each person fits into the larger picture; and (h) warn certain employees that they must improve.

Appraisal interviews are usually conducted on a scheduled basis, such as every six months or once a year. Normally the immediate supervisor will initiate and conduct the interviews, although some firms place this responsibility upon a staff member farther up the organization chart. Appraisal interviews should not be equated with correction, or disciplinary, interviews. In the appraisal interview the overall job and the employee's relation to it are investigated, whereas in disciplinary interviews some specific incident or series of incidents that calls for correction is considered.

Correction Interview

Although the terms *disciplinary interview* and *reprimand interview* have long been used to describe a type of face-to-face situation, we agree with Holm, who states:[9]

. . . "correction" suggests a more positive approach. It suggests that the purpose should not be merely to discourage undesirable behavior, but to encourage the substitution of desirable behavior.

When work is improperly or poorly done, when directions or instructions are not followed, when normal protocol is overlooked, when employees waste time or are chronically tardy or absent, or when they do not comply with necessary regulations, a correction interview is called for. It should be an occasion for an objective evaluation of the error or problem and a search for a remedy, in preference to an accusation or an indictment of the offending person.

Interviews of almost every type should be conducted in a place that is free from distractions and where full attention of each of the parties can be given. A cardinal principle for the correction interview especially is that it be conducted in private, where others cannot see or hear.

A major obstacle to the successful interview, and especially the correction interview, is the bias of the interviewer. He must be exceedingly careful to examine and acknowledge his own prejudices and biases so as to minimize the likelihood of their "getting in the way" of his objectivity. He must accept the respondent's attitudes and feelings, although the behavior, which may be an expression of these attitudes and feelings, perhaps cannot be condoned. To "accept" attitudes and feelings merely means that the interviewer realizes that the respondent possesses them. Only when the interviewer can understand the attitudes and feelings that give rise to the behavior that needs correcting can he be objective in his judgments.

The good interviewer will seek information from the respondent regarding the problem, encouraging him to talk about it himself rather than bombarding him with "facts" and "proof." Frequently, when an offender tells his own version of the offense, he begins to discover that he was in the wrong and may even offer suggestions for correction. This permits him an opportunity to save face. A person generally will be more likely to change his attitudes and behavioral patterns when he arrives at the consciousness of the need to change by himself than when lectured to by someone else. This does not always occur, but no harm can be done in giving this technique a fair trial.

Corrective action is more likely to be accepted by the offender if the interview can be focused upon the act rather than upon the person. Statements that tend to induce resentment or put the respondent on the defensive immediately should be avoided. The ultimate goal should be to reach a mutually satisfying solution to the problem.

Counseling Interview

The counseling interview usually is one that investigates some personal problem of the respondent with a view to arriving at a solution that will overcome the problem. Social workers, lawyers, clergymen, marriage counselors, industrial psychologists, and teachers are among those who normally conduct interviews of this type.

Much that we have said concerning the correction interview is applicable here. Objectivity is of paramount importance, and judgments should be made only after the interviewer has a complete understanding of the situation. Again, if the solution to the problem can be brought out from the respondent himself, the solution probably will be more satisfying and acceptable to him.

Exit Interview

Employees quit jobs for a great number of reasons. The alert manager wants to discover whether these reasons might have been avoidable and could be corrected in the future. He wants to know whether a misunderstanding, an unfortunate circumstance over which the company had no control, or a policy or operation of the firm might have caused the employee to quit. To discover possible problems an increasing number of firms in American industry conduct exit interviews with employees who voluntarily terminate their jobs. One purpose is to attempt to discover the real reason the person is quitting and to get from him any suggestions he might have for improvement in company policy, company benefits, job responsibilities, working conditions, salary, and so forth. Another purpose might be to sustain a favorable image of the company in the eyes of an employee who is about to leave.

Many departing employees are reluctant to give the real reasons for their leaving or to discuss their job or the company. The respondent must be made to realize that he is not being reprimanded or "put on the spot." Rather, he should be made to feel that he is an important member of the firm and one who can benefit the organization. It takes a skillful interviewer, however, to conduct a valuable exit interview with many departing employees.

The time for the exit interview is important. Obviously, it should be near the end of the employment period, but not on the final day, if that can be avoided; on the day the employee is leaving his mind is likely to be too full of other matters to be particularly helpful. Infrequently, if ever, are fired employees interviewed, although on occasion employees who have been dismissed through no fault of the company (due to loss of government contracts, for example) are asked to participate in an exit interview.

Other Interviews

The other types of interview will be treated only briefly here.

The sales interview is for the purpose of bringing about some specific action on the part of the respondent. The sales interview must not be considered one that merely sells a tangible product: it may "sell" an idea or concept or policy, or it may be for the purpose of changing the respondent's attitude toward an organization or person. The principles of persuasion discussed throughout this book apply to the sales interview.

The grievance interview is termed by Holm[10] "a correction interview in reverse, with the subordinate seeking improved conditions or behavior rather than the superior." Many of the principles discussed in connection with the correction interview apply, except that the role of the interviewer usually is the subordinate or the union representative in a business organization. The student who goes to a professor's office with a complaint will find himself in the role of the interviewer in a grievance interview.

Information-gathering interviews are common and range from very casual talks to formal interview situations. The student who needs information to complete a term-paper assignment may interview the student-body president, a business executive, or a politician. Market analysts and pollsters are in business to gather information and do so by means of the interview. Doctors, lawyers, and clergymen often are involved in this type of interview.

Other types of interview are consulting interviews, for exchanging information and ideas or solving problems, and induction interviews, for assisting in the orientation of newly hired employees. These types involve principles previously established.

PREPARATION FOR THE INTERVIEW

Success in an interview is seldom the result of chance. Although many interviewers unfortunately enter the interview situation with little or no planning, the most successful interviews are those for which preparation has been made. The interviewer should determine his objective, analyze the situation, plan the organization and content, and provide the proper physical setting.

Objective

The specific objective of any interview will be (1) to secure or give information, (2) to induce change or cause some action to take place, or (3) to solve problems or make decisions. Do you want to get all the information possible from this respondent in this area? Do you want the respondent to see the situation in a new light? Do you want to have both of you arrive at a mutually acceptable solution to a problem? Do you want your respondent to vote for your candidate? Do you want him to accept your plan for reorganization? You must determine in advance the anticipated outcome of the interview.

We mentioned previously that an interview must be flexible. You must be prepared for an occasional change of objective. For instance, you may set out only to gather information but then discover from the information gathered that there is a problem you had not anticipated; now your objective shifts to finding a solution to the problem.

Whether you are interviewer or respondent, determine in advance what you hope to achieve from the interview.

Analysis

Analyzing the situation in preparation for an interview cannot be stressed too strongly. Too many times interviews are arranged on the spur of the moment or are entered into without sufficient knowledge of the situation. Know as much as possible about the other participant in the interview. This applies equally to interviewer and respondent. In an employment interview the interviewer should know something about the applicant or at least what information he can gather from the application form. David Phillips states:[11]

The interviewee also should do some advance planning whenever possible. In many interviews it is quite probable that certain questions will be asked or certain areas covered. In an employment interview, for instance, the interviewer will be interested in the applicant's education, experience, and personality traits as they apply to the position under consideration. The candidate should therefore consider his qualifications in light of the position desired and be prepared to answer questions of this nature. This preparation should result in more complete and precise answers that will make for a more effective interview. If an employee of a company is being interviewed about a certain suggestion he has made for a change in production methods, he should have his reasons and support clearly in mind in an organized fashion so that the information and arguments he presents will be clear and effective. The uncertainty as to the questions and procedures to be followed in an interview does not mean that the interviewee cannot and should not prepare. Any advance thinking and planning he may do will usually pay off in better answers and better questions on his part.

General preparation is possible. Each party should secure as much pertinent background information as possible in advance of the interview. By their doing so, much time during the interview can be saved and the advance planning of the structure of the interview can be more efficiently accomplished.

Structure

Although one of the characteristics of an interview is that it is flexible, the general organization should be planned in advance. In a previous section of this chapter we suggested that the limitations and boundaries of the content area be considered before the interview takes place. The interviewer should ask himself such questions as these: What is the scope of the content area? What are the essential aspects that must be treated in the interview? What are the areas that are not important and therefore should be eliminated? How much in depth is it necessary to go? If these questions are considered in advance, the interview will be more likely to achieve its specific goal in a minimum of time.

The next step in planning the structure of the interview is deciding on the sequence of the important points to be covered. There is usually some logical order in which material should be considered.

However, the interviewer must remember that there should always be room for flexibility. But the interviewer who gives careful consideration to the sequence of the areas to be covered will usually discover that the interview will naturally flow fairly well in this same sequence.

It is usually unwise to write out *all* the questions that you might feel obliged to ask during the interview. Such a practice tends to make the interview inflexible, to lessen the rapport that might otherwise be established between the participants, and to reduce the need of listening carefully on the part of the interviewer. Nevertheless, a few key questions concerning major areas to be covered will prove helpful.

When the object of an interview is to induce change, the content and sequence of the questions are especially important. Let us assume that a supervisor has to ask an employee to change certain on-the-job behavior. It may first be necessary to determine whether the employee actually knows what the acceptable behavior is; this can be established through questioning. Next, the supervisor needs to determine whether the employee is aware of his own incorrect behavior. Then he must be made to see the need for change. Finally, the supervisor must get from the employee a commitment to initiate the desired change. It is true that a stern rebuke and a gruff order might accomplish the desired change in less time, but desirable employee relations with management would probably suffer.

The interviewer must be prepared to reword any questions to suit the atmosphere of the interview, the interests of the respondent, and any information previously obtained during the meeting. A detailed discussion concerning the wording and selection of questions will be found later in this chapter.

After specific objectives are determined, the situation analyzed, background material gathered, and the organization of the interview planned, it is wise to formulate an introductory statement concerning the objectives and content area. True, there will be some social amenities as the two participants meet for the interview, but too often these are prolonged because the interviewer has not planned carefully how the interview is going to progress from the greeting stage to the content-discussion stage. Getting started on the content area is probably the most difficult task, but advance planning will make the task much easier. We shall discuss specific suggestions for the opening phase of the interview in a later section of this chapter.

Proper Physical Setting

Sometimes the physical setting is beyond the control of either interviewer or respondent, but frequently it is under the control of one or the other. When a doctor interviews a patient in his own office, for example, the physical situation is controlled by the interviewer; when an opinion gatherer calls to interview a housewife in her home, the physical situation is in the control of the respondent. In either case a good deal can be done to promote rapport. The ideal situation includes comfortable chairs, an airy room, indirect lighting, absence of interfering noises or other distractions, easy access to needed records, and surroundings that put both respondent and interviewer at ease. One of the most common sins of inexperienced interviewers is placing the respondent with the light in his face, which not only makes him uncomfortable but prevents him from seeing the facial expressions of the interviewer.

Certain physical factors that apply to either party can materially affect the outcome, especially if they represent status symbols. When one party sits in a swivel chair (generally more comfortable than a straight chair), has the vantage position behind a desk, and has framed diplomas hanging conspicuously on the wall, the other party may feel at a disadvantage. This is not to say that the person in whose office the interview is taking place should be deprived of comforts or stripped of all status symbols when these are an accepted part of his work situation. However, differences in status between interviewer and respondent should not be emphasized or made conspicuous.

One successful personnel administrator makes it his custom to move away from his desk and sit at a table across from the respondent. Typical comments of respondents he has interviewed are of this nature: "I thought I'd be afraid to talk to him, but I really enjoyed it" and "I don't know why I was worried before I went in."

Other items that affect the physical setting and often can be controlled are the time of day, which is important when interviewing a person in his home, the length of the interview, and the amount of privacy. Such distractions as telephone calls or other interruptions and blaring radios or television should be avoided, if at all possible.

THE STRUCTURE AND CONTENT OF THE INTERVIEW

Some interviews are more highly structured than others, depending on the formality and specific objectives; however, all interviews have these three phases in common: an opening, a main part, or body, in which the basic content is considered, and a termination, or closing. We shall now discuss these stages separately and offer suggestions for the conduct of each.

The Opening

The introductory phase should be as brief as possible, taking no more time than is necessary to accomplish the social amenities and to introduce the content area:[12]

Depending upon prior relationships between the parties, the opening phase of an interview may be brief or its development may require some time. Old friends can get down to business at once, whereas strangers or persons between whom relations are strained may find developing productive relationships to be time consuming.

One of the first principles to be considered is that of establishing rapport between the two participants. An overextended period of social amenities, however, may do just the opposite: it may create additional tensions. If an employee has been called in to the supervisor's office, he may have apprehensions concerning the reason for his summons. With each moment that the supervisor inquires about the employee's golf game, the health of his wife, and the success of his son in college, apprehensions are likely to increase. The employee is probably thinking: "It must be something pretty bad; he doesn't want to start talking about it. I wish he would tell me what's on his mind so I can begin thinking of my defense."

Establishing rapport is of utmost importance to a successful, cooperative, productive interview. Sincerity on the part of both participants is the best ingredient. Almost universally interviewers are admonished to put the respondent at ease. We agree wholeheartedly with this principle. However, we also agree with Balinsky and Burger, who believe that such an admonition has often been as harmful as it has been helpful.[13] When the interviewer works so hard to accomplish this purpose that his techniques are obvious and his insincerity shows, more tensions will be created than reduced, and the desired rapport will not be established. Be sincere, be yourself, whether you are interviewer or respondent. This will help, more than will any other technique, to put both participants at ease.

The purpose and aims of the interview should be explained in the opening phase. This is the introductory statement, suggested earlier, that should be prepared carefully in advance. For the interviewer this is as important as in a speech before a large audience. Responses will not be relevant if objectives are hidden. On the other hand, caution should sometimes be observed that the objective is not stated too abruptly and quickly. The supervisor who opens an interview with the question, "Fred, why can't you keep your crew producing like Jack's?" is apt to put Fred immediately on the defensive. It may be many minutes before rapport can be established.

The opening of an interview should accomplish essentially the same purposes as the introduction in a speech. It should establish rapport between the interviewer and respondent, should gain the favorable attention and cooperation of the respondent, state the subject and objectives, and establish the interviewer's point of view.

The Body

This, of course, is the main part of the interview situation. It will be the longest phase; in many half-hour interviews this stage might well consume 27 or 28 minutes. This is the portion of the interview that attempts to accomplish the specific purpose previously determined.

The body normally consists primarily of questions being asked and responses given. Although we have designated one of the participants interviewer and the other respondent, questions may at times be asked by the respondent and answers given by the interviewer. Let us now consider some of the types of question that are found in interviews.

Direct Question

The direct question, or closed question, usually is employed for eliciting specific information or facts. It permits the respondent little or no freedom of selection in his response, since the boundaries of the response are normally implied in the question. Such questions as "When did you work for XYZ Company?" and "What was your major area in college?" are typical of the direct, or closed, question, as are most questions that call for either a "Yes" or a "No." Little information, other than specific facts or observations, can be obtained from such questions; little information concerning attitudes and values of the respondent can be gained.

Open Question

This type of question broadens the scope of the response and may reveal information or suggest areas that the interviewer had not anticipated. It asks the respondent to "talk about" something and usually elicits a longer response. The interviewer is much more likely to be able to assess attitudes and values than from the closed question. Such a question usually forces the respondent to engage in deeper thinking. Such questions as "What do you consider the most beneficial aspects of this plan?" and "What type of curriculum do you think would be most beneficial to you?" fall into this category, as do any "tell me about" questions. The interviewer must give a great deal of thought to this type of question, however, to avoid waste of time and to ensure that the interview will not go off on unnecessary and unproductive tangents. Questions that are too open and too broad in scope can defeat the purpose of the interview.

Laundry-List Question

One writer has suggested a type of question that he calls the "laundry-list question," which can be employed in connection with the open question. He explains it as follows:[14]

Applicants almost invariably find some areas more difficult to discuss than others. Confronted with a question that requires considerable analysis, they frequently "block" and find it somewhat difficult to come up with an immediate response. In such a situation, the interviewer comes to the applicant's assistance with a laundry-list type of question. As the name implies, this type of question suggests a variety of possible responses and permits the subject to take his choice. If the subject blocks on the question, "What are some of the things that a job has to have in order to give you satisfaction?", the interviewer may stimulate his thinking by such a laundry-list comment as, "You know some people are more interested in security; some are frankly more interested in money; some want to manage; some want an opportunity to create; some like a job that takes them out-of-doors a good bit of the time— what's important to you?" Given a variety of possible responses, the applicant is normally able to marshal his thinking and supply a considerable amount of information.

Yes-Response Question

Questions that suggest a point of view on the part of the interviewer and call for agreement with a "yes" answer are yes-response questions. This is the type frequently used in the sales interview and other persuasive interviews, but they yield little or no information, either objective or subjective. Such questions as "Don't you agree that you could use these books many times to good advantage?" or "You do agree that the company policy is right, don't you?" or "Wouldn't it be a better plan to write the term paper early in the semester than to wait until the night before it is due?" are examples of the yes-response question. They are dangerous in information-gathering interviews, because they evaluate the answers before they are given. Such questions may have their rightful place in sales interviews, but they should be used sparingly, if at all, in correction, appraisal, or counseling interviews. To ask, "You know what you did was wrong, don't you?" would elicit a "yes" answer if the respondent wanted to please the interviewer or quickly conclude the meeting, but it would not necessarily mean that any attitudes were changed or that the response was even true. What we said earlier concerning the benefit of allowing the respondent to come to a decision through his own mental and emotional processes is certainly applicable here.

Mirror Question

The mirror question is used often by the skilled interviewer. It uses one response as a "stepping stone" to another question, probing more deeply or asking for an explanation or expansion of a statement just made. Care should be taken not to use it too frequently; if the respondent is forced to defend or explain every statement he makes, he will become more and more reticent to respond, resulting in the suppression of much useful information. However, this type of question should be employed when something needs to be explored further, or when there is doubt about what was actually meant by the response. Furthermore, it helps in giving the interview a natural "flow" and provides more continuity to the meeting. An example of this type of question is found in this situation: After the response, "I think students should have the option of being graded on a pass/no-pass basis," the interviewer might ask this mirror question, "Do you think that this should apply to all courses, even in the major area?"

Loaded Question

The loaded question is one that is filled with emotionally charged language or concerns a "touchy" subject. "When are you long-hairs going to cut out this nonsense?" to a college fraternity member and "Why do you union people keep making unreasonable demands?" to a union member would be considered loaded questions. This type of question, which tends to reveal the interviewer's bias, will undoubtedly bring about an emotional response but will seldom provide much information; in fact, it may terminate all cooperative communication. Some interviewers use the loaded question intentionally to make the respondent angry enough to reveal his true feelings, but that is dangerous at best.

Hypothetical Question

The hypothetical question deals with a hypothetical situation, an imaginary instance. It is sometimes used to elicit sentiments, values, and aspirations of respondents. "Let us assume that you were the instructor, what would you do?" and "If you were the fraternity social chairman, how would you attempt to achieve greater participation in the social activities?" are examples of this type. When posed as hypothetical questions, they must be truly hypothetical; if you have reason to believe that a student violated a school regulation, do not use such an approach with him as "Suppose that one of the students violated a school regulation. . . ." This is not hypothetical, and it will undoubtedly be regarded as a direct accusation—"sugar-coated" but still an accusation—and any rapport you may have achieved will be lost.

Silence

Although silence in itself is not a question, it sometimes may be substituted for a question to good advantage in an interview. It might be called an *implied* question. A brief silence can indicate to the respondent that the interviewer feels there is more to be said on the subject; because he feels somewhat uneasy about the silence, the respondent will search his mind for further information in order to ease the tension. Pauses may be very beneficial to both parties of an interview, providing them with opportunities to stop and reflect upon what has been said. With practice an interviewer can learn to estimate the length of these periods of silence to allow them to be long enough to be productive but not so long that continuity is lost and rapport is reduced.

The Closing

The closing of an interview is essentially the same as the conclusion of a speech, though generally shorter. Although there is a temptation after the main body of material has been covered to let the interview lapse into nothing more than social conversation, the conclusion performs several specific functions. It may summarize the material covered, suggest areas of agreement, determine follow-up activities, settle another time for meeting, or merely evaluate the progress made. The conclusion should be brief but not abrupt. A great amount of random conversation or a complete lack of any conclusion may undermine whatever progress has been made during the interview.

The respondent should be aware of cues that indicate the interview is terminated. If either party says, "Well, I believe I have all the information I need," the next step is to utter a brief "Thank you," and rise. A suggestion concerning the time of the next session, if one is needed, the presentation of forms to be filled out at home, a statement by the interviewer as to when the respondent may expect to hear from him, a statement indicating that the planned time for the interview has elapsed, and a gracious expression of appreciation—any one of these is a cue that the interview is over. Visual cues also must be observed. If the interviewer begins to look at his watch frequently, checks his appointment calendar, pushes back his chair and rises and, certainly, if he goes to the door and opens it, the respondent should understand that the interview has ended or is about to end.

Any interview, whether the specific purpose has been achieved or not, should end on a positive note. This is stressed in the following quotation:[15]

"Where do we go from here?" is a better ending for the interview than a perfunctory close or summary of what has been covered in the course

of the consultation. Some explicit statement of implementation, some indication of further discussion in the future, or some assurance of the continued concern of management in the information sought or expressed—such communicative devices demonstrate that effective interviews seldom conclude with a period. *Successful interviews in management organizations more often conclude with a question mark or a comma or a colon. Otherwise, a feeling that everything has been said would be left with both participants, and the door to future essential interviewing on the same subject might be closed and locked.*

If there has been adequate and well-thought-out prior planning by the interviewer, he will know when the specific goal has been achieved or when the session has ceased to be productive. With practice he can learn how to make an effective, mutually satisfying, and graceful termination of the interview.

STYLE IN THE INTERVIEW
Chapter Seven dealt with style in communication. A rereading of that chapter and of the following treatment should be beneficial to the interview participant.

Verbal Communication
Since word meanings and usage differ with socioeconomic status, age, cultural background, occupation, and geographical location, a given word may have different meanings for interviewer and respondent. Therefore, use words with "shared" meanings whenever possible, define unfamiliar words, and when words have two or more meanings, indicate the one intended. Guard against words that discourage the free flow of communication because they are not in good taste, are outmoded, represent inaccuracies as seen by the other person, are mispronounced and hence misunderstood, are too general, or have negative connotations.

Shared language is the maximal language understood by both participants. The description of a pain or an illness given by a patient to his doctor would not involve the same vocabulary as that used between two doctors. Two mechanical engineers would have a larger shared vocabulary than an engineer and a stenographer. But the size of the shared vocabulary is not the major consideration in successful communication; what is necessary is that adequate sharing of *meaning* take place. A good interviewer will acquaint himself with some of the jargon that might be used by the respondent, but he will not attempt to *use* jargon himself unless he is quite familiar with it and accustomed to using it. To use jargon with which one is unfamiliar is to run the risk of appearing ridiculous and insincere. When jargon of the trade or profession is a "natural" part of the vocabularies of both participants, however, its use can aid in communication.

Bypassing presents one of the major difficulties in interviewing. One writer has offered this definition:[16] "Bypassing . . . is the name for the miscommunication pattern which occurs when the *sender* (speaker, writer, and so on) and the *receiver* (listener, reader, and so forth) *miss each other with their meanings.*" Bypassing is likely to occur when different meanings can be attributed to the word ("grass," for example) or when different words are used to express the same thing. The wise communicator will avoid bypassing by his careful selection of words that convey the meanings he intends and by listening, not merely to the words he hears used, but also to the contexts in which they are employed.

Careful attention to the wording of questions can make the difference between a successful and an unsuccessful interview. Avoid putting the respondent "on the spot." Help him to "save face" wherever possible. One writer suggests[17] that questions be "softened" by such introductory phrases as "Is it possible that," "Would you say that," "What prompted your decision to," "How did you happen to," and "Has there been any opportunity to." He also suggests[17] qualifying phrases that help to remove bluntness in questions by suggesting *degree* rather than the concept of wholly good or bad: "might," "perhaps," "to some extent," and "somewhat." The left-hand column of the list below contains a number of questions taken from actual interviews, in which the words and phrases that tend to block effective communication are italicized. The right-hand column restates these questions somewhat more acceptably. It is obvious that the revised questions would reduce the probability of putting the respondent on the defensive, thereby encouraging more cooperative communication.

1. When would I *get my first raise?*	What is the company's salary schedule?
2. Do you think your proposal action is *wise?*	How will your proposal action aid in solving the problem?
3. I cannot understand how I got such a grade. Did you *really read* my paper?	I cannot understand how I got such a grade. On what questions did I do poorly?
4. Have you given any *careful consideration* to possible solutions?	What consideration have you given to possible solutions?
5. Have you any *logical support* for your statement?	What support do you have for your statement?
6. Were you *fired* from your previous job?	Why did you leave your previous job?

7. How can I *get ahead* in   What are the opportunities for ad-
   your company?   vancement in your company?

Nonverbal Communication

Perhaps in no other communicative situation is the attention to non-verbal communication more important than in the face-to-face inter-view. We have treated this aspect of communication in Chapter 7; let us consider briefly here some of the specific types of nonverbal communi-cation of which the interview participant must be aware.

Each participant should train himself to "listen" not only to what is said, but to what is *not* said. Facial manifestations, such as frowns, shifting of the eyes, and involuntary smiles, aid the listener in assessing "real" meanings behind the words spoken. Bodily movement, too, can convey meanings. Watch for tightening and relaxation of muscles, changes in position of hands, and observable mannerisms. Animation as one speaks and listens, or the lack of it, can assist in the interpretation of attitude. Although nonverbal behavior can add meaning to a commu-nicative act, caution in interpretation must be observed. Many of the observable cues might be the result of excessive nervousness or some pressures outside the interview situation. One can, however, with train-ing and practice, learn to "listen" to nonverbal communication as an aid to better understanding of the other participant.

SUGGESTIONS FOR PARTICIPANTS

The following suggestions, which in a sense summarize this section, should aid both interviewer and respondent in creating conditions conducive to success in the interview.

For Both Participants

1. Provide comfortable and cheerful physical surroundings.
2. Try to equalize status relationships.
3. Keep distractions to a minimum.
4. Concentrate both physically and mentally on the matter at hand.
5. Look pleasant and appear interested in the other person; smile.
6. Show by your facial expression that you are reacting to what has been said; avoid nonverbal manifestations of dis-approval.
7. Speak directly to the other person.
8. Try to control nervous mannerisms.
9. Avoid too much warm-up (opening).
10. Avoid too lengthy a closing.
11. Avoid premature evaluation and judgment.

12. Identify your own prejudices, and attempt to keep them out of the interview situation.
13. Avoid arguing.
14. Analyze the situation in advance, and plan ahead.
15. Keep the purpose of the interview constantly in mind.
16. Avoid excessive note taking and excessive use of prepared notes.
17. Listen carefully and objectively.

For the Interviewer

1. Show by actions that the respondent is welcome if he has come to your office for the interview.
2. Have a tentative structure for the interview planned.
3. Do not keep looking at your watch.
4. Avoid any actions that suggest boredom, lack of interest, disbelief, or opposition.
5. Have any needed equipment, supplies, or literature readily available.
6. Ask types of question that will best achieve the objectives.
7. Be willing to understand the respondent's attitude and behavior, even though you may not approve.
8. Delay evaluation or judgment until you have all the information.
9. Wait patiently for answers; do not interrupt.
10. Your responsibility is, in the words of Balinski and Burger, to:[18]

Probe,	not cross-examine
Inquire,	not challenge
Suggest,	not demand
Uncover,	not trap
Draw out,	not pump
Guide,	not dominate

For the Respondent

1. Take cues from the interviewer on degree of formality.
2. Sit down only when asked to do so.
3. Be prepared to take notes, if it is necessary to record information.
4. Don't smoke unless invited to do so.
5. Leave promptly when the interview is over.
6. Be neat and conservative in your appearance.
7. Prepare ahead of time by anticipating questions that might be asked.

8. Answer questions honestly and completely.
9. Don't attempt to bluff; be willing to say, "I don't know."
10. Generally attempt to expand your responses beyond a simple "yes" or "no."
11. Be polite, but friendly.
12. Keep your emotions in check.
13. Be sincere—be yourself.

EXERCISES

1. Interview a person who uses interviewing as a tool of his profession as, for example, a personnel director, newspaper reporter, social worker, or probation officer. Your purpose will be to secure information concerning what he considers good techniques and major barriers in interviewing.

2. Watch an interview conducted on television. To what extent are the principles considered in this chapter followed? How could the interview have been improved?

3. How would you "soften" the following questions to make them less blunt?
   a. Why did you switch from Psychology to Management?
   b. Why did you have trouble with your Sociology teacher?
   c. Are you going to continue with these poor study habits?
   d. Don't you know that what you did was wrong?
   e. Now what are you going to do about it?

4. Interview two people in your class to discover interesting things in their backgrounds, special interests, hopes for the future, etc. Use only *direct* questions in the first interview; use *open* and *mirror* questions in the second. Analyze the amount and quality of information secured from each.

5. Assume that you are to interview someone on your campus. This might be the football coach, an instructor, the dean of your college, or a student leader. Plan the general purpose and the specific questions you will ask.

6. Write out a plan for an interview that you might conduct for *each* of these purposes: (1) to gather information, (2) to induce change, and (3) to solve a problem or make a decision. Your plan should include the introductory statement (after the social amenities are over), the sequence of the major areas to cover, and the termination.

7. Analyze an interview in which you recently participated. What was the nature of your planning? What did the other participant do that either facilitated or hampered communication?

8. Make a list of all the physical cues you can think of that might be involved in an interview situation. Compare your list with the lists of several others in the class.

ADDITIONAL READINGS

Balinsky, Benjamin, and Ruth Burger, *The Executive Interview*, New York, Harper & Row, 1959.

Fear, Richard A., *The Evaluation Interview: Predicting Job Performance in Business and Industry*, New York, McGraw-Hill, 1958.

Fenlason, Anne F., Grace B. Ferguson, and Arthur C. Abrahamson, *Essentials in Interviewing*, rev. ed., New York, Harper & Row, 1962.

Goyer, Robert S., W. Charles Redding, and John T. Rickey, *Interviewing Principles and Techniques: A Project Text*, Dubuque, Ia., Brown, 1964.

Hariton, Theodore, *Interview! The Executive's Guide to Selecting the Right Personnel*, New York, Hastings House, 1970.

Holm, James N., *Productive Speaking for Business and the Professions*, Boston, Allyn & Bacon, 1967, chap. 8.

Kahn, Robert L., and Charles F. Cannell, *The Dynamics of Interviewing*, New York, Wiley, 1957.

Kelly, Joe, *Organizational Behaviour*, Homewood, Ill., Irwin, 1969, pp. 378–388.

Keltner, John W., *Interpersonal Speech-Communication: Elements and Structures*, Belmont, Calif., Wadsworth, 1970, chap. 12.

Peskin, Dean B., *Human Behavior and Employment Interviewing*, New York, American Management Association, 1971.

Roethlisberger, F. J., and William J. Dickson, *Management and the Worker*, Cambridge, Harvard Univ. Press, 1950, chaps. 9, 10, 12, 13.

Tacey, William S., *Business and Professional Speaker*, Dubuque, Ia., Brown, 1970, chap. 9, pp. 132–144.

Zelko, Harold P., and Frank E. X. Dance, *Business and Professional Speech Communication*, New York, Holt, Rinehart & Winston, 1965, chap. 7, pp. 142–157.

Zelko, Harold P., and Harold J. O'Brien, *Management-Employee Communication in Action*, Cleveland, H. Allen, 1957, pp. 93–101.

NOTES

[1] Keith Davis, *Human Relations at Work*, 2nd ed., New York, McGraw-Hill, 1962, p. 401.

[2] Robert S. Goyer, W. Charles Redding, and John T. Rickey, *Interviewing Principles and Techniques: A Project Text*, Dubuque, Ia., Brown, 1964, p. 6.

[3] James N. Holm, *Productive Speaking for Business and the Professions*, Boston, Allyn & Bacon, 1967, p. 233.

[4] Annette Garrett, *Interviewing: Its Principles and Methods*, New York, Family Service Association of America, 1942, pp. 13–14.

[5] Holm, *op. cit.*, p. 224.

[6] Dean B. Peskin, *Human Behavior and Employment Interviewing*, New York, American Management Association, 1971, p. 10.

[7] Newell C. Kephart, *The Employment Interview in Industry*, New York, McGraw-Hill, 1952, p. vii.

[8] Norman R. F. Maier, *The Appraisal Interview: Objectives, Methods, and Skills*, New York, Wiley, 1958, p. 3.

[9] Holm, *op. cit.*, p. 217.

[10] *Ibid.*, p. 218.

[11] David C. Phillips, *Oral Communication in Business*, New York, McGraw-Hill, 1955, pp. 181–182.

[12] Holm, *op. cit.*, p. 234.

[13] Benjamin Balinsky and Ruth Burger, *The Executive Interview*, New York, Harper & Row, 1959, p. 30.

[14] Richard A. Fear, *The Evaluation Interview: Predicting Job Performance in Business and Industry*, New York, McGraw-Hill, 1958, pp. 92–93.

[15] Ted J. McLaughlin, L. P. Blum, and D. M. Robinson, *Communication*, Columbus, Merrill, 1964, p. 209.

[16]William V. Haney, *Communication and Organizational Behavior: Text and Cases*, rev. ed., Homewood, Ill., Irwin, 1967, p. 216.

[17]Fear, *op. cit.*, p. 98.

[18]Balinski and Burger, *op. cit.*, p. 59.

CHAPTER SIXTEEN
COMMUNICATING IN DISCUSSION GROUPS

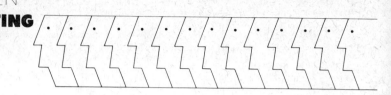

The whole purpose of democracy is that we may hold counsel with one another, so as not to depend upon the understanding of one man, but to depend upon the counsel of all.

Woodrow Wilson

The complex nature of present-day social, economic, scientific, and political problems, the need for the best possible resources—in both ideas and methods—in solving these problems, the greater reliance on group processes in democratic decision making, and the necessary interdependence among persons in group situations—all these and other factors have given increased significance to the need for effective communication in all types of discussion groups.

We constantly participate in some form of discussion. We plan a vacation with the family, make decisions for entertaining guests at our home, or engage in serious exchange of ideas on some political topic with friends. In college you engage in class discussions, confer with instructors, or participate in some student-faculty committee. During a business day one may engage in labor-management negotiations, confer on a company sales policy, discuss the merits of one's products with prospective buyers, or work with others in the solution of some interpersonal problem.

The teaching and use of group discussion methods is now commonplace in the areas of religion, the military, civic groups, education, governmental agencies, scientific research and development, counseling and therapy, business and industry, agriculture, labor, and certain other professions. It is literally true that the effectiveness with which problems are solved, understandings reached, and personal adjustments made depends in large part on how effectively the skills of discussion are used.

Our aim in this chapter is to give you an overview of the nature and functions of the discussion process itself, its values in a democratic society, the characteristics of groups in which discussion is used effectively, and the actual conduct of discussion. Our concern is to help you understand how effective communication can improve the use of group discussion.

THE NATURE OF GROUP DISCUSSION

Many interactional processes take place within human groups: acculturation, associative and dissociative activities, communication, therapy, modification of individual personalities, and learning and problem solving are examples. These processes are not necessarily mutually exclusive. Our concern in this chapter is with still another group process, discussion, which may at times partake of some of the elements of all of the above. We define discussion as the *purposeful, systematic, oral* exchange of *ideas, facts, and opinions,* which occurs in a *group* whose members *share in its leadership.* Let us look at this definition more closely.

Purposeful

We do not consider idle conversation to fall within the purview of this definition. When people meet for the specific purpose of discussing a topic, they are concerned about some form of outcome: reaching a decision, learning, resolving a difference, achieving some other group goal, or providing some ego satisfaction for the individual members of the group. A group may sometimes have a social goal, such as the development of good feeling, but this, too, is a means of achieving other serious projects.

Of the six elements or dimensions of discussion, clarity of purpose is perhaps the most important. At any rate, a group will accomplish little without a well-defined goal. Ideally, the purpose of a discussion is known in advance, decided upon at the outset, clearly defined, accepted by the group, reviewed frequently during the discussion, and restated for concurrent by the members at the close of the discussion.

Systematic and Logical

Ideally, discussion uses rules of logic and clear thinking, it follows the generally accepted sequence of steps in reflective thinking, it employs meaningful and clear language, it seeks freedom from bias, and it gives all discussants the opportunity for optimal participation. Sometimes, however, the thinking of the group members is far from logical; the solution to a problem may be considered before all the facts have been presented, or progress may be blocked because what is said is misunderstood. The ideal, nevertheless, should always be our goal.

Oral Process

The exchange of ideas in discussion takes place through speech. Therefore, the participants must have some proficiency in oral communication. Certainly all comments should be heard and understood, language should be pertinent and clear, and voice and gesture must be used effectively. As in a speaking situation, the content must be adapted to the discussion goal, and audiovisual resources should be used if they contribute to goal achievement. All possible channels of communication should be kept open.

Content

Effective discussion requires the use of all available facts and opinions, including points of view of both experts and laymen. Discussion should never be, as its critics sometimes charge, "a pooling of ignorance." The content should be significant, dealing with matters that in some way affect the lives of the participants.

Study and research that results in a thorough problem analysis, utilization of all pertinent resources, exploration of all possible solutions, and consideration of the implications of the accepted solution is a *sine qua non* of effective discussion.

Group Process

Discussion involves both person-to-person and person-to-group relationships. More than in most other speaking situations, the participants are concerned with matters of status, group standards and loyalties, internal cohesion, and the ego needs of individuals who participate. Like all the other elements, this dimension also varies from one discussion to another. At best the interpersonal relations contribute maximally to the unity of the group; at worst the group process is characterized by disharmony, disagreement, and seemingly unresolvable conflict.

Leadership

In all discussion there must be an element of leadership. Ideally, the leadership function is shared and not the sole responsibility of one person. The current concept of leadership is that, since leadership is related to the diverse tasks that must be carried out in discussion, many persons may therefore share in leading a discussion. Thus, "leadership" may mean assisting in the planning and preparation stages of a discussion, performing some assigned task in the discussion itself, such as making periodic summaries, or serving as an evaluator. Under certain conditions, as when a group is largely inexperienced in discussion techniques, or when it has a limited time to arrive at a consensus, a single leader is named. Later in this chapter we shall consider the various leadership styles and the leadership contributions that may be made by group members, in addition to the functions to be performed by the designated leader. That is, we believe that discussion should permit every discussant to share in the performance of leadership to the extent of his ability.

THE FORMS OF GROUP DISCUSSION

Now that we have briefly considered the components of any discussion, let us look at some of the formats in which discussion occurs. There are a number of bases for the classification of discussion groups, including purpose, size, degree of formality, and many others. A classification most frequently used by writers on discussion and group processes is that of the mode of exchange of ideas—the manner of interaction, private or public. We believe this division has the most practical value for the student in understanding what actually takes place in discussion.

The Private Group

By a "private" discussion, sometimes called "informal," "round-table," "closed-group," or "small," we mean any discussion that takes place without an audience. All the members are participants. Private discussion usually *does take place* in small groups, generally of not more than fifteen or twenty. The members are seated in a face-to-face situation; each member is in direct eye contact with all of the others.

The person calling the meeting usually indicates the purpose, or the purpose may be decided by the group. All members of the group take an active part; there should be no nonparticipants, since the members are selected or are in the group because they are highly homogeneous in knowledge about the subject, willingness to contribute, status, and desire to reach the group's goal. There should be no spectators. Neither should anyone be considered a special authority, unless he has been called in as a special resource person. The procedure and atmosphere of the group are characterized by informality, a relaxed attitude, permissiveness, and feelings of security. Members remain seated while speaking, first names are frequently used, and a spirit of goodwill and friendly objectivity should prevail. Although the members may have prepared in advance for the discussion, the contributions are usually short, participation is fairly well equalized among the members and, ideally, the pattern of contributions should follow a sequence that contributes maximally to group productivity. What we have just been saying might be stated briefly by saying that all group members contribute to the "input," so that the "output" will be maximized.

Leadership functions, unless there is a designated leader, usually are performed by the various members of the group. When there is a willingness on the part of each member to let others participate, when the members have a sense of responsibility for making progress, and when the group can and does make procedural decisions that contribute to productivity, private discussion can be an effective tool in a democratic society.

A review of the conditions necessary to make private discussion effective might be summarized by these suggestions for the participants:

1. Be sure that you and the other members understand the purpose of the discussion.
2. Speak whenever you have a contribution to make. Study and think about the topic in advance. Your experience and knowledge probably will be different from those of the other discussants.
3. Be sure that you understand the meaning of what is being said.
4. Listen critically and thoughtfully to others. Be prepared to apply the tests of evidence and opinion to your own contributions and those of others.
5. Let the other person have his chance to participate, too. Optimal participation by all is the goal.
6. Try to make sure that the group has all the resources available to achieve its goals.
7. Share leadership functions with the other members of the group. Draw reticent members into the discussion when you can.
8. Do what you can to develop goal-oriented or group-oriented interaction.
9. Chart the progress the group is making toward its goals. Do this yourself by occasional summaries, or ask others to perform this function.
10. Do what you can to develop a permissive, secure, and cordial atmosphere. If you disagree with someone, be friendly about it.
11. Be flexible in your thinking on the topic. Be ready to present your own ideas forcibly, but be ready to change your position if new facts or interpretations warrant a change.
12. Do what you can personally to keep the channels of communication open.
13. Always keep the purpose of the discussion in mind, especially at the close. Be sure plans are made for future meetings or action, if necessary.

There are numerous reasons why you should be familiar with the private-discussion format. Two are especially important. First, it is the type most frequently used, both in school and outside. You perhaps participate daily in several informal, private discussions: in seminar classes, in larger classes when small groups make plans for some class activity, in student committee meetings, in your home with your family, or in purposeful meetings with friends. Outside school the private discussion is a frequently used tool in decision making and is a preparation for larger public meetings involving discussion.

Perhaps the most significant reason for study and practice in informal discussion is that one learns many of the skills needed for effective communication in many life situations. This is the primary aim of most of the "sensitivity training" programs being conducted both on and off college campuses. Improved skill in dealing with other people is needed by all of us.

The Public Discussion Formats

The three public types of discussion most frequently used are the panel-forum, the symposium-forum, and the lecture-forum. A brief description of each type follows.

The Panel-Forum

The panel-forum is a staged discussion in which a group of persons, usually not more than seven or eight, including a chairman, carry on a discussion on an announced topic before an audience. After the panel has conversed for a specified period, members of the audience are permitted to ask questions or make limited comments of their own. The panel members are seated so they may see each other and still view the audience.

Usually they are selected because they have some special knowledge about the topic or are in a position to secure some information. Advance preparation is necessary, and the panel members usually find it advisable to meet for planning purposes one or more times. At these planning meetings the members become acquainted, determine a tentative pattern for the discussion, make special assignments for research, and decide on procedures.

The discussion is informal. There are no set speeches, contributions are brief—seldom more than a minute or two—and all members contribute about equally. The chairman opens the discussion by introducing the panel members. He then states the topic, indicates something of its importance, and suggests possible aspects to be considered. He should also announce any special rules to be followed, before the discussion begins.

The panel interaction in a panel-forum is essentially an informal discussion that is staged before an audience. Potter and Andersen state:[1]

The function of the panel is to provide expert analysis of a problem— including the raising of significant issues and presentation of pertinent facts and opinions—prior to the forum period, so that the understanding of the listeners will be increased and their thinking focused and sharpened. The forum period provides the opportunity for the audience members to call attention to points overlooked by the panelists, raise questions about matters already considered, present needed facts, suggest applications, and even give vent to feelings.

When the panelists are aware of the fact that they are appearing before an audience and must be heard at all times and appear as if speaking to the listeners, and at the same time conduct an informal, lively analysis of the topic among themselves, then the panel-forum can be a useful public form of communication.

The panel-forum has many values. It is useful in raising the important issues of a problem in the early stages of its analysis, and it can be used in crystallizing public opinion when a decision on a solution to a problem must be reached. It provides the opportunity for a wide variety of views to be presented to the audience.

The Symposium-Forum
The symposium-forum is also a staged form of discussion, in which a number of speakers, seldom more than five, present prepared speeches on the selected topic, audience participation following. A chairman introduces the speakers, states the topic, indicates rules of procedure, makes transitional remarks in presenting successive speakers, handles the question-and-answer period, and concludes the program. The speakers address the audience just as they would in a formal platform situation and speak without being interrupted by the other speakers, although sometimes they engage in a brief panel type of discussion immediately after their talks. The essential difference between the panel-forum and the symposium-forum is that the latter involves set speeches whereas the former requires the factual information to be presented informally, as in conversation. Both are attempts to engage in group thinking; neither is a debate, although conflicting points of view are often considered.

The symposium-forum, with its planned speeches, obviously is more informative than the panel-forum and serves better to crystallize thinking on a topic. When it is desirable to have factual material and carefully considered opinion presented on different aspects of a problem, the symposium-forum is the better choice.

The chairman of a symposium-forum introduces the topic, points out its importance, and sometimes indicates the point of view of the speakers. He announces any rules that will be followed, introduces each speaker, and usually makes some pertinent remarks between speeches, to show the relationships of the subject matter presented. He moderates the forum session; he suggests or outlines any "next steps," such as additional meetings, decisions, and action to be taken; and he performs the usual social amenities required in closing.

The Lecture-Forum

The lecture-forum is a symposium-forum with only one speaker. A forum period following the lecture gives the audience an opportunity to comment and ask questions.

The discussion period in each of these programs serves to clarify dubious points, supply additional information, resolve differences among the speakers themselves, answer audience questions and, especially, give the audience the sense of having participated in the program.

GROUP DISCUSSION IN A DEMOCRATIC SOCIETY

The tradition of discussion in this country is an old one. Since the days of the early New England town meetings, group deliberation, debate, and persuasive speaking have been the tools used in making decisions affecting the public welfare. This is the only way that a democracy can be permanently successful, for if the majority of the people are unconcerned or uninformed about public issues, decisions are necessarily made by a few and are not necessarily made in the interest of the majority. This is the path that has led in our day to pseudodemocratic decision making, secret parleys on matters of public concern, nonviolent and violent dissent, forms of subversion and anarchy, and even wanton destruction and armed conflict. The decision making of one or a few leads eventually to dictatorship, in which the interests of the people are subverted in the interests of the ruling elite.

We stated in Chapter One that the voices of the younger generations must make themselves heard, if the vital issues of the day are to be solved. This chapter is designed to aid them in participating more actively in discussions that affect their private or public life.

The Functions of Group Discussion

Briefly, discussion serves individual needs and aids in implementing group goals.

Meeting Individual Needs

The *group* goals of discussion are usually stated in advance or determined early in any given discussion. Most frequently they are overtly expressed. It is sometimes more difficult to state explicitly the role group discussion serves in meeting individual needs. Nevertheless, we may generalize by saying that participation in discussion meets individual needs that are goal, group, or ego centered.[2] Let us consider briefly the distinction among the three needs.

Sometimes a person becomes a member of a group—or maintains his membership in it over a period of time—because of *goal-centered* needs. That is, he feels he is making some contribution to the stated purposes of the group, to the *accomplishment of its goals.* This is true of the active church member who doesn't tithe and the inactive one who does tithe, the person who joins a fraternity or sorority, the activist who participates in nonviolent or violent confrontations, or the student who serves on some student or student-faculty committee. In each case the individual wants to contribute to the goals of his group: he pays dues, if any, does menial or important assigned tasks, solicits others to become members, joins in fund-raising campaigns, attends annual conventions, or accepts every opportunity to tell others about the accomplishments of *his* group. By his participation he is meeting a personal need to contribute to an organization whose values, norms, and purposes he accepts. This person is known by his works.

Sometimes participation in a group and in its discussions and activities serves the *group-centered* needs of an individual. Group-centered activities are those which contribute to the *maintenance of the group* as an identity. The individual performs acts that help the group maintain its morale, continue working as a cohesive unit, resist disintegrating pressures from either inside or outside, enhance its prestige and influence, participate in acts designed to make other members feel that the group is making progress towards its goals, reduce tensions among the members, or help to resolve differences that may be calamitous. In a discussion group the communication that is group-centered is easy to spot. Such expressions as "It seems to me we have actually accomplished a lot so far; let's review," "I believe there is a compromise that will provide benefits for both views expressed here today," or "What we have been saying makes good sense, let's follow up on it," are types of communication intended to—and able to—give the group a sense of accomplishment, resolve differences, or prod the members to further activity.

Finally, individuals perform acts that meet *ego-centered* needs. These are the things a person does to enhance his personal status or deflate that of others, work off aggression, defend his personal security, or isolate himself from the group. Ego-oriented needs may be of a positive nature. There is a saying that "the kingmaker cannot always be king." Some people get their ego satisfactions by what they can do for others and are willing to remain "backstage."

We believe we may safely generalize and say that the discussion that takes place within a group, at whatever level it may be, and many of the related decisions and actions that result, serve mainly the psychological needs of the individual. A summary of this point of view is expressed by two authors of a book on discussion methods. They state:[3]

. . . Individuals are drawn into groups, continue to function in them, and find their greatest satisfaction from psychological forces, the most important of which may be the sense of "belonging"—being an integral part of an ongoing group activity. Riesman points out that some individuals join groups because they are "outer directed"—that is, they are in need of external support for their ego; he is critical of the lack of "inner-directed" maturity of many or most Americans. Eric Fromm, a psychiatrist concerned with this lack of inner resources, considers such dependence on others as a form of "escape from freedom"—a psychological retreat from individuality. Whyte sees much the same tendency to conform, to "belong," to find a justification and defense of the self in dependence upon the group, upon group standards, upon group membership—what he slightingly describes as the "tyranny" of the group.

Such "group-oriented" behavior has many implications in our consideration of discussion groups, but the first important fact to consider is the actual presence of such drives toward dependency and belongingness. It is a major thesis of this book that the seemingly contradictory needs of "belongingness" [which is a form of conformity] and of "individuality" can be maintained only through democratic discussion. Only through democratic processes can the individual in a group maintain his integrity as a person.

Implementing Group Goals

In view of the widespread use of discussion, there can be little question about its value in helping to achieve group goals. To emphasize this point we need only look at some of the types of group in which discussion takes place.

Discussion occurs in various *occupational* groups: scientific research and development teams, medical and rehabilitation groups in hospitals, management staffs in industry, the captain and officers on a ship, and the faculties of colleges.

Learning groups employ discussion widely. For example, it is the primary means of communication in the family group, in on-the-job training groups, in youth groups, in which skill training is a part of the program, as in the Boy Scouts or Girl Scouts, in home study groups such as the Great Book classes, and in the many types of instructional groups in our educational system.

Discussion also occurs in *avocational* groups. The members of these groups engage in activities and discussions that cover the gamut of man's interests.

Another type of group that engages in a great deal of discussion is the *community organization*, which might include luncheon clubs, Town Hall groups, or such organizations as B'nai B'rith and the Congress of Parents and Teachers.

Aiding in Decision Making

There are many ways by which decisions are reached in a representative form of government: by administrative ruling—as certain rulings made by the President—by voting in an election, by compromise in labor-management negotiations, or by integration in discussion when the final decision reflects an amalgam of the viewpoints of many. In each instance the decision makers are influenced by some form of rhetorical presentation or analysis of the problem involved, the most significant being persuasive speaking, discussion, and debate.

To understand the role of discussion—the concern of this chapter—we need first to look at the complete process of democratic decision making and then to focus on the specific functions discussion performs.

Discussion in a democracy is a tool of analysis, decision making, and problem solving, all leading to group or individual action on vital public issues. Such action usually results after the individuals and groups involved have proceeded through a series of stages, which we call "deliberation" or "study-action continuum."[4]

STUDY-ACTION CONTINUUM

1 A problem situation arises.	2 The problem is located and defined.	3 Study and research are carried out.	4 The problem is discussed by parties involved.
8 The action is evaluated.	7 Action is taken.	6 Decisions are made.	5 Alternative solutions are debated.

The stages in such a continuum are not always as clear-cut as the accompanying diagram suggests, nor are they always mutually exclusive; at times steps 1 and 2 merge; steps 3 and 4 may occur concurrently; frequently the discussion and debate steps overlap or there is no debate; a discussion often stops at step 6, no action being taken, or action may be taken prematurely; in many instances the final step, evaluation, is completely omitted. In general, however, effective decision-making follows the cyclical sequence indicated. Individuals or groups recognize a problem on which action should be taken—the need for a public parking lot near a new shopping center, for example. The problem is located and defined, and its local implications are determined. Various groups, committees, and agencies study and discuss the problem as a preliminary to determining solutions. Let us say that one solution involves placing the lot on land belonging to the high school; that solution is then debated prior to community action. If the proposal is approved, the responsible agencies take appropriate action to implement the decision. This action is often evaluated later to determine whether it is proving adequate and in the best interests of the people.

We have said that persuasive speaking, discussion, and debate are three important tools in democratic decision making. What roles do these forms of group communication play in the deliberation continuum?

Discussion is vital as long as there is need for inquiry on which later decisions will be based; debate follows logically when all avenues of investigation have been explored and it becomes necessary to determine the majority wish. The essence of discussion is reflective thinking—the search for answers that have not been predetermined. Discussion is the process of cooperative inquiry in which decisions and commitments to action are held in abeyance until the ramifications of all possible solutions can be investigated. The content of discussion includes all facts and opinions that bear on any solution. In discussion you consider every point of view before it is eliminated.

The essence of debate, in contrast, is intentional thinking—arguing for the acceptance of an answer its supporters believe best. Debate is the process of competitive advocacy, in which opposing points of view are supported; its content includes only those facts and opinions which back either the affirmative or negative side. In debate you argue for a single point of view.

When a consensus is reached without debate, the group may take action as soon as the discussion seems to be finished. The discussion step itself, however, can seldom, if ever, be eliminated. It is always necessary to have some deliberation on a problem to be sure that all facts have been considered, all parties heard, all viewpoints considered.

Otherwise, whatever action is taken might prove ill advised and hasty. Discussion ensures cooperative inquiry on controversial issues prior to decision making.

Let us briefly review how discussion and debate differ in philosophy and procedure.

Discussion is:	Debate is:
1. A reflective thought process	1. An intentional thought process
2. Inquiry at its best	2. Advocacy at its best
3. Cooperative in nature	3. Competitive in nature
4. Inclusive in its use of all available resources	4. Exclusive in the use of resources
5. Somewhat flexible in procedure	5. Somewhat formal in procedure
6. Not limited to the support of a single point of view	6. Limited, in that support must reflect either an affirmative or negative viewpoint
7. Designed to reach a group consensus	7. Designed to result in a group vote

We have now looked at the broad picture of democratic decision making and have contrasted discussion and debate as two important rhetorical techniques in the analysis and resolution of public issues. It is now well to ask what specific functions discussion plays in a democratic society.

Aiding in Problem-Solving

When we say that discussion is used in problem solving, we use *problem* in its broadest sense, to include the resolution of differences, the settling of a grievance, decision making on a wide range of topics, and the formulation of policies. Any problem situation that requires the application of the principles of analysis leading to some solution comes within the purview of the term *problem-solving*. Effective problem-solving discussion still relies on the principles of reflective thinking set forth some sixty years ago by John Dewey. These are, briefly, (1) awareness of a problem, (2) the location and definition of the problem, (3) suggestion of possible solutions for the problem, (4) rational elaboration of the suggested solutions, and (5) experimentation or testing which will lead to the verification or rejection of the solutions selected in the preceding phases.[5] Let us look at the steps in this process.

Awareness of the Problem. Our awareness of most problems is greater when they touch us in a personal way. If our own needs or those of our family or associates are at stake, we want to do something about it. When our principles are assailed, we stand up for the right as we see it. When facts are unknown, contradictory, or vague, we want to know the truth of the matter. But only when we see such personal implications do we begin the process leading to the resolution of a problem. Awareness of a problem sometimes comes in the nature of a revelation, suddenly. On the other hand, it may result from experiences over a long period of time.

There are three different types of problem: those of fact, of value, and of policy.

In a problem of fact we are concerned with the truth of a statement, the ramifications of a fact, or the extent to which available facts support a given conclusion. Thus, juries are asked to determine whether an accused person actually did commit an alleged crime. The results of an innovation in safety controls for landing airplanes may need to be studied. A state crime commission may wish to determine the causes, extent, and results of drug uses. Answers to such questions may require research, experimentation, and individual study, but discussion also is always involved.

With problems of value we are concerned with certain questions: What is desirable? What is proper? What is best? Value judgments concern the desirability of some concept, institution, process, person, or thing. Such questions as the following are examples:

How worthwhile will membership in the Common Market be to Great Britain?
Are present television programs improving in quality?
Are our present foreign-aid programs as valuable as they should be?
How valuable have our Peace Corps programs in Latin American countries been?
What are the relative values of nonviolent and violent confrontations with authority in changing policies?
What would be the benefits to the student body if the campus newspaper moved off campus?

The problem of policy asks different questions: What action should be taken? How should this be done? It deals with such questions as these:

What action should be taken to curb juvenile delinquency?
What should be our national farm policy about parity?
What should be done to conserve our water resources?

What should management in plant X do about the new union
contract just submitted?

Many high school students participate annually in discussion
tournaments. Their topics usually are problems of policy, in which a
shift from the status quo is advocated.

Locating and Defining the Problem. Perhaps the greatest problem in
discussion is that we are frequently not aware of exactly what is
included in the subject under discussion. Once we recognize that a
problem exists, our task is to locate and define it. If you are a foreman
facing a slowdown on the assembly line, you need to know whether the
problem is human or mechanical. If you are to discuss a subject of your
choice in class—say student-faculty relations—you will first have to
designate some specific immediate problem: freshman orientation, graduate counseling, class relationships, or sponsorship of extracurricular
activities.

The reason for concern about locating the problem is that we
must be sure that the real problem is being discussed. In a discussion
about education the focus of the subject would first have to be
determined. Shall it be adult education, higher education, vocational
education, or secondary education? It will almost certainly be necessary
to narrow these questions still further in order to get at a specific
problem. The question might prove to be "What are the respective roles
of the state colleges and the universities in undergraduate training?"

Locating and defining a problem also means that all terms used
and, possibly, the implications of the topic must be understood. If
there are different ideas within the group about the meaning of a topic,
immediate attention must be given to arriving at some consensus. For
example, in dealing with the question of federal aid to education, it
would first be necessary to agree upon what is meant by "education."
Is it private or public or both? Elementary level or all levels? Formal
education only or informal as well?

Studying the Problem. Once the problem has been located and defined
the next step is study and analysis. This means an examination of its
history, insofar as it bears on the problem, and the causes and present
state of the problem, with perhaps a consideration of future effects. In
the problem-solving sequence the analysis demands rounding up every
available fact and opinion bearing on the problem: its history, the issues
involved, and their ramifications.

Establishing the Criteria for Solutions. At this point in the analysis of
the problem—before possible solutions are suggested—it is essential that

the criteria of quality solutions be established. This phase of the reflective-thinking process is often overlooked by discussion groups, resulting in a needless waste of time. An example of the wisdom of setting up the criteria before suggesting the solutions is found in the family discussion of what make and type of new car to buy. If the major criterion is low initial cost, no time should be spent looking at Lincoln Continentals or Cadillacs. If large carrying capacity is the major criterion, it would be useless to spend time inspecting or considering a Pinto, a VW "bug," or a Toyota Corona. In any problem-solving discussion the criteria for the decision or the solution should be considered before the specific solutions are offered. After this step is completed, the group may wish to redefine the problem.

Suggesting Possible Solutions. After the group has determined the specific problem to be solved and the conditions that govern any acceptable solution, suggestions of possible solutions are in order. None should be ignored, even though at first glance it may seem far fetched or impossible. As solutions are suggested, it is a good idea to list them on a blackboard before considering the implications of any one. Each must then be considered thoroughly.

Partial solutions should not be overlooked. Resolving a problem sometimes is a step-by-step process. Keep in mind also that solutions do not always arrive "full blown." In its early stages a solution may be vague, too inclusive, or temporary.

Exploring Possible Solutions and Selecting the Best. Judgment should be withheld until all possible solutions can be considered. This insistence on suspended judgment is essential in all reflective thinking. All hypotheses must be tested, both to insure that the final decision is the best and to avoid having a "pet" solution imposed by a part of the group. Any best solution should always be considered as tentative at the time of its adoption—it can only apply under existing or anticipated circumstances. New conditions will probably necessitate an altered solution. Many solutions in discussion are made by people who are biased or who act hastily, and hence we cannot expect any given solution to be perfect. It is therefore often advisable to evaluate a given decision some time later, and to alter it if change seems advisable.

Implementing Learning Process
Besides its function in problem-solving, discussion serves an educational function. Groups often come together for the sole purpose of increasing their understanding of a topic; they also are formed for the purpose of learning personal skills, such as critical thinking, improved speaking and

listening, or improvement in some needed motor skill. In college seminars, on-the-job training groups, military briefing sessions, professional conferences, and home study groups, discussion serves these purposes primarily. In some situations, of which the many training programs in group development held throughout the country are foremost examples, group discussion serves primarily as a means of helping people learn how to get along better with others, of helping in personality growth and support, and of overcoming personality problems. These groups seek to aid individuals in improving their relations with others rather than gaining in personal skills or knowledge.

The stress on discussion as a learning device is steadily increasing. There is little doubt that under certain conditions it is superior to other techniques as a learning technique. This has been established by research studies, surveys of the effectiveness of adult-education study groups and workshops, reports of classroom experiments, and analyses of the results of the use of discussion as a learning device in such areas as agriculture, business and industry, the armed forces, religious education, and agencies of criminal control, investigation, and rehabilitation.[6]

The discussion method is capable of providing the climate and conditions essential for learning. If a person is to be motivated to learn, he must have constructive interaction with his fellow learners, critical yet supportive evaluation from others, opportunity for experimentation in new ways of thinking and behaving, tasks that challenge his growing intellectual abilities and that are progressive in difficulty and complexity, and a climate that encourages the development of his individuality.[7]

Discussion can provide—although frequently it does not—certain other conditions needed for effective learning: the stimulus to achieve, security when achievement does not come up to the individual's or the group's own standards, a balance between feelings of dependency and self-reliance, some relationship to previous experience, and relevancy to the individual's needs. One writer makes this last point in this statement:[8]

The discussion method supports the general goals of teaching. Through discussion, the teacher can make subject matter alive for the student by confronting him with problems and situations that require personal effort to resolve. Discussion gives the student greater responsibility for learning. Additionally, it trains him to play a more effective role in his society, where interaction in small groups is so important. The typical classroom is directed to the convenience of the teacher as he directs the students in the mastery of material. The teacher's goals may not necessarily accord with those of the student. To do a more effective job of teaching it is necessary for the teacher to discover what the student wants to gain from his learning and find ways in which subject matter can be made more meaningful in terms of student-centered needs.

Serving as Therapy

The literature on the use of the discussion group as a therapeutic device reflects several trends: (1) the practice of group therapy is increasing in the treatment of a wide range of personal problems, from severe cases of mental and personality disorders to mild forms of deviant or ineffective interpersonal behavior; (2) there is an increasing theoretical or philosophical acceptance of the belief that the concept of the "dynamics of the group" is central to the therapeutic process; (3) there is a growing understanding among speech educators, psychologists, and clinical therapists that, although group processes may in some situations be supportive of individual growth and behavioral change, there are distinct differences between a "training group" and a "therapy group" in makeup, procedures, and goals.

The terms *T-groups,* or "training groups," and *therapy groups* are sometimes used synonomously, and certainly the two types have some characteristics in common. They are both experiences that bring about greater insights into intrapersonal and interpersonal behavior and create some behavioral change in the individuals involved. In both types the groups undergo a series of stages in development from inception to termination, beginning with various degrees of interpsychic tensions, the development of mutually constructive interpersonal rapport accompanied by a seeking for goal structure, and ending with feelings of relief, which accompany successful group action.[9] The individual affective states that accompany these developmental stages vary from anxiety, frustration, hostility, and reluctance to give up traditional or "back home" ways of behaving, to feelings of cooperation, ego satisfaction, and acceptance of self and others.

There are, however, significant differences between T-groups and therapy groups. The membership or "target populations" differ. The members of an intensive therapy group are screened by clinical and diagnostic procedures. At times selective personality criteria are applied for exclusion.[10] At one extreme of the continuum—the therapy group—members suffer from extreme or deeply rooted personality or psychosomatic problems; at the other extreme—the T-group, or laboratory group—membership is drawn from professional workers in public health, education, religious education, industrial relations, social work, and the military. The membership of a T-group is usually heterogeneous in nature, although members may be drawn from the same profession or organization.

The authors of a text on T-group training indicate further differences:[11]

While there are some obvious similarities between the T group and the therapy group—in part because any effective education has therapeutic overtones—the T group differs in a number of important ways. It tends to utilize data about present behavior and its consequences rather than delving into genetic causes. It tends to deal with conscious and pre-conscious behavior rather than with unconscious motivation. The T group makes the important assumption that persons participating are well rather than ill.

T-groups are limited in time from two or three days to two months at the most; therapy groups may continue over periods of eighteen to thirty months. T-groups are generally directed primarily toward learning needs; therapy groups are directed toward personality change. The T-group seeks to train individuals who in turn might train others; the therapy group focuses primarily on what happens to the individual member of the group. The T-group and therapy groups utilize somewhat different types of evaluation and research techniques. T-groups—although their methods do not follow traditional teaching methods—are closely linked to the educational milieu; therapy groups are the psychologist's and psychiatrist's tools for the treatment of mental or personality maladjustments. Finally, to a much greater degree than in a therapy group, the T-group is less concerned with the "inner workings" of the individual and more with his "outer workings"—the ways in which he relates to other people.

Therapy groups are purposely unstructured, placing on both therapist (leader or trainer) and group members pressures to discover their respective roles vis-à-vis each other. Since there are no agenda or external tasks to perform, and the leader or therapist is usually nondirective, deep tensions are likely to develop. The members must learn to free themselves of leader dependency, develop greater sensitivity to others and awareness of self, establish forms of action acceptable to the group, and develop patterns of behaving that progress from ego to group or goal centeredness.

You will undoubtedly participate in some type of therapy or training group during your college career or after graduation. You need to recognize that the goals are different from those in problem-solving discussions, the situation usually is completely unstructured, different and deeper tensions are likely to develop, and you will need to develop new interpersonal and goal-seeking skills. Whatever traumas may result, the experience will still be worthwhile if the groups are conducted properly.

The material in this section has been presented to acquaint you with the characteristics of T-groups and therapy groups. Individuals possessing a good background in their profession and a thorough understanding of leadership principles and group methods might be satisfactory leaders or trainers in T-group situations, but only highly trained psychologists or psychiatrists should attempt to lead a therapy group. The individual confronted with possible membership in a therapy group would do well to investigate its leadership before joining.

Securing Commitment

Members of a discussion group usually have a strong feeling of commitment to carry out decisions made by the group. Their sense of commitment comes about in several ways, each of which exerts an increasing amount of pressure on the individual to conform to the decisions made by the group.

At one extreme, a person will act in conformity with the group's action patterns because of his personal attraction to the group or because of his approval and acceptance of the group's goals. There is no group pressure on the individual; his commitment to the group and its purposes comes solely from the ego satisfactions he gets from membership. His participation in the discussions of the group—general meetings, committees and so forth—may be infrequent, but he still supports the group.

At a second level, we find that group members feel a strong commitment to carry out the wishes of a group when they have participated in the process of decision-making. The decision to act is still a personal one, but the individual is psychologically committed to go along with a decision he has helped to make. Numerous research studies have confirmed this hypothesis. Two studies dealt with changes in food habits made by housewives during World War II. In the first study the aim was to increase the use of beef hearts, sweetbreads, and kidneys, and the second aimed to increase the home consumption of either fresh or evaporated milk.[12] In both studies groups of women either listened to a persuasive speech urging the desired change or participated in a discussion starting with "what housewives in general might do" and then considering what the individuals in the discussion groups might do. In the first study 3 percent of the housewives listening to the lecture made changes in their food-using habits, whereas 32 percent of those in the discussion groups changed. In a study dealing with industrial workers the psychologists Lester Coch and John French, Jr., demonstrated that when the workers took part in decision-making small-group discussions, the changes in industrial methods were more successfully introduced. These authors concluded:[13]

It is possible for management to modify greatly or remove completely group resistance to changes in methods of work and ensuing piece rates. This change can be accomplished by the use of group meetings in which management effectively communicates the need for change and stimulates group participation in planning the changes.

In several other studies the same general conclusion has been reached, namely that "performance was superior and attitudes more favorable when subjects followed plans they had developed for themselves."[14] Although other recent research raises the question whether discussion alone, without some accompanying decision, is the crucial factor in achieving individual commitment to action, we may say with confidence that discussion as a decision-making tool contributes to a person's willingness to act in ways in agreement with the tenor of the discussion.[15] Thibaut and Kelley summarize the point we have been making in these words:[16]

If general participation in developing and planning a goal means heightened understanding of it and commitment to it, the group problem-solving process may be more economical in the long run than one that begins with the most expert thought and advice.

A third level of getting commitment to conform is when the group itself exerts pressure on the individual. Again, numerous research studies confirm this conclusion.[17] Although the specific hypotheses tested in these studies varies, there is sufficient evidence to conclude that, when a group is relatively cohesive and attractive to its members, when communication relative to change is shared by all, when majority opinion is known to be in favor of a change, when the members have a shared perception of the need for a change, and when pressures for change are relevant to the basis of attraction to the group, then individual members feel highly motivated to conform to the influences of the group.

Training Others in Personal Skills
A concomitant of the seven functions of group discussion we have just considered is that it trains individuals in needed skills of communication, critical thinking, creativity, personal adjustment and growth, and interpersonal relations and also provides them with a wealth of knowledge on topics having both personal and interpersonal implications. Each individual needs to develop these skills and gain more useful knowledge. A discussion group may be planned and conducted with these goals as primary ones, or they may be considered secondary, hoped-for results from a discussion designed to achieve some other

purpose. In the next section, dealing with the values of discussion, we consider further some ways in which discussion serves the individual.

The Values of Group Discussion

In each of the previous sections of this chapter we have stated explicitly or suggested by implication some of the values of discussion. Let us now look at the values of discussion in a somewhat different light. What are its values that cut across individual and group bounds? We consider four.

Emotional Expression and Development

This value may be considered a continuum ranging from catharsis—getting something off one's chest, a form of letting off steam—to considered, purposeful contributions related to the specific nature of the developing discussion. In between we find the expression of emotions such as anxiety, insecurity, fear, mistrust, dependency, and withdrawal, or mistaken conceptions of the self-image. Whatever the nature of the emotional maladjustment or deviance from the norm, the individual needs to express his feelings. He discovers that others have many of the same fears and anxieties and gets support from the group. He learns, perhaps for the first time, that others perceive him differently from the way he does himself; under a permissive and helping discussion climate he can begin the climb back to reality. At times it is important for the individual to learn how others have handled problems of marital relations, drug use, child guidance, and mental health; such problems may be studied in a discussion group. At other times the individual's need is merely to understand better how to relate to others in job situations or to get along better with subordinates, peers, or superiors. Through role playing the group member has an opportunity to practice needed skills and behavior patterns, develop greater sensitivity to others and, hopefully, modify his own ways of behaving.

It is extremely important that the expression of emotions be permitted in a discussion group. As early as 1938 Elliott wrote,[18] "It is usually essential . . . that at some time the strong emotion be expressed with whatever vehemence the individuals feel." Current writers on group processes agree. They see the expression of deep-rooted emotions or surface feelings as serving to release tensions, provide a necessary base for the analysis and development of individual personality and the group's health, eliminate or reveal hidden agenda so they can be dealt with, and give input data that will enable the group to analyze and possibly improve its goal-seeking methods.

Input in Problem Solving

One of the values of discussion in all its functions is that there is a wider range of input—information, opinions, and other resources—than when an individual must, for example, solve a problem alone or try to discover why he is unable to work effectively with others. Two or more persons in a group will increase proportionally the number of communication skills, facts, creative talents, critical-thinking abilities, and new ways of looking at the analysis of a problem or its solution. Some persons are skilled in goal-oriented participation; others have group-centered orientations. This assures a needed balance between focus on content and process, which is said by many authorities to be essential.

The assumption that people can learn through interaction with others is one of the reasons for the initiation and spread of T-groups. The authors of the primary text describing this method state:[19]

. . . Each individual may learn about his own motives, feelings, and strategies in dealing with other persons. He learns of the reactions he produces in others as he interacts with them. From the confrontation of intentions and effects, he locates barriers to full and autonomous functioning in his relations with others. Out of these he develops new images of potentiality in himself and seeks help from others in converting potentialities into actualities.

None of these values is possible when an individual functions unilaterally; he must engage in interaction with others whose perceptions and interpretations differ from his own.

The authors of a well-known text on discussion methods state the case this way:[20]

It is not without good reason that the cliché, "Two heads are better than one," has been so often repeated. One can cite personal experience and the testimony of others, as well as experimental evidence, to document the proposition that many problems can be solved more effectively through the interplay of several minds than by people working alone. . . .

. . . in a complicated world, where problems take on so many dimensions, even the most intelligent individuals find it difficult to encompass all aspects by themselves.

Examination of Evidence and Thinking

Potter and Andersen, quoted previously, have considered some of the attitudes they believe are essential to effective problem solving. Two of them are the development and maintenance of a reflective approach and the maintenance of a critical attitude toward the quality of the discussion.[21] These writers suggest that, if the goal of discussion is to achieve the best possible solution, each discussant must give equal hearing to all points of view, regardless of his personal prejudices, and that "thoroughness, an insistence upon accuracy, skepticism based on considered judgment, . . . and, above all, a willingness to hold decisions in abeyance until all solutions have been explored" are important ingredients of discussion. They make this suggestion for the discussant.[22]

Listen critically and thoughtfully to others. Seek the other person's point of view; probe for new information and opinion. But don't accept unsupported generalizations. Remember: use your critical faculties when listening.

This is good advice, but we should add, "Remember: use your critical faculties when speaking."

Earlier in this chapter we compared the characteristics of discussion and debate and indicated that critical thinking at its best was essential to both of these rhetorical forms. The use of the best methods of research and analysis, forms and tests of reasoning, forms and tests of opinion, the checking of fallacies in reasoning and objectivity, and an adherence to ethical standards are essential for effective discussion problem solving.

There are limits to the extent to which an individual can or will be critically objective in his participation,[23] but it is necessary to interact with others before we can be sure of the quality of our reasoning and evidence. We all have some faulty ways of thinking, some prejudices and biases, and some personal interests that we may not perceive as conflicting with those of the other members of the group. When our cognitive and affective behaviors are scrutinized by others, group productivity usually is improved.

Motivation and Involvement

A fourth significant value of discussion is that it can assure maximal motivation and involvement of the group members. Again, we realize that practice does not always measure up to the ideal or desired standard. But there is no rhetorical technique that has greater potentiality on this point. A democratic leader who is permissive and patient, members who know and accept their responsibilities in discussion, a leader-member relationship that establishes a balance between goal- and group-centered behavior, and a topic that is related to the need-value systems of all participants—these and other factors can provide the conditions essential for motivation and involvement. Even in large meetings shy members can be helped to contribute when appropriate procedures are used. When leadership is considered a function of the group instead of one of a single "leader," and when the members have minimal feelings of defense and maximal feelings of security, the ego satisfaction the discussant gets from participating assures productive involvement.

THE NATURE OF SMALL-GROUP DISCUSSION

To understand how the process of discussion proceeds most effectively it is well to consider briefly the nature of small groups in which discussion may occur. We are concerned with two aspects of the small group: its structural and its interactional dimensions. We shall consider selected structural characteristics and interactional patterns that will aid you in understanding the forces functioning both inside and outside the small group. This understanding of theoretical concepts of small-group structure and functioning—call it the psychology and sociology of the small group—should help you in becoming a more effective discussion group member. As a point of reference we cite the following definition of the small group:[24]

A group refers to a face-to-face or co-acting interaction system *in which successive interactions determine its structure, identity, and content and contribute to the satisfaction of certain needs of the members of the system. Or we may say that* a group, *given certain dimensions of space and time and reflecting more or less unchanging characteristics in its population, serves through the interactions of its members to satisfy some of their basic needs and drives.*

Structural Dimensions

As a small group begins its life cycle, input is composed of what the members bring to the group as individuals and what they bring as a group.

Individual Characteristics

The *size* of small groups varies from two (the dyad) to fifteen or twenty or even more. As the group becomes larger, the interrelationships among its members change. Greater size increases many aspects of the complexity of the group. The number of possible interpersonal relationships increases geometrically, which decreases the number of opportunities for contributing that the individual can make. This in turn decreases member satisfaction.[25] More time is required to reach consensus, and there is a greater likelihood that splinter (conflicting) groups will develop. In small groups there is a tendency for feelings and sentiments to be emphasized more. That is, the affective component of the content is considered as well as the substantive component.

At some level in the increase in the size of a group a point is reached where formalization of procedures begins: leadership roles become specialized, rules and regulations for process are established, control and patterns of communication develop, locomotion toward group goals is necessarily slowed down, and leaders in large groups tend to be stricter in their relations with the members.

A concise summary of the results of discussion in small groups (two, three, and four members) and large groups (five, six, and seven members) is presented in research done by Slater.[26] Small groups had more time for problem solving, greater efficiency, more concentration on the job and more accomplishment, less competition and isolation of group members from discussions, and more satisfaction with positions in the group. Although those experimental groups might all be considered "small," there seems to be evidence supporting the generalization that an increase in size changes the functioning of a group. Speaking of optimal size for productive discussion groups, Bass states:[27]

The optimum size shrinks to two when only simple, solitary judgments are required, where adding members mainly adds redundant information to the groups. For single, uncomplicated judgments a two-man panel seems to do the best job, since interaction interferences are minimized. Two-man groups have been found more accurate and satisfying than those of three or four in size in a variety of such simple judging operations.

The *sex* of the members of a discussion group is another factor that *may* have some influence on small-group processes. The authors have been unable to find research studies dealing directly with the relation between the sex of the participants and such factors as productivity, attitude change, and leadership characteristics, but we believe that the sex of group members must be given consideration. In our experience in the conduct of discussion in classes, we have noted few significant differences between male and female students in knowledge of discussion skills, critical thinking ability, variety of interest in subject matter, or effectiveness in interpersonal relations. However, there seem to be marked differences in attitudes on some topics, less willingness on the part of women in classes to assume voluntarily leadership positions in discussion groups, and a tendency of women to do a more detailed analysis of a topic. Review the section on "Language of Sexuality" in Chapter Seven.

Another input each discussant brings to a small group is his *expectations and needs.* They may relate to the covert or overt goals of either the group or the individual. It is obvious that only infrequently do the private and public goals of the group and all its members coincide. When the group's goals are clear and are accepted by the members, when the members feel secure in expressing their expectations, feelings, and opinions on the subject, when there is general agreement about the extent, ability, and nature of commitment to act on group decisions made, and when the members know that some rewards will accrue from any action taken, then group productivity usually is high.

It is important, too, to note that the individual's expectations and needs in participating in small-group discussions are related to the "hierarchy of roles" within the group. Some persons wish to stay "behind the curtain," while others have a need to be "in front of the footlights." This applies in discussion as well. It suggests the need for a variety of leadership tasks, an emphasis on democratic leadership climate, the opportunity for training and growth in leadership experiences, a minimum of feelings of defense and anxiety in interpersonal relations, and cohesive locomotion toward group goals.

A fourth input from each member of a small discussion group is his *communicative skills.* It is hard to generalize on this point, but on the basis of our experience with a wide variety of adult groups outside the classroom and within we believe that individual heterogeneity of communication skills is usually the case in discussion groups. Skills of analysis, logical reasoning, objectivity, ability to speak effectively to several or to many, willingness to speak out on the subject, power of concentration, creative thinking ability, and knowledge of the subject matter usually vary. All these differences limit the potential effectiveness of the discussion and impose restrictions on the leader or leadership team. The pace of the discussion must be slowed down, greater effort must be made to secure maximal involvement, more attention must be devoted to process and, again, a wide variety of functional roles must be planned to provide for a maximal use of the communicative skills the group members possess.

If we believe that speech is the primary medium of communication in small-group activity, then it is apparent that the discussion leader should be aware of the typical communication lacks that individuals have, that the discussion-group member should assume greater responsibility for more effective communication in discussion, and that the student of discussion should seek to improve his communicative skills.

Group Characteristics

Four group structural dimensions are of particular significance: the purpose, the autonomy of the group, the role structure within the group, and the developmental stages in the life cycle of the group.

The *purpose* of a group may be overt or covert, predetermined or emergent, or some combination of these. Sometimes the goals of discussion groups are outlined in general terms and must be explicitly determined by the group. This was the situation with the fifteen-member Wage-Price Stabalization committee appointed by President Nixon in 1971. Their responsibility was to slow down the rate of inflation; their discussion task was to find the best means, acceptable to the labor, management, and public representatives on the committee, of accomplishing this task. The explicit statement of the goals of a group is sometimes its most difficult task. It should be clearly stated, be relevant to the problem as defined, be generally acceptable to the group's members, and be possible of achievement.

A second group membership characteristic is the *autonomy* of the group. By this we mean the degree to which a group functions independently of other groups and occupies an independent position in the conduct of its decision-making affairs. The autonomy of a group is reflected in its right and responsibility for determining its own actions, its freedom from regulations imposed by a parent or outside group, the minimal amount of influence exerted on its members by their reference groups, and the responsibility it carries for its own acts. Few small discussion groups have complete autonomy. A local chapter of the AAUN, VFW, BPOE, AFL-CIO, NAACP, or YMCA must conduct its affairs somewhat in line with the regulations established by its respective national organization. The external organizations, of which a local group is a part, are roughly equivalent to what Homans—in his theory of groups—calls the "external system." The external system brings forces to bear on a small group that determine or modify the internal processes of a group. These forces, according to Homans, are physical activities, sentiments or feelings, and verbal interactions.[28]

Each small discussion group needs to know the boundaries of its autonomy, if it is to be maximally effective. The unstructured nature of the T-group at the beginning of its life cycle reflects some of the characteristics of a completely autonomous group, a group that determines its own content, disciplines or otherwise controls its own members, is usually cut off from ties to the "outside" world, gets little, if any, direction from its "trainer," and has a minimum of role differentiation.

Learning groups, especially in the classroom, have a reasonable degree of autonomy, except for content. The problem here, however, is to get students to assume the roles they must play in an autonomous group, when the instructor permits or persuades them to make their own decisions about content, procedures, teacher-student relations, and grading.

The *hierarchical relationships* in a group constitute another group characteristic. This refers to the differentiation of roles within the group. Sometimes these roles are stable, clearly differentiated, few in number, established by the "rules" of the group, and specific as to function, and persons playing the roles continue "in office until their term expires." Discussion in such a group is more or less formalized and may even be guided by "rules of order." There are other groups in which strict role relationships develop but are the result of on-going interactions within the group. Gangs, play groups, some athletic teams, work groups, inmates of penal institutions, and communes develop modes and customs of behavior, clearly differentiated leader and member roles, and rules of discipline generally accepted by the membership. Discussion in these groups may be formal or informal, permissive or restricted (depending on the character of leadership), and goal-centered or group-centered. The role structure, even when the climate of the group is autocratic, is designed to maintain group cohesiveness and goal achievement.

The hierarchical relationships in still other groups develop from the interpersonal interactions within the group but have somewhat different characteristics The roles are still functional, but they are performed successively by different persons within the group, are not always clearly differentiated, and follow procedural rules that are flexible and can be easily changed by the membership; if there is a "leadership" figure, he usually plays a "helping" rather than a "directive" role.

An understanding of group roles, role functions, and role relationships is essential for effective discussion.

A fourth group characteristic with important implications for effective discussion is the *development stage* of the life cycle of the group. This may refer to the stages in the problem-solving sequence considered earlier in this chapter, to the changing stages of group growth such as occur in T-groups, to the developmental task stages that occur in primary groups such as the family, to the structured task-oriented progression in the classroom, or to the well-defined steps in the organization of a formal group such as a local chapter of a national fraternity. As a student you will be primarily concerned with discussion as it occurs in a problem-solving sequence, in T-group development, or in the typical classroom.

We have already pointed out the stages in the problem-solving discussion sequence. You have had many experiences that can guide you in classroom discussions. It may be well for you to be aware, at least, of the life cycle of training groups. Although different researchers have stated that the stages in the development of a T-group follow different patterns,[29] there seems to be some agreement about what happens when a group of strangers meets for the first time in a situation in which they must define their own tasks and attempt to achieve them in a relatively unstructured interaction pattern. The report by Thelen and Dickerman is an adequate generalized summary of T-group development. They suggest that groups go through four rather distinct stages in their life cycle:[30] (1) an effort by the individual members to satisfy their ego needs and establish with others in the group relations that are similar to their "back home" stereotypes, (2) a period of frustration and conflict created by the stereotyped ways of behaving in the first stage and a rebellion against the "leaders," (3) the beginning and establishment of feelings of cohesiveness and responsibility for satisfying individual and group needs, and (4) a stage of mature goal-centeredness and sensitivity to the rights of others. The focus is on group productivity and the satisfaction of ego needs.

Any discussion is influenced by many factors, including both the individual and group characteristics we have considered. To be aware of these structural dimensions of a small discussion group is a first step in understanding how to contribute maximally to any discussion.

Interaction Dimensions

A small group has both structure and interaction dimensions. We now consider two of the latter: patterns of participation and leadership.

Participation Patterns

There are a number of ways of classifying participation patterns in a small discussion group. We shall consider briefly four of them. The patterns are not mutually exclusive, but each involves different modes of participation on the part of both leader and discussants.

Cooperation versus Competition. The classic study that differentiates between the two concepts of cooperation and competition and the effects of each upon small (face-to-face) group functioning is that of Deutsch.[31] Deutsch says a cooperative group has "promotively interdependent goals." This is defined as meaning that, if the goals of one individual are reached, the goals of all other members can be reached to some degree. A competitive group has "contriently interdependent goals." That is, if a goal or "goal region" is reached by one individual or by a portion of individuals, the other individuals will be unable to reach their respective goals. In discussion a promotive interdependence is the ideal situation, each individual working for goals that are mutually satisfying to all.

Much has been written about the need for cooperation in small-group discussion and the distinction between cooperative and competitive discussion. We believe difference of opinion in discussion is needed, provided the varying points of view are used as a basis for securing the "best" solution. But a competitive attitude, as defined by Deutsch, can do much to destroy the effectiveness of discussion. A useful contrast of the divergent characteristics of cooperative and competitive discussion is given by Potter and Andersen.[32] We present an adaptation of this material below.

If discussion is to be effective, the *participation pattern* must:

Be cooperative	*not*	Competitive
Be in agreement on goals		Divided as to goals
Follow an orderly problem- solving sequence		Reflect subjective, often nonlogical thinking
Make constructive use of conflict		Be divided as to goals
Give all participants a chance to satisfy their ego needs		Limit the satisfaction of ego needs to a few
Reflect a willingness of all to accept responsibility for accomplishing group tasks		Develop a disregard for individual responsibility for the group's goals
Move toward feeling of reli- ance on the group members		Move toward feeling of reli- ance on the leader
Encourage freedom of expression		Inhibit expression of ideas
Make optimal use of all resources		Limit the use of available resources
Develop feelings of security and cohesiveness		Allow feelings of threat and defense
Permit the group to make procedural decisions		Limit procedural decisions to one or a few

Group, Goal, or Self Orientation. In a previous section dealing with the use of discussion as a means of meeting individual needs, we explained briefly the differences among these three patterns of participation. Goal-oriented behavior patterns seek primarily the accomplishment of the group's goals. Group-oriented behavior seeks primarily to maintain the group as an identity, including concern about its morale, cohesion, and autonomy. Ego-oriented behavior seeks primarily to enhance the self-interests of the individual. An excellent article written by Benne and Sheats[33] describes these patterns of participation. We give below only the captions of the behaviors listed in their classification.

Goal-oriented behavior includes:
1. Goal-setting activity
2. Process-related activity
3. Seeking information and opinion

    4. Giving information and opinion
    5. Reasoning activity
    6. Evaluating activity
    7. Synthesizing activity
Group-oriented behavior includes:
    1. Encouraging activity
    2. Compromising and mediating activity
    3. Improving communication patterns
    4. Tension-reducing activity
    5. Follower activity
    6. Cathartic activity
    7. Reality-testing activity
Self-oriented behavior includes:
    1. Aggressive behavior
    2. Obstructing activity
    3. Recognition-seeking activity
    4. Withdrawal activity
    5. Competitive activity
    6. Play-boy activity
    7. Special-interest solicitation

It should be obvious that a combination of goal-oriented and group-oriented patterns of participation will result in greater group productivity.

Task Orientation versus Process Orientation. Task and process orientations as patterns of behavior are closely akin to the goal and group orientations described previously. A person who is essentially task oriented moves steadily toward goal achievement with little consideration for what may be happening to the group in the process. He focuses on the logical analysis of the problem, ignores the feelings of the individual group members, pushes always toward "getting the task done," frequently may impose his own will on the group, and is somewhat inflexible in his consideration of what he may consider to be irrelevant issues or suggestions. By contrast, the process-oriented individual is less concerned about the immediacy of goal achievement. He focuses on the smoothness with which the group functions. He wants procedural questions answered before he will discuss the subject matter. Protocol, group membership, length of meetings, agenda priorities, and even seating arrangements may be considered before he is ready to exchange views on the problem the group must solve. In recent years we have seen many instances of the failure of international conferences to achieve their avowed goals because of the insistence on making decisions about what are almost insignificant procedural matters before the general purpose of the meeting is taken up. Although procedural matters are important and are sometimes given too little consideration, they cannot become the tail that wags the dog.

Nondirection versus Direction. Nondirective and directive participation patterns have greater implications for therapy groups than for problem-solving groups and apply more to what the leaders do than to membership behavior. The student and practitioner of discussion should nevertheless know the distinction between the two.

Nondirective behavior patterns are unstructured (or at least appear to be), do not seem to follow a systematized pattern of problem solving,[34] have leaders who give little if any "direction" to the discussion, place little control on the equalization of participation, and give little concern to progress toward goals or the charting of what progress occurs; if leadership emerges, it comes from the group, or the group continues without apparent leadership; and there is little concern about sensing and acting on the will of the group.

Directive participation patterns are the converse of these. An attempt is made to define goals clearly, progress toward goals is systematized and evaluated by the group, group members assume more responsibilities, and the leadership is shared and directed toward goals.

Both nondirective and directive participation patterns have advantages and disadvantages. Nondirective participation gives freedom to the group members, but it can end in chaos. Directive participation assures greater productivity but can end in the autocratic takeover of the group by one or a few of the members. The rule of thumb, apparently, is to seek the best from both forms of member behavior.

Leadership Patterns

It is probably true that there are as many leadership patterns in small-group discussions as there are leaders. We therefore limit our analysis of this subject to dimensions and styles of leadership that affect the effectiveness and productivity of discussion.

Leadership Dimensions. Influence, or power, is one dimension of leadership. Influence is the nature and extent to which an individual persuades or leads others. Influence is more than group belongingness. Bonner states in this connection:[35]

Not all individuals, however, are satisfied with group belongingness as such. Some desire not only to belong but even more to influence, persuade, or lead others. In some people these motives exceed the need for acceptance. Belongingness as such is for them only a means whereby they may direct and influence others. When the need to dominate is powerful, authoritarian control becomes the central gratification. When it is softened by a consideration for the well-being of others, democratic leadership is a normal consequence. In the latter case, dominance loses its aggressive properties, and the individual finds satisfaction in being an instrument for the achievement of goals collectively.

A second dimension of leadership patterns is *communicative skill.* In discussion this is no less important than in the interview and in platform speaking. Audibility, logical and creative expression, concision, informality while being forceful, vocal variety, well-documented evidence and opinion, critical listening ability, and a willingness to share in the communicative transaction are but a few of the skills needed. In fact, most of what we have said in this text is related to the communicative skills needed in discussion.

Effective *guidance and control* is a third dimension of leadership in discussion. Productive discussion stays on the beam. This is the responsibility of the discussants, too, but it is a primary leadership function. Guidance and control do not need to be applied in a dictatorial manner; rather, the dimension of leadership should assist the group to determine its goals, establish priorities for the agenda, ensure relatively equal participation, press for continued progress toward the goals, chart the progress made, and try to reach a consensus agreeable to all. Guidance and control should be democratic, not autocratic.

Informality and flexibility constitute a fourth dimension of discussion leadership. Although agenda should be prepared in advance, the leader must be willing to digress if the group wishes. The cathartic value of a brief digression sometimes saves valuable time later in a discussion. Restrictive and seemingly autocratic enforcement of rules can negate the potential of a productive group. A willingness to share the leadership roles, secure maximal involvement of all members, assimilate new members readily, and provide opportunity for the release of tensions is an indication of a flexible leadership.

Finally, *training skill* is the fifth important dimension of leadership. One of the generalizations that may be conclusively made on the basis of the research, theoretical conceptualization, and practice in the area of group processes is that people can be trained for more effective leadership in groups. We believe this, and we believe further that it is a responsibility of the "leaders" of a discussion group to train the membership in leadership skills. When it is feasible, the best discussion leader helps others assume leadership roles and "works himself out of a job."

Leadership Styles. The studies conducted under Lewin's direction on leadership under different social climates—democratic, autocratic, and laissez-faire (unorganized)—have become a landmark for students and practitioners of discussion.[36] Reports of these studies have appeared in almost every text dealing with small-group discussion processes. The types of leadership behavior observed in the studies are described by White and Lippitt as follows:[37]

"Autocracy" here implies a high degree of control by the leader without much freedom by the members or participation by them in group decisions, while both "democracy" and "laissez-faire" imply a low degree of control by the leader. "Democracy" is distinguished from "laissez-faire," however, by the fact that in it the leader is very active in stimulating group discussion and group decisions, while in laissez-faire he plays a passive, hands-off role.

Because of the philosophical and practical implications of the adoption of any one of these leadership roles in discussion, we have listed below some generalizations about each type, which may guide you when you play a leadership role in discussion.[38]

In a *democratic-leadership climate* we may expect to find the following.

1. Policy decisions are made by the group, encouraged and assisted by the leader.
2. Activity plans are made by the group, technical advice being provided by the leader when needed.
3. Member satisfactions are gained in making own decisions.
4. Members grow in self-confidence and self-acceptance.
5. Leaders and members function as peers.
6. Emphasis on status decreases and emphasis on respect for others increases.
7. Listening improves, with a resultant greater acceptance of the ideas of others.
8. Little stress is placed on discipline, unless imposed by the group. The leader's relation to the members is friendly, helping, and tolerant.
9. There is a fundamental belief on the part of the leader that the members can attain their own ends by using their own resources.
10. Subgroup assignment and task decisions are left up to the group.
11. Responsibilities are placed on all members.
12. Status in the group is earned by the contribution made to the achievement of the group's goals; praise from the leader is objective and factually based.

In an *autocratic-leadership climate* we may expect to find the following.

1. Activity plans are made by the leader, with some uncertainty on the part of members about what the next steps may be.
2. All policy decisions are made by the leader.
3. Member frustrations may increase, unless productivity is high, resulting from high standards set by the leader.
4. Member discontent may develop when leaders seek dominance for its own sake.
5. Considerable status differences exist between leaders and members.
6. Aggressive status-seeking activities develop among members who have need of status.
7. Members listen carefully to leader's instructions; they may pay little attention to what others say, unless productivity is at stake.
8. Considerable stress is placed on discipline and on getting the job done.
9. There is a fundamental belief on the part of the leader that constant direction is necessary for goal achievement.
10. Subgroup assignment and task decisions are made by the leader.
11. Limited responsibility is placed on all members; members are chosen for specific tasks.
12. Status comes from praise from the leader, which is usually personal and subjective.

In a *laissez-faire–leadership climate* we may expect to find the following.

1. Members of the group are given help in activity plans by the leader only when he is asked.
2. The group has complete freedom to make policy decisions without any help or guidance from the leader.
3. Members do not know what is expected of them and develop disunity and dissatisfactions.
4. Members have little sense of accomplishment.
5. Few contacts exist between leader and members. Little friendship for the leader develops.
6. Status-mindedness develops, resulting in competitive hostility.

7. Members focus primarily on their own concerns. Listening to others' comments is infrequent.
8. There is no concern for discipline. Members develop self-assertiveness without regard for others.
9. There is little concern for group goal achievement.
10. Comments by leader on member activities are infrequent. No attempt is made by leader to interfere with group's activities.
11. Leader places no responsibilities on members, who are left to develop activities if they wish.
12. Development of feelings of unity, self-confidence, or friendliness lacking.

We believe the democratic type of leadership produces the best results under most circumstances. However, there are times when a group must be "guided" and other times when it must be "left alone."

THE CONDUCT OF GROUP DISCUSSION

Effective discussion must be well planned and well conducted and have a meaningful conclusion. In this section we consider three facets of discussion that contribute to group-discussion productivity: leadership functions, member responsibilities, and process evaluation.

The Functions of Leadership

The reader may have noted that we have talked about "leaders" and "leadership" throughout this chapter. Primarily our concern has been with the leadership function. Our belief is that, although a leader may be designated to perform a certain task in discussion, the productivity is greater, more individual needs are met, cohesion is stronger, and the commitment to action is greater when leadership functions are shared by all members of the group. We therefore define leadership on a functional basis; that is, anything a member does that contributes to goal achievement is considered the performance of a leadership task.

This division of leadership functions—or of responsibilities—applies to both formal (public) and informal (private) discussions. Usually leadership functions should be shared. However, in some circumstances the leadership function is better centralized. For instance, groups inexperienced in discussion usually find the steady direction of a single leader helpful. When time is limited, excessive division of leadership responsibility tends to slow progress. However, the suggestions that follow assume that, in general, responsibility will be shared as much as possible.

Among the functions to be performed in any discussion—formal or informal—are getting started, securing participation, making progress, guiding, creating a permissive atmosphere, and closing.

We now turn to a consideration of the various leadership functions that must be performed in the conduct of a discussion.

Providing the Beginning

Some discussion groups are called together "at a moment's notice," but most of the participants know about them well in advance. In the latter case careful planning and preparation is a must. The members of a private discussion or the panelists or speakers in a public discussion should be selected well in advance of the meeting. Publicity and promotion, if needed, must be considered. If films are to be shown, technicians may be needed. Many other tasks, besides, may need to be performed, especially in public discussion. The topic outlines are the joint responsibility of the panel members and moderator or of the members and leaders of an informal discussion group. Only in the most exceptional cases should the outline of points to be considered in a discussion be made by any one person.

In preparing for a panel-forum you need at least one planning meeting, at which moderator and panel members together agree on the procedures for governing the program, develop outlines, and assign individual members phases of the topic for special study. When panel members are chosen for special knowledge on some aspects of the topic, as is often the case, they are assumed to be responsible for those aspects in the panel discussion. A brief rehearsal before the program is always helpful, especially for beginners. However, even the most experienced television panels almost always run through the discussion beforehand to ensure a measure of smoothness. At the very least they should agree on the first few points to be considered.

In a private discussion some consideration should be given to rules of procedure before a discussion of the topic itself.

The opening of any discussion program is extremely important. If the group members do not know each other, they should be introduced, unless the size of the group makes this inadvisable. Self-introductions usually are advisable in informal discussions. The moderator usually introduces panel members or symposium speakers to the listeners.

To start the discussion the moderator or leader announces the procedures to be followed—time schedules, recess periods, order of speaking, length and nature of audience contributions, and any other pertinent items. If they have not been determined in advance, he gets agreement from the group members on what these should be. He also states the purpose of the discussion, points out its significance, suggests something of the issues involved, and makes the first step in beginning the discussion. The last may be a statement of the first point to be considered, a general question to all panelists or group members, or a specific question to some selected person. There should always be advance agreement on the first steps in a discussion, as to both order of speaking and content.

In opening a discussion it is important to create an atmosphere in which members will not only feel free to participate but also feel a responsibility to participate.

When the moderator or leader gets early agreement on the rules of procedure, impresses listeners with the significance of the topic, makes clear to all his own role as neutral guide, and develops an atmosphere in which the participants have confidence, the discussion usually is off to a good start.

Providing Optimal Participation

Members of a discussion group, whether private or public, have a resource potential that must be tapped if the discussion is to be most effective. Hence, everyone involved should be concerned with both the quantity and quality of participation. It is usually fairly easy to get every one to participate if each member is made to feel that his contributions are wanted and his personality respected. Obviously, it is hardly to be expected that all will participate equally; occasional silences should not be disturbing. At the same time the moderator or leader should not permit anyone to monopolize the discussion.

The discussion chairman will find the following suggestions helpful:

1. Recognize a person who hasn't talked in preference to one who has.
2. Don't feel obliged to comment every time a member makes a contribution. Refer questions to the group, unless you are the only person who has the answer.
3. Don't push the discussion too fast. In discussion you must start where the group members are and move them only as fast as they will go.
4. Try to get talkative members to assume responsibility for getting reticent persons to speak.
5. In stimulating the discussion avoid questions that can be answered with only "yes" or "no."
6. Summarize or clarify when necessary, to keep the discussion from slowing down.
7. Test the information and evidence presented.
8. Keep the discussion "on the beam."

Guiding for Progress

All members of a discussion group should be familiar with the steps in logical thinking and should follow them. Moreover, progress is greatly aided by effective transitions from one point to another and by frequent summaries. It is not necessary to talk out every point considered, but the group should not move on to another point as long as there is still considerable interest in the one being discussed. Effective discussion leaders and members point out areas of agreement and disagreement, clarify points when needed, and constantly keep the major goal in mind. It helps, too, to point out progress toward that goal from time to time.

Discussion is not always all sweetness and light. Differences of opinion should be not only expected but welcomed and used as the basis of necessary study and analysis, to further integration rather than conformity. If conflicting opinions are respected, people are more likely to feel that they can talk freely. In other words, progress in discussion should never be at the expense of any individual member. It goes without saying that the leader should never take sides; a member could easily lose his sense of security if the leader is on the other side.

Positive guidance is achieved when the leader or members do certain things themselves or encourage others to do them. Negative guidance keeps certain things from happening. Occasionally summaries by the moderator and clarifying statements by group members would be positive guidance. Avoiding such disturbing factors as digressions, conflicts between persons rather than about ideas, and monopoly of the discussion by a few, would be negative guidance. The discussion chairman, particularly, should try to guide and direct rather than control. At times he may have to make procedural decisions, give factual information, or suggest phases of the topic that might be considered. However, he should do this in the interest of progress and not to express a personal point of view.

An aid to guidance is the discussion outline, if one can be prepared in advance. It is not essential to follow every point in the outline exactly, but it serves as a tentative guide for the discussion, the major points to be covered, and the particular phases of the topic for which group or panel members are responsible. Its function is comparable to that of a speech outline, ensuring that all significant points are included and that they are covered adequately; it also guides the group members during the discussion. The preparation of such an outline usually stimulates study on the topic, crystallizes thinking, conserves time in the actual discussion, and generally increases the effectiveness of group thinking.

Discussion outlines vary a good deal. Some consist merely of a series of questions the moderator will ask the panel members. Others list the major points tentatively selected for consideration. An outline may also indicate in some detail the pattern of thinking to be followed. Whatever its form, the sequence of points should follow the progression of the problem-solving steps considered earlier. Those five steps are sometimes condensed into three considerations essential in any discussion: What is the problem? What are the possible solutions? What is the best solution?

A brief discussion outline on the subject of providing adequate medical care might look like this:

How Can Adequate Medical Care Be Provided in Our Community?
    I. What is the problem?
        A. How does the need for medical care affect the individual?
        B. How does the provision of medical care affect the doctor?
        C. What are the community-wide implications of the need for adequate medical care?
        D. What national implications must be considered?
    II. What can be done about it?
        A. In what ways are existing services adequate?
        B. Would the promotion of group hospital and medical-care plans help?
        C. How can community-supported free or low-cost services be provided?
        D. In what ways can Medi-Cal and Medi-Care help?
    III. What action can be taken now?
        A. Expand local hospital facilities?
        B. Stimulate the adoption of group health plans?
        C. Expand state and federal aid for health and hospital care?

In one discussion in which this outline was used the panel members decided that the expansion of the hospital facilities through the use of city funds and the promotion of group health plans were the two best immediate steps that could be taken. A different group in another discussion situation might agree on some other "best" solution.

Ensuring Objectivity
We have remarked that any good discussion must embody the principles of reflective thinking, starting with an analysis of a problem and presenting all available information pertaining to it, before decisions are made. Critical objectivity is the essence of reflective-thought processes.

All members of a discussion group, and especially the leader, can help to establish this attitude of critical objectivity. They can refuse to reject ideas that superficially appear irrelevant or unimportant. They can refuse to be side-tracked by purely tangential ideas. They can insist on considered judgments rather than unsupported assertions. They can make every effort to be impersonal, tolerant, critical of premises and conclusions, fearless in facing facts, and free from emotional bias.

Creating the Atmosphere

Both physically and psychologically much can be done to create an atmosphere conducive to discussion. First, of course, there should be concern for members' comfort, seating arrangements, acoustics of the meeting room, heat and ventilation, availability of materials, proper use of visual aids, and times to recess. Although the leader usually appoints someone to handle these matters, sometimes they all fall on the discussion chairman.

The psychological task of creating a permissive atmosphere is not so simple. Too frequently discussion is overly serious and even dull. Although we would hardly approve of conducting it on a light or frivolous level, it should nevertheless be an enjoyable experience. Leader and members should treat it as such and help to make it pleasurable for all. Some of the leader's responsibilities along this line have already been mentioned, but they can certainly bear repetition. He should make sure that the members know each other and that they feel free to use first names. He should also try to have them avoid status symbols. Members should never feel pushed. Furthermore, they should be called on to establish group standards. The chairman should always keep members informed of their own progress and give them the feeling that they are contributing effectively to the accomplishment of group goals.

It is also helpful to have each member feel protected and encouraged to make his maximal contribution. If the leader knows the members, he usually can draw them out. Some have facts they should be encouraged to present; others have analytical skills that should be utilized. Those with special facility in speaking should be stimulated to encourage others to contribute.

Effecting Closure and Follow-up

As the discussion nears its end, the leader should summarize, or have others summarize, the progress made, indicate differences that remain unresolved, review decisions made, and point out action that is warranted. He should indicate how reports of the discussion may be secured or will be distributed and suggest readings that may help the discussants prepare for the next meetings.

The leader should scrupulously watch that prearranged time limits are observed; nothing takes the edge off a good discussion more than failure to end on time. He should make sure that those responsible for future planning are aware of their duties and that arrangements for possible future evaluations or discussions are made. In closing he thanks the participants for their contributions.

Participant Responsibilities

We have previously considered the various types of participation patterns that reflect the mode of behavior of individuals in discussion. Let us now look at some of the specific responsibilities of the discussants.

Preparing for Participation

It is probably a truism to say that each member should prepare himself to be a valuable member of the group; and yet this cannot be said too often. He can seek information and opinions of others in advance of the discussion, he can study and do research himself, he should attend all preliminary planning meetings, he should come to the discussion with ideas and questions in mind, he should assist in the preparation of any needed materials and, finally, he should familiarize himself with the discussion methods to be used. Every individual has a unique background, which makes his particular contribution valuable, since no one else can see the problem from exactly the same point of view.

Communicating Effectively

Obviously, discussion reaches its greatest effectiveness when each member is an effective speaker. At the very least, individual contributions should be easily heard, clear, brief, to the point, and accurate. Facts must be supported, opinions well considered, and the ideas presented well organized. Whatever is said should be said in a lively, conversational style. It is fully as important, when he is not speaking, that each member take a lively interest in what the others are saying.

The content of one's contributions is as important as his articulateness in speaking. All types of supporting material should be used: statistics, quotations, sound reasoning, generalizations, applications of principles, definitions, testimony, summaries, or clarification of points made. Content presentations should, of course, be regarded as a major responsibility of each member of the group.

Contributing Systematically

Effectiveness usually is increased when all members understand the process of reflective thinking. They should then be able to identify the stage of the discussion at any time and contribute accordingly. Contributions should relate to what has previously been said, deal with the specific point under consideration, and be directed toward the overall goal. As already remarked, differences of opinion should be welcomed and dealt with constructively as bases for clarification and integration. Rules of evidence and opinion should be followed, and reasoning should be sound.

Maintaining Friendly Attitudes

It almost goes without saying that each member of a discussion group should demonstrate a sense of fair play and conduct himself with decorum, treating others as he would like to be treated himself. The sure ways of spoiling the occasion are to monopolize the time, refuse to contribute, complain, encourage personality conflicts, be on the defensive, and try to be the center of attention at all times. A good way to make yourself a wanted person in a discussion group is to show interest in what others say and to be considerate of them. Be willing to do the tasks needed by the group; assume your share of responsibility for making progress. Don't let the chairman do it all!

Conditions are rarely the same in any two discussion groups. At times it may be your lot to be chairman, but do not consider it your prerogative to hold this position in every discussion. At times you may be able to help others grow in leadership skills, and at other times you may learn from them. Flexibility, willingness to subordinate self, attentiveness at all times, positiveness when needed, and sensitivity to others are invaluable skills for every participant in a discussion.

Process Evaluation

A third essential for the effective conduct of discussion is process evaluation, a consideration of (1) how well the group progressed toward its goal, or the *content,* (2) how effective was the planning, or the *procedures,* and (3) how well the members worked together, or the *individuals and the group* itself. Discussion can be improved only when the members are concerned about their progress and eager to improve.

Evaluation should be a continuous process. The specific nature of the evaluation should be considered in advance of the discussion, and tools for evaluation should be prepared.[39] If progress is blocked during the discussion, some effort should be made to determine the cause. Finally, some form of post-meeting evaluation should be made. The following questions should suggest some of the trouble spots in discussion.

Of Content

Evaluation of the content of a discussion implies concern for the group's progress toward established goals. It can be judged by such questions as the following.

Were the goals clearly established at the outset of the discussion? Did all members understand and accept the goals? If not, why not?

Were priorities established in the accomplishment of the goals?

Were enough resources available to make needed decisions leading to goal accomplishment? If not, what additional resources were needed? Where could they have been obtained?

Was adequate use made of resources available to the group?

Was progress toward goals too fast? Too slow? Why?

Was the discussion always relevant to the topic?

What aspects of the topic received insufficient consideration? Too much consideration?

Did the group understand and make effective use of problem-solving techniques in achieving their goals?

Of Procedures

Frequently progress is hampered because the members of a group do not work well together or do not know how to carry on a discussion. Such questions as the following will focus attention on procedures:

Were preparation and planning effective?

Was the atmosphere conducive to group progress and growth?

Were responsibilities shared?

Was there effective communication among the members?

Did hidden conflicts block the progress?

Were members dependent on the leader? Could leadership tasks have been performed by other members of the group?

Was effective use made of special discussion techniques such as role playing, brainstorming, and problem census?

Was there a balance between emphasis on content and process?

Of Individuals and the Group

Discussion is fruitful for the individual only when he gets some personal satisfaction from participation. This satisfaction partly comes from the fulfillment of ego needs and partly from the fact that he has been able to contribute to group goals. The following questions focus attention on such problems:

Did each member make his maximal contribution?

Did each member seem interested in the discussion?

Was each member secure in the group?

Did the group function on a mature level? If not, why not?

Were the group needs being met?

Did the group have enough cohesion to withstand external pressures?

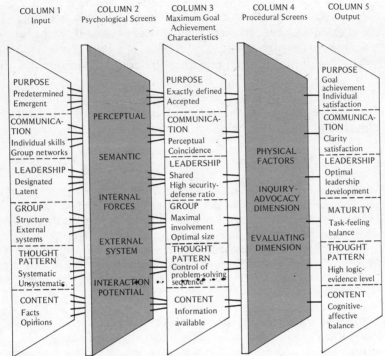

COLUMN 1
Input

COLUMN 2
Psychological Screens

COLUMN 3
Maximum Goal
Achievement
Characteristics

COLUMN 4
Procedural Screens

COLUMN 5
Output

FIGURE 16-1. Model of small-group discussion.

Were appropriate decisions made on follow-up activities? Were specific assignments made?

A MODEL OF SMALL-GROUP DISCUSSION

By way of summary of this last section on the conduct of discussion, and to bring together in a unified way much of what we have considered in the entire chapter, we present a model of discussion that shows the nature of its input, process, and output; see Figure 16-1. The content that follows is a modification of an article written by one of us.[40]

Column 1 represents the six components of any discussion, which we treated in the first section of this chapter. Beneath each component are listed the characteristics that circumscribe that component. Together the six components represent the individual and group inputs in discussion. Column 2 represents a number of socio-psychological processes through which all inputs are screened as discussion begins. The screens act as filters of both what is said and what is heard. Column 3 represents some of the necessary process characteristics that each input component must have for maximal goal achievement. Column 4 represents three important procedural screens that affect the on-going discussion process. Column 5 represents some of the essential characteristics each component must possess if the output is to be considered maximally effective.

The horizontal lines connecting the columns suggest that at the outset of any discussion each individual functions unilaterally, that their functions gradually converge toward a greater maturity of the group and more goal-centeredness, and that eventually the individual goals almost completely coincide with the group goals.

EXERCISES
1. List a number of typical situations in which you participate in informal discussion. Are these situations similar or do they differ? Do they all have the components (dimensions) of discussion outlined in the first section of the chapter? Comment on your findings in class.
2. Select a vocation or profession in which you are interested. Make a list of situations in which you might participate in discussion if you were actually engaged in that vocation or profession. How large a role does discussion play in this occupation?
3. Comment on the following statements:
    a. Discussion and debate are essential tools of a democracy.
    b. Democracy extends only as far as the sound of a man's voice.
    c. There is little evidence that the average person can discuss anything intelligently.
    d. The characteristics of most discussions are manipulation and control.
    e. The decisions made by a few carefully chosen persons are better than decisions made through discussion.
4. Make a list of things that act as blocks to effective discussion, listing them under planning and preparation, leadership, participation, logic of discussion, and evaluation.
5. Be prepared to discuss in class your reaction to the six dimensions of discussion listed in this chapter. Do you believe that all are an essential part of every discussion?
6. Assume that you have been asked to serve as chairman of a panel forum. Make a list of things you would do in preparing for the discussion.
7. We have stated that group discussion meets some of a person's ego needs. How does this apply to you? What values or benefits do you gain by participating in discussions?
8. How has discussion helped in meeting the goals of some of the groups to which you belong? Comment in class on your reactions to this question.
9. Think critically of the learning discussion groups of which you are a member. Do they conform to the criteria one would expect of this type of discussion group?
10. Prepare a five-minute speech in which you give your reactions to the use of discussion in democratic decision-making. Give as many illustrations as you can to support your views.

11. In this chapter it has been indicated that discussion and debate are essential democratic tools. Join four of your classmates in preparing a symposium-forum on how these two processes are used in some area of our national life such as religion, labor-management relations, education, business and industry, scientific research, and the military. Your instructor will help you to find helpful references. Plan for four five-minute symposium speeches, and have one of your group serve as moderator. Allow at least twenty minutes for audience participation.

12. Carry out the following exercise in cooperation with three or four of your classmates. Select any topic from the list given below, or pick some other topic of interest to the members of your group. Prepare to participate in a class panel-forum on the topic. Decide in your group who your moderator should be, and assign any specific duties that may be necessary.

    a. How can teacher-student relations be improved in this college?
    b. How can juvenile delinquency be eliminated in this community?
    c. What effect will the Watergate affair have on political campaigns?
    d. How can television programming be improved?
    e. What can be done to ensure academic freedom in the colleges?
    f. How can the cost of college education be reduced?
    g. What can we do to lessen racial intolerance among college students?
    h. How can we improve our relations with Latin-American countries?
    i. How can we improve the quality of our representatives in foreign countries?
    j. How can we best meet the needs of the "exceptional" children in our secondary schools?
    k. What can be done about closing the "credibility gap" between the people and our governmental officials?
    l. How can the judicial system in this country be improved?

13. Make a list of five problems of value with which young people are concerned. Make two other lists of five topics of value and of policy that have campus implications. Compare your lists with those of two other classmates. How do they compare?

14. Contact one of the speech pathologists in your school, and determine whether he uses group therapy in dealing with speech ailments. Get his reactions concerning the values of group therapy, and report your findings to the class.

15. Do you believe that participating in a decision that affects you increases your commitment to the action planned?

16. The text suggests that the number of participants, the individual's expectancies and needs, the sex of the members, communicative skills, group purpose, group autonomy, hierarchical relations, and the life cycle of a group are functionally related to the success of a small-group discussion. What is your reaction? Be prepared to comment on your reactions in class.

17. Write out a two-page statement of what you consider to be the characteristics of an ideal leader for a small-group discussion.

18. Have you ever participated in discussion groups in which the leadership was autocratic? Democratic? Laissez-faire? Comment in class on the exact differences among the leaders.

19. Work with five of your classmates on this exercise. Select some topic you

believe would be suitable for class discussion. Together work out a complete discussion outline for the subject. Prepare to discuss the topic before your classmates.

20. Study the model of small-group discussion presented in this chapter. Give your reactions to it in class. In what ways should the model be changed?

ADDITIONAL READINGS

Andersen, Martin P., "The agree-disagree discussion guide," *Speech Teacher*, 8 (no. 1, Jan. 1959), 41–48.

Barnlund, Dean C., "Our concept of discussion: Static or dynamic?" *Speech Teacher*, 3 (no. 1, Jan., 1954), 8–14.

Bonner, Hubert, *Group dynamics: Principles and applications*, New York, Ronald, 1959, chaps. 2, 3, 6, 8, 12.

Cartwright, Dorwin, and Alvin Zander, *Group dynamics: Research and theory*, 2nd ed., New York, Harper & Row, 1960, chaps. 3, 9, 19, 25.

Davis, James H., *Group Performance*, Reading, Mass., Addison-Wesley, 1969, chaps. 1, 3, 4, 5.

Ewbank, H. L., and J. Jeffery Auer, *Discussion and Debate*, 2nd ed., New York, Appleton, 1951, chaps. 2, 4, 15, 16, 18, 19, 20, 21.

Gulley, Halbert E., *Discussion, Conference, and Group Process*, 2nd ed., New York, Holt, Rinehart & Winston, 1968, chaps. 1, 2, 3, 4, 8, 9, 10, 11, 14, 17.

Haiman, Franklyn S., *Group Leadership and Democratic Action*, Boston, Houghton Mifflin, 1951, chaps. 4, 5, 7, 8.

Haiman, Franklyn S., "The specialization of roles and function in a group," *Quart. J. Speech*, 43 (no. 2, Apr. 1957), 165–174.

Paulson, Stanley F., "Pressures toward conformity in group discussion," *Quart. J. Speech*, 44 (no. 1, Feb. 1958), 50–55.

Phillips, Gerald M., *Communication and the Small Group*, Indianapolis, Bobbs-Merrill. 1966, chaps. 1, 3, 4, 5.

Sattler, William M., and N. Edd Miller, *Discussion and Conference*, 2nd ed., Englewood Cliffs, N.J., Prentice-Hall, 1968, chaps. 3, 4, 5, 7, 10, 11, 13, 14, 15, 17.

Shepherd, Clovis R., *Small Groups: Some Sociological Perspectives*, San Francisco, Chandler, 1964, chaps. 3, 4.

Thonssen, Lester, "The social values of discussion and debate," *Quart. J. Speech*, 25 (no. 1, Feb. 1939), 113–117.

NOTES

[1] David Potter and Martin P. Andersen, *Discussion: A Guide to Effective Practice*, 2nd ed., Belmont, Calif., Wadsworth, 1970, p. 155.

[2] These are frequently called functional roles of group members or participation patterns. We consider these concepts in detail in a later section in this chapter.

[3] Potter and Andersen, *op. cit.*, p. 15.

[4] See Andersen, Martin P., *A Study of Discussion in Selected Wisconsin Adult Organizations and Public Agencies*, unpublished Ph.D. dissertation, Univ. Wisconsin, 1947, pp. 26–32; and Halbert E. Gulley, *Discussion, Conference and Group Process*, Holt, Rinehart & Winston, 1960, pp. 8–12.

[5] John Dewey, *How We Think*, Boston, Heath, 1910, pp. 67–78.

[6] See Abbott Kaplan, *Study-Discussion in the Liberal Arts*, The Fund for Adult Education, 1960, pp. 128–138; Edmund de S. Brunner, David S. Wilder, Corrine Kirchner, and John S. Newberry, Jr., *An Overview of Adult Education Research*, New York, Adult Education Association of the U.S.A., 1959, pp. 163–176; Robert E. Palmer and Coolie Verner, "A comparison of three instructional techniques," *Adult Education*, 9 (no. 4, Summer 1959), 232–238; Laurence F. Kinney, "Perspective for discussion,"

Adult Education, 11 (no. 1, Autumn 1960), 3–11; R. O. Beckman, *How to Train Supervisors*, 4th rev. ed., New York, Harper & Row, 1952, pp. 10–19; Lois E. Le Bar, *Focus of People in Church Education*, Westwood, N.J., Fleming H. Revell. 1968, pp. 163–207; John G. Geier, Robert F. Forston, and Charles Urban Larson, "Small group discussion versus the lecture method: A study in individual decision making," *Western Speech*, 34 (no. 1, winter 1970), 38–45; and Harry Sharp, Jr., and Joyce Milliken, "Reflective thinking ability and the product of problem-solving discussion," *Speech Monographs*, 31 (no. 2, June 1964), 124–127.

[7]See Martin P. Andersen, "The roles of the teacher of discussion," *Quart. J. Speech*, 46 (no. 2, Apr. 1960), 176–188; Leland P. Bradford, "The teaching-learning transaction," *Adult Education*, 8 (no. 3, Spring 1958), 135–145; Jack R. Gibb, "A climate for learning," *Adult Education*, 9 (no. 1, Autumn 1958), 19–21; and Gerald M. Phillips, *Communication and the Small Group*, Indianapolis, Bobbs-Merrill, 1966, pp. 52–65.

[8]*Ibid.*, Phillips.

[9]See Dorothy Stock Whitaker and Morton A. Lieberman, *Psychopathy and Group Process*, New York, Atherton Press, 1965, pp. 117–132; Herbert Thelen and Watson Dickerman, "Stereotypes and the growth of groups," *Educ. Leadership*, 6 (no. 5, Feb. 1949), 309–316; Matthew B. Miles, *Learning to Work in Groups*, New York, Bureau of Publication, Teachers College, Columbia Univ., 1959, pp. 87–92; George R. Bach, *Intensive Group Psychotherapy*, New York, Ronald, 1954, pp. 198–200, 268–273; B. Aubrey Fisher, "Decision emergence: Phases in group decision-making," *Speech Monographs*, 37 (no. 1, Mar. 1970), 53–66; and Leland P. Bradford, Jack R. Gibb, and Kenneth D. Benne, *T-Group Theory and Laboratory Method*, New York, Wiley, 1964, pp. 253–270.

[10]See Bach, *op. cit.*, pp. 18–22.

[11]Bradford et al., *op. cit.*, p. 2.

[12]Kurt Lewin, "Group decision and social change," in Guy E. Swanson, Theodore Newcomb, and Eugene L. Hartley, eds., *Readings in Social Psychology*, rev. ed., New York, Holt, Rinehart & Winston, 1952, pp. 459–473.

[13]Lester Coch and John R. P. French, Jr., "Overcoming resistance to change," *Human Relations*, 1 (no. 4, 1948), 531.

[14]B. M. Bass and H. J. Leavitt, "Some experiments in planning and operating," *Management Sci.*, 9 (1952), 574–585.

[15]See John Mann, *Changing Human Behavior*, New York, Scribner, 1965, pp. 90–91; Gardner Lindzey and Elliot Aronson, eds., *The Handbook of Social Psychology*, 2nd ed., vol. IV, Reading, Mass., Addison-Wesley, 1969, pp. 84–88.

[16]J. W. Thibaut and H. H. Kelley, *The Social Psychology of Groups*, New York, Wiley, 1959, p. 272.

[17]Jack Brehm and Leon Festinger, "Pressures toward uniformity of performance in groups," *Human Relations*, 10 (no. 1, 1957), 85–91; Leonard Berkowitz, "Group standards, cohesiveness, and productivity," *Human Relations*, 7 (no. 4, 1954), 509–519; Robert R. Blake, Milton Rosenbaum, and Richard A. Duryea, "Gift-giving as a function of group standards," *Human Relations*, 8 (no. 1, 1955), 61–72; Dorwin Cartwright, "Achieving change in people: Some applications of group dynamics theory," *Human Relations*, 4 (no. 4, 1951), 381–392; and S. E. Asch, "Effects of group pressure upon the modification and distortion of judgments," in H. G. Guetzkow, ed., *Groups, Leadership and Men*, Pittsburgh, Carnegie Press, 1951, pp. 171–190.

[18]Harrison Sackett Elliott, *The Process of Group Thinking*, New York, Association Press, 1938, p. 171.

[19]Bradford et al., *op. cit.*, p. 2.

[20]Dean C. Barnlund and Franklyn S. Haiman, *The Dynamics of Discussion*, Boston, Houghton Mifflin, 1960, pp. 326–327.

[21]Potter and Andersen, *op. cit.*, pp. 119–122; 120.

[22]*Ibid.*, p. 60.

[23]See Barnlund and Haiman, *op. cit.*, pp. 326–333, for a statement on this point.

24Potter and Andersen, *op. cit.*, p. 12.

25James A. Schellenberg, "Group size as a factor in success of academic discussion groups," *J. Educ. Sociol.*, 33 (no. 2, 1959), 73–79; and A. Paul Hare, "Intraction and consensus in different sized groups," *Am. Sociol. Rev.*, 17 (no. 3, June 1952), 261–267.

26P. E. Slater, "Contrasting correlates of group size," *Sociometry*, 21 (no. 2, 1958), 129–139.

27Bernard M. Bass, *Organizational Psychology*, Boston, Allyn & Bacon, 1965, p. 203.

28See George C. Homans, *The Human Group*, New York, Harcourt, 1950.

29See Bradford, et al., *op. cit.*, pp. 396–400.

30Thelen and Dickerman, *op. cit.* See also W. G. Bennis and H. A. Shephard, "A theory of group development," *Human Relations*, 9 (no. 4, 1956), 415–437; Matthew B. Miles, *op. cit.*9; R. M. Powell, "An experimental study of role taking, group status, and group formation," *Sociol. Soc. Res.*, 40 (no. 3, 1956), 159–165; and Michael S. Olmstead, *The Small Group*, New York, Random, 1959, pp. 82–88.

31Morton Deutsch, "A theory of co-operation and competition," *Human Relations*, 2 (no. 2, 1949), 129–152.

32Potter and Andersen, *op. cit.*, p. 56.

33Kenneth D. Benne and Paul H. Sheats, "Functional roles of group members," *J. Soc. Issues*, 4 (Spring 1948), 41–49. The reading of this complete article is highly recommended.

34See Ernest G. Bormann, *Discussion and Group Methods*, New York, Harper & Row, 1969, p. 285, for an excellent statement on the nature of "trial and error" problem-solving discussions.

35Hubert Bonner, *Group Dynamics: Principles and Applications*, New York, Ronald, 1959, pp. 47–48.

36See Ralph K. White and Ronald O. Lippitt, *Autocracy and Democracy*, New York, Harper & Row, 1960; and R. Lippitt, "An experimental study of the effect of democratic and authoritarian group atmospheres," *Univ. Iowa Studies Child Welfare*, 16 (no. 3 1940), 43–195, Ames, Iowa, University of Iowa Press.

37White and Lippitt, *op. cit.*, p. 12.

38These lists have been adapted from a variety of sources, including the references in note 39. See also Potter and Andersen, *op. cit.*, pp. 84–85; Hubert Bonner, *op. cit.*, pp. 178–190; Kurt Lewin, Ronald Lippitt, and Ralph K. White, "Patterns of agressive behavior in experimentally created 'Social Climates'," in C. G. Browne and Thomas S. Cohn, *The Study of Leadership*, Danville, Ill., Interstate Printers and Publishers, 1958, pp. 296–303; and C. G. Browne, " 'Laissez Faire' or 'Anarchy' in Leadership," also in Browne and Cohn, *op. cit.*, pp. 304–309.

39Potter and Andersen have developed a wide variety of evaluation and measuring instruments for use in assessing the success of a discussion. See also William M. Sattler and N. Edd Miller, *Discussion and Conference*, 2nd ed., Englewood Cliffs, N.J., Prentice-Hall, 1968, pp. 473–488.

40Martin P. Andersen, "A model of group discussion," *Southern Speech J.*, 30 (no. 4, Summer 1965), 279–293.

APPENDIX:
**SELECTED
SPEECHES
FOR STUDY
AND
ANALYSIS**

DECLARATION OF WAR[1]

The following speech was presented by President Franklin D. Roosevelt to a joint session of Congress on December 8, 1941, in response to the attack on Pearl Harbor the previous day.

Yesterday, December 7, 1941—a date which will live in infamy—the United States of America was suddenly and deliberately attacked by naval and air forces of the Empire of Japan.

The United States was at peace with that nation and, at the solicitation of Japan, was still in conversation with its government and its Emperor, looking toward the maintenance of peace in the Pacific. Indeed, one hour after Japanese air squadrons had commenced bombing in Oahu, the Japanese ambassador to the United States and his colleague delivered to the Secretary of State a formal reply to a recent American message. While this reply stated that it seemed useless to continue the existing diplomatic negotiations, it contained no threat or hint of war or armed attack.

It will be recorded that the distance of Hawaii from Japan makes it obvious that the attack was deliberately planned many days or even weeks ago. During the intervening time the Japanese Government has deliberately sought to deceive the United States by false statements and expressions of hope for continued peace.

The attack yesterday on the Hawaiian Islands has caused severe damage to American naval and military forces. Very many American lives have been lost. In addition American ships have been reported torpedoed on the high seas between San Francisco and Honolulu.

Yesterday the Japanese government also launched an attack against Malaya.

Last night Japanese forces attacked Hong Kong.

Last night Japanese forces attacked Guam.

Last night Japanese forces attacked the Philippine Islands.

Last night the Japanese attacked Wake Island.

This morning the Japanese attacked Midway Island.

Japan has, therefore, undertaken a surprise offensive extending throughout the Pacific area. The facts of yesterday speak for themselves. The people of the United States have already formed their opinions and well understand the implications to the very life and safety of our nation.

As Commander-in-Chief of the Army and Navy, I have directed that all measures be taken for our defense.

Always will we remember the character of the onslaught against us.

No matter how long it may take us to overcome this premeditated invasion, the American people in their righteous might will win through to absolute victory.

I believe I interpret the will of the Congress and of the people when I assert that we will not only defend ourselves to the uttermost but will make very certain that this form of treachery shall never endanger us again.

Hostilities exist. There is no blinking at the fact that our people, our territory, and our interests are in grave danger.

With confidence in our armed forces—with the unbounding determination of our people—we will gain the inevitable triumph—so help us God.

I ask that the Congress declare that since the unprovoked and dastardly attack by Japan on Sunday, December 7, a state of war has existed between the United States and the Japanese Empire.

ICH BIN EIN BERLINER[2]

The following speech was presented by President John F. Kennedy from the steps of the city hall, June 26, 1963, to a public gathering in the Rudolphe Wilde Platz, Berlin, where he was honored by Chancellor Adenauer and Mayor Brandt.

I am proud to come to this city as the guest of your distinguished Mayor, who has symbolized throughout the world the fighting spirit of West Berlin. And I am proud to visit the Federal Republic with your distinguished Chancellor who for so many years has committed Germany to democracy and freedom and progress, and to come here in the company of my fellow American, General Clay, who has been in this city during its great moments of crisis and will come again if ever needed.

Two thousand years ago the proudest boast was "civis Romanus sum." Today, in the world of freedom, the proudest boast is "Ich bin ein Berliner."

I appreciate my interpreter translating my German!

There are many people in the world who really don't understand, or say they don't, what is the great issue between the free world and the Communist world. Let them come to Berlin. There are some who say that communism is the wave of the future. Let them come to Berlin. And there are some who say in Europe and elsewhere we can work with the Communists. Let them come to Berlin. And there are even a few who say that it is true that communism is an evil system, but it permits us to make economic progress. *Lass'sie nach Berlin kommen.* Let them come to Berlin.

Freedom has many difficulties and democracy is not perfect, but we have never had to put a wall up to keep our people in, to prevent them from leaving us. I want to say, on behalf of my countrymen, who live many miles away on the other side of the Atlantic, who are far distant from you, that they take the greatest pride that they have been able to share with you, even from a distance, the story of the last 18 years. I know of no town, no city, that has been besieged for 18 years that still lives with the vitality and the force, and the hope and the determination of the city of West Berlin. While the wall is the most obvious and vivid demonstration of the failures of the Communist system, for all the world to see, we take no satisfaction in it, for it is, as your Mayor has said, an offense not only against history but an offense against humanity, separating families, dividing husbands and wives and brothers and sisters, and dividing a people who wish to be joined together.

What is true of this city is true of Germany—real, lasting peace in Europe can never be assured as long as one German out of four is denied the elementary right of free men, and that is to make a free choice. In 18 years of peace and good faith, this generation of Germans has earned the right to be free, including the right to unite their families and their nation in lasting peace, with good will to all people. You live in a defended island of freedom, but your life is part of the main. So let me ask you, as I close, to lift your eyes beyond the dangers of today, to the hopes of tomorrow, beyond the freedom merely of this city of Berlin, or your country of Germany, to the advance of freedom everywhere, beyond the wall to the day of peace with justice, beyond yourselves and ourselves to all mankind.

Freedom is indivisible, and when one man is enslaved, all are not free. When all are free, then we can look forward to that day when this city will be joined as one and this country and this great Continent of Europe in a peaceful and hopeful globe. When that day finally comes, as it will, the people of West Berlin can take sober satisfaction in the fact that they were in the front lines for almost two decades.

All free men, wherever they may live, are citizens of Berlin, and, therefore, as a free man, I take pride in the words *Ich bin ein Berliner.*

ALFIE

The following speech by Larry Schroeder, a student at California State University, Fullerton, was given in the Fall of 1967 to a class in Speech Communication, California State University, Fullerton.

One of the better movies recently produced was about a British fellow named Alfie. The theme song from this movie has become popular and is familiar to most people. The motion picture was impressive because of the significance of the comment that it made. Alfie was an interesting fellow. Here was a man who seemed to have everything going for him. He got what he wanted and he got away without complications. He lived with one woman for a while, long enough for her to bear his child, but when he became bored, he left. A friend of his was in the hospital. Alfie had an affair with his wife. She became pregnant but an abortion solved the problem.

Even though Alfie treated people shabbily, he appeared to many as the epitome of a guy who "had it made." He never got emotionally hung up. You'd think then that Alfie would be happy about life, but the movie ended on a different note. Alfie wasn't satisfied. He was unhappy. He was defeated and he didn't know why. His final comment was, "What's it all about?"

This is the question that I pose for you. Whether your name is Alfie, Bill or Virginia, what is it all about?

In an attempt to answer this question, let us look first at some examples of animal life. The lower forms such as worms, lizards or snakes possess only the faculty of sensation. That is, they can react in an automatic fashion to stimuli. An example of this would be the avoidance of pain. In the laboratory the pain-pleasure mechanism is the motivating force in experiments with rats.

Higher forms of animal life have an added quality. They possess the ability to perceive. They are able to retain and relate sensations. In its highest form this means awareness of environment and ability to react to it as a whole rather than to isolated sensations. Man is the highest form of life on earth. Man is different from lower animals, for he is able to translate perceptions into conceptions. Therefore we must conclude that man has the ability to reason. We must conclude also that reason has something to do with his being here. It provides the ability to communicate with other human beings.

Now let us take a look at man from another point of view. You have heard of Peking Man. You have heard of the findings of Leakey in the Odival Gorge of Kenya—men who lived 3 million years ago—and one of the most interesting findings is that men lived together. As far back as anthropologists are able to trace the history of man, they find that he has banded together. We can assume that one of the initial reasons for this was to obtain safety and protection. We also know that this is not the only reason why man lives communally.

Communication is associated with communal living. A speaker and a listener are provided. Pictographs, signs, even words are symbols and through them man communicates. Because he can reason, because he can communicate, man is not alone.

Let us ask now what man does with this ability to communicate. At this point we are forced to conclude that communication is the basis of organized society. We can answer the question by looking at ourselves. We express ourselves to others through speech, the written word or art forms. We inform, we persuade, we inspire. What we are doing is relating ourselves to others. We are sharing our thoughts, our feelings, our personalities. This is what the cave man was doing when he painted pictures on the wall of his home. This is the purpose of drama and dance. Why does man live together and what is the purpose of his communication? It is the means by which he relates himself to others.

It is only natural to ask why is this so important. Dr. Harry Sullivan in his book *Conceptions of Modern Psychiatry* talks about avoidance of loneliness because as Sullivan states, "we have a desire to touch one another and to be physically close." A good example of this is that of a child snuggling up to its mother. Coming home to a cold empty house is not what most of us would consider a comforting feeling.

Man has a hierarchy of needs and values and not until one is satisfied will he seek satisfaction for the next. Primary among these are the physiological needs and the safety needs. In our society they are reasonably easy to gratify. This is particularly true in cultures where the basic rights and needs of people are considered on an economic as well as a political basis. Once these physiological and safety needs are gratified, the next to emerge are the love and affection and belonging needs. An important thing to remember is that the love needs are reciprocal. That is, they involve both giving and receiving love.

In his book, *A Theory of Human Motivation*, Dr. A. H. Maslow states that the thwarting of the love need is the most common cause of maladjustment.

All right then, what's this all about? Simply stated, man can reason, man can communicate, man can meet his physical needs, but this is not enough. Whether his name be Alfie, Bill, Virginia—it doesn't matter—man needs to love and to be loved. Looking at it from this point of view, the evolution of the "hippie" movement is an understandable protest against a loveless environment.

Let's go back to where we started. Alfie represents what is wrong with many of us today. Alfie lost his capability to love. He didn't know how to relate closely to anyone. As a result his whole life was empty and meaningless. If life is going to have any meaning for you and for me, we've got to reach out, make contact and we've got to care. We all need love. *This* is what it's all about. This is what *living* is all about. . . . The love of man and God. . . . The love of man for all men. . . . The love of a man for a small child. . . . The love shared between a man . . . and a woman.

NOTES

[1]In *Congressional Record*, 77th Congress, 1st Session, vol. 87, part 9, Washington, D.C., U.S. Government Printing Office, 1941, pp. 9504–9505.

[2]In *Public Papers of the Presidents of the United States*, "John F. Kennedy: Containing the Public Messages, Speeches, and Statements of the President: January 1 to November 22, 1963," Washington, D.C., U.S. Government Printing Office, 1964, pp. 525–552.

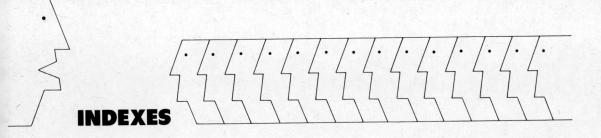

INDEXES

NAME INDEX

SUBJECT INDEX

74 75 76 9 8 7 6 5 4 3 2 1